Sustainable Development Policy and Administration

PUBLIC ADMINISTRATION AND PUBLIC POLICY

A Comprehensive Publication Program

Executive Editor

JACK RABIN
Professor of Public Administration and Public Policy
School of Public Affairs
The Capital College
The Pennsylvania State University—Harrisburg
Middletown, Pennsylvania

Assistant to the Executive Editor
T. Aaron Wachhaus, Jr.

Available Electronically

Principles and Practices of Public Administration, edited by Jack Rabin, Robert F. Munzenrider, and Sherrie M. Bartell

Sustainable Development Policy and Administration

edited by

Gedeon M. Mudacumura
Pennsylvania State University
Middletown, Pennsylvania

Desta Mebratu
United Nations Environment Programme
Nairobi, Kenya

M. Shamsul Haque
National University of Singapore
Singapore

Taylor & Francis
Taylor & Francis Group
Boca Raton   London   New York

A CRC title, part of the Taylor & Francis imprint, a member of the
Taylor & Francis Group, the academic division of T&F Informa plc.

Published in 2006 by
CRC Press
Taylor & Francis Group
6000 Broken Sound Parkway NW, Suite 300
Boca Raton, FL 33487-2742

International Standard Book Number-10: 1-57444-563-4 (Hardcover)
International Standard Book Number-13: 978-1-57444-563-3 (Hardcover)
Library of Congress Card Number 2005028874

Library of Congress Cataloging-in-Publication Data

Sustainable development policy and administration / edited by Gedeon M. Mudacumura, Desta Mebratu, M. Shamsul Haque.
     p. cm. -- (Public administration and public policy ; 118)
Includes bibliographical references and index.
ISBN 1-57444-563-4 (alk. paper)
    1. Sustainable development--Government policy. 2. Economic development--Environmental aspects. 3. Environmental policy. 4. Economic policy. I. Mudacumura, Gedeon M. II. Mebratu, Desta. III. Haque, M. Shamsul. IV. Series.

HC79.E5S86697 2006
338.9'27--dc22   2005028874

informa
Taylor & Francis Group
is the Academic Division of Informa plc.

Visit the Taylor & Francis Web site at
http://www.taylorandfrancis.com

and the CRC Press Web site at
http://www.crcpress.com

Foreword

The United Nations (UN) Conference on Human Environment held in 1972 represents the turning point in the environmental thinking of the global community. This conference, which subsequently led to the establishment of the United Nations Environment Programme (UNEP), for the first time recognized the importance of environmental management and the use of environmental assessment as a management tool. Even if the link between environmental and developmental issues did not emerge strongly in the conference outcomes, there were clear indications that the form of economic development would have to be altered. Around the same period, a group of eminent scientists and concerned citizens gathered in Rome to look at the global environmental crisis that was expanding at an alarming rate. This group, later to be known as the Club of Rome, produced a comprehensive report on the state of the natural environment. This report emphasized that the industrial society was going to exceed most of the ecological limits within a matter of decades, if it continued to promote the kind of economic growth witnessed in the 1960s and 1970s.

The fact that environment and development could not for long remain in a state of conflict gradually became apparent after the 1972 UN Conference on the Human Environment. In the following years, terms such as *environment and development*, *development without destruction*, and *environmentally sound development* evolved. The term *ecodevelopment* appeared in the UNEP review in 1978. By this time, it was recognized internationally that environmental and developmental ideas needed to be considered concurrently. Throughout the 1980s, there had been a number of initiatives that focused on understanding the linkages between environment and development. The most significant of these undertakings was the work done by the World Commission on Environment and Development (WCED), which was established by the UN. The work of WCED culminated in the publication of its 1987 report, *Our Common Future*, better known as the "Brundtland Report." This report provided a major political turning point that gave the concept of sustainable development great geopolitical significance and transformed it into a catchphrase of global policy making.

The United Nations Conference on Environment and Development that was held in 1992 provided the basic framework for the promotion of sustainable development through the adoption of Agenda 21 and a number of declarations that provided the basis for global environmental governance. The thousands of community-based, government-led, and private sector initiatives that were undertaken in the 1990s in the context of Agenda 21 made significant contribution to the promotion of sustainable development objectives. The World Summit on Sustainable Development (WSSD) held in 2002 provided a new impetus to the global movement for sustainable development. The WSSD process led to the launching of numerous global and regional partnerships aimed at the promotion of the broad objectives of global sustainability through concrete project implementations. It also adopted the Johannesburg Plan of Implementation, which outlined the key measures that need to be undertaken at the national, regional, and international levels in order to tackle the challenges of meeting the needs of the current generation while maintaining a balanced environment for future generations.

Despite the significant progress that has been made since the UN Conference on Human Environment, the global community is still facing huge challenges in terms of global sustainability. As was underlined in the Johannesburg Plan of Implementation, addressing these challenges would require a fundamental shift in both our institutional and individual ways of thinking. The Plan recognized the crucial role that education plays for the promotion of sustainable development. On the basis of the call made by the WSSD, the United Nations General Assembly declared the years 2005 to 2014 the United Nations Decade on Education for Sustainable Development.

The elaboration of concepts and tools and the compilation of replicable cases of applications are important prerequisites for sound education for sustainable development. The publication of this *Sustainable Development Policy and Administration* is expected to contribute to the further development of the knowledge base that is required for programs on education for sustainable development. The combination of the sections on conceptual review, policy and institutional analysis, and sectoral cases of applications enhances its utility. I also believe the reader will benefit from the broad area of topics combined with key sectoral focus and geographical coverage of cases.

Klaus Töpfer
Executive Director
United Nations Environment Programme

Preface

The multidimensional sustainable development phenomenon has been the subject of theoretical and pragmatic discourses during the last two decades. While such discourses highlighted sustainability as one of the major objectives of all development policies, ensuring a sustainable mode of development may imply a continuous search for adequate means and ways to address the persistent problems of food shortages and starvation in marginalized regions of the world, the increasing incidence of man-made and natural disasters, the failure to reduce environmentally hazardous activities, and other dynamic development challenges that represent a global threat to sustainability. Ultimately, since the initial sustainability principles were devised in efforts to improve on those of conventional economic development, which were primarily conceived to achieve economic growth without appropriate consideration of other development dimensions, a call to revisit the underlying premises of sustainable development should aim at unraveling ongoing processes of unsustainable activities while ascertaining holistic strategies to overcome recurring challenges locally and worldwide.

This book seeks to provide a learning resource describing some major policy and administration issues that are critical to understanding the multiple dimensions of sustainable development. The running theme of all contributions underscores the urgent need of promoting the broad objectives of global sustainability while shedding light on relevant insights to tackle the challenges of meeting the needs of the current and future generations. Realizing that the United Nations General Assembly declared the period 2005–2014 the United Nations Decade on Education for Sustainable Development, this timely volume, *Sustainable Development Policy and Administration*, which brings together diverse contributions dealing with the multiple facets of development, represents a rich reference document for graduate students, professors, scholars, and public and private development managers interested in the emerging field of sustainable development.

The editors who assumed the final responsibility to coordinate the various manuscripts take this opportunity to acknowledge the talented contributors who shared willingly their research on major sustainable development issues. Similarly, the editors thank Dr. Jack Rabin, Executive Editor of the Public Administration and Public Policy series (Taylor & Francis Group LLC), for accepting our proposal and offering valuable suggestions during the publication process. The editors would like also to thank Dr. Klaus Toepfer, the executive director of the United Nations Environment Programme (UNEP), for contributing the Foreword of the book. Last but not least, Naomi Lynch, the production editor, deserves special recognition for her commitment to get this project done on time.

Gedeon M. Mudacumura
Desta Mebratu
M. Shamsul Haque

Contributors

Getachew Assefa
Royal Institute of Technology, Stockholm, Sweden

Anthony Barclay
Economic Community of West African States (ECOWAS), Abuja, Nigeria

Noorjahan Bava
University of Delhi, Delhi, India

Tracy Berno
Christchurch Polytechnic Institute of Technology, New Zealand, and University of the South Pacific, Suva, Fiji

Patricia A. Cholewka
Columbia University, New York, USA

Berhe T. Costantinos
United Nations Development Program, New York, USA

O.P. Dwivedi
University of Guelph, Guelph, Canada

Björn Frostell
Royal Institute of Technology, Division of Industrial Ecology, Stockholm, Sweden

Eric Goewie
Wageningen University, Wageningen, the Netherlands

Kathryn Gow
Queensland University of Technology, Brisbane, Australia

M. Shamsul Haque
National University of Singapore, Singapore

Patricia A. Hippler
Pennsylvania State University, University Park, Pennsylvania, USA

Renu Khator
University of South Florida, Tampa, Florida, USA

Nadejda Komendantova-Amann
Sustainable Development Research Institute, Vienna, Austria

Josef Leitmann
The World Bank, Washington, DC, USA

Watana Luanratana
Bangkok Metropolitan Authority, Bangkok, Thailand

Ralph Luken
UNIDO, Vienna, Austria

Desta Mebratu
United Nations Environment Programme, Regional Office for Africa, Nairobi, Kenya

Britta Meinke-Brandmeier
Darmstadt University of Technology, Darmstadt, Germany

Graham Miller
University of Surrey, Guildford, England

Paul C. Mocombe
Florida Atlantic University, Boca Raton, Florida, USA

Gedeon M. Mudacumura
Pennsylvania State University, University Park, Pennsylvania, USA

Lucio Munoz
Independent Researcher/Consultant, Vancouver, British Columbia, Canada

Heather Nel
University of Port Elizabeth, Port Elizabeth, South Africa

Kala Saravanamuthu
University of New England, Armidale, New South Wales, Australia

Stephen G. Schwenke
Ethics and Public Management Programme, Makerere University, Kampala, Uganda

Júlio da Silva
Embrapa, Clima Temperado, Pelotas, Brazil

Rui Melo de Souza
Embrapa, Clima Temperado, Pelotas, Brazil

C. Visvanathan
Asian Institute of Technology, Bangkok, Thailand

David Walker
Pennsylvania State University, University Park, Pennsylvania, USA

João Pedro Zabaleta
Embrapa, Clima Temperado, Pelotas, Brazil

Andrew A. Zekeri
Tuskegee University, Tuskegee, Alabama, USA

Table of Contents

SUSTAINABLE DEVELOPMENT: MAJOR DIMENSIONS AND THEORETICAL FRAMEWORKS

Chapter 1

Rethinking Sustainable Development Policy and Administration

M. Shamsul Haque and Gedeon M. Mudacumura

CONTENTS

Revisiting Sustainable Development: Why?

In the current age, one of the most critical human concerns shaping the global discourse on the current mode of development or progress has been related to the question of its eventual sustainability. During the recent three decades, the debate on a sustainable mode of development has gained increasing significance through the worldwide proliferation of conferences, seminars, reports, books, and journals as well as conventions, protocols, and institutions. In the process, the idea of "sustainable development" has been reified almost into an "ideology" in both developed and developing nations (Crabbé, 1997, p. 1). Thus, in one form or another, most international institutions, national governments, and local communities tend to base their development policies and programs on sustainability as one of the major objectives. In fact, some of the largest global forums organized in recent years have been related to worldwide environmental concerns and sustainability objectives, which include the Stockholm Conference on the Human Environment (1972), the Ottawa Conference on Conservation and Development (1986), the United Nations Conference on Environment and Development or the Earth Summit in Rio de Janeiro (1992), and the World Summit on Sustainable Development in Johannesburg (2002).

From these global forums attended by heads of states or their representatives from countries all over the world emerged major conventions and protocols for the protection of the environment and the realization of sustainable development. For example, the Vienna Convention on the Protection of the Ozone Layer (1985) stressed the need for intergovernmental cooperation to protect the ozone layer; it was reinforced further by the Montreal Protocol on Substances That Deplete the Ozone Layer (1987), which provided specific guidelines for identifying the causes and remedies of ozone depletion. Another related measure is the Madrid Protocol (1991), which identified Antarctica as a "natural reserve" and emphasized the protection of its environment from commercial ventures pursued by various countries.

However, some of the most comprehensive protection measures emerged from the Earth Summit (1992), including the Convention on Biological Diversity, the Framework Convention on Climate Change, the Rio Declaration (for sustainable development), and the Agenda 21 (prescribing specific preventive and remedial measures) (Haque, 2000; Reid, 1995). Another of the most widely known international measures for environmental protection and sustainability is the Kyoto Protocol (1997), which has generated worldwide debate and controversy. With regard to greenhouse gases, the Kyoto Protocol defines the emissions limits and targets to be followed by various categories of countries (excluding developing countries) within the specific time frame (Sheeran, 2004). Thus, since the publication of *Our Common Future* by the World Commission on Environment and Development headed by Gro Harlem Brundtland (WCED, 1987), which emphasized and popularized the idea of sustainable development, some of these major international initiatives or measures have been undertaken.

Unfortunately, these international initiatives have been quite ineffective in addressing environmental degradation and ensuring a sustainable mode of development. In particular, the industrialized countries have failed to realize their promises to reduce voluntarily environmentally hazardous activities (such as emissions) that represent a global threat to sustainability (Sheeran, 2004). On the other hand, the current process of economic development, based on rapid industrialization, urban expansion, and hazardous production and consumption, continues to worsen the unsustainable conditions of air pollution, chemical contamination, land degradation, ozone depletion, deforestation, biodiversity loss, global warming, and so on (Haque, 2000; Flint, 2004). These unsustainable conditions are not isolated from the changing patterns of climate, increasing incidence of natural disasters, and growing problems of food shortages and starvation in different parts of the world (Guimaraes, 2004; Haque, 1999a). Thus, the significance of revisiting sustainable development not only lies in the proliferation of global forums, conventions, institutions, and publications in this regard; it is also evident from the failures of such initiatives to address the continuing process of unsustainable activities and overcome the new challenges to sustainable development worldwide.

Controversies over Sustainable Development

To address the problems of unsustainability mentioned, it is necessary to attain certain global consensus on the concepts, approaches, models, and strategies of sustainable development. But there are too many controversies over the issue that need to be resolved. *First,* there are some major approaches of sustainable development that are mutually incompatible or contradictory. For example, the *utilitarian* approach prescribes the welfare trade-off between generations and suggests that there is no need for changing current economic activities that cause greenhouse gases, if the benefit from these activities exceeds the harm done by such activities to future generations in terms of global warming (Anand and Sen, 1994). On the other hand, the *ethical* approach to sustainable development is concerned for welfare inequality between generations and emphasizes that it is the "moral obligation" of the current generation enjoying welfare to maintain the capacity and opportunity of future generations to have equivalent welfare. It is also stressed by some scholars that future generations are entitled to or have rights to the same level of environmental quality and resources enjoyed by the current generation. In this regard, Anand and Sen stress the moral obligation to do justice to the poor and deprived population in the current generation itself.

It is obvious that because of its narrow focus on the combined total welfare of the current and future generations, the utilitarian approach to sustainable development is not only insensitive to the needs of future generations, it is also quite indifferent to the environmental implications of economic activities as long as such activities maximize human welfare or benefit. On the other hand, although the ethical approach does address the question of intergenerational equality in welfare, it remains human-centered in terms of its emphasis on the maintenance of environmental resources for human species without much concern for environmental sustainability as an end in itself, which can be observed in various traditional cultures or belief systems. Thus, in studying sustainable development, it is necessary to emphasize environmental sustainability not only for the current and future generations (including all classes and groups in each generation), but also for the environment itself.

Second, there is also controversy over the various dimensions and components of sustainable development. In terms of dimensions, in existing studies, there are tendencies among some scholars and experts to emphasize "economic" sustainability that focuses on the implications of development activities for environmental costs. Some of them stress "environmental" sustainability that prescribes the realization of development in line with biotic capacity and resource constraints; others draw attention to "social" sustainability that supports people's active involvement in managing environment and development (see Estes, 1993; Reed, 1996; Haque, 1999b). However, these major economic, social, and environmental dimensions of sustainable development are mutually complementary rather than exclusive. For instance, in pursuing development, one needs to consider its environmental costs, make sure that it does not put excessive pressure on environmental capacity, and ensure its implementation based on people's participation. In addition, there are cultural and attitudinal dimensions of sustainable development, including people's lifestyles and consumption patterns, that greatly affect environmental resources and conditions. In fact, one major challenge to sustainable development today is the environmentally hazardous modern lifestyle based on endless consumerism that has expanded worldwide in the current age of globalization. Thus, in both theory and practice of sustainable development, it is crucial to stress its multidimensional nature.

Similarly, there are some major perspectives of development in existing literature that tend to focus on specific components of sustainability. For instance, the so-called ecosimplification perspective shows concern for the current situation of diminishing plant and animal species, which is likely to cause the loss of biodiversity, simplification of the complex ecosystems, and thus further ecological imbalance. On the other hand, the "contamination" perspective focuses on the sustainability challenge or environmental threat posed by the biochemical contamination of land, air, and water, whereas the "natural-resource-consumption" perspective explains how such a challenge may have been created by the reductionist assessment of environmental resources in terms of their consumption value (see Haque, 1999; Hempel, 1996). Once again, there should not be any conflict among these perspectives, each of which stresses one major set of components constituting the overall sustainability. There is a need for a more holistic perspective that emphasizes the significance of simultaneously resolving the problems of sustainability caused by biodiversity loss, biochemical contamination, utilitarian valuation of natural resources, and so on.

Third, there is a major controversy in terms of priority between the two major goals—economic growth and environmental sustainability—pursued today by almost all nations. While economic growth remains the most dominant development agenda for most countries, many critics stress its adverse environmental outcomes caused by growth-driven industrial expansion, resource depletion, and hazardous production. However, there are arguments supporting the view that economic growth could be an effective means for achieving sustainable development: "Sustainability requires alleviation of poverty, a decline in fertility, the substitution of human capital for natural resources, effective demand for environmental quality, and a responsive supply. These changes cannot take place on a sustainable basis without growth" (Crabbé, 1997, p. v). In reconciling this debate, *Our Common Future*, or the Brundtland Report, emphasizes the kind of economic growth that is conducive to the sustainability of the environmental resource base (World Commission on Environment and Development [WCED], 1987). In this regard, it is necessary to highlight that it is hardly possible to expand modern economic growth without depleting natural resources and diminishing environmental sustainability.

In fact, the current global fetish for rapid economic growth based on expansive industrialization, urban development, and hazardous consumption—pursued or reinforced by market-led reforms (e.g., deregulation, liberalization, privatization, corporatization, and antiwelfarism)—has created havoc for environmental sustainability (Haque, 1999a). As a result, the reexamination of economic growth as a national and international development agenda became quite prominent at both the Earth Summit in Rio de Janeiro and the World Summit on Sustainable Development in Johannesburg. However, in both developed and developing nations, policy makers are quite reluctant to compromise their growth-driven development objectives. Even the recent prescription for tradable emissions permits is unlikely to abate unsustainable economic growth, because under this system, the affluent nations not only can continue their economic activities and expand emissions by purchasing such emissions permits from poor countries, but can also relocate their hazardous industries in these less industrialized countries. In short, while economic growth continues to be the primary national goal for most countries, its adverse implication for sustainable development remains largely unresolved.

These are a few examples of some major controversies in sustainable development approaches, perspectives, and priorities. There are many other conceptual, theoretical, and structural dilemmas, which are addressed by various authors in this volume. The point here is that these basic controversies or dilemmas need to be resolved in order to delineate effective policies and institutions for sustainable development, which require a thorough reexamination of the issue. In fact, there are divergent views over policy options and institutional challenges, which are analyzed in the remaining sections of this chapter.

Institutional Challenges for Sustaining Development

Despite multiple interventions from various public and private institutions at the local, national, and international levels, the development research community has not yet sorted out the relevant sustainable development strategies and the main factors leading to sustainability. It is worth recalling that sustainability principles were devised in efforts to improve on those of conventional economic development, which were primarily conceived to achieve economic growth without appropriate consideration of other development dimensions: social, cultural, ecological, political, and spiritual (Kelly, 1998; Mudacumura, 2004). Such a narrow focus could have been one of the main constraints preventing development researchers from suggesting adequate solutions (deLeon, 1992; Dryzek, 1990; Haque, 1999b; Stiglitz, 1998).

A close look at the history of exploitation of natural resources and current environmental deterioration should indicate the seriousness of prioritizing the economic dimension over the development dimensions mentioned. Thus, as stated at the beginning of this chapter, rethinking the underlying premises of sustainable development is no longer an option but a necessity if one takes into account the urgency of preventing the "society from sailing by a wrong compass, at the expense of the environment" (Hueting, 1992, p. 255) or implementing "decisions made on the basis of curious blend of ideology and bad economics" (Stiglitz, 2002: xiii).

In light of the preceding concerns, the institutions engaged in furthering sustainable development face the challenging task of determining the necessary and relevant information to identify, implement, and evaluate sustainable development policies geared toward meeting the needs of the current generation without compromising the welfare of future generations. To minimize the likelihood of devising irrelevant solutions requires governments, communities, and the private sector at different levels to work collaboratively in the design and implementation of sustainable development policies. Such collaboration may allow decision-making institutions to integrate valid and reliable information related to multiple development dimensions in the identification of objectives, the design of policies, and the evaluation of courses of action. As Forrester (1994, p. 249) remarked, most misbehavior of corporate, social, and governmental systems arises from the dependence on erroneous intuitive solutions to complex behavior, and failing to capture information about the structure and behavior of the system in which development decisions are being made will most likely lead to ineffective policy design. In fact, removing conceptual barriers through interdisciplinary cooperation and cultivation of systems thinking is one of the best strategic approaches to improving the design of development policies (Saeed, 1994).

Besides the challenge of devising adequate solutions, most scholars and practitioners of development management agree that problems of implementing, managing, and institutionalizing development activities remain serious and pervasive (Rondinelli, 1982), and the majority of international development agencies acknowledge that carefully planned and systematically analyzed projects are worthless unless they can be implemented effectively (World Bank, 1983). As emphasized earlier, relevant information plays a critical role in the effective implementation of sustainable development policies. Compiling such information must not be restricted to the empirical methods since, as the World Bank (1998, p. 1) acknowledges, "the empirical base of decision making is weak."

Actually, the complex interrelationships surrounding sustainable development issues make obsolete the traditional management approaches structured on rigid, deterministic control, which assume a high degree of knowledge about what needs to be done and of certainty in a world in which the correct solutions are not always clear, and the only certainty is a high degree of uncertainty (Rondinelli, 1982). As such, institutions involved in the implementation of sustainable development strategies should embrace the concept of multiagency networks (Mudacumura, 2002). Premised on a continually evolving consensus among network members, this management approach can preclude simple solutions devised by any agency acting alone. With sustainability being beyond the reach of individual agency, this approach makes sense when each implementing agency recognizes that there are no easy solutions and no single solution for multidimensional sustainable development problems. Ultimately, addressing such problems requires a sustained multi-institutional approach to generate a range of plausible, implementable solutions (http://www.scienceinafrica.co.za/).

Furthermore, the multiagency network environment stresses the importance of continuous feedback and action to suit the ongoing needs of the multiple development stakeholders whose active involvement is vital in the implementation of sustainable development policies. Concretely, the active involvement of all development stakeholders can foster creative thinking while generating ownership and motivation of the people to honor the cultural and spiritual traditions of all network members. Indeed, Goulet (1980, p. 488) observed that a growing chorus of voices, in rich and poor countries alike, proclaims that full human development is not possible without regard for essential moral values.

Consequently, building networks of development institutions can create an enabling environment for empowering all development stakeholders, providing them with the opportunity to share the information while collectively devising strategies to distribute equitably global resources, a sine qua non condition for sustaining development on a global scale. "If sustainable development is to be realized, it has to be built on the consent and support of those whose lives are affected" (http://globalknowledge.org).

From this context, the empowerment of network members may constitute a development management strategy that is necessary for the generation and use of local/traditional knowledge. As Stone (1966) remarked, a great deal of untapped, traditional knowledge and experience is available in respect to the development of effective organizations to manage comprehensive development programs. Because of their complexity, sustainable development issues require the knowledge, commitment, and action of multiple stakeholders, in particular, the laypeople who bring valid perspectives to decision making (Beierle, 1999). In fact, "most development analysts now maintain that developmental wisdom is lodged not in government bureaucracies. but in local communities and institutions" (Hyden, 1997, p. 4).

Furthermore, such development management requires fostering consensus among all vested interests, in particular, grassroots organizations. Thus, allowing diverse groups and individuals to have their own cultural contexts and local narratives taken into account fits with the concept of decentralized participatory decision making, an approach that improves the implementation of sustainable development strategies, which, in turn, could lead to increased economic growth and social justice (U.S. Foreign Assistance Act of 1973). Among other features of this decentralized participatory decision making are a strong scientific base, extensive involvement of stakeholders, a proactive and holistic approach to issues, and the integration of a wide range of regulatory and nonregulatory solutions (Randolph and Bauer, 1999). Specifically, active citizen participation is needed for the organization and functioning of development activities for the main purpose of guarding against abuses of state power (Hyden, 1997). Moreover, promoting a development management that fosters participatory decision making is the right strategic approach to attack the root causes of development failures. In fact, it has been found that effective development management is one of the prerequisites for removing the structural barriers that limit people's ability to get out of poverty (United Nations Development Programme, 1996; World Bank, 1998).

Therefore, development institutions have to shift their focus from reductionist development management to a management premised on holistic thinking, a process that falls in line with the need to revisit sustainable development foundations. This shift to holistic thinking might enable the networked institutions implementing sustainable development policies to explore the multiple development dimensions, ensuring particularly that the cultural achievements of all societies and civilizations of the world are not overlooked. Furthermore, such holistic thinking can provide development stakeholders with the opportunity to match words with deeds, a process that the United Nations development agencies had failed to accomplish five years after the Earth Summit in Rio de Janeiro (Ismail, 1997).

Along the same line, this suggested development management implies identifying a core development value that opposing groups in the "North" and "South" agree on, a core value that can enable both groups to make decisions that integrate the multiple development dimensions. Ultimately, achieving such integration involves coordination, negotiation, and compromise for the sake of ensuring a good quality of life for current and future generations, the cornerstone of sustainable development.

Similarly, as indicated earlier, effective implementation of sustainable development strategies can emerge from broad-based network organizations linking the public and private development entities on different geographical levels. Such global networks could rely on information provided by multidisciplinary teams of scholars, practitioners, think tanks, grassroots organizations, and all agencies interested in furthering sustainable development.

Particularly, the multidisciplinary dialogue should address the potential risks of subscribing to narrow perceptions of reality, which have been inadequate for dealing with complex sustainable development problems. Specifically, the dialogue should rely on the holistic approach to ascertain a deeper understanding and appreciation for how development problems are identified, defined, and solved. This multidisciplinary dialogue should address the contending issues among development theorists in different disciplines, all working within their own methodological traditions and using often incompatible analytical tools and techniques. This dialogue could awaken the rationalists who still believe that complex social problems can be understood in their entirety through systematic analysis and solved through comprehensive planning (Lindblom, 1965). In fact, the uncertainty of development problems combined with the complexity of relationships between developing nations and international development institutions make it nearly impossible to plan, analyze, and manage projects in highly rational and systematic ways (Rondinelli, 1982).

Moreover, the broad-based management decisions reached through networks would ensure that local communities reach beyond their individual interests in future development to account for national and global needs. Broadening the decision-making process can allow network members to devise development management strategies with built-in mechanisms reflecting two guiding principles: transparency and accountability. Such principles can ensure that development management decisions are geared toward building sustainable and healthy communities in which all resources are shared equitably.

To recap, most scholars and practitioners acknowledge that sustainable development problems are closely interconnected and interdependent so that they cannot be understood using the "chop up and study the parts" reductionist method of current academic disciplines and government and nongovernment development institutions. "Such an approach will never resolve any of our difficulties but will merely shift them around in the complex web of social and ecological relations" (Capra, 1982, p. 26). Therefore, the interconnectivity of sustainable development issues requires all institutions at the local, national, and international levels to join efforts through global development network organizations, working collectively in the design and implementation of sustainable development policies. Such active collaboration among development institutions can take advantage of creative synergies to achieve outcomes that might be impossible for any development institution to achieve alone.

In This Volume

In light of the preceding discussion, the contributing authors explored various aspects of the multidimensional sustainable development phenomenon, focusing primarily on issues pertaining to policy and administration. This edited volume reflects insights from scholars and practitioners with a broad range of development experiences in various nations of Africa,

Asia, Australia, Europe, and the Americas. These geographically distributed contributions make this volume an exceptional compilation of global research on pertinent sustainable development issues.

While recognizing the inability to analyze all the multiple facets of sustainability thoroughly and systematically, this volume strives to present the contributions of diverse scholars and practitioners in a coherent structure of chapters categorized and arranged into the following sustainable development themes: major dimensions and theoretical frameworks, policies and institutions, national and regional experiences, current and future challenges, and alternatives and recommendations. A brief synopsis of the chapters is provided under each theme.

Part I. Sustainable Development: Major Dimensions and Theoretical Frameworks

The dynamic and multifaceted concept of sustainable development has been the subject of intense research in both developed and developing countries during the last two decades. In this first section, Shamsul Haque explores how the concept of sustainable development has become one of the most significant global issues in terms of academic discourse and practical policy debate, arguing that its conceptual clarity and consensus remain a basic precondition for meaningful debate and effective policy formulation. Despite series of discussions, analyses, and critiques in an enormous number of books, journals, and global conferences, there are still considerable disagreements over the idea of sustainable development. Haque presents existing concepts and definitions of sustainable development under some major categories and examines their limitations in terms of their tendencies to be empiricist, reductionist, unilinear, human-centric, and even hegemonic. He concludes with some suggestions with a view to articulate a more comprehensive and holistic concept of sustainable development that could create an effective foundation of future discourse and policies.

Along the same line, Berhe Costantinos elaborates on the underlying premises of the sustainable development concept while underscoring its nexus with governance policy. Concretely, he highlights how the global community has tried to build parallels between poverty and human destitution with the governance regimes that exist in poor nations, a governance program based on pillars of support aimed at strengthening civil society and various coordinates of government and governing institutions. He further acknowledges the challenges of transitioning to a sustainable development path despite the current democratically favorable contemporary global conditions. In probing the sustainable development–governance nexus, Costantinos focuses his research on the evolving "political theory" of governance in which polity seeks mechanisms to convert political preferences to sustainable development administration; sustainable development policy analysis, formulation, and management protocols making public policy accountable, transparent, and predictable to the local/global community; and establishment of the conceptual, operational, and functional nexus among sustainable development theory, policy, and tools and sustainable development administration in relation to assets and capital. In his final analysis, Costantinos notes that the comprehension of governance as a sustainable development tool is imprecise simply because the concept is still evolving.

Indeed, Daly (1996) recognized how this evolving sustainable development concept had risen in a decade to the prominence of mantra or a shibboleth since the 1987 publication of *Our Common Future,* a report produced by the WCED. Since then, thousands of initiatives have been undertaken at local, national, and global levels in an attempt to address different aspects of the environmental challenges. However, their impact in shaping "our common future" on a more sustainable basis seems to be minimal when measured against the enormity of the global environmental challenges. This has led to an increasing level of frustration and disenchantment, even among the different groups promoting the concept of sustainable development. Desta Mebratu's chapter attempts to present a new framework for sustainability and sustainable development by looking at the conceptual precursors. Among other precursors, he alludes to the African tradition, which views man not as the master of the universe but as the center, the friend, the beneficiary, and the user who must live in harmony with the universe, obeying the laws of natural, moral, and mystical order. If these laws are unduly disturbed, man suffers most.

Mebratu further reviews the most relevant systems and evolutionary principles that constitute the conceptual frameworks of sustainability. He views systems as thoroughly man-made and defines a specific system as the point of view of one or several observers. Thus, utilizing systems thinking for the concept of sustainability requires revitalizing the specialized systems thinking based on the principles and spirit of general systems thinking. Considering the complexity of the environmental challenges, Mebratu suggests that the conceptual limitations may be overcome through the combined application of the General Systems Theory and the General Evolutionary Theory, whose basic principles are the following: (1) evolution is an irreversible and nonlinear change of both natural and man-made systems in domains far from thermodynamic equilibrium; (2) the direction of evolution is characterized by an increasing ability of organisms and systems to sense and assess the state of the environment, to learn appropriate responses, and to transmit this knowledge to succeeding generations; and (3) systems with organized complexity can only be understood by looking at their dynamic interrelationships (feedback), a process that is more than linear summation of cause–effect chains.

While Mebratu looks at the systems concept of sustainability, Mudacumura goes a step further to suggest a general theory of sustainability after considering the growing dissatisfaction over what is known about the underlying premises of development. Several scholars have labeled such knowledge as practically irrelevant, theoretically impoverished, ideologically prejudiced, and narrowly focused—lacking multidisciplinary perspectives. The absence of a clear theoretical and analytical framework makes it difficult to determine whether the new policies will indeed foster an environmentally sound and socially meaningful form of development.

Keeping in mind current large-scale global development changes, Mudacumura's chapter alludes to the previous models of development, which failed to devote serious attention to the phenomenon of sustainability, and presents his general theory of sustainability, which attempts to bridge the economic, social, cultural, political, ecological, and spiritual dimensions of development while giving equal consideration to each dimension. Three overall insights derived from his general theory of sustainability conclude his chapter: (1) societal empowerment, which connotes a process by which individuals may gain mastery or control over their own life with democratic participation in the life of their community while providing the opportunity for citizens to feel their own worth, be all they can be, and see the same worth in other people; (2) global networking, which creates an enabling environment for solving complex development issues, since global networking rests on the premise that active collaboration among organizations engaged in promoting development may take advantage of creative synergies to achieve outcomes that are impossible for anyone to achieve alone; and (3) holistic thinking, an emerging approach that provides a better analogy for understanding society and its complex issues, in particular, the interrelationships among the six dimensions and the two theoretical boundaries of the general theory of sustainability. As the ingredients of a cake are inexplicably intertwined and are necessary for full flavor, so are the development dimensions interconnected and indispensable for sustainable development.

Ultimately, addressing sustainable development issues implies thinking holistically, that is, looking at the big picture (the whole phenomenon of sustainability) while maintaining awareness of the interconnected dimensions of development.

O. P. Dwivedi and Renu Khator, authors of the last chapter in the first section, looked at the major global development milestones, tracing the initial large-scale attempts to sustain development from the 1972 Stockholm Conference, which heightened worldwide awareness of pollution problems. These problems emerged in reaction to the publication of *The Limits to Growth,* a study that underscored the urgency to control the present growth trends in world population, industrialization and pollution, food production, and resource depletion. Until that time, the pollution problem was seen as a by-product of industrialization, and the authors refer to Indira Gandhi, former prime minister of India, who coined the concept of "pollution of poverty" while arguing that poverty and need are the greatest polluters.

The world gathering in Sweden led to the establishment of environment ministries, departments, and agencies worldwide, thus putting the environment on the international agenda. It further laid the foundation for the next United Nations (UN) Conference on Environment and Development (UNCED), also known as the Earth Summit, held in 1992 in Rio de Janeiro. The summit adopted Agenda 21, a blueprint for sustainable development, with agreed common vision for growth, equity, and nature conservation for future generations, and created a new agency, the UN Commission on Sustainable Development, to collect data on environmental and development activities and to monitor individual and collective progress of nations toward achieving the goals set forth in Agenda 21.

Ten years after the Rio conference, the anticipated progress had been much slower to materialize than hoped. The state of the world's environment remained very fragile, while the vast majority of human beings still lived in conditions of unbearable deprivation and squalor. Dwivedi and Khator note that these issues were the focus of the third global development milestone, the UN-sponsored Millennium Summit, in 2002. It was hoped that by the time nations assembled in South Africa, concrete and practical steps would be agreed on to deal with the core relationship between human society and the natural environment. The authors contend that the summit missed the opportunity to respond seriously to the injustice of disparity between the rich's easy access to resources and what is left to the poor, to halt the continuing assault on the ecological well-being of Mother Earth, and to do something concrete to help improve the life of the marginalized of the planet.

The following section elaborates on specific policies and institutions aimed at fostering sustainable development. Policy makers have been struggling with issues ranging from ever-growing proportion of city dwellers, the challenges of sustaining farming operations while bridging farming and tourism, and the role of government and nongovernmental institutions in promoting sustainability.

Part II. Sustainable Development: Policies and Institutions

Josef Leitman's chapter underscores the current trend toward an urbanized world, substantiating his arguments with current urban population statistics and highlighting that more than half of the world's population will be living in cities and towns by the end of the first decade of the 21st century. As the engines of national and regional economic growth, urban areas are the world's most important consumers of resources, generators of waste, and, consequently, sources of environmental problems. Population and economic growth are partly responsible for creating externalities—more people making more things demand more resources and generate more waste. The resulting set of environmental problems consists of inadequate access to environmental infrastructure and services, pollution from urban wastes, natural resource degradation, exposure to environmental risks, and global environmental issues.

Addressing such urban environmental problems requires the interaction of numerous public, private, not-for-profit, and household stakeholders; each group has its own interests and patterns of behavior, which lead to varied and sometimes conflicting actions and viewpoints. Thus, realizing that one quarter to one third of all urban households in the world live in absolute poverty, any policy geared toward the improvement of urban environmental problem must not overlook the importance of reducing poverty, which interacts with the urban environment. In tackling the broader issue of vulnerability of the urban poor, Leitman suggests a three-pronged approach: (1) a propoor orientation in the options for solving other security problems, for example, slum upgrading and lifeline utility pricing as alternatives for increasing access to services and infrastructure; (2) growth-with-equity strategies that create an enabling environment for more urban poor to reduce their economic vulnerability; and (3) political rights and participation so that the problems of poverty are articulated and recognized in the political arena.

Sustaining the urban population requires policy makers to understand what it takes to sustain farming operations, which supply food, a key element on the hierarchy of physical needs. The chapter coauthored by Eric Goewie, Júlio da Silva, João Pedro Zabaleta, and Rui Melo de Souza attempts to answer the empirical question, "What is sustainable farming?" The authors echo the same problem raised by previous contributors regarding the multitude of definitions of sustainability, reiterating the challenge to quantify this concept since nobody knows the specific needs of future generations. Narrowing their focus on farming, the authors view its aim as striving for minimal disturbance of production conditions in soil, crops, and animals, reminding the reader that the use of synthetic compounds and various tillage methods could reduce soil fertility. They further allude to the sustainability of agricultural production systems, which are related to the potential of self-restoration of production factors used for farming. Thus, sustainability may be a function of the possibilities for self-restoration inside a farm.

Concretely, land use is in a state of sustainable development if the farmers permanently strive for equilibrium between what they apply to and what they remove from their land. One of the main findings of their research is that organic management of land use systems substitutes external inputs with organic inputs, which are obtained from natural resources such as biological nitrogen fixation, biological control of pests, and maintenance of a high level of permanent soil fertility. Such resources are found in farm- or forest-bound ecosystems, and the management of such systems is ecosystems oriented and pays attention to the self-organizing properties of the ecosystems concerned.

While Gowie and colleagues explore the type of knowledge needed for sustainable farming, Tracy Berno's chapter highlights the need to bridge sustainable agriculture and sustainable tourism for the sake of enhancing sustainability. Considering that tourism has had few salient benefits for those in the rural regions, Berno proposes to expand the backward economic linkages by increasing the amount of local agricultural products used in the tourism industry, a suggestion that calls for a joint optimization of three related areas of sustainability: sustainable agriculture, sustainable cuisine, and the tourism industry. By focusing on the more sustainable production and use of agricultural products in the tourism sector, along with enhancing the economic benefit, a reduction in "product miles" and other wastes can be realized.

The author further notes that experiencing a country's products is essential to understanding its culture. As such, sustainable cuisine is becoming an intricate part of an authentic travel experience, and the development and promotion of sustainable cuisine through the operation-alization of the "farm-to-restaurant" concept can support sustainable agri-culture by increasing demand for local products, as well as contributing to the overall ethos of sustainable tourism. In a nutshell, the chapter explores the relationships of sustainable agriculture, sustainable cuisine, and the tourism industry, particularly as it relates to sustainable tourism. Means for increasing the linkages among these three areas of sustainability are discussed, and the barriers and facilitators to implementing the farm-to-restaurant concept are identified.

So far, the contributors in this second section of the book have geared their focus on policy issues related to urban population and sustainable agriculture and tourism. The remaining contributions shed light on the role of government and nongovernmental institutions in furthering sustainable development. In that respect, Heather Nel discusses how local governments in partnership with nongovernmental organizations (NGOs) are becoming frontline development agencies capable of bringing about the social and economic welfare of local communities in South Africa. Municipalities, she argues, work together with local communities to find sustainable ways to meet their needs and improve the quality of their lives. In this context, municipalities are required to devise integrated development plans that form the framework for development projects within the local government sphere.

Her chapter devotes attention to the need for active community participation in project conception, as well as the various mechanisms or strategies that are utilized by South African municipalities to bring about integrated development. With respect to the strategies to enhance community participation within the local government sphere, she elaborates on the need for municipal–community partnerships in South Africa with specific reference to engaging NGOs in local development initiatives. Despite the benefits of engaging such community partners in the conception and implementation of development projects, the author notes that the balance of power still often lies in favor of local government and suggests the need for training and capacity building of both civil society organizations and local government managers to rectify this situation. She recommends that both parties to the partnership should have a clear understanding of their respective roles and responsibilities with respect to planning and implementing sustainable development projects within the local government sphere.

Nel's contribution focuses on the microlevel of local government; Noorjahan Bava takes a macroperspective to explore India's march toward sustainable development, a challenging process in governance throughout the world. For Bava, sustainable development is about human endeavors for the realization of the development ideals and goals of intergenerational equity, intergender equity, and intranational and international equity. She further sees sustainable development as a multidimensional concept, which entails ecological, socioeconomic, and politicocultural sustainability. As a process, sustainable development denotes all efforts made by the people individually and collectively and by the government at various levels aimed at the fulfillment of the basic needs of life with scope for improvement in the quality of life. This process must establish and maintain synergy between development and environment; that is, concern for conservation of natural resources and ecological balance should be integrated into developmental plans and strategies. Bava examines all these theoretical issues, addresses people's participation in sustainable development and the performance failures, and alludes to some empirical findings on India's performance on the sustainable development front. She concludes her chapter on a pessimistic note that India has to walk many miles before achieving sustainable development. With this brief background on policies and institutions, the contributors in the following section gear their focus on national and regional sustainable development experiences.

Part III. Sustainable Development: National and Regional Experiences

Addressing the challenges of microfinance in Asia, Kathryn Gow first notes the increasing growth of microfinance schemes, which are making a remarkable difference in the life of individuals who have access to microcredit loans. These individuals are often women, and their only alternative (outside loans from families) has been to borrow cash from traditional moneylenders; this process in turn leads them to be exploited and locks them into the continuing cycle of poverty because of very high interest rates.

Gow's chapter focuses primarily on the goals, objectives, and strategies for microfinance schemes and the overarching policies that have allowed them to flourish. The author points out that since most microfinance programs are conducted in rural areas, public policy on rural development has a vital influence on the support, funding, and regulation of poverty alleviation and rural development strategies. She further remarks that the presence of microfinance institutions in rural areas may be preventing rural people from migrating to the cities in search of work; the more people leave a community, the more the remaining community suffers from the absence of those human resources and their income. Undoubtedly, policies that facilitate microfinance schemes and institutions need to have strategies that ensure the review of the management and monitoring of such activities within an overarching conceptualization of sustainability.

As Gow focuses on the microfinance experiences in Asia, Patricia Hippler investigates how American citizens, through a variety of tools, are turning their communities around and generating optimism for the sustainable future. Her chapter examines the value of a participatory approach to sustainable neighborhood revitalization and underscores the critical role of participation in sustainable development efforts. She further outlines some of the more common tools to facilitate participation, provides examples of participation efforts in various cities across the country, and concludes with an important discussion of the limits and constraints of participation, as well as some suggestions to overcome the challenges.

Following the challenges of revitalizing the urban cities in North America, the third chapter in this section looks at the experience of sustaining rural development in Nigeria, the most populous country in Africa. Indeed, Andrew Zekeri reiterates that contemporary trends in the rural areas of many African countries seem to demand bold initiatives in rural policy and a concerted effort in sustainable rural development policy, highlighting how a comprehensive and effective rural policy has been an elusive goal and sustainable rural development policy has become more of a rhetoric exercise than a reality at both national and international levels. He further notes that searching for a sustainable rural development policy for Africa in the 21st century requires a critical review of previous rural development policies and projects to identify the major pitfalls. Such a review can suggest directions for a new agenda to apply social science research and education in the search for sustainable development policy and administration.

Concretely, his chapter examines the impact of an agricultural development project on rural farmers and their farming system, paying attention to the adoption of recommended farm practices and reasons why the project failed to alleviate poverty and to increase domestic output of agricultural products. The chapter further identifies some of the essential elements of sustainable rural development that are used as criteria for assessing the performance of the World Bank–sponsored agricultural development project. Zekeri presents finally some policy implications of the findings and lessons learned for sustainable rural development in the 21st century.

Similarly, in searching for development solutions for depressed rural areas in the United States of America, David Walker explores how various states turned to prisons as an engine for local economic development when traditional underpinnings of rural economies—including farming and resource extraction—were eroding. He argues that changing public policies toward drug abuse, crime, and incarceration resulted in an explosion in the number of state and federal prisoners after the mid-1970s, prompted rural communities to compete for prisons with hopes of attracting jobs and rebuilding their economy. Envisioning recession-proof prosperity and growth guaranteed by steadily increasing incarceration rates, as well as multiplier effects to spur new businesses, rural communities all over the country offered a variety of inducements to attract prisons.

Walker, moreover, reviews the growing body of research that indicates how the tangible economic benefits of prison construction to host communities are negligible and may even be negative in some cases. Meanwhile, the social costs of hosting a prison remain largely overlooked in cost–benefit assessments since those costs are difficult to measure. Furthermore, the author expands on the future prospects of rural prison economies, which are increasingly uncertain, and underscores that prisons have turned out to be unreliable engines of rural economic development.

Along the lines of regional and national sustainable development experiences, the chapter authored by Watana Luanrata and C. Visvanathan emphasizes the crucial issues of waste management in the metropolis of Bangkok, underscoring how spills of waste, dust problems during transport, and malodor from transfer stations and landfill sites constitute some of the technical problems encountered in waste management, problems about which affected citizens have complained. Moreover, waste collectors and scavengers work in an unhealthy environment, which creates a serious social problem. The authors suggest additional sustainable measures based on the legal, financial, and technical instruments and motivation to exert control in the waste generation, sound collection system, market for recycle and reuse, dissemination of information and environmental education, a monitoring system for the proposed activities, and pilot projects.

As Luanrata and Visvanathan deal with waste management problems in the Bangkok metropolitan area, Britta Meinke takes a macroperspective in studying the international hazardous waste trade. In her chapter, she documents how the transboundary movements of hazardous wastes are a phenomenon of the industrialized world and are legitimized with free trade and labor sharing in waste disposal among states with the same economic and environmental standards. Meinke further notes how the poorest countries in the world joined the group of potential importing countries for hazardous wastes, highlighting the extent to which the new "importing countries" usually lacked the financial, technical, legal, and institutional capacity for monitoring trade in hazardous waste and preventing illegal imports. Ultimately, controlling the transfrontier movement of hazardous wastes requires governments and international organizations to support efforts to achieve an effective international regime, here conceived as sets of implicit or explicit principles, norms, rules, and decision-making procedures around which actors' expectations converge in a given area of international relations.

The chapter provides insights on how international environmental regimes can contribute to sustainable development, supporting the argument that in some issue areas, states establish and maintain not only global regimes but also regional ones to ensure effective protection of the environment. She alludes to the Basel Convention on the Control of Trans-Boundary Movements of Hazardous Wastes and Their Disposal signed in March 1989 by 35 countries and the European Community. The provisions of the Basel Convention cover the generation, management, and disposal of hazardous wastes.

Thus far, the chapters in this section have dealt with microfinance in Asia, neighborhood revitalization in the United States, rural development in Sub-Saharan Africa, rural development in the United States, waste management in Bangkok, and international hazardous waste trade. In the last chapter of this section, Paul Mocombe looks at the institutionalization of poverty in the Third World using the case of Grenada. Starting with the argument that some developing countries' governments sell their countries and people to foreign investors in nontraditional export sectors through the establishment of export-processing zones (EPZs), which are labor-intensive manufacturing centers involved in the import of raw materials and the export of factory products, Mocombe claims that such export-processing arrangements leave these countries and their citizens at the mercy of foreign manufacturers. He further attempts to shed light on globalization and its necessary outcome—the institutionalization of poverty throughout the Third World—within the relational signs of the Protestant ethic, interpreting the impact of globalization from the context of the Grenadian government, which has adopted (forcefully) this way of life. As for any new phenomenon, the pros and cons of the impact of globalization have been the subject of serious debate in recent years, and the following section alludes to some of the arguments when addressing sustainable development's current and future challenges.

Part IV. Sustainable Development: Current and Future Challenges

For the last two decades, development researchers have attempted to ascertain the factors that prevent development from being sustainable while searching for plausible strategies leading to sustainability. Some make the simplistic "one size fits all" development approaches the scapegoat of the majority of, if not all, development failures. Others view the current practice of identifying cause-and-effect linkages for a multifaceted phenomenon such as sustainable development and devising appropriate policies as the challenging task confronting development scholars. Overall, the state of the art in both the theory and the practice of implementing sustainable development policies in both the "North" and "South" is still deficient.

Since translating policy reforms and program intentions into results that ultimately produce benefits and better lives for citizens is the heart of sustainability endeavors, Gedeon Mudacumura reviews the development literature, exploring the challenges of implementing sustainable development policies in both developed and developing countries. One of the critical challenges has been the language and terminology gap between theorists and practitioners, and bridging this gap may lead to developing both wider and better understanding of implementation factors and the process linking policy goals to outcomes. Similarly, policy makers and public managers face the challenge of sustaining policy reforms beyond the launch phase so that those policy changes, whose benefits rarely appear in the short term, can bear fruit. The author further looks at the fragmented nonlinear nature of the policy process, and elaborates on policy implementation in a multiorganizational context, putting more emphasis on the crucial interactions of development organizations committed to various forms of social change and development leading to strong sustainable communities.

Building on his experience in less developed countries (LDCs), Anthony Barclay contends that the pursuit of human development has been and remains exceedingly challenging because of the complexity of the issues, the peculiarities of contexts, and the enormity of the constraints. Thus, if sustainable development is to have any substantive operational significance, it must be defined more concretely to reflect contextual and spatial specificity. Otherwise it would serve only as an abstraction of limited pertinence to comprehending the dynamics and profound complexities of the issues concerning the improvement of human development.

From that perspective, Barclay's chapter addresses the challenges of improving human development, discussing sustainable development in the context of governance with reference to African countries in general, and Liberia in particular, within a political economy framework. From an institutional perspective, the author views governance and political economy as sustainable development's contextual features. He further presents the sustainable development challenges faced by most African countries, highlighting the Liberian situation as a case study to provide an empirical content. His emphasis on Liberia provides a credible indication through which one may understand the dramatic downward spiral of Liberia's socioeconomic conditions and the imperative for recovery along a path of sustainable development. To achieve this end, Barclay suggests a people-centered approach to institutional development in which capacity building prioritizes personal development so that progress and achievement may be realized not by the personalization of the issues, but rather by individuals' and groups' character, competence, and genuine commitment.

Besides the challenges of bridging the gap between theorists and practitioners, and the imperative of improving human development through capacity building, Getachew Assefa and Bjorn Frostell acknowledge the challenges of devising appropriate technologies with minimal negative impacts on the environment. Considering the current growth of world population and the shrinking of nonrenewable resources, the authors argue that the application of technologies will continue to increase in line with the quest for commensurate carrying capacity of the Earth.

In light of the rapid evolution of science and technology that leads to increased energy and resource consumption and environmental pollution,

Assefa and Frostell allude to the 1972 Stockholm Conference, which brought to light the undesirable impact of technologies. Among other areas of concern, the conference underscored the need for understanding and controlling the man-made changes in the major ecological systems, the need for accelerating the dissemination of environmentally sound technologies and for developing alternatives to existing harmful technologies, and the need to avoid commitment to new technologies before adequately assessing their environmental consequences. Of the approaches and tools proposed to assess different impacts of technical systems, technology assessment (TA) has won institutional recognition since its inception, and the Congressional Office of Technology Assessment (OTA) in the United States was founded with the aim to study technological change and provide early indications of the probable positive and negative impacts of the application of technology. The authors elaborate on the concept of TA, pointing out the limitations associated with conventional TA. Current activities at the international level are also presented.

Similarly, the chapter by Ralph Luken and Nadejda Komendantova-Amann addresses the challenge of assessing the outcomes of sustainable development strategies in developing and transitional economies. One of the recommendations of the Rio Conference required countries to jointly optimize their various sectoral economic, social, and environmental policies and plans for the sake of achieving sustainable development. In that context, most developing country governments have made efforts to draw up national sustainable development strategies, and the last World Summit on Sustainable Development (WSSD) in Johannesburg called for the completion and the beginning of the implementation of those strategies by 2005.

With regard to recent assessment of industry-related issues, the authors refer to the International Forum on National Sustainable Development Strategies, which discussed the experiences in formulating national sustainable development strategies and highlighted a number of obstacles in the realization of these strategies such as the inability of many countries to develop a clear approach to the issue or to create effective assessment mechanisms; a proliferation of policies, activities, and institutions focusing on different sustainable development concerns but with no or little coordination among ministries or agencies; and the inadequate sharing of the experience gathered.

Given the dearth of information about the role of industry in sustainable development, the United Nations Industrial Development Organization (UNIDO), as part of its preparatory activities for WSSD, requested national experts in 18 developing and transitional economies to report on the extent to which recent changes in industrial, environmental, and technology policies have more closely aligned industrial development objectives with sustainable development objectives. The experts were also requested to assess the impact of industry (manufacturing in particular) on sustainable development, roughly over the period 1990 to 2000, to report on obstacles encountered in enhancing the positive and reducing the negative impacts of industry on sustainable development, and to put forward proposals for enhancing the contribution of industry to sustainable development.

Thus, Luken and Komendantova-Amann use the 18 national reports and international data sources to ascertain the impact of industry on sustainable development in the 18 countries. Considering the qualitative nature of the economic, social, and environmental data in these national reports, the assessment draws only on data available from international organizations. The authors characterize available industry-relevant data on all three dimensions of sustainable development—social, economic, and ecological—and then elaborate on trends in a few of the identified parameters to give a sense of what happened on each of the three dimensions over the period 1990 to 2000 and present an integrative index using a methodology similar to the one used by the United Nations Development Program in constructing the Human Development Index. The chapter concludes with a summary of the perceptions of the country experts about the obstacles to enhancing the socioeconomic impacts and mitigating the negative environmental impacts of industry on sustainable development.

In terms of ascertaining the current and future challenges to sustainable development, G. Miller and Tracy Berno's chapter reviews the changing conceptualizations of the tourism industry, particularly as they relate to sustainable tourism. Currently, tourism is the world's largest economic sector and its economic importance is indisputable. Tourism is one of the top five export categories for 83% of all countries in the world and the main source of foreign exchange for at least 38% of countries. Tourism is the only international trade in services in which the LDCs have consistently had surpluses compared with the rest of the world. Between 1980 and 1996, LDCs' positive balance in the travel account rose from US$4.6 billion to US$65.9 billion. This was driven primarily by the growth of inbound tourism to countries in Asia, the Pacific Islands, and Africa.

Moreover, the authors argue that having identified the potentially negative environmental impacts of tourism and having moved beyond a simple recognition of the economic benefits of tourism, development planners now need to advance beyond the reactionary interpretation that sustainable tourism (ST) is synonymous with ecotourism. This requires a more sophisticated understanding of the tourism industry that integrates the industry with other sectors of the economy and seeks further stakeholder involvement to promote sustainable development. The chapter concludes by presenting a discussion of the need to facilitate this conceptual shift through the development of indicators that can assist monitoring of whether tourism is moving toward or away from sustainability.

The last chapter in this section underlines the challenges facing health-care managers in the newly independent nations of the former Soviet Union. Patricia Cholewka analyzes these countries' health-care systems between 1991 and 2001 and highlights how health-care managers accustomed to a controlled command economy had a hard time in embracing the management premises of the free-market economy. Judged by Western health-care management models, the health-care systems in the newly independent nations of the former Soviet Union were incapable of meeting patient care standards within the dynamic, business-oriented, and consumer-driven environments of more established democratic countries. Among other constraints, these countries lacked adequate funding for advanced medical technology, relied on outdated clinical practice standards and administrative protocols, lacked comparable academic knowledge and an unbiased research base, and dealt with an entrenched bureaucracy that perpetrated a static health-care culture focused on therapeutics instead of disease prevention.

Cholewka's chapter presents a brief retrospective review of some of the intrinsic constraints influencing resistance to health-care change, the anticipated changes to these systems, and the actual program outcomes. She discusses the challenges of restructuring the inherited pro-Communist system's style, while profiling both unresolved and ongoing health-care issues that should be acknowledged in order to devise appropriate policies geared toward a sustainable health-care system. Sustaining the health-care system, she argues, requires paying attention to health-care financing, improving quality of health services, and mobilizing citizens and communities for better health.

Part V. Conclusion: Alternatives and Recommendations

Thus far, the chapters in this volume have looked at various aspects of the sustainable development phenomenon, pointing out some relevant concerns that need in-depth examination. The authors contributing to this last section shed light on some alternatives and specific recommendations for sustaining development. Concretely, Stephan Schwenke assesses the World Bank's new urban strategy created after the Bank realized that urban development activities could and should have a greater impact in raising the living standards of the poor and promoting equity. His chapter highlights how life is extremely tough in the urban areas in LDCs of the world, where the severity of poverty and the deprivation of opportunities constitute a profound moral challenge, a problem often overlooked by the rich and powerful in the South and in the more advanced, industrialized, and postindustrial economies of the world. His assessment raises several legitimate questions such as "Is it morally permissible to maintain distinct and inferior standards for people just because they are poor? If not, who would enforce a more equitable standard? Are there moral obligations that we have—as individuals and governments, North and South—to overcome deprivation and uphold a more uniform standard of dignity in the urban South? And why has so little been said, when discussing urbanization in the South, concerning such moral dimensions?"

The author explores the new urban strategy from ethical and moral perspectives and suggests some explicit amendments including the recognition of universal human dignity, the embracing of a process of moral analysis within governance processes, and the institutionalization of popular participation based on the moral equality of all persons. In this manner, each city might gradually move toward an explicit, integrated, and localized articulation of *the livable city* ideal, influencing development strategies and governance processes qualitatively, and providing the essential motivation for sustained beneficial change.

Whereas Schwenke narrows his focus to the World Bank's new urban strategy, the chapter authored by Lucio Munoz attempts to broaden the scope of sustainable development by bridging public and private interfaces. He introduces a framework that allows one to state the necessary and sufficient conditions for the existence of long-term full human rights–friendly development and describes the dilemmas that are generated when moving away from full human rights friendliness.

Concretely, Munoz's framework is based on whether or not development processes are fueled by the interaction of local and international human rights–friendly businesses and governments. Such a framework allows an appreciation of the structure of development processes when interacting business and government actions are considered to be human rights–unfriendly, or partially human rights–friendly, or totally human rights–friendly. The author describes the main human rights interfaces of businesses and governments to point out the need to work toward the promotion and implementation of proactive private–public human rights–friendly development models that are based on the notion of self-interest and regulation consistency. Using qualitative, comparative theoretical tools, Munoz shows how business self-interest can be framed to be human rights–friendly through effective monitoring and enforcement, and highlights the dilemmas generated when relaxing local and international monitoring and enforcement mechanisms partially or totally.

Munoz's chapter uses qualitative comparative analysis to underscore the need for businesses and governments to jointly optimize their collaboration for the materialization of human-centered development. Shifting the focus to the foundation principles of accounting, Kala Saravanamuthu evaluates accounting's contributions to the development of analytical tools that should promote innovation and implementation of sustainable practices. She recognizes the underlying connection between information and the decision-making process and argues that it can no longer be assumed that "better" information will always results in greater optimality. Her chapter adds an ethical dimension to March and Simons's satisficing decision processes. Information, she contends, refers to analytical data, which involve rethinking how accounting represents business performance because management decisions can either (further) aggravate or mitigate the impact of business activities on the fragile socioecological environment, which has already been ravaged by organizational practices that have prioritized economic growth above everything else.

Acknowledging that society does not have the luxury of postponing ethical issues until it has generated "enough" money, Saravanamuthu examines the ethics behind the various definitions of sustainable development and assesses a number of competing interpretations with regard to the meaning and implications of sustainability while attempting to make sense of the pertinent question regarding managers' accountability under an ethos of sustainable development. In her critique of accounting's contribution to the sustainability debate, she draws on a European study of environmental management accounting practices and the most recent Global Reporting Initiative to determine whether accounting is living up to contemporary societal expectations: that is, to engender socioenvironmentally conscious decisions.

In the concluding chapter of this volume, Shamsul Haque looks at the critical impacts of inequality on sustainable development, contending that current studies on sustainable development encompass its major dimensions, causes, and implications, which are embedded in its diverse concepts, approaches, models, and even policies. However, a major component of existing research are the "causes" challenging sustainability or leading to unsustainability. Some of these common causes include environmental predicaments, population explosion, modern economic growth, industrialization and urban expansion, and human poverty.

His chapter recognizes these causes of unsustainable development but stresses another more serious but overlooked cause—various forms of inequality within and between nations such as economic inequality, consumption inequality, social inequality, political inequality, and cultural inequality—attempting to explain how these major forms of inequality may have caused greater harm to the environment and sustainability than the other widely discussed causal factors. The chapter concludes with a recommendation that these major forms of inequalities must be resolved to a certain extent in order to ensure a meaningful form of sustainable development in all nations and regions.

References

Anand, S., and Sen, A. (1994). Sustainable Human Development: Concepts and Priorities. Occasional Paper, July 1994. New York: Human Development Report Office, United Nations Development Programme.

Beierle, C.T. (1999). Using social goals to evaluate public participation in environmental decisions. *Policy Studies Review*, 16(3/4): 75–103.

Capra, F. 1982. *The Turning Point: Science, Society and the Rising Culture*. New York: Simon & Schuster.

Crabbé, P.J. (1997). Sustainable Development: Concepts, Measures, Market and Policy Failures at the Open Economy, Industry and Firm Levels. Occasional Paper No. 16, October 1997. Ontario: Industry Canada.

Daly, E.H. (1996). *Beyond Growth*. Boston: Beacon Press.

DeLeon, Peter. (1992). The democratization of the policy sciences. *Public Administration Review*, 52(2): 125–129.

Dryzek, J.S. (1990). *Discursive Democracy: Politics, Policy Science, and Political Science*. Cambridge: Cambridge University Press.

Estes, R.J. (1993). Toward sustainable development: From theory to praxis. *Social Development Issues*, 15(3): 1–29.

Flint, R.W. (2004). Sustainable Development: What Does Sustainability Mean to the Individual in the Conduct of Their Life and Business? In: Mudacumura, G.M., and Haque, S.M., eds., *Handbook of Development Policy Studies*. New York: Marcel Dekker.

Forrester, J.W. (1994). Systems dynamics, systems thinking, and soft OR. *System Dynamics Review*, 10: 245–256.

Goulet, D. (1980). Development experts: The one-eyed giants. *World Development*, 8: 481–489.

Guimaraes, R.P. (2004). The Dilemmas of Sustainable Development: Politics, Institutions and Social Participation. In: Mudacumura, G.M., and Haque, S.M., eds., *Handbook of Development Policy Studies*. New York: Marcel Dekker.

Haque, M.S. (1999a). The fate of sustainable development under the neoliberal regimes in developing countries. *International Political Science Review*, 20(2): 199–222.

Haque, M.S. (1999b). *Restructuring Development Theories and Policies: A Critical Study*. Albany: State University of New York Press.

Haque, M.S. (2000). Environmental discourse and sustainable development: Linkages and limitations. *Ethics & the Environment*, 5(1): 1–19.

Hempel, L.C. (1996). *Environmental Governance: The Global Challenge*. Washington, D.C.: Island Press.

Hueting, Roefie. (1992). Growth, Environment, and National Income: Theoretical Problems and a Practical Solution. In: Ekins, P., and Max-Neef, M. eds., *Real-Life Economics: Understanding Wealth Creation*. London: Routledge, pp. 255–264.

Hyden, G. (1997). Civil society, social capital, and development: Dissection of a complex discourse. *Studies in Comparative International Development*, 32(1): 3–30.

Ismail, R. (1997). Five years after Rio and still questions left unanswered. *Reuters*, June 28, 1997, p. B14.

Kelly, K.L. (1998). A systems approach to identifying decisive information for sustainable development. *European Journal of Operational Research*, 109: 452–464.

Lindblom, Charles E. (1965). *The Intelligence of Democracy*. New York: Free Press.

Mudacumura, G.M. (2002). Towards a General Theory of Sustainability: Bridging Key Development Dimensions through a Multi-Paradigm Perspective. Doctoral dissertation, Pennsylvania State University, Harrisburg.

Mudacumura, G.M. (2004). Development Agenda for the 21st Century. In: Mudacumura, G.M., and Haque, S.M., eds., *Handbook of Development Policy Studies*. New York: Marcel Dekker.

Randolph, J., and Bauer, M. (1999). Improving environmental decision-making through collaborative methods. *Policy Studies Review*, 16(3/4): 168–191.

Reed, D. (1996). *Structural Adjustment, the Environment, and Sustainable Development*. London: Earthscan.

Reid, D. (1995). *Sustainable Development: An Introductory Guide*. London: Earthscan.

Rondinelli, D.A. (1982). The dilemma of development administration: Complexity and uncertainty in control-oriented bureaucracies. *World Politics*, 35(1): 43–71.

Saeed, K. (1994). *Development Planning and Policy Design: A System Dynamics Approach*. Avebury, England: Aldeshot.

Sheeran, K. (2004). Equity and Efficiency in International Environmental Agreements: A Case Study of the Kyoto Protocol. In: Mudacumura, G.M., and Haque, S.M., eds., *Handbook of Development Policy Studies*. New York: Marcel Dekker.

Stiglitz, J. (1998). *Towards a New Paradigm for Development: Strategies, Policies, and Processes*. Geneva: UNCTAD.

Stiglitz, J. (2002). *Globalization and Its Discontents*. New York: W.W. Norton.

Stone, D.C. (1966). Guidelines for training development administrators. *Journal of Administration Overseas*, 5(4): 229–242.

United Nations Development Programme. (1996). *Human Development Report*. New York: Oxford University Press.

World Bank. (1983). *World Development Report 1983*. Oxford: Oxford University Press.

World Bank. (1998). *Assessing Aid, What Works, What Doesn't and Why*. Oxford: Oxford University Press.

World Commission on Environment and Development. (1987). *Our Common Future*. Oxford and New York: Oxford University Press.

Chapter 2

Limits of "Sustainable Development" as a Concept

M. Shamsul Haque

CONTENTS

Introduction and Background

In recent years, the growing worldwide concern for a sustainable mode of progress or development has led to a proliferation of academic discourse and policy debate on the issue, which in turn has created a greater need for articulating the meanings of sustainable development, reconciling its diverse connotations, and reaching a conceptual consensus in this regard. The significance of this conceptual clarity and consensus lies in the fact that the vast field of development studies, in which sustainable development is a recent addition, is replete with irreconcilable ideological differences, theoretical impasse, and policy controversies. In addition, compared to well-established and widely debated topics in economic development, the question of sustainability is relatively new in terms of its systematic study, and that newness also signifies the need for its proper conceptual clarification.

However, in the evolution of sustainable development as a concept, it is possible to discern some major events and stages. In the 1960s, international conferences such as the Ecological Aspects of International Development Conference in Washington, D.C. (1968), and the UNESCO Biosphere Conference in Paris (1968) emphasized the significance of environmental sustainability in pursuing economic development (Barrow, 1995, p. 369). During this period, it was increasingly realized that there are serious limits of environmental capacity to assimilate wastes created in the process of economic growth (Crabbé, 1997). In this regard, several case studies on development projects pointed out the limits of economic growth and stressed the need for finding alternatives to balance economic growth with environmental concern. This emerging focus on environmental questions, which implied the growing challenge to the sustainability of prevailing modes of development, became more globally recognized because of the United Nations Conference on the Human Environment (1972) attended by 119 countries, which resulted in the *Stockholm Declaration on the Human Environment* as well as *Action Plan for the Human Environment*, which emphasized more environment-friendly development plans and strategies and more effective environmental assessment and protection at the national and international levels (Reid, 1995).

While this increasing realization of the environment–development linkage represented significant progress in advancing the principle of sustainability, it was the International Union for the Conservation of Nature (IUCN) that in 1980 formally introduced the term *sustainable development*, especially through its report *World Conservation Strategy: Living Resources Conservation for Sustainable Development* (IUCN, 1980). In this IUCN report, the concept of sustainability stressed the need for integrating natural conservation and economic development, preserving biodiversity, and taking care of the biosphere for the current and future generations (IUCN, 1980; Mebratu, 2000). In 1986, the IUCN also organized the Ottawa Conference on Conservation and Development, which paid attention to the significance of people's basic needs, self-determination, social justice, and ecological integrity for sustainable development (Reid, 1995). To a great extent, these IUCN initiatives represented a precursor to subsequent efforts to conceptualize sustainable development, including the definition provided by the report of the World Commission on Environment and Development (WCED).

For this widely known WCED report *Our Common Future*, which is also known as the Brundtland Report (named after Gro Harlem Brundtland, who headed the WCED), sustainable development is "development that meets the needs of the present without compromising the ability of future generations to meet their own needs" (WCED, 1987, p. 8). In articulating such a concept of sustainable development, the Brundtland Report not only emphasizes the satisfaction of basic needs (e.g., food, water, energy, sanitation) for the current and future generations, it also requires a change toward a new pattern of economic growth that is equitable and sustainable (Crabbé, 1997; Mebratu, 2000). The report also stresses the need for attaining a sustainable level of population, reorienting technology, conserving resources, and pursuing participatory development (WCED, 1987). The Brundtland Report played a crucial role in establishing sustainable development as a global model, and to a great extent, shaped the agenda for the subsequent debates at the UN Conference on Environment and Development or Earth Summit (1992), the Kyoto Conference (1997), the World Summit on Sustainable Development (2002), and so on. Among these recent events, however, it is the Earth Summit that became one of the most effective means to reinforce the significance of environmental sustainability and generate global awareness of the environment–development relationship. The major outcomes of this Earth Summit, including the Convention on Biological Diversity, the Convention on Climate Change, the Rio Declaration, and Agenda 21, draw attention to the importance of some major dimensions of environmental sustainability in pursuing socioeconomic development (Haque, 2000).

During the period since this Earth Summit, sustainable development has been illustrated and advocated through many other conferences, workshops, books, journals, and reports. Despite the proliferation of such debates and publications, there are critics who argue that the concepts of sustainable development remain quite vague, contradictory, confusing, and overlapping (Daly 1996; Langhelle, 1999; Thomas, 1990). This conceptual ambiguity has allegedly become a source of disagreement rather than consensus (Daly 1996; Holmen, 2001). It is argued that the connotations of sustainable development based on individual interpretations have become so diverse that the concept has often been "misused" and become almost "meaningless" (Holmen, 2001). In this regard, it is necessary to articulate a more comprehensive concept of sustainable development in order to have any meaningful discourse and effective policy agenda on the issue. It is pointed out by Sachs (1991) and Lele (1991) that the imprecise concepts of sustainable development may lead to conflicting policies, and its inconsistent interpretations need to be overcome if it is to be accepted as a "meaningful paradigm" of development. This chapter examines the existing interpretations of sustainable development, evaluates their major limitations, and concludes by offering some suggestions to reach a comprehensive view on the concept.

Existing Interpretations of Sustainable Development

During recent decades, the number of concepts or interpretations related to sustainable development almost exploded across academic disciplines as well as among national and international policy circles, although the actual conceptual differences among them seem to be quite superficial (Crabbé, 1997; Langhelle, 1999). This proliferation of sustainable development concepts offered by academics, policy experts, and international institutions has become quite unmanageable and may require some classification of such fragmented, overlapping, and repetitive concepts into broader conceptual categories. In general, most existing concepts of sustainable development can be categorized into three major perspectives: (1) the human-centric perspective, which emphasizes the primacy of human economic needs and values (for both current and future generations); (2) the ecocentric perspective, which stresses the inherent value or goodness in environmental sustainability beyond human needs; and (3) the dualistic perspective, which tends to focus on both human needs and environmental concerns.

First, under the *human-centric perspective,* which is also known as the anthropocentric paradigm, the idea of sustainable development emerged as a means to express the concern for the continuing satisfaction of human needs across generations, which increasingly appeared to be under challenge by the worsening ecological disorder and rapid resource depletion. In this regard, the IUCN report emphasized the conservation of resources with a view to overcoming the deteriorating ecological condition challenging human development (Atkinson, 2000). More importantly, the Brundtland Report clearly expressed the primacy of human needs of the current and future generations in its definition of sustainable development, an anthropocentric view (Langhelle, 2000, p. 300; WCED, 1987, p. 8). For this Brundtland Report, which has been one of the most frequently cited sources of the sustainability concept since its publication in 1987, the "exploitation of resources" should be consistent with present and future human needs (WCED, 1987, pp. 8–10).

Since the publication of this report, there has been a significant expansion of conceptual debate on sustainable development dominated by such a human-centric perspective for which the main focus is on the maintenance of the ecological support system needed for the continuing survival of the human species (Liverman et al., 1988). In particular, the emphasis is on how to maintain the availability of necessary natural resources and conducive living atmosphere for future generations by ensuring that the current rates of resource use and waste disposal do not exceed the rates of resource regeneration and waste absorption (Pearce, 1988). The "thoroughput" approach of Daly (2002) also holds this view of sustainable development by stressing the principle that the "physical flow from nature's sources" (which passes through the economy and returns to "nature's sinks") should not decline and the ecosystem's regenerative capacity should be sustained, so that the access of future generations to the ecosystem's resources remains at least equivalent to that of the present generation.

Within the human-centric perspective, there is also the neoclassical economic interpretation of sustainability. For this neoclassical approach, the problems of environment are largely caused by the lack of its proper valuation, for which it is necessary to treat the environment as a commodity in order to make sure that it is not freely overused and thus is protected more effectively (Redclift and Benton, 1994). Once the environment as a commodity is appropriately priced by creating the supply and demand curves, most societies will adopt protection measures, which would eventually be favorable to sustainable development (Jacobs, 1994; Moffat, Hanley, and Wilson, 2001). In line with this neoclassical approach, some scholars highlight the need for assessing environmental assets and transactions and increasing utility over time (OECD, 2001). This main tenet of the neoclassical approach implies the instrumental value of the environment (commodity) to human needs (utility). On the other hand, those who analyze sustainable development in the context of poorer developing countries also favor the human-centric perspective; they prescribe self-reliant economic progress, improvements in people's living standards, and satisfaction of basic needs as a means to stop environmental degradation and enhance sustainable development, because poverty and scarcity often compel people to become overreliant on ecological resources (Barbier, 1987; Tolba, 1987).

Second, the *ecocentric perspective* represents an understanding of sustainable development that is almost the opposite of the human-centric perspective in terms of its overwhelming emphasis on the significance of ecology as an end in itself rather than as a means for satisfying present and future human needs. However, there are some major theoretical strands within this perspective, including the so-called deep ecology, ecofeminism, and ecosocialism. The proponents of deep ecology, including its founder, Arne Naess, are critical of the human-centric perspective (also known as "shallow ecology") and its tendency to dichotomize human species and nature, assess the environment in terms of its use value to human concerns, and so on (Dias, 2002). For this deep ecology approach, there is no separation between humans and natural environment, all species have equal rights to life, and all should live in harmony (Li, 1996). Thus, this approach emphasizes the Earth's richness in biodiversity and equality among all species forming the land community (Mebratu, 2000). It also believes in the intrinsic value of nature and its living beings and nonliving objects irrespective of whether they are useful or valuable to human species (Li, 1996).

On the other hand, for those who advocate the ecofeminist view introduced by Francoise d'Eaubonne, the contemporary ecological crisis is a consequence of an existing male-dominant system that exploits both women and nature (Dias, 2002, p. 205). Proponents seek to explain the linkages between the subjugation of women and subjugation of nature (Warren, 1993). They believe that the replacement or elimination of such a male-dominant system, which poses threats to women and nature, is the main solution to this problem. The ecocentric perspective is also endorsed by the proponents of ecosocialism, which is similar to the so-called social ecology introduced by Murray Bookchin. The main contention of ecosocialism is that the realization of sustainable development is hardly possible under the capitalist market system, which is largely responsible for ecological destruction, and that this capitalist development has to be replaced with an ecology-driven socialist development (Mebratu, 2000).

Third, the *dualistic perspective* tends to pay attention to both the human and ecological dimensions of sustainable development. Some authors emphasize the need for recognizing the crucial relationship between the "economic system" and the "ecological system" in order to ensure both the continuity of human life and the diversity of ecological conditions (Constanza, Daly, and Bartholomew, 1991; Norton, 1992). Because of this linkage between human existence and the ecological system, the challenge is how to maintain the basic human living condition without jeopardizing the ecological system that supports that condition. This argument regarding the human–ecology relationship in sustainable development is strengthened further by stressing the interaction and interdependence between human needs and ecological integrity. It is believed that the goals of economic development and ecological sustainability can be mutually reinforcing rather than contradictory (Lele, 1991).

In line with the dualistic outlook on sustainable development, there are authors whose policy stance is to make sure that human economic activities remain within the ecological bounds, that the ability of nature to provide the life-support system is recognized and respected, and that the role of environmental inputs in raising the quality of life is appreciated (Norton, 1992; Pearce and Watford, 1993). Greater importance is also given to the maintenance of a self-sustaining ecological system while pursuing human development (Norton, 1992). However, the mode development itself may need to be changed—and that may require serious compromises in economic growth that involves harmful practices—in order to maintain ecological sustainability. In this regard, there have emerged certain reform efforts within the traditional human-centric perspective, such as the so-called anthropocentric reformism, which is less concerned about the anthropocentric outlook in relation to environmental problems and pays more attention in this regard to hazardous human practices that "stem from ignorance, greed, illegal behavior, and shortsightedness" (Dias, 2002, p. 205).

From the preceding analysis, it can be understood that the dualistic perspective on sustainable development attempts to stress the importance of both human progress and ecological sustainability, instead of focusing too much on the use of the environment to satisfy present and future human needs (as in the human-centric perspective) or on the intrinsic value of the ecological system above human needs (as in the case of ecocentric perspective). The use of this dualistic perspective can be found not only in conceptual and theoretical literature; it is also pursued in some empirical studies on sustainable development emphasizing its operational indicators. For instance, in presenting the sustainability indicators, Kade-kodi (1992) covers human quality-of-life indicators (e.g., life expectancy, health standard, income level, and consumption pattern) as well as ecology-related indicators (e.g., atmospheric temperature, air and water quality, forest cover, plant and animal species, and soil quality).

Shortcomings of Existing Interpretations

In the preceding discussion on sustainable development, the chapter has explained the major categories of its conceptual interpretations falling under the human-centric, ecocentric, and dualist perspectives. These interpretations have their own limitations or drawbacks pointed out by various critics, which need to be examined in order to articulate a meaningful understanding of sustainable development. In this regard, this section attempts to examine some of the major limits of existing concepts or interpretations.

First, with regard to human-centric interpretations, many critics argue that this perspective on sustainable development is too utilitarian and tends to assess the value of nature in terms of its utility to satisfy human needs. Despite the emphasis on intergenerational equity, the fact remains that the focus is mainly on equity among human generations without much concern for other species, and human needs and preferences tend to be the utmost priority for most proponents of this perspective (Toman, 1992). The extent of such a utilitarian outlook is more intensive in the neoclassical economic approach to sustainability, which suggests that it is possible to deplete nonrenewable resources if adequate investment is made in alternative resources for future generations (Heyes and Liston-Heyes, 1995). In addition, although this perspective is strongly in favor of intergenerational equity, it seems to be relatively indifferent to the significance of resolving the severe inequality that currently exists between the rich and poor citizens and between the developed and developing countries. Sustainability ethics requires consideration of distributive justice (Guimaraes, 2001) not only for future generations but also for current societies and nations.

The human-centric perspective is also accused of being too concerned with economic growth: it prescribes policies and strategies in favor of economic growth that often causes rapid resource depletion and worsen ecological disorder (Haque, 2000; United Nations Development Programme, 1996). For some authors, the Brundtland Report itself expected to have "a new era of economic growth" and showed a certain bias toward it without specifying how such growth could be environmentally sustainable (Reid, 1995; WCED, 1987). It is this preference for continuing economic growth inherent in the mainstream human-centric concept of sustainable development for which many environmentalists dislike the concept (Holmen, 2001). It is argued further that sustainable development seems to worry about how environmental problems may affect economic growth rather than how this growth can affect the environment.

Second, there are also some major limits of the ecocentric perspective on sustainable development, although it attempts to overcome some of the shortcomings found in the human-centric view. For some authors, this perspective is quite unrealistic or impractical, because it tends to discourage humans from utilizing any nonrenewable natural resources, and that is quite unlikely to happen in the real world (Heyes and Liston-Heyes, 1995). In addition, although the proponents of ecocentrism assess the value of nature in terms of its very existence independently of human use and consciousness of it, the critics argue that such value has no relevance to humans and that it becomes valuable only when humans come in contact, recognize its intrinsic qualities, and often take action to conserve its integrity (Li, 1996). It is also observed that there are some contradictions inherent in the ecocentric perspective. In particular, this perspective considers human population a part of nature as other species are and believes all of them have an equal right to live; however, one of its main proponents (Arne Naess) seems to violate this principle by supporting artificial population control (Li, 1996).

In addition, the extreme goal of some advocates of ecocentrism to preserve everything "natural" without disruption by human action may overlook the fact that there are certain aspects of nature (e.g., various diseases and disasters) that do not always favor the survival of many species. As Holmen (2001) mentions, if there had been no human action or if all choices were surrendered to the fate determined by nature for the past centuries, then what we could still expect to be "natural" perhaps would be poverty, crop failures, tuberculosis, infant mortality, mass migration, and so on. Moreover, for some critics, although the supporters of the ecocentric perspective like to preserve unspoiled nature and its plant and animal species and want to enjoy the healing effect of such naturalness or "primitiveness" in developing societies, the people of these countries themselves want to overcome this status of "primitiveness" (Holmen, 2001). They may even interpret such an ecocentric position as an effort of international institutions such as the United Nations to manipulate developing countries to accept the environmental agenda set by Western nations (Crabbé, 1997, p. 5).

Third, although the ecocentric perspective, despite the limits mentioned, provides an alternative view on sustainability, the current national and international debates, conventions, and institutions are largely dominated by the human-centric perspective, often in its most utilitarian form. It can be easily observed that for two decades, the human-centric proposition on sustainable development presented by the Brundtland Report (*Our Common Future*) has been most dominant, and today a full-fledged "profession has grown up around that proposition" (Taylor, 2002, p. 2). The aftermath of the Brundtland Report has seen the emergence of some major competing definitions of sustainable development. Although these views are classified into so-called strong definitions and weak definitions, most of them remain in line with the report's human-centric outlook in terms of their common emphasis on the centrality of human needs for present and future generations, although they may differ in terms of how they prioritize the intergenerational trade-off in natural resources (Pearce and Warford, 1993; Taylor, 2002).

In the practical operationalization of sustainable development, the dominance of the human-centric perspective remains strong in environment-related conventions and protocols (e.g., the Vienna Convention, the Montreal Protocol, the Convention on Biological Diversity, and the Kyoto Protocol) as well as major institutions (e.g., the United Nations Environment Programme, the UN Commission on Sustainable Development, and the Secretariat of the Convention on Biological Diversity). In most such cases, there is hardly any scope for the assumptions or beliefs found in deep ecology, ecofeminism, or ecosocialism: they are largely guided by the mainstream or conventional meaning of sustainability, which advocates the survival of human species across generations through maintaining the Earth's life support systems and adopting appropriate policies and institutions in this regard (Liverman et al., 1988).

Fourth, the existing perspectives on sustainable development tend to be quite reductionist in terms of their narrow focus mainly on material human needs and environmental concerns—that is, the economic and ecological realms of development—while overlooking social, political, cultural, and ethical dimensions. But for some scholars, the realization of overall sustainability is highly dependent on social reality (e.g., poverty and inequality), political structure (e.g., scope for people's participation), cultural values and ethics (e.g., belief in conservation), and even socio-psychological needs (e.g., desire for nonmaterial peace and contentment) (Guimaraes, 2004; Haque, 1999b; Taylor, 2002).

With regard to the reductionist tendency in the sustainability debate, some have observed that this model is relatively indifferent to the role of cultural norms in development, that environmental sustainability must be a part of the larger socioecological system, and that a broader definition of sustainable development should cover all the ecological, social, economic, political, and cultural spheres of sustainability (Corson, 1994; Crabbé, 1997; Haque, 2000). But the dominant human-centric perspective on sustainability is more concerned for the continuing survival of the human species without much attention to how the realization of this sustainability can be affected by other human dimensions such as society, politics, and culture. Similarly, the narrow focus of the ecocentric perspective on the ecosystem as an autonomous entity appears to exclude these other dimensions of development.

Finally, the preceding perspectives on sustainable development tend to present their respective views as universal, and they remain quite contextless in terms of their indifference to contextual variations that affect the possibility of sustainability itself. The generalization of the dominant human-centric view of sustainability into a universal development concept is done by separating the environment–development nexus from the societal context, which varies among nations (Redclift, 1988). This tendency represents the common Western tradition in which an artificial dichotomy is made between nature and society and the ecosystem is presented as a contextless category in order to claim the scientific reliability and universal validity of Western environmental knowledge (Norgaard, 1988). There are some serious shortcomings in such decontextualized interpretations of sustainability. For example, the main focus of sustainable development on the continuing satisfaction of human needs across generations ignores the fact that the perception of such "needs" itself varies among cultures and among generations (Haque, 2000). What are considered parts of basic necessity in developed nations such as the United States (e.g., personal computers and private cars) might be viewed as luxurious consumption items in poorer developing countries such as India. What are accepted as normal consumption goods by the present generation (e.g., electricity, telephone, television) could be perceived as parts of an affluent lifestyle by the previous generation.

With regard to the outlook on nature, whereas the Western assumption of the nature–society dichotomy encourages control over nature by expanding science, technology, and industry, the Eastern or traditional belief in nature–society coexistence prescribes living in harmony with nature (Haque, 2000; Norgaard, 1988). Historically, before the Western colonial intervention, the indigenous cultural values in Africa, Asia, and Latin America were largely in favor of environment-friendly principles such as prudent use of resources and care for nature and the ecosystem (Haque, 2000). The above cross-cultural and intergenerational variations in the concepts of human need and ecology are often ignored in much of the current discourse on sustainability. In this context, it is not surprising that developing countries often consider sustainable development an ideology used by developed nations to stifle their economic progress (Crabbé, 1997). Regarding the parochial understanding of, and contextual diversity in, sustainable development, Redclift (1988) mentions that the current environmental discourse remains ethnocentric, and that sustainability takes different meanings in postindustrial and transitional societies.

Concluding Remarks

First, one major challenge to building a comprehensive concept of sustainable development is to create a synthesis or reconciliation between human needs and the ecology. Although the dualistic perspective tries to present a balanced view, it offers mostly a technical summation of some of the essential tenets of the human-centric and ecocentric perspectives rather than a more creative framework based on the dynamic interaction and interdependence between the human species and the ecosystem. There are some authors, however, who attempt to bridge this gap by stressing the interaction and connectivity between the two (Gladwin et al., 1995). Guimaraes (2001) emphasizes the need for maintaining the integrity of nature and preserving biodiversity (giving equal rights to all species) at the same time, and for this the author prescribes a shift from anthropocentrism (human-centrism) to biopluralism. The point here is that there is a need for working out an appropriate framework based on a creative synthesis between human needs and ecological needs.

Second, as discussed, the existing perspectives on sustainability focus on intergenerational equity while largely overlooking the issue of intragenerational equality among classes and nations. My other chapter in this volume discusses the point that interclass and international inequalities constitute one of the most critical causes of environmental unsustainability.

It is not only the rich who contribute to environmental degradation by consuming hazardous goods, it is also the poor who create pressure on environmental resources by clearing forest, overcultivating land, and so on. Guimaraes (2001) mentions that people in extreme poverty are unlikely to have any concern for environmental sustainability because of their own vulnerable condition. The main contention here is that the concept of sustainable development must go beyond intergenerational equity and incorporate the principle of equality within and between nations.

Third, the current perspectives are mostly concerned with human needs and/or ecological problems, and this parochial outlook needs to be overcome by covering the social, political, cultural, and spiritual dimensions of sustainability in order to construct a more comprehensive and holistic concept of sustainable development (Mudacumura, 2004). Some authors emphasize the significance of relating ecological sustainability to economic sustainability (e.g., poverty eradication and distributive justice), political sustainability (e.g., equality in sharing power), cultural sustainability (e.g., shared values and customs), and so on (Brown et al., 1988; Crabbé, 1997; Mudacumura, 2004). This multidimensional view on sustainable development is more likely to be effective in explicating the complex nature of sustainability.

Finally, the concept of sustainable development should overcome the tendency to claim universal applicability and recognize contextual diversity. It is emphasized by some authors that as the importance of biodiversity, the idea of sociodiversity should be taken into account, multiple identities and values should be appreciated, and diverse political settings should be recognized in a new paradigm of sustainability (Guimaraes, 2001). In other words, the concept of sustainable development should be flexible enough to consider the contextual variations among societies (Redclift, 1988). Before the emergence of the sustainability debate since the mid-1980s, there emerged diverse traditions of development theories (e.g., modernization theory and dependency theory) as well as alternative views on development such as "self-reliant development," "authentic development," "just development," and "emancipatory development" (Engel, 1990; Haque, 1999a). Although some of these development theories and perspectives were comprehensive, context-sensitive, and multidimensional, their prominence has declined perhaps because of the growing dominance of sustainable development as a new global model despite the limitations discussed. It is possible that the proponents of the sustainability model may have something valuable to learn from these earlier traditions of development thinking.

References

Atkinson, A. (2000). *Promoting Sustainable Human Development in Cities of the South: A Southeast Asian Perspective.* Geneva: United Nations Research Institute for Social Development.

Barbier, E. (1987). The concept of sustainable economic development. *Environmental Conservation* 14(2).

Barrow, C.J. (1995). Sustainable development: Concept, value and practice. *Third World Planning Review* 17(4): 369–386.

Brown, B.J. et al. (1988). Global sustainability: Towards measurement. *Environmental Management* 12(2).

Constanza, R., H.E. Daly, and J.A. Bartholomew (1991). Goals, agenda and policy recommendations for ecological economics. In R. Constanza (ed.), *Ecological Economics: The Science and Management of Sustainability.* Washington, D.C.: Island Press.

Corson, W.H. (1994). Changing course: An outline of strategies for a sustainable future. *Futures* 26(2): 206–223.

Crabbé, P.J. (1997, October). *Sustainable Development: Concepts, Measures, Market and Policy Failures at the Open Economy, Industry and Firm Levels.* Occasional Paper No. 16. Ontario: Industry Canada.

Daly, H.E. (1996). *Beyond Growth.* Boston: Beacon Press.

Daly, H.E. (2002). Sustainable development: Definitions, principles, policies. Speech delivered at the World Bank, April 30, 2002, Washington, D.C.

Dias, C.M.M. (2002). Sustainable development: The anthropocentric epistemology. In Stefan C.W. Krauter (ed.), *RIO 02—World Climate & Energy Event,* Proceedings of RIO 02. Rio de Janeiro: Imprinta Express.

Engels, J.R. (1990). Introduction: The ethics of sustainable development. In J. Engel and J.G. Engel (eds.), *The Ethics of Environment and Development: Global Challenge, International Response.* London: Belhaven, pp. 1–23.

Gladwin, T.N., J.J Kennelly, and T. Krause (1995). Shifting paradigms for sustainable development: Implications for management theory and research. *Academy of Management Review* 20(4): 874–907.

Guimaraes, R.P. (2001). The politics and ethics of sustainability as a new paradigm for public policy formation and development planning (I). *International Journal of Economic Development* 3(3).

Guimaraes, R.P. (2004). The political and institutional dilemmas of sustainable development. In Gedeon Mudacumura and M. Shamsul Haque (eds.), *Handbook of Development Policy Studies.* New York: Marcel Dekker.

Haque, M.S. (1999a) *Restructuring Development Theories and Policies: A Critical Study.* Albany: State University of New York Press.

Haque, M.S. (1999b). The fate of sustainable development under the neoliberal regimes in developing countries, *International Political Science Review* 20(2): 199–222.

Haque, M.S. (2000). Environmental discourse and sustainable development: Linkages and limitations. *Ethics & the Environment* 5(1): 1–19.

Heyes, A.G., and C. Liston-Heyes (1995). Sustainable resource use: The search for meaning. *Energy Policy* 23(1): 1–3.

Holmen, H. (2001). The unsustainability of development. *International Journal of Economic Development 3* (1).

International Union for the Conservation of Nature (1980). *World Conservation Strategy: Living Resources Conservation for Sustainable Development.* Gland, Switzerland: IUCN.

Jacobs, M. (1994). The limit to neoclassicism: Towards an Institutional Environmental Economics. In M. Redclift and T. Benton (eds.), *Social Theory and the Global Environment.* London: Routledge.

Kadekodi, G.K. (1992). Paradigms of sustainable development. *Development* 3: 72–76.

Langhelle, O. (1999). Sustainable development: recovering the essence and ethics of *Our Common Future. International Political Science Review* 20(2).

Langhelle, O. (2000). Sustainable development and social justice: Expanding the Rawlsian framework of global justice. *Environmental Values* 9: 295–323.

Lele, S.M. (1991). Sustainable development: A critical review. *World Development* 19(6): 607–621.

Li, H.L. (1996). On the nature of environmental education (anthropocentrism versus non-anthropocentrism: The irrelevant debate). In Frank Margonis (ed.), *Philosophy of Education 1996.* Champaign: Philosophy of Education Publication Office, University of Illinois at Urbana-Champaign.

Liverman, D.M., M.E. Hanson, B.J. Brown, and R.W. Merideth (1988). Global sustainability: Toward measurement. *Environmental Management* 12(2): 133–143.

Mebratu, D. (2000). Strategy Framework for Sustainable Industrial Development in Sub-Saharan Africa: A Systems-Evolutionary Approach. Doctoral Dissertation, International Institute for Industrial Environmental Economics, Lund University, Lund, Sweden.

Moffatt, I., N. Hanley, and M.D. Wilson (2001). *Measuring and Modeling Sustainable Development.* London: Parthenon.

Mudacumura, G.M. (2004). Conclusion: Development agenda for the 21st century. In G. Mudacumura and M.S. Haque (eds.), *Handbook of Development Policy Studies.* New York: Marcel Dekker.

Norgaard, R.B. (1988). Sustainable development: A co-evolutionary view. *Futures* December, pp. 606–620.

Norton, B.G. (1992). A new paradigm for environmental management. In R. Costanza, B.G. Norton, and B.D. Haskell (eds.), *Ecosystem Health: New Goals for Environmental Management.* Washington, D.C.: Island Press. pp. 23–41.

OECD. (2001). Policies to Enhance Sustainable Development. Paris: OECD

Pearce, D. (1988). Optimal prices for sustainable development. In D. Collard, D. Pearce, and D. Ulph (eds.), *Economics, Growth and Sustainable Environment.* London: MacMillan.

Pearce, D.W., and J.J. Warford (1993). *World Without End.* Washington, D.C.: Oxford University Press.

Redclift, M. (1988). Sustainable development and the market: A framework for analysis. *Futures* December, pp. 635–650.

Redclift, M., and Benton T. (1994). *Social Theory and the Global Environment.* London: Routledge.

Reid, D. (1995). *Sustainable Development: An Introductory Guide.* London: Earthscan.

Sachs, W. (1991). Environment and development: The story of a dangerous liaison. *The Ecologist* 21(6): 252–257.

Taylor, J. (2002). *Sustainable development: A dubious solution in search of a problem.* Cato Policy Analysis Series, No. 449, Washington, D.C.: The Cato Institute.

Thomas, W.M. (1990). *Green Development.* London: Routledge.

Tolba, M. (1987). *Sustainable Development—Constraints and Opportunities.* London: Butterworth.

Toman, M.A. (1992). The difficulty in defining sustainability. *Resources* 106: 3–6.

United Nations Development Programme (1996). *Human Development Report, 1996.* New York: Oxford University Press.

Warren, Karen J. (1993). Introduction. In Michael E. Zimmerman et al. (eds.), *Environmental Philosophy: From Animal Rights to Radical Ecology.* Englewood Cliffs, NJ: Prentice-Hall.

World Commission on Environment and Development (1987). *Our Common Future.* Oxford: Oxford University Press.

Chapter 3

Sustainable Development and Governance Policy Nexus: Bridging the Ecological and Human Dimensions

Berhe T. Costantinos

CONTENTS

Introduction

The 21st century has ushered in a time of unprecedented global wealth and extraordinary opportunities, but poor nations have yet to benefit from this. In this globalization of prosperity and plenty, an important dimension that features prominently in the poverty discourse is the relative contribution and weight of international mechanisms for promoting sustainable development (SD). An array of declarations, communiqués, and action programs notwithstanding, the human development crisis and progress toward human security continues unabated. Massive militarization and persistent armed conflicts, economic crisis manifested by absolute poverty, and a vicious sociopolitical environment have rendered societies and polities tragic scenes of present-day human crisis,[1,2] rendering whole populations chronically dependent on international food aid charity.

Fittingly, the global community has tried to build parallels between SD and governance in poor nations. Not surprisingly, and invariably, international development assistance to these nations is being redesigned to include governance programs that are based on pillars of support aimed at strengthening civil society and the various coordinates of government and governing institutions. The effort requires that we pay careful attention not only to specific objectives pursued by promoters of SD—the distinctive agendas, interests, and concepts that determine the domain of their activities—but also to the framework of political thought, discourse, and action, through which stakeholders translate these specific organizational elements into a broader pattern of ideas and apply them to SD.

The first step consists of a description of the central component of the SD strategy in objective terms. This involves noting problems of political and social change identified and solutions offered, that is, the articulation of SD issues, goals, tasks, mechanisms, and activities. The second step is analysis of the SD strategy—examination of its sources, elements, features, and limitations and its implications for SD.[3]

This chapter demarcates the agency and ideological purview that address the multidimensional, multisectoral, and multitrack policies, strategies, and processes to create the holism enshrined in SD, which can only be achieved through the sustainable livelihoods synergy—resilience, economic efficiency, social equitability, and ecological stability. In this faith, governance for SD links directly to the formation of ecological, social, economic, and political capital in terms of collective ideology, action, organization, and leadership to ensure people's participation in SD as citizens of a political society.

Research Inquiry

Civil societies everywhere have risen to the challenge to end these brutal regimes. The end of the eighties marked the dismantling of power oligarchies that presided over humankind's most appalling era of distress and despair. As we entered the decade of the nineties, ordinary citizens witnessed a unique era emerging in human history, testifying to the systematic disintegration of totalitarianism and with it the miraculous reprieve of humanity, which tend to relegate earlier "great" events in history to the back of the stage.[4] Nevertheless, even under democratically favorable contemporary global conditions, historical, ideological, and strategic characteristics internal and external to the societal change process still make the transition to a sustainable development path a costly exercise.[5] There is no simple or immediate identification of the transition problems as they actually are; there is only a definition of them from a certain perspective and toward a certain "resolution." The intergenerational SD perspectives in currency constitute few among other actual or possible perspectives, though dominant ones to be sure. Recognition of this fact would represent a significant improvement in our consciousness and praxis.

The key inquiry focuses on whether the endowment of institutions in civil society and state is conducive to sustainable development. In probing the SD–governance nexus, the theme of discourse and inquiry will converge on establishing the conceptual and operational linkages among SD theory, policy, and tools and SD administration in relation to assets or capital. It endeavors to evolve a "political theory" of environmental governance as the applied realm of politics (agency, ideology, and process), in which polity seeks mechanisms to convert political preferences to SD administration and make SD policy analysis, formulation, and management accountable, transparent, and predictable to communities.

Current Policy Realities of Human Adaptive Strategies

Environmental Governance without Vision and Development without Vision

Development efforts in many developing nations over recent decades have been frustrated by the complex and multifaceted nature of change because of a number of inherent contradictions among the various issues and actors and their differing perspectives. In order to understand the specific constraints of and opportunities for SD, analysis of the following contradictions can be useful for understanding the context and issues, and for defining opportunities for constructive action: central control vs. decentralized control, statutory rights vs. customary rights, modern knowledge systems vs. endogenous knowledge systems, and formal institutions vs. endogenous institutions.[6]

Poor nations are still predominantly characterized by rural production systems and premodernity development cultures. Although there are still relatively strong endogenous cultures and institutions,[7] the long-term exclusion from political power has denied these institutions possibilities for the accumulation of knowledge and experience in serving as a link between indigenous and modern knowledge systems and incapacitating leadership helpless to present viable policy alternatives.[8] In the creation of the nation-state, independent governments have tended to impose authority on local people. This has resulted in support for the nationalization of natural resources and policies that take little account of local needs and interests. In the forestry sector, this has too often been reflected in the approach to forest management that excludes local people and emphasizes forest utilization for commercial purposes only. This approach has resulted in the undermining of local capacities to manage natural resources sustainably and led to a situation in which people are forced to cope as best they can even if this threatens their long-term survival. This has stifled local initiatives, broken down indigenous systems, and created an attitude of resignation among communities, which in turn present a challenge to efforts for revival of local control. Conflict arises because central authority attempts to retain control by imposing official structures and co-opting local leaders.[9]

Recent attempts to compensate for the shortcomings of centralized management have had equally negative consequences. The new resource tenure regimes continue to discriminate against customary and traditional resource management cultures however sustainable, favoring instead the modern, formal sector and those having access and connections to the central authorities. Statutory systems of natural resource ownership and management are based on government decrees and statutes that rarely have reference to people's aspirations, hence their alienation from public interest. Very often, "people are denied access to or have no knowledge of these statutes until they are legally enforced and take their toll in courts and police actions."[10] In addition, statutes provide the ground for officials to take control of people's resources; very often accumulation of power in the hands of one or few officials who can decide the fate of natural resources and people without due regard to environmental considerations results. These local officials are only accountable to higher officials and local people have no control over their actions.[11] Enabling laws and policies on paper are not necessarily enforced, either because they are disregarded by officials or because they are unenforceable.

By comparison, customary systems, rules, and procedures (very often unwritten) often establish accountability and link the rights and responsibilities that govern resource management, thus providing a basis for conflict resolution. These systems have been enriched through evolution over many generations (where they have not disintegrated through marginalization). Individual decisions concerning natural resource management and utilization are based on a "legal" framework that has reference points to the optimal exploitation of these resources, and transgression is punishable by cultural laws and the regulations that legitimize the latter. Individual and collective accountability to communal and intra- and intergenerational interests is very high.[12] Communal tenure and management systems are complex and adaptive. The user rights provided by these systems are often strong and confer a high degree of tenure security on individuals.[13]

Local people in many communities from different sectors of society understand and relate to resources according to their respective knowledge systems, and their management practices reflect these systems. While the power of the modern sector stems, in part, from improved communication, it has largely excluded the traditional sector. This has been compounded by the difficulty of communication across cultures and knowledge systems, and by ignorance of the very existence of other ways of seeing, understanding, and managing natural resources.[14] As a result, the modern profit-based way (which narrowly sees the utilization of a few products and species) of understanding resource management has prevailed and dominated and determined how resources have been managed.

> Conditions for pastoralists in recent years have worsened considerably. Ever increasing areas that were once communal pastures have been lost to pastoral production. Irrigation schemes, small scale farming and mechanized agriculture have withdrawn large tracts of the most productive land for nonpastoral use. Food production per head and living standards for pastoralists have fallen. Future incomes and welfare are further threatened by increased degradation of land while a growing conflict of interests is pitting pastoral communities against governments, against each other, and against each other, and against other land users. These conflicts do not usually manifest themselves as large scale armed conflicts although this has sometimes been the case, particularly in West Africa; they are more structural

and hidden. They are nonetheless violent in their impact of forcing people from their homes and in the violations of human rights which can follow from evictions, as has recently been experienced in Kenya. Historically, pastoral groups have managed conflicts over resources through tried and tested traditional systems. However, with tenure reform and the alienation of pastoralists from their lands, customary methods of negotiation, arbitration and adjudication are breaking down in competition with more omnipotent forces. The rapid transformation of pastoralism is increasingly shifting control over land to small, male-dominated elites, some from within pastoral societies but mostly from agricultural, urban, and civil service or military backgrounds. The vast majority of herders, impoverished and politically deprived, find themselves with neither enough animals nor sufficient access to rangeland and water to sustain their livelihoods. Under these conditions men become either hired herders for absentee herd owners, migrate out of pastoral areas for waged labor, while women remain at home, assuming greater responsibility for the management of herds and flocks, or are expected to fend for themselves without any animals for as long as men are away.[15]

Different biocultural realities give rise to different resource management systems. Endogenous resource management systems vary according to their specific contexts, defining the specific uses and users of the various resources within the community, functioning as reservoirs of traditional knowledge, preserving customary rights and responsibilities within societies, enforcing them, transmitting them from generation to generation, and (where not entirely marginalized by the modern sector) governing the utilization and conservation of resources. These institutions have been evolving and continue to adapt to changing conditions and develop new mechanisms. These institutions offer important organizational potential as the formal institutions have come to dominate, marginalize, and even eradicate the endogenous institutions.[16]

It is necessary to acknowledge the cultural diversity that contains the knowledge necessary to maintain it. Local technical knowledge is a reflection of the context-specific. It is necessary to acknowledge the linkages between local knowledge and context-specific management of resources. By maintaining this array of culturally embedded technical knowledge and the corresponding ecosystems, it becomes possible to sustain healthy and productive local resource management for the benefit of local livelihoods, possibly leading to more sustainable resource management at the national and regional levels. Throughout many developing nations, governments, donors and other development agents are becoming increasingly aware of customary management, customary rights, endogenous institutions, and the existence of different knowledge systems and community governance systems. There is also a growing recognition and understanding of the potential for linking to and supporting these in an effort to realize sustainable resource management and development, and the need to try overcome the constraints described above. In short, endogenous institutions and resource management systems represent a latent resource; providing potential alternatives where modern approaches have not attained expectations or counterpoints/correctives for mainstream development approaches.[17]

Theories of development have evolved useful tools over the past six decades: modernization theories (1950s, early 1960s), dependency theories (late 1960s, early 1970s), the world economy view (late 1970s, early 1980s), basic needs approaches (late 1970s), and the alternative modes of production and sustainable livelihoods that are directed at empowerment and human development (1970s to 1990s),[18] culminating in an increasing awareness of the necessity to reconcile the contradictions described in order to ensure sustainable management of natural resources. This awareness lies behind the current encouraging trend in which institutions at all levels are becoming willing to acknowledge the management potential of endogenous institutions and the necessity to base development efforts on local aspirations and to use the local potential as a bridge between endogenous and formal institutions. Thus an important challenge concerns the strengthening of civil society, a process requiring a broader approach and time perspective than are prevalent in approaches in currency today, the process of the retrieval of community history and adaptive strategies that lead to sustainable livelihoods[19] within a robust and historically sedimented framework. The approach aims to restore the salience of decision making and provide an integrated framework for diverse goals.

The SD approach can be described at three levels: a set of normative goals and poverty eradication and empowerment processes. It is also presented as an integrative concept that aims simultaneously to maintain or enhance resource productivity of the poor; secure their ownership of and access to assets, resources, and income earning activities; and ensure adequate stocks and flows of food and cash to meet basic needs.[20] UNDP defines SD as a combination of poverty eradication, empowerment and participation, and sustainable development. However, the essence of the concept is not in its normative goals, but in a broader perspective that gives rise to these goals. This is evident from the way the two operative words are defined in literature: *sustainability* is premised on decision

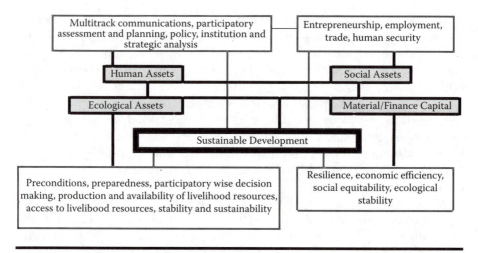

Figure 3.1 Participation synergy in RBA sustainable livelihoods programme framework. (From Titti and Singh, 1996, p. 24.)

making that reflects a balance among economic efficiency, ecological integrity, and human well-being (including equity considerations); *livelihoods* are the assets, activities, and entitlements by which people make a living, and sustainable livelihoods are derived from people's capacity to access options and resources and use them to make a living in a way that does not foreclose options for others to make a living, either now or in the future (see Figure 3.1).[21]

Defining the Ecological–Human Nexus in Policy Analysis

Context

Sustainable development policy analysis and formulation concern the practical approach to be adopted with regard to the integration and interface between the social–political, ecological, and economic realities of human development. The purposes of this section are the following:

- To recontextualize the interfaces among the economic efficiency, ecological stability, political, and social equitability dimensions of "citizen participation" within the context of the sustainable development construct, grounding the value-added dimensions in a major paradigmatic shift that such interfaces and integration bring to light

- To define the process and strategic dimensions to sustainable development policy interfacing and the distinctive roles of organizations and their vested interests and the extent to which these two independently and collectively influence policy analysis, formulation, and management
- To evolve a concrete understanding of the policy nuances of the sustainable development construct as a multitrack, multistakeholder holistic approach to the strategic planning and management process to mainstream the interface between and within economic, social, and ecological dimensions of integration and sustainability in all facets of capital development and accumulation at national, subnational, and local community levels

What are the added values of the sustainable development construct? A complete coverage and analysis of the programs that deal with and lead to social equitability, economic efficiency, ecological sustainability, and coping and adaptive strategies and theories is well beyond the scope of this chapter. It is however useful to address, early on, the incremental effect that each area contributes to the unfolding synergy advanced by the sustainable development construct arising from empowerment (individual, social, economic), sustainability (technological, environmental, social–cultural, economic, institutional), resilience (ability to withstand shocks and stresses), and adaptive governance systems (power dynamics, resource management, dispute resolution, devolutionary decision making on entitlement, strategic planning, and management). We can define these thematic areas in relation to the development of human, social, physical, and natural capital.

We distinguish the sustainable development added value in the development of human capital that is a necessary condition for citizens to participate meaningfully in self-empowered action from the administrative and managerial call for human resources development that is targeted at a very useful but narrow focus on human skills development toward a certain employment. The sustainable development construct underpins the synergy that is created by various interventions to promote people's participation as citizens of a political society.[22] Today, impoverished nations are going through a revolution giving way to renewed awareness for an enabling political climate that promotes the new realism of sustainable human development (SHD). The multidimensional, multisectoral, and multitrack input that is required as one of many outputs to create the holism enshrined in the SD can only be achieved through the SD synergy—resilience,[23] economic efficiency, social equitability, and ecological stability.[24] In this view, empowerment for participatory development goes beyond the restricted goal of generating awareness (which may invariably result in various degrees of empowerment that could also lead to anarchy) but links directly to the formation of social capital in terms of collective ideology, collective action, organization, and leadership to ensure access to political contestation and entitlement.

The policy implications of augmenting human capital through economic efficiency are far reaching. Economic efficiency as an input into the human capital formation process, on the one hand, and as an output of a complex series of social, economic, technological, moral, and managerial decisions and actions, on the other, is indeed a strong value-added component of the SD synergy. Such empowered participation is directed at evolving macro- and micropolicies that address the human development and human security dimension of SHD. Microlevel policy analyses that modulate economic efficiency as it relates to human capital development are informed by imperatives that promote indigenous knowledge as a base for human capital development; the introduction of contemporary knowledge to boost indigenous thinking; the moral and psychological imperative to be able to produce with internal assets, resources, and means; the introduction of external resources that can be sustained by internal assets in the long term; the enhancement of human capability to recover from shocks and stresses; and micropolicies that address the dimensions of vulnerability (human) and proneness (physical and natural environment).[25]

Macro- and mesolevel policies that will be influenced by micropolicies include constitutional provision of a bill of rights. Although a bill of rights should be firmly entrenched in the constitution, the negative terms in which many of these rights are provided have become a source of divergence in many nations. The bill does not cover the full range of rights and freedom guaranteed under the international Bill of Rights, such as equality before the law, the right to take part in the government, an enforceable right to compensation for unlawful arrest or detention, the right to leave one's country, and gender equality. Further, the enjoyment of these rights and freedom is made subject to a number of limitations: respect for the rights and freedom of others and the public interest. In another arena, we have decentralization policies that would create the local enabling environment for human development. For the purpose of our analysis, the concept of decentralization is used in the context of the transfer of legal, administrative, and political authority to make decisions and manage public functions from the central government to field organizations of those agencies, subordinate units of government, semiautonomous public corporations, areawide development authorities, functional authorities, autonomous local governments, or nongovernmental organizations.[26]

The policy analysis and formulation issues that are addressed under natural assets are metric relationships between, on the one hand, sustainability, management, and resilience and, on the other hand, economic efficiency, social equitability, and ecological stability. The impact of environmental problems is particularly manifested in poor land-use systems. Policy synergy can ensure environmental stability by providing a micropolicy basis for the following activities: [27]

- Energy flow through farming systems is considered as a whole to ensure maximal economy (economic efficiency) in order to prevent long-term deterioration in the natural resources, specifically soil and forests; production systems are resilient enough to withstand drought.
- Farming practices are sufficiently diversified to be conducive to sustainability and stability by ensuring that soil fertility is being maintained so that there are a supply and recycling of nutrients; soil conservation practices are durable; production is diversified on any given farm or within an area, and irrigation systems are properly maintained to prevent salinity and situation problems.
- Diversified cropping is used for pest control; crop genetic diversity is maintained and understood.
- Trees are included in the system for animal maintenance and fuel wood supply.
- Livestock is managed in a way that prevents damage of the environment by use of adequate food and water for the type and number of livestock; the feeding system does not compete with organic matter inputs to the soil; no further expansion of livestockd in competition with food production is allowed.
- Policies that promote soil fertility are maintained by using crop rotation, promoting traditional farming practices, and introducing new technologies that offer adequate soil conservation; use of fertilizers does not replace other management practices such as use of manure and residue to maintain soil fertility.
- Farming practices such as soil conservation, soil fertility, and management of soil moisture are encouraged to leave a good resource base for generations to come.
- Population is adjusted to carrying capacity, and grazing for animals is managed in a sustainable manner not harmful to the environment; land-use planning avoids use of marginal, fragile areas so as to minimize environmental deterioration; income generation activities that are promoted will not be harmful to the environment.

Agency, Political Ideology, Strategy, and Process in SD

Agency

Agency refers to the full range of significant participants and their activities and relations to sustainable development policy formulation and management. Participants include potential as well as actual domestic as well as international actors. Micropolicies such as sustainable agriculture that require a reorientation to traditional and indigenous means of farming demand that some old habits generated by "extension-oriented agriculture" die. Some stakeholders in state and government will find this a difficult choice to make. The following are the undercurrents that determine the scope and nature of agency-specific needs, imperatives, and causes for interaction in a "participatory development" exercise that is prognostically dominated by certain stakeholders.[28]

The basic point here is that the extent and nature of livelihood sustainabilities are conditioned by the breadth of the range of available participants and the degree of uncertainty and complexity that characterize their agency and functional relations. In reality a rich associational life characterizes many traditional societies.[29] But the richness of such forms of associational life does not imply the presence of a strong civil society. The kinds of associations prevalent in the context of authoritarian or hegemonic regimes tend to reflect the weak character of the state.[30] Informal associations are characterized by fragmentation and disengagement from the state institutions. While associations exist, they have not developed more formal structures and do not openly present themselves in the public area. The weakness of the state means that few incentives have existed to form autonomous organizations to engage with the state; rather the "exit" option has prevailed as individuals have preferred to remain outside the reach of state institutions.[31]

At the structural level, a certain hierarchy of agency and activity is evident within the network of participants, such that some actors assume primary position relative to others that are by comparison relegated to be limited players. This characterizes the "enabling environment" for SD that is modulated and, at times, mediated by a number of distinctive and shared additional elements. This includes concepts and rules of government, national and cultural values, traditions of political discourse and arguments, and modes of representation of specific individual interests, needs, and issues.[32] These elements, or complexes of elements, tend to assume varying forms and enter into shifting relations of competition, cooperation, and hegemony during the exercise of participation. Generally, the broader the range of ideological elements at play and the more varied and uncertain their relations, the greater the possibilities of process openness and transparency that can exist.[33]

But many questions that need to be addressed in the sustainable development policy linger: Does "participatory development" enter local processes as an external ideology, constructing and deploying its concepts in sterile abstraction from the immediacies of indigenous traditions, beliefs, and values? The sustainable livelihood construct adds value to traditional "participatory development" projects and programs as it bases its assumptions on historically rooted community knowledge and experience.[34]

- In the case of rural communities, those that are "out of reach" in particular, do ideas addressing participation conflicts come into play in total opposition to, or in cooperation with, historic values and sentiments? The sustainable livelihood construct adds value to traditional participatory paradigms by the very fact that communities build norms in participation based on their cultural adaptive strategies. The spiritual dimensions of community unity and strength, for instance, have enabled people to organize themselves and realize their potential and power as individuals and communities, working toward the kind of self-reliance and self-determination that are essential conditions of interdependence.[35] Kinship, unity of purpose, and oneness among community members facilitate the task of effective organizational action, which is in turn expedited by organizational structures and leadership based on unity. Community organization members cherish shared perceptions and common cultural values on how they perceive themselves in relation to their environment. They also share common ideology—definition of goals, policy statements, formulation of strategies, and planning.[36]

- Two intellectual traditions provide the theoretical framework within which the discussion is occurring: the Marxist perspective and a political interactive framework.[37] The Marxist-inspired discourse seeks to understand the configuration of social forces in the context of the always impending social transformation of society on the basis of the balance of such forces. Some of the critical issues raised in this discourse are the historical and class role of civil society in social transformation and its relationship to the forces of production and the state. The political interaction perspective, on the other hand, presumes that the state–society relationship is central to understanding the political dynamic of Africa. It is a synthesis of conventional analysis of African politics, which attempts to deconstruct the contentions of previous sociological and anthropological analyses and reinterprets them within the problematic of the state–society nexus. Characteristically it eschews a predetermination of the locus of power in any of the public or private spheres. Otherwise known as the political choice framework, it derives its theoretical leitmotif from the recognition of multiple factors at work on the African political scene and tracing of their diverse dynamics over time. The neoliberal orthodoxy's offshoots of this tradition have tended to treat civil society as if it were a replacement of class analysis. In order to unpack some of the superogatory aggregation of class categories, proponents have striven to expose a broader range of social relationships, strategic options, and behavior patterns within and among classes and, by that means, mitigated the theoretical effect of structural determinism, which usually accompanies class analysis.

■ The inspiration for the spiritual dimensions arises from shared values, vision, and resources of a community; demanding common tasks that build a community and the momentum for radical citizen participation; realism about what it means to be human depends on shared values; and the primacy of partnership among human communities. The concept of participatory development as it is envisaged today aims to renew these ideas of partnership political processes involving the society as a whole by at last giving due recognition to the role of local populations.[38]

■ In the struggle over the establishment of participatory rules of engagement, do leading stakeholders equate the articulation of their ideas and agenda with the production of broad-based concepts, norms, and goals that should govern the direction of national development at all levels? The sustainable livelihood construct adds value to traditional participatory paradigms by including the whole arena of multitrack communications.

■ Do participatory processes signify change in terms of the transformation of the immediate stuff of a stakeholder-specific partisan agenda into a new kind of coevolutionary activity, an activity mediated and guided by objective and critical policy analysis, formulation and management standards, rules, and principles? The main issue in state institution–citizen relations is whether or not state institutions have the capacity and the will to relate to citizens and citizen groups on the basis of mutual respect, autonomy, equality, and trust. The sustainable development adds value to traditional participatory paradigms by including the whole arena of civic education. The evidence for this assertion is the virtual absence of civic education training as a key component of many participatory development programs and projects. It is fundamental to the sustainable development construct that civic education—learning about and appreciating one's rights, duties, obligations, and responsibilities as a citizen and the immediate rules, laws, and governance structures within which one exercises citizenship—be the first and fundamental step in development participation.[39]

In the light of these questions, it is possible to draw a conceptual distinction between two levels of articulation of ideology in policy analysis, formulation, and management process and to note the implications of their relations for process openness. There are, first, representations of specific interests, identities, needs, wishes, goals, claims, and demands in policy formulation and management, differences in different individuals, groups, and communities. These are to be distinguished from a second level of production and circulation of collective ideology, in which broad-based concepts, principles, and rules take shape and come into play in the analysis, formulation, and management of policies for sustainable development.

Operative Ideology

Operative ideology relates to complexes of ideas, beliefs, goals, and issues that can enter cooperative play (the underlying thesis of participatory development and poverty elimination discourse) or competitive contestation and governance reform (which the sustainable livelihood construct underpins). It includes alternative definitions of societal vulnerabilities and problems and varying solutions offered for them. Beyond the sphere of agency, therefore, opportunities, possibilities, and problems of sustainable development can be grasped in terms of the related domain of ideology. Ideological elements and constructs might be seen as the very constitutive structure of sustainable development process openness and closure. Participatory development as a specific field of action should apply to "decisions concerning collective or individual measures, made through organizations and affecting social groups lack access to political expression."[40]

Process and Strategy

Micropolicy management, as closely linked as it is with macropolicy management, demands a multistakeholder, multitrack communications strategy that constantly informs stakeholders of their policy choices and options. We can analyze sustainable development as a dynamic interaction of strategy and process. The dynamics of interplay between processes and strategy in a livelihood system, where assets change hands spontaneously, is dependent on the specific social agency and political ideology. Social capital development that is based on perfect order devoid of conflict (a normal element of social cohesion, often serving as an important impetus for positive social change) cannot exist unless we assume absolute

zero-sum human interaction. Hence, as a way of overcoming these difficulties, we may theorize sustainable development as the dynamic interaction of strategy and process.

The hypothesis is based on the following assumptions: Whereas external resources are crucial to national development, policy analysis, formulation, and management in sustainable development must proceed from
the acknowledgment that all those involved in the process must and
should broaden their perception and realize that the people are the key
to sustainable development. The so-called poor have adaptive strategies
that have been outmoded through policies and actions of governments
and international trade. It is easy to follow the current trend within the
international community and advocate the participatory approaches as
desirable tools to promoting SD, and it is not difficult to make normative
judgments about how development practitioners, people, and donors
should behave if livelihoods are to be sustainable—the poor must participate in decision making. But it is not so easy to conceptualize a participatory multistakeholder system, within which the sustainable
development strategy is grounded, as a working process that is balanced
against strategy to determine what makes for real, as opposed to vacuously
formal, process. This is particularly the case where the "giver" strata (the
state, donors, nongovernmental organizations [NGOs]) tend to view the
relations of their particular agenda with their broader roles and responsibilities of helping the poor as relatively simple and direct, unproblematically reducing the latter to the former.[41] It is possible to see it as the
playing out of objective and critical standards, rules, and concepts of
political conduct in the goals and activities of all participants.[42]

The issue here is not simply one of "application" of rules to particular
activities, nor of dissolving agent-catered strategies into "objective" principles and norms. It is rather the production or articulation of self-
development process elements and forms within and through the strategic
(and nonstrategic) activities of various participants. Highlighting the mutually constitutive and regulative articulation of strategy and process, we
shift the center of analysis away from the two as separate formations that
enter only externally into relations with each other. This shift of analytical
focus serves to emphasize the critical point that the task of broadly
structuring sustainable development, as a gender-sensitive self-empower-
ing change mechanism, is more important than that of promoting it within
the specific program design of a particular agency's "participatory development" agenda.[43] The latter, which is manifested in a variety of efforts
ranging from community diagnostics to implementation of community-
based donor-funded programs, is or should be only a second-order
concern compared to the former, which is primarily a strategic tool adopted

by communities and individuals to enhance their adaptive strategies that are important in the transition to a more fulfilled livelihood.

Beyond the sphere of political agency, possibilities and problems of posttransition conflicts can be grasped in terms of the related domain of ideology. Ideological elements and constructs might be seen as the very constitutive structure of process openness and closure. Political transitions will commonly be characterized by a number of distinctive and shared additional elements, including concepts and rules of government, national and cultural values, traditions of political discourse and arguments, and modes of representation of specific interests, needs, and issues. These elements, or complexes of elements, will tend to assume varying forms and to enter into shifting relations of competition, cooperation, and hegemony during political reform. Generally, the broader the range of ideological elements at play in a transition to democracy, and the more varied and uncertain their relations, the greater the possibilities of process openness and transparency.

As do political organizations and the activities to which they are often tied more or less closely, transitional ideological constructs tend to be unsettled and, at times, unsettling. Particularly at the initial stages of political transition, they are more likely to be uncertain rather than stable structures of ideas and values. This has the effect of opening up the reform process, of freeing the process from simple domination by any one organized actor or coalition of actors. Yet ideological elements and relations take shape and come into play within a hierarchy of global and local agencies and groups. A determinate order of institutions, powers, interests, and activities operate through complexes of transition ideas and values, filling out, specifying, anchoring, and often shortcutting their formal content or meaning.[44] This may impose ideological as well as practical limits on the extent to which and how democratic reform processes can be opened up or broadened.

Thus, the fact that external promoters or supporters of developing nations' conflict management projects often do not efficiently realize the following in practice: (1) that the potential of the ideas and goals they promote raises the issue of whether the ideas in question may be fundamentally constrained at the moment of their conception; (2) that the volume of their interventions is not nearly proportional to their impact raises the issue of implementation by the very institutions and technocratic structures that ground their articulation; and (3) that although the explicit concepts of good governance and capacity building for conflict management that current international initiatives operate may be consistent with goals of "empowerment" of indigenous communities and individuals, of enhancing local institutional and human capacities, the initiatives tend to work toward these goals in narrow technocratic and managerial terms.

The initiatives seem to equate technocratic rationality and capacity with totality of institutional purposefulness and strength.[45]

Objectives and Expected Results of the SD–Policy Nexus

The pillars of support for governance in developing nations are based on strengthening civil society and the various coordinates of government and governing institutions. Capacity support of the civil society, political parties, and business community will focus on civic education, political participation and conflict management, communications, information management, and the media.[46] Support of the legislature at the federal and state levels will enhance an enabling environment and support to the judiciary, rule of law, and access to justice. Support of the executive will be in the form of continuing reform of the civil service, defining of the role of the military, police, and security forces, and strengthening of the administrative capacity and resource base of state and local governments. Finally, support will take the form of streamlining economic governance through economic and financial management at the federal and state levels and promoting transparency, accountability, and integrity in the public and private sectors.[47]

1. Support of civil society, civic groups, the business community, aimed at public enlightenment and political participation: the main thrust of this strategic objective is to promote and support broad-based political participation. The objective of the component is to ensure the active political participation of all relevant stakeholders, particularly of grassroots women, men, and youth and civil society organizations (CSOs). The program is designed to enable them to assess their problems and opportunities, action planning and project identification, and implementation, monitoring, and evaluation of activities. In keeping with its functions of strengthening civil society and fostering a dynamic relationship between state and civil society, a major preoccupation of the program would be the promotion of a rights culture among the population. It aims to address developing nations' paradox of scarcity amid plenty that shows up in the strengths and weaknesses of various movements and the contests for social space, legitimacy, domination, and resistance. It addresses that fragile structure and organization of developing nations' civil society that are susceptible to fractious politics driven by personality, ethnicity, fundamentalism, competition, corruption, and nonaccountability.[48] It aims to reduce poverty

by empowering people as the most viable path to developing nations' holistic development. The focus of this strategic objective is to ensure the active political participation of all relevant stakeholders, particularly of grassroots women, men, and youth and their corollary civil society organizations; to enable these stakeholders to assess their problems and opportunities and to build their capacity to plan, identify, implement, monitor, and evaluate projects and activities, strengthen the relations between state and civil society, and promote a rights culture among the population.

Capacities building to enable CSOs to function as legitimate representatives of society through creation of mechanisms for them to exist legally and function as a counterweight to the other powers will be achieved by developing legislation and supporting policies that allow the smooth registration of CSOs; institutionalizing self-regulating mechanisms in the state to protect CSOs from undue interference will have a significant impact on the democratization process. Developing institutions, mechanisms, and procedures that undertake public opinion surveys, plebiscites, and referenda will involve CSOs in decision making; civic education can provide training as a key component of local, district, and national development programs. In addition, CSOs will have developed the capacity to act as intermediaries for their members with the federal structure, the state governments, and other stakeholders. This will be achieved through a variety of actions and outputs. These include developing organizational capacity to enhance the effectiveness of the organization at achieving its stated objectives; building the human and material resources of the organization vis-à-vis membership, technical skills, and adequate budgets; developing the organizational complexity of an organization's internal structure; and engendering organizational cohesion through the sharing of common values, goals, and organizational culture among an organization's leaders and members. Developing, refining, and maintaining participatory methods, tools, and techniques enable stakeholders to participate actively in the program. Such methods, tools, and techniques for participatory assessment and planning, implementation, and monitoring, which purposefully and meaningfully gender disaggregated relevant data and information on socioeconomic characteristics, already exist. This process can be achieved by data that are developed and available and regularly reviewed, monitored, and updated to reflect experience and new thinking.

2. Support of the legislature is implemented to create an enabling environment for sustainable development; the two most urgent tasks in developing nations are to pursue democracy and to reduce poverty. The lawmakers of the country have the vanguard role in developing constitutional, policy, and legislative and administrative rules for poverty reduction and sustainable human development. These must include the bill of rights that will enable every developing nation to have a livelihood security that must be guaranteed by a democratic state. The aim here is to strengthen the capacity of the national and the state legislatures to fulfill their three constitutional roles—lawmaking, representation, and oversight, and the internal structure and organization of the legislatures and the role of political parties within them. Capacity building for an elected legislature to develop and proclaim sustainable development policies aims at ensuring that the legislature understands its role and its historical responsibility. This will be achieved by training in democratic governance, good governance, the legislative process and rules of parliament, lobbying, formulation and observance of codes of conduct, and visits to other countries to observe and share experiences with other legislators; developing a training course to upgrade the skills of legislators in the functions outlined; and developing awareness among elected officials by their spending a minimum specified amount of time in their electoral district. Capacity building for the legislature to have oversight over executive policy-level management depends on the following activities, to give members of the legislature at all levels sufficient access to information and technical resources to enable them to make informed decisions. This will be achieved by providing a database containing reference material to parliamentarians, developing systems whereby public opinion can be made known to members of the legislature, including support to develop their constituency, developing the capacity of the legislature to draft and introduce legislation or amendments to existing legislation on specific subjects.

3. Support of the judiciary, rule of law, and access to justice requires capacity-building programs to make them more effective in administering justice and law enforcement. The judiciary is an instrument to fight corruption, abuse of power, drug scandals, and illegal involvement of the security forces in politics. In addition the unjust society created by successive military regimes can only be redeemed through systematic capacity development of the justice system in developing nations. The focus here is on strengthening the capacity of the judiciary to serve its function as a neutral and

unimpeachable arbiter of justice, increasing access to justice in the population, and improving the rule of law upstream and downstream.

4. Capacity building for economic and financial management at the federal and state levels focuses on strengthening the capacity of the state and local governments to enhance their decentralization and political representation of the public and to enable them to design and manage the services they offer. It also strengthens the capacity of developing nations' financial institutions at the federal and state levels to promote efficient economic and financial management and encourage private sector growth and international confidence. This will be achieved by defining and delineating procedures, norms, and legislation that make government officials subject to the rule of law, including regulations prohibiting acceptance of bribes or kickbacks.

5. Capacity building for legal and regulatory frameworks to educate institutions and civil society organizations is achieved by developing administrative norms to control grand corruption and graft, developing a system of checks and balances to ensure that such regulations are adequately enforced, developing curricula and systems for public education to fight corruption, developing media awareness to fight corruption and graft, and establishing a code of practice for professionals at all levels. The legislature and the judiciary have the historical mandate and duty to control corruption.

6. National and local capacities are developed for community systems that enable stakeholders to articulate needs, to create opportunities, and to share knowledge and create consensus for governance and sustainable development. The expected output here is that communications systems for poverty alleviation and sustainable development are established. Actions to achieve this result are to identify key communication tracks and channels at national, district, and community levels; to assess the effectiveness and efficiency of various informal and formal channels and tracks, including radio, libraries, the Internet, and theater; to identify institutional linkages for effective flow of communication between districts and local areas and between districts and national institutions; and to support the establishment and operationalization of a multitrack communications system center. Feedback mechanisms on policy between local communities and decision makers will also be established. This will be achieved by linking participatory development exercises with developed communication systems; empowering stakeholders to control decision-making processes; linking participatory processes with civic education programs, though gender, population,

health, environment, and human rights information fed into the communications systems.

7. Support of cross-cutting issues—gender and human security; governance research, extension, and communication; human rights; and cultural renewal—is provided by strategic focus on increasing social harmony, protecting the environment, improving security, and improving the status and contribution of women in developing nations' society and politics. The following results are expected from this intersectoral work:

Development of local governance action plans that represent the true development aspirations of the people and processes that enhance their livelihoods. This will determine how we understand, investigate, and articulate means to exploit actual and potential linkages between indigenous, adaptive knowledge and contemporary knowledge and technology. This will enhance smallholders' productivity through technology development, dissemination, and enhanced use, as a means of improving livelihood availability at the household level. Consensus and linkages between the program and other livelihood security-related programs, projects, and activities of stakeholders and partners that strive to achieve livelihood security can be created. This will be achieved by strengthening at the local government level and relevant units of government ongoing policy formulation and analysis, program formulation, and implementation of environmental action plans and the comanagement programs as they relate to natural resource use.

Tools and processes that create an enabling environment for policy analysis, formulation, and management are developed. Within this context, the specific focus on policy analysis and development of an enabling environment is to provide tools for creating a framework for the analysis of existing policies, policy gaps, and omissions; ensuring a coherent policy environment, institutional analysis, and formulation of new policy choices; improving on old policies, including alternative policies; designing a national policy framework conducive to a continuous and participatory process, including legal instruments to recognize CSOs, community-based organizations (CBOs), and other groups often marginalized in decision-making processes; and establishing a code of practice for partnership building with provisions for continuous improvement with respect to participatory approaches.

Enhancement of capacity for wise decision making at the national level that responds to actual conditions throughout the country and the concerns expressed by the people. This will be done through improved analysis, formulation, and advocacy of government policies and programs in support of the program; enhanced decision-making capacity that promotes the program at the local government levels; and building of capacity of local organizations and individuals at the local government and household levels to make wise decisions that promote the program and enhance gender balance and equity. Immediate objectives in this arena are development and operationalization of a national gender program; enhanced coordination, relevance, and effectiveness of supporting agencies to government and other partners in integrating gender into development programs; and gender analysis and gender-responsive program and project design.

SD networking—SD networking faces many limitations in the sphere of institutional development. Networkers have been unable to establish a clear and coherent voice regionally on issues that are crucial to our work, or to the interest of the communities we profess to serve. This contravenes the ideals, standards, and rules of effective networking management process. It also encourages well-meaning individuals to alienate themselves from the process, rather than participate in it and work to improve it. Although many proposals for remedial action have been formulated, real commitment to collaborative processes at the interorganizational level has always been limited. Mobilizing the action required has also remained a daunting challenge, as many practical and structural constraints militate against commitment by individual groups to interorganizational initiatives nationally and regionally.[49]

An increased awareness of this problem has led us to question the nature of the relationship that has existed among us, providing a significant impetus for change in our network development consciousness and practice. It is foreseen that there will be a need for periodic review of this process to encourage SD to open forums for such initiatives, as they pave the way toward consensus and alliances for empowerment.

The aim of such a collaborative effort is the development of an organic network that will cement the SD ideals in every SD network, member, facilitator, networker, community of persons, and institution with which we network. This is intended to build true networking that would unite the national program with a continentwide network that would facilitate linkages and exchange of activities. It is a statement of institutional principles and ethics for practice, designed as a reference document for all SD networks and practitioners, to enhance the forests, trees, and people nexus at the intraorganizational and interorganizational levels. It encourages qualitative improvement in our relationship by contributing to ongoing SD networks' and practitioners' commitment to the use of high standards of networking management practices; encouraging SD networks and practitioners to develop a collective capacity for advocacy to articulate the needs of the constituencies we serve effectively; serving as a guide document for improving the partnership between professionals and practitioners and our collaborators, by setting out institutional modalities aimed at enhancing the present pattern of pluralistic networking as an instrument of multitrack communication; supporting the establishment and operation of an effective process of institutional strengthening and horizontal linkages among network partners; fostering a genuine commitment of both SD networks and practitioners and our partners to a locally driven approach to the challenges of the nexus; and helping to focus the attention of resourceson improving the human environment by eradicating the grinding poverty witnessed in many quarters today.[50]

- Objective 1: Share knowledge systems, tools, technology, and adaptive strategies that people developed on their own long before donors, NGOs, and political powers came into being. Expected outputs are an interactive database on institutions, publications, case studies, and planned activities and national programs that take the lead in capitalizing on the wealth of information generated in national programs and developing SD disciplines throughout the network.
- Objective 2: Help to overcome language barriers by institutionalizing cost-effective but determined language lessons that would allow easier communications. Outputs are training needs analysis and identification of trainees and training packages and modalities in language lessons for all regions identified.
- Objective 3: Initiate immediate advocacy networking, research collaboration, and interregional consultation activities on all existing information on national SD activities. Outputs are a compiled listing (however irregular) of all existing publications, institutions, ongoing activities in all SD regions and governments and of international finance institutions (IFIs), donors, and multinationals sensitized about key issues affecting marginalization of local communities in plans in whose formulation they have not participated, with the

aim of improved interregional cooperation and consultation through exchange visits to study specific issues and formalization of relationships among network collaborators.

■ Objective 4: Develop information communication mechanisms on key initiatives with a view to coordinating activities that reinforce each other for a meaningful continental impact. Tracks, channels, and levels of communication are identified and clear designations of tracks of cooperation, dependency, services, and conflict, where any may arise, among interregional network stakeholders are specified.

Winding Up the Discourse on the SD–Governance Nexus

The underpinning of the SD–governance nexus is designed to address the twin priorities of poverty reduction and promotion of sustainable livelihoods, on the one hand, and the social, political, and economic dimensions of governance on the other. The objective is to affect human development through the synergy of complementing upstream activities with downstream–local community-level projects that ensure sustainable livelihoods. The downstream activities also include promoting small enterprises, improving access of the rural and urban poor to basic services, creating new jobs, improving agriculture, and supporting community-based projects.

Accordingly, the overall aim of capacity-building initiatives is to help individuals become more focused on taking charge of their own situations and working toward changing their own conditions. This cannot be achieved through single "training" sessions. Instead, the program will endeavor to establish a continuity of presence until the capacity that is to be instilled is fully internalized by the ultimate beneficiary. This will be done by establishing domains of capacity building. A core group of people will be required in each domain of capacity building to continue the activities over the necessary period. The core group will be expected to develop capacity-building modules that meet the specific requirements of the target group or groups in its domain. Each module will require a group of facilitators to work together over the required time frame to implement the various activities specified therein. This process will be facilitated through the multitrack communication network, by allowing two-way (or multitrack) communication to emerge between and among stakeholder groups.

Capacity-building activities under the program will emphasize complementarity with other activities required to fully achieving objectives. This recognizes that capacity building in itself is not enough to remove the underlying constraints and obstacles to development. The program will start from the premise that building capacity is a necessary, but not a sufficient condition for achieving the program objectives. Substantive capacities at national and state levels will be built to create a sense of national ownership of policy decisions. Capacity gaps and aims have been identified for each capacity building target at three levels: policy and program, institutions and coordination, and human resources.

- Promotion of dialogue, public enlightenment, and cultural renaissance: Dialogue will include stakeholders in the political scene in forums that can resolve potential areas of conflicting ideas in a nonadversarial manner. This also aims at strengthening the national capacity to develop, manage, and deliver a national civic education program that will be linked with human rights groups and official democratic institutions. At this level, the aim will be to develop a national civic education policy that clarifies the roles of official democratic institutions in civic education efforts as well as provides a framework for the design, planning, and delivery of an effective and independent civic education program. A second objective will be to assist in the development of a civic education program, targeting various segments of the society, including schools, churches, civil society, the police, prisons, and the media. Gender equality issues should be included in the training material in civic education.[51]
- Institutional development: The aim will be to increase the capacity of civic education and human rights institutions to perform effectively their functions. Interinstitutional consultation and coordination mechanisms among all institutions concerned, including those in the areas of human and civic rights, will be strengthened in the development of civic education messages, implementation, monitoring, and evaluation. This will promote commitment and support for civic education activities by all stakeholders. Capacity building will target the human resources of various institutions involved in civic education and the protection of human rights. Trainers, administrators, planners, and policy makers will benefit from training (local and on the job) to allow the smooth operation of the institutions and programs.
- Ensuring parliamentary mechanisms: This capacity-building target aims at improving the effectiveness of parliament and strengthening the institution's ability to interact with the various branches of government and society. The policy framework and legislation pertaining to these capacities are considered adequate; hence the

focus will be placed on other aspects of capacity building. This capacity-building target aims at enhancing national capacities in planning and conducting elections at the national and local levels.

■ Local governance and development management: This aims at developing the software for strengthening governance at the state levels. It is designed to strengthen the capacity of the communities, their representative institutions, and intermediary organizations to participate, in a positive and constructive manner, in the decision-making process. Organization and institution will be enhanced at the local government level to enable local governments to analyze the constraints and opportunities they face in their day-to-day life; propose and plan activities relevant to local conditions, which address the identified problems (using methods, techniques, and technologies appropriate to local conditions such as participatory approaches (RRA, PRA, LLPA, DELTA, etc.)[52] that have evolved over a long period in local communities; be major partners in the implementation of the priority actions; and play a key role in the monitoring and evaluation of all activities, so that appropriate refinements can be made to ensure they remain appropriate to local circumstances and to ensure their sustainability; provide or ensure access to decentralized, local level services and goods from both public agencies and the private sector; facilitate the flow of information and resources from the national level down, and from the local government level up, and ensure strong linkages between national policies and strategies and local-government level plans and action.

■ We need to design a "more comprehensive asset-based strategy, one which might involve virtually the entire community in the complex process of regeneration … processes, basic building blocks of a community's assets combined into a strong and dynamic community building strategy, disciplines of community organising, community economic development and community-based planning inform this whole community strategy, appropriate convenors for this process, providing it with the leadership which invites investment and vision. The steps are mapping completely the capacities and assets of individuals, citizens' and local institutions; building relationships among local assets for mutually beneficial problem-solving within the community; mobilising the community's assets fully for economic development and information sharing purposes; convening as broadly representative a group as possible for the purposes of building a community vision and plan and leveraging activities, investments and resources from outside the community to support asset-based, locally-defined development."[53]

■ Extension, communication, and research: This strategy involves the need for cutting-edge research on the architecture of the modern nation-state, and relations among the state, civic organizations, and the market. It also involves determining the competence and structure of local, regional, and national state institutions and authorities; election systems and processes; financial control and transparency of government spending in a modern democratic state; functioning and funding of political parties; the relations among the media, businesses, the NGO sector, and the government; the role of the civil society and its socioeconomic partners (trade unions, entrepreneurs' associations) in economic and political life and in decision-making processes; the judiciary system in a modern democracy, human rights in a society in transformation, culture, tradition, and renewal; economic growth and globalization; the importance of the economics of the poor; and democratic management of ethnic conflict.

The chapter has endeavored to show that the convergence and amalgamation of the security, economic, and sustainable development agenda signify a negotiating trend toward defining an adaptive paradigm to a new world order. This convergence reflects an emerging consensus on the mutually reinforcing role of political governance and SD. Nonetheless, the comprehension of governance as an SD tool is imprecise because the concept is still evolving. Hence, SD hinges, to a significant degree, on the configuration of governance (political) rules and institutions in state and civil society. This has important implications for social change and hence poverty reduction.

One way of conceptualizing forces of social change is in terms of different forms of "capital"—applied here in the broadest sense as resources or assets that may be utilized to achieve social objectives. For the purposes of conceptualizing poverty-relevant social change, seven forms of capital are particularly relevant: human, economic, social, political (which includes the network of informal and formal political alliances that confer decision-making authority and sources of violence and means of enforcing social norms and maintaining social relationships), and environmental (natural resources). Changes in any one of the forms of capital interact in complex ways with other forms of capital to constitute poverty-relevant social change. Analyses based on different forms of capital may very well lead to similar policy prescriptions. Hence combinations of the following reasoned poverty reduction strategies that have direct implications on begetting sustainable livelihoods (SL) are recommended:

1. We focus our antipoverty strategies primarily on human capital development that links investment in education, health, and nutrition with SL. Policies, strategies, and action plans to enable human development must perforce play a leading role.

2. Second are those mechanisms that increase the primary income of the poor, with emphasis placed on factors that increase the level or price of output and the returns received by poor producers, whereby output is a function of factors of production (land, labor, and physical) capital and financial capital (credit and technology). Increasing output entails increasing the volume, distribution, and productivity or changing the relative prices of factor inputs.

3. Finally, human security, governance, and rights-based poverty reduction promises to cap the entitlement and equity arenas. Sadly, it has been primarily and narrowly reckoned in technocratic terms to refer to public sector management issues (e.g., civil service reform), in public policy terms (market liberalization, privatization), etc. Needless to say, human security is "protecting the vital core of all human lives in ways that enhance human freedoms and human fulfilment—it is protecting fundamental freedoms—freedoms that are the essence of life … build on people's strengths and aspirations … protecting people from critical and pervasive threats … using processes that build on people's strengths and aspirations … creating political, social, environmental, economic, military, and cultural system that together give people the building blocks of survival, livelihood and dignity."[54] In its present use, it embodies three basic principles: *inclusiveness, lawfulness,* and *accountability.*

In the globalization of public policies we are forced to review some issues in the relations among global SD, the nation-state, governance, and citizenship. "The emergence of the modern understanding of citizenship in the West was associated particularly with the advent of capitalism and of centralized nation states in the sixteenth to seventeenth centuries. Citizenship was finally given voice as a massively influential political concept in the seventeenth and eighteenth centuries by the events of the English, American and French Revolutions. The rights announced by these revolutions, their concepts of liberty, equality and fraternity and their attempts to found the modern nation state constitutionally on the will of the people helped to construct the modern Western conception of citizenship." Hence, citizenship will need to go beyond the nation-state, grasping structural complexities that emerge and the new postindustrial and postnational dynamics influencing citizenship from the family and local levels to the transnational level and the intergenerational sphere. [55]

Poor nations need to expedite citizenship development by enlarging people's choices and expanding human capabilities. The three essential capabilities for human development are that people lead long and healthy lives and are knowledgeable about and have access to the resources needed for a decent standard of living. If these basic capabilities are not achieved, many choices are simply not available, and many opportunities remain inaccessible. But the realm of human development goes further: essential areas of choice, highly valued by people, range from political, economic, and social opportunities for being creative and productive to enjoyment of self-respect, empowerment, and a sense of belonging to a community. Human development leads to the realization of human rights—economic, social, cultural, civil, and political.

The crux of the challenge is to create, retain, and put to productive use people who have those qualities throughout the economy. It is basically about having the ability and willingness to identify, sequence, and execute human-centered development priorities and programs in the face of limited human, financial, and institutional capacities. It boils down to formulating and executing national and sectoral policies that would enhance aggregate commitment, willpower, and capacities to mobilize, develop, motivate, encourage, and utilize all segments of the population. Meeting this challenge is synonymous with meeting the development challenge at large. The results, under all probability, would lead to the creation of a strong nation, active in both domestic and world transactions. The overall objective is to develop a critical mass of human qualities and ensure their effective participation in the development process in order to provide, consolidate, expand, and sustain the required base for development within a rapidly shrinking and competitive global environment.

Abbreviations and Acronyms

ALF	Africa Leadership Forum
AS	Adaptive Strategies
AU	African Union
BHN	Basic Human Need Approach
CBD	Capacity-Building Domain
CBM	Capacity-Building Module
CBO	Community-Based Organizations
CHED	Centre for Human Environment and Development
CoP	Communities of Practice
CSOs	Civil Society Organizations
EGS	Employment Generation Schemes
EU	European Union

GCA	Global Coalition for Africa
ICA	Income–Consumption Approach
ICT	Information Communication Technology
IGAD	Inter-Governmental Authority on Development
IMF	International Monetary Fund
IPR	Intellectual Property Rights
IFI	International Finance Institutions
IT	International Trade
KM	Knowledge Management
M&E	Monitoring & Evaluation
MIS	Management Information Systems
MTAs	Multilateral Trade Agreements
MTCS	Multi-Track Communications Systems
NGO	Nongovernmental Organization
NRM	Natural Resources Management
PAPSL	Participatory Assessment and Planning for SL
PMESL	Participatory Monitoring and Evaluation for SL
PMSC	Programme Management, Support and Coordination
PPA	Participatory Poverty Assessment
PPISL	Participatory Implementation for SL
PRSP	Poverty Reduction Strategy Paper
RBA	Rights/Asset-Based Development
SAP	Structural Adjustment Programme
SL	Sustainable Livelihoods
SLA	Sustainable Livelihoods Approach
SSA	Sub-Saharan Africa
TRIPS	Trade Related Intellectual Property Rights
UNGA	United Nations General Assembly
WB	World Bank
WTO	World Trade Organization

References

1. www.unep.org/Documents/Default.Print.asp?DocumentID=52&ArticleID=51-26k-; see also Costantinos, BT (1993), "The Horn of Africa: Human Migration and Adaptation to Marginal Environments, Emerging Paradigms and Political and Environmental Dimensions to Participatory Counter-Desertification Measures," Intergovernmental Negotiating Committee on the Convention for Desertification, Bamako/Paris.
2. Costantinos, BT (2000), Policy Analysis, Formulation, and Management in Sustainable Livelihoods: An Issues Paper, paper developed for the United Nations Development Program BDP as a think piece and working paper on expanded SL program development.

3. Costantinos, BT (1997, 2), Building in-country capacity for sustainable democracy, Zambia Case Study—International Institute for Democracy and Electoral Assistance (Mission Report), pp. 2–3.

4. Copstantinos, BT (1997), "Strategic approaches to building capacity for community-based conflict management," backgrounder prepared for the Malawi SLP, PAPSL tools, UNDP/GoM, Malawi, http://www.carnegie.org/sub/pubs/corp.html.

5. See Costantinos, BT (1996), "Political transitions in Africa: An Ethiopian case study," ALF/GCA Washington, Addis Ababa, pp. 22, 24, 234, where it has been underpinned that the passage to democracy in developing nations is political development problematique. This is not merely because of the challenges of balancing the desire for an immediate democratic transition with the reality of initiating a democratic transition in nations and states with a limited democratic experience, an underdeveloped civil society, and high levels of illiteracy. It is also fact that the transition was bound to have shortcomings that stem in part from historical and structural conditions marked by authoritarian and militarist tradition for a good part of our history.

6. Forest Trees and People Report (1994), pp. 5–9; Costantinos, BT (2000), "Policy Analysis, Formulation, and Management in Sustainable Livelihoods: An Issues Paper," paper developed for the UNDP BDP as a think piece and working paper on expanded SL program development.

7. Developing nations are also unique in their ecological and cultural diversity, manifested, for example, by their more than 2,000 languages. Recently, the linkages between biological and cultural diversity have been increasingly acknowledged in the development agenda.

8. Politicians, as are chieftains, are groomed in the neopatrimonial style of politics; the linkages are fragmentary and on a dyadic basis. The problem with clientelistic exchanges is that they remain highly personal and do not contribute to the creation of forms of trust and reciprocity beyond those narrow relations. Finally, both cultural structures that allow for the articulation and aggregation of interests in society are rudimentary.

9. Costantinos, BT (2000); FTPP (1994), pp. 5–9; www.unep.org/Documents/Default.Print.asp?DocumentID=52&ArticleID=51-26k-.

10. Ethiopian Government (1975), "Proclamation to Make All Rural Lands Public Property," Addis Ababa.

11. Forest Trees and People (1994), p. 5.

12. Costantinos, BT (1997, 2), "Local Institutions, Farmers' Local Knowledge, Research and Practice in Ethiopia: A Primer on Sustainable Livelihoods," paper presented to International Conference on Creativity and Innovations at Grassroots for Sustainable Natural Resources Management, Institutional Innovations—Ahmedabad, January, pp. 10–14.

13. Forest Trees and People (1994); see also http://www.undp.org/fssd/approach.htm. Although communal management systems are also susceptible to co-optation by dominant individuals and groups, accountable and transparent management is more likely to be found within decentralized systems.

14. Costantinos, BT (1997, 2).
15. Lane, CR, ed. (1995), "Custodians of the Commons," EARTHSCAN Publications, p. 5.
16. Forest Trees and People (1994), pp. 5–6.
17. Lane CR, ed. (1995); Forest Trees and People (1994), p. 7.
18. See Colfer, C, Pierce, J, Gill, DW, and F (1988), "An Indigenous Agricultural Model from West Sumatra: A Source of Scientific Thought for Agricultural Systems," 26 (2): 191–209; also see Jorgensen, DL (1989), "Participant Observation: The Methodology for Human Studies," London: Sage Publications; O'Brien, PJ (1975), "A Critique of Latin American Theories of Dependency," in Oxaal, I, et al., eds., "Beyond the Sociology of Development," London: Routledge & Kegan Paul; Ghai, DP (1977), "What Is the Basic Needs Approach to Development All About?," in Ghai, DP, et al., "The Basic Needs Approach to Development," Geneva: ILO; Sandbrook, R (1982), "The Politics of Basic Needs," London: Heinemann; Lipton, M (1977), "Why Poor People Stay Poor: Urban Bias in World Development," Cambridge, Mass: Harvard University Press.
19. http://www.undp.org/fssd/approach.htm; UNDP (1998), Sustainable Livelihoods, Executive Board Note—New York. UNDP defines the SLA as an integrated package of policy, technology, and investment strategies together with appropriate decision-making tools that are used together to promote sustainable livelihoods by building on local adaptive strategies. The approach seeks to overcome the limitations of earlier "participatory approaches." Its value added arises from several features. These include the provision of an integrated framework in which aspects of several earlier approaches come together synergistically; assessment of community assets, adaptive strategies, and livelihood activities as the entry point; and strong emphasis on the questions of sustainability in economic, environmental, and social terms. Governance and policy questions and their interlinkages are addressed in a cross-sectoral and holistic manner by focusing impacts analysis on the totality of the livelihood system and its sustainability rather than on sectors and examining the interlocking nature of macro- and microlinkages, sectoral policies, and social policies with governance arrangement. This broad definition takes on specific and operational meaning mainly at the household or community level in the biophysical and socioeconomic contexts in which they are located.
20. Banuri, T, and Holmberg, J (1992), "Governance for Sustainable Development: A View from the South," London: IIED.
21. Titti and Singh (1996) (1995), "Adaptive Strategies in Arid and Semi-Arid Lands," IISD Resources Paper, pp. 23–34; UNDP (1998); Costantinos, BT (1998).
22. Costantinos, BT (2000); see also http://www.undp.org/governance/, http://www.carnegie.org/sub/pubs/corp.html, www.unep.org/Documents/Default.Print.asp?DocumentID=52&ArticleID=51-26k-.

23. Stresses and shocks arise from, inter alia, natural resources degradation; the population resource balance and biological carrying capacity; social conflicts; disabling policies, parasitic states, market manipulations; slow-onset naturally induced stresses and shocks—drought, pest infestations, postharvest losses, epidemics, and pandemics; rapid-onset naturally induced stresses and shocks.

24. Hardman, M, and Midgely, J (1981),"The Social Dimensions of Development," New York: Wiley; Cardoso, FH "Dependence and Development In Latin America," *New Left Review*, July–August. Sunkel, O (1969), "National Development Policy and External Dependence in Latin America," *Journal of Development Studies*, Vol. 6, no. 1.

25. http://www.undp.org/governance/, http://www.carnegie.org/sub/pubs/corp.html, www.unep.org/Documents/Default.Print.asp?DocumentID =52& ArticleID=51-26k-.

26. See McCracken, J, and Pretty J "Glossary of Terms in Sustainable Agriculture," IIED Gatekeeper Series No. London.

27. Costantinos, BT (1999), "Social capital and adaptive conflict management: Legal and policy framework, natural resources–based conflict management typologies, and lessons learned for mainstreaming best practices," A Centre for Human Environment Research Programme supported by FTPP Ethiopia, the Commission of the European Union and Studies under the International Institute of Sustainable Development, p. 12.

28. Costantinos, BT (1996), "Political Transitions in Africa: An Ethiopian Case Study," ALF/GCA, Washington, Addis Ababa.

29. Chazan, N (1999), "Politics and Society in Contemporary Africa," Colorado, p. 32.

30. http://www.undp.org/governance/.

31. Op. cit.

32. Costantinos, BT (1996).

33. Costantinos, BT, et al. (1997), **"Building in-country capacity for sustainable democracy, Zambia Case Study"**—International Institute for Democracy and Electoral Assistance, (Mission Report).

34. Op. cit. More specifically, it has tools to record community responses on what has been the impact of ecosystem, socioeconomic, and political changes on livelihoods. What are the demographic, socioeconomic, cultural, and political responses (adaptive strategies) of communities to these changes? Are there differential responses between men and women? What informs these responses: Traditional, contemporary knowledge and practices or the integration of the two? Internal and external technological innovations? Have these responses led (or do they have the potential to lead) to sustainable livelihoods? What kinds of interventions (communication and outreach strategies, technological innovation, etc.) are needed to enhance community responses so that they lead to sustainable outcomes? What is the process by which communities and external change agents integrate contemporary and indigenous knowledge in pursuit of adaptive strategies that lead to sustainable livelihoods? What economic, ecological, social, cultural, or political environment contributes to the evolution of

successful adaptive strategies (best practice)? To what extent does this environment impact positively or negatively on poverty alleviation, employment generation, and social cohesion? What indicators can be used to measure progress? What role can external agents play in developing indicators and reinforcing adaptive strategies? And what kinds of policy changes are needed to support the evolution or enhancement of adaptive strategies that lead to sustainable livelihoods?

35. Spretnak, C (1996), "State of Grace—the Recovery of Meaning in the Post Modern Age," San Francisco: Harper, pp. 33–39.
36. Kanyinga, K "The Social Political Context of the Growth of NGOs in Kenya," in Fibbon, P (ed.), "Social Change and Economic Reform in Kenya," pp. 48–49.
37. Chazan, N (1999), "Politics and Society in Contemporary Africa," Colorado.
38. Fowler, A (1989), "CSOs and Development in Kenya: Interim Results of a Survey," paper presented for the workshop Into the Nineties: CSOs during the Current Development Plan and Beyond, IDS and KNCSS, Nairobi.
39. Op. cit.; see also Costantinos, BT (1995), "Participation in development and citizenship: Taking stock of the ideology and practice," paper presented to the first networking conference, Society for Participatory Development, SPADE, Ethiopia.
40. Costantinos, BT (1996), p. 232; see also Fowler, A, Campbell, P, Pratt, B (1992), "Institutional Development and CSOs in Africa: Policy Perspectives for European Development Agencies," INTRAC, Oxfam, UK, pp. 19–20, 22.
41. Op. cit.
42. Op. cit.; also for general reference see http://www.undp.org/governance/.
43. Op. cit.
44. See Singh, JS (1977), "A new international economic order: Towards a fair distribution of the world's resources," New York: Praeger; Bagwahati, JN (1977), "The New International Economic Order: The North South Debate," Cambridge, Mass.: MIT Press; Tinbergen, J (1978), "RIO: Reshaping the International Order: A Report to the Club of Rome"; Lewis, WA (1978), "The Evolution of the International Economic Order," Princeton: Princeton University Press; ILO (1976–1977), "Employment Growth and Basic Needs: Meeting Basic Needs Strategies for Eradicating Mass Poverty and Unemployment," Geneva.
45. Ibid.
46. Ibid.
47. Costantinos, BT (1997), "Strategic approaches to building capacity for democratic transition in Africa," backgrounder prepared for the International Advisory Group on Capacity Building, International IDEA, Stockholm, p. 12.
48. Op. cit.
49. Op. cit.; see also Furtado, C (1971–1972), "Development under Development." Berkeley: University of California Press; Fowler, A and R James, "The Role of Southern CSOs in Development Cooperation," Occasional Paper Series No. 2 INTRAC, Oxford, UK; Fowler, A (1992), "Striking a Balance," Oxford ; Ng'ethe Njuguna (1989), "In Search of CSOs: Towards

a Funding Strategy to Create NGO Research Capacity in Eastern and Southern Africa," Occasional Paper No. 58, Institute for Development Studies, University of Nairobi, Nairobi, Kenya; Korten, DC (1987), "Third Generation NGO Strategies: A Key to People-Centered Development," *World Development*, Vol. 15 (Supplement), pp. 145–159.

50. Ibid.
51. Costantinos, BT (1999) "Is good governance evaluable? Concepts, strategic and processual elements, and analytical limitations in evaluating national political and economic governance," ECA, Sept. 21–23, Addis Ababa, Ethiopia.
52. Bratton, M (1989), "The Politics of Government–NGO Relations in Africa," *World Development* Vol. 17, pp. 569–589; Costantinos, BT (1999).
53. Kretzmann, JP, and McNight, JL (1993), "Building communities from inside out—a path towards finding and mobilizing community assets," Chicago: ACTA Publications.
54. UN Commission on Human Security (2003), "Human Security Now: Protecting and Empowering People," New York: OUP; www.un.org/publications.
55. Korsgaad, O (1995), "Adult Education, Democracy and Globalisation," *Journal of World Education* 2.

Chapter 4

Systems Concept of Sustainability and Sustainable Development

Desta Mebratu

CONTENTS

Introduction

Although contemporary environmentalism started to emerge in the 1960s, its effect spread to every corner of the world in the 1980s, leading to an upsurge of the environmental movement throughout the world. This attracted increased attention from national and international political machineries, and growing interest and curiosity within the academic community. As we enter into the beginning of the third millennium, we find ourselves overwhelmed by complexities unprecedented in human history (Mebratu, 2000). Today, mankind has the capacity to produce far more information than anyone can absorb, to foster far greater interdependency than anyone can manage, and to accelerate change far faster than anyone has the ability to keep pace (Senge, 1990). Parallel to (or as a result of) this unprecedented labyrinth of complexity, we have myriad systemic dysfunctions, each with its own ecological, economic, and social dimensions, that do not have simple causes or solutions.

It has been nearly a decade since the terms *sustainable development* and *sustainability* "rose to the prominence of mantra or a shibboleth" (Daly, 1996) after the 1987 publication of the United Nations– (UN-) sponsored World Commission on Environment and Development (WCED) report *Our Common Future*. Despite its reported vagueness and ambiguity, the WCED definition of sustainable development has been highly instrumental in developing a "global view" with respect to our planet's future (Mebratu, 1998).

Since then, thousands of initiatives have been taken at local, national, and global levels in an attempt to address different aspects of the environmental challenges. A number of encouraging local outcomes have ensued from these activities. However, their impact in shaping "our common future" on a more sustainable basis seems to be minimal when measured against the enormity of the global environmental challenges. This has led to an increasing level of frustration and disenchantment, even among the different groups promoting the concept of sustainable development (Mebratu, 1998). It is in this context that the enhancement of the conceptual clarity of sustainability and sustainable development becomes of vital importance. This chapter attempts to present a new conceptual framework for that concept. To this end, the first section looks at the conceptual precursors for sustainability and sustainable development. This is followed by a review of the most relevant systems and evolutionary principles that constitute the conceptual frameworks that are going to be used. The last two sections describe sustainability and sustainable development in terms of the preceding chapters.

Conceptual Precursors on Sustainability

The WCED definition of sustainable development is taken as a starting point for most current discussions on the concept. The WCED report, which is also known as the Brundtland Commission Report, constituted a major political turning point for the concept of sustainable development. But it is neither the starting point nor the possible end of the conceptual development process (Mebratu, 1998). As with any conceptual process governed by general evolutionary theory, there are some significant conceptual precursors that led to the WCED's definition of sustainable development, which in turn was followed by other conceptualization efforts (Mebratu, 1998). This section focuses on reviewing the historical and conceptual precursors of the concept of sustainable development.

Religious Beliefs and Traditions

Historically, religions have taught us to perceive and act on nonhuman nature in terms of particular human interests, beliefs, and social structures (Mebratu, 1998). To assess religion's view of nature and to see how contemporary theology deals with the environmental crises, we must attend with care to the full range of writings and practices that religious traditions offer. Many writers have found the Judeo-Christian writings about "man's right to master the Earth" an essential source of the havoc wreaked by Western societies upon the Earth. Other religious environmentalists have discovered environmentally positive passages in classic texts, and they claim that Judaism and Christianity are more environmentally minded than they seem at first glance (Kinsley, 1996).

Besides the dominant religions of East and West, there are numerous indigenous beliefs and traditions that were used as the basis for traditional coping mechanisms long before the rise of any religious beliefs (Mebratu, 1998). One still can find numerous cases of such beliefs, based on indigenous traditions and values, that are used as the basis of community life. In Hawaiian thought, there are close parallels between humans and nature (Dudley, 1996). Hawaiians traditionally have viewed the entire world as being alive in the same way that humans are alive. Similarly, there was no such thing as emptiness in the world for a Lakota Indian (Mathiessen, 1984). Even in the sky there were no vacant places. Life was existent everywhere, visible and invisible, and every object imparted great interest to life.

In the African view, the universe is both visible and invisible, unending, and without limits (Mbiti, 1996). Events come and go in the form of minor and major rhythms. For African tradition, man is not the master of the universe: "He is only the center, the friend, the beneficiary, and the user.

For this reason, he must live in harmony with the universe, obeying the laws of natural, moral, and mystical order" (Mbiti, 1996). If these are unduly disturbed, it is man who suffers most.

In general, the following are the major conclusions that can be drawn from the analysis of religious and traditional beliefs on sustainability and sustainable development (Mebratu, 1998):

- A critical review of the writings on both sides leads to the conclusion that religions have neither been simple agents of environmental degradation nor unmixed repositories of ecological wisdom.
- Although they have different contexts and structures, all of the indigenous traditions and beliefs have the core element of the importance of living in harmony with nature.
- An important lesson to be drawn from indigenous traditions and beliefs is the "holistic vision" that is inherent in all of the beliefs and the importance attached to being in constant communication with nature.
- Whatever environmental value we may find in the teachings of the different religions of East and West, and the indigenous traditions and practices, it would be unrealistic to advocate any of these traditions as the basis for addressing the environmental crises of the 21st century.
- Nonetheless, traditional wisdom has much to offer in terms of living in harmony with nature and in society, and this is one of the fundamental tenets of the concept of sustainability.

Economics and the Theory of Limits

Toward the end of the 18th century, many of the evil effects of the industrial revolution had surfaced. Unemployment, poverty, and disease were already problems calling for remedial treatment. Contrary to the ideas of William Goldwin (1756–1836) and the marquis de Condorcet (1743–1794), Thomas Malthus said that the vices and misery that plague society are not due to evil human institutions, but to the fecundity of the human race (Oser and Blanchfield, 1975). This belief led to his theory of population dynamics. According to Malthus's theory, population, when unchecked, increases geometrically while subsistence increases arithmetically, at best (Oser and Blanchfield, 1975). Together with David Ricardo (1772–1823), who fundamentally agreed with his population theory, Malthus expressed his "environmental limits thinking" in terms of the limits on the supply of good-quality agricultural land and the resultant diminishing returns in agricultural production (Pearce and Turner, 1990).

For Malthus, the fixed amount of land available meant that as the population grew, diminishing returns would reduce the per capita food supply. The standard of living would be forced down to a subsistence level, and the population would cease to grow. Diminishing returns set in, not so much because of absolute scarcity, but because of the varying quality of available land. The fundamental shortcoming of this theory is that, in both cases, "the subject of diminishing returns was defined on the basis of keeping the total production curve fixed" (Pearce and Turner, 1990). In reality, technical innovations, such as the use of fertilizers, have shifted the total production curve upward, increasing output per unit of input and offsetting the tendency toward diminishing returns. Still, the Malthusian theory of "environmental limits" may be considered a precursor to the concept of sustainable development (Mebratu, 1998).

Political Economy and the "Scale" of Organization

Looking back at the history of political economics, one finds the "subterranean tradition" of organic and decentralist economists, among whom Ernest F. Schumacher could be cited as the principal one. According to Roszak (1989), it would be no exaggeration to call Schumacher the Keynes of postindustrial society, by which he meant a society that has left behind its lethal obsession with those megasystems of production and distribution that Keynes tried so hard to make manageable. The first work of Schumacher appeared in 1959, *The Crucial Problems of Modern Living*. His works culminated in international recognition and fame after the first publication of his famous book *Small Is Beautiful* in 1979. The themes addressed in this book included the following:

- Sharp criticism of overorganized systems as destructive of the human spirit and of the planet alike
- Concern about the rapid depletion of natural resources and the corresponding destruction of the environment
- Concept of intermediate or appropriate technology and the importance of human scale, perhaps the concept for which the book is best known
- Failure of traditional economics to include incommensurable "noneconomic factors" in the policy-making process
- Need for human beings to be close to the nurturing land, in both fact and spirit (McClaughry, 1989)

Although the book contains a number of controversial and debatable ideas, Schumacher's concern about the exhaustion of the planet's resources gave new impetus to a whole generation of environmental defenders

(Mebratu, 1998). His effort of looking at the economic, ecological, and social aspects of a given system added a new dimension to the discourse on the "scale of organization." Some experts believe that the concept of appropriate technology defined as technology that takes heed of the skill, levels of population, availability of natural resources, and pressing social needs defined by the people themselves is the immediate precursor to the concept of sustainable development. According to DuBose and associates (1995), "sustainable development can be traced back at least as far as the mid-1960s, when appropriate technology was promoted as the way to help develop the lesser developed countries."

Post-Stockholm Conference Trends

The 1972 UN Conference on Human Environment in Stockholm, which recognized the "importance of environmental management and the use of environmental assessment as a management tool" (DuBose et al., 1995), represents a major step forward in the development of the concept of sustainable development. Even if the link between environmental and developmental issues did not emerge strongly, there were indications that the form of economic development would have to be altered (Mebratu, 1998).

In the years following, the terms *environment and development, development without destruction*, and *environmentally sound development* evolved and finally, the term *ecodevelopment* appeared in the United Nations (UN) Environment Program review in 1978. By this time, it became recognized internationally that environmental and developmental ideas needed to be considered concurrently. According to Tryzna (1995), however, the first major breakthrough in conceptual insight was that of the International Union for the Conservation of Nature (IUCN).

If the IUCN takes the credit for using the term *sustainable development* for the first time, the WCED, through its report *Our Common Future* (1987), provided the major political turning point that made the concept of great geopolitical significance and the catch-phrase it has become today (Holmberg, 1994). The report of WCED, also known as the Bruntland Commission Report, contains the key statement of sustainable development, which is defined as "development that meets the needs of the present without compromising the ability of future generations to meet their own needs" (WCED, 1987). This definition marks the concept's political coming of age and establishes the content and structure of the present debate (Kirkby et al., 1995). The conceptual definition of the Brundtland Commission Report contains two key concepts (Mebratu, 1998):

- The concept of "needs," in particular the essential needs of the world's poor, to which overriding priority should be given
- The idea of limitations imposed by the state of technology and social organization on the environment's ability to meet present and future needs

The commission underlined the strong linkages among poverty alleviation, environmental improvement, and social equitability through sustainable economic growth. Not surprisingly, since it may be interpreted in so many different ways, the Brundtland Commission's definition of sustainable development has received very wide acceptance. As noted by Pearce and colleagues (1989), "It fits nicely into political sound bites compared with its predecessor's 'eco-development'; it is something to which everyone can agree, like motherhood and apple pie." According to Daly (1996), having consensus on a vague concept, rather than disagreement over a sharply defined one, was a "good political strategy." In the late nineties, however, this initial vagueness was no longer a basis for consensus, but a breeding ground for disagreement.

Post-WCED Trends

Since the definition and subsequent popularization of the term by WCED in 1987, numerous efforts have been made by different groups, organizations, and individuals to capture the meaning of the concept. Although it is a cumbersome task to cover exhaustively all the definitions that have mushroomed over the years, in broad terms the existing variety of definitions of sustainable development can be categorized into three major groups, depending on the constituent representation reflected in their presentation (Mebratu, 1998). These are (1) the institutional version, (2) the ideological version, and (3) the academic version.

All of these definitions are based on acceptance that the world is faced with an environmental crisis and that we must make a fundamental change to overcome this crisis. Instead of focusing on the semantics used in the different groups of definitions, Mebratu (1998) reviewed the major groups of definitions with respect to the following questions: What is identified as the source of the crisis? What is the core approach to the solution? What is the proposed solution platform? What is the key instrument for the solution?

For the institutional version, the definitions given by WCED, the International Institute of Environment and Development (IIED), and the World Business Council for Sustainable Development (WBCSD) can be taken as representative. A synoptic comparison of these definitions shows that they all share the same definition of sustainable development, which

Table 4.1 Comparative Analysis of the Institutional Version of Sustainability

Institution	Drivers	Solution Epicenter	Solution Platform	Instruments (Leadership)
WCED	Political consensus	Sustainable growth	Nation-state	Governments and international organisations
IIED	Rural development	Primary environmental care (PEC)	Communities	National and international NGOs
WBCSD	Business interest	Eco-efficiency	Business and industry	Corporate leadership

Source: Mebratu, 1998.

is very much based on *need satisfaction,* with a wide spectrum of interpretation. As can be seen from Table 4.1, the differences in interpretation are reflected in their differences regarding the identification of the *epicenter* of the solution, the *solution platform,* and the *leadership center* for actualizing the solution. These factors are very much influenced by the *institutional objectives,* which are the direct reflection of the interests of the establishment (Mebratu 2000).

At the ideological level, although there are some factors that indicate the emergence of a distinct green ideology, the environmental versions of classic ideologies such as liberation theology, radical feminism, and Marxism are the dominant ones. Although the conceptual basis of eco-theology, ecofeminism, and ecosocialism are rooted in very different liberation theories (as may be seen from Table 4.2), there is a striking structural similarity among these versions in the identification of the source of the environmental crisis, the solution epicenter, and the role of leadership (Mebratu, 1998).

In the academic version, the economist, ecologist, and sociologist conceptualizations reflect the response of the scientific community to the challenge of the environmental crisis of the 21st century. In general, the academic versions exhibit conceptual shortcomings of one type or another that are related to their reductionist epistemological foundations and reflected in their solution frameworks (Mebratu, 2000). Although the increasing acceptance of the interdisciplinary nature of the issue by the scientific community is a source of encouragement, there is a danger that the prevailing conflicts of views about the environmental crisis, which arise from being locked within the reductionist way of thinking, may harden into inflexible and polarized oppositions (Redclift and Woodgate,

Table 4.2 Comparative Analysis of the Ideological Version of Sustainability

Ideology	Liberation Theory	Source of the Environmental Crisis	Solution Epicenter	Leadership Center
Eco-theology	Liberation theology	Disrespect to divine providence	Spiritual revival	Churches and congregations
Eco-feminism	Radical Feminism	Male-centred (Androcentric) epistemology	Gynocentric value hierarchy	Women's movement
Eco-socialism	Marxism	Capitalism	Social egalitarianism	Labour movement

Source: Mebratu, 1998.

Table 4.3 Comparative Analysis of the Academic Version of Sustainability

Academic Discipline	Drivers (Epistemological Orientation)	Source of Environmental Crisis	Solution Epicenter	Instruments (Mechanism of Solutions)
Environmental economics	Economic reductionism	Undervaluing of ecological goods	Internalisation of externalities	Market instrument
Deep ecology	Ecological reductionism	Human domination over nature	Reverence and respect for nature	Bio-centric egalitarianism
Social ecology	Reductionist-holistic	Domination of people and nature	Co-evolution of nature and humanity	Re-thinking of the social hierarchy

Source: Mebratu, 1998.

1994) (see Table 4.3). The source of the problem is that each discipline approaches the other in a reductionist fashion, seeking to impose its view of goals and procedures on the decision-making process (Tryzna, 1995). In this respect, there is a growing consensus about the need for a new way of scientific thinking based on radical revision of existing approaches, with the objective of transcending the pervasive "dualism" of subject–object, mind–matter, nature–society, and so on, that dominates modern thinking (Clarke, 1993).

The Conceptual Framework

The alternative conceptual framework proposed in this chapter is based on the key principles of systems evolution and information theories. The following section discusses the key principles used as the basis. This is followed by a discussion on the principle of hierarchies and interactions as a source of dynamic complexities.

Systems Evolution and Information

One of the most deeply buried metaphors of science is the concept of a "thing" or "part" that can be separated cleanly from other things or parts. The metaphor is so deep that we seldom know when we are using it (Weinberg, 1975). Our use of the "part" or "thing" metaphor is closely allied to our experience of physical space, and particularly to our experience of "boundaries." Thus, the "thing" is separated from its environment by an imaginary boundary, and the interaction between the "thing" and its environment is described in terms of distinct "input–output" relationships.

Problems particularly arise because the choice of boundaries will be very much influenced by the specialized way of thinking and principles, by past experiences, and, most of the time, by the purpose of the specific system exercise (Mebratu, 2000). Although the boundary metaphor more easily permeates systems thinking through diagrams than through analogical statements, it has led to the derailing of the very purpose of systems thinking: overcoming the limitation of reductionist simplicity in the organized complex region (Weinberg, 1975).

According to specialized systems thinking (Weinberg, 1975), systems are thoroughly man-made, and the definition of a specific system is the point of view of one or several observers. Utilizing systems thinking for the concept of sustainability requires revitalizing the specialized systems thinking on basis of the principles and spirit of general systems thinking. The key element of this revitalizing process, in this context, is the redefinition of the concept called *system* (Mebratu, 2000).

With respect to the relationship between evolution and information, Ayres (1994) indicated that all physical processes and transformations (including phylogenic evolution) can be described in terms of two fundamental information quantities. These are, respectively, pure uncertainty-reducing or distinguishability information (D information) and evolutionary survival–relevant information (SR information). According to Ayres, D information is a quantity that exists independently of any reference system or observer and hence is an extensive variable. Thus, it can be regarded as a fundamental variable for describing the natural world. In contrast,

SR information is the information that is relevant to the evolutionary selection process and is definable only in terms of a specific local system. Hence, it is an intensive variable.

The combined application of general systems thinking and general evolutionary theory provides a new framework of systems, which include the following variables:

- A unit is any organized physical entity with a specific functional purpose and manifestation. Each unit is characterized by the D information embodied within it.
- An environment is the field of significance of a unit within which it conducts its functional purposes and exhibits its manifestations. The field of significance (the environment) is characterized by the SR factors, which have multiple dimensions.
- There is a dynamic linkage between the unit and its environment that is exhibited through the complex web of interaction. The interaction within and between the D factors and the SR factors defines the functional capacity of the system.
- A system is the totality of a physical unit, its environment as a field of significance, and the interaction between the units and their environment.
- Evolution, as the processing, accumulation, and transferring of survival-relevant (SR) information, maximizes the embodiment of D information (diversity, complexity, and stability) (Mebratu, 2000).

To illustrate the unit and system relationship with an example, an individual person can be described as both a unit and a system. His or her identity as a unit is defined by the distinguishability information that has been organized in the form of deoxyribonucleic acid (DNA).[1] This sets the boundary condition for what it can be and what it cannot be. The surroundings within which the individual exists will provide the field of significance within which the individual functions as a system. Similar analogies can be made for industrial and social units and systems.

Hierarchy and Interaction: Source of Dynamic Complexity

According to the general model of organized complexity (Checkland, 1993), there exists a hierarchy of levels of organization, each more complex than the one below, and each level characterized by emergent properties at the lower level. Thus, entities that are whole at one level of the hierarchy simultaneously become parts of the higher level of entities (Mebratu, 2000). Thus, a given system exhibits the properties of being a whole and a part at a given moment in time. An individual person is a whole on its own and a part of the family, which is a higher system in the social hierarchy.

Figure 4.1 depicts the cosmic hierarchy developed based on this principle. The model is based on the presence of both horizontal and vertical hierarchy, clearly indicating that the existence of a specific level in the hierarchy is strictly dependent on the existence of the earlier level in the vertical and in the horizontal hierarchy. The following are the major features of the cosmic hierarchy (Mebratu, 2000):

- The horizontal hierarchy depicts the universe hierarchy that is divided into abiotic, biotic, social, and economic cosmoses in the order of their precedence. Thus, the abiotic cosmos is the basis for the existence of the universe, and the economic cosmos is the last element in the hierarchy.
- The vertical hierarchy depicts the hierarchy within the cosmos. Each cosmos has a base element, which serves as a basis to the specific cosmos and as a linking element of the specific cosmos with the earlier cosmos in the hierarchy.
- Thus, the basic units, which are the atoms of the abiotic cosmos, the cell of the biotic cosmos, the human being of the human universe, the firm of the economic cosmos, and the family of the social cosmos, are the critical elements that keep the whole universe together through their vertical and horizontal functions.
- This structure leads to the conclusion that any tampering with respect to the core elements has to be done with utmost care since it has two-dimensional effects in both the horizontal and vertical directions of the cosmic hierarchy.[2]
- Market, as the socioeconomic institution through which information is exchanged, holds a prominent position in defining the functional efficiency of any given socioeconomic system.
- The key principle of the natural universe is evolution; the governing principle of the human universe is social transformation. The combined principle of the natural and human universe is, however, coevolution.

The relationships and interactions among the different aspects of the cosmic universe are described by the cosmic matrix (Table 4.4). The cosmic matrix is composed of the cosmic processes, measurable flows, regulating mechanisms, nonstable parameters, and nondesirable outcomes (Mebratu, 2000). The cosmic processes are those processes that inherently determine stability within the cosmic regimes, and the measurable flows are characteristic parameters or flows that define the nature of the cosmic processes. The regulating mechanisms are the cosmic mechanisms through

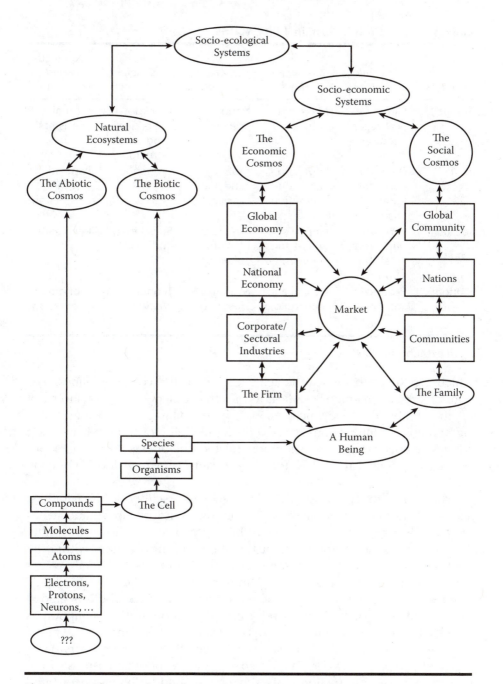

Figure 4.1 The cosmic hierarchy. (From Mebratu, 2000.)

Table 4.4   The Cosmic Sustainability Matrix

Cosmos	Cosmic Process	Measurable Flows	Regulating Mechanisms	Nonstable Parameters	Nonregulated Outcomes
Abiotic	Geophysical regeneration	Mass and energy	Natural cycles	Breakdown of cycles and seismic structures	Natural disasters
Biotic	Reproduction and metabolism	Population and consumption	Mobility and succession	Overshoots	Population crash/ extinction
Social	Participation and distribution	Empowerment and welfare	Structural transformation	Social inequity	Revolution
Economic	Production and exchange	Capital and technology	Market adjustment	Economic inflation	Economic depression

Source: Mebratu, 1998.

which a cosmic steady state is achieved within the cosmic regimes. The nonstable phenomena are indicators of effects of persistent offshoots of the measurable flows beyond the steady-state limit as a result of a feedback lag and cosmic interactions that override the ability of the feedback loop within the specific cosmos. The nonregulated outcome is the spontaneous corrective mechanism that restores the system to a new level of steady state.

The cosmic process of the abiotic cosmos is described as the geophysical regeneration that is based on thermodynamic principles, and it has mass and energy as its major measurable characteristic flows (Mebratu, 2000). The cosmic performance of the abiotic cosmos is kept within the limit of a steady state through the various natural cycles such as the water and nitrogen cycles. On the other hand, the cosmic process of the biotic cosmos is the combined effect of reproduction and metabolism guided by the principles of evolution, and it has population and consumption as the characteristic measurable flows. The cosmic performance of the biotic cosmos is kept within the limit of a steady state through the primary effect of mobility and succession. With respect to the economic cosmos of the human universe, production and exchange, guided by human needs and aspirations, are identified as its cosmic process; capital (both natural and human) and technology (both natural and human) are the measurable parameters. The cosmic performance of the economic cosmos is regulated by the continuous adjustment of the market.

Participation and distribution measured by the level of empowerment and welfare are identified as the cosmic processes that constitute the social cosmos of the human universe. The cosmic performance of the social cosmos is kept within the limit of sustainability through structural trans-formation of governance that goes hand in hand with the economic cosmos.

Excessive accumulation and depletion, population, and consumption overshoots; economic inflation; and social inequity are the nonstable parameters for the abiotic, biotic, economic, and social cosmos, respec-tively, indicating an unstable situation (Mebratu, 2000).

The corresponding corrective phenomena of these undesirable out-comes, from the point of view of cosmic stability, are natural disasters such as earthquake, droughts, and floods for the abiotic cosmos. Similarly, sudden population crashes and gradual extinction of species are the corrective mechanisms for the biotic cosmos, and economic depressions and revolutions are corrective mechanisms for the economic cosmos and the social cosmos, respectively. Although each cosmic system is treated separately for the sake of convenience and clarity, in the actual case there will be a varying second-degree effect of one cosmic system over the other depending on the level of hierarchy within the cosmic hierarchy (Figure 4.1). However, this does not rule out the possibility of the existence of an independent region of an abiotic cosmic system that is beyond the reach of the human universe.

Considering the complexity of the environmental challenges, it is proposed that the conceptual limitations may be overcome through the combined application of the general systems theory and the general evolutionary theory. The basic principles of systems and evolutionary theories that are adapted to this research are (Mebratu, 2000) the following:

- Evolution is an irreversible and nonlinear change of both natural and man-made systems in domains far from thermodynamic equi-librium (Malaska, 1991).
- The direction of evolution is characterized by an increasing ability of organisms and systems to sense and assess the state of the environment, to learn appropriate responses, and to transmit this information to succeeding generations (Ayres, 1994).
- Systems with organized complexity can only be understood by looking at their dynamic interrelationships (feedback), a process that is more than linear summation of cause–effect chains (Check-land, 1993).

These and other relevant principles of general systems and evolutionary and information theories are used as the basis to develop an alternative conceptual framework for sustainability and sustainable development, which is presented in this chapter.

Sustainability: As a Systemic Property

In the preceding section, we saw the cosmic interaction that is built upon the vertical and horizontal interactions of the four cosmic components. The properties at the system level will be quite different from the cosmic properties because no unit system could be distinctly categorized in one or the other cosmos. In other words, systems exhibit a four-dimensional property (abiotic, biotic, social, and economic), with a varying degree of one or the other cosmic properties, as a manifestation of cosmic interaction (Mebratu, 2000). When we divide the cosmic interactions in accordance with the vertical hierarchy of the cosmic hierarchy (Figure 4.1), we find that the foundation for the cosmic interaction is the interaction between the abiotic and biotic cosmoses, laying down the basis for any kind of systems sustainability.

The definition of the concept of sustainability within the context of this chapter is based on the following two assertions (Mebratu, 2000). First, every unit has a given functional capacity, which follows an initially increasing and later decreasing pattern with time. This is in line with the ontological (life cycle) pattern of development that covers the ascendancy, climax, and retrogression phases. The second assertion is that every system has a succession function that enables the system to sustain its functional capacity through alternative cycles of succession. Sustainability is, therefore, the maintenance of a given level of systemic function that reconciles with the principal feedback loops of natural cycles and succession through the proper combination of unit functional capacity and succession time (Mebratu, 2000). As such, sustainability can be considered as the driving force behind any systemic function.

Plotting the functional capacity of a system over its lifetime gives the sustainability curve for a given system. Figure 4.2 depicts the functional capacity of a system with time, each curve representing the functional path of the system over its lifetime and the successive curves representing the successive systems. The area under each curve represents the total functional capacity of a system over its lifetime. The slope of the sustainability curve indicates the state of functionality, of the system. A negative slope stands for a decline in functionality and a positive slope indicates an increase in the functionality functions. In either of the cases, having a significant peak and trough is an indication of a persistent systemic

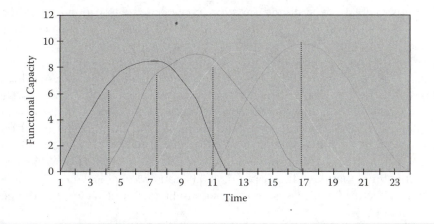

Figure 4.2   Functional capacity of successive systems. (From Mebratu, 2000.)

dysfunction, and systems with a persistent negative slope are heading toward a crash or extinction.

The following principles of sustainability, based on the preceding discussion, can be drawn from the figure (Mebratu, 2000):

- Every system has an initially increasing and then decreasing unit functional capacity as a function of its lifetime. The path of ascendancy and retrogression is determined by the level of interaction between the D factors and the SR factors of the system that are defined by the field of interaction.
- A certain level of systemic function is maintained through an alternative succession of unit systems, and either the vertical movement of the unit functional capacity or the horizontal movement of the system succession time frame can be affected by this level.
- The SR information of each generation is transformed to D information of the successive generation through the successive cycles of evolution (for the natural) and innovation processes (for the man-made) (see Figure 4.2).
- Any systemic function that is within the limit of the stability factors of natural cycles and biotic succession is sustainable, and any systemic function that exceeds the limits of the stability factors is unsustainable.
- Unidirectional phenomena that result in an increased unit functional capacity irrespective of the limits of the feedback loops lead to unsustainable systemic function, which results in some type of a crash.

A given level of systemic function can be achieved in two different paths (Mebratu, 2000). The first path, which has an insurmountable physical limitation that is related to the SR factors, is pushing the unit functional capacity peak upward, irrespective of changes in the physical limits. This could exceed the physical limits and lead to undesirable down crashes of the functional capacity and a subsequent loss in capacity. The second path is keeping the functional capacity increment in pace with the change in the physical limits and manipulating the time frame of the succession cycle to keep the systemic functional performance at a steady-state level. Although this approach might result in lower functional capacity per unit time than the first option, it potentially enables the system to achieve a better level of systemic sustainability without facing the danger of crashes.

Units belonging to the natural universe have built-in mechanisms of feedback loops that balance the total effect of positive and negative feedback loops, thereby maintaining systemic sustainability in accordance with the second option. On the other hand, the human universe has the tendency to generate units that lack such a balance between positive and negative feedback loops, thereby leading to the tendencies of exceeding physical limits. The organizing principles that underlie sustainable systems are the presence, the maintenance, and the production of microscopic diversity that results in an ecological structure (Mebratu, 2000).

According to Allen (1994), ecological structure emerges over time, as the types of behavior present in our possibility space increase and become more complex. The survival of the whole system may depend on the system's effective adaptation to external events, and the survival of the individuals of which it is composed may require success in the internal adaptive processes. As evolution proceeds, it gradually switches from introducing adaptations that deal with the external world to introducing adaptations that succeed within the internal environment. This is just the normal process of the development of ecological structures (Allen, 1994).

When some successful innovation occurs in the system, some new source of positive feedback has been discovered. In natural ecosystems, this would result in the "success" of some populations for a time, during which their prey would decline in numbers and their wastes would build up. However, in the natural example, after some time, a variant of another population would "discover" that it could "use" this newly successful population and its accumulation of waste. This is because any special concentrations of matter that have high free energy are potential sources of food for other populations. After a further period, the initial innovative population would have been reincorporated into the ecosystem, and the challenge that it offered initially would have been met by the internal diversity of the population of the ecosystem (Allen, 1994).

This is lacking for human ecosystems. The first reason is the interval between the human innovation process and the ecological evolution process, which is not sufficient to allow an ecological response, particularly as we keep changing what we are dumping on the environment at a faster rate. The second reason, however, is the earlier tendency of using dispersion as our method of getting rid of wastes. Instead of accumulations building up and becoming a potential source of raw material for some unknown future process, the waste is dispersed into the soils, the oceans, and the atmosphere.

On the basis of the preceding model of systemic function, one can identify the following three major possible scenarios in systemic evolution (Mebratu, 2000):

- *Scenario one:* Most systems are functioning under some level of feedback lags between the intensive factors of the SR block. Thus, most systems will exhibit an oscillating sustainability curve with positive and negative slopes. This is especially intense in the case of man-made systems.
- *Scenario two:* A persistent negative slope of function represents an increasing mismatch between the D factors and the SR factors. Such a scenario may lead to the bifurcation of the system, resulting in a new level of compatibility between the D factors and the SR factors.
- *Scenario three:* In some cases, systems might be faced with a mismatch within the extensive factors of the D block that leads to the complete failure of the feedback mechanism as a source of corrective measure. Such a scenario is detrimental to the sustainability of the systemic function and will, in most cases, lead to extinction of the system.

In terms of the preceding discussion, sustainability can be defined as a systemic property of maintaining an incremental functional capacity of a given system through successive generations (Mebratu, 2000). As such, every ecosystem strives to maintain a positive increment in terms of its functional capacity. The core element of sustainability is functional sustainability rather than systemic sustainability. The sustainability of systems can be achieved through an evolutionary succession of the systems that results in the maintenance of the functional capacities of the systems. Systems are always in a dynamic and an irreversible state of evolution; systemic functions are either progressing or regressing, depending on the evolutionary path followed by the system. In conclusion, it can be said that sustainability is the governing principle in any systemic interaction and is to systems what thermodynamics is to units (Mebratu, 2000).

Sustainable Development as a Societal Process

The increasing global economic disparity witnessed over the last few decades discouraged the notion of fulfilling development aspirations through the conventional development paths. As a result, the expectation of and the demand for something new have grown, questioning the basic assumptions behind the dominant theory of growth. Malaska (1991) argues that the concept of growth has many dimensions and thus we need not give up the use of the concept itself but only a unidimensional interpretation of "gaining weight," or its meaning as extensive growth. Hence, attention should be given to the meaning of *intensive growth* and *regenerative growth* as the necessary elements of transformational dynamics of development.

According to Malaska (1991), each new stage of development has within it the seeds of further change. This is a basic idea of transformational dynamics, and it also underlies evolution and feedback. Accordingly, development means self-organizing, changing orders emerging as a result of nonlinear, nonequilibrium processes triggered by local fluctuations, and not merely of perennial global equilibrium (Malaska, 1991). The onset of nonequilibria can be triggered by comparatively small local fluctuations, originating within the local subsystem or from the outside. Once established, the fluctuations become amplified and spread in the domain of the subsystems. Then they constitute a sizable force capable of modifying macrobehavior. A mechanism for local nucleation and fluctuations is thus vital.

Development nucleation can only materialize around some perceived needs so far left unsatisfied. The mode of production (agricultural, industrial, etc.) is merely a manifestation of changing material orders to fit with the desire to satisfy such needs (Malaska, 1991).

Bifurcation is introduced into social processes because of the inability of the faculty of the dominant social and economic orders to facilitate new emerging needs and values, thus creating the evolutionary dynamic, propelling humanity from the past toward the future.

According to Ayres (1994), one of the most significant evolutionary innovations of humans was the extrasomatic storage and processing of information. The first step in this direction, of course, was the invention of pictographs and written language, and the creation of books and libraries. This was followed only in the very recent past—historically speaking—by the introduction of technological devices to enhance the human sense and the human brain. It is interesting to note that the economic system is effectively defined by the scope of its internal communication system: the price system. Market prices are the signals by which the market regulates itself.

Nevertheless, Ayres (1994) states, "The economic system lacks a well-developed mechanism for sensing the condition of the environment in which it is embedded. This is a fundamental weakness that also threatens the long-run survival of human civilization, unless it can be rectified by the creation of new 'sensory organs' via conscious sociopolitical processes."

According to evolutionary thinking, biological evolution is a process of accumulating "useful" genetic information. The best measure of evolutionary progress is the ability to store and process information in the brain and/or central nervous system (Mebratu, 2000). Similarly, social evolution is a process of accumulating "useful" cultural information that is used for social purposes, passed on via social processes, and stored in different forms of social capital. In both cases the term *useful* must be understood as that which assists survival and growth. As stated by Ayres (1994), "The direction of evolution is characterized by an increasing ability of organisms and systems to sense the state of the environment, to assess its risks and opportunities, to learn and remember appropriate responses, and to transmit this useful information to other individuals in the community and to succeeding generations."

Thus, sustainability can be interpreted as follows for social systems:

- The continuous transformation of SR information in the form of cultural transformation is the basis for social evolution.
- The pace and path of societal evolution are functions of the ability of sensing, processing, and accumulating SR information of the society.
- Ecological factors constitute the major, but not the only, part of the SR information that led to the agricultural and industrial transformations.
- The D information that was discussed in an earlier section constitutes the entity factors of a social system while the SR information constitutes the significance factors.

Figure 4.3 presents the sustainable development model that is based on the principles discussed in the preceding sections. The principal factors of the entity (distinguishability) factors of societal systems are ecological space, demography, and culture, and the multiple interactions of these factors define what a given social system is: its process of becoming and the nature of its evolutionary path (Mebratu, 2000). The ecological space defines the possibility space for societal evolutionary process. In terms of a society, this is given by the source and sink functions of the natural environment. The source function includes the services provided by the natural environment as a source of material and energy inputs for societal

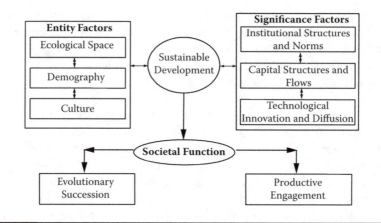

Figure 4.3 The sustainable development model. (From Mebratu, 2000.)

activities, and the sink function covers services provided by the natural environment as a recipient of emissions and discharges of socioeconomic activities. Demography stands for the overall distribution of population and the nature of human settlements in a given ecological space. Culture constitutes the accumulated SR information of a given society through evolutionary succession. As such, culture can be considered as the DNA equivalent of societal systems.

The significance factors of a societal system are the factors that provide the field of significance for a given societal system to fulfill a given societal function; the multiple interactions of these factors determine the nature of information flow in different forms. The principal significance factors for a societal system are institutional structures and norms, capital structures and flows, and technological innovations and diffusions (Mebratu, 2000). The institutional structures and norms of a given social system provide the basis for the field of significance. But it also includes the hierarchical influence that is defined by the hierarchical requirements imposed by the different levels of the hierarchy within the social cosmos (Figure 4.1). The capital structures and flows, as determined by the type(s) of the dominant property right regimes, are other significance factors that determine the nature of the field of significance (Mebratu, 2000). The technological innovation and diffusion factor, which has a direct linkage with the cultural aspect of the entity factor, is another factor that determines the nature of the field of significance for a given society.

The interactions between the entity factors and the significance factors of a given social system constitute the bases for fulfilling societal functions (Mebratu, 2000). While there are numerous attributes and functions that could be listed under societal functions, all of these functions can be broadly categorized under the function of evolutionary succession and productive engagement. As part of the broader universe that is driven by evolutionary succession, achieving evolutionary succession becomes the inherent principal function of any societal system. On the other hand, as a distinct entity from the natural universe, productive engagement becomes the other principal function of any societal system. The principal functions of evolutionary succession and productive engagement will take different forms of expressions and attributes depending on the nature of the entity factors and the nature of interactions among the entity and significance factors (Mebratu, 2000).

The productive engagement function of a given society is based on two fundamental processes (Mebratu, 2000). The first process is the process of preparing a given member of the society for the function of productive engagement. While this process takes different forms, the essence of the process is based on the transfer of the accumulated SR information and the building up of capacity to identify, process, accumulate, and transfer survival-useful information to the next generation. Depending on the nature of the society, there are a number of parameters that determine the path of this process. Traditional and indigenous societies conduct this process mainly through "word of mouth," while education and research are the major instruments for modern societies to conduct this process.

The second fundamental process of the productive engagement process is the actual engagement of a social entity in socially useful and productive activities. This is very much dependent on the socioeconomic structure of the specific society that constitutes the basis for the division of labor and responsibility within the society (Mebratu, 2000). In most traditional and indigenous societies, every member of the society has some kind of responsibility. Gender and age hierarchy are the key elements that largely determine the nature of the division of labor in traditional and indigenous societies. On the other hand, education and specialized skill are the critical elements that determine the nature of the division of labor in modern societies and societies in transition. In either of these cases, it can be said that the ability to process and transform SR information is the core element in determining the nature of the division of labor in a given society. The fundamental prerequisite for fulfilling the productive engagement function of a society is avoiding a mismatch between the process of preparing for productive engagement and the structure of productive engagement.

Similarly, the evolutionary succession function is composed of two fundamental processes (Mebratu, 2000). The first process refers to the process of evolutionary succession as a species. This involves maintaining the required socioecological balance between societal activities and the natural ecosystem that provides the basis for any socioeconomic activities. The sustainability indictor principles that are applied by the natural step program cover this aspect of the evolutionary succession. The explicit principles are (1) substances extracted from the lithosphere must not systematically accumulate in the ecosphere; (2) society-produced substances must not systematically accumulate in the ecosphere; (3) the physical conditions for production and diversity within the ecosphere must not become systematically deteriorated; (4) the use of resources must be efficient and just with respect to meeting human needs (Azar et al., 1996).

The second process refers to the process of evolutionary succession as a society. This involves maintaining the required socioeconomic balance within the global hierarchy. Thus, the fulfillment of both the socioecological and socioeconomic requirements is essential for achieving the function of evolutionary succession for any society. Moreover, the continuous interaction of the functions of evolutionary succession and productive engagement determines the path of development of a given society (Mebratu, 2000).

The optimality of the interaction within and between the entity (extensive) factor and the significance (intensive) factor is defined by the effectiveness of the feedback and corrective mechanisms (Mebratu, 2000). An increasing weakness in the feedback and corrective mechanism indicates an increasing mismatch between or within the extensive and intensive factors. On the basis of the preceding discussion, sustainable development can be defined as

> a societal process of maintaining an optimum interaction between the entity and significance factors of a given society with an objective of providing productive engagement for its members and ensuring the evolutionary succession of the society. (Mebratu, 2000)

In parallel with the three-systems scenarios of sustainability discussed earlier and based on the concept of sustainable development presented in this section, one can identify the following three prevailing global scenarios (Mebratu, 2000).

- *Scenario one:* The increasing mismatch between the intensive factors has become more evident between the rate of technological innovation and diffusion and the corresponding changes in institutional structures and norms. More specifically, the advance that has been made in the areas such as information technology and biotechnology in recent years is causing a major shakeup in the domain of institutional structures and norms at the global level by fundamentally influencing the societal ability to process and transform information. The ongoing controversy on the corporate desire to patent genetically modified organisms can be cited as a case of mismatch of all three elements of the significance factor. The technology transfer and diffusion process in the South is also influenced by the gap between technological innovation and diffusion factors and institutional structures and norms. In this context, reorienting the technological innovation and diffusion processes with the necessary changes in institutional structures and norms is one of the key steps for promoting sustainable development at the global level.

■ *Scenario two:* The liberalization trend, which is mainly driven by the goal of maximization of profit as its principal goal, is intensifying the mismatch between the intensive and extensive factors of societies at different levels. This is manifesting itself in a wide range of crises, including increasing unemployment due to corporate down-sizing and shrinking national economies due to continuous marginalization of economies of the developing world. The creation of global alliances through strategic integration is costing thousands of jobs, especially in the industrialized countries. The increasing power of the World Trade Organization in the name of trade liberalization is affecting the lives of millions throughout the world, and more significantly, farmers in the developing world. These aspects are very critical, especially for the situation in developing countries. In this context, there is a strong need to overcome some of the major global constraints that are currently in place, in terms of international trade, in order to make progress toward global sustainability.

■ *Scenario three:* There is strong evidence indicating that we are moving toward a mismatch of the extensive factors of our society. The mismatch between ecological space and demography has already started to become a global threat because increasing segments of the global population live in areas already declared to be ecologically deficit areas. The effect of this mismatch manifests itself in global environmental challenges such as global warming and desertification, to mention two. Furthermore, the mismatch within the intensive factors is being further aggravated by the mismatch between the intensive and extensive factors and within the extensive factors. Thus, the sustainable development agenda should address all three levels of mismatch, within both the global and local contexts.

While the promotion of sustainable development may take different forms depending on the kind of the social system, the fulfilment of the following conditions is a fundamental requirement for achieving sustainable development by any society (Mebratu, 2000):

- *Reducing* the mismatch between the major factors of significance by avoiding any significant feedback lag within the social system
- *Resolving* the mismatch between the entity and significance factors of the system
- *Avoiding* any mismatch within the entity (extensive) factors of the social system

Conclusion

In general, it is important to note that humans have no single instinctively prescribed mode of life, but a range of variable "material cultures." The socioecological consequences and conditions of human–environmental interactions are a function of each specific mode of social life as defined by the interaction between the entity and significance factors (Mebratu, 2000).

Thus, as stated by Redclift and Woodgate (1994), it is entirely feasible that there may be numerous possible, but qualitatively distinct, directions for future sustainable development. Each will have to observe the boundary conditions that are defined by the entity factors, but there is no necessity that society will require a return to rustic simplicity, material deprivation, or narrow-minded localism.

Finally, the history of science shows that new ways of scientific thinking are related to the development of new paradigms. The discussion presented in this chapter introduces a new dimension of scientific thinking in the sustainability debate by using the general systems, general evolutionary, and information theories as the bases. As pointed out by Thomas S. Kuhn (1962), "To be accepted as a paradigm, a theory must seem better than its competitors, but it needs not and in fact never does, explain all the facts with which it can be confronted." It is believed that the conceptual framework presented in this chapter could be further developed and lead to better understanding of sustainability and sustainable development.

Notes

1. DNA is that part of the cell where all genetic information of a living organism is stored.
2. According to this model, one does not need to develop a complicated mathematical model or plead for ethics to show the danger of casual tempering with nuclear technology and genetic engineering.

References

Allen, P.M. (1994). Evolution, sustainability, and industrial metabolism. In R.U. Ayres and U.E. Simonis (eds.), *Industrial Metabolism: Restructuring for Sustainable Development*, pp. 78–102. Tokyo: United Nations University Press.

Ayres, R.U. (1994). *Information, Entropy and Progress: A New Evolutionary Paradigm*. New York: American Institute of Physics.

Azar, C., Holmberg, J., and Lindgren, K. (1996). Socio-ecological indicators for sustainability. *Ecological Economics*, 18/2, 89–112.

Checkland, P. (1993). *Systems Thinking, Systems Practice*. Chichester, England: John Wiley & Sons.

Clarke, J.J. (1993). *Nature in Question*. London: Earth Scan Publications.

Daly, E.H. (1996). *Beyond Growth*. Boston: Beacon Press.

DuBose, J., Frost, J.D., Chamaeau, J.A., and Vanegas, J.A. (1995). Sustainable development and technology. In D. Elms and D. Wilkinsin (eds.), *The Environmentally Educated Engineer*, pp. 73–86. Canterbury: Center for Advanced Engineering.

Dudley, M.K. (1996). Traditional native Hawaiian environmental philosophy. In R.S. Gottlieb (ed.), *This Sacred Earth*. New York: Routledge.

Holmberg, J. (ed.). (1994). *Policies for a Small Planet*. London: Earthscan.

Kinsley, D. (1996). Christianity as ecologically harmful. In R.S. Gottlieb (ed.), *This Sacred Earth*. New York: Routledge.

Kirkby, J., O'keef, P., and Timberlake L. (1995). *Sustainable Development: The Earthscan Reader*. London: Earthscan.

Kuhn, T.S. (1962). *The Structure of Scientific Revolutions*. Chicago: The University of Chicago Press.

Malaska, P. (1991). Economic and social evolution: The transformational dynamics approach. In E. Laszlo (ed.), *The New Evolutionary Paradigm*. New York: Gordon & Breach Science.

Matthiessen P. (1984). *Indian Country*. New York: Penguin Books.

Mbiti, J.S. (1996). African Views of the Universe. In R.S. Gottlieb (ed.), *This Sacred Earth*. New York: Routledge.

McClaughry, J. (1989). Preface. In E.F. Schumacher (ed.), *Small Is Beautiful*. London: Harper Perennial.

Mebratu, D. (1998). Sustainability and sustainable development: Historical and conceptual review. *Journal of Environmental Impact Assessment (EIA) Review*, 18, 493–520.

Mebratu, D. (2000). Strategy Framework for Sustainable Industrial Development in sub-Saharan Africa. Doctoral dissertation, Lund University, Lund, Sweden.

Oser, J., and Blanchfield W.C. (1975). *The Evolution of Economic Thought*. New York: Harcourt Brace Jovanovich.

Pearce, D.W., Markandya A., and Barbier E.B. (1989). *Blue Print for a Green Economy*. London: Earthscan.

Pearce, D.W., and Turner. R.K. (1990). *Economics of Natural Resources and the Environment*. New York: Harvester Wheatsheaf.

Redclft, M., and Woodgate G. (1994). Sociology and the environment. In M. Redclift and T. Benton (eds.), *Social Theory and the Global Environment*. London: Routledge.

Roszac, T. (1989). Introduction. In E.F. Schumacher, *Small Is Beautiful*. New York: Harper Perennial.

Senge, P.M. (1990). *The Fifth Discipline—the Art and Practice of the Learning Organizations*. New York: Doubleday.

Tryzna, T.C. (1995). *A Sustainable World*. Sacramento: IUCN.

Weinberg, M.G. (1975). *An Introduction to General Systems Thinking*. New York: Wiley-Interscience.

World Commission on Environment and Development (1987). *Our Common Future*. London: Oxford University Press.

Chapter 5

Sustaining Development: The Road from Stockholm to Johannesburg

O. P. Dwivedi and Renu Khator

CONTENTS

First Two Decades of the Global Environmental Movement

The month of June (5–16) in 1972 saw a gathering of many world leaders in Stockholm to discuss the environmental issues in a systematic and comprehensive manner. Until that time, the planet Earth was treated as an unchanging backdrop to all kinds of human unrestricted activities. The Stockholm Conference raised several questions such as the following: Is global pollution a problem of poverty or a cause of affluence? What is the share of responsibility by the wealthy North in degrading the environment? Can there be international responses to environmental problems that can impel nation-states to abide by international agreements and conventions? In addition to these questions, there was a clear divide between the poor South and the rich North. Perhaps it is better to trace the background of these questions raised at the Stockholm Conference.

While preparations were being made for the first United Nations (UN) conference on the environment, a most heated debate in the history of environmental concern was occasioned by the publication in 1972 of the book *The Limits to Growth*. The Club of Rome, founded in 1968, sponsored this study, which sold 4 million copies within 4 years. The club commissioned the Massachusetts Institute of Technology to use systems dynamics. Using systems modeling as a technique, the report argued effectively that there was an urgent need to control the present growth trends in world population, industrialization and pollution, food production, and resource depletion if we wish to save our Earth from a planetary-proportion disaster (Meadows et al., 1972).

Thus, the UN conference started on the note of an apocalyptic horizon when on June 5, 1972, after 2 years of preparatory work, it began an international discourse at the Royal Opera House in Stockholm, Sweden. The conference was divided into two blocs: the industrialized nations and the poor countries. The latter were led by India, Philippines, Kenya, and China. The inaugural speech by the prime minister of Sweden set the tone of the conference with the statement of fact that each individual in the industrialized countries draws, on the average, 30 times more heavily on the limited resources of the Earth than his fellow man in the developing countries (Caldwell, 1984, p. 50).

The conference produced the four major cornerstones of the first international framework for addressing environmental issues: (1) the Stockholm Declaration, consisting of 26 principles; (2) the Action Plan for the Human Environment, with three specific components: an environmental assessment program, environmental management activities, and supporting measures; (3) a plan to establish the United Nations Environment Programme; and (4) a voluntary Environment Fund. The main achievement of the Stockholm Conference was heightening worldwide awareness of pollution problems. Until that time, the pollution problem was seen as a by-product of industrialization. But it took the courage and leadership of Indira Gandhi, the prime minister of India, to widen the concept with her allusion to the "pollution of poverty." She was the only head of government aside from the prime minister of the host nation Sweden to attend the conference. She declared: "We do not wish to impoverish the environment any further and yet we cannot for a moment forget the grim poverty of large numbers of people. Are not poverty and need the greatest polluters?" (Gandhi, 1972, p. 2). For her, India's environmental plight "compounded to seemingly unmanageable proportions by poverty, squalor and ignorance, shows why environmental problems must be treated as an integral part of the development strategy in this case, tackling poverty, unemployment, disease and ignorance simultaneously" (India, 1972).

Other developing nations joined India in emphasizing that poverty was the worst form of pollution. For example, from India's viewpoint, just as the pollution of air and water, accumulation of wastes, urban blight, loss of wildlife, and dereliction of land and forests were examples of environmental degradation in the industrialized nations, so were the various companions of poverty such as disease, malnutrition, hunger, and squalor in the developing nations. To India and a host of poor nations, a sustainable "environment" was a society in which people would not go hungry, water would be easily accessible and free from disease-carrying germs, sanitary conditions would be at acceptable levels, and the basic needs of the populace would be fulfilled, without despoiling nature of its beauty and of the freshness and purity so essential to all human beings (Dwivedi, 1997, p. 52).

The ideological differences between the poor and wealthy nations were not removed, but "ameliorative and evasive strategies adopted by the developed nations postponed the day of actual confrontation" (Caldwell, 1984, p. 51). The following were the conference outputs: (1) The Declaration on the Human Environment with 26 principles, (2) Recommendations for Action (109 in number), and (3) Other Resolutions, such as celebrating the World Environment Day on June 5 every year, convening a second UN Conference on Human Environment, and condemning nuclear tests carried out in the atmosphere. But the main achievement of the Stockholm Conference was the legitimization of environmental issues as an object of national and international policy. It impelled the national governments to start creating administrative mechanisms for environmental protection.

Along with many industrialized nations, developing countries such as India, Philippines, and Indonesia established ministries of environment. For example, India, after establishing a mechanism at the federal level to examine and provide policy guidelines on controlling pollution, amended its 1976 constitution to obligate government "to protect and improve the environment and to safeguard the forests and wildlife of the country" (Dwivedi, 1997, p. 61). A major victory for the poor nations was Recommendation 109, which stated that "it should further be ensured the preoccupation of developed countries with their own environmental problems should not affect the flow of assistance to developing countries and that this flow should be adequate to meet the additional environmental requirements of such countries" (quoted from Ontario, Canada, 1974, p. 132). On December 15, 1972, the UN General Assembly adopted the various recommendations from the Stockholm Conference and established a new international environmental monitoring agency, the UN Environment Programme (UNEP), with its head office in Nairobi, Kenya.

The Stockholm Conference started a new wave of environmentally conscious international conventions and treaties such as Prevention of Pollution from Ships (MARPOL) signed in London on November 2, 1973, and Convention on the Conservation of Antarctic Marine Living Resources, Canberra, May 20, 1980. In 1980, the UN General Assembly decided to celebrate the tenth anniversary of the Stockholm Conference in May 1982. The conference agreed that national governments have been slow in implementing full measures for environmental protection, as there is a mixed record of achievement. Nevertheless, it was thought that by the next environmental decade (that is by 1992), there ought to be overall good progress.

Thus, a foundation was laid for a next UN conference to be held in 1992. There is no doubt that the world gathering in Sweden three decades ago was a watershed. The conference inspired nations and green activists everywhere. It also led to the establishment of environment ministries, departments, and agencies worldwide. It put the environment on the international agenda. Finally, the event also led to the creation of the World Commission on Environment and Development (WCED), also called the Brundtland Commission, which reported in 1987 and internationalized the term *sustainable development*.

The 1992 Earth Summit in Rio

It was exactly 20 years later, in 1992, when the international community gathered for Earth Summit in Rio de Janeiro, Brazil. The Rio Summit, formally known as the United Nations Conference on Environment and Development (UNCED) and popularly dubbed Earth Summit, was the second UN conference on the environment. On the surface, the progress from the first gathering to the second gathering was remarkable. In comparison to the Stockholm Conference, where only two heads of state were in attendance, 116 heads of state attended the Earth Summit. In contrast to 134 nongovernmental organizations (NGOs) in Stockholm, members of 7,892 NGOs from 167 countries were present in Rio (Bryner, 1999, p. 157). Similarly, instead of a handful of journalists from the North at the 1972 conference, 8,000 journalists coming from all over the world covered the 1992 Earth Summit on a daily basis.

The format of the Earth Summit also exhibited inclusivity that was absent in 1972. For instance, many NGOs and private organizations were given seats at the table, and many more were able to influence the process by a parallel venue offered by the Green Forum. Needless to say, any recognition for the NGOs was nonexistent during the Stockholm Conference. The demographic distribution of participants at the two meetings is equally revealing: Whereas only one tenth of the participants in 1972 were from the South, one third of them represented the South in 1992. Without a doubt, one can argue that by 1992, the environmental issue had come of age and had taken the center place on the world stage.

The Earth Summit took place in a world that was significantly different from the one that existed in 1972. During the 20 years, the Cold War had ended, the Soviet Union that led the boycott of the Stockholm Conference was no longer a player, the global market was emerging at a rapid speed, scientific advances had brought nations together, the Internet had boosted the power of epistemic communities, and many environmental disasters had taken place outlining the futility of national borders in regard to environmental problems (Khator, 1995). All of these changes had generated a new level of public awareness and urgency that, among other factors, helped shape the scope of the Earth Summit and broadened its appeal, visibility, and scope.

By 1992, with the conceptual breakthrough provided by the Brundtland Commission, the summit demonstrated that environmental protection could no longer be regarded as a luxury of the rich only. Rather, environmental factors would have to be integrated with economic and social issues, which then must become a central part of the policy-making process in all countries. It was very clearly expressed by many who attended the summit that the time had come for rich industrialized nations, which had benefited immensely from their wasteful ways of economic progress, to help the developing world combat poverty so that these poorer nations did not have to go through polluting the world in order to achieve that kind of economic progress. To this end, the summit adopted Agenda 21, a blueprint for sustainable development, with an agreed common vision for growth, equity, and nature conservation for future generations.

Agenda 21, despite its rhetorical significance, served one crucial function—for the first time, it formalized the expectation of a North–South partnership (Rio Documents, 2002, p. 125). The 800-page document outlined commitments from nations to internalize environmental costs, address poverty, change consumption patterns, include women and indigenous people in decision making, undertake environmental assessments, build capacity in developing countries, strengthen scientific knowledge, and bridge the data gap (UN Secretary General, 2001). The Earth Summit also created a new agency, the UN Commission on Sustainable Development, to collect data on environmental and development activities and to monitor individual and collective progress of nations toward achieving the goals set forth in Agenda 21.

Although significant positive changes occurred during the 20 years from the Stockholm Conference to the Rio Earth Summit, many issues remained unchanged. Exclusion of the South and its perspective, which was questioned by Gandhi in 1972, remained a serious challenge during and after the Earth Summit. Many nongovernmental and governmental delegates left the summit viewing the glass as half empty rather than as half full when the summit failed to deal with real issues. It was widely believed that despite all the symbolic attention to the needs of the South, the ultimate success of Agenda 21 depended on the willingness of the North to provide funds and know-how to the South, but the structure to produce such willing behavior could not be established.

Furthermore, despite all the efforts of international agencies to create opportunities for the South, trade patterns continued to be skewed in favor of the North, limiting the ability of the South to fund its own needs. Consumption patterns also remained intact, leading the North to continue on its destructive path and tempting the South to follow the same road. The Earth Summit took baby steps toward building global cooperation, but the feelings of tension and distrust between the North and the South remained and were reflected even during the 1997 Kyoto Conference on Global Climate Change (Conca and Dabelko, 1998).

The 2002 World Summit in Johannesburg

By the year 2002, when another gathering of world leaders took place on the general issue of the environment, a realization surfaced that the three main pillars of sustaining the world—environmental protection, social development (also called human development), and economic prosperity—cannot be kept separate. Even economists started saying that all five kinds of capital (natural, social, financial, human, and physical) that shape human progress are interconnected. Another understanding developed that the role of business and NGOs should not be viewed as separate from the total process of governance; instead there should be a partnership of governing institutions, business, and NGOs. Finally, an awareness dawned on people that poverty and environmental quality are interlinked, that the poor should not be blamed for degrading the environment, and that they should not be on trial, as was the case at Rio meeting (Verolme, 2002).

However, people all over the world had realized that the anticipated progress has been much slower. Environmental destruction had not been arrested and the state of the world's environment remained very fragile. Instead, high consumption and a materialistic pattern of societal behavior kept on taxing the Earth's natural life-support systems. It was also clear that the wealthy nations, in particular, did not keep the promise they made in Rio—either to protect their own environment or to help the developing world defeat poverty.

The old situation continued when 20% of humanity kept on enjoying privileges and prosperity undreamed by others; when the model of development prescribed by the West and such international agencies as the World Bank and International Monetary Fund (IMF), was unable to control poverty and destitution; when the wasteful ways of the rich countries kept on exacting a heavy toll on the planet and its resources; and when the vast majority of human beings still lived in conditions of unbearable deprivation and squalor (Ermen, 2002, p. 62). All these issues were discussed during the UN-sponsored Millennium Summit in 2002, and it was hoped that by the time nations assembled in South Africa, concrete and practical steps would be agreed on to deal with the core relationship between human society and the natural environment.

The Johannesburg Summit, called the World Summit on Sustainable Development (WSSD), took upon itself to discuss five specific areas (UN, 2002b):

1. *Water and sanitation* were the primary issue mainly because more than 1 billion people do not have access to safe drinking water, about 2 billion people do not have proper sanitation facilities, and about 3 million people die each year of diseases caused by unsafe water.

2. *Energy* is essential not only for living but also for development. And yet 2 billion people do not have any access to a proper energy source for their daily use. Is it not strange that 20% of the world population uses more than 70% of the world energy produced?

3. *Health* is intimately linked with the environmental conditions. But more than 1 billion people breathe unhealthy air, and as a consequence, more than 3 million people die each year of air pollution. Many tropical diseases are closely linked with polluted water sources and poor sanitation.

4. *Agricultural productivity:* About two thirds of the world's agricultural land is degraded either because of overuse of pesticide, overgrazing, desertification, or natural disasters. Unless the human encroachment on forests, grasslands, and wetlands is reversed, agricultural productivity will not be increased.

5. *Biodiversity protection and ecosystem management* are declining at an unprecedented rate; half of the tropical rain forests and mangroves are gone, 75% of marine fisheries stock is gone; monoculture and bioseeds are further affecting the biodiversity pool; and each country is reporting the continuing decline of its biodiversity genetic pool.

Thus, when the nations met in South Africa from August 26 to September 4, 2002, there were doubts whether expectations since the Rio Summit of 1992 would be met. In the end, the WSSD was able to negotiate and adopt two main documents: (1) The Plan of Implementation and (2) the Johannesburg Declaration on Sustainable Development.

The Plan of Implementation has identified the following issues needing immediate world attention: poverty eradication, changing unsustainable patterns of consumption and production, protecting and managing the natural resource base of economic and social development, globalization and sustainable development, health and sustainable development, small island states and their sustainable development, sustainable development for Africa; regional initiatives for Latin America, Asia, and Pacific, Western Asia, and Europe; and an institutional framework and means of implementation. Finally, the Johannesburg Declaration issued at the end of the summit (1) outlines the progress made from the UNCED (Brundtland Commission report in 1987) to the WSSD in 2002, (2) highlights challenges and expresses a commitment to sustainable development, (3) underscores the importance of multilateralism, and (4) emphasizes the need for speedy implementation (UN, 2002a, 2002c).

Verdict on WSSD

Although it is really too soon to pass any verdict on the summit, it can be said that the WSSD was a missed opportunity. Of course, there were some modest gains such as that the NGOs could participate fully, unlike in 1992, and that some countries tried very hard to rope in all big players to agree on the plan of action for poverty removal and substantial financial help to debt-ridden nations. Nevertheless, this summit could have been a turning point because the global meeting could have responded seriously to the injustice of the disparity between the rich, who have easy access to resources, and what is left to the poor; it could have taken strong steps to halt the continuing assault on the ecological well-being of Earth; and it could have tried to do something concrete to help improve the lives of the marginalized of the planet.

It was also clear that rich nations were not about to make commitments that would undermine their position of privilege and respond with urgency to global ecological threats. Similarly, the multinational corporations that benefit most from the current economic model of governance would not let their countries barter away their power and influence. However, it was clear that everyone was talking about sustainable development, which had become by this time a household term and a celebrated paradigm.

Sustainable Development

The term *sustainable development* was popularized by the work of the World Commission on Environment and Development (WCED), popularly called the Brundtland Commission, in the mid-1980s, but its origins date back to the 18th and 19th centuries when foresters in Europe used the word *sustainable* to voice their concern about the clear-cutting methods of logging (Dwivedi et al., 2001, p. 220). Because the forests were not regenerating adequately, the foresters wanted to ensure that trees were planted to replace the ones logged. Canada's earliest documented commitment to sustainability planning was the designation of Canada's first national park, Banff, in 1885 (Dwivedi et al., 2001, p. 220). Over time, a number of actors have struggled for increased attention to the preservation of nature as a moral and ethical imperative.

Environmental concerns gained international attention during the Brundtland Commission. The commission brought more than a conservation or environmental preservation perspective to the table. Instead, it was concerned with merging environmental sustainability with social and economic development, recognizing the nature of inequality and its relationship to resource availability. The Norwegian prime minister, Gro Harlem Brundtland, chaired the Brundtland Commission. The secretary general of the commission was a Canadian named Jim MacNeill. The commission played an important role in shaping how the various nations would develop and address environmental and economic policies.

From the Brundtland Commission emerged a document, *Our Common Future*, in which sustainable development was defined as meeting the needs of the people today without jeopardizing the needs of future generations (WCED, 1987). The term *sustainable development* is premised on a long-term view of development and of environmental integrity.

The WCED stressed the active participation of various actors (i.e., governments, NGOs, and community members) to ensure sustainable development but paid specific attention to the need for economically viable solutions and management of natural resources in environmentally sound ways. Sustainable development, as an increasingly popular concept, offers a framework for the integration of environmental policies and development strategies. The increasing importance attached to environmental sustainability and social and economic development, as noted by the Brundtland Commission, solidified sustainable development as a guiding principle.

The Brundtland Commission Report, released in 1987, helped pave the way toward the important United Nations Conference on Environment and Development (UNCED). The commission defined *sustainable development* as "development that meets the needs of the present without compromising the ability of future generations to meet their own needs" (WCED, 1987, p. 43). Naturally, this is an imprecise statement that raises more questions than it answers. Whose needs are being met? What are the limitations imposed by technology—or by our awareness of the possible harmful effects of technology—when we go about meeting these needs? Will future generations even perceive needs as we do presently? A great deal of controversy has surfaced regarding the true meaning, if a universal one can be found, of this term.

To critics, the term *sustainable development* means nothing more than "business as usual," and the third point, with its redistributive connotations, was never a serious promise in the first place. Critics point to the proliferation of the use of the term *sustainable development* (SD) among industrial lobbyists and strategists, the international community's wide usage of the term in various proclamations that fail to force states to actually change policies, and its adoption by multilateral lending institutions, such as the World Bank, that have checkered histories in the areas of environmental impact assessment.

Indeed, some critics argue that the term is in fact self-contradictory. Can "development," as we have come to know it, and which is primarily based on overtaking nature, using it, and reconstructing it to serve our ends (this is the *utilitarian* perspective on nature), really be sustainable in the long term? Sharachchandra Lele argues sustainable development "is being packaged as the inevitable outcome of objective scientific analysis, virtually an historical necessity that does not contradict the deep-rooted normative notion of development as economic growth. In other words, SD is an attempt to have one's cake and eat it too" (Lele, 1991, p. 619). There is also a tendency to view the term as purposively misleading, lulling citizens into the false belief that things are being done to benefit the environment in the long term although, in fact, little is taking place. In short, critics view the term as an erroneous label at best, and as a purposefully misleading one at worst.

If we think seriously about the implications of SD, it is a fairly demanding concept. It demands restraint from current activities many value as the producers of wealth, and for the sake largely not of people of industrialized nations or others today, but of future generations whom we will never personally know. This may be seen as a great sacrifice in a consumer culture, especially among those without children (or plans to have them). And, as Edith Brown Weiss argues, it also entails that we accept the concept of group rights, as opposed to individual rights: "Intergenerational planetary rights [are] group rights ... in the sense that individuals hold these rights as groups in relation to other generations—past, present and future" (Weiss, 1993, p. 344).

The problem, again, is that there is no universal perception of just what the needs of these groups will be; or even, for that matter, what type of environmental problems they will be facing even if we do very little else to damage the current ecosystems that sustain us. Beyond this, there are many fundamental disagreements about what types of activities merit condemnation or approval.

During the 1992 UNCED, sustainable development was brought into another forum of international planning and policy process. The UNCED, or the Earth Summit, as it was commonly called, offered a venue for heads of states, representatives from UN agencies, and NGOs to discuss and debate the challenges of sustainable development. Following the Earth Summit, the United Nations Commission for Sustainable Development (CSD) was created in December 1992. The purposes of the commission were to ensure effective follow-up of UNCED and to monitor and report on implementation of the Earth Summit agreements.

The CSD has 53 members and operates as a functional commission of the United Nations Economic and Social Council. Each year, the CSD holds a meeting to address progress in meeting the agreements of Agenda 21, one of the documents that emerged out of the 1992 UNCED. Over 50 ministers and more than 1000 NGOs participated in the commission's work. As central to its mandate, the commission ensures that sustainable development issues are visible and addressed within the UN system (United Nations Commission on Sustainable Development, 1999).

However, the term *sustainable development* is not without its critics. Disagreements over the meaning of the term continue today as the phase is criticized for having a veneer of environmental respectability while promoting continued unsustainable economic growth. Despite the disagreements over the meanings and definitions, the concept has become a central feature in many nations' environmental policy planning. For example, in the case of Canada, the federal government has decided to integrate the concept of sustainable development into federal legislation by amending the Auditor General Act, which established the commissioner of the Environment and Sustainable Development (Environment Canada, 2000).

Sustainable Development: New Paradigm for Decision Making

Sustainable development is an important concept in environmental policy making. However, the relevance of sustainable development as a "new paradigm for decision making" and its potential to challenge "existing decision-making practices" are thwarted by a diminishing supply of resources required to translate policies into action. Essentially, sustainable development is a "process" that implies change. Therefore, in order to comprehend the true needs and objectives of an interdependent, environmentally sound, sustainable future, we must be able to maintain flexibility consistent with the dynamism found within the (re)conceptualization of sustainable development.

The concept of sustainable development has fundamentally changed the nature and scope of the debate about the environment and its relationship to development (Dwivedi, 1997). In the past, whenever a new situation emerged, it was added onto the concept of economic development. The concept of sustainable development, however, has superseded the entire notion of economic development; as a result, the pursuit of economic growth can no longer be our core value. Rather, it is now part of a larger picture, and our central concern must be to integrate economic and environmental concerns in a viable development strategy. The World Commission on Environment and Development has stated: "We have in the past been concerned about the impacts of economic growth upon the environment. We are now forced to concern ourselves with the impacts of ecological stress ... upon our economic prospects" (WCED, 1987, p. 5).

In essence, sustainable development, as a general principle, must ensure that it be the duty of all peoples and their governments to protect, conserve, preserve, and pass on to future generations nature's heritage and the legacy of human civilization, while preventing all deliberate measures and acts (of individuals and states) that might harm or threaten that heritage. This concept, linking development and environment, envisions a policy based on government recognition that long-term economic growth is possible only if a nation sustains its natural environment and cultural heritage, adopts an integrated approach to sustainable development, and recognizes the interconnectedness of scientific, technological, social, cultural, and economic dimensions.

Furthermore, the concept requires that the country maintain a balance of its human resources, cultural property, and its natural heritage, so that its people may live in ecological harmony. These perspectives require a better, more comprehensive definition of the concept:

> Sustainable development obliges humanity to use, develop, manage, and care for the environment and planetary resources in a manner that supports the stewardship of all creation (including all natural resources, and the welfare of all living beings), and the continuity of cultural and spiritual heritage of each community, as well as the maintenance of harmony between people and nature for present and future generations. (Dwivedi, 1997, p. 28)

It does not matter how complex or simple a definition is so long as it conveys the meaning it is supposed to claim. In the case of sustainable development, it not only presents a new paradigm for decision making in all sectors of society and at all levels from the global to the local, it also "challenges existing decision making practices insofar as it demands both the integration of economic, environmental, and social considerations; and attention to the long run consequences for future generations of present-day decisions and policies" (Bell, 2000, p. 1).

Furthermore, the sustainable development concept implies a fusion of two imperatives: the right to develop (economically, socially, politically, and culturally) and the need to sustain the environment. In other words, all future development must be achieved in a sustainable and equitable manner. Thus, the concept denotes a balance between sustainability and equitability: Sustainability brings environmental concepts into the development process, and equitability injects developmental matters into national and international environmental protection efforts (IUCN, 1995, p. 42). The concept also implies intragenerational equity between rich and poor, taking the needs of all people into account, especially through the transfer of resources to poor communities and regions.

At the global level, however, we must consider how these needs can be taken into account, given that some continue to overconsume natural resources in order to maintain their version of quality of life, while the majority of the world's population continues its onslaught on natural resources in response to hunger and poverty. Unless we unite these two approaches and operationalize them through our governing institutions and through personal commitment, our present crises will persist, and human development, about which we all worry, will be difficult to sustain.

Sustainable Development: The Next Challenge

Progress in human development has been extraordinary during the past 50 years because, on average, people in developing nations are healthier, wealthier, better fed, and more literate. And this has all happened during our lifetime. Life expectancy has risen, great advances have been made in primary education, and food sufficiency has been achieved in several countries. Nevertheless, wide disparities are also evident. For example, the amount spent by Europeans on mineral water in 1 year is enough to provide primary education in developing countries for the next 10 years because there are still 1 billion people who cannot read and write, and among them two thirds are women; or when we talk about wealth, we should note that the income gap between the top 20% nations and the bottom 20% poorer nations rose from a proportion of 30:1 in 1960 to 78:1 in 1994. Thus, human development has not kept an even pace.

Amartya Sen considers human development as a process of expanding the real freedom that people enjoy; and a process that enhances people's choices and thus raises their level of well-being (Sen, 1999, p. 36). From this perspective, substantive freedom includes the capacity to avoid deprivations such as starvation, undernourishment, or premature mortality. It also includes acquiring basic education and skills to be gainfully employed, as well as the freedom to participate in political, economic, and social systems. It means building up capacity for people to make decisions.

At the same time, it must be noted that human development and economic growth are mutually reinforcing, because for the development to be sustainable, both should accelerate in tandem. This requires (1) receiving the basic services (such as education, primary health care, adequate supply of food, clean water, and sanitation); (2) participating in the implementation as well as design of developmental programs created in their name and for them if the resources are to benefit the most needy (especially women and other marginalized persons); (3) recognizing the need for greater cooperation of all sectors of human development including spiritual well-being; (4) being proactive in the global economy because globalization disproportionately favors those who have expertise, power, and the capacity to compete in the global market (Kagia, 2002).

Action Agenda for Sustainable Development

The following strategies are offered as closing reflections on the sustainable development paradigm.

Encourage the Evolution of the Sustainable Development Paradigm from Its Existing Latent Policy State

The concept of sustainable development is yet to emerge from its continuing status as a latent policy paradigm because a fully developed policy paradigm provides a series of principles or assumptions that guide future actions and suggest a framework of achieving results. Despite its two-decades-long existence, sustainable development remains a latent paradigm because "it does not yet have the coherence of earlier paradigms such as Keynesian economics or the liberal economic-growth paradigm" (Doern and Conway, 1994, p. 235). Nevertheless, the concept is bound to persist because of the following reasons:

■ Its meaning is vague enough to attract all kinds of ideologies and thought processes such as traditional conservation movements, green parties, environmental nongovernmental organizations (ENGOs), religious organizations and faith groups, industrial and commercial interests, and labor movements: nearly everyone.

■ It has acquired international legitimacy among scientists, resource economists, public choice theorists, and scholars around the globe, as such the concept appears to have attained universal validity.

■ It has been used as the fundamental idea not only by the Brundtland Commission and IUCN, but also by all international development aid agencies such as the World Bank, the United Nations, and the International Monetary Fund.

■ It has a mass following among poor and wealthy people, who see in it their hopes and dreams.

■ It conjures a relationship between North and South by including factors such as equity, needs, and responsibility for universal care and *Sarvodaya* — social and spiritual upliftment of all together (Dwivedi, 1990, p. 210).

Establish an Explicit Framework of Individual and Collective Duties and Responsibilities

Environmental protection can take many forms. Individuals make countless decisions over the course of their lives, and when taken in the aggregate, clearly these decisions have a great impact on environmental health. Along the same line, as time passes and more and more people become aware of the importance of their actions, they take adaptive measures. For example, the Canadian recycling programs are a success in some regions precisely because people have decided to use them, sorting their garbage and refraining from disposing of newspapers and other easily recyclable products.

Thus, we have to keep this individual responsibility in mind when discussing sustainable development, and challenge ourselves further to find new solutions beyond recycling. This quite likely involves a new set of values concerning consumer behavior and the reduction of consumer goods. Further, the leaders of the private sector make decisions that influence the level of pollution that is released in the atmosphere and into rivers and other "sinks." These decisions are often prompted by government regulations, but they can be made at the level of individual initiative also. In short, it is important to realize that individual responsibility is vital to both sustainable development and the pursuit of human security.

Have Each Country Develop a Governmentwide Sustainable Development Strategy

Because of the multidisciplinary nature of sustainable development and environmental issues, the responsibility for environmental protection cannot be left to only one government department; all departments must coordinate their activities within a central framework. An integrated strategy for sustainable development and environmental protection (SDEP) should be adopted and secured by governmentwide enforcement. The integration of SDEP considerations requires both vertical and horizontal linkages. *Vertical linkage* means that the country has an integrated SDEP mechanism, which involves federal, state, and local governments united by common themes—ecosystem protection, pollution control, health, equity, respect for nature, concern for the needs of future generations, natural resources, historical and cultural properties, and so on. Such an integrated, sustainable development system, providing for full accountability for the allocation and expenditure of resources, may not be easy to operationalize. Instead, it may be desirable, therefore, first to institute a well-functioning, horizontal coordinating mechanism within the central government, and only then to attempt to develop an integrated approach. Such an approach, especially for developing nations, requires (1) an appointment of an interministerial committee for sustainable development and environmental protection, (2) a dependable monitoring mechanism, and (3) an establishment of a central office to oversee the overall operation of the strategy. Such a central office could be called a commission of the environment and sustainable development. Such an approach may assure the interconnection and coordination of various policy fields currently managed by different ministries and avoid the compartmentalized approach to sustainable development and environmental protection and conservation that results in fragmented decision making. That kind of framework might create an environment that does the following:

- Ensures early and effective consultation in the entire area of sustainable development and environmental protection
- Assures a full and open sharing of information among ministries, departments, and public sector undertakings on all matters relating to sustainable development and the environment (SDE)
- Advises government and parliament on matters relating to SDE in order to prevent duplication and to ensure proper enforcement
- Minimizes conflict among ministries, departments, and other agencies on activities that involve SDE
- Maximizes cooperation with state governments and, through them, with local governments

Establish an Integrative Approach Eliciting Support from all Stakeholders

For these two approaches to work effectively, it is important to appreciate the role of a nation's cultural and spiritual heritage, which entreats people to live in harmony with nature. The authors believe that by bringing religious, cultural, traditional, and secular domains together we can wage a successful fight to protect the environment. Furthermore, only by enlisting the assistance of all societal forces will we be able to work together for sustainable development.

Understand the Impact of Globalization on Sustaining Our Global Village

Of course, globalization offers great opportunities, but at the same time, we should know about its negative, disruptive, and marginalizing effects. Globalization appears to have divided the worlds between the connected, which have a monopoly on almost about everything, and the majority on the fringes, who are isolated and have practically nothing (Dwivedi, 2003). It seems that globalization has created an international order in which a group of privileged people control all political and economic powers, while the rest continue to be poor and marginalized (Dwivedi, 2003). Would it not be fair and just if the global actors of international development aid show sensitivity, vision, and the right kind of leadership? Perhaps globalization ought to become a process whereby all the citizens of this global village feel that they are equal in sharing together the prosperity, natural resources, as well as liabilities confronting every one of them. Without this collaborative and cooperative partnership between the North and South, would the 21st century be any different from what we have already gone through?

Protect Both the Human-Created and Nature-Gifted Biosphere Diversity

Globalization, as noted, is creating a trend toward the homogenization of many activities, such as management of business (including interfering with the management of state machinery), trade and commerce, education and research, communications, and technology transfer. But this trend, which is bringing, on the one hand, uniformity of context, perspective, and style of doing things, is, on the other hand, happening at the expense of the world's diversity of not only thought and action but also variety of species, grain stock, and the universe. It seems that this trend of monoculture of thought and action may also weaken those nations that are commercially less powerful. As more and more genetically modified organisms (GMOs), biotechnology, and biogenetics are being pushed by the multinational corporations of the West onto the developing nations, the indigenous variety and diversity are going to lose out. Sustainable development means protecting the world's creative and indigenous variety and diversity by developing socially just and ecologically sustainable means for the conservation and use of biodiversity through imaginative environmental governance (UNESCO, 2002).

Immediately Recognize the Southern Input

There is no doubt that scholars in the North have dominated the environmental thinking, but such conceptual linkages have been developed without sufficient foundation in Southern realities, sufficient consultation with Southern intellectuals and researchers, and integration of developing country perspectives (Dwivedi and Nef, 2004, p. 84). Consequently, Northern research and policy recommendations on environmental security and sustainable development issues are generally skewed without encompassing the full range of global questions (Dwivedi and Nef, 2004). It is not that Northern academic and policy-making institutions are unaware of Southern problems, but "they have failed to produce a working strategy to prevent conflict related to environmental stress" (Mendez, 2002, p. 9). Sometimes developing countries have also banded together to present a common front at international forums against the North-led environmental issues. Nevertheless, without developing a global agenda that is driven by a Southern perspective and without including Southern input, any international effort is doomed.

Enhance Global Sustainability

The Johannesburg Summit was to build a new ethic of global sustainability, a new common plan of action, and to agree on developing a greater sense of mutual care and responsibility. Instead, much has been left to regional cooperation and national action. It is here where the North and South will have to sit down together and formulate a global strategy for sustainable living.

Lessons that we ought to learn from the Rio and Johannesburg meetings are to implement what was promised during the Rio and Johannesburg meetings before making further pledges; and that these promises (including treaties, conventions, or agreements) require financial commitments. And most important, the United States ought to set an example rather than continuing its disappointing record of not ratifying various environmental treaties and conventions.

For sustaining our world and for the well-being of all, it is imperative that first poverty is eliminated, the economic status of women is improved, and children are educated, because in the final analysis, peace on Earth and sustainable development for all will be possible only when a global integrated agenda operationalizes the listed goals. This is the hope and vision of sustainable development for and during the 21st century. We would like to conclude by referring to the groundbreaking Brundtland Commission Report, written in 1987, which shed a new light on the concept of development as one of *sharing, caring, protecting, and conserving:*

> The Earth is one but the world is not. We all depend on one biosphere for sustaining our lives. Yet each community, each country strives for survival and prosperity with little regard for its impact on others. (WCED, 1987, p. 27)

References

Bell, D.V.J. (2002). Canada's Commissioner of the Environment and Sustainable Development: A case study. York Centre for Applied Sustainability. Retrieved from http://iisd.ca/measure/scipol/case2.doc.

Bryner, Gary C. (1999). Agenda 21: Myth or reality. In: Vig, Norman J., and Axelrod, Regina S., eds., *The Global Environment*. Washington, D.C.: CQ Press, pp. 157–189.

Caldwell, Lynton K. (1984). *International Environmental Policy: Emergence and Dimensions*. Durham, N.C.: Duke University Press.

Conca, Ken, and Geoffrey D. Dabelko (1998). Twenty-five years of global environmental politics. In: Conca, K., and Dabelko, Geoffrey D., eds., *Green Planet Blues: Environmental Politics from Stockholm to Kyoto*. Boulder, Colo.: Westview, pp. 1–16.

Doern, Bruce G., and Thomas Conway. (1994). *The Greening of Canada*. Toronto, Canada: Toronto University Press.

Dwivedi, O.P. (1990). Satyagraha for conservation: Awakening the spirit of Hinduism. In: Engel, J. Ronald, and Engel, Joan Gibb, eds., *Ethics and Environment and Development: Global Challenge and International Response*. London: Belhaven Press, pp. 201–212.

Dwivedi, O.P. (1997). *India's Environmental Policies, Programmes, and Stewardship*. London: Macmillan Press.

Dwivedi, O.P. (2003). New leadership in the global village. In: Boyer, J. Patrick, ed., *Leading in an Upside-Down World*. Toronto: Dundurn Group, pp. 189–195.

Dwivedi, O.P., J.P. Kyba, Peter Stoett, and Rebecca Tiessen (2001). *Sustainable Development and Canada*. Peterborough, Canada: Broadview Press.

Dwivedi, O.P., and J. Nef (2004). From development administration to new public management: The quest for effectiveness, democratic governance, governability, and public morality. In: Sanjeev Reddy, P.L., Singh, Jaideep, and Tiwari, R.K., eds., *Democracy, Governance and Globalization*. New Delhi, India: Indian Institute of Public Administration, pp.71–91.

Environment Canada (2000). Sustainable development information system. Retrieved from http://www.sdinfo.gc.ca.

Ermen, Raymond van (2002). Economic cooperation: A new world order. In: *Survey of the Environment: 2002*. Chennai (Madras), India: The Hindu, pp. 61–64.

Gandhi, Indira (1972). Address at the UN Conference on Human Environment, Stockholm, Sweden, June 14, 1972. New Delhi, India: Department of Science and Technology.

India, Commission on Human Environment. (1972). *Indian National Report, 1971*. (Abridged by Washington, D.C.: Woodrow Wilson International Center for Scholars, Environment Series 201.)

IUCN, Commission on Environmental Law. (1995). International Covenant on Environment and Development, (Draft), Gland, Switzerland: IUCN.

Kagia, Ruth (2002). Prospects for accelerating human development in the twenty-first century. In: Ginkel, Hans van, Barrett, Brendan, Court, Julius, and Velasquez, Jerry, eds., *Human Development and the Environment: Challenges for the United Nations in the New Millennium.* Tokyo, Japan: United Nations University Press, pp. 63–75.

Khator, Renu (1995). Managing the environment in an interdependent world. In: Garcia-Zamor, Jean-Claude, and Khator, Renu, eds., *Public Administration in the Global Village.* Westport, Conn.: Praeger, pp. 83–98.

Lele, S. (1991). Sustainable development: A critical review. *World Development,* 19, no. 6, 607–621.

Meadows, D.H., D.L. Meadows, J. Randers, and W.W. Behren (1972). *The Limits to Growth: A Report for the Club of Rome's Project on the Predicament of Mankind.* New York: Universe Books.

Mendez, Ariel (2002). Exploring linkages between environment, development and sustainable peace. *PECS News,* no. 6, pp. 9, 15.

Ontario, Canada (1972). *Towards an Environmental Action Plan.* Toronto: Government of Ontario.

Rio Documents (2002). *Looking Ahead: Editorial.* Chennai (Madras), India: The Hindu Survey of the Environment, pp. 125–127.

Sen, Amartya (1999). *Development as Freedom: Human Capability and Global Need.* New York: Alfred Knopf.

UNESCO (2002). Enhancing Global Sustainability. Report of the Preparatory Committee for the World Summit on Sustainable Development, New York, March, 25 2002. Retrieved from http://undesdoc.unesco.org/images/0012/001253/125351e.pdf.

United Nations (2002a). Johannesburg Summit 2002. New York. Retrieved from http://www.johannesburgsummit.org/html/whats_new/feature_story39.htm.

United Nations (2002b). The road from Johannesburg: What was achieved and the way forward. Retrieved from http://www.un.org/esa/sustdev/media/Brochure.PDF.

United Nations (2002c). *Report of the World Summit on Sustainable Development.* Document A/CONF.199/20. New York: United Nations.

United Nations Commission on Sustainable Development. (1999). About commission on sustainable development. Retrieved from http://www.un.org/esa/sustdev/csdgen.htm.

UN Secretary General (2001). Implementing Agenda 21. Report to the UN Commission on Sustainable Development, New York. Retrieved from http://www.johannesburgsummit.org/html/documents/no170793sgrepnt.pdf.

Verolme, Hans J.H. (2002). From Rio to Johannesburg: A European perspective. In: *Environmental Change and Security Project Report.* Washington, D.C.: Woodrow Wilson International Center for Scholars, pp. 5–7.

Weiss, Edith Brown (1993). Intergenerational equity: Towards an international legal framework. In: Choucri, N., ed. *Global Accord: Environmental Challenges and International Responses.* Cambridge, Mass.: MIT Press, pp. 333–354.

World Commission on Environment and Development (1987). *Our Common Future.* New York: Oxford University Press.

Chapter 6

Toward a General Theory of Sustainability

Gedeon M. Mudacumura

CONTENTS

Introduction

The popularization of the sustainable development phenomenon raised a growing dissatisfaction over what is known about the underlying premises of development. In fact, several scholars labeled such knowledge as practically irrelevant, conceptually Eurocentric, theoretically impoverished, ideologically prejudiced, paradigmatically bankrupt, philosophically parochial, and narrowly focused—lacking multidisciplinary perpsectives (Braun, 1990, p. 55; Edwards, 1989, p. 121; Goulet, 1983, p. 610; Haque, 1999a, p. 5; Leys, 1996, p. 7; Mathur, 1989, p. 470; Mudacumura, 2002, p. 39; Palmer, 1978, p. 95; Pieterse, 1991; Preston, 1985, p. 4; Wiarda, 1981, p. 191).

Haque (1999), moreover, argued that the increasing global concern for rethinking development and reexamining the traditional mode, based on the logic of industrialism, reinforced the focus on the question of sustainability, and the global crisis that resulted from widespread industrialization shifted thinking toward sustainable development (Daly, 1991; Reid, 1995). Similarly, a special session of the United Nations (UN) General Assembly concluded that the "overall trends for sustainable development are worse today than they were in 1992" (UN, 1997, para. 4). Those closely connected to the global financial institutions acknowledge that macroeconomic policy and international free trade alone are not improving development prospects for the world's poor, and that chronic impoverishment and environmental degradation reinforce each other to create increasingly unstable social and ecological systems (Camdessus, 2000; Sachs, 1999).

Recently, several influential development stakeholders have sympathized with the need to change established structures while revisiting the development models. World Bank (WB) president Wolfensohn (1999) called for an "integration of effort" and expanded partnerships among groups (aid agencies, other financial donors, the private sector and nongovernmental organizations), as well as a sharing of knowledge, in order to produce a new integrated plan for development.

Along the same line, Camdessus, the former director general of the International Monetary Fund (IMF), recognized the failure of macroeconomics to solve systemic poverty and the need to advance well beyond debt forgiveness to empower underdeveloped economies. Recommendations for alleviating poverty include new institutional alliances, new investment in breaking the poverty cycle, and equity in the distribution of intellectual property and the patenting of knowledge, which has the central role in determining prosperity (Sachs, 1999).

This chapter will briefly allude to the previous models of development, which failed to devote serious attention to the phenomenon of sustainability. The author further presents his general theory of sustainability, which attempts to bridge the economic, social, cultural, political, and, ecological dimensions of development in order to achieve a multidisciplinary understanding.

Historical Background of Sustainability

To appreciate fully the variety, complexity, and pervasiveness of development problems, Meier (1995) reminded us to be aware of their historical perspectives since this was one of the best safeguards against taking a superficial view of development problems. In addition, the proposition that particular human practices would prove unsustainable surfaced in literature going back to the ancient Greeks, in the last 200 years (Malthus, 1820); and particularly in the period since World War II (Brown, 1954; Carson, 1962; Meadows et al., 1972).

Recently, *sustainability* became a catchword capturing the attention not only of environmental scientists and activists but also of some mainstream economists, social scientists, and policy makers (Holdren et al., 1995). This phenomenon gained greater attention during the United Nations Conference on Environment and Development (UNCED) in Rio de Janeiro (1992), where world leaders demonstrated that no one group of nations could continue progressing while the majority of its people remained hungry and poor (Dwivedi, 1994). Among the three landmark documents adopted during the 12-day conference were the Rio Declaration, which called for eradication of poverty worldwide; Agenda 21, which spelled out over 120 initiatives to be put into action between 1992 and the year 2000; and the Statement of Principles on Forests. The Preamble of Agenda 21:1.1 of the Rio Declaration began on a foreboding, but optimistic note:

> Humanity stands at a defining moment in its history. We are confronted with a perpetuation of disparities between and within nations, a worsening of poverty, hunger, ill health and illiteracy, and the continuing deterioration of the ecosystems on which we depend for our well-being. However, integration of environment and development concerns, and a greater attention to them will lead to the fulfillment of basic needs, improved

living standards for all, better protected and managed ecosystems and a safer, more prosperous future. No nation can achieve this on its own; but together we can—in a global partnership for sustainable development.

Income disparity between the "haves" and the "have-nots" was demonstrated clearly from the United Nations Development Programme's (UNDP) statistics on global distribution of income. The statistics showed that the richest 20% of the world's population received 82.7% of the total world income, while the poorest 20% got only 1.4% (UNDP, 1992).

Recent statistics highlight that the world has deep poverty amid plenty. Of the world's 6 billion people, 2.8 billion—almost half—live on less than $2 a day, and 1.2 billion—a fifth—survive on less than $1 a day (World Development Report, 2000/01). According to the final report of the World Commission on the Social Dimension of Globalization, released in February 2004, the income gap between the richest and poorest countries is widening significantly, rising from US$212 versus US$11,417, respectively, in 1960–1962 to US$267 versus US$32,339 in 2000–2002. Specifically, most of the countries of the world that were poorer in 2000 than in 1990 are in Sub-Saharan Africa, according to the United Nations Development Programme's Human Development Report 2003. Ultimately, these statistics revealed that global economic growth had hardly filtered down, and optimism that so-called modern development would have floated a rising tide of people on an upward spiral of wealth and prosperity was misplaced (Pezzoli, 1997). Despite five decades of international development efforts, the hard fact remains that one in five living on this planet—or over 1 billion persons—is existing in conditions of "absolute poverty" and is thus unable to feed, clothe, and house himself or herself in a manner that can sustain health and human dignity.

The Rio Conference further stressed that human beings, in their quest for economic development and enjoyment of the riches of nature, had to come to terms with the reality of resource limitation and the carrying capacities of ecosystems and had to take account of the needs of future generations (International Union for the Conservation of the Nature [IUCN] 1980). This international concern for stewardship fit with Ruskin's (1849) insight and reminded us that God has lent us the Earth for the span of our lives, that the Earth belongs as much to those who are to come after us whose names are already written in the book of creation as to us. Ruskin further warned that we have no right, by anything that we do or neglect, to involve future generations in unnecessary penalties or deprive them of benefits that are in our power to bequeath.

In light of the preceding and other development initiatives mostly geared toward exploration of other development dimensions, the 1980s is considered a turning point that ushered in a new development era (Daly, 1991; Haque, 1999; Leys, 1996). The international development community recognized the negative impact of economic development models on the environment, the increasing number of people living below the poverty level, and the political crises resulting from unsustainable development policies. As Norgaard (1994:1) maintained:

> Development, with its unshakable commitment to the ideas of progress, is rooted in modernism and has been betrayed by each of its major tenets. Attempts to control nature have led to the verge of environmental catastrophe. Western technologies have proved inappropriate for the needs of the South, and governments are unable to respond to the crises that have resulted.

This new development era brought about different views of sustainable development.

Diverse Views of Sustainability

Sustainable development is a very problematic phenomenon because its language and definitions differ according to the ideological perspectives of groups advocating sustainability (McManus, 1996). For instance, Di Castri (1998) noted the excessive use and loose meaning of the term *sustainable development*. Hundreds of definitions of this phenomenon have been proposed, and they have quite different connotations. For example, sustainable development has been variously conceived as vision expression (Lee, 1993), value change (Clark, 1989; Farrell, 1999), moral development (Rolston, 1994), social reorganization (Gore, 1992), and transformational process (Viederman, 1994) toward a desired future or better world.

Nevertheless, sustainable development was defined most influentially by the World Commission on Environment and Development (the Brundtland Commission) as "development that meets the needs of the present without compromising the ability of future generations" (WCED, 1987, p. 8). The "needs" included food, water, shelter, education, health care, and employment.

This seminal definition of sustainable development is translated usually into the simultaneous satisfaction of three objectives: economic efficiency, environmental protection, and social justice (Castri, 1995; Healey and Shaw, 1993; Pearce et al., 1990; Sadler and Jacobs, 1989). As such, sustainability depends on dynamic relationships between people in the same society and from different societies, between people and their technology and other species and their shared natural environment

(Downs, 2000). From this perspective, the Brundtland Commission's definition shifted the focus from a monodimensional to multidimensional view of development.

Although criticized, the Brundtland definition reiterated Ruskin's (1849) stewardship concerns, emphasizing the responsibilities of the current generation to the future while admonishing the future to determine how best to use its inheritance from the past (Howe, 1997). Similarly, Solow (1992, p. 15) extended the Brundtland definition to highlight the duty imposed by sustainability. This duty is not to bequeath to posterity any particular thing but rather to endow posterity with whatever it needs to achieve a standard of living at least as good as one's own and to look after the next generation similarly.

In addition, Pronk and Haq (1992) introduced the concept of fairness in their conception of sustainable development by emphasizing the rationale for economic growth. Thus, sustainable development should provide fairness and opportunity for the entire world's people, not just the privileged few, without further destroying the world's finite natural resources and carrying capacity.

Furthermore, elaborating along the lines of equity, Briassoulis (1999) viewed sustainable development as a form of development that allows the pursuit of well-being by present-living generations, while caring about the legitimate right of future generations to develop their own welfare. Thus, intra- and intergenerational justice in the distribution of the costs and benefits of development should be a basic, albeit a most thorny, aspect of sustainable development (Briassoulis, 1999).

Moreover, Liou (1999) expanded on the sustainable development phenomenon by stressing a broader scope of total development, which considers human resources development, the balance between environmental protection and economic growth, the appreciation of cultural differences, the cultivation of local administrative systems, and the importance of performance accountability. Similarly, the underpinnings of sustainability are captured in Carley and Christie's (1992, p. 48) definition of sustainable development as a "continuing process of mediation among social, economic and environmental needs which results in positive socioeconomic change that does not undermine the ecological and social systems upon which communities and society are dependent."

In addition, sometimes sustainable development refers to a managerial and operational process meant to improve patterns of stability and adaptability of current development (Beckerman, 1994). More often, sustainable development evokes an alternative, ideological model of development that is opposite and inherently contradictory to present practices (Redclift, 1987).

Notwithstanding the extraordinary growth of the sustainability literature in the past few years, much of the analysis and discussion of this phenomenon remained mired in terminological ambiguities as well as in disagreements about facts and practical implications (Lele, 1991; Reid, 1995). Thus, Tolba (1984) lamented that sustainable development had become an article of faith often used, but little explained. The U.S. National Academy of Engineering further noted that sustainable development would remain little more than a slogan unless disciplines interested in development could provide operational concepts that improve the economy and the environment (Warnick and Ausubel, 1997).

Moreover, other scholars have acknowledged the lack of a rigorous theoretical framework. "The absence of a clear theoretical and analytical framework makes it difficult to determine whether the new policies will indeed foster an environmentally sound and socially meaningful form of development," Lele (1991, p. 608) asserted. Consequently, theorists and practitioners have been grappling with the sustainability phenomenon for at least the past two decades, and Jacobs (1993) believed that no one has been able to fully explore this complex phenomenon.

Skolimowski (1995) thought that despite its ambiguity, the phenomenon of sustainable development struck a middle ground between more radical approaches; that is, the phenomenon turned out to be palatable to everybody, but raised crucial issues when one recalls how earlier models of development largely failed to meet the needs of the present in both North and South over the past 50 years. (The terms *North* and *South* are used, respectively, to refer to industrialized countries and countries with little industrialization, commonly known as developing countries).

Finally, Sadler and Jacobs (1989) asserted that the sustainability of the human enterprise, in its broadest sense, depends on technological, economic, political, and cultural factors as well as on environmental ones. Scholars and practitioners in the different relevant fields tended to see different parts of the picture and think in terms of different time scales, often using the same words to mean different things (Holdren et al., 1995).

Brief Review of Key Precursors of Sustainable Development

To understand sustainable development, it is useful to introduce briefly some key economic development theories recognized as the precursors of sustainability. For instance, Myrdal (1968) conceived economic development as nothing less than the upward movement of the entire social system, or the attainment of a number of ideals of modernization. Moreover, Black (1966) viewed the ideals of modernization as comprising productivity, social and economic equalization, modern knowledge, improved institutions and attitudes, and a rationally coordinated system of policy measures that can remove undesirable conditions in social systems that have perpetuated underdevelopment.

With the preceding ideals in mind, different models intended to move backward, underdeveloped nations to acceptable levels of economic development were devised. The following discussion centers on six diverse theories and models of economic development: (1) linear-stage theory, (2) Harrod-Domar growth model, (3) structural-change models, (4) international-dependence models, (5) neoclassical counterrevolution model, and (6) new growth theory.

Linear-Stage Theory

Theorists of the 1950s and early 1960s viewed the process of development as a series of successive stages of economic growth. In fact, Rostow (1990) described the transition from underdevelopment to development in terms of a series of stages through which all countries must proceed. His rationale was built on the idea of economic growth based on a dynamic theory of production rooted in the flow of changing technologies and the history of particular societies.

His analysis allowed him to generalize that economic development can be characterized by five successive stages: traditional society, preconditions for takeoff, takeoff, drive to maturity, and, the age of high mass consumption. Rostow's development stages also can be compared to Adam Smith's development sequences of hunting, pastoral, agricultural, commercial, and manufacturing stages (Meier, 1995).

Rostow defined the traditional society as one whose structure is developed within limited production functions, based on pre-Newtonian science and technology and on pre-Newtonian attitudes toward the physical world. In this context, Newton was used as a turning point in history when philosophers of science came to believe that the world was subject to a few knowable laws and was systematically capable of productive manipulation.

Building on that belief, Rostow conceived traditional societies in such a way that increases in output were predictable. Since traditional societies engaged mainly in farming operations, by expanding acreage, improving irrigation systems, introducing new crops and improvising other technical innovations, particularly in trade and industry, the productivity of farming operations would increase.

A typical traditional society devoted a very high priority to clan connections, which played a large role in social organization. In terms of cultural values, traditional societies generally valued what might be called a "long-run fatalism." The latter consisted of the assumption that the range of possibilities open to one's grandchildren would be just about what it had been for one's grandparents. In other words, traditional societies had a clear concept of what current development scholars refer to as *intergenerational equity*.

Thus, Rostow's theory, according to Kuznets (1971), adopted a unidirectional view of development in which a stage materializes, runs its course, and never recurs. Kuznets viewed Rostow's linear-stage theory as a conception of long-term economic change that implies (1) distinct time segments, characterized by different sources and patterns of economic change; (2) a specific succession of these segments, so that b cannot occur before a, or c before b; and (3) a common matrix, in that the successive segments are stages in one broad process—usually one of development and growth rather than of devolution and shrinkage (Kuznets, 1971).

The assumption that all economies tend to pass through the same series of stages is one of the major critiques of the linear-stage theory. According to Meier (1995), maintaining that every economy always follows the same course of development, with a common past and the same future, is to overschematize the complex forces of development and to give the sequence of stages a generality that is unwarranted.

Harrod-Domar Growth Model

Todaro (1996) contended that the mobilization of domestic and foreign savings in order to generate sufficient investment to accelerate economic growth is the prerequisite for development takeoff. This Harrod-Domar growth model consisted of an economic mechanism by which more investment leads to more economic growth. The underlying assumption is that additional investment would always increase the total level of income, which would in turn lead to higher demand for consumer goods. In this way, investment stimulates economic growth and increases national wealth, which will, eventually, trickle down to the poor.

Both the linear-stage theory and the Harrod-Domar model emphasized the concept of economic growth. As Todaro (1996) remarked, these approaches implicitly assumed the existence of well-integrated commodity and money markets, highly developed transport facilities, a well-trained and educated workforce, the motivation to succeed, and an efficient government bureaucracy to convert new capital effectively into higher levels of output. The "unrealistic" nature of most of these assumptions led to the development of the structural-change models.

Structural-Change Models

Todaro (1996) argued that the main hypothesis of the structural-change models is that development is an identifiable process of growth and change whose main features are similar in all countries. Among other characteristics, the structural-change models stressed the shift from agricultural to industrial production, the steady accumulation of physical and human capital, and the change in consumer demands from an emphasis on food and basic necessities to desires for diverse manufactured goods and services (Fei and Rannis, 1964). Furthermore, a country's resource endowment and its physical and population size and its access to external capital, technology, and international trade are key constraints that must be properly addressed (Chenery and Syrquin, 1975).

One of the most discussed structural-change models, which dominated the literature of the development process during the 1960s and early 1970s, was Lewis's (1955) theory of two-sector surplus labor. Lewis's model focused on the mechanism by which underdeveloped economies transform their domestic economic structures from having a heavy emphasis on traditional subsistence agriculture to a more modern, urbanized, and industrially diverse manufacturing and service economy (Fei and Rannis, 1964).

Lewis's rationale was that the surplus of labor in the rural agricultural sector could be absorbed gradually by a high-productivity, modern industrial sector (Lewis, 1954). The Lewis model was used as the rationalization for the growth of cities and urban industries as people migrated from farms and small towns, as well as for the decline in family size and overall population growth as children lost their economic value when parents substituted child quality (education) for quantity (Todaro, 1996). A good illustration of the impact of Lewis's model is China's current migration of labor from its more prosperous coastal provinces to cities, which has made it more difficult to double-crop land. In fact, many villages no longer have enough able-bodied workers to make this quick transition—and the double-cropped area is shrinking as a result (Brown, 2004).

In reaction, Third World and Western development scholars, dissatisfied with Western growth development models, initiated research that led to the international-dependence models, the focus of the next discussion.

International-Dependence Models

The proponents of international-dependence models argued that structural-change economists failed to identify the critical factors in a nation's development process and (more importantly) diverted attention from the real factors in the global economy that maintained and perpetuated the poverty of developing nations (Todaro, 1996). Moreover, this new school of thought viewed underdeveloped countries as beset by institutional, political, and economic rigidities, both domestic and international, while also being caught up in a dependence and dominance relationship with rich countries (Todaro, 1996).

More specifically, Dos Santos (1969) conceived dependence as a conditioning situation in which the economies of one group of countries are linked to the development and expansion of others. This relationship of interdependence between two or more economies, or between such economies and the world trading system, turns into a dependency relationship when some countries can expand through "self-impulsion" while others, being in a dependent position, can only expand as a "reflection" of the expansion of the dominant countries; this situation may have positive or negative effects on the dependent countries' immediate development (Dos Santos, 1976).

Along the same lines, Baran (1975) realized that whether rich nations are intentionally exploitative or unintentionally neglectful, the coexistence of rich and poor nations in an international system dominated by unequal power relationships between the center (the developed countries) and the periphery (the less developed countries) renders attempts by poor nations to be self-reliant and independent difficult and sometimes even impossible. Another major preoccupation is that within developing countries the small elite ruling class that enjoys high incomes, social status, and political power perpetuates the system (knowingly or not) of inequality through ill-conceived socioeconomic policies. In fact, Leys (1975) and others documented that the Third World's continuing and worsening poverty was attributable to economic policies of the industrial capitalist countries embraced by the small but powerful elite groups in the less developed countries.

Generally, the advocates of international-dependence models rejected categorically traditional Western economic growth theories. Instead, they put more emphasis on international power imbalances and on needed fundamental economic, political, and institutional reforms, both domestically and worldwide.

In reaction to international-dependence models, free marketers devised the neoclassical counterrevolution model, discussed next.

Neoclassical Counterrevolution Model

The neoclassical counterrevolution school of thought emerged to counteract the theoretical premises advanced by the proponents of the international-dependence models. The central argument of the neoclassical counterrevolution model was that underdevelopment results from poor resource allocation, which is due to incorrect pricing policies and too much state intervention by overly active developing nations' governments.

Moreover, convinced that state intervention in economic activity slows the pace of economic growth (Little, 1982), the proponents of the neo-classical counterrevolution model suggested freer markets and the dismantling of public ownership, state planning, and government regulation of economic activities as the correct economic solutions to underdevelopment. The free marketers also asserted that liberalization of national markets draws additional domestic and foreign investment and, thus, increases the rate of capital accumulation (Todaro, 1996). However, markets are eminently suitable for the pursuit of private interests, which may conflict with what serves the common interest, and markets' time perspective is usually rather short (Soros, 2000; Stokke, 1991).

Recalling that early development economics assigned to the interventionist state a key role in correcting market failures and ensuring economic efficiency, growth, macroeconomic stability, and social development, the neoclassical counterrevolution model brought a dramatic shift, as the state came to be seen as a barrier rather than a driving force in the development process (Mohan and Stokke, 2000). Moreover, in the 1980s, the Bretton-Wood Institutions (World Bank and IMF) promoted market liberalism as the most efficient mechanism for delivering economic and social development within a global market system.

One of the critiques of the neoclassical counterrevolution model was that its assumptions concerning markets in developing nations were totally unrealistic (Todaro, 1996). In fact, the harmful neoliberal policies pushed by the IMF for the past 20 years have neither increased per capita economic growth rates to where they had been in the 1960s and 1970s nor substantially reduced poverty in the global South (Rowden, 2004). Criticisms, moreover, highlighted that information was limited, markets are fragmented, and many the economies of developing nations were still non-monetized (Arndt, 1988). The dissatisfaction with the neoclassical counterrevolution model led to the development of the new growth theory.

New Growth Theory

Also known as the endogenous growth school of thought, the new growth theory was the newest school of development theory during the latter half of the 20th century (Stern, 1991). The new growth theory departed from strict adherence to the dogma of free markets and passive governments (Haque, 1999b).

Despite the challenge to economic growth posed by resource scarcity, the advocates of the new growth theory believed that new ideas and technologies have enormous potential to rearrange or to reorganize raw materials or physical resources to enhance productivity and growth (Romer, 1990). New growth theorists also viewed knowledge as a form of capital as distinguished from physical capital, claiming that although the amount of knowledge created from additional investment in research gradually declines, this investment eventually leads to higher returns in terms of goods produced (Romer, 1986).

Furthermore, behind all forms of new ideas, knowledge, and technologies is human capital. "Among the major variables contributing to economic growth, the key factor remains the stock of human capital (creative and capable human resource), not the total population," Haque (1999a, p. 64) asserted. Romer (1990, p. 99) further contended that an economy with a larger stock of human capital would experience faster growth.

From a theoretical perspective, the new growth theory emphasized the role of innovative ideas, new knowledge, human capital, and technological progress to overcome stagnation and to create wealth. In fact, the new growth theory explained technological change as an endogenous outcome of public and private investments in human capital and knowledge-intensive industries, such as computer software and telecommunications. The main failing of this theoretical framework was its focus on economic growth without much concern for issues such as class inequality and environmental problems caused by industrial growth (Daly, 1991; Haque, 1999a; Reid, 1995).

In summary, the authors of the theories and models discussed put particular emphasis on the economic dimension, overlooking the multidimensional nature of sustainable development. Indeed, several scholars have argued that failing to study the phenomenon of sustainable development and its multiple facets has created metadevelopment problems that are a cluster of very closely interconnected problems (Chisholm, 1997; Haque, 1999a; Leys, 1996; Reid, 1995; Stiglitz, 1998). Thus, any attempt to solve any aspect of the sustainable development problem is unlikely to be successful unless its multiple facets are treated simultaneously.

Lack of a General Theory of Sustainability

Thus far, this brief literature review has discussed a variety of diverse views of sustainability and a number of economically based development theories. Despite numerous studies on sustainable development and its importance, there does not exist a general theory of sustainability grounded on a solid, interdisciplinary framework.

Furthermore, existing theories and models of sustainable development seem incapable of explaining associated problems, such as poverty, inequality, and the ecological crisis (Dopfer, 1979). In fact, current sustainable development theories often are considered as a basic component of the global problem because they contain ideological and institutional devices that enhance the process of intellectual bureaucratization and perpetuate domination and exploitation (Addo et al., 1985, p. 4; Harrod, 1982, p. 3; Sheth, 1987, p. 53).

In light of these major shortcomings of sustainable development theories, Apter (1987), Dopher (1979), Haque (1999a), Leys (1996), and others called for a thorough reexamination of sustainable development's theoretical foundations. Some development scholars are specifically calling for the deconstruction of any Eurocentric prejudices, and the building of a more unifying theory of sustainable development that takes into account the multiple facets of development (Edwards, 1989; Mathur, 1989; Mudacumura, 2002; Nuscheler, 1988; Pieterse, 1991, Redclift, 1987; Wallerstein, 1989; Weigel, 1989).

In addition, as a solution to the theoretical crisis of the late 1970s, Reuveny (1979, p. 54) suggested reexamining the premises of the leading Western theories of development in order to develop new theories based on revised premises. One revision was removing the epistemological dominance of economic empiricism over most sustainable development theories, which may lead to the exclusion of noneconomic dimensions (political, social, and cultural) from the sustainable development discourse (Kay, 1991; van Nieuwenhuijze, 1982).

Similarly, the global development network recently organized an international conference (http://www.gdnet.org/tokyo2000/agenda.php). Its main theme was "Beyond Economics: Multidisciplinary Approaches to Development." By looking beyond economics, sustainable development thinkers acknowledged their long-held monodirectional focus on economics while dealing with a multidimensional phenomenon. Such acknowledgment justifies the need to build a general theory of sustainability grounded on diverse disciplines.

In the same vein, the World Bank's Electronic Conference highlighted the lack of a consistent and comprehensive theory of sustainability (http://www.worldbank.org/devforum/forum_cdf.html). Moreover, the Panos Research Institute conducted another Electronic Conference, in which sustainable development issues were debated. The lack of the existence of a multifaceted theory of sustainable development was one major observation (http://www.worldbank.org/devforum/forum _globalization.html).

Despite two decades of research on sustainable development, a general theory of sustainability grounded on a solid, interdisciplinary framework is still a gap in the sustainability literature. Existing theories of sustainable development do not explain the multifaceted problems such as poverty, inequality, politics, and ecological crises.

Moreover, it is time for the reexamination of the premises of the leading Western theories of sustainable development in order to remove the epistemological dominance of economic empiricism, which has led to the exclusion of noneconomic dimensions. The following section underlines the major tenets of the general theory of sustainability, which bridges economic, political, social, cultural, spiritual, and ecological dimensions of development. As Holling (1995) noted, building usable and useful theory is not an academic luxury, but a practical necessity, particularly in times of profound change. Thus, we may argue that devising the general theory of sustainability is timely when one keeps in mind current large-scale global development changes.

Tenets of the General Theory of Sustainability

This section describes briefly the six key dimensions that compose the general theory of sustainability and alludes to intragenerational equity and intergenerational equity, two theoretical boundaries of the general theory of sustainability. The former denotes that the fair distribution of development resources starts with the current generation, while the latter expands the concept of just distribution of resources to decisions pertaining to the welfare of future generations. For interested readers, Mudacumura (2002) provides an in-depth analysis of the general theory building method and detailed explanation of the key dimensions and theoretical boundaries, which are beyond the scope of this chapter.

The Economic Dimension

This author defines the *economic dimension* as a dynamic structural change process that preserves cultural values and human dignity, while exploring the interconnected relationships geared toward improving people's economic welfare at the local, national, and global levels (Mudacumura, 2002). Improving economic welfare for all the people implies the recognition of interconnected relationships and the realization that economics is only one part of the toolkit needed to achieve economic sustainability. Along the same train of thought, particular emphasis on "global equity," here conceived as determined efforts for redistribution of global financial resources, underlines the importance of considering the interrelationships among ecological, cultural, political, economic, spiritual, and social dimensions at the local, national, and global levels, a prerequisite for the materialization of the dynamic, structural changes in a global economy (Mudacumura, 2002).

Furthermore, as emphasized in the definition, interconnectedness explains the relevance of keeping together the main development dimensions, particularly when one recalls the fragmentary approaches of contemporary development scholars and their lack of appreciation of interlinked development dimensions (Leys, 1996). Similarly, acknowledging "interconnectedness" in development can explain the failures of previous development approaches that were premised on reductionist thinking, that is, the belief that all aspects of complex phenomena can be understood by reducing them to their constituent parts and by looking for mechanisms through which these interacted (Capra, 1982; Corbridge, 1998).

The definition of the economic dimension, moreover, highlights "human dignity," conceived as the ability of individuals to work and earn decent wages that enable them to take care of themselves and their families. It is a known fact that an economic system with a large number of undernourished and unemployed people at the bottom end of a long social ladder can never provide a firm basis for political or economic development (Bava, 2000). Specifically, a sociopolitical–economic system in which there are inequality, poverty, and unemployment (and hence no scope for dignified human life for all people) can never be regarded as an economically sustained society (Bava, 2000).

In brief, emphasizing intricate development issues leads to the need to explore further the extent to which fostering economic sustainability fits with improving people's participation in policy making, preserving cultural practices, and promoting global equity and societal welfare—key premises of the social dimension, discussed next.

The Social Dimension

Mudacumura (2002) conceived the social dimension as consisting of a participatory decision-making system through which empowered people devise strategies aimed at fostering global equity and preserving cultural practices, while recognizing the complex challenges of securing current and future generations' welfare. Specifically, the social dimension capitalizes on people as a key asset in any development effort who, when empowered, unleash their thinking processes, making them active participants in the identification of a community's complex development issues (Mudacumura, 2004a).

Furthermore, empowered individuals at the grassroots levels can design suitable development policies that not only foster global equity but also preserve local cultural practices. Empowered people produce effects and can exert their will against opposition (cf. Arendt, 1986). Such empowerment hinges on the existence of an environment that promotes open and nondistorted communication, that is, an environment in which local citizens participate as equals in the deliberation of issues affecting their lives. As Sen (1999) asserted, people directly involved must have the opportunity to participate in deciding the appropriate development options that might foster global equity, searching for meaningful realization of equality not only for elites who own the majority of resources but also for the vast multitude who do not possess such resources (Mudacumura, 2004a).

Thus, grassroots participation connotes a process whose objective is to enable the vast multitude to initiate action for self-reliant development and acquire the ability to influence and manage change within their societies, including shaping global equity decisions that ultimately affect their lives. Such a process entails an active and sustained role in determining how development resources should be generated and evenly distributed, a determining factor that explains the importance of the social dimension (Mudacumura, 2004a).

In fact, experience has demonstrated that participation in decision making improves the quality, effectiveness, and sustainability of development strategies (UNDP, 1997). Thus, enabling grassroots citizens to play major roles in development decision-making processes is a backbone of the social dimension.

The social dimension, in addition, emphasizes the preservation of local cultural practices. Chambers (1997) noted that acknowledging the values of local cultures and ensuring that cultural practices are not overlooked constitute one strategic approach to sustainable development. Historically development programs that ignored the relevance of local cultural practices failed (Cernea, 1993).

Finally, empowered people working with institutions engaged in sustaining local development pay attention to local cultural practices because culture is intrinsically part of development (Mudacumura, 2004b). As such, cultural preservation cannot materialize without a decentralized system of governance and an effective intersectoral collaboration, two key components of the political dimension discussed next.

The Political Dimension

The political dimension can be understood as a decentralized effective system of governance in which the interlinked, embedded, symbiotic relationships between public and private development stakeholders' concerns are taken into account while devising development strategies (Mudacumura, 2002). This definition underscores the crucial importance of effective political systems of governance that enable the private and public sectors to collaborate while carrying forward development functions for governance, here conceived as the manner in which power is exercised in the management of a country's economic and social resources for the ultimate goal of improving societal welfare (Mudacumura, 2004a).

The preceding definition puts emphasis on the effective system of governance to underline the increasing attention to good governance, a sine qua non for promoting strategies geared toward the betterment of the population at large. Good governance, therefore, implies improving the quality of services and leadership at the local level with decision making decentralized at the grassroots levels.

Specifically, decentralization shifts the development responsibilities to grassroots organizations and local authorities, thus bringing decision-making processes closer to the people who become the agents in their own change. As such, decentralizing the decision making allows people to be active change agents, a process that might lead to the sustainability of local development (Mudacumura, 2004b).

Decentralization further draws attention to the importance of accountability and participation within a democratic political framework in enhancing public capacity (Doyal and Gough, 1991). Such enhancement includes channels for the public to voice their needs, to influence policy making, and to ensure that those charged with implementing policy remain accountable to those whose livelihoods and future they will affect (Currie, 1992).

Additionally, effective systems of governance imply collaboration between public and private development stakeholders who are responsive and accountable to the global population and pay particular attention to development strategies focused on increasing meaningfully the well-being of all the people (Mudacumura, 2004a). Since neither public nor private development stakeholders have access to the necessary skills, resources, knowledge, and contacts to further development on their own, the collaboration between both sectors is a prerequisite for achieving sustainable development goals. Intersectoral collaboration is thus critical for fostering global solidarity, cultural awareness, and human dignity, key determinants of the cultural dimension.

The Cultural Dimension

This *cultural dimension* is defined as the genuine way in which a community of people acknowledges their complex shared values, beliefs, customs, and skills, and determines to preserve the cultural practices that underpin the community members' synergetic relationships for the sake of maintaining human dignity, while promoting global solidarity (Mudacumura, 2002). This definition points to a community's way of acknowledging the key elements of people's cultural practices, underlining that a people's commitment to preserving cultural practices may go beyond local boundaries. Such commitment to preserve a local culture also may enable individuals to recognize the relevance of human dignity (Mudacumura, 2002).

Specifically, recognizing human dignity entails acknowledging the main beliefs and values to which individuals pay most attention. Such recognition may further individual self-respect and resistance to exploitation and domination, thus offering real meaning to other values that make people's lives more productive in their communities.

Moreover, cultural practices point to the existence of a general set of rules that control the behavior of individuals through recourse to shared values (Gross and Rayner, 1985). Shared values may thus create a cultural awareness that, in turn, may explain how individuals with the same core values can initiate building global solidarity, here conceived as a way of preventing any forces that would destroy the global population's cherished values and beliefs.

Furthermore, commitment to global solidarity can help recognize cultural differences, while minimizing the risks of divorcing the concrete experiences of a people from their local context. Similarly, community members who are open and receptive to new development insights that do not conflict with their cultural practices may discover that this cultural awareness can be a dynamic source to sustain local development.

Along the same train of thought, the definition of the cultural dimension alluded to the concept of interconnectedness to underscore the extent to which creative expression, traditional knowledge, and other cultural practices are integral parts of people's lives in diverse societies. As stated earlier, since it can be argued that culture permeates all aspects of life, any development process must be embedded in local culture for development to be sustainable. In brief, the integration of cultural practices and people's lives emphasizes the interconnection between culture and development. From this perspective, we can argue that culture is the most fundamental element of development.

The discussions have so far addressed the economic, social, political, and cultural dimensions, providing a definition for each dimension and explaining the extent to which the dimensions are interrelated. It is worth highlighting that social, political, economic, and cultural dimensions come into play in a number of ways when addressing ecological and spiritual dimensions.

The Ecological Dimension

The ecological dimension underscores a holistic decision-making approach that strives to make sense of the interlinked and symbiotic natural and cultural resources that must be preserved while addressing current and future generations' societal welfare (Mudacumura, 2002). The definition emphasizes the interlinked relationships existing in the natural world. Such interrelationships point to the fact that efforts geared toward improving societal welfare are intrinsically dependent on human interactions with the natural world.

Concretely, we may argue that the interlinkages between people and the natural world justify the relevance of paying attention to people's culture, particularly when ecological and cultural well-being are indistinguishable. The interconnectedness of people and nature explains the indispensability of searching for adequate means of creating a sustainable society without destroying natural life-support systems.

Furthermore, the impacts of uncontrolled human interactions with natural subsystems may jeopardize these symbiotic relationships, thus leading to potential ecological crises. Attempts to prevent ecological crises imply the necessity to emphasize the importance of bringing human development into harmony with the natural environment without jeopardizing the welfare of current and future generations.

Additionally, it is worth recalling that saving the planet and its people from impending ecological crises constitutes the underlying theme of the ecological dimension. Such a theme further underscores the importance of recognizing the welfare interdependence between generations, since each generation has an obligation to protect the productive, ecological, and physical processes that are needed to support future human welfare (Norton, 1996).

Along the same line, the ecological dimension's definition underscores the holistic thinking approach, which recognizes that the whole system is greater than the sum of its subsystems (Kast and Rosenzweig, 1972). Such a holistic approach may explain the interrelated ecological issues that transcend life experiences and capabilities of individuals and communities. The holistic thinking approach thus enables development stakeholders to make sense of interconnectedness; empowerment, and the productive good life, which also are basic components of the spiritual dimension of development.

The Spiritual Dimension

The *spiritual dimension* is defined as a transcendental value system that connects the self with other interrelated subsystems and functions synergically with the rest of our human faculties through inner-transformational changes leading to productive, good lives (Mudacumura, 2002). This definition points to a transcendental value system that fosters symbiotic interrelationships in which the individual exists and functions as a central part of the integrated, whole system. Specifically, the individual is part of a global community consisting of intricately balanced, interdependent parts and processes (Mudacumura, 2004).

Moreover, as active agents in shaping the global environment, individuals may strive to balance the interdependent parts and processes, a balance without which the survival of mankind can be compromised.

Similarly, looking at spirituality as transcending all human subsystems and containing revitalizing power may explain the extent to which people's selfish or careless motives may be changed.

It further sheds light on how changed individuals may live productive, good lives in the global community. In this context, a *productive, good life* means living a complete life, not dying prematurely, having good health, being nourished adequately, and possessing adequate shelter (Nussbaum, 1990). Again, such dynamic, transformational changes leading to a productive, good life underscore the necessity of paying attention to the harmonious relationships that should exist between individuals and the natural environment.

Moreover, we may argue that the inner-transformational changes suggested by the definition of the spiritual dimension are premised on an understanding of the relations of parts to the whole, and of past to present to future (Engel, 1998). Such an understanding might explain why spiritually led citizens work together on faith-based issues, trying to regain their self-worth while living productive, good lives.

Productive, good lives also involve reaching "spiritual fulfillment," a balance between individuals and their surrounding environment. Without a desire for spiritual fulfillment, one might question whether people can lead productive, good lives characterized by peacefulness, joy, happiness, enlightenment, and creative expression, all of which may provide the mental pathways leading individuals away from material consumption and wealth accumulation to a higher level of satisfaction and purpose (Cobb, 1995; Daly, 1991).

The spiritual dimension, moreover, might explain the need to go beyond accumulating material wealth without considering the effects of that accumulation on the quality of the human condition (Gondwe, 1992), for the underlying rationale of the spiritual dimension is a focus on people's redemptive, inner-transformational changes that may produce renewed individuals, socially accountable to both current and future generations. This rationale fits with Tawney's (1920) argument that a healthy society comprises people who are trustees in the discharge of a social purpose.

The spiritual dimension further highlights the importance of empowerment, a process whose purpose is to expand people's capabilities. Such an expansion involves an enlargement of choices and an increase in freedom (UNDP, 1996). In fact, empowerment underscores that a learning and organizing process exists that allows people to define their development objectives, assess the implications of development options available to them, and assume responsibility for actions to achieve their agreed-upon objectives.

Finally, the spiritual dimension emphasizes that we should think holistically. It is worth remembering that holism is concerned with interconnections, interrelationships, and long-term underlying systemic patterns (Wheatley, 1992). Thus, relying on holistic thinking may explain how an individual may connect with other interrelated subsystems while operating in a symbiotic, global environment.

In summary, a close examination of the underlying premises of the discussed dimensions of development calls for bridging the multiple dimensions while giving equal consideration to each dimension. Concretely, three overall findings may be inferred from this general theory of sustainability: (1) societal empowerment, (2) global networking, and (3) holistic thinking.

Societal Empowerment

In a world plagued with interwoven and self-perpetuating problems, development is primarily about people's education and organization. Specifically, empowerment may give people a sense of security through participation in debates geared toward improving the overall societal welfare.

Thus, societal empowerment connotes a process by which individuals may gain mastery or control over their own lives with democratic participation in the life of their community. Concretely, societal empowerment may provide the opportunity for citizens to feel their own worth, be all they can be, and see the same worth in other people. To that extent, empowering the whole society means raising people's consciousness and critical thinking processes to increase self-confidence and the ability to play an assertive role in the decisions of the community (Zimmerman and Rappaport, 1988).

Considering that citizens are the beneficiaries, as well as the victims, of all development activities (Cernea, 1993; Schumacher, 1977), empowering citizens also may be a crucial step toward societal empowerment, a sine qua non for sustainable development. Furthermore, in discussing the interrelationships among the six dimensions of this general theory of sustainability, the relevance of people's empowerment was emphasized, pointing to the need for training people, enabling them to be active participants in the design, implementation, and evaluation of development strategies affecting their lives.

Despite the worldwide presence of different international development agencies and the UN's development programs, empowering people with the objective of increasing societal welfare has not been given adequate consideration. In fact, DeLancey (1994, p. 296) concluded that the combined efforts of the UN and of developing countries' governments, donor nations, and nongovernment organizations have been woefully inadequate in improving societal welfare. Puchala (1995) further commented that in spite of numerous development undertakings, missing the goal of investing in humans was one of the main causes of development failures.

Therefore, keeping in mind past development failures, this general theory of sustainability underscores the importance of societal empowerment, emphasizing the potential impacts it could have on furthering development once empowered people exchange strategic development insights through a global network of development organizations.

Global Networking

Global solidarity may imply a clear recognition of the nonexistence of boundaries to our environment and the increasing interdependence among people and nations. Building on this research's findings, this general theory of sustainability highlights the need for development stakeholders to work cooperatively within and between countries, striving to bridge the ecological, economic, social, political, cultural, and, spiritual dimensions while devising comprehensive development strategies.

Similarly, the current trend toward globalization and the magnitude of political, ecological, and socioeconomic, cultural, and spiritual challenges underscore the imperative to build a global network of development organizations. As such, networking all development organizations from local to global levels may create an enabling environment for solving complex development issues, thus providing opportunity for people to enjoy productive, good lives, for global networking rests on the premise that active collaboration among organizations engaged in promoting development may take advantage of creative synergies to achieve outcomes that are impossible for any one to achieve alone. Ultimately, networks are necessary to link the innovative agendas of research institutions, governments, industries, and grassroots organizations that are aimed at clarifying and implementing approaches to sustainable development (Pezzoli, 1997).

Moreover, as this general theory of sustainability's interrelationships highlighted, the interconnectivity and dynamic nature of development problems make them immune to simple solutions. Development strategies may thus fail to materialize if development stakeholders overlook the multidimensionality of development problems.

Similarly, the increasing global interdependencies and the interconnectedness of development issues call for an interorganizational action to search for concrete solutions toward a more desirable future. This means bringing together all institutions of development stakeholders at the local, national, and global levels to achieve a better coordination of development activities so as to foster sustainable development.

Furthermore, coordinating the insights from diverse development stake-holders implies adopting multiple strategic approaches to deal with problems. Networking development organizations can, therefore, help by matching the multiple and interdependent development problems while focusing on a shared vision of what is good for the community at the local, national, and global levels, a process that requires embracing a holistic thinking approach, the third main finding of this research.

Holistic Thinking

Holism refers to an attitude that recognizes that (1) the whole is greater than the sum of its parts, (2) reductionist analysis never tells the whole story, and (3) the abstractions necessary to design mechanistic models conflict with reality (Kast and Rosenzweig, 1972). Similarly, previous discussions alluded to the philosophical background of the mechanistic approach, highlighting the extent to which scholars from diverse disciplines acknowledge the emergent holistic thinking, which provides a better analogy for understanding society and its complex organizations (Hwang, 1996; Kauffman, 1995; Kiel, 1991; Sterman, 1994; Wheatley, 1992).

The post–Second World War era, however, witnessed the emergence of the holistic thinking approach when scholars and policy makers in both developing and developed nations struggled with the crucial issue of development. As Bava (1993) argued, the centrality of the sustainable development phenomenon to governments' public policies, combined with the spurt in developmental theory building during the Cold War, paved the way for the genesis of the holistic thinking approach.

In light of the interrelationships among the six dimensions and the two theoretical boundaries of this general theory of sustainability, dealing with complex development issues that cannot be broken down into parts or managed by any single mind may require embracing a holistic thinking approach. Moreover, it is worth reiterating the importance of looking at the interconnected social, economic, political, ecological, cultural, and spiritual dimensions of development. As the ingredients of a cake are inexplicably intertwined and are necessary for full flavor, so are the development dimensions interconnected and indispensable if development is to be sustainable.

Ultimately, addressing development issues implies thinking holistically, that is, looking at the big picture (the whole phenomenon of sustainability) while maintaining awareness of the interconnected dimensions of development.

Conclusion

This chapter looked at some of the major economic development theories that preceded the sustainable development paradigm. Despite the firm commitment of early economic development theorists to push for economic growth, current economic development statistics reveal that most poor nations, which embraced the growth paradigm, still fight for economic survival. Strong critics go to the extent of labeling the advocates of the failed growth models as wanting to sustain the unjust domination over the global South they enjoyed in colonial days (Ambrose, 2004).

Recalling that building usable and useful theory is not an academic luxury, but a practical necessity, devising a general theory of sustainability is timely when one keeps in mind the current trend toward globalization, particularly the large-scale global development challenges. The chapter further alluded to the shortcomings of analyzing complex development policies by relying on the reductionist policy research approach and suggested adopting a comprehensive and holistic analysis approach to capture the multiple facets of the sustainability phenomenon.

The discussion, moreover, addressed the need for global development networks that foster participatory decision making while devising comprehensive development strategies that integrate the identified key development dimensions. Such networks would involve all development stakeholders and preclude simple solutions implemented by any development organization acting alone. .

In a nutshell, the general theory of sustainability underscores the need to broaden our paradigmatic lenses while devising and analyzing strategies intended to promote sustainable development. These strategies, however, should aim at improving societal welfare in a changing and competitive world in which the persistence of extreme poverty is not compatible with the underlying theme of sustainable development.

References

Addo, Herb. (1985). *Development as Social Transformation: Reflections on the Global Problematique*. Boulder, Colo.: Westview Press.

Ambrose, Soren. (2004). We Dream a World: Resisting & Surviving Six Decades of the IMF & World Bank. 50 Years Is Enough Network. *Economic Justice News*, January 2004.

Apter, David Ernest. (1987). *Rethinking Development*. Beverly Hills, Calif.: Sage Publications.

Arendt, H.W. (1986). Communicative power. In S. Lukes., ed., *Power*. Blackwell: Oxford.

Arendt, H.W. (1988). Market failure and underdevelopment. *World Development*, 16 (February 1988).

Ascher, William. (1999). Resolving the hidden differences among perspectives on sustainable development. *Policy Sciences*, 32: 351–377.

Baran, Paul. (1975). *The Political Economy of Neocolonialism*. London: Heinemann.

Bava, N. (1993). *Development and the Social Science Method: An Interdisciplinary and Global Approach*. New Delhi: Uppal Publishing House.

Bava, N. (2000). Paradigms of development. In N. Bava, ed., *Public Policy and Administration: Normative Concerns*. New Delhi: Uppal Publishing House.

Beckerman, W. (1994). Sustainable development: Is it a useful concept? *Environmental Values*, 3: 191–209.

Black, C.E. (1966). *The Dynamics of Modernization, a Study in Comparative History*. New York: Harper & Row.

Braun, Gerald. (1990). The poverty of conventional development concepts. *Economics*, 42: 55–66.

Briassoulis, Helen. (1999). Sustainable development and the informal sector: An uneasy relationship? *Journal of Environment and Development*, 8(3): 213–237.

Brown, Harrison. (1954). *The Challenge of Man's Future*. New York: Viking.

Brown, L. (2004). China's shrinking grain harvest: How its growing grain imports will affect world food prices Retrieved from http://www.earth-policy.org/Updates/Update36.htm.

Camdessus, M. (2000). Speech to the United Nations Conference on Trade and Development (UMCTAD) in Bangkok. *IMF Survey*, 29(4): 50–53.

Capra, F. (1982). *The Turning Point: Science, Society and the Rising Culture*. New York: Simon & Schuster.

Carley, M., and Christie, I. (1992). *Managing Sustainable Development*. London: Earthscan.

Carson, R.L. (1962). *Silent Spring*. Boston: Houghton Mifflin.

Castri, F. (1995). The chair of sustainable development. *Nature and Resources*, 31(3): 2–7.

Cernea, Michael M. (1993). The sociologist's approach to sustainable development. *Finance & Development*, 33(4): 11–13.

Chambers, Robert. (1997). *Whose Reality Counts? Putting the First Last*. Bath, England: The Bath Press.

Chenery, Hollis B., and Syrquin, Moshe. (1975). *Patterns of Development: 1950–1970*. London: Oxford University Press.

Chisholm, Rupert F. (1997). Building a Network to Foster Economic Development. *International Journal of Public Administration*, 20(2): 451–477.

Clark, W.C. (1989). Managing planet earth. *Scientific American*, 261(3): 47–54.

Cobb, John B., Jr. (1995). Toward a just and sustainable economic order. *The Journal of Social Issues*. 51(4): 83.

Currie, B. (1992). Food crisis and prevention: An analysis in the Indian context. *Contemporary South Asia*, 1(1): 93–111.

Daly, H.E. (1991). From empty-world economics to full-world economics: Recognizing an historical turning point in economic development. In R. Goodland, H.E. Daly, S.E. Serafy, and B. von Droste., eds., *Environmentally Sustainable Economic Development: Building on Brundtland.* Paris: UNESCO.

DeLancey, M. (1994). *Historical Dictionary of International Organizations in Sub-Saharan Africa.* Metuchen, J.J.: Scarecrow Press.

Di Castri, F. (1998). Ecology in a global economy. In B. Gopal, P.S. Pathak, and K.G. Saxena., eds., *Ecology Today: An Anthology of Contemporary Ecological Research.* New Delhi: International Scientific Publications.

Dopher, Kurt. (1979). *The New Political Economy of Development.* New York: St. Martin's Press.

Dos Santos, Theotonio. (1969). The crisis of development theory and the problem of dependence in Latin America. *Siglo,* 21.

Dos Santos, Theotonio. (1976). The crisis of development theory and the problem of dependence in Latin America. In Henry Bernstein., ed., *Underdevelopment and Development.* New York: Penguin.

Downs, Timothy J. (2000). Changing the culture of underdevelopment and unsustainability. *Journal of Environmental Planning and Management,* 43(5): 601–621.

Doyal, L., and Gough, I. (1991). *A Theory of Human Need.* Basingstoke, England: Macmillan.

Dwivedi, O.P. (1994). *Development Administration, from Underdevelopment to Sustainable Development.* New York: St. Martin's Press.

Edwards, Michael. (1989). The Irrelevance of development studies. *Third World Quarterly,* 11(1): 117–135.

Engel, J.R. (1998). The faith of democratic ecological citizenship: *The Hastings Center Report.* Hastings-on-Hudson, 28(6): 31–41.

Farrell, A. (1999). Sustainability and decision-making: the EPA's Sustainable Development Challenge Grant Program. *Policy Studies Review,* 16(3/4): 37–73.

Fei, John C.H., and Ranis, Gustav. (1964). *Development of the Labor Surplus Economy: Theory and Policy.* Homewood, Ill.: Irwin.

Gondwe, Derrik K. (1992). *Political Economy, Ideology, and the Impact of Economics on the Third World.* New York: Praeger.

Gore, Albert. (1992). *Earth in the Balance: Ecology and the Human Spirit.* Boston: Houghton Mifflin.

Goulet, Denis. (1983). Obstacles to world development: An ethical reflection. *World Development,* 11(7): 609–624.

Gross, J., and Rayner, S. (1985). *Measuring Culture.* New York: Columbia University Press.

Haque, M.S. (1999a). *Restructuring Development Theories and Policies: A Critical Study.* Albany: State University of New York Press.

Haque, M.S. (1999b). The fate of sustainable development under neo-liberal regimes in developing countries. *International Political Science Review,* 20(2): 197–218.

Harrod, Jeffrey. (1982). Development studies: From change to stabilization. In B. de Gaay Fortman., ed., *Rethinking Development*. Hague: Institute of Social Studies.

Healey, P., and Shaw, T. (1993). Planners, plans and sustainable development. *Regional Studies*, 27(8): 769–776.

Holdren, J.P., Daily, Gretchen, C., and Ehrlich, Paul R. (1995). *The Meaning of Sustainability*. Washington, D.C.: The World Bank.

Holling, C.S. (1995). Barriers and bridges to the renewal of ecosystems and institutions. In Lance Gunderson, C.S. Holling, and S. Light., eds., *Barriers and Bridges to the Renewal of Ecosystems and Institutions*. New York: Columbia University Press, pp. 3–34.

Howe, Charles W. (1997). Dimensions of sustainability: Geographical, temporal, institutional, and psychological. *Land Economics*, 73(4): 597–607.

Hwang, S.W. (1996). The implications of the nonlinear paradigm for integrated environmental design and planning. *Journal of Planning Literature*, 2: 167–180.

International Union for the Conservation of Nature and Natural Resources. (1980). *World Conservation Strategy: Living Resource Conservation for Sustainable Development*. Switzerland: Gland.

Jacobs, M. (1993). *The Green Economy: Environment, Sustainable Development and the Politics of the Future*. Vancouver, BC: University of British Columbia Press.

Kast, F.E., and Rosenzweig, James E. (1972). General systems theory: Applications for organization and management. *Academy of Management Journal*, December, 447–465.

Kauffman, S. (1995). *At Home in the Universe: The Search for the Laws of Complexity*. London: Viking.

Kay, C. (1991). Reflections on the Latin American contribution to development theory. *Development and Change*, 22(1): 31–68.

Khator, Renu. (1998). The new paradigm: From development administration to sustainable development administration. *International Journal of Public Administration*, 21(12): 1777–1801.

Kiel, D. (1991). Lessons from the nonlinear paradigm: Applications of the theory of dissipative structures in the social sciences. *Social Science Quarterly*, 72: 431–442.

Kuznets, Simon. (1971). Notes on stage of economic growth as a system determinant. In Alexander Eckstein, ed., *Comparison of Economic Systems, Theoretical and Methodological Approaches*. Berkeley: University of California Press.

Lee, K.N. (1993). *Compass and Gyroscope: Integrating Science and Politics for the Environment*. Washington, D.C.: Island Press.

Lele, S. (1991). Sustainable development: A critical review. *World Development*, 9: 607–621.

Lewis, Arthur W. (1954). Economic development with unlimited supply of labour. *Manchester School*, 22: 139–191.

Lewis, Arthur W. (1955). *Theory of Economic Growth*. London: Georges Allen and Unwin.

Leys, Colin. (1975). *Underdevelopment in Kenya: The Political Economy of Neo-colonialism*. London: Heinemann.

Leys, Colin. (1996). *The Rise and Fall of Development Theory*. Bloomington: Indiana University Press.

Liou, Kuotsai Tom. (1999). Administrative reform and economic development: Concepts, issues, and the national experience. *Policy Studies Review*, 16(2): 1–18.

Little, Ian. (1982). *Economic Development: Theories, Policies, and International Relations*. New York: Basic Books.

Malthus, T.R. (1820). Principles of Political Economy. Quoted in Daly, Herman E. (1991). *Steady-State Economics*. Washington, D.C.: Island Press.

Mathur, G.B. (1989). The current impasse in development thinking: The metaphysics of power. *Alternatives*, 14(4): 463–479.

McManus, P. (1996). Contested terrains: Politics, stories and discourses of sustainability. *Environmental Politics*, 5(1): 48–73.

Meadows D.H., Meadows D.L., Randers, J., and Behrens, W.W. III. (1972). The Limits of Growth. *A Report for the Club of Rome's Project on the Predicament of Mankind*. New York: Potomac Associates Book.

Meier, Gerald M. (1995). *Leading Issues in Economic Development*. New York: Oxford University Press.

Mohan, G., and Kristian Stokke. (2000). Participatory development and empowerment: The dangers of localism. *Third World Quarterly*, 21(2): 247–268.

Mudacumura, G.M. (2002). Towards a General Theory of Sustainability: Bridging Key Development Dimensions through a Multi-Paradigm Perspective. Ph.D. dissertation, Pennsylvania State University, Harrisburg.

Mudacumura, G.M. (2004a). Development agenda for the twenty-first century. In G. Mudacumura and S. Haque, eds., *Handbook of Development Policy Studies*. New York: Marcel Dekker.

Mudacumura, G.M. (2004b). The role of nongovernmental organizations in rural development. In G. Mudacumura and S. Haque, eds., *Handbook of Development Policy Studies*. New York: Marcel Dekker.

Myrdal, Gunnar. (1968). *Asian Drama, an Inquiry into the Poverty of Nations*. New York: Pantheon.

Norgaard, R.B. (1988). Sustainable development: A co-evolutionary view. *Futures*, 20(6): 606–620.

Norton, B.G. (1996). Integration or reduction: two approaches to environmental problems. In A. Light and E. Katz, eds., *Environmental Pragmatism*. London: Routledge, pp. 105–138.

Nuscheler, Franz. (1988). Learning from experience or preaching ideologies? Rethinking development theory. *Law and State*, 38: 104–125.

Nussbaum, M. (1990). Aristotelian social democracy. In R. Douglass, G. Mara, and H. Richardson, eds., *Liberalism and the Good*. New York: Routledge.

O'Riordan, T. (1993). The politics of sustainability. In R.K. Turner, ed., *Sustainable Environmental Economics and Management: Principles and Practice*. London: Belhaven.

Palmer, N.D. (1978). Development: The need for an effective dialogue. In Sudesh Kumar Sharma., ed., *Dynamics of Development*. Delhi: Concept.

Pearce, D., Barkier, E., and Markandya. (1990). *Sustainable Development of Economics and Environment in the Third World.* Aldershot, Hauts: Edward Elgar.

Pezzoli, Keith. (1997). Sustainable Development: A Transdisciplinary Overview of the Literature. *Journal of Environmental Planning and Management,* 40(5): 549–574.

Pieterse, J.N. (1991). Dilemmas of development discourse: The crisis of developmentalism and the comparative method. *Development and Change,* 22(1): 5–29.

Preston, P.W. (1985). *New Trend in Development Theory.* London: Routledge and Kegan Paul.

Pronk, Jan, and Mahbubul, Haq. (1992). *Sustainable Development: From Concept to Action. The Hague Report.* New York: United Nations Development Program.

Puchala, Donald J. (1995). *The Ethics of Globalism.* Providence, RI: Academic Council of the United Nations System.

Redclift, M. (1987). *Sustainable Development: Exploring the Contradictions.* London: Methuen.

Reid, D. (1995). *Sustainable Development: An Introductory Guide.* Earthscan: London.

Reuveny, J. (1979). Development theory: Marxist challenge and non-Marxist response. *International Problems,* 18(1–2): 47–57.

Rolston, H. (1994). *Conserving Natural Value.* New York: Columbia University Press.

Romer, Paul M. (1986). Increasing returns and long run growth. *Journal of Political Economy,* 94(5): 1002–1037.

Romer, Paul M. (1990). Endogenous technical change. *Journal of Political Economy,* 98(5): 71–102.

Rostow, W.W. (1990). *The Stages of Economic Growth, a Non-Communist Manifesto.* Cambridge: Cambridge University Press.

Rowden, Rick. (2004). Succession underscores IMF's outdated structure. *The Financial Times,* March 9, 2004.

Ruskin, John. (1849). Quoted in Richard Douthwaite. (1993). *The Growth Illusion: How Economic Growth Has Enriched the Few, Impoverished the Many, and Endangered the Planet.* Tulsa, Okla.: Council Oak Books.

Sachs, J. (1999). Helping the world's poor, *The Economist,* 14 August, pp. 17–20.

Sadler, B., and Jacobs, P. (1989). A key to tomorrow: On the relationship of environmental assessment and sustainable development. In P. Jacobs and B. Sadler, eds., *Sustainable Development and Environmental Assessment: Perspectives on Planning for a Common Future.* Quebec: Canadian Environmental Assessment Research Council, pp. 3–31.

Schumacher, E.F. (1977). Small Is Beautiful, Economics as if People Mattered. *Harper Perennial.*

Sen, Amartya. (1999). *Development as Freedom.* Oxford: Oxford University Press.

Serageldin, Ismael. (1996). Sustainable development: From theory to practice. *Finance and Development,* 33(4): 3.

Sheth, D.L. (1987). Alternative development as political practice. *Alternatives*, 12(2): 155–171.

Skolimowski, H. (1995). In defence of sustainable development. *Environmental Values*, 4: 69–70.

Solow, Robert. (1992). An almost practical step toward sustainability. An invited lecture on the occasion of the fortieth anniversary of Resources for the Future, October 8, Washington, D.C.

Soros, George. (2000). *Open Society: Reforming Global Capitalism*. Boston: Little, Brown.

Sterman, J.D. (1994). Learning in and about complex systems. *Systems Dynamics Review*, 10: 291–330.

Stern, Nicholas. (1991). Public policy and the economics of development. *European Economic Review*, 35(2/3): 241–254.

Stiglitz, Joseph. (1998). *Towards a New Paradigm for Development: Strategies, Policies, and Processes*. Geneva: UNCTAD.

Stokke, Olav. (1991). Sustainable development: A multi-faceted challenge. The *European Journal of Development Research*, 3(1): 8–31.

Tawney, R.H. (1920). *The Acquisitive Society*. New York: Harcourt Brace & World.

Todaro, Michael P. (1996). *Economic Development. Reading*, Mass.: Addison-Wesley.

Tolba, M.K. (1984). The premises for building a sustainable society. Address to the World Commission on Environment and Development, Nairobi. United Nations Environment Program.

United Nations. (1997). Statement of Commitment. United Nations Commission on Sustainable Development, Overall Review and Appraisal of the Implementation of Agenda 21, Report of the 7th Session A/S-19/29, 27th June, paragraph 4. Online at http://www.un.org/esa.

United Nations Development Programme. (1992). *Human Development Report*. New York: Oxford University Press.

United Nations Development Programme. (1996). *Human Development Report*. New York: Oxford University Press.

United Nations Development Programme. (1997). *Who Are the Questions-Makers? A Participatory Evaluation Handbook*. New York: Office of Evaluation and Strategic Planning.

United Nations Development Programme. (2003). *Human Development Report*. New York: Oxford University Press

van Nieuwenhuijze, C.A.O. (1982). *Development Begins at Home: Problems and Prospects of the Sociology of Development*. Oxford: Pergamon Press.

Viederman, Stephen. (1994). The Economics of Sustainability: Challenges. Paper presented at the Governor's Conference on Ecosystem Management, Orlando, Florida, September 21, 1994.

Wallerstein, Immanuel. (1989). The capitalist world economy: Middle-run prospects. *Alternatives*, 14(3): 278–88.

Weigel, Van B. (1989). *A Unified Theory of Global Development*. New York: Praeger.

Wheatley, M J. (1992). *Leadership and the New Science: Learning about an Organization from an Orderly Universe*. San Francisco: Berrett-Koehler.

Wiarda, H.J. (1981). The ethnocentrism of the social science: Implications for research and policy. *The Review of Politics*, 43(2): 163–197.

Warnick, I., and Ausubel, J. (1997). Industrial ecology: Some directions for research. Program for Human Development, Rockefeller University. Retrieved from http://phe.rockefeller.edu.

Wolfensohn, J.D. (1999). A Proposal for a Comprehensive Development Framework, Discussion Draft, Washington, D.C.: World Bank.

World Commission on Environment and Development. (1987). *Our Common Future*. Oxford: Oxford University Press.

World Development Report. (2000/01). Retrieved from http://www.world-bank.org/poverty/wdrpoverty/

Zimmerman, Marc A. and Rappaport, Julian. (1988). Citizen participation, perceived control, and psychological empowerment. *American Journal of Community Psychology*, 16(5): 725–750.

SUSTAINABLE DEVELOPMENT: POLICIES AND INSTITUTIONS

Chapter 7

Urbanization and Sustainable Development Policy and Administration

Josef Leitmann

CONTENTS

Introduction

We are on the verge of an urbanized world. By the time we complete this first decade of the 21st century, more than half of the world's population will be living in cities and towns. At the beginning of the 19th century, only 3% of the world was urban, and by 1900, this had only grown to just under 14% (Population Reference Bureau, 2003, p. 1). Cities are increasingly where the world's population, including the poorest people, will reside. At the same time, urban areas are more and more the engines of national and regional economic growth. Thus, they are the world's most important consumers of resources, generators of waste, and, consequently, sources of environmental problems.

In the half-century since 1950, the world's urban population rose from 750 million to 2.9 billion persons. The population of urban areas is expected to grow by 1.8% annually between 2000 and 2030, or nine times as fast as the 0.2% rate for rural areas. Over 60 million people are added to urban populations each year, or more than 1 million per week. By the year 2030, 60% of the world's population will live in cities and towns. More than 90% of this increase will occur in cities of the developing world (United Nations Population Division, 2002, p. 1). Figure 7.1 indicates how urbanization differs according to geographic area; it suggests that Africa and Asia are urbanizing most quickly.

These cities currently generate more than half of economic wealth in the developing world and accounted for 80% of gross domestic product (GDP) growth during the past decade (World Bank, 2002a; Data Table 2). Population and economic growth are partly responsible for creating exter-

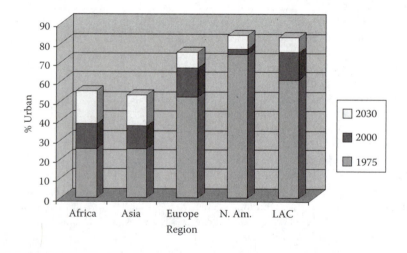

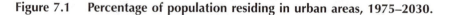

Figure 7.1   Percentage of population residing in urban areas, 1975–2030.

nalities—more people making more things demand more resources and generate more waste. Other variables are also critical, such as lifestyles, wealth distribution, natural and spatial factors, and governance systems. The resulting set of environmental problems consists of inadequate access to environmental infrastructure and services, pollution from urban wastes, natural resource degradation, exposure to environmental risks, and global environmental issues. A huge number of people are affected by urban environmental degradation: 1.1 billion people live in cities that have unhealthy air quality; 590 million have inadequate sanitation; and 280 million city dwellers do not have access to safe drinking water (Leitmann, 1999, pp. 61–63).

The Dynamics of Urbanization and Environmental Change

Environmental change occurs when one moves from rural to urban settings for a number of different reasons. On average, cities tend to have worse air quality, less ultraviolet radiation, more fog, greater cloudiness, more precipitation, a higher temperature, less humidity, and lower wind speeds than surrounding rural areas. Important factors influence these and other environmental characteristics that make cities different. Primary determinants include (1) a city's level of economic development, (2) rapid demographic change, (3) natural and spatial factors, and (4) the institutional setting. The interaction of these variables constitutes the dynamics that link urbanization and environmental change.

Economic Development

A simplistic model of the relationship between economic growth and the urban environment would suggest that as cities become wealthier, they consume and throw out more. Thus, economic growth should lead to greater environmental degradation from higher resource use and higher waste generation per capita. However, the evidence shows that this is only partially true. As cities grow economically (as measured by per capita income), they do produce more municipal waste and carbon dioxide emissions per person (McGranahan et al., 2001).

However, urban concentrations of particulate matter decrease with growing wealth, as do sulfur dioxide emissions (after a period of increase). Importantly, the percentage of the population with access to safe drinking water and adequate sanitation increases dramatically with economic growth. This more complicated picture can be understood if we add some information to the simplistic model.

Consumption and waste do increase with economic growth. At the same time, as cities become richer, they have more resources (financial, technological, and human) to solve certain problems and a more educated and wealthier population, who increasingly demand a better quality of life (Bartone et al., 1994). Thus, citizens demand (and can increasingly pay for) piped water, sewerage, and air that does not have health-threatening pollutants such as fine particulates, sulfur dioxide, and lead. Municipal and sometimes national governments sooner or later respond to this demand, and, with higher revenues from economic development, they have the resources to provide water, remove wastes, and clean the air for more of the urban population. Benefits also extend beyond the wealthy and educated classes to a broader group of citizens. Emissions of municipal solid waste and carbon dioxide increase on a per capita basis partly because there is greater consumption of energy and other resources, and partly because these are externalities that usually do not directly affect the health and well-being of urban residents in the short term.

Thus, as cities develop economically, the nature of environmental risks faced by their populations undergoes a transition. This is graphically shown in Figure 7.2. In the poorest cities, household sanitation problems are most severe; they are also local, immediate, and health-threatening.

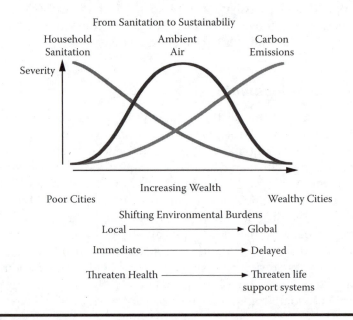

Figure 7.2   The urban environmental transition in cities.

As cities develop economically, household sanitation improves, but ambient air quality deteriorates and carbon dioxide emissions begin to grow. In the wealthiest cities, household sanitation is usually excellent and air quality has improved, but emissions of greenhouse gases continue to rise; in these cities, problems are more global in nature, have a delayed impact, and threaten life support systems (McGranahan et al., 2001).

Demographic Factors

Rapid population growth is especially important for the urban environment in developing country cities. As a city grows, there is a greater concentration of people, industry, commerce, vehicles, energy consumption, water use, waste generation, and other environmental stresses. Cities that are doubling every 10 to 20 years thus must rapidly mobilize resources to manage and mitigate the impacts of these stresses.

The scale of the problem can often exceed the capacity of local government to collect, treat, and dispose of municipal sewage and solid wastes; the capacity of authorities to control dangerous wastes and emissions; and the capacity of nature to assimilate all of these wastes. An analogous scale problem exists on the input side as a result of the concentrated resource consumption taking place in urban areas. Urban demand for fossil fuels, water, food, minerals, timber and fuelwood, and other resources often has impacts on distant peoples, watersheds, and forests. These problems can exist for large cities and megacities, where the magnitude of resource consumption and waste generation is enormous and the jurisdictional situation is often complex. They can also affect smaller and medium-sized cities that may not have the capacity or the resources to respond to rapid changes in population and the nature of environmental problems.

Natural and Spatial Factors

Two key conditions that affect the nature of the urban environment are the features of the ecosystem(s) where a city is located and the patterns of land use. A city's surrounding ecosystem(s) can have important consequences for the degree and nature of environmental problems faced in an urban area. This includes the geography, topography, vegetation, and climate where a city is located. For example, London has not suffered from malaria because it is not located in a tropical ecosystem where the mosquito vector can thrive. Air pollution in Mexico City and Los Angeles is intensified because of natural and climatological features in those cities that result in thermal inversions. The built environment in a city also constitutes a sort of ecosystem that affects air quality, energy consumption, temperature, wind speed, and water management.

Urban land use decisions are critical determinants of environmental quality. At some point in their existence, most cities have experienced distortions in land markets. Poorly functioning land markets, combined with ineffective land management policies and practices, have resulted in degradation of environmentally fragile lands (for example, wetlands and coastal resources), occupation of hazard-prone areas (for example, steep slopes, flood plains, and vacant land adjacent to polluting industries or waste disposal sites), air pollution, congestion and accidents, and the loss of cultural and historical resources, open space, and prime agricultural land (Bernstein, 1993).

Density and spatial patterns of development also have important implications for various environmental outcomes. For example, high-density development can achieve economies of scale in infrastructure provision but impose higher costs associated with congestion (for example, the rapid spread of communicable disease due to crowding or increased incidences of accidental injuries) if the development is not well planned and provided with adequate infrastructure. Lower-density development outside the central city means reduced congestion in residential areas, but higher costs for infrastructure provision, and in the absence of adequate public transport, higher levels of air pollution from automobile traffic. The concentration of industry in relatively few locations is another factor that imposes serious environmental consequences. In the metropolitan areas of Bangkok, Lima, Mexico City, Manila, and Sao Paulo, for example, industrial pollution, including the impacts of poorly managed hazardous wastes, imposes serious health impacts in the areas of the country where there are the highest concentrations of population (Bartone et al., 1994).

Institutional Setting

There are a number of institutional factors that influence urban environmental outcomes in cities. First, the composition, interests, relative power, and interactions of stakeholders are important. Next, the relationship of jurisdictions to key environmental problems in a city has serious consequences. Finally, the degree to which there is intersectoral coordination will affect how cross-media environmental problems are managed.

To a large extent, the nature of urban environmental problems is determined by the interaction of numerous public, private, not-for-profit, and household stakeholders, each group having its own interests and patterns of behavior (Leitmann, 1999, pp. 86–88). The varied and sometimes conflicting actions and viewpoints of these actors can add to other constraints on improving environmental quality and human security.

Ideally, levels of responsibility and decision making should correspond to the scale of an environmental problem. However, actual jurisdictional arrangements usually do not adhere to this principle. For example, municipal authorities are normally responsible for solid waste management, but their usually inadequate approaches to disposal have important spillover effects for neighboring jurisdictions within a region or metropolitan area. A second jurisdictional factor is that urban institutions are often not the only stakeholders with the power to address environmental problems within their jurisdictions. For example, leaded gasoline may be causing health problems in a particular city, but the authority to regulate fuel composition usually rests with the national government. Thus, cities usually cannot solve many of their environmental problems by themselves but must enter into partnerships with different levels of government, with the private sector, and with the community.

Managing the urban environment requires both policy makers and managers to take into account the complex cross-media effects of urban pollution. Any plans to improve one environmental medium (air, water, or land), therefore, should consider the potential effects of that intervention on other media. For example, sewage treatment plants may clean up the flow of wastewater but produce large quantities of sludge that will have to be disposed of safely on land. In light of cross-media effects, relevant jurisdictions and institutions should carefully coordinate to ensure that problems are effectively addressed. Failure to do so can result in both cross-media pollution problems as well as a loss of resources spent on ineffective actions, for example, investments in surface drainage without parallel improvements in solid waste collection and disposal, or the development of a sewage treatment plant without parallel control of industrial pollution.

Human Development Issues

The main human development issues that have emerged from urbanized environmental challenges are (1) greater vulnerability of the urban poor, (2) problems of inadequate access to basic services, (3) exposure to natural and anthropogenic risks, and (4) insecurity from global environmental threats.

Vulnerability of the Urban Poor

One quarter to a one third of all urban households in the world live in absolute poverty (United Nations Human Settlements Programme, 2001). Poverty interacts with the urban environment in two ways: the actions of low-income groups have consequences for the environment and the poor are disproportionately affected by many environmental problems. Briefly, the following are some of the effects of poor groups on the urban environment:

- *Migration*—in developing countries, it is often the rural poor who migrate to cities and accelerate urban population growth. This accelerated growth stresses the ability of municipalities to provide environmental services as well as to collect and treat wastes.
- *Squatting*—lack of disposable income combined with dysfunctional land markets in many developing cities often results in the growth of illegal settlements. Often, these settlements are located on land that is environmentally sensitive or hazard-prone. The development of irregular settlements also makes it difficult to provide squatters with access to environmental services and infrastructure efficiently.
- *Lack of options*—when services and infrastructure are not available or are too costly (see later discussion), then low-income households and neighborhoods may be forced to act in ways that harm the environment and themselves. For example, if solid waste is not regularly collected, then it may be dumped or burned, contributing to the spread of disease vectors, air pollution, and flooding (Leitmann, 1999, p. 67).

The poor are more seriously affected by a range of urban environmental problems. Foremost among the environmental concerns of the urban poor are health problems resulting from a substandard living environment that does not protect them from human excreta and other wastes, indoor air pollution, or natural hazards. Intraurban studies confirm that the mortality and morbidity rates of gastrointestinal and respiratory infections and malnutrition are significantly higher for the urban poor than for other urban residents (McGranahan et al., 2001). So too are the resulting costs of health care and productivity losses. Among the urban poor, there are several particularly vulnerable groups: children, women, adolescents, cottage industry workers, the disabled, and the elderly. These groups are particularly exposed because they lack the economic ability to invest in mitigating measures and pay for services, knowledge about alternatives, and the political strength to push for environmental improvements. They also tend to spend more time at home, where exposure to polluted water, poor indoor air quality, disease vectors, crowded conditions, and poor sanitation may be the greatest (McGranahan et al., 2001). In industrialized countries, this inequitable exposure to environmental risks has helped spawn the "environmental justice" movement.

The poor are most affected by environmental risks in cities for a variety of reasons. The first has to do with location. The neighborhoods or areas where poor people can afford to live are often undesirable pieces of real estate because they are located near industrial areas, are exposed to high levels of air and water pollution, and may be more subject to damage by natural hazards (Leitmann, 1999, p. 15). Second, poor communities often lack the political power to pressure for a cleaner environment or to obtain environmental services such as clean and reliable water supply, sanitation, waste collection, and drainage. Finally, the poor often cannot afford coping mechanisms to mitigate negative environmental impacts, for example, using pumps to evacuate flood waters, taking vacations out of the city during severe air pollution days, or drinking bottled water.

Access to Basic Services

The most critical urban infrastructure and services from an environmental perspective are the water and sanitation systems, solid waste management, drainage, and transportation (see Table 7.1). A set of important environmental problems occurs, mostly with negative health consequences, when people do not have adequate access to these facilities and when their quality is poor.

Table 7.1 Options for Addressing Poor Access to Environmental Infrastructure and Services

Poor Access to Environmental Infrastructure and Services	(P = Policy; I = Investment)
Serviced land and shelter	P: Clarify property rights; reduce unneeded regulations, government involvement, and subsidies for land market
	I: Upgrade slums; develop sites and services projects
Water supply, sanitation, drainage, solid waste collection, energy	P: Incentives for demand management; reduce subsidies and recover costs; target subsidies for the poor; strategic planning; introduce affordable standards; coordinate between sectors; use new infrastructure to guide land use; design with nature
	I: Use appropriate technologies; expand access to basic services; increase use of private and community resources; improve operations and maintenance

Modified from Leitmann, 1999.

Around the world 280 million city dwellers do not have access to safe drinking water near their homes, and 590 million urban residents do not have access to adequate sanitation; although 70% of the urban population has access to some form of sanitation, only about 40% are connected to sewers (Leitmann, 1999, p. 61). In poorer cities, the pollutant that takes the highest toll on health is human waste. The World Health Organization (WHO, 2000, pp. 1172–1282) estimates that 1.7 million children under the age of 5 die each year in the developing world of diarrheal diseases, largely because of poor sanitation, contaminated drinking water, and related problems of food hygiene; an estimated one million fewer children would die from diarrheal diseases each year if all people had access to adequate water and sanitation facilities. Infectious and parasitic diseases linked to water quality and quantity are the third leading cause of productive years lost to health problems in the developing world. Diarrheal death rates are typically about 60% lower among children who live in households with adequate water and sanitation facilities than among those in homes without such facilities (Leitmann, 1999).

From half to two thirds of household solid waste in lower-income cities is not collected (World Resources Institute, 1996, p. 70). At the same time, solid waste management consumes 20% to 40% of municipal budgets in poorer cities (United Nations Centre for Human Settlements, 1996, p. 270). Uncollected waste is then informally dumped or burned in neighborhoods. This situation provides a breeding ground for disease-carrying pests and causes localized air pollution. The lack of basic solid waste services in crowded, low-income neighborhoods is an important contributor to disease among the poor, though much less so than the pathogens associated with poor water and sanitation. In wealthier cities, collection rates improve and approach 100%; however, the volume grows and the waste composition changes, creating disposal problems (World Bank, 2002b, p. 112).

Inadequate storm water drainage has a number of negative impacts. Flooding that is exacerbated by poor drainage can result in death caused by drowning, burial in landslides, or collapsing houses. Flooding results in economic harm through property damage, road congestion, disruption of public services, and lost employment. In many poorer cities, sewage and sullage (gray water) are removed by drains. Flooding can spread wastewater in communities, with resulting health effects. Standing water, resulting from poorly drained rainwater, provides ideal conditions for outbreaks of insect-borne diseases.

Insufficient access to safe and reliable transportation can be a major environmental problem. Increasing motorization, poorly functioning public transportation, badly maintained roads, lack of walkways and cycle paths, poor traffic management, and lack of enforcement and education contribute

Table 7.2   Options for Addressing Natural and Human Hazards

Natural and Human Hazards	(P = Policy; I = Investment)
Natural hazards	P: Enable land markets; existence and enforcement of land use and building codes; disincentives for occupation of high-risk areas; disaster mitigation and preparedness planning; incentives for disaster-resistant construction techniques I: Forecasting and early warning of predictable hazards; public awareness campaigns about risks and mitigation
Human-induced hazards	P: Environmental zoning I: Improve emergency response capacity; public awareness

Modified from Leitmann, 1999.

to traffic congestion, road accidents, and air pollution, with associated health and economic losses. The cost of road accidents in developing countries, two thirds of which occur in urban areas, is 1% to 2% of GDP or $65 billion annually according to the World Health Organization (WHO, 2003, p. 1), reflecting high fatality and injury rates and property damage.

Environmental Hazards

Environmental hazards (Table 7.2) have natural and human sources, as well as the interaction of the two. Almost 2 billion people were affected by disasters during the 1990s, 80% of whom lived in Asia (United Nations Centre for Human Settlements, 2001). Many cities are subject to significant loss of life and property from natural sources such as earthquakes and floods, as well as wildfires, tropical storms, mudslides, and volcanic eruptions. For example, the average annual loss from earthquakes in Turkey, mostly in urban areas, is estimated at 0.8% of GNP. Up to 50 of the fastest growing cities in the developing world are located in earthquake zones (World Bank, 2002b, p. 116). Damage from the 1988 flooding in the Rio de Janeiro metropolitan region was estimated at over $900 million, and the 1998 flooding in Wuhan left 200,000 people stranded while causing an estimated $480 million in damage (Leitmann, 1999, p. 70).

Human sources of environmental risk in cities include accidents caused by industries, municipal facilities, traffic, and fires. Over the past four decades, the number of human-made disasters has tripled (United Nations Centre for Human Settlements, 2001). Perhaps the most notorious urban industrial accident was the 1984 disaster in Bhopal, which claimed thousands of lives and led to the destruction of a swathe of homes and industrial facilities. This hazard was exacerbated by the failure to control settlement around the chemical plant. In 1992, powerful explosions caused by liquid hexane that was dumped into the municipal sewer system killed over 200 people, injured 1,000 others in Guadalajara, and damaged homes, streets, and commercial buildings (World Bank, 1998, p. 12). Traffic accidents claim thousands of lives in some of the world's largest cities each year. The situation is particularly striking in developing cities with fewer cars per capita but higher accident rates. In India, there are more fatalities each year from road accidents than in the United States, although India has one twentieth the number of motorized vehicles (United Nations Centre for Human Settlements, 1996). The loss of life and property from fires that are intentionally or accidentally set plagues virtually every city in the world; the problem is worsened by insufficient preventive measures (e.g., public education and enforced building codes) and low emergency-response capacity (e.g., inadequate fire-fighting capability and medical facilities).

Human actions can deepen and widen the impact of many natural hazards. Loss of life and property from earthquakes is heightened when unsafe buildings are constructed in areas of high seismic activity or when cities are not prepared to handle emergencies. Similarly, the damage from flooding is intensified when people settle in floodplains, drainage is inadequate, or uncollected solid waste is disposed of in existing drains.

Global Threats

Although many of the environmental effects of urban areas tend to be local, cities can have important consequences for environmental problems of a global nature and can also be seriously affected by global problems (see Table 7.3). Examples include the following:

- *Greenhouse gases*—Cities consume 80% of the world's fossil fuels. Consequently, cities such as Canberra, Chicago, and Los Angeles have carbon dioxide emissions that are six to nine times greater per capita than the world's average and 25 times (or more) than those of poorer cities such as Dhaka (United Nations Centre for Human Settlements, 1996). One estimate suggests that 40% of total CO_2 emissions in North America are from 50 metropolitan areas (World Resources Institute, 1996).
- *Sea level rise*—If cities are a primary contributor to global warming, they can also be its victim. Most U.S. coastal cities, Buenos Aires, Rio de Janeiro, Hamburg, London, St. Petersburg, Venice, Lagos, Bombay, Bangkok, Hong Kong, Shanghai, and Sydney are among

Table 7.3   Options for Addressing Global Environmental Threats

Global Environmental Threats	(P = Policy; I = Investment)
Land-based sources of marine pollution	P: Introduce water pricing and effluent charges; subsidize sewage treatment; plan and manage watersheds I: Improve monitoring and enforcement; develop facilities for reusing wastewater; introduce clean technologies
Greenhouse gas emissions	P: Remove energy and vehicle subsidies; introduce road and emissions charges; integrate transport, land use and road planning; least-cost energy planning; improve traffic management I: Develop clean technologies, renewable energy, district heating, energy-efficient buildings, substitution to cleaner fuels, nonmotorized transport, vehicle maintenance, and related public awareness campaigns; improve performance of public transit
Land and ecosystem degradation	P: Remove artificial shortages of land and subsidies on natural resources; identify critical areas for protection; incentives for sustainable use of sensitive areas; ecolabeling; resource-efficient building standards; promote compact land use I: Improve monitoring and enforcement of land use controls; purchase sensitive and valued lands; resources for urban greening and andagriculture

Modified from Leitmann, 1999.

the places that would be seriously affected by flooding due to a rise in sea levels.

■ *Climate change*—Projections of the impact of changing global climate on European cities suggest that Berlin will experience a warmer and wetter climate that could exacerbate smog and acid rain, Volgograd could suffer from spring flooding and summer dust storms, and Liverpool could be affected by malfunctioning sewers cause by the impact of increased rainfall on its tidal river.

■ *Pollution of international waters*—Land-based sources of marine pollution have been an important cause of degrading international waters. Urban wastes usually constitute the major component of these land-based sources (Leitmann, 1999, pp. 73–74).

Finally, although physically more remote, even the preservation of biodiversity has two important urban dimensions. First, much of the demand for threatened plant and animal species comes from the urban economy.

Second, the political, financial, and intellectual support for protecting biodiversity is usually based in cities. Just think how many wildlife parks and other environmental groups are headquartered and have their membership base in urban areas.

Options for Improving the Sustainability of Urbanization

Cities can and should address these environment-based threats to human development. There is a range of policy and investment options for improving access to environmental infrastructure and services, reducing the risks posed by environmental hazards, and diminishing the contribution that cities make to global environmental problems. These options are summarized in Tables 7.1, 7.2, and 7.3. The broader issue of vulnerability of the urban poor needs to be tackled by a three-pronged approach: (1) a pro-poor orientation in the options for solving other security problems (e.g., slum upgrading and lifeline utility pricing as alternatives for increasing access to services and infrastructure), (2) growth-with-equity strategies that create an enabling environment for more urban poor to reduce their economic vulnerability, and (3) political rights and participation so that the problems of poverty are articulated and recognized in the political arena.

These options for increasing the sustainability of urban development can also be viewed as sets of policy instruments, that is, regulatory policy, economic incentives, direct investment, property rights, land use controls, and information, education, and research. Each is briefly described with select examples of its application in cities.

Instruments for environmental regulation consist of discharge standards, permits and licenses, land and water use controls, and public health codes. They are essential for preventing or reducing the degradation of air, water, and land resources. Regulation requires both rules and an effective system of monitoring and enforcement. By themselves, regulatory instruments can be inefficient and costly to enforce. On the positive side, they yield predictable results and are necessary to establish a baseline of acceptable behavior. Santiago (Chile) uses environmental regulation to cope with air pollution emergencies: in a state of emergency, 80% of vehicles that run on leaded gas are banned from circulating and factories that are major emitters of air pollutants can be closed down (Inter Press Service, 1998). In addition, all new vehicles must use lead-free gasoline.

Economic incentives for managing the urban environment include user charges, resource pricing, pollution taxes, congestion charges, grants and subsidies, tax credits, rebates, and fines. These instruments often involve applying direct costs on polluters (the Polluter Pays Principle) such as industrial effluent charges for air or water pollution based on the amount and toxicity of discharges. However, they can also involve indirect charges, for example, the taxation of fuel use can be a powerful indirect instrument for controlling air pollution because of the relationship between fuel use and emissions. In comparison with regulations, economic instruments are more efficient and flexible. They can also increase equity, generate revenue, and continuously exert pressure on polluters. Economic instruments are rarely used alone; they typically rely on and reinforce regulations. For example, the city of Brisbane (Australia) has a set of regulations to protect the rich biodiversity of its bushlands. These are supplemented with two economic instruments: a ratepayer fee raises over $5 million a year for bushland acquisition and maintenance, and landowners who agree to protect private bushland from development can receive up to a 50% reduction in their general ratepayer levy (International Council for Local Environmental Initiatives, 1996).

Direct investment is one of the most powerful tools that a city can use to protect, improve, or rehabilitate the environment. Revenues can be raised for municipal investment in a range of environmental infrastructure and services such as water purification and distribution, wastewater treatment, drainage, sanitary landfilling, and public transportation. Cities can also acquire land to increase recreational opportunities and protect sensitive ecosystems. Additionally, municipalities can encourage other stakeholders to make investments that improve environmental management. For example, the environmental and other investments in upgrading slums can unleash private resources for environmental improvement. Some of the key investment options are summarized in Tables 7.1, 7.2, and 7.3.

Clarifying property rights can greatly improve management of air, water, and land resources. Better definition of water rights can be used to promote water conservation, defining and allocating discharge rights can help control air and water pollution, and providing secure land tenure can increase both public and private investment in housing and infrastructure improvements. For example, the opportunity to own land gave slum residents in Solo (Indonesia) the incentive to upgrade their plots and neighborhoods, resulting in key improvements to water supply, drainage, sanitation, solid waste management, and urban greening (Leitmann, 1999, p. 254).

There is a range of land use controls that can be used to manage the urban environment, including environmental zoning, acquisition, expropriation, easements, land exchanges, purchase or transfer of development rights, land readjustment, and guided land development. Land use controls can be effectively combined with infrastructure provision to guide development away from environmentally sensitive areas; this was done in metropolitan Jakarta to protect the city's key watershed. Land use controls can also be blended with investment in public transportation and roads to reduce congestion and air pollution, as was done in Curitiba, Brazil (Rabinovitch and Leitmann, 1996).

The final set of tools—information, education, and research—are essential for developing awareness and knowledge of the urban environment. Information about a city's environmental situation can be acquired using techniques such as rapid assessment, geographic and land information systems, and environmental assessment. Access to this and other information, via educational initiatives, underpins public consciousness of the urban environment. Research is essential to close knowledge gaps about the urban environment. Good research should yield information on the characteristics of media-specific environmental problems, the dynamics of environmental degradation, and the magnitude and distribution of impacts.

Policy instruments are more effective when they are used in mutually supportive packages. The way that various instruments are selected and used to reinforce each other will depend on a number of factors: (1) urgency of the problem that needs to be addressed; (2) political, social, and institutional acceptability of the solution; (3) cost and anticipated benefits; (4) degree to which low-income and vulnerable groups benefit; (5) compatibility with existing administrative, legal, political, and fiscal regimes; (6) ease of monitoring and enforcement; and (7) harmony with the city's overall development strategy.

Another way of considering which policy options are most appropriate is to link them to objectives that can differ according to a city's level of development. For example, a low-income city may place greater priority on the objective of improving citizen access to environmental services and infrastructure. Thus, it would pursue policy options such as regulation (enforcing the legalization of connections to networks), direct investment (obtaining funds to expand networks), and land use controls (regularizing spontaneous settlements to lower the costs of infrastructure and service provision).

Beyond these factors, several principles can be applied to assist in selecting policy instruments for managing the environment. These principles are (1) look for win–win solutions in which two or more problems are solved or both the environment and the economy benefit, (2) choose the options that address the environmental problems of the poor and vulnerable groups in a city, and (3) seek cost-effective approaches that pay their way. These principles are elaborated with examples in the following.

Win–win situations occur when a policy option or package solves more than one problem or meets both environmental and economic objectives. Curitiba (Brazil) is famous for its win–win approach to problems. For example, the problems of flooding, housing exposed to environmental hazards, and lack of green space were solved by a program to resettle riverbank dwellers, create artificial lakes, and turn these spaces into parks. Floods are now a thing of the past, and green space rose from 0.5 to 50 m³ per citizen during a 20-year period of rapid population growth (Leitmann and Rabinovitch, 1996). Win–win options that can yield both environmental and economic returns include incentives to support low-polluting or environment-related industries, investment in energy efficiency and water conservation measures, modernization of industrial equipment and processes, and recycling or reuse of wastes.

As many urban environmental problems disproportionately affect the poor and vulnerable, who are least able to cope with or escape from risks, environmental solutions should, at a minimum, benefit this segment of society. In fact, a triple-win approach is advocated in the urban policies of international aid agencies: urban development should help to alleviate poverty, be environmentally sustainable, and contribute to economic productivity (World Bank, 2002b). One way of ensuring that low-income groups benefit is to target a package of management options on the environmental problems of low-income neighborhoods.

The benefits and costs of policy options being considered should be as explicit as possible. In the case of win–win solutions, both environmental and economic benefits should be calculated. Distributional consequences (who benefits) should also be estimated in order to determine whether the poor will gain or lose. On the cost side, interventions that match cost to users' ability and willingness to pay should be favored. Policy options that pay their own way by recovering costs are inherently more financially sustainable than those that must be subsidized. However, cost recovery can conflict with an emphasis on serving the poor, so targeted subsidies or cross-subsidization may be warranted in particular cases. Overall, the identification of options requires creativity so that the full range of costs and benefits is considered.

Conclusion

The pace and style of urbanization have increased human exposure to a number of environmental risks. The dynamics of urbanization and environmental change are driven by a number of factors: the quality of consumption, production, and economic growth; a city's ability to cope with population growth; relations between ecosystems and land use patterns; and governance arrangements. These dynamics have resulted in a set of human security issues—increased vulnerability of the urban poor, problems of inadequate access to services, greater exposure to natural and anthropogenic risks, and heightened global environmental threats.

Fortunately, the urbanizing world can draw from a range of policy options to increase security, manage the environment, and improve the quality of life in cities.

References

Bartone, Carl, Janis Bernstein, Josef Leitmann, and Jochen Eigen, 1994. Toward environmental strategies for cities: Policy considerations for urban environmental management in developing countries, UMP Policy Paper No. 18, Washington, D.C.: World Bank.

Bernstein, Janis, 1993. Land use considerations in urban environmental management, UMP Discussion Paper No. 12, Washington, D.C.: World Bank.

Inter Press Service, 1998. First Smog Emergency in Santiago Since 1992, Inter Press Service, May 21, 1998.

International Council for Local Environmental Initiatives, 1996. Economic instruments to improve environmental performance: A guide for local governments, Toronto: ICLEI.

Leitmann, Josef, 1999. *Sustaining Cities: Environmental Planning and Management in Urban Design.* New York: McGraw-Hill.

McGranahan, G., P. Jacobi, J. Songsore, C. Surjadi, and M. Kjellén, 2001. *The Citizens at Risk: From Urban Sanitation to Sustainable Cities.* London: Earthscan.

Population Reference Bureau, 2003. Patterns of World Urbanization, Retrieved from www.prg.org.

Rabinovitch, Jonas, and Josef Leitmann, 1996. Improving the quality of urban life: Curitiba challenges conventional wisdom, *Scientific American* 274(3).

United Nations Centre for Human Settlements, 1996. *An Urbanizing World: Global Report on Human Settlements*, London: Oxford University Press.

United Nations Human Settlements Programme, 2001. *The State of the World's Cities Report 2001.* Nairobi: UNCHS.

United Nations Population Division, 2002. *World Urbanization Prospects: The 1999 Revision.* New York: United Nations.

World Health Organization, 2000. Special theme—child mortality, *Bulletin of the World Health Organization*, 78(10), 1172–1282.

World Health Organization, 2003. Road safety is no accident, *Newsletter on Road Safety*, No. 1, November 2003.

World Bank, 1998. Mexico: The Guadalajara Environmental Management Pilot, Report No. 18071-ME, Washington, D.C.: World Bank.

World Bank, 2002a. *Beyond Economic Growth: Meeting the Challenges of Economic Development.* Washington, D.C.: World Bank.

World Bank, 2002b. Incubators for Change? Urban areas as centers for innovation and transformation, in *World Development Report 2003.* New York: Oxford University Press.

World Resources Institute, 1996. *World Resources 1996-97: The Urban Environment.* New York: Oxford University Press.

Key Web Sites

Environment and Urbanization journal (www.iied.org/human.html)
International Center for Local Environmental Initiatives (www.iclei.org)
The Urban Environmental Management Virtual Library (www.gdrc.org/uem)
UN Centre for Human Settlements/Habitat (www.unchs.org)

Chapter 8

What Is Sustainable Farming?

Eric Goewie, Júlio da Silva, João Pedro Zabaleta, and Rui Melo de Souza

CONTENTS

Introduction

Sustainability is an issue that has inspired policy makers, teachers, and scientists. However, most of them got into problems when trying to make this notion applicable. Rigby and Caceres (2001) identified more than 386 definitions of sustainability. This is not surprising as the notion of *sustainability* was introduced as something that has to be referred to the needs of future generations (United Nations Conference on Environment and Development, 1992). The Dutch Scientific Counsel for Governmental Policy, the WRR (1994), shows that sustainability is hard to quantify, as nobody knows what future generations actually need. At best, the WRR states that we might talk about "sustainable development" only. In other words, present generations must leave some part of their available natural resources for the benefit of future generations. Goewie (2002) observes that sustainability is not a question of energy saving or efficient use of natural resources only, but that it is an attitude as well. Röling (2002) says that such an attitude is dependent on humankind's willingness to leave certain amounts of natural resources untouched.

Kremers (1993) examined 40 interpretations of sustainability related to agricultural land use. He categorized them by means of the Multifaceted Structured Entity Modelling (Rozenblit and Ziegler, 1986), an electronic tool for classification and weighing of soft data, such as notions, descriptions, definitions, and interpretations. He demonstrated that most descriptions for sustainability of agricultural production systems are related to potentialities of self-restoration of production factors used for farming. So "sustainability" could be a function of the possibilities for self-restoration inside a farm (see Table 8.1). Indeed, Smeding (2001) demonstrated that biodiversity inside farms increases the longer they are managed organically. Is there more evidence for it? The next section gives an answer.

Table 8.1 Dominating Items Found among Forty Descriptions of Sustainability

Sustainability is related to:
An everlasting and achievable management objective
Cyclic processes
Application of renewable natural resources only
Biodiversity as carrier of self-organization in ecosystems
"Polluter pays" principles
Energy balances

Kremers, 1993.

Biodiversity and Possibilities for Self-Restoration of Natural Resources

The aim of farming—control of conditions for the production of top levels of biomass (a limited number of crops and animals)—is that of striving for minimal disturbance of production conditions in soil, crops, and animals (Porceddu and Rabbinge, 1997). Natural differences in soil fertility are reduced through the use of synthetic compounds and various tillage methods. Natural differences in one crop become leveled by means of herbicides and with homogeneity among varieties. We may assume therefore that the biodiversity of mainstream (capital-intensive) farms must be low. So the possibilities for self-restoration of farm-bound natural resources have no meaning for the farmers involved. All production concerned is primarily the result of efficient use of external inputs.

So, the soil of such farms is considered as nothing more than a substrate necessary for bearing some kind of production. But is the inverse true as well? Is it reasonable to assume that increasing biodiversity contributes automatically to the development of more self-restoration of farm-bound living production factors such as soil fertility and prevention of diseases or pests? We will address this question by way of three lines of approach:

- The relation between biodiversity and the type of soil use
- The relation between biodiversity and the development of a farm as an agroecosystem
- The relation between biodiversity and the possibilities for self-restoration inside agroecosystems.

Relation between Biodiversity and the Type of Soil Use

Grime (1979) demonstrated an optimal connection between species diversity and the standing crop: The maximal standing crop is correlated with production limiting factors (stress) and/or with removal of the subsoil biomass (disturbance). Bakker and van Wieren (1995) concluded that a low-standing crop and species diversity could cohere with limitations in production such as very dry, dark, salt, or nutriment-poor substrate. So a high-standing crop and low species diversity could cohere with nutrient rich substrates, where only some quickly growing species eliminate moderately growing species easily. Naveh and colleagues (in Bakker, 1989) found high species diversity in overgrazed pastures. He explained that phenomenon by assuming that heavy grazing during long periods induces evolutionary changes along with the introduction of new species. The latter ones settle more easily the more the vegetation is kept open. Huston (1979) demonstrates that the production of slowly growing standing crops

Table 8.2 Overview of Characteristics of Two Popular Farming Systems

	Description	Year Round Soil Coverage	Grow Rapidity of the Standing Crop	Number of Commodities per Farm	Soil Fertility of Production Land	Farmbound Biodiversity
Organic farming	Low-standing crops (slow-growing), low harvest regime	High	Slow and controlled growing	High	Low	High
Mainstream farming	High-standing crop (fast-growing), high harvest regime	Low	Fast and forced growing	Low	High	Low

combined with their removal at low frequencies induces high species diversity. Species diversity remains low, however, when fast-growing standing crops are combined with high harvest frequencies inside a farm.

Both situations correspond with an organic and a mainstream farm production system, respectively (Mäder et al., 2002). Table 8.2 shows the difference between the types of farms.

Relation between Biodiversity and the Development of a Farm as an Agroecosystem

An ecosystem left to its own devices evolves gradually toward its next succession under simultaneous leveling of abiotic variations of the soil involved (Odum, 1971). Figure 8.1 shows that an ecosystem becomes exhausted when it is prevented from evolving to its next succession phase and drops back to its preceding succession phase (Bakker, 1989; Tilman, 1988). In other words, an ecosystem can only be kept in one and the same succession phase when external inputs are introduced continuously. Another possibility is that we stimulate the ecosystem to produce higher amounts of the nutrients required by itself. That is the situation in organic farms (see Table 8.2). The manager of an organic farm must therefore enhance biodiversity in order to become able to produce all required inputs.

Our conclusion is that a mainstream, capital-intensive farm is comparable with a pioneer ecosystem in which natural differences in fertility of

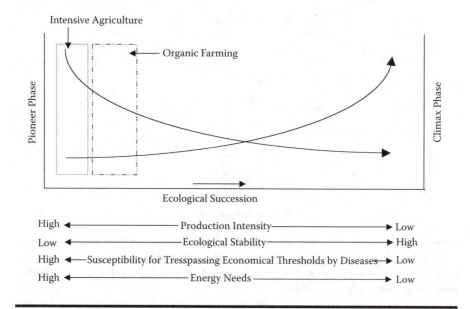

Figure 8.1 Succession phases in the development of ecosystems according to Odum (1971) and De Zeeuw (1998). From an ecological point of view, intensive agriculture (very much dependent on external synthetical inputs) is comparable with an ecosystem in its pioneer phase. Organic farmers replace synthetical external inputs by ecological principles (e.g., animal manure, leguminoses, predation) on purpose. Such a system focuses on maintaining (management) of food chains among organisms. From an ecological point of view, organic farms could therefore be considered as ecosystems in a phase directly after the pioneer phase.

soil are leveled by means of external synthetic inputs. That makes rapid growth and removal of biomass possible, thus preventing the increase of farm-bound biodiversity. Similarly, an organic farm is comparable with the succession phase after the pioneer phase, as natural differences in soil fertility fluctuate with the extent of crop rotations involved. So there must be a positive correlation with the complexity of soil use.

Relation between Biodiversity and the Potentiality for Self-Restoration inside Agroecosystems

Ecologists contrast system approaches concerning life phenomena with mechanistic approaches advocated by classical agroecologists. In system approaches, it is more important to pay attention to the mutual relations among system elements rather than to the individual elements (fixed structures) themselves. Life processes determine structures of organisms and ecosystems. Machinelike concepts start only from the structure of the

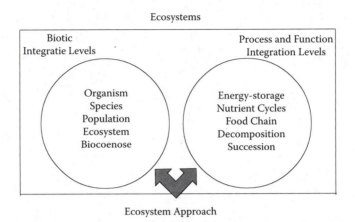

Ecosystems

Biotic Integratie Levels — Organism, Species, Population, Ecosystem, Biocoenose

Process and Function Integration Levels — Energy-storage, Nutrient Cycles, Food Chain, Decomposition, Succession

Ecosystem Approach

Figure 8.2 Ecosystems may be investigated along two different points of view: either from the structuring elements involved or from the system conditioning processes. (Anonymous, 1993.)

system. Machines follow the law of cause and effect: When they break, there is a cause. Functioning of organisms is determined by cyclic running information streams (feedback loops). Disturbances may originate in more than one site and reinforced by positive feedback or become extinct by negative feedback mechanisms. The first play a part in learning and evolution processes, the latter in regulation of physiological processes (e.g., body temperature, blood pressure).

Living beings and ecosystems are open systems. That means that they must exchange energy and matter with their surroundings constantly. By doing so they keep themselves far from their thermodynamic equilibrium. Once they are dead they follow the second law of thermodynamics, and their structure progresses from order to disorder.

The stability of organisms and ecosystems is not invariable, although very dynamic (Verhoef and Daan, 1995; Altieri, 1995). They keep their structures despite permanent variation and interchange of elements. Many variables are mutually dependent and oscillate between an upper and a lower limit, even when there is no disturbance. This condition (homeostasis) is very flexible. It has many alternatives for interplay with its surroundings (Figure 8.2). So there is dependence on the environment, while there is also a relative autonomy, that is to say, maintenance of organisms' structure. Immunologic deficiencies among animals and human beings demonstrate that systems autonomy is weak.

Life phenomena such as immunity and homeostasis are part of self-regulation (Rossignol et al., 1998). A living system adapts itself to changes in its environment as long as the regulation is not beyond its normal fluctuations of homeostasis (e.g., enhanced pulsation or loss of turgidity during dry weather). When a variable is pushed toward its limit, there is talk of stress. In such cases, the variable loses its elasticity and is no longer able to adapt. When situations of stress continue, adaptation occurs by complete and irreversible changes in the physiologic features of the system (e.g., development of resistance against chemicals). If more extreme adaptations are required, genotypical changes become necessary. They provide ecosystems with more possibilities for variation or room for flexibility. They are irreversible, however, for those individuals that are part of the ecosystem concerned. Self-renewal by self-regulation is a very important aspect of living systems. Organic farmers know how to manage such processes. They especially use the following methods:

- Organic matter (e.g., manure, plant extractions) is applied instead of synthetic chemicals (Habets and Oomen, 1997).
- Special organisms are used for natural production of required substances, such as nitrogen fixing bacteria by leguminous plants or phosphate mineralization by VA-Mycorrhiza (Dekkers and Van der Werff, 2001; Lee, 2002).
- Farm bound food webs are reinforced (Lee, 2002; Smeding, 2001).

We may conclude again that a strong relation exists between biodiversity and possibilities for enhanced self-regulation of farm-bound natural resources.

What implications do the preceding conclusions have for our possibilities of making sustainability in farming measurable? This question will be answered in the following sections.

Quantification of Sustainable Land Use

Stoyke and Waibel (1994) tried to make sustainable development of production farms quantifiable. They state that sustainable development of production farms is strongly related with farmers' skill in reducing the amount of nonrenewable natural resources necessary for production with simultaneous maintenance of the farm's profitability. Van Leeuwen (1993) introduced the term *restorability* of natural resources. He defined restorability as the regeneration of affected populations and ecosystems to the situation before the situation of impairing. Restoration of impaired ecosystems costs money and must be considered as costs of renewing natural resources. Goewie and Van der Ploeg (1996) postulated that there is a relation between the reduction of nonrenewable resources in land use and the maintenance of profitability of that same land. That relation is tightened by an orthogonal basis. The relation concerned is a hyperbola representing all different rates of sustainable land use.

A relation between sustainability (S) and self-organization of a living system (s) was assumed. So

$$S \approx f(s) \tag{a}$$

In the preceding section, it was determined that the number of possibilities for self-regulation inside a production farm is proportional to its level of biodiversity (b).
So

$$s \approx f(b) \tag{b}$$

Substitution of (a) by (b) results in

$$S \approx f(b) \tag{c}$$

Consider this equation for a production farm: one using and one not using synthetic chemicals. We may expect that biodiversity in the farm using synthetic chemicals will be lower than in the farm that does not apply synthetic chemicals (Zadoks, 1993; Stoyke and Waibel, 1999). Let us compare both situations. First we consider the situation for a farm that uses synthetic chemicals, and then we do the same for an organic farm, one that does not apply synthetic chemicals at all.

When a farmer uses synthetic chemicals, we must expect that biodiversity on his farm (number of species per square meter) will be low (Eijsackers et al., 1995). So low biodiversity must be a function of the high expenses (E) that a farmer must incur for synthetic chemicals. So

$$b \approx f(1/E_{\text{synthetic chemicals}}) \approx f(1/E_{\text{external inputs}}) \tag{d}$$

When a farmer does not use synthetic chemicals, we must expect that biodiversity on his farm will be high (Kenmore, 1991; Van Schoubroeck, 1999; Smeding, 2001; Lee, 2002). This implies that more species will compete for the same natural resources, such as nutrients, water, or space (Ittersum and Rabbinge, 1997). According to Figure 8.1, such competition will result in lower production per hectare. Lower production, or in other words, higher loss of harvest, also implies lower income. Financial losses might be quantified by taking into account current market prices (Haan et al., 1993; Waibel, 1999). So a loss of harvest, expressed in kilograms (kg) per hectare (ha) times the market price of the mainstream commodity involved, could indicate the reduction of income. This figure could be considered as the price that a farmer has to pay if he wishes to produce organically (without synthetic chemicals).

In this case, the farmer has to rely on biological control systems, on possibilities for crop rotation (rational application of predators and antagonists), and on organic manure, available at his own farm. We call such farm-bound natural resources *internal input*. Our way of reasoning permits us to conclude that the price for the farmer's confidence in his farm-bound natural resources is quantifiable, namely, in the reduction of the actual production times the market price of the commodity involved. So

$$b \approx (E_{\text{farm bound natural resources}}) \approx f(E_{\text{internal inputs}}) \tag{e}$$

Substitution of equation (e) in (d) results in

$$E_{\text{internal inputs}} \approx 1/E_{\text{external inputs}} \tag{f}$$

This is a hyperbola, shown graphically in Figure 8.3.

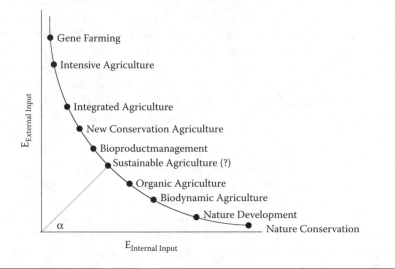

Figure 8.3 Graphical presentation of equation (f). The curve sets all types of agricultural land use that were realized in practice or has been mentioned in the literature. The position of each type of agricultural land use, indicated at the hyperbola, is arbitrary. The summit must be of a special meaning. The figure makes two points clear. First, a high production goal cannot meet demands for sustainability, and a low production goal cannot meet demands for profitability. Second, integrated and agroecological agriculture are two types of agricultural land use with differing priorities. Integrated farming gives an accent on profitability with sustainability as a side product. Agroecological agriculture does the opposite. It seeks profitability after having set the principles for sustainability. Which is better is a matter of political and ethical decision making.

Measuring Sustainability in Farming Systems

Figure 8.3 provides us an interesting opportunity for making a certain amount of sustainability measurable. Therefore, we have to consider the tangent of the hyperbola. So

$$\alpha = E_{\text{external inputs}}/E_{\text{internal inputs}} \qquad \text{(g)}$$

Both expenses (E) are quantifiable, so α must be knowable. When α > 45°, then the farming system involved must be considered as unsustainable (the farm consumes proportionally too much of irreversible natural resources). When α < 45°, then the farming system involved must be considered as sustainable (the farm leaves proportionally sufficient irreversible natural resources). But what happens if α = 45°?

When α = 45°, we expect that $E_{\text{external inputs}}$ = $E_{\text{internal inputs}}$, or in other words, a loss of income will be compensated by a similar reduction in costs. That happens if the tangent touches the hyperbola at its summit. At this point, the hyperbola establishes a type of land use that we could call *sustainable agriculture*. Specifically, the internal farm-bound natural resources are dynamic enough to buffer applied external inputs and to compensate for income reduction due to lower production ambitions. The summit of the hyperbole thus sets a form of agricultural land use that must be also sustainable from a farm social–economic point of view.

This hypothesis also offers an interesting starting point for governmental policy making. For the situation in which α = 45°, entrepreneurs could make their farm more sustainable by themselves without loss of profitability since costs are lowered without loss of produce. However, when α > 45° and the government wants to make agriculture more sustainable, then it will have to subsidize. In the case of α < 45° and government unwillingness to subsidize, market prices should increase. When neither subsidies nor elevated market prices are possible and the government compels sustainability by laws and regulations, then the farmer pays the bill, which is not an acceptable option either (see Figure 8.4).

Strengths and Weaknesses of the Concept

Figure 8.5 shows the hyperbola $E_{\text{internal inputs}} \approx 1/E_{\text{external inputs}}$ at a randomly chosen site of the abscissa and ordinate. But what does it mean when the hyperbole appears at other sites between the abscissa and ordinate? We consider four situations, when the hyperbola appears close to the origin (of abscise and ordinate), far from the origin, moved away over the ordinate from the origin, and moved away over the abscissa from the origin.

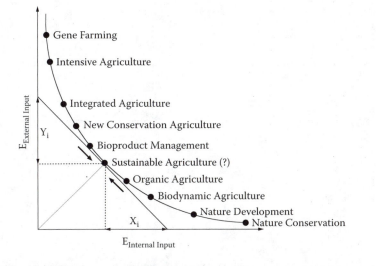

Figure 8.4 The summit of the hyperbola indicates where agricultural land use fully buffers applied external inputs in a farming system. We may expect that such buffering helps maintain self-organization in farm-bound natural resources. So, the type of land use involved must be of a sustainable nature. Thus sustainable farming is the theoretical optimum between the already existing "integrated agriculture" on the one hand and "organic agriculture" on the other. A "sustainable farm" practically comes into existence when the growing efficiency of external inputs in integrated systems, on the one hand, and the growing effectiveness of productive capacities of farm-bound natural resources, on the other, meet. We consider sustainable agriculture therefore as a mix of the best of both types of land use and as acceptable, from a societal point of view, because the loss of income, due to the reduction of harvest, is compensated by an equal reduction of costs. If not, then the price of food should increase or the government must subsidize.

If the hyperbola shows up close to the origin of abscissa and ordinate and if its summit has the same distance to both axes, we may conclude that the reduction of external inputs, in compensation for the loss of production, makes no sense. Here, we encounter a situation of exhaustion. Farming in such a situation is undesirable. We find such forms of land use south of the Sahara in Africa (Sanchez et al., 1995). This happens when soils have no form of buffering of water and nutrients. Availability of water or nutrients decreases quickly to a minimum (Figure 8.5a).

If the hyperbola shows up far from the origin of abscissa and ordinate and if its summit also has the same distance to both axes, we may conclude the following. A reduction of external inputs for the compensation of a loss of production only makes sense if market prices are high or if the government subsidizes. Here we encounter a situation where agriculture

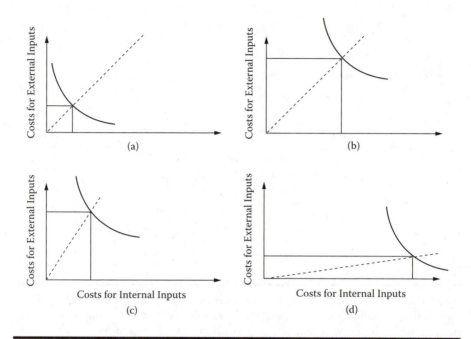

Figure 8.5 Four positions of the hyperbola representing the sets of all types of agricultural land use realized in practice. Situation a (left, above) represents a situation in which reduction of external inputs is almost useless, as farming must happen in a resource poor (exhausted) production situation. Situation b (right, above) represents a situation in which reduction of external inputs is fully compensated by market prices. Situation c (left, below) represents the present situation of mainstream or integrated farming. Situation d (right, below) represents the situation of organic farming.

fully functions according to a free market system. In such a market, the consumer compensates all costs involved with the production of his food, including the costs for cleaning the environment, protecting of nature, and maintaining a health-care system (Haan et al., 1993). Such a situation is comparable with the market for industrial goods. All external costs involved with industrial production are paid by industries themselves. Industries finally charge the consumer. Here, the polluter pays principle has been fully realized (Figure 8.5b).

If the hyperbola is moved over the ordinate, away from its origin, we encounter the present situation of mainstream agriculture. This kind of land use is dependent on synthetic external inputs, water, capital, and, in the near future, transgenic organisms. In the last 15 years, agricultural sciences, forced by the new insights from environmental and medical sciences (Vito and Birnbaum, 1993), developed new types of agricultural land use (Figure 8.5c). Farming has become more and more efficient

(Haverkort et al., 1997). That is to say, farmers can produce the same with smaller amounts of external inputs. The resulting type of agricultural land use is known as *integrated agriculture*. The basic principle in present agricultural research assumes that the ratio output (O) versus input (I) should tend to 1, or

$$O/I \xrightarrow[\Delta T = \infty]{} 1 \tag{h}$$

Computer modeling facilitated by electronic information systems made this principle achievable. The resulting farming systems became capital intensive and more friendly to the surroundings of the production sites involved. Profitability of such farms has to come from making the most of upscaling (Ploeg, 1999). So integrated farming must result in large farms that fully separate land use for agriculture and land use for nature (WRR, 1992). There are signs that this kind of land use will not be accepted by the society (Anonymous, 1996). Consumers and environmental protection organizations fear permanent dependency on chemicals and multinationals. Consumers' resistance to gene technology in open field systems or unfriendly kinds of animal husbandry might be another herald (De Jonge and Goewie, 2000).

If the hyperbola is moved over the abscissa, away from its origin, we encounter the present situation of organic land use (Figure 8.5d). This kind of land use fully depends on available farm-bound natural resources. In the last 10 years, much research has been done in this field. The basic principle followed by this so-called organic agriculture is that the farmer is not allowed to introduce more nutrients (external inputs in general) to his land than his crop or husbandry will remove by harvest or selling of meat or milk. In other words, the farmer must produce under the strict condition of input (I) equal to output (O) right from the beginning that he decided to turn his farming system into an organic one, or

$$O - I \underset{\Delta T = 0}{=} 0 \tag{i}$$

Biology and ecology as sciences and facilitated by information technology made this principle fully applicable. Figure 8.5 shows these possibilities.

Conclusion

Our description of sustainability in farming accommodates various realistic types of land use. Land use is in a state of sustainable development if the managers involved permanently strive for equilibrium between what they apply to and what they remove from their land. So ecosystems will not be burdened in an irreversible way. Integrated management of land use systems strives for that equilibrium by trying to produce the same with decreasing amounts of external inputs involved. Organic management of land use systems substitutes external inputs with organic inputs. Organic inputs are obtained from natural resources such as biological nitrogen fixation, biological control of pests, or maintaining of a high level of permanent soil fertility. Such resources are found in farm- or forest-bound ecosystems. Management of such systems is therefore ecosystems oriented and pays attention to the self-organizing properties of the ecosystems concerned.

Another conclusion refers to the kind of scientific research needed. Up to now, most agricultural research has been organisms (e.g., crops, animals, pests) oriented (Goewie, 1997). So we learn more about less or we spend more money on less needed knowledge. Sustainable development of agriculture needs systems-oriented knowledge. This demands a less disciplinary- or commodity-oriented attitude of researchers and research institutes.

Acknowledgments

This chapter began as a discussion with scientists of EMBRAPA Clima Temperado, the Brazilian research organization for agriculture and nature in the state of Rio Grande do Sul, Brazil, and with the farmers of the same state. The authors are grateful to Dr. Bonifacio Nakasu, general director of EMBRAPA Clima Temperado, Pelotas, RS, Brazil, for his kind hospitality and support. We thank Dr. Lee of the Horticultural Research Centre of the University of Bogotá, Jorge Tadeo Lozano in Colombia, Professor Dr. Oldeman of the Wageningen University, and Dr. Romeijn of Treemail Publishers for reading the manuscript and for providing useful suggestions and improvements.

References

Altieri, Miguel A. (1995). Plant disease ecology and management. In: Altieri (ed.), *Agroecology: The Science of Sustainable Agriculture*. Boulder, Colo.: West-view Press, IT Publications, pp. 307–320.

Anonymous (1993). Hoofdlijnen van ecosysteemgericht ecotoxicologisch onder-zoek (Mainlines of ecosystem research for ecotoxicology). Raad van het Milieu en Natuuronderzoek (RMNO), Report RMNO 91, p. 21.

Anonymous (1996). The declaration of Cork: A living countryside: Conclusions of the European Conference on Rural Development, Cork, Ireland, November 1996, pp. 7–9.

Bakker, J.P. (1989). *Nature Management by Grazing and Cutting.* Dordrecht: Kluwer Academic.

Bakker, J.P., and S.E. van Wieren (1995). Natuurbeheer. In: Bakker, K., J.H. Mook, and J.G. van Rhijn (eds.), *Oecologie.* Bohn: Stafleu Van Loghum, 1995, p. 661.

De Zeeuw, Dick (1998). Plattelandsontwikkeling en duurzame landbouw in een tijd van globalisering (Regional development and sustainable agriculture in a time of globalisation). Editor: IMSA Institute, Amsterdam, pp. 20–21.

Dekkers, T.B.M., and P.A. van der Werff (2001). Mutualistic functioning of indigenous arbuscular mycorrhizae in spring barley and winter wheat after cessation of long-term phosphate fertilization. *Mycorriza* 10: 195–201.

Eijsackers, H., J.C. Duinker, and T.E. Cappenberg (1995). Oecologische effecten van milieuverontreiniging, de negatieve zijde van ons menselijk handelen (Ecological impact of environmental pollution, the negative side of human action). In: Bakker, K., J.H. Mook, and J.G. van Rhijn (eds.), *Oecologie.* Bohn: Stafleu Van Loghum, 1995, pp. 617–646.

Goewie, E.A. (1997). Multifunctioneel agrarisch grondgebruik als instrument (Multifunctional agricultural land use as a tool). In: Ingrediënten voor een duurzame samenleving (Ingredients for a sustainable society). The Hague, the Netherlands: Council for Research on Environment and Nature (RMNO), p. 75.

Goewie, E.A. (2003). Organic agriculture in the Netherlands: developments and challenges. NJAS, *Wageningen Journal of Life Sciences* 50: 153–170.

Goewie, E.A., and J.D. van der Ploeg (1996). Doelen van de landbouw (Goals of agriculture). In: Themadagen P.E., Wageningen, P.A. Haverkort (eds.), Hoe ecologisch kan de landbouw worden? (How ecological can agriculture become ?). AB-DLO, Thema 3, pp. 1–15.

Grime, J.P. (1979). *Plant Strategies and Vegetation Processes.* Chichester, England: Wiley

Haan, M. de, S.J. Keuning, and P.R. Bosch (1993). Integrating Indicators in a National Accounting Matrix including Environmental Accounts (NAMEA): An Application to the Netherlands. Voorburg: Centraal Bureau voor de Statistiek.

Habets, A.S.J., and G.J.M. Oomen (1997). N-DICEA: Modelling nitrogen dynamics in crop rotations in ecological agriculture. *Quantitative Approaches in System Analysis* 10: 73–79.

Haverkort, A.J.H., Van Keulen, and M.I. Minguez (1997). The efficient use of solar radiation, water and nitrogen in arable farming: Matching supply and demand of genotypes. In: M.K. van Ittersum and S.C. van de Geijn (eds.), *Perspectives for Agronomy. Adopting Ecological Principles and Managing Resource Use.* Elsevier Sciences bv, pp. 191–200.

Huston, M. (1979). A general hypothesis of species diversity. *American Naturalist* 113: 81–101.

Ittersum, M.K. van, and R. Rabbinge (1997). Concepts in production ecology for analysis and quantification of agricultural input-output combinations. *Field Crops Res.* 52: 197–208.

Kenmore, Peter E. (1991). How rice farmers clean up the environment, conserve biodiversity, raise more food, make higher profits. Indonesia's IPM: A Model for Asia. FAO Rice IPC Programme Report, Philippines, pp. 34–45.

Kremers, J.H. (1993). Duurzame landbouw (Sustainable agriculture). MSE Model. M.Sc. thesis, Department of Informatics, Agricultural University Wageningen, pp. 15–30.

Lee, R.A. (2002). Interactive design of farm conversion: Linking agricultural research and farmer learning for sustainable small scale horticulture production in Colombia. Published Ph.D. thesis, Wageningen University, The Netherlands. 293 pp. http://library.wur.nl.

Mäder, Paul, Andreas Fliessbach, David Dubois, Lucie Gunst, Padruot Fried, and Urs Niggli (2002). Soil fertility and biodiversity in organic farming. *Science* 226: 1694–1697.

Odum, E.P. (1971). *Fundamentals of Ecology.* New York: Holt-Saunders Press.

Ploeg, Jan-Douwe, van der (1999). De empirische variatie in I/P relaties (The empirical variation in input/output relations). In: *De virtuele boer* (The virtual farmer). pp. 180–200.

Porceddu, E., and R. Rabbinge (1997). Role of research and education in the development of agriculture in Europe. *The European Journal of Agronomy* 7: 1–13.

Pretty, J.N. (1995). *Regenerating Agriculture: Policies and Practice for Sustainability and Self-Reliance.* London: Earthscan; Washington, D.C.: National Academic Press; Bangalore: Action Aid, p. 23.

Rigby, D., and D. Caceres (2001). Organic farming and the sustainability of agricultural systems. *Agricultural Systems* 68: 21–40.

Röling, Niels (2002). Stop de landbouw-tredmolen (Stop the agricultural treadmill). Resource. *Magazine van de Wageningen Universiteit & Researchcentrum* 5: 4.

Rossignol, Martial, Line Rossignol, Roelof Odeman, and Soraya Benzine-Tizroutine (1998). *Struggle of Life or the Natural History of Stress and Adaptation.* Treebook 1, Treemail, Heelsum, The Netherlands.

Rozenblit, J.W., and B.P. Ziegler (1986). Entity-based structures for model and experimental frame construction. In: Elzas, M.S., T.I. Oren, and B.P. Zeigler (eds.), *Modelling and Simulation Methodology in the Artificial Intelligence Era.* Amsterdam: Elsevier Science Publishers BV North Holland.

Sanchez, P.A., A.M.N. Izac, I. Valencia, and C. Pieri (1995). Soil fertility replenishment in Africa: A concept note. Nairobi, Kenya: ICRAF, pp. 2–5

Smeding, Frans W. (2001). Steps towards food web management on farms. Published Ph.D. thesis of the Wageningen University, The Netherlands, pp. 5–29. http://library.wur.nl.

Stoyke, C., and H. Waibel (1994). A contribution towards more sustainable farming systems. In: J.B. Dent and M.J. McGregor (eds.), Rural and Farming Systems Analysis. *European Perspectives,* pp. 145–158.

Tilman, D. (1988). Plant strategies and the dynamics and structure of plant communities. Published Ph.D. thesis, Rijksuniversiteit van Groningen, Groningen, The Netherlands.

United Nations Conference on Environment and Development (1992). Promoting sustainable agriculture and rural development. Agenda 21, Chapter 14, June 14, 1992..

Van Leeuwen, C.J. (1993). Over ecotoxicologische grenzen. *Intreerede bij de Rijksuniversiteit van Utrecht*, pp. 28–29.

Van Schouwbroeck, Frank (1999). Learning to fight a fly: Developing citrus IPM in Bhutan. Published Ph.D. thesis, Wageningen University, Wageningen, The Netherlands. http://library.wur.nl.

Vandermeer, John (1990). Notes on agroecosystem complexity: Chaotic price and production trajectories deducible from simple one-dimensional maps. *Biological Agriculture and Horticulture* 6: 293–304.

Verhoef, H.A., and S. Daan (1995). Oecofysiologie van dieren (ecophysiology of animals). In: Bakker, K.J.H. Mook and J.G. van Rhijn (eds.), *Oecologie*. Bohn Stafleu Van Loghum, Houten/Diegem, pp. 175–199.

Vito, M.J. de, and L.S. Birnbaum (1995). Toxicology: Special issue on biological mechanisms and quantitative risk assessment, *Toxicology* 102: 115–123.

Waibel, Hermann, and Gerd Fleisscher (1999). Kosten und Nutzen de chemischen Pflanzenschutzes in der Deutschen Landwirtschaft aus gesamtlicher Sicht. Wissenschaftsverlag Vauk Kkiel, KG, 329 pp.

Wetenschappelijke Raad voor het Regeringsbeleid (WRR) (1992). Grond voor keuzen: Vier perspectieven voor de landelijke gebieden in de Europese Gemeenschap (Land for choices: Four perspectives for countrysites in the European Union). Reports to the Government No. 42, 203 pp.

Wetenschappelijke Raad voor het Regeringsbeleid (WRR) (1994). Duurzame risico's: een blijvend gegeven (Sustainable risks: A permanent datum). Reports to the Government No. 44, 216 pp.

Zadoks, J.C. (1993). Cultural methods. In: J.C. Zadoks (ed.), *Modern Crop Protection: Developments and Perspectives*. Wageningen, The Netherlands: Wageningen Press, pp. 165–166.

Chapter 9

Bridging Sustainable Agriculture and Sustainable Tourism to Enhance Sustainability

Tracy Berno

CONTENTS

Introduction

Many of the efforts undertaken to maximize the economic benefits derived from tourism have concentrated on increasing the number of tourist arrivals, the average length of stay, and the overall expenditure of tourists. Despite boosting the overall gross domestic product (GDP) of less developed countries (LDCs), tourism has had few salient benefits for those in the outlying (rural) regions. One potential way of enhancing the economic benefits of tourism to a destination is to expand the backward economic linkages by increasing the amount of local agricultural products used in the tourism industry. Not only does this contribute to positive economic benefits, but it also contributes to the articulation and mutual support of three related areas of sustainability: sustainable agriculture; sustainable cuisine (also known as "slow food"), and the tourism industry, thus supporting sustainable tourism.

All tourists eat while they are on holiday, and food is a significant area of tourist expenditure. By focusing on the more sustainable production and use of agricultural products in the tourism sector, along with enhancing the economic benefit, a reduction in "product miles" and other wastes can be realized. It has also been found that increasing numbers of travelers are stating that local products are a key aspect of their travel experience and that they believe that experiencing a country's products is essential to understanding its culture. Sustainable cuisine is becoming a key part of an authentic travel experience. The development and promotion of sustainable cuisine through operationalizing the "farm-to-restaurant" concept can support sustainable agriculture by increasing demand for local products, as well as contributing to the overall ethos of sustainable tourism.

In terms of sustainability, the level of imported agricultural products can affect the social and economic impacts of tourism. From an economic point of view, there is an urgent need for the tourism sector, especially in LDCs, to optimize their use of locally produced agricultural goods.

This chapter considers the relationship among sustainable agriculture, sustainable cuisine, and the tourism industry, particularly as it relates to sustainable tourism. Means for increasing the linkages among these three areas of sustainability will be discussed. Barriers and facilitators to implementing the farm-to-restaurant concept will also be explored through the consideration of the Fiji Grown—From Farm-to-Table concept.

Sustainable Tourism: Bringing Food into the Equation

Because the tourism industry is reputedly the largest industry in the world and one of the most significant economic sectors, the need to address its sustainability is critical. As discussed by Miller and Berno (2005), as many areas of sustainable development have been, sustainable tourism was originally approached from an environmental management platform. However, over the intervening years, a more holistic approach to sustainable tourism has emerged, one that considers a broad range of stakeholders and the multisectoral nature of the tourism industry.

The concept of sustainable tourism has contributed to an increased interest in the use of local resources in tourism development and the idea that host communities should benefit as much as possible from tourism in terms of income and employment opportunities. Despite this broadening of the conceptualization and operationalizaton of sustainable tourism, scant attention has been paid to an essential component of the tourism industry and tourist experience—that of the relationships among food production, food consumption, and sustainable tourism.

Food and Tourism

Food is an essential component of tourism. It may seem obvious, but it warrants mention that 100% of tourists eat when they travel, and dining is consistently in the top three most popular tourist activities (National Restaurant Association [US], 2003). It is estimated that food represents one third of total tourist expenditure (Belisle, 1983). Yet for many countries, particularly LDCs, food represents one of the highest areas of economic leakage in tourism. The degree to which tourism in a country relies on imported foods can significantly affect the social and economic impacts of tourism. Importing foods results in a loss of foreign exchange earnings and lost opportunities to expand and modernize local food production and processing. This may result in a loss of local income and employment (Telfer and Wall, 1996).

Despite an abundance of locally produced foods and food products, in many LDCs much of the food served in the tourism sector is imported. There are many reasons for the reliance on imported agricultural products. Availability, price, consistency, and quality of local products are some of the reasons cited (Telfer, 2000). Others have suggested that tourists demand foods that are often not grown in the host region or are hesitant to try local foods or cuisines (Gomes, 1997). Also posing threats to sustainability are the "international" menus (which often include parodies of local dishes rather than authentic local food) favored by many large hotels and resorts and the proliferation of transnational fast-food and restaurant chains at the expense of small locally owned enterprises (Swarbrooke, 1999; Torres, 2003).

Despite these impediments, however, the benefits of tourism to a destination can be enhanced by expanding the backward economic linkages by increasing the amount of local foods used by the tourism industry (Telfer and Wall, 1996). Creating and strengthening these back linkages between tourism and the food production sectors can provide a proximate market for locally produced products, while enhancing tourists' experiences by providing them with the opportunity to consume high-quality local produce (Boyne, Williams, and Hall, 2001). Enhancing linkages between agriculture and tourism presents significant opportunities for stimulating local production, retaining tourism earnings in the locale and improving the distribution of economic benefits of tourism to rural people (Torres, 2003).

The benefits of increased linkages between tourism and agriculture go beyond just "what is on the plate" and include the generation of a range of both direct and indirect demands for agricultural products and services related to tourism (Fox and Cox, 1993). These interactions are summarized in Table 9.1. These demands can result in a variety of positive outcomes, including a reduction in product miles and other wastes (for further discussion on product miles and waste reduction see The Logistics Business, 2003; Food Initiatives Group, 2003; Treesponsibility, 2003; Pirog, Van Pelt, Enshayam, and Cook, 2001); enrichment of localities and economic links; more attractive, vital, and viable rural areas; a more vibrant and locally distinctive tourism; and greater economic and social well-being for the host community (Gordon, 1999).

Linking Sustainable Cuisine and Sustainable Agriculture

Despite Gomes's (1997) observation that some tourists are reluctant to try local foods and cuisines, an increasingly significant number of travelers are stating that food is a key aspect of the travel experience and that they believe experiencing a country's food is essential to understanding its culture (Condé Nast Publications, Inc., and Plog Research, 2001, cited in Deneault, 2002). In the wake of globalization and the "homogenization" of tourism experiences, increasing numbers of tourists are seeking authentic experiences. Food, or gastronomy, is one means of expressing authentic local culture or heritage (Haukeland and Jacobsen, 2001; Richards, 2002).

The increasing appeal of gastronomy and locally sourced cuisine in tourism results in part from processes in society at large. People's interests in food quality, ecological concerns about the needs for increased sustainable agricultural practices, health and nutrition concerns, a more sophisticated knowledge of food and beverages, and acquired information

Table 9.1   Tourism and Agriculture Interactions

Production Related	*Consumption Related*
Direct	*Indirect*
Production of the food that tourists eat, including aspects such as:	Tourists' consumption of food, including aspects such as:
Agri- and horticultural food production	Food choices
Sustainable agricultural systems	Service sector management studies
Food processing	Food safety
Supply chain management	Impacts on destinations' food consumption
Impact on destinations' food production	
Indirect	*Indirect*
Land, labor, and capital: competition and complimentarity between the tourism and food production sectors	Tourists' consumption of agricultural landscapes and settings
Creation and maintenance of landscapes and settings	Food as a destination image component or marketing and promotion tool
Creation of facilities	Consumption of agritourism products and services such as farm parks and visitor attractions
Mutually beneficial transport improvements (i.e., tourism related transport improvements that enhance agricultural distribution)	

Adapted from Boyne, Williams, and Hall, 2002.

about different cuisines are impacting tourists' expectations and behaviors when they travel (Haukeland and Jacobsen, 2001).

This movement toward "authentic" regional or local cuisine is not exclusive to the domain of tourism. In response to the growth of fast foods, the concept of slow foods or sustainable cuisine has emerged. Believing that in the name of productivity, contemporary society ("Fast Life") has changed humans' ways of being, threatening the environment and landscapes, the sustainable cuisine movement considers that the defense against these unsustainable practices should begin with the redis-covery of regional foods and cooking. The movement has progressed from a sole focus on pure gastronomy toward ecology and a dedication to sustaining the land and farmers who produce artisanal foods. "The 'eco' part of [this] ecogastronomic movement necessitate[s] a new focus on education of the entire food continuum, from soil to table" (Martins, 2001, p. xiv). Thus the slow-food movement makes the critical linkage between sustainable agriculture and sustainable cuisine.

Sustainable cuisine is a pattern of eating that derives from a sustainable food system and supports the goals of such a system. Sustainable cuisine is an approach to gastronomy that ensures, rather than compromises, the ability of future generations to enjoy an abundant, nourishing, wholesome, flavorful, and safe food supply. Toward this goal, sustainable cuisine features foods that are grown in environmentally responsible ways and that are processed, marketed, and consumed as close as possible to the farms on which they were grown (Wilkins, 1999).

Sustainable cuisine promotes local food economies, "system[s] of producing, processing and trading, primarily of organic and sustainable forms of food production, where the physical and economic activity is largely contained and controlled within the locality or region where it was produced, which delivers health, economic, environmental and social benefits to the communities in those areas" (Sustain, 2002, p. 4) (Figure 9.1).

The tourism industry can take advantage of the growing interest in sustainable food systems and sustainable cuisine by promoting and using more local products throughout the industry, while meeting travelers' needs for an authentic, high-quality experience. By forging stronger linkages between agriculture and tourism through the development and promotion of sustainable cuisine, a symbiotic relationship between these sectors can be established.

The Farm-to-Restaurant Concept

By adopting the principles of sustainable cuisine, critical linkages between the tourism industry and sustainable agriculture can be forged, thus furthering a holistic approach to sustainable tourism (see Figure 9.2).

One way of operationalizing the articulation among the areas of sustainable agriculture, sustainable cuisine, and the tourism industry is through the development and promotion of the farm-to-restaurant concept, which can support sustainable agriculture by increasing demand for local products. The farm-to-restaurant concept promotes a high-quality tourism product through a value chain, which supports the use of local agricultural products within the tourism industry (Berno, 2003; Center for Corporate Citizenship at Boston College [CCCBC], 2002). The farm-to-restaurant concept does not have to stop at the dining experience. As indicated in Table 9.1, it can also lead to a range of related direct and indirect agritourism activities and products, including floriculture, food festivals, farm visits, factory tours, and value-added products, such as souvenir food merchandise, thus further enhancing the benefits to the local community.

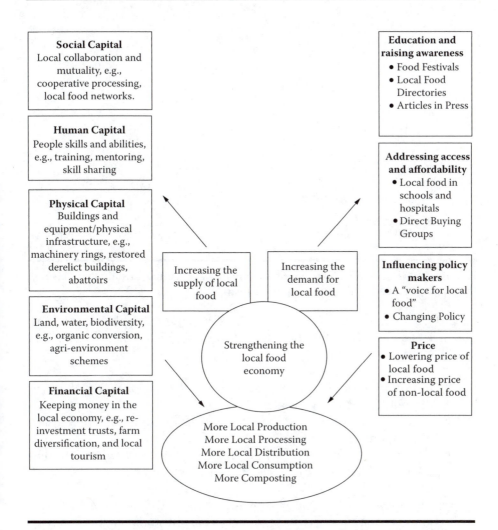

Figure 9.1   Economic framework for strategic interventions and determinants of the supply and demand for local food. (From Sustain, 2002, p. 5. With permission.)

The farm-to-restaurant concept does not involve the farmers and restaurateurs. As in most initiatives to support sustainable development, to operationalize the farm-to-restaurant concept successfully, a broad range of stakeholders must be involved. These include interests such as relevant government ministries (e.g., tourism, agriculture, fisheries, environment), national food production, pastoral and agricultural associations, providers of tourism and hospitality education, chefs and/or hotel management, national and local tourism organizations, communities of interest (rural producers, individuals with relevant expertise, etc.), and others with interests in rural development and the agricultural and tourism sectors.

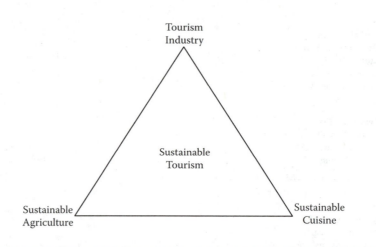

Figure 9.2 The relationships among sustainable agriculture, sustainable cuisine, the tourism industry, and sustainable tourism.

Just as the farm-to-table concept has a range of stakeholders, the beneficiaries of successful implementation are equally broad. They include the following:

- *Regional agricultural producers and the regional rural sector* through increases in production and sales of local products
- *Regional tourism and hospitality students* through additional training opportunities
- *Providers of regional tourism and hospitality education* through additional training materials and expert training (e.g., master's classes)
- *Employees in the tourism and hospitality sector* through improvements in the tourism food products available and increased training opportunities
- *Hotels* through improvements in the range and quality of tourism food products available, opportunities for professional development of staff, opportunities for niche marketing of local cuisine and potential agritourism associated with local production
- *National and regional hotel associations* through improvements in the tourism food products available, opportunities for professional development of members, and marketing opportunities for regional cuisine
- *Regional and national tourism organizations* through improvements in the overall tourism product, opportunities for niche marketing of regional cuisine, and potential agritourism associated with local production

■ *Regional governments* through increased sustainable rural development, revenue from the sale of local products, and the potential to develop additional niche markets (regional cuisine and agritourism)
■ *Tourists* through improved range and quality of foods available, enhanced cultural experiences through eating local products, niche market of regional cuisine, and agritourism
■ *Tourism and hospitality academic community* through additional knowledge and information about the links among sustainable rural development, agricultural production, and the tourism industry (Berno, 2003).

Implemented well, the farm-to-table concept links sustainable agriculture, sustainable cuisine, and the tourism industry, resulting in positive outcomes for a broad range of beneficiaries.

Situating the Linkages within the Context

Despite the potential positive benefits of a concept such as farm-to-restaurant, as discussed, increasing the linkages between tourism and agriculture has numerous challenges that must be overcome. There is no simple formula for increasing the use of local agricultural products in the tourism industry. As Torres (2003) points out, the examination of tourism and agriculture must be situated within the local farming development context of the host country destination.

There are numerous examples of successful strategic alliances between primary agricultural producers and the tourism industry. For example, the broad-based community development Hui Mea'ai project in Kauai, Hawaii, teaches producers to grow, market, and distribute top-quality agricultural products. The products are then sold to tourism operators or partners such as the Kauai Marriot Hotel, which incorporate the products into innovative dishes, highlighting the regional cuisine. The project started in 1998, and in that first year of operation, sold 5,834 pounds of produce. By 1999, sales had increased to 32,498 pounds. As of 2002, there were 56 growers involved in the cooperative, supplying 25 local tourism operators (CCCBC, 2002).

Not all tourist destinations have the benefit of the technology, transport infrastructure, or technical advice to support a large-scale cooperative such as the one in Kauai, hence the importance of considering the context. Kleins Camp in Tanzania, for example, is one of the most remote safari camps in Tanzania. Fulfilling its requirements for fresh produce without relying on costly imported goods required an innovative approach. In this context, the solution was in the form of the establishment of a small garden outside the staff village to supplement the weekly supplies being brought in from town. One staff member was employed to run the garden and plans were developed to pay for the vegetables once the garden was established. The gardener now employs two people to help him meet the needs, and the Kleins Camp supplies all the other camps in the Serengeti and two local villages. The gardener is no longer on the payroll as he is able to support himself through the profits of the operation (Gordon, 1999).

The examples presented illustrate how a well-planned, contextually appropriate agriculture and tourism project can meet with success over the longer term. However, in many instances, there are challenges to the successful sustainability of these types of projects. The case of Fiji's Fiji Grown—From Farm-to-Table is discussed next to give an example of some of the situational factors and issues that need to be addressed in promoting the articulation of sustainable agriculture, sustainable cuisine, and the tourism industry.

Fiji Grown—Implementing the Farm-to-Restaurant Concept

In global terms, the countries of the South Pacific* account for only 0.15% of the world's international tourist arrivals, but this small number is enough for tourism to be the mainstay of the region's economy. For many small South Pacific island states with minimal exploitable natural resources, tourism is one of their only (if not the only) development options.

Traditionally, tourism to the South Pacific has been predicated on the "Sun, sea, sand" image associated with larger-scale mass tourism. In the South Pacific, this form of tourism has often resulted in a high degree of economic leakage and poor multiplier effect. So, despite boosting the overall GDP of South Pacific nations, tourism has had few salient benefits for those in the outlying (rural) regions.

One area of tourism in the South Pacific that has experienced a high degree of economic leakage is the food and catering sector. As do many small island developing nations, Fiji experiences a high degree of leakage of the tourism dollar (the most recent estimate is over 60% [Tourism Council of the South Pacific (TCSP), 1990]), and much of that is attributed to leakage through imported foodstuffs in the hotel and resort sector. Both the Ministry of Tourism (2002) and the South Pacific Tourism Organisation (SPTO) (2003) have identified a need to increase the linkages between

---

* Members of the South Pacific Tourism Organisation (SPTO).

tourism and agricultural production to address the retention of tourism revenue.

From an economic point of view, there is an urgent need for the tourism industry in Fiji to optimize the use of locally produced food. Despite this need, however, significant impediments inhibit the increased use of local products in the tourism sector. These barriers include the need to prepare local foods in ways acceptable to the tourist palate, a lack of confidence of chefs in the use of local foods for tourist consumption, and irregular availability and poor quality control in the production processing and distribution of local food products for the tourism sector (Berno, 2003; Fiji Hotel Association, 1999; Naikatini, 1999).

In an attempt to address the problem, in 1986 the then Tourism Council of the South Pacific (now the South Pacific Tourism Organisation) commissioned the writing of a tropical foods cookbook for hotels, *Cooking the South Pacific Way—A Professional Guide to Fiji Produce.* To ensure supply of local products to support the recipes in the book, the project was linked with primary agricultural production, with an expectation that the Ministry of Agriculture would assist through encouraging the increased production and supply of the foods discussed in the book. The projected outcome of this effort was for hotels to be able to obtain adequate local products to help reduce the reliance on imported fruits and vegetables.

Fifteen hundred copies of the book were produced and distributed throughout the region, most in Fiji. The recipes appeared to be useful to chefs, and most hotels began to use some locally grown vegetables on a more regular basis. However, many chefs complained that the supply of local fruits and vegetables was irregular and of inconsistent quality. Unfortunately, essential linkages among hotel chefs, purchasing officers, and the Ministry of Agriculture lacked coordination, and the project, despite its initial encouraging success, was not sustainable.

It has now been 15 years since the book went out of print. Recent research (Cummins, 2002; Fiji Hotel Association, 1999) suggests that many chefs currently working in the tourism industry lack the knowledge and skills to use tropical foods in Western-type menus. There is now an urgent need to revisit the project and support its implementation with an efficient local food supply system, thus both supporting the rural production sectorand reducing economic leakage in the tourism industry. A situational analysis, however, reveals that there are barriers that must be overcome before the Fiji Grown concept can be implemented and sustained.

A Situational Analysis of the Fiji Context

Fiji is a small island nation, comprising over 300 islands, with a population of just fewer than 750,000. The majority of the population is almost evenly split between indigenous Fijians and Indo-Fijians (the descendents of indentured laborers taken to Fiji in the late 1880s to work in the sugarcane fields). There are also small minorities of Chinese, Europeans, and other Pacific Islanders resident in Fiji. The tourism industry attracts approximately 400,000 visitors to Fiji per annum, most of whom stay in resorts in the drier west of the main island of Viti Levu, which is also the area of the highest agricultural production.

As a result of the composition of the population, there are a number of cuisines in Fiji, many of which have been adopted and adapted from other cultures. Indo-Fijian, Chinese, and indigenous Fijian cuisines are all available, as are foods from many Western and Asian traditions. Most of these foods are represented in some form on the menus of the hotels and resorts, though for the most part, menus reflect a bias toward "Western"-style foods, which often require imported ingredients. The Pacific Islands, including Fiji, however, are not generally highly regarded for their cuisine, and it would be fair to say that they are not considered to be a destination for culinary tourism. When one thinks of Fiji, it is inevitably the ubiquitous "sun, sea, sand" image that comes to mind, rather than culinary experiences.

Despite this, there are opportunities to increase the linkages between tourism and agriculture through the development of a distinctive sustainable cuisine, a "Fiji–Pacific cuisine." A brief strengths, weaknesses, opportunities, and threats (SWOT) analysis highlights some of the facilitators and barriers to forging articulations among sustainable agriculture, sustainable cuisine, and the tourism industry in Fiji.

Strengths

The Fiji context offers potential for improving the variety, quality, and value of the food experience.

- An abundance of well-trained chefs working in the industry
- Increasing interest in organic production in the agricultural sector
- Strong linkages between cuisine and culture in Fiji
- Food a year-round, 24-hour-a-day product
- Food almost unexploited in terms of a tourism attribute in Fiji
- Broad range of good local products (food and floriculture) available

Weaknesses

- Nonexistent or poor international perception of Fiji–Pacific cuisine
- Lack of a clearly defined Fiji–Pacific cuisine

- Many local treatments of food products unacceptable to the tourist palate
- Lack of resources for education and training on the preparation of indigenous products for the tourism sector
- Lack of organization(s) focusing on the development of local products as part of the overall Fiji tourism product
- Need for public and private sector stakeholders to form new strategic alliances and partnerships in order for Fiji Grown to work
- Need to market internationally the concept of Fiji Grown

Opportunities

- Work with stakeholders to develop and implement fully the Fiji Grown concept
- Promote sustainable cuisine to tourists by working with industry and producers to create local and export-ready products
- Increase Fiji Grown promotional activities and partnerships with the industry (major hotels, destination marketing organizations, transport, and accommodation sectors)
- Creation of "value-added" products such as souvenir food items, and farm tours
- Capitalize on the excellent growing conditions in Fiji to grow both indigenous products as well as high-demand exotics

Threats

- Lack of sustainability of previous initiatives
- Lack of confidence of some chefs in the use of local foods for tourist consumption
- Tourist preferences for familiar (i.e., non-Pacific) foods
- Irregular availability and poor quality control in the production, processing and distribution of local food products for the tourism sector
- Budget constraints that make it difficult for some operators to adopt Fiji Grown (e.g., use of fresh flowers and fruit baskets in hotel rooms, flower garlands upon arrival etc.)
- Negative perception of food in Fiji that may make promotion of the concept of Fiji Grown challenging (Berno, 2003)

The Way Forward for Fiji Grown

It is clear that the potential exists in Fiji to forge stronger relationships between the agriculture and tourism industries, and there are some examples of successful relationships active in this area. For example, several of the "top-end" boutique resorts in the country have developed distinctive Fijian cuisines, and several grow their own organic produce to support their requirements. These resorts have excellent international reputations for the quality of their foods. However, because of their exclusivity, the impacts of their initiatives on the Fiji tourism industry as a whole are relatively minor.

On the other end of the scale, budget "backpacker"-type accommodations often source much of their food products locally, as this is often a less expensive option than purchasing costly imported goods. Additionally, many small-scale backpacker operations in Fiji are indigenously owned and managed. As such, staff often do not have the training or skills to use exotic ingredients and therefore rely on local products cooked in more traditional ways. As with the boutique end of the tourism industry, however, backpackers comprise only a small share of the in-bound tourism market.

The majority of in-bound tourism to Fiji can be described as mass tourism. This is often the most difficult sector of the tourism industry in which to make inroads in terms of introducing sustainable cuisine. Even in this area, however, some producers have been successful in increasing their supplies to the larger resorts. One initiative has seen the formation of a local agricultural cooperative that now supplies fresh produce directly to the Outrigger Reef Resort, one of the largest resorts in the country. Another successful initiative, spearheaded by the executive chef of one of the larger chains of hotels in the country, the Tanoa Group, has led to the use of more local ingredients on the menus throughout the properties in the group (Berno, 2003).

On this larger scale, there are numerous salient benefits to a broad range of stakeholders should a sustainable Pacific cuisine be successfully developed and implemented industrywide. Fiji Grown has the potential to contribute to sustainable rural development, support the agricultural sector, and reduce economic leakage by addressing the ongoing need to increase the production and use of local products in the main mass tourism sector through: (1) developing sufficient, reliable, high-quality local foods for hotels; (2) training chefs in the cooking and presentation of local produce; (3) providing chefs and tourism and hospitality educators with education and training about local food recipes suitable for modern hotel menus; (4) introducing the "Healthy Food" concept as an integral component of tourism and hospitality education and hotel catering; (5) using local high-quality cuisine as a marketing tool for hotels adopting the program; while

(6) ensuring that the health and nutrition of rural producers is not compromised by the diversion of food supplies to the hotels (Berno, 2003).

However, lessons learned from past efforts, as well as the situational analysis, suggest that the way forward for Fiji Grown requires careful consideration of the particularities of the Fiji context. The successful linkages already achieved can serve as examples of how the Fiji Grown concept can be implemented and sustained. Further work and research, however, are required to take the initiative countrywide.

Conclusion

One of the most important areas of the tourism industry is that of food production and consumption. Ironically, however, despite the fact that all tourists eat as part of their tourist experience, this is an area that has received little attention in the tourism literature. Much has been written about sustainable tourism, yet few initiatives have been undertaken to consider the relationship between sustainable agriculture and sustainable tourism. Yet not only can better linkages between agriculture and tourism result in higher levels of economic retention, they can contribute significantly to the ethos of sustainable tourism.

Increasingly, as destinations seek to differentiate themselves in the market, a distinctive local cuisine can be used as a tool for promotion. This further serves to reinforce the increasing desire of tourists for "authentic" experiences. What could be more authentic than partaking of regional cuisine, prepared with fresh regional ingredients? Sustainable cuisine, which supports sustainable agriculture, can be an integral tool for sustainable tourism.

As Boyne, Williams, and Hall (2001, p. 5) point out,

> where destination areas' [high-quality] food and beverage [and other] production are utilized to strengthen the tourism product, and tourists are encouraged to purchase and consume locally produced [products], thereby stimulating local primary production sectors, we see a bi-directional development process—food production for tourism *and* tourism for food production.

References

Belisle, F.J. (1983). Tourism and food production in the Caribbean. *Annals of Tourism Research*, 10: 497–513.

Berno, T. (2003). Fiji grown: From farm to restaurant. Keynote address presented at the FAO/Ministry of Agriculture Fiji Grown Workshop. February 26–28, Korolevu, Fiji.

Boyne, S., Williams, F., and Hall, D. (2001). Rural tourism and food production: Opportunities for sustainable development. Paper presented at the RICS Foundation Roots 2001 Conference. November 12–13, London. Retrieved from http://www.rics-foundation.org/publish/download.aspx?did=2768.

Boyne, S., Williams, F., and Hall, D. (2002). The Isle of Arran Taste Trail. In: Hjalager, A., and Richards, G., *Tourism and Gastronomy.* London: Routeledge, pp. 91–113.

The Center for Corporate Citizenship at Boston College (2002). *A Productive Partnership: The Kauai Marriott Resort and Beach Club and the Kauai Food Bank.* Boston: The Center for Corporate Citizenship.

Cummins, K. (2002). Agriculture, Food and Nutrition in the Developing World. Unpublished manuscript.

Deneault, M. (2002). *Acquiring a Taste for Cuisine Tourism: A Product Development Strategy.* Ottawa: Canadian Tourism Commission.

Fiji Hotel Association (1999). Report on a Survey to Determine the Kinds and Amounts of Locally Produced Foods Used by Fiji Hotels and Resorts. Unpublished report.

Food Initiatives Group (2003). Getting the taste for healthy, sustainable food in greater Nottingham. Retrieved from http://groundworkgreaternottingham. org.uk/fig/local/food_miles.html.

Fox, M., and Cox, L.J. (1993). Linkages between agriculture and tourism. In: Khan, Olsen, M., and Var, T., eds., *VNR's Encyclopedia of Hospitality and Tourism.* New York: Van Nostrand Reinhold, pp. 910–917.

Gomes, A.J. (1997). Integrating tourism and agricultural development. In: France, L., ed., *The Earthscan Reader in Sustainable Tourism.* New York: Earthscan, pp. 187–195.

Gordon, C. (1999). Food—the world on our plate—but is it sustainable? *Green Hotelier,* 15: 16–19.

Haukeland, J.V., and Jacobsen, J.K.S. (2001). Gastronomy in the periphery: Food and cuisine as tourism attractions at the top of Europe. Paper presented at the 10th Nordic Tourism Research Conference, Vasa, Finland, October 18–20, 2001. Retrieved from http://padua.wasa.shh.fi/konferens/abstract/a6-haukeland.pdf.

The Logistics Business (2003). Reducing food miles—Green propaganda or sound business sense? Retrieved from http://www.logistics.co.uk/db_pdf/reducing_food_miles_69.pdf.

Martins, P. (2001). Introduction. In: Petrini, C., ed., *Slow Food. White River* Junction, VT: Chelsea Green Publishing, pp. xiv–xv.

Miller, G.A., and Berno, T. (2005). Towards sustainable tourism: Moving beyond ecotourism. In: Mudacumura, G.M., Mebrutu, D., and Haque, M.S., eds., *Handbook of Sustainable Development Policy and Administration.* New York: Marcel Dekker, pp. 535–555.

Ministry of Tourism (2002). Fiji: The contribution of the tourism sector to the economy. In: United Nations Economic and Social Commission for Asia and the Pacific, Committee on Transport, Communications, Tourism and Infrastructure Development, Fourth Session, November 13–15, Bangkok. Bangkok: UNESCAP CTCTID, pp. 12–19.

Naikatini, U. (1999). Brief—Local Foods in Hotel Project. Unpublished Fiji Ministry of Agriculture manuscript.

National Restaurant Association (2003). Travel and tourism facts. Retrieved from http://www.restaurant.org/tourism/facts.cfm.

Pirog, R., Van Pelt, T., Enshayan, K., and Cook, E. (2001). *Food, Fuels and Freeways*. Ames, IA: Leopold Center for Sustainable Agriculture.

Richards, G. (2002). Gastronomy: An essential ingredient in tourism production and consumption? In: Hjalager, A., and Richards, G., eds., *Tourism and Gastronomy*. London: Routeledge, pp. 3–20.

South Pacific Tourism Organisation (2003). *Regional Tourism Strategy for the South and Central Pacific. Part 1: Strategy for Growth*. Suva: SPTO.

Sustain (2002). *Sustainable Food Chains Briefing Paper 1: Local Food; Benefits Obstacles and Opportunities*. London: Sustain.

Swarbrooke, J. (1999). *Sustainable Tourism Management*. London: CABI.

Telfer, D.J. (2000). Tastes of Niagara: Building strategic alliances between tourism and agriculture. *International Journal of Hospitality and Tourism Administration*, 1(1): 71–88.

Telfer, D.J.; and Wall, G. (1996). Linkages between tourism and food production. *Annals of Tourism Research*, 23(3): 635–653.

Torres, R. (2003). Linkages between tourism and agriculture in Mexico. *Annals of Tourism Research*, 30(3): 516–566.

Tourism Council of the South Pacific (1990). *Economic Impact of Tourism in Fiji*. Suva: TCSP.

Treesponsibility (2003). Food miles: How far has your food travelled? Retrieved from http://anderson.ath.cx:8000/treesponsibility/art013.html.

Wilkins, J.L. (1999). Sustainable food systems. In: Frenza, J.P., ed., *Earth Pledge Foundation Sustainable Cuisine White Papers*. New York: Earth Pledge Foundation, pp. 12–16.

Chapter 10

Sustaining Development Projects through Nongovernmental Organizations in Municipal–Community Partnerships

Heather Nel

CONTENTS

Introduction

In terms of recent legislation in South Africa, there is a strong focus on progressively building local government into an effective, frontline development agency capable of bringing about the social and economic uplifting of local communities. Municipalities are no longer mere providers of services such as water and electricity. Rather, the emphasis has shifted to developmental local government, whereby it is the central responsibility of municipalities to work together with local communities to find sustainable ways to meet their needs and improve the quality of their lives. In this context, municipalities are required to produce integrated development plans that form the framework for development projects within the local government sphere. Within this framework, municipalities need to initiate and design development projects together with local communities.

In this regard, the Constitution of the Republic of South Africa (1996, Act 108) indicates the objectives of local government in Section 152 as to ensure the provision of services to communities in a sustainable manner and to encourage the involvement of communities and community organizations in the matters of local government. Furthermore, the Constitution stipulates the developmental duties of municipalities in Section 153. In this regard, it is stated that a municipality must structure and manage its administration, budgeting, and planning processes to give priority to the basic needs of the community and to promote the social and economic development of the community.

It is, therefore, apparent that the Constitution upholds and entrenches the right of existence of local government, especially in respect to ensuring sustainable development. The White Paper on Local Government (1998, Notice 423) is another policy framework that has significant implications for local government in South Africa. The White Paper puts forward a vision of "developmental local government" that centers on working with local communities to find sustainable ways to meet their needs and improve the quality of their lives. The White Paper provides the following approaches to assist municipalities to become more developmental:

- Integrated development planning and budgeting
- Performance management
- Working together with local citizens and partners

Evidently, planning and management for development must also combine—integrate—key aspects of development such as social, economic, environmental, ethical, infrastructural, and spatial. Achieving such integration requires municipalities to mobilize the participation, commitment, and energies of residents and stakeholders by establishing participatory processes that are constructive and effective.

This chapter devotes attention to the need for active community participation in project conception, as well as the various mechanisms or strategies that can be utilized by South African municipalities to bring about integrated development. With respect to the strategies to enhance community participation within the local government sphere, particular emphasis will be placed on the need for municipal–community partnerships in South Africa with specific reference to the need to engage nongovernmental organizations (NGOs) in local development initiatives. Before delving into the analysis, it is worth clarifying the characteristics of development projects.

Characteristics of Development Projects

Oosthuizen (1994, p. 42) defined a *project* as any undertaking with a known starting point and specific objectives by which completion is identified. Similarly, Kerzner (1992, p. 2) considered a project to be any series of activities that has a specific objective to be completed within certain specifications; has defined start and end dates; and consumes resources such as finance, personnel and equipment.

Atkins and Milne (1995, pp. 3–5) distinguish between conventional and development projects. It is asserted that development projects extend the project activities, output, and time frame beyond the scope of conventional projects by encouraging and assisting the beneficiary community to participate actively in the project and to take ownership, insofar as possible, of the asset created; maximizing the short-, medium- and long-term project benefits to alleviate poverty in a sustainable and replicable manner; using the project as a vehicle for training and building the capacity of the local community; enhancing employment opportunities through the use of labor-intensive technologies; and minimizing negative environmental impact and thereby enhancing sustainability.

It is interesting to note from the preceding that development projects are primarily characterized by an emphasis on engaging the beneficiary community in those attempts by local government to meet basic needs. Added to this, development projects are furthermore characterized by attempts to create jobs and build the capacity of beneficiary communities in a sustainable, viable, and transparent manner.

To facilitate such attempts, municipalities can make use of the project management cycle as a framework within which to manage development projects. This project management cycle comprises various interrelated and interdependent phases, namely, (1) *project conception*, whereby the need for a development project is identified and a project proposal is formulated; (2) *project preparation*, whereby a project proposal is subjected to a series of stringent feasibility analyses before being submitted to a higher authority for appraisal; (3) *project implementation*, whereby the actual work is done to give effect to the objectives of the project; and (4) *project evaluation*, whereby the effectiveness and efficiency of the project in terms of goal attainment are determined (Nel, 1999).

The discussion in this chapter focuses on the need for community participation in managing local development projects. Thus, it is essential for municipalities to identify, formulate, and implement project proposals that meet community needs, but through the widest possible consultation with and participation of community members.

Community Members and Project Development Management

Chandler (1988, p. 175) defines *community participation* as the direct involvement of the local community in the processes of policy formulation, administrative decision making, and program implementation. Furthermore, Scruton (1982, p. 345) implies that decisions made should involve and be acceptable to those affected by them. Thus, the making and implementation of decisions relating to development in the local government sphere should not be done in isolation of the local community being served.

Braun (2003, p. 188) asserts that the demand for participation of the people affected by development projects is neither incidental nor unfounded. In this regard, there has been a sobering realization that no matter how technically correctly they are planned and however well intended in economic terms, development projects often fail because they were planned and executed in a top-down fashion "amid serene disregard of the real-life conditions of the people affected." The result is that the target groups cooperate only haltingly, demonstrate at times a great deal of apathy, and manifest "project resistance." Participation is therefore advocated as an instrument to increase and stabilize project success and sustainability.

In this respect, Brown (1995, p. 46) adds that *community participation* can be defined as an active process by which beneficiary or client groups influence the direction and execution of a project rather than merely being consulted or receiving a share of the benefits. This definition has some important implications for the project management cycle. It implies that (1) the context of participation is the definition of the scope of the project, after which technical and managerial aspects need to be decided on by the project manager and the project team; (2) the community affected by the proposed project is the focus in that the acceptance by community members of the project is crucial to the eventual success of the management of the project; (3) community participation involves collective action by the community as a group or a couple of groups, and a major task for the project manager is ensuring that the community is organized in a manner whereby it can act in concert to advise on issues relating to the project.

It is added that in eliciting participation from beneficiary communities, the municipality needs to engage in a two-way communication process with the community concerned. This basically entails engaging the community in project conception to determine their needs and expectations, and being responsive to identified community needs, and informing the community of progress being made in projects undertaken to meet these needs.

Community and participation are linked in such a way as to render ideas of community unsustainable without the processes of participation to reinforce and develop a collective sense of identity, interest, and place (Smith and Beazley, 2000, p. 858). In an attempt to encourage a more enlightened dialogue on community participation, Arnstein (1969) developed a typology, or ladder, of community participation. This typology identifies eight levels of participation moving from nonparticipation, through degrees of tokenism, to the higher levels whereby citizens gain increasing levels of decision-making power. This typology is illustrated in Figure 10.1.

Although this typology provides a helpful starting point for an analysis of community participation, Burns and associates (1994, p. 161) identify a number of problems with this model. First, it is argued that Arnstein's typology should not represent the rungs of the ladder as equidistant, in that experience has shown that it is far easier to climb the lower rungs than to scale the higher ones. Second, it is necessary to distinguish more clearly between participation and control. In this respect, these authors identify four spheres of citizen power: individual, neighborhood, local governance, and national governance. It is pointed out that it is quite possible for citizens to enjoy a high degree of power within the second sphere yet comparatively little within the third. This may be due to municipalities' jealously maintaining control over strategic and policy-making matters. Alternatively, citizens may be denied power within the third sphere because local strategic powers have been absorbed by the national government. It is worth noting that "whoever controls strategy controls the script, because resources and operational practices tend to flow from the former and not the other way around" (Burns et al., 1994, p. 159).

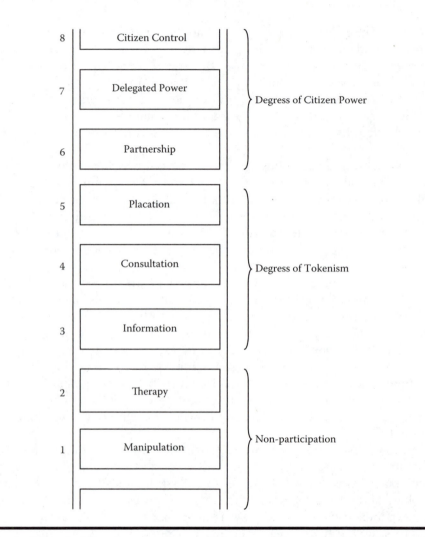

Figure 10.1   Ladder of community participation. (From Arnstein, 1969, p. 216.)

With respect to community participation, it is helpful to distinguish between informing and consulting and decentralized decision making. Davis (1997, p. 31) elaborates by defining *consultation* as an exchange between citizens and their government, between those who make policy and those affected by policy choices. However, consultation does not involve any fundamental shift in ultimate responsibility for decision making in that decisions are still made by the municipality. Thus, local government retains control, even when delegating some choices to the community.

Closely related to consultation is informing. Progressive municipalities have recognized that sound approaches to community involvement need to be supported by high-quality information. Clearly, a prerequisite of meaningful participation by the community is the provision of clear, understandable information about local decisions and policies and the reasons for these, as well as the services to which they are entitled. In other words, citizens should be consulted about the level and quality of services they receive and, where possible, be given a choice about services that are provided, as well as full and accurate information about services to which they are entitled.

However, it should be noted that beneficiary communities tend to react negatively to proposals that affect them and have been identified and formulated without their involvement. The result is skepticism of the community in respect to the motives and intentions of the local government managers, especially when it appears that all the important decisions have already been made. In this respect, a top-down approach to community participation whereby local government managers merely inform communities of decisions already taken without their involvement needs to be avoided. Furthermore, a paternalistic approach to consultation should be guarded against since communities resent the attitude that professionals "know what is best" for them. Finally, consultation and information should not be utilized merely to legitimize decisions made by the local council. Rather, community members need to be engaged in making decisions relating to development projects to be undertaken by the municipality.

To facilitate this, community participation may take on the form of decentralized decision making. This involves the local authority committing itself to taking into account the views of the community before decisions are made. This further requires a transfer of at least some power, and citizens acquire genuine bargaining influence. However, Section 32(2) of the Municipal Structures Act stipulates that any delegation or instruction (1) must be in accordance with the Constitution; (2) be in writing; (3) be subject to any limitations, conditions, and directions the local council may impose; (4) include the power to subdelegate a delegated power; (5) not divest the council of the responsibility concerning the exercise of the power; and (6) be reviewed when a new council is elected.

The *Integrated Development Planning Manual* emphasizes that the IDP process is an integrated approach to development planning with all sectors and functions working together in pursuit of a common vision. Community participation must be structured to enhance interaction of the various sectors. Structures that represent a wide range of sectoral interests and expertise will stand a greater chance of developing holistic sustainable solutions. This should in turn foster greater cooperation and coordination between a wide range of development agencies and establish a culture of integration across municipal departments.

In this regard, an effective decentralized decision-making process will be characterized by representative attendance at workshops and public meetings, the filtering of information down to the man and woman in the street, few incidents of conflict during meetings and workshops, and continuous progress in the planning process. Moreover, a large measure of consensus between stakeholders and role players; clear mandates for participants; clear, supported terms of reference for all participants; and clear and agreed-to codes of conduct for all participative sessions are other characteristics of such decentralization.

In short, a halfhearted approach to community participation will not deliver these results. Municipalities need to give community participation careful thought and make full use of all available resources to assist with the process. Some municipalities will require more complex community participation processes than others. For instance, large municipalities with a history of tension or conflict between various community groups will need processes that take this history into account. In such cases, municipalities might include a community participation facilitator to assist with the process. At the same time, community participation must not become an obstacle to development. Elected municipal counselors are the legitimate representatives of the community. At certain points, municipal councils will have to make difficult decisions and demonstrate clear leadership.

In light of the preceding, it is imperative that municipal role players are aware of the various forms of community participation, since this will inform decisions as to which strategies of participation are the most appropriate in a particular project setting.

Forms of Community Participation

The White Paper on Local Government indicates that municipalities require active participation by citizens at four levels, namely: (1) as voters—to ensure maximal democratic accountability of the elected political leadership for the policies they are empowered to promote; (2) as citizens who express, via different stakeholder associations, their views before, during, and after the policy development process in order to ensure that policies reflect community preferences as far as possible; (3) as consumers and end users, who expect value for money, affordable services, and courteous and responsive service; and (4) as organized partners involved in the mobilization of resources for development via for-profit businesses, non-governmental organizations, and community-based organizations (Republic of South Africa, 1998b).

For the purposes of this discussion, attention will be devoted to the involvement of local communities in development initiatives in the form of partnerships.

Partnerships

A partnership is a further step toward handing control of a decision from local government to the community in that it provides some measure of joint decision making. Partnership is often achieved through advisory boards and representative committees designed to provide continuing expert and community input. Community representatives on an advisory board can provide policy makers with direct and unfiltered views, while local government representatives are given the opportunity to explain their approach and objectives.

Smith and Beazley (2000, p. 861) provide an interesting typology of partnerships as they relate to urban regeneration initiatives in the United Kingdom. These authors indicate that partnerships represent a collective attempt to add value to, or derive some mutual benefit from, activities that individual actors or sectors would be unable to attempt alone. In addition, they are promoted as the solution to difficult problems and have the potential to allow local needs to be identified and addressed, give local people a voice, and empower local communities leading to greater social justice.

However, it is common to find examples of partners being drawn into the process after the design for the particular project has been established by the lead agency, in this case, the municipality. Clearly, this type of partnership represents an imbalance of power between the partners involved and is essentially exclusivist in structure. In this respect, the typology referred to is worth noting since it depicts the type of partnerships that may evolve within the local government sphere, depending on the degree of power granted to community partners (see Table 10.1).

Table 10.1 Typology of Partnerships

Shell	Nominal involvement of partners. The leader is dominant and partners have little involvement in any stage of the process.
Consultative	Partnership remains strongly controlled by the leader, but partners are consulted to some extent and allowed to make changes at the margin.
Participative	Partners have increased and often equal access to the decision-making framework and their views frequently shape policy.
Autonomous	The partnership develops an independent identity in which partners are fully integrated. All partners have equal access and mechanisms exist to ensure genuine and sustained involvement.

Source: Smith and Beazley, 2000, p. 861.

The White Paper on Local Government goes beyond merely engaging community partners in the making of decisions pertaining to development. The White Paper stipulates that municipalities can utilize partnerships to promote emerging businesses, support NGOs and community-based development organizations (CBDOs), mobilize private sector involvement, and promote developmental projects that are initiated but not necessarily funded by local government (Republic of South Africa, 1998b). Essentially, this involves service delivery partnerships that entail a range of creative methods through which municipalities can mobilize external capacity and resources for the development of the area.

Matovu (2002, p. 27) writes that, in Africa, it is clear that local governments are weak in the provision of services and civil society, including NGOs, has the potential to provide services. This represents a missing link in joining the two parties and demonstrates the need to facilitate the forging of partnerships. This writer adds that, in theory, a vibrant civil society can contribute to effective institutional development and democratic decentralization, enhance the responsiveness of government institutions, increase the information flow between government and the people, make development projects more sustainable, and enhance accountability and transparency—all of which constitute good governance.

It is worth noting in this respect that interaction with NGOs and CBDOs could prove to be instrumental in facilitating empowerment and sustainable development in that these organizations fulfill a vital role in (1) capacity building or ensuring the acquisition of skills and competence within disadvantaged communities and thereby reducing a culture of dependency and (2) allowing or generating the ability among members of disadvantaged communities to participate effectively in the process of development planning (Davies, 1993, pp. 40–41).

Davies (1993, pp. 42–43) adds that NGOs, CBDOs, and other civil society organizations (CSOs) such as civic associations require a facilitating environment in which to operate. In particular, these organs of civil society need support from municipalities, at least to the extent that their role in development is acknowledged and understood. In encouraging such a mutually supportive relationship, local government managers can be instrumental by (1) providing opportunities (for example, through training) for local NGOs and CBDOs to strengthen their capacity in servicing development needs within the communities being served, (2) expanding information-sharing and networking activities with local NGOs and CBDOs in respect to development initiatives, and (3) encouraging national government and multilateral agencies to channel more aid to NGOs and CBDOs with a recognized ability to undertake development projects effectively and efficiently.

These factors are reflected in a report on municipal–community partnerships (MCPs) issued by the Department of Provincial and Local Government (www.local.gov.za). This report supports the shift away from the municipality as the sole service provider to the role of a leader and facilitator of development, working in collaboration with a multiplicity of community partners. Successful MCPs are understood as service delivery and governance mechanisms that include three key elements, namely, enhancing the organizational effectiveness of local government, extending basic services to address areas of greatest unmet needs and poverty, and promoting community empowerment and the deepening of the social contract at a local level.

This MCP report suggests that the following sectors should be prioritized as the lead components of an MCP strategy within the local government sphere in South Africa: (1) basic services such as water and sanitation, refuse collection, roads, and environmental maintenance; (2) social housing in metropolitan areas, cities, and towns; (3) local economic development strategies; and (4) revenue management, including billings and revenue collection. Irrespective of the sector(s) in which MCPs are established, it is crucial that the local government create an enabling environment to ensure the success of community partnerships.

Conducive Environment for Municipal–Community Partnerships

The IDP manual highlights that the IDP process introduces a new system of planning in local government. It is important that sufficient capacity be developed to undertake the process effectively and efficiently. The process requires new skills of professionals and municipal council members alike and demands a shift in both attitude and approach.

The participants in the planning process represent a wide variety of interest groups with different interests and backgrounds. The various role players need to enter the planning process on an equal footing. This implies that the role players in the planning process need to be empowered in order to ensure that their contributions are meaningful. Training requirements may include training on the integrated planning approach and procedures; training on a wide variety of development issues, such as transport, housing, environment, tourism, and health; and training on the management and coordination of the process.

Fredericksen and London (2000, p. 233) add that partnerships between government and CSOs have proved to be central to long-term neighborhood revitalization in many settings in the United States. However, it is argued that in their haste to contract with community partners, such as

NGOs and CBDOs, municipalities may not be considering the real possibility that such organizations do not have the capacity to deliver services or effectively manage development projects over time. It is recommended that particular attention be devoted to key elements such as the leadership and vision, management and planning, and operational support, including skilled staff and adequate infrastructure of the organizational capacity of CSOs when engaging in empowerment strategies.

Morris (1995, p. 424) supports this and argues that governance should be reassessed and improved through a number of interrelated actions, including engaging with and involving the community in partnerships with government. She writes that NGOs play a crucial role in terms of promoting greater participation by citizens in decision making and acting as gatekeepers in longer-term agendas ranging from protecting citizens' rights to ensuring sustainable and equitable development.

Furthermore, Box and colleagues (2001, p. 616) support this notion of substantive democracy and write that in the search for an alternative to the market-based model of public administration, a central element should be a collaborative relationship between citizens and public administrators. The emphasis of this collaborative model is on giving citizens the knowledge and techniques they need to deal with public policy issues and providing an open and nonthreatening forum for deliberation and decision making.

Teisman and Klijn (2002, p. 198), moreover, concur by stating that partnerships can be seen as new governance schemes that aim to manage the increased interdependencies among all kinds of societal actors. These authors write that the partnership concept may be linked to the trend toward network forms of government in which public actors, such as municipalities, take their interdependencies with other actors into account and try to solve governance problems through cooperation rather than through central steering and control. According to Ferreira (2002, p. 19): "You cannot build a community from the top down or from the outside in. The only way to build a community is from the inside out—local people come together, hold hands and look in one direction—come together and start to invest in themselves and their resources in creating a better future."

Nalbandian (1999, p. 191) shifts the focus to local government managers and asserts that the prevalence of MCPs is requiring managers to lead by example to help pave the way for the establishment of these partnerships. It is noted that there has been a change in direction in terms of local government management away from professional elitism toward a community paradigm. It appears that local government managers need to be able to move in this direction if they are to maintain their effectiveness and influence. There is therefore a need to capacitate local government managers in the areas of community building, facilitative leadership, managing of diversity, and problem solving.

The report on MCPs referred to earlier summarizes by highlighting the key cross-cutting activities that are required to develop an enabling environment for successful MCPs. These activities include the establishment of a training and *capacity-building program* to empower CSOs and enhance municipal capability to work on MCPs, the need for *research and development* and the production and dissemination of international and local knowledge and best practices with respect to MCPs, and the need for a national Municipal Services Partnership (MSP) policy and establishment of a national MCP fund to support all of those activities.

The *World Development Report* (2000/2001, pp. 110–111) points out that particular attention needs to be devoted to empowering the poor to participate in local governance through NGOs and CBDOs. However, it is recognized that major impediments to organization by poor communities are lack of time, resources, information, and access to outside sources of help. Added to these are the physical constraints on collaboration such as geographic dispersion and poor transport and communications infrastructure. Ethnic and other social divisions are another impediment. Emmett (2000) adds that the concerns of social capital are of special interest in South Africa, where key institutions such as the family and community have been subjected to profound processes of disintegration. Among the symptoms of this disintegration are family breakdowns, high unemployment, high crime rates, despair, and acceptance of the victim image.

In light of the preceding, it is particularly important that municipalities in South Africa attempt to create an environment that is supportive of MCPs. The *World Development Report* (2000/2001, p. 111) indicates that municipalities can facilitate greater collaboration between them and local communities by reducing obstacles to collective action in communities. To foster developmental synergies between NGOs and local government, it is recommended that the latter generate community demand for better service delivery through intensive dissemination of information; make available to communities the information and technical, marketing, credit, and other support they need to implement development projects; and train and motivate their staff to focus on managing overall strategy while providing technical support, regulations, and facilitation.

King, Feltey, and Susel (1998, pp. 323–325) concur by summarizing the actions required of municipalities to enhance *authentic participation*, which is defined as "deep, continuous involvement in administrative processes with the potential for all involved to have an effect on the situation." Such authentic participation implies the ability and opportunity of local communities to have an impact on decisions relating to local governance and development initiatives. Giving effect to such participation requires a three-pronged approach, namely one that seeks (1) to empower and educate community members by designing processes whereby citizens know that their participation has the potential to have an impact, where a representative range of citizens are included, and where there are visible outcomes; (2) to reeducate local administrators to equip them to deal with the change in their role as expert managers to one of cooperative partners. This implies providing training in process and interpersonal skills such as communication, listening, team building, meeting facilitation, and self-knowledge; and (3) to enable administrative structures and processes not only to democratize formal institutions and procedures, but also to make room for nonbureaucratic discourse by providing appropriate levels of resources and changing job descriptions of local administrators to include reference to the facilitation of community participation.

Evans (1996, p. 1120) asserts that although it is not a "magic bullet," partnerships between local government and the community lie at the heart of the development process. Similarly, Evans points out that this synergy is based on complementarity involving mutually supportive relations between local government and its citizens. Such a complementary relationship is characterized by the roles of local government and civil society remaining distinct, while the former provides inputs to assist local communities in carrying out development initiatives in a sustainable and effective manner.

Evans (1996, p. 1124) further concedes that while stocks of social capital are important to the creation of synergy, he believes that the key issue involves "scaling up" or the movement of NGOs and other civil society organizations away from parochial identities to more encompassing forms of organization that are politically and economically efficacious. In addition to increasing the power of local communities, scaling up can have a number of benefits for the development process in general in that it allows for greater economies of scale, increases the possibilities of intersectoral collaboration, provides for larger pools of skills from which development projects can draw, and may allow for the employment of permanent paid staff instead of unpaid volunteers (Emmett, 2000).

Conclusion

This chapter has explored the role of local government in engaging local communities in the management of development projects through forging municipal–community partnerships with civil society organizations. In this respect, it was pointed out that local government has been assigned a developmental role in the sense that legislation stipulates that municipalities will be expected to create conditions of participatory governance, whereby their citizens are given real opportunities to participate in and influence the outcomes of development initiatives. In fulfilling its developmental role, it was proposed, local government should adopt a project management approach whereby municipalities identify needs and initiate various development projects that will meet these needs in a sustainable manner. Thus, it was argued that it is essential for municipalities to identify, formulate, and implement development projects that meet community needs, but through the widest possible consultation with and participation of community members.

In addition, it was pointed out that community participation can assume various forms and that it is important that municipalities decide in advance which model they are going to adopt when embarking on the management of development projects. Along the same lines, the chapter discussed the issue of community participation, which implies consulting the community on proposed development initiatives and projects; informing the community of local decisions and the reasons for these, as well as the services to which they are entitled; and decentralizing decision making, whereby local government transfers some of its power to make development decisions to community bodies such as local development forums or ward committees.

Moreover, it was emphasized that community participation should be defined as the active process by which beneficiary or client groups influence the direction and execution of a project rather than merely being consulted. This implies that the municipality engages the community in identifying and implementing projects that will meet their needs and expectations through strategies such as municipal–community partnerships. Such partnerships are endorsed by the White Paper on Local Government as a mechanism by which local authorities can harness external capacity and resources to undertake development projects.

In a South African context, MCPs mostly target CSOs, including NGOs, as alternative service providers and partners with local government in the effort to meet community needs. Despite the benefits of engaging such community partners in the conception and implementation of development projects, it was found that the balance of power still often lies in the favor of local government. To rectify this situation, the final section of this chapter devoted attention to the role of local government in empowering the community and in creating an enabling environment in which MCPs can succeed. Most important, the need for training and capacity building of both CSOs and local government managers was stressed. Both parties to the partnership need a clear understanding of their respective roles and responsibilities with respect to planning for and implementing sustainable development projects within the local government sphere in South Africa.

References

Arnstein, S.R. (1969). A ladder of citizen participation. *Journal of the American Institute of Planners*, 35: 216.

Atkins, H., and Milne, C. (1995). Role of Consultants in Development Projects. Development Bank of Southern Africa.

Box, R.C., Marshall, G.S., Reed, B.J., and Reed, C.M. (2001). New public management and substantive democracy. *Public Administration Review*, 61(5): 616.

Braun, G. (2003). Participation as a process: A success story of the education system in Yemen. *Development and Cooperation*, 30(5): 188.

Brown, C.J. (1995). Project scoping through public participation. *Project Pro*, 5(4): 46.

Burns, D., Hambleton, R., and Hoggett, P. (1994). *The Politics of Decentralisation: Revitalising Local Democracy*. London, MacMillan.

Chandler, R.C. (ed.) (1988). *The Public Administration Dictionary. Second Edition*. Santa Barbara, CA: ABC-Clio.

Davies, B. (1993). Empowering the poor: Capacity-building in the eastern Cape. *Indicator South Africa*, 11(1): 40–43.

Davis, G. (1997). Rethinking policy making: A new role for consultation? *Administration*, 45(3): 31.

Emmett, T. (2000). Beyond community participation? Alternative routes to civil engagement and development in South Africa. *Development Southern Africa*, 17(4).

Evans, P. (1996). Government action, social capital and development: Reviewing the evidence on synergy. *World Development*, 24(6): 1120–1124.

Ferreira, J.N. (2002). Realising effective integrated development through partnerships between local government and stakeholders. *Government Digest*.

Fredericksen, P., and London, R. (2000). Disconnect in the hollow state: The pivotal role of organizational capacity in community-based development organizations. *Public Administration Review*, 60(3): 233.

Kerzner, H. (1992). *Project Management: A Systems Approach to Planning, Scheduling and Controlling. Fourth Edition*. New York. Van Nostrand Reinhold.

King, C.S., Feltey, K.M., and Susel, B. (1998). The question of participation: Toward authentic public participation in public administration. *Public Administration Review*, 58(4): 323–325.

Matovu, G.W.M. (2002). Africa and decentralization: Enter the citizens. *Development Outreach*, 4(1): 27.

Morris, P. (1995). Democracy, governance and partnerships with institutions of civil society and the private sector. *Development Southern Africa*, 12(3): 424.

Nalbandian, J. (1999). Facilitating community, enabling democracy: New roles for local government managers. *Public Administration Review*, 59(3): 191.

Nel, H.J. (1999). A Project Management Approach to the Implementation of Development Programmes at Local Government Level. Unpublished Doctoral thesis, University of Port Elizabeth.

Oosthuizen, P. (1994). *The Silent Revolution: Project Management—How to Make Business Work*. Arcadia, ME: PM Publishers.

Republic of South Africa (1996). Constitution of the Republic of South Africa, 1996 (Act 108 of 1996). Pretoria: Government Printer.

Republic of South Africa (1998a). Local Government: Municipal Structures Act, 1998 (Act 117 of 1998). Pretoria: Government Printer.

Republic of South Africa (1998b). White Paper on Local Government, 1998 (Notice 423 of 1998). Pretoria: Government Printer.

Scruton, R. (ed.) (1982). *Dictionary of Political Thought.* London: Pan Books.

Smith, M., and Beazley, M. (2000). Progressive regimes, partnerships and the involvement of local communities: A framework for evaluation. *Public Administration: An International Quarterly,* 78(4): 858–861.

Teisman, G.R., and Klijn, E.-H. (2002). Partnership arrangements: Governmental rhetoric or governance scheme? *Public Administration Review,* 62(2): 198.

World Development Report (2000/2001). *Making State Institutions More Responsive to Poor People.* Chapter 6, Oxford University Press, World Bank, Washington, D.C., pp. 110–111.

http://www.local.gov.za/DCD/Integrated Development Planning Manual. Department of Constitutional Development, Republic of South Africa.

http://www.local.gov.za/DCD/Integrated Development Planning for Local Authorities: A User-Friendly Guide. Department of Constitutional Development, Republic of South Africa.

http://www.local.gov.za/DCD/Municipal-Community Partnerships. Department of Constitutional Development, Republic of South Africa.

Chapter 11

Sustainable Development in India

Noorjahan Bava

CONTENTS

Introduction

This study of India's march toward sustainable development (SD), including other millennium goals, is carried out at two levels—conceptual and empirical. For the purpose of the study, SD is treated as a key concept in social sciences and as a challenging process in governance everywhere. As a concept, SD signifies human endeavors for the realization of the development ideals and goals of intergenerational equity, intergenderal equity, and intranational and international equity. As a multidimensional concept, SD entails ecological, socioeconomic, and politicocultural sustainability.

As a process, SD denotes all efforts made by the people individually and collectively and by the government at various levels aimed at the fulfillment of the basic needs of life with scope for improvement in the quality of life. This process must establish and maintain synergy between development and environment; concern for conservation of natural resources and ecological balance should be integrated into developmental plans and strategies. All these theoretical issues are examined in the first part of the chapter; the following parts address, respectively, people's participation in SD and performance failures. The second section deals with some empirical findings on India's performance on the SD front, and the concluding section ends on the pessimistic note that India has to walk many miles before achieving SD.

Conceptual Framework of the Study

One of the time-honored concepts in social sciences, *development* became the focus of many theories at the hands of academics and the center of world politics, administration, diplomacy, economics, and international trade everywhere after the emergence of the Third World at the end of World War II. It became the idiom of the latter half of the 20th century.

The addition of sustainability to the notion of development has not only enriched the latter but also catapulted it into an idiom of the 21st century and one of the eight millennium goals of the world.

Since the 1970s, the issue of SD has become one of the most urgent and critical challenges facing humankind and all nations—both developed and developing. The challenge that causes grave concern to all right-thinking men and women in general and policy makers, planners, environmentalists, scholars, and the United Nations (UN) in particular is the gigantic problem of ensuring the survival of the planet Earth. Human endeavors involving mindless and reckless pursuit of creation of wealth sans concern for protection of nature have pushed the Earth to the brink of extinction. Other contributing factors to this universal dilemma are human greed; reckless adventures; war between nations for peace, power, prosperity, security; and pursuit of policies of laissez-faire, crass commercialism, colonialism, imperialism, modernism, and developmentalism by governments of Western and non-Western nations (Bahuguna, 1993; Bava, 1997, 1999; Gaan, 1993; Roy, 1993). As a result, the existence of the blue spaceship called the Earth is threatened by depletion of renewable and nonrenewable resources; destruction of the world's biosphere and biodiversity—flora, fauna, forest cover, animal species, and marine life; water, land, air, and noise pollution; and ecological degradation leading to depletion of the ozone layer, buildup of greenhouse gases, rise in sea level, global warming, climate change, desertification, droughts, and floods.

Conceptualization of SD

The concept of SD, which emerged at the Stockholm Conference in 1972, was popularized by the World Conference on Environment and Development (WCED), 1987 (also known as the Brundtland Report or *Our Common Future*), and the Rio Declaration on Environment and Development (Agenda 21). SD represents a paradigm shift from unregulated, indiscriminate, rapacious exploitation of natural resources for economic (material) development to adoption of environment-centered, ecologically sound development paths, policies, and strategies. SD denotes environment-friendly development, economic growth with social and gender justice in every state and equity, and equality among nations; among regions, groups, segments, genders, and sectors within nations; and between generations (Bava, 1984, 1993; Misra, 1993; Weidner, 1977).

Both "sustainability" and "development" are evolving and multidimensional concepts. The controversy between conservation and development that raged during the 1970s spawned the view that both were competing and contradictory concepts. Conservationists emphasized the need to conserve the natural resources in protected areas—national parks and wildlife sanctuaries from which human economic activities should be excluded. Developmentalists, particularly from Third World countries, on the other hand, maintained that they could not afford the luxury of nature conservation at the cost of human and economic development (Bava, 1997). This view was emphasized by the Indian prime minister Indira Gandhi at the UNCHE (1972), when she said that "poverty is the biggest polluter" of environment in developing countries.

The 1980s witnessed a major change in attitudes as both sides admitted that environment and development are *synergic in nature* and therefore are not contradictory but complementary to one another. The view that conservation is required for SD and vice versa came to be universally accepted. It means for achievement of the goal of SD and optimal use of natural resources, environment concerns, challenges, and constraints are required to be integrated in planning, designing, and implementing development projects at all levels. The envisaged benefits, goals, and objectives from development activities can be fully realized only if they are environmentally sustainable, socially sound, gender equitable, and designed and executed with wholehearted participation of the public. By *public* we mean the target public, the general public, citizen groups, civil society bodies, and nongovernmental organizations as well as the industries, the market, and the media. If environment concerns and challenges are to become integral parts of the development process, it is necessary to use an integrated, holistic systems approach and a decentralized, democratic, people's participation orientation to SD plans, policies, and programs (Bava, 1984).

SD stands for *simultaneous* protection of natural environment and promotion of human welfare and well-being. SD is the process of planning and implementation of ecologically sustainable economic development policies that facilitate meeting the basic needs of all the people of the present and future generations and provides opportunities to all to satisfy their aspiration for better quality of life and for release of their creative potentialities (Dhanagare, 1992; Misra, 1993).

In other words, while planning for SD, planners and policy makers must ensure "macrocoherency" to prevent ecological degradation and decay and "microcoherency" so that rights, needs, and interests of local people in general and the more marginal groups in particular are protected (Utting, 1994). From this perspective, the tendency of some economists to treat environment as an "externality" to the production process and therefore difficult to quantify in terms of national economic accounting cannot be justified. It is imperative that environment impact assessment (EIA) of development projects be taken as seriously as a production target. From a systems point of view, "sustainable" development implies that it is necessary to recognize the interface between the ecosystem and the sociocultural and politicoeconomic system, which will vary from society to society, and from nation to nation at all levels.

SD is a dynamic process of meeting the basic needs of all people with scope for improving the quality of life of human beings within and between nations (*intranational and international equality*) in ways that sustain and protect the natural environment—the biosphere and biodiversity. Specifically, SD should mean (1) the sustainability of the biophysical–chemical environment; (2) sustainability of human development, the latter sustaining the former; and (3) the sociocultural and politicoeconomic sustainability (Fuwa, 1995). Similar notions of SD are echoed in the definition of SD as development that meets the needs of the present without compromising the ability of future generations to meet their own needs (WCED, 1987). For the International Union for Conservation of Nature (IUCN, 1991), SD is improving the quality of human life within the carrying capacity of supporting ecosystems. SD is economic growth that provides fairness and opportunity for all the world's people, not just the privileged few, without further destroying the world's finite natural resources and carrying capacity (Pronk and Haq, 1992).

There is a general consensus that SD is not a static concept but a dynamic process to be carried on by all the people of a society engaged in developmental tasks in tune with their genius, sociocultural values, and perspectives at all levels. SD also demands that in every modern nation, the state, citizens, civil society groups, industry, market, and government and nongovernmental organizations and international agencies engaged in developmental activities at local, subregional, regional, national, and global levels ensure that the basic needs of all people are met. While basic needs for some include food, clean water and air, clothing, shelter, health, education, and employment, for others they also include opportunities to improve the standard of life and release of the creative potentialities of people. However, this endeavor should be carried out within the limits set by *the carrying capacity and self-supporting, fragile ecosystems so that SD is possible for the present and future generations—for all the peoples of the world.*

Dimensions of SD

The burgeoning literature on SD reveals that members of different academic disciplines tend to emphasize their respective disciplinary thrust when conceptualizing the key concept. For instance, economists emphasize the maintenance and improvement of the living standard of people. Environmentalists, ecologists, and scientists express concerns about preserving the adaptability and functions of the entire ecological and biophysical systems. Geographers and anthropologists focus on the viability of social and cultural systems. And political scientists urge the need to establish a political order based on the foundation of democracy, equality, liberty, justice, fraternity, rule of law, nonviolence, and human rights at all levels.

But the fact remains that in any discussion of environmental sustainability social, political, economic, and cultural issues come into play in a number of ways (Lele, 1995). Similarly, Holling (1995) warns that the biophysical dimensions of SD cannot be separated neatly from the economic and social dimensions. Any attempt to ignore the interlinkages among these factors is bound to encourage piecemeal strategies of investments that would fail to improve the status of people. While partial policies fail, integrated and holistic policies may have a chance to succeed. However, it is necessary to separate and examine each aspect for purely analytical purposes and for better grasp of the problems involved in each of them. Far more than environment-friendly technology, SD involves paradigm change: changes in lifestyles and attitudes toward nature and style of development. It calls for political, social, economic, cultural, and ethical changes, and the concept needs to be looked at from diverse perspectives (Bava, 1997).

Environmental and Ecological Sustainability

Natural scientists say that all ecosystems are characterized by five features: *integrity, complexity, stability, diversity,* and *resilience.* If any of them is weakened or jeopardized, the system collapses. The ecosystem is integrated; all its constituent elements are so interdependent that destruction of any one harms the whole system. Land, soil, water, air, vegetation, temperature, pressure, and all plant and animal species (flora and fauna), including microorganisms, constitute one integrated whole.

The integrity of the ecosystem depends on its *carrying capacity, assimilative capacity,* and *renewability.* The carrying capacity is the ability of an ecosystem to feed a certain population of humans and animals. Use of any resource beyond its carrying capacity will threaten its stability. Technology cannot always be of help. In the case of land, for instance, economists have worked out the carrying capacity in terms of net primary productivity (NPP). The NPP of land is fast declining because of deforestation and overgrazing.

The assimilative capacity of an ecosystem is directly linked to its carrying capacity. All systems, including the ecosystem, have a metabolic process to remove waste. Although a certain amount of waste discharged in soil, air, or water will be purified by the natural process, problems like ecological degradation and decay can arise, disrupting the integrity of the ecosystem, if wastes such as industrial effluents (mercury, acids, atomic wastes) and nonbiodegradable wastes (plastic) accumulate beyond the metabolic capacity of the system to assimilate. The wastes have to be treated before they are released, or their quality and quantity have to be controlled.

The recharging capacity of the ecosystem is another characteristic very closely dependent on the assimilative capacity of the system. All renewable resources need time to recoup and regenerate. If the assimilative capacity is damaged, renewability of the system will be adversely affected (Bava, 1997; Misra, 1993).

The third dimension of natural environment is biodiversity. Conservation of biodiversity is the foundation of SD. Biodiversity consists of three components (1) *genetic diversity*, (2) *species diversity*, and (3) *ecosystem diversity* (Misra, 1993). *Genetic diversity* refers to the sum total of chromosomal information carried by individual plants and animals. It is true that if the practice of monoculture (growing only a particular variety of crop or plant) is followed for long, the gene bank of the crop (variety and diversity) maintained by nature will be lost to humanity forever. This applies to all vegetation and animals. Likewise, if virgin forests are destroyed, human beings will never know how many varieties of plants and animals are lost forever.

A heavy responsibility, therefore, falls on humanity to ensure environmental *stewardship*: protection of the natural environment. Human beings must be concerned about conservation of biodiversity because all of the plant and animal species are *interdependent* and constitute a gene pool of great importance. In order to conserve biodiversity, the natural ecosystems and whatever is left of the modified ecosystems must be protected. Biodiversity entails *biosphere reserves*, which are areas of terrestrial and coastal ecosystems. These reserves are rich in biodiversity and cultural heritage and encompass unique ecosystems, which are representative of major biogeographic zones of the world.

Man-made ecosystems (forests, parks and sanctuaries, and wildlife reserves) should be planned now so that nature can regenerate in its normal course. Diverting forestland for agricultural purposes is considered to be unsound practice from the perspective of biodiversity, on which depends the continued productivity of agriculture and forestry. The issue of environmental sustainability also involves the question of *sustainable use of both renewable and nonrenewable resources*. Sustainability does not necessarily imply maintaining some static state, but rather maintaining the resilience and capacity of the ecosystems to adapt to change.

The general state of the physical environment is to a large extent determined by living organisms. For instance, the presence of free oxygen in the environment is the result of biological photosynthesis, and living organisms play a major role in the biochemical cycles of such elements as sulfur, calcium, nitrogen, and phosphorus. Limits on the sustainable use of physical processes in the environment are related to both additions and subtractions of materials. The most important mechanism by which materials are removed from the environment is the alteration of ecosystems: deforestation, drainage of wetlands, and the conversion of grasslands into degraded pastures. These activities decrease the size of the original habitat, altering the ratio between the habitat's edge and its interior, thereby resulting in higher rates of species extinction. Such activities also increase the distances between patches of habitat, thereby lowering recolonization rates of species (Bava, 1997).

Sociocultural Sustainability

Humans are an integral part of the natural environment; human *population* constitutes the fourth aspect of ecological sustainability. Here lies one of the major challenges before planners and policy makers, particularly in developing countries. The crux of the problem lies in the fact that both population and the carrying and assimilative capacities of the ecosystem depend on the *man–land ratio*. If human population increases without a corresponding increase in natural resources, the carrying capacity of the ecosystem, that is, the quality and the quantity of natural resources, will be reduced. The problem becomes more acute in predominantly agrarian countries such as India, where more people depend on agriculture for their livelihood. Unless the growth rate in population is arrested so as to keep pace with the rate of economic growth, it is bound to affect the fragile ecosystem adversely and result in ecological crisis as predicted by Malthus.

An important aspect of social sustainability is cognizance of the close relationship between poverty and environmental degradation. The poor and women among the poor suffer the consequences of environmental degradation most because they are the most vulnerable and least able to avoid or mitigate the consequences. The ratio of per capita income is 150:1 between the top and bottom 20th percentiles of the world population.

Basically, the greatest proportion of the poor live in *rural* areas. This is true not only of the world as a whole but also of all developing countries. According to the World Resources Institute, the rural poor constitute 69% in Sub-Saharan Africa, 74% in Southern Asia, and 60% in Latin America. It has been found that rural areas woefully lack necessary conditions for human development—facilities, amenities, and essential infrastructure for sustenance of a decent standard of life—that exist in urban areas. Unemployment, illiteracy, low productivity of land and labor, unequal ownership of land and other assets, coupled with poor socio-economic status, rain-fed agriculture, and lack of effective administration also contribute to poverty in rural areas. According to the 1992 World

Bank Report, soil degradation and desertification increasingly affect the rural poor. Increasing dependence of the rural and tribal poor on meager land and forest for fuel, food, fodder, and medicines further aggravates the problem.

Migration of rural people to urban areas does not solve problems. On the contrary, it results in growth of slums, unregulated colonies, increasing pressure on existing civic amenities, crime, and law and order problems. These problems result in environmental degradation and pollution in towns and cities. The 1992 World Bank Report indicates that 1.7 billion people go without sanitation facilities; 1.2 billion people live in urban areas in developing societies who do not meet World Health Organization (WHO) standards on dust and smoke. The use of firewood, charcoal, and dung—the primary source of fuel in these societies—endangers the health of 400 million to 700 million people, especially women and children. Automobile emissions also leads to air pollution and respiratory problems in children and adults alike.

The fact is that in most developing nations, it is not merely the quality of life but life itself that is at great risk because of environmental degradation caused by poverty. Developing countries are faced with poverty caused by their colonial past, population explosion, lack of resources for meeting the basic needs of life, and unjust and exploitative policies pursued by industrialized countries in economic and trade-related matters with these nations through the World Bank, International Monetary Fund (IMF), and World Trade Organization (WTO). In addition, the wasteful and unsustainable lifestyles of people in developed countries have been contributing to ecological degradation throughout the world.

Socially SD thus calls for (1) eradication of poverty, hunger, diseases, malnutrition, unemployment, and illiteracy of three fourths of the world's population, who live in developing nations; (2) ending of inequality between men and women within every nation and inequality between nations; (3) equitable sharing of the world's resources between rich and poor nations; (4) and pursuit of such policies by governments at local, national, regional, and international levels to ensure protection of cultural, social, and biological diversity. Monoculturism in human, plant, or animal species is a known threat to their survival; as such, it must be eschewed at all costs (Bahuguna, 1993). The World Bank, which has now launched the Bio-Diversity Action Plan, has, for the past 40 years, been financing the destruction of genetic diversity in the Third World. It has financed the Green Revolution, which replaced genetically diverse indigenous cropping systems in the Third World with vulnerable genetically uniform monocultures. In fact, the continued spread of genetic uniformity is perversely viewed as a means for "biodiversity conservation" in the program of the World Bank (Vandana Shiva, 1988, 1991).

Economic Sustainability

Man must stop ravaging the Earth in the name of economic development. Mahatma Mohandas Gandhi observed, "There is enough for the people of the world to meet their need but not their greed." Man has become so acquisitive that there has developed a dichotomy between the planet Earth and the human freedom to ravage it. A contradiction between anthropocentric and cosmocentric views of the universe seems to constitute the substructure of the present-day concept of economic development (Gaan, 1993).

Economic sustainability calls for greater use of renewable energy than nonrenewable energy sources such as fossil fuels—oil and natural gas, coal, and atomic energy. It also demands effective changes in lifestyles of people and practices and policies of governments of industrialized nations. A study estimated that the production of the chemical used in the refrigeration industry, chloroflourocarbons (CFCs), was 1.2 million tons in 1991. Out of this, the richest country in the world, the United States, with a population one fourth that of India, alone produced 300,000 tons, which was 50 times India's emission level of 6,000 tons, a bare 0.6% of the global emissions. The Montreal Protocol, which made a clarion call for reduction of CFCs by all countries, puts developing nations like India in a big dilemma, for these countries cannot meet the tall commands of the protocol without the transfer of the right technology and funds for meeting the incremental costs for switching over to the new technology. In the case of India, for instance, the required fund amount was a whooping Rs.15 billion at 1989 prices. This is why the protocol was changed in favor of the developing nations at the London meeting. As the European Community representative stated before the UN General Assembly: "Industrialized countries need to assist developing countries in their environment related efforts, *inter alia* by the provision of additional financial resources and also by facilitating access to and transfer of, environmentally sound technologies on a *fair and most favorable basis* [emphasis added]."

Economically, SD thus demands both attitudinal and policy changes of developed countries and cooperation with the developing nations. The nations in the South need the technologies of the Western countries so that they can profit more directly from their own resources, diversify production, and reduce environmental pollution. This calls for modifications in the intellectual property rights regime; indigenous capacity building, through access to relevant scientific and technical information training; and development of existing technologies (Bava, 1997).

Political Sustainability

Environmentally synergic economic development hinges on the effective performance of the role and functions of political institutions, which include state, government, administration, and bureaucracy, as well as people and civil society bodies. They must work toward the establishment and maintenance of a *democratic polity,* which rests on the foundation of liberty, equality, cultural diversity (pluralism), justice, fraternity, rule of law, human rights, and citizen participation in the process of governance and development at all levels.

Politically, SD signifies respect for and adherence to the principle of equality and justice governing the relations between men and women; among different groups, segments, and regions; among various sectors of the economy within a nation; and between rich and poor nations of the world. It calls for a new international world order in which the prevailing North–South divide in matters of international trade and aid, transfer of technology, and information and resource sharing gives way to a more equitable and humane world order. The developing nations are understandably concerned that their socioeconomic development can be constrained by the policies of the governments and lifestyles of people in the North. The latter are concerned with biodiversity conservation, particularly *in situ* conservation, which demands the setting aside of protected areas to ensure a continued supply of components of biodiversity—actual and potential raw materials for plant breeding, for new medicines, and for the wider biotech industry (the North's commercialized conservation). The nations in the South do not want to forgo their development or that of their people by acceding to the demands of the North. Further, experience reveals that those who benefited most from the utilization of biodiversity were not the owners or the "curators" of this biodiversity but those who possess the technology and have access to the markets to profit from it: the industrialized countries and their multinational corporations. Justice lies in giving protection and remuneration to the providers of the genetic resources, the farmers and other local people, who, through their pursuit of agriculture, forestry, and other production systems have been the curators of such biodiversity for centuries.

As Vandana Shiva (1991) asserts, the Third World people and forest dwellers participate in the ecological processes of reproduction of biodiversity. They are in fact participating in the biological renewal of life; through their cultures and lifestyles they simultaneously achieve "production" and "conservation," categories that in industrial civilization are "separate and opposed." These dualistic and separated categories, she observes, underlie the approach of *Conserving the World's Biological Diversity* (World Bank Report, 1992). The major shortcoming of such an approach gives rise to the view that the problem is that of the South and the solution is that of the North. She further observes that unless this polarity and dualism are removed, the conservers of the world's biological diversity will be treated as those who threaten it and the predatory systems that "consume" biodiversity as raw material to the point that extinction will be perceived as essential to programs of conservation. "This logic should be turned upside down and inside out" (Shiva, 1991).

People's Participation in SD

Aristotle defined *citizenship* as participation of the citizens in the management of public affairs, particularly in the administration of justice and holding of offices. People's participation in public life is the cornerstone of both democracy and decentralized development. Electoral participation of citizens to form or change a government or their role as people's representatives, as legislators, and as members of the ruling party or the opposition or as makers of public policy constitutes only limited participation in representative democracies. Genuine participation of all citizens in the process of governance at all levels and their continuous interest in and enthusiasm for matters of public interest on a day-to-day basis are the requisites of a vibrant, participatory democracy.

In democracies, the people, the citizens, have to be *the subject and object of development programs*. In the context of SD, people's participation signifies the involvement of the public—the targeted group as well as the general public—in the various interfaces of the decision-making process. These include the stages of forecasting, planning, formulation, implementation, monitoring, and evaluation of development policies, plans, programs, and projects. Wholehearted and total involvement of the public in the decision-making process is the sine qua non of successful administration of SD (Bava, 1984, 1993).

Democracies are eminently suited to promote SD because of the freedoms, rights, openness, access to information, and infinite opportunities for citizen participation in sustainable development activities both individually and collectively through civil society, nongovernmental organizations (NGOs), social and environment groups, and activists (Payne, 1995). The goal of SD requires the total involvement of people, government, industry, market, media, private and public agencies, women's groups, and conservation activists.

A decentralized, participatory approach to conservation and environmental stewardship is also an essential requirement to provide dynamic support to local communities to maintain bio-diversity, cultural diversity, and equitable development. Local communities everywhere must be allowed to play a major role in managing and benefiting from the natural resources on which their livelihood and culture depend (Schmandt, 1994). SD projects will only work if local residents, through education and participation, accept the need for change and perceive that their own interests will be served by such participation. This will only happen if they become full partners and stakeholders in the process of finding and implementing new solutions.

As India's experience with the centrally sponsored scheme of community development in the 1950s demonstrated, projects proposed by outside experts will not attract the cooperation and trust of local people, on which working solutions depend. This is because outsiders, including local government officials, tend to operate from a distance and are often ignorant of the concerns and priorities of the local people.

Effective public participation is critical to development and conservation efforts in every state. Inclusion of citizens' voices in decision making promotes governmental accountability and increases the likelihood that decisions will be based on the felt needs of the people who are directly affected by them. Promoting people's participation is, in effect, promoting the democratic process—fostering transparency, utilizing a wide base of opinions to strengthen decisions reached, and ensuring public support for them. Further, it can help overcome deficiencies associated with governments.

In addition, local citizens' intimate knowledge of environmental threats and violations of law can help broaden government's considerations and heighten awareness. By investing their time, energy, and resources, local citizens can supplement government's efforts to monitor and enforce environmental laws. However, people's participation requires the recognition of their environmental rights, clear environmental standards, access to information, genuine opportunities for participation, and an independent and well-informed judiciary to enforce their rights (www/world bank.org/html. Indiaprogram).

As Misra (1993) succinctly puts it:

> Sustainable development is not the business of the government and private companies alone. It is the business of the people in general. It is a process which has to be initiated at each level of human endeavor and life. It involves individuals, families, communities, corporate bodies, nations and the global society. It has to be a movement. It calls for *mass participation of people* because it involves paradigmatic change which is difficult to bring about unless great many people get involved [emphasis added].

SD in India: Empirical Findings

Foundation of India's SD Policies and Administration

SD in India rests on four pillars, the foremost among them being the Republican constitution of India. It provides for a parliamentary democracy, with fundamental human rights for all the citizens to realize their cherished values of liberty, equality, and fraternity. The exercise of these rights has to be consistent with the territorial integrity and sovereignty of the nation. It also provides for the rule of law and an independent judiciary to protect the constitution and the rights of the citizens. Second, as a developing nation, India believes in the sovereign right to equality among nations and the right to development for her people and the country as a whole. Third, India is a member of the UN and signatory to international laws, conventions, treaties, agreements, and Declarations on Human Rights, Conservation of Biosphere and Biodiversity, Sustainable Development, and so on. India is committed to all its international responsibilities, including promotion of understanding, peace, security, and cooperation among nations. Fourth, for the people and government in India, the concept of SD translates into *synergy between environment and development for the realization of intra- and intergenerational equity, intergenderal equity, and international and intranational equity.* In India, the world's largest functional democracy, the formulation, implementation, and evaluation of SD policies is the joint responsibility of the government, its citizens, people, industry, market, civil society and community organizations, and the media at all levels.

In its report *Our Common Future,* the WCED (1987) identified eight key issues of SD: (1) population and human resources, (2) industry, (3) food security, (4) species and ecosystems, (5) urban challenges, (6) managing of the commons, (7) energy, and (8) conflict and environmental degradation. Although there are very close interlinkages among these aspects, this chapter confines itself to India's performance in protection of environmental and ecological sustainability in the country since 1950, when the constitution was promulgated.

In India, the credit goes to all the three branches of government—the executive, legislature, and judiciary at central and state levels—as well as NGOs and social and environmental activists for developing, enforcing, monitoring, and evaluating the field of environment law (EL). The role of administration in environmental management is very critical.

Causes of Environmental Degradation in India

Because India is a developing nation, the political leaders, planners, and policy makers, led by Prime Minister Nehru, gave the highest priority to an *anthropocentric* approach to national development. They had to redeem the promises made to the people during the freedom movement to provide a life of dignity and honor each citizen of Free India. Toward this end, they adopted a constitution that guaranteed each citizen the cherished values of human rights, consisting of freedom, equality, fraternity, and individual dignity, and conscientiously chose a *democratic paradigm of governance and development.* India followed the path of planned economic development with social justice. Many 5-year plans were launched after 1950 to uplift the teeming millions from poverty, unemployment, disease, illiteracy, and ignorance (Bava, 1984). Development of agriculture, industry, and infrastructure received the highest priority in the national agenda for progress, prosperity, and peace.

Industrial Policy Resolutions adopted by the government of India, the first in 1947 and the second in 1956, led to a large-scale industrialization and multipurpose river valley projects in the country. The Green Revolution, in the mid-1960s, no doubt increased agricultural productivity manifold, but it also led to large-scale use of chemical fertilizers, pesticides, and insecticides and intensive use of irrigation water for double and multiple cropping in some areas. All these factors, coupled with urbanization, commercialization, mining, and construction of megadams and reservoirs, ushered in an era of increasing pollution, dwindling forest resources, deforestation, and rehabilitation of people uprooted from the dam sites.

In addition, India's environmental problems also result from the use of poor-quality coal as an energy source. Approximately 70% of coal contributes to considerable environmental degradation. The thermal power stations, industries, factories, and harmful automobile emissions from vehicles and the use of noncommercial sources of fuel from coal briquettes, paddy husk briquettes, animal dung, and trash as sources of energy contribute to serious air pollution. Water pollution is due to improper disposal of waste in rivers, streams, and coastal areas. Massive growth of population in postindependence India with attendant poverty, growing unemployment and underemployment, malnutrition, ill health and illiteracy greatly contributed to environmental degradation in the country.

International Cooperation for SD in India

The Ministry of Environment and Forest (MOEF), Government of India, also serves as the nodal agency in the country for promoting international cooperation in the sphere of SD by implementing the United Nations Environment Programme (UNEP), South Asia Co-operative Environment Programme (SACEP), and International Centre for Integrated Mountain Development (ICIMOD) and for following up on the United Nations

Conference on Environment and Development (UNCED). It is also entrusted with the issues relating to multilateral bodies such as the Commission on Sustainable Development (CSD) and Global Environment Facility (GEF) and of regional bodies such as the Economic and Social Council for Asia and Pacific (ESCAP) and South Asian Association for Regional Co-operation (SAARC) on matters pertaining to environment.

The World Summit on Sustainable Development (WSSD), held from August 26 to September 4, 2002, at Johannesburg, South Africa, reviewed and appraised the progress toward sustainable development and the commitments made 10 years earlier at Rio and forged a cohesive set of global partnerships to achieve comprehensive implementation of Agenda 21. In this context, the following documents were produced by the ministry: (1) Agenda 21—An Assessment; (2) Empowering People for Sustainable Development; (3) Toward Sustainability—Learning from the Past, Innovating for the Future; and (4) Sustainable Development—Learning and Perspective from India. An Indian delegation led by the minister of environment and forests attended the summit and adopted the Plan of Implementation and Johannesburg Declaration.

India also participated in the 22nd Session of Governing Council/Global Ministerial Environment Forum (GMEF) of UNEP held February 3 to 7, 2003, at Nairobi, Kenya, which addressed the state of the environment and contribution of UNEP to various environmental challenges. The follow-up actions arising from WSSD, in the field of international environmental governance, and linkages among and support of environment-related conventions were also discussed.

The Environment Ministry's Global Environment Cell (GEC) with United Nations Development Program (UNDP) assistance continued to provide technical and scientific inputs in the process of project formulation including those for Global Environment Facility (GEF) assistance. Twelve projects are under implementation, of which one has been completed. Under the India Canada Environment Facility (ICEF), 21 projects have been approved so far with a total outlay of Rs.1.625 billion.

A new plan has been incorporated in the tenth 5-year plan for preparation of State of Environment (SOE) reports. The objective behind this scheme is to highlight the upstream and downstream linkages with environmental issues besides creating a baseline document.

India ratified the Kyoto Protocol, which was adopted in 1997 committing the developed countries to reduce their emissions of greenhouse gases by an average of 5.2 percent during 2008–2012 with reference to 1990 level of emissions.

India hosted the Eighth Conference of the Parties to the United Nations Framework Convention on Climate Change from October 23 to November 1, 2002, at New Delhi. Over 4,300 delegates from all over the world attended the conference, making it one of the biggest international events of its kind ever held in the country. The minister of environment and forests was elected the president of the Conference of the Parties on October 23, and he led the negotiations at the conference, which successfully completed negotiations in several critical areas. Parties agreed on the rules and procedures for the Executive Board of the Clean Development Mechanism under Kyoto Protocol, as well as simplified procedures for small-scale projects. The conference concluded guidelines for reporting and review under Kyoto Protocol after 3 years of intense negotiations. It adopted the New Delhi Work Programme, relating to education, training, and public awareness, for 5 years, and set a time frame for operationalization of the Special Climate Change Fund by 2003 at the next Conference of the Parties the following year. Most important, the conference adopted the Delhi Ministerial Declaration, which firmly establishes the link between climate change and sustainable development and brings out the importance of adaptation. The high point of the conference was the speech of Prime Minister Attal Behari Vajpai, in which he outlined the basic tenets of the Indian perspective on the ongoing climate change negotiations.

During 2000 and 2001, six projects in the renewable energy sector were endorsed by India for implementation as Clean Development Mechanism Projects under the Kyoto Protocol. Implementation of these projects would help in attracting foreign investments in such projects in the country as well in accessing more efficient technologies.

India fervently observes World Environment Day on June 5 every year and the International Day for the Protection of the Ozone Layer on September 16. A set of newly designed posters, special covers, and stickers and the fifth edition of the book *The Montreal Protocol, India's Success Story* were released on the occasion. An exhibition of ozone-friendly products developed by industry with assistance from the Montreal Protocol Multilateral Fund was also organized. One of the companies exhibited refrigerators that operate very efficiently with hydrocarbon as a refrigerant.

During the year 2000–2001, seven investment projects for Foam, Commercial Refrigeration, and Aerosol and three noninvestment projects at a cost of US\$13,866,127 were approved by the executive committee of the Montreal Protocol Multilateral Fund. Four producers of CFCs—SRF Limited, Gujarat Fluorochemicals Limited, Navin Fluorine Industries, and Chemplast Sanmar Limited—signed a pledge reiterating their commitment to the Montreal Protocol on Phasing Out Ozone Depleting Substances on May 2, 2002.

Under the World Bank–assisted Environment Management Capacity Building (EMCB) Project, the EIA subcomponent, the mining subcomponent, the ambient air quality monitoring subcomponent, the development of standards subcomponent, the environment law component, and the environmental research subcomponent were continued during the year. An environmental information service (ENVIS) subcomponent was also implemented to broaden the ambit of ENVIS by including various subject areas, themes, local conditions, and issues and to establish a nationwide network for environmental information.

During 2000 and 2001, under World Bank assistance Delhi Urban Environment and Infrastructure Improvement Project was launched jointly by the Ministry of Environment and Forest and the Delhi government with Japanese assistance. The UNDP-assisted Global Environment Cell in the MOEF provides scientific and technical inputs to project formulation including those of the GEF, and so far 13 projects of GEF–Small Grants Programmes have been funded.

India was represented at the various meetings of the United Nations Framework Convention on Climate Change by the officials of the Ministries of Environment and External Affairs June 12 to 15, 2000, in Bonn, Germany, and September 11 to 15, 2000, in Lyon, France. An Indian delegation led by the minister of power also attended the Sixth Conference of Parties to the Framework Convention on Climate Change November 13 to 25, 2000.

The minister of environment and forest attended the First Global Ministerial Environment Forum of the UNEP in New York from April 24 to May 5, 2000, as well as the ESCAP Ministerial Conference on Environment and Development, September 4 and 5, 2000, in Japan.

People's Participation in SD through Local Self-Government and Decentralized Development

Mahatma Mohandas Gandhi, the father of the nation, said, "Real India lives in the villages." He, therefore, gave the pride of place to rural development and advocated a decentralized, democratic model of development in which every village would be the unit of planning to reach the goal of self-sufficiency. He emphasized full and active participation of all the adult villagers in the *gram sabha* (village assembly) and *panchayat* (village council) in making decisions affecting their life. The Seventy-Third Amendment of the Constitution of India (1993) has rejuvenated the three-tier *Panchayat Raj* (village democracy) system with gram sabhas and panchayats at the village level, and block and district panchayats at the intermediate and apex levels as units of local self-government and catalysts of rural development (Bava, 1997, 2004).

All states (save a few) of the Indian federation have a constitutional body called panchayats to channel participation of the rural citizens in self-governance (grassroots democracy) and decentralized rural development.

With a view to strengthen the Panchayati Raj, the state legislatures have devolved powers, functions, and finances to the panchayats at village, block, and district levels. The District Planning Committee is required to make and execute integrated plans for development in both rural and urban areas with social justice and with full participation of the panchayat members. Panchayati Raj is a great success in West Bengal and Kerala, where political, economic, and financial powers have been devolved on the panchayats by the state governments, whereas in other states not only is devolution of power to the local government bodies inadequate, but also there is lack of political will at the state level to part with power (Bava, 2004).

People's Participation through NGOs and Civil Society

Since India's seventh five-year plan, it has been the policy of the government—both central and state—to involve NGOs in the process of *decentralized development in a phased manner* (Bava, 2003). A large number of NGOs, citizen groups, civil society bodies, and individuals participate in the process of development planning and administration.

A number of successful instances of people's participation and involvement through local government bodies, NGOs, and individual citizens in SD in general and environmental protection in particular have come to light in many states (Chaube and Chakrabarty, 1999). "There are numerous instances of village regeneration through peoples' participation" (Agarwal, Narain, and Sen, 1999).

Sukhomajri Village in Haryana

One outstanding example of community land management working wonders is that of Sukhomajri, a dry village on the foothills of the Shivaliks in Haryana. The villagers took it on themselves to rejuvenate the land through the "cyclical mode of development" under the inspiration of a soil scientist, P. R. Mishra. This model of people's participation is based on the philosophy that "if villagers reinvest their savings from regenerated land for further ecological improvement, it will result in a cyclical growth." Thanks to the phenomenal success of this experiment in participatory community land regeneration and development, there are concrete, visible signs of green fields with dancing crops. Irrigation waters flowing from the dams through canals have brought smiles to the face of the villagers of Sukhomajri because they have banished poverty and malnutrition.

Many factors are responsible for the success of Sukhomajri. These include: willing, continuous, and wholehearted participation of the village people; Haryana Government's Forest Department allowing the villagers to manage the watershed, and distributing high-yielding seeds and fertilizers; good relationship between the government and the local people; villagers' ready implementation of the decisions to protect the hills from grazing through self-restraint, and protecting the trees and grass with zeal. In addition, institutional support was given by three different bodies—the Central Soil and Water Conservation Research and Training Institute (CSWCRTI), Haryana Forest Department, and the Ford Foundation, who teamed up to assist the Sukhomajri villagers develop their own institutions for watershed protection and equitable water distribution from earthen dams. Sukhomajri's success has spread to six more villages—three in Haryana (Nada, Logarh, Bunga) and three in Punjab (Relmajara, Nada, and Gochar) and to Bihar as well.

Jhabua, Madhya Pradesh

The participatory community land management approach has also transformed Jhabua, a poor tribal district of Madhya Pradesh, into a sea of greenery and prosperity. "This is an outstanding example, as it represents the effort of a State Government to involve the people in the management of their land and water resources on a very big scale, with excellent results. Unlike Sukhomajri, where bureaucratic interference soon started having negative effects, in Jhabua, the people are involved in the concept, planning, implementation, and management of land and watershed activities. There is good coordination among the district officials and the villagers (Agarwal, Narain, and Sen, 1999). True, greed for power and money, alcoholism, and other social vices hamper common welfare. Fortunately, Sukhomajri and Jhabua have shown that it is not impossible to do away with these evils and create ideal villages, if villagers are made the "focus" of their development work.

The two experiments in participatory development have one big difference: In Haryana, "the politicians were not interested in the Sukhomajri experiment as it was a case of people bypassing them and taking care of their own development" (Agarwal, Narain, and Sen, 1999). At the beginning, some local leaders did not like the idea of officials going directly to the people. This was the reason behind transferring a former chief conservator of forest, Gurunam Singh, in 1975. Further, the political patronage for joint forest management was not high in Haryana. That is why it does not feature in the government's agenda. Now things have improved. "When politicians know of the project and its impact, they show interest," says S. K. Singh, chief conservator of forest, Haryana. But in the case of Jhabua, the secret of success lies in *the political will* shown by the then Madhya Pradesh chief minister, Dig Vijay Singh, who believes that *people should be directly involved in solving their own problems.*

In 1985, Jhabua was just a poor tribal district. Thirteen years later, the land was being nursed back to life with great care. Trees are beginning to grow and there is grass all around. Dug wells are overflowing with water in a place that was chronically drought prone in the 1980s. It is the result of political will, combined with bureaucratic competence and commitment and people's participation (Agarwal, Narain, and Sen, 1999).

Some of the other outstanding instances of successful participation of large groups of people in environment protection movements are the Chipko Movement, led by Sundarlal Bahuguna in Uttar Pradesh, and the Appiko Movement (literally meaning "embrace the trees"), led by the Samaj Privartana Samudaya (Society for Social Change) in Karnataka. The regeneration of dry villages through construction of earthern dams, check dams, and water storage tanks for rainwater, harvesting and raising of crops like cashew nuts, through people's participation in the form of *shramdhan* (free labor) as in the village Raeligaon Siddhi in Maharashtra, Alwar district, in Rajasthan and in Tamil Nadu, are only a few other instances (IJPA, No. 3, 1989).

Bihar

An excellent example of citizen participation and involvement in the area of environmental protection is that of an Indian college teacher turned environmental activist in the State of Bihar popularly known as Guddu Baba (real name is Vikas Chandra)—the "high priest of the Ganga." In three years since 1996, this man's crusade has reaped rich dividends. He brought the plight of the river Ganga (Ganges) to the notice of the Patna High Court and, since then, with the help of the judiciary, has helped stem the pollution of the river. His achievements include getting three defunct water treatment plants running in the state capital, Patna; stopping dead bodies from being dumped into the river by Patna Medical College Hospital (PMCH) by people who believe in water burial and by the very poor, who cannot afford the cost of cremation; and getting two of the defunct crematoriums functioning. Guddu Baba has also succeeded in getting the patient's meal allowance raised from Rs.3 daily to Rs.25 in PMCH through a court order. He also succeeded in his efforts to cremate the dead with dignity by ensuring that an incinerator was installed, instead of the PMCH's throwing the corpses into the river. He organized a human chain of 100 people to create awareness in the people and local authorities of the need to keep the Ganga clean. As recognition of his yeoman service, the Environment Department of Delhi University has invited Guddu Baba to create awareness among the students.

Delhi

In Delhi, the Aravali Ridge is the only natural barrier between the desert of Rajasthan and Delhi. Thanks to the 30 check dams built by the Forest Department and people, Aravali's desert vegetation has disappeared and verdant patches of broadleafed trees have started growing again. These are indigenous species like *Anogysis pendula,* which have reappeared in the Asola forest area. "The Aravali species are fast reappearing, replacing the desert species that is over-running the forests here," says Deputy Conservator of Forests (South) R. S. Prashant.

According to an NGO, Sristi, "Regular recharge of ground water can be ensured by a better undergrowth and tree cover by retaining the Ridge as a natural forest and not as a park. According to a wild life department official, the replacement of the narrow-leafed desert vegetation with the broad-leafed trees helps in many ways. Because the bigger leaves are better carbon sinkers, they can absorb more pollution and release oxygen. It will also add to the green cover of the city and lead to a rise in the water table. It will also help prevent soil erosion by having a firmer grip on the topsoil. The Asola experiment, therefore, needs to be replicated in other parts of the Ridge."

According to a study by Saurabh Sinha of the Centre for Science and Environment, who carried out an impact assessment on rainwater harvesting in certain parts of the city: "In Jamia Hamdard University, the pre-monsoon level was 45 meters below ground level (mbgl). The post monsoon level was 38 mgbl. In Janaki Devi College, the water table had risen from 35.8 to 22.1 mbgl. The quality of the water too has improved. There are other benefits also—now there is no water logging and the cost of running tube wells has come down since with each meter's fall in the water table, an additional 0.4 kilo watt of energy is required to pump out the same amount of water (TOI, Jan. 29, 2003). It is also heartening to note that the Delhi Metro Rail Project is now ISO 14001, certified as eco-friendly metro rail. This makes it the first mass rapid transport system in the world to get this certification in the construction stage."

The government of India has taken many measures toward conservation of natural resources, including forestry and wildlife, biodiversity, and biosphere conservation; environmental impact assessments; prevention and control of pollution; Ganga and Yamuna River action plans; and regeneration and development and environmental research (MOEF Annual Report, 2000-2001).

Performance Failures and Shortcomings

Air Pollution

The National State of the Environment Report, 2001, prepared for the UNEP by the government of India, lists five main areas: land degradation, biodiversity, air pollution, freshwater management, and hazardous waste management. It has identified air pollution, specifically vehicular pollution, as one of the priority areas and has made recommendations. The "practical strategies" outlined to reduce emissions and congestion and to check air pollution are promotion of mass transport systems, traffic planning and management, taxes on fuels and vehicles, further tightening of emission norms and fuel quality specifications, and promotion and use of alternative fuels, as in compressed natural gas (CNG), liquid petroleum gas (LPG), propane-, or battery-operated vehicles.

The report rightly says that vehicular pollution control in metropolitan and smaller cities deserves top priority because, in India, millions of people breathe impure air contaminated by dreaded pollutants, resulting in pulmonary diseases, allergies, and even death. In Delhi, one of the more polluted capitals in the world, virtually no initiative to clean the air has come from the government. Every order has come from the Supreme Court, be it on unleaded petrol, phasing out of old commercial vehicles, introduction of CNG, or tightening of emission norms.

The MOEF, the national implementing agency for the report, has not implemented the recommendations. Nor is there any evidence that the Union Finance Ministry is aware of the intrinsic link between the economy of the country and its environment, for, if it had that awareness the Union Budget for 2003–2004 would not have levied higher excise duties on auto CNG and lowered diesel prices—the very opposite of the environmental requirement. Nor was there any fresh initiative in the budget on the promotion of renewable energy sources such as hydro, wind, or solar power (TOI, March 11, 2002).

Water Pollution, Groundwater Depletion, and Freshwater Scarcity

In a performance review of the Yamuna Action Plan (YAP) by IIT-Roorke, sponsored by the MOEF, the report says that it is "a well-conceived" plan but suffers from many shortcomings in its implementation. It mentions that "some drains that dump waste water into the Yamuna have not been intercepted; some new pollution points have come up; the main problem areas are Muzaffarnagar, Yamunanagar, Agra, and Faridabad; sewer cleaning has remained erratic; local bodies are unable to provide data on the

Table 11.1 Levels of Water Pollution in Delhi

Pollutants	Present Level	Maximal Permissible Limit
Nitrate	174 mg/L	100 mg/L
Sulfate	680 mg/L	100 mg/L
Fluoride	3 10 mg/L	1.5 mg/L
Mercury	4.60 µg/L	1 µg/L
Arsenic	69.5 µg/L	50 µg/L

use of sewer cleaning machines; sewage treatment plants are working in most places but remain underused and power cuts are frequent" (TOI, Feb. 3, 2003). The report continues to say that although the riverine states are responsible for operation and maintenance of assets, Uttar Pradesh (UP) has failed to provide any funds. Throughout UP and Haryana, there is no planned utilization of the nutrient-rich treated effluent for irrigation. Gas collection and use are minimal. Although community toilets have been set up, user charges are high. Haryana is ahead of UP in completing infrastructure work, but plants do not have enough sewage to treat. Further, treated effluent is being discharged into drains and biogas utilization is poor. Above all, the YAP has failed in invoking people's participation and creating awareness.

In Delhi, water pollution is alarming. A recent study conducted by the Guru Gobind Singh Indraprastha University reveals that pollutants have trickled down the troubled waters of the Yamuna and led to the drying up of Delhi's aquifer system. It has also revealed that the concentration of arsenic, mercury, nitrates, sulfates, and dissolved salts in the capital's groundwater exceeds permissible limits, as Table 11.1 shows.

The quantity of pollutants detected in the groundwater, in turn, affects the health of the people, since the excessive presence of dissolved salts in water affects the kidneys, nitrates can trigger the "blue-baby" syndrome, sulfates can cause gastric problems, and fluorides can lead to fluorosis and dental disorders. The contaminated water can also cause cancer, liver and kidney damage, and neurological and reproductive disorders. In Kerala, studies have directly linked the use of the pesticide Endosulfan to cancer of the testicles, prostate gland, and breast. Children are the most vulnerable because they do not have a fully developed immune system to fight these toxins. Experts say that the presence of mercury and arsenic beyond the permissible limit is a matter of "grave concern."

The Delhi Water Board (DJB), the local body responsible for supplying drinking water to city households, has woefully failed to enforce stringent quality control and effective purification methods. Studies show that only 18 out of 33 tests prescribed by the Bureau of Indian Standards for drinking water are reportedly being carried out. Tests for the presence of mercury, cadmium, selenium, arsenic, lead, zinc, ionic detergents, mineral oil and pesticides are not conducted at all by DJB.

In fact in 1996 an Indo-Dutch study of the Yamuna river water had found pesticides like DDT, aldrin, dieldrin, heptachlor and BHC in the river water being supplied as drinking water. Then again Indian Toxicological Research Institute in Lucknow had found pesticide residue in almost all essential commodities of life and also found that people of Delhi had the world's highest levels of DDT accumulated in their body fat. (*Sunday Hindustan Times*, Feb. 22, 2003)

The excessive and alarming presence of these harmful substances in groundwater is attributed to the continuous discharge of sewage and industrial effluents into the river Yamuna. Subsequently, they seep into the groundwater aquifer, which, being sandy in nature, allows pollution to spread at a rapid rate. A study says that another problem involves the strength of Delhi's freshwater flow. If pumping activities continue with the current frequency, the city's supply of freshwater will mingle with saline water and Delhi's groundwater reserves could turn completely saline. Sixty-seven sites have been identified as hydrographic stations to be monitored through piezometers. "We are examining the 'draft' and 'recharge' aspects, says the official" (TOI, Jan. 31, 2003).

It was only after the Center for Science and Environment, a Delhi-based NGO, made public its alarming finding that the bottled and packaged drinking water sold by various brand companies contained pesticide residue that the Delhi government banned their sale and cancelled the license of these companies. It included Bisleri International, Noida, as well. Earlier inspections by the Bureau of Indian Standards led to action against eight plants, including one each of Pepsico, Bisleri, and Ion-exchange.

Groundwater Woes

According to the chairman of the Central Pollution Control Board, D. K. Biswas, "As groundwater levels, under pressure from the growing population, go down, the concentration of harmful toxins in water increases. Sewage pollution also increases." Groundwater is not an endless resource, and rainwater harvesting is becoming the only alternative of meeting the water requirement of a growing population. Recognizing this, rainwater harvesting has been made mandatory in several cities in Haryana and Punjab. As far as national capital is concerned, groundwater is critical in south and southwest Delhi districts, where tube wells were banned in 2002. Groundwater has not improved in places where water-harvesting systems are in place in Delhi, for instance, at the Jawaharlal Nehru University (JNU) and Indian Institute of Technology (IIT). In fact, ground-water fell in JNU by 2.5 m in January 2003. Sanjay Van, a forest area in the southwest, is the only place where groundwater has been constant. Its postwinter level was 1.08 m in 2003. The water-harvesting system will not work immediately. Although the government of Delhi has banned bore wells, the law has not been effectively enforced. Delhi citizens have failed to obey the law and have bribed the officials of the Delhi Municipal Corporation to allow them to bore wells in an illegal manner.

According to a research study by Saurab Sinha of the Center for Science and Environment, some parts of Haryana and Punjab are faced with a peculiar problem—the water table is rising and falling simultaneously. This phenomenon is caused by the overexploitation of deep aquifers in these areas. For instance, Dera Bassi near Chandigarh used to have a shallow water level till a few years ago, and the farmers were a happy lot. But over time, industries dug deep tube wells. Even farmers followed suit. "As a result, the level of water in the shallow aquifers (up to 30 m deep) is rising, and the level in the deeper aquifers is falling," said Central Ground Water Board, Northern Regional Director M. D. Nautiyal.

What are the impacts of this drying up of the deep aquifers? "We are facing problems of broken roads, unstable building foundations, flooded basements and poor sewerage," according to a respondent of the area. Several trees were uprooted in Mukhtsar, the cotton crop was destroyed, thousands of precious trees like sesame and keekar were destroyed," stated Mukhtsar District Forest Officer S. P. Singh.

The remedy to this problem lies in conservation of water at deeper levels, say the officials of the Central Ground Water Board (CGWB). They advised the authorities to build harvesting structures in such a way that water from the upper aquifers is directed to the fast-depleting lower aquifers. They are asking people to harvest water at deeper levels to solve the problem.

Large areas of Haryana and Punjab are also facing severe depletion of groundwater. In 1995, over 50% of the "dark" overexploited blocks were located in six states, including Punjab and Haryana, according to then union agricultural minister Ajit Singh. In dark blocks, the groundwater exploitation is over 85% of the amount recharged, whereas in overexploited blocks over 100% of the amount recharged is drawn. In Punjab, 93 out of 138 blocks are dark or overexploited, whereas in Haryana the numbers are 41 out of 110 blocks. As a result of this, the cost of drawing water is increasing as more power is required. Moreover, the use of fertilizers is increasing and the soil is getting degraded.

Conclusion: India's March toward SD and Millennium Goals

Intergenerational Equity

India's efforts toward achievement of the eight Millennium Goals, including SD, are a mixed bag of impressive fulfillment in some areas and failure in others. As far as the achievement of the goal of *intergenerational equality and equity* is concerned, India is striving hardly and consistently to ensure that the basic needs of life of the present generation are met without compromising the capacity of the future generation to meet theirs. This is partly evident from the fact that India achieved a sustained economic growth of 5% to 5.5% during 1998–2003 and partly from the recent decision of the government of India to repay the country's public debt amount secured on small interest rates. Definitely, India has to go miles to realize full environmental sustainability, but the present track record is an encouraging sign that the nation is moving in the right direction.

Intranational Equity

In terms of the UNDP's Human Development Index (HDI, 2003), which measures the achievements of countries on the basis of indicators such as life expectancy, educational attainment, income levels, and political and economic participation of citizens, India has slipped three notches from 124 to 127 in the ranking of countries on development. India's performance on the SD front is not very rosy. As far as the first Millennium Goal—reducing by half the number of people living on less than a dollar a day—is concerned, the report states, "India is home to the largest number of hungry people at 233 million." However, the report quickly adds that with sustained economic growth, India and China—two of the world's most populous countries—can reach the goal. While China's economy moved 150 million people out of poverty from 1990 to 2000, India averaged a growth rate of a 4%

It is ironic that despite India's food security being quite good, with government food warehouses overflowing with wheat and rice, millions of people go without food. The public distribution system that was recently reorganized to serve the people below the poverty line is most inefficiently administered. To make matters worse, there is inordinate delay in lifting of the grains by the state governments and widespread corruption in the Food Administration. The net result is that there are several states like Orissa, where people living in tribal and drought-prone areas die of starvation, though the government denies such reports (TOI, June 25–27, 2003).

According to the report of the Economic Survey 2002–2003, the poverty ratio in India had declined from 54.9% in 1973–1974 to 36.0% in 1993–1994 because of the success of the poverty alleviation programs. The poverty ratio further declined to 26.1% in 1999–2000. While the proportion of poor in the rural areas declined from 56.4% in 1973–1974 to 27.1% in 1999–2000, the decline in urban areas was from 49% to 23.6%. In absolute terms, the number of the poor declined to 260 million in 1999–2000, with about 75% of these being in the rural areas.

> Wide inter-state disparities are visible in the poverty ratios between rural and urban areas as also in the rates of decline of poverty. Among major States, Orissa, Bihar, West Bengal and Tamil Nadu had more than 50 percent of their population below the poverty line in 1983. By 1999–2000, while Tamil Nadu and West Bengal had reduced their poverty ratios by nearly half, Orissa and Bihar continued to be the two poorest States with poverty ratios of 47 and 43 percent respectively. In 1999–2000, 20 States and Union Territories had poverty ratios, which were less than the national average. Among other States, Jammu and Kashmir, Haryana, Gujarat, Punjab, Andhra Pradesh, Maharashtra and Karnataka also succeeded in significantly reducing the incidence of poverty. (Economic Survey, GOI, 2002–2003)

Great disparities in income, infrastructure, and economic development exist not only among various regions of the country but also sharp inequalities prevail among different segments and groups of the people of India. Among the minorities, the Indian Muslims who constitute the largest minority group, are the most socially and economically backward people. Whereas the constitution of India has provided 15 and 7.5% reservation for the Scheduled Castes and Scheduled Tribes, respectively, in the seats of parliament/state assemblies, educational institutions, and public employment, there is no such reservation for the Muslims. In a few states like Tamil Nadu, Muslims are also treated as backward class and are given reservation in educational institutions and in government jobs. The year 2004 being an election year in India, states like Rajasthan and Madhya Pradesh have provided for reservation for upper caste people on economic ground.

While atrocities, crimes, and violence against scheduled castes and tribes have been perpetrated by members of the upper castes for decades in independent India, Muslims have also suffered from Hindu militant and fundamentalist elements and outfits, resulting in large-scale communal killings, violence, arson, and heavy loss of property. States most affected by communal riots are UP, Maharashtra, Karnataka, and Tamil Nadu, particularly since the demolition of the Babri Masjid (mosque) on December 6, 1992, and in Gujarat in the post-Ghodra anti-Muslim riots in February–March 2002. Communal riots had taken place many times in the past, but these most recent holocausts were abetted by those in political power. Recent instances of violent attacks against the Christians, who are a small minority group in the country, also threaten and weaken the *secular democratic fabric of the pluralistic Indian society.*

Intragender Equity

As far as educational development is concerned, the UNDP report says that in India, "40 million children, more than one third of the world's total are not in primary school." According to *Census of India*, 2001, the literacy rate in the country is 65.38% (75.85% for males and 54.16% for females). Among states, Kerala is on the top with 90.92% in the country, and it also tops both in male (94.20%) and in female (87.86%) literacy. Mizoram (88.49%) and Lakshadeep (87.52%) follow. Bihar with a literacy rate of 47.53% ranks the last in the country, preceded by Jharkand (54.13%) and Jammu and Kashmir (54.46%). The literacy rate of Bihar is also the lowest for males (60.32%) and females (33.57%).

At the national level, the female literacy rate is 54.16% ; there are 495.7 million females and 531.3 million males in the country. The sex ratio in the country has always remained unfavorable to females. In addition, the plight of the "girl child" is worsening day by day. In the male-dominated Indian society, the female child is discriminated against in the fulfillment of all the basic needs of life. The practice of female foeticide is increasing at an alarming rate in some states, such as Tamil Nadu, Punjab, and Haryana.

Despite the law banning sex discriminating tests, clinics, doctors, and people violate the law with impunity. Violence and crime against women are on the increase. There is no *gender equality in family, social, economic, political, and administrative life for the women of India.* The Women's Reservation Bill, which aims at 33% reservation for Indian women in the parliament and state legislatures, has been scuttled for the fifth time in the parliament because of lack of consensus among the major political parties.

Although 33% reservation for women has been made in the seats and positions of chairpersons of the local government bodies as a result of the Seventy-Third and Seventy-Fourth Amendments, empirical evidence reveals that women representatives are facing many challenges in their role performance. This only indicates that male politicians are yet to accept gender equality gracefully in real political life. No doubt India has had a woman prime minister, Indira Gandhi; a woman deputy chairperson of the Rajya Sabha (upper house of parliament) in Dr. Najma Heptulla; and women ministers and governors; however, participation of women in the process of governance and administration is very limited in the country. While electoral (exercising the right to suffrage) participation of women in large numbers takes place in most elections to parliament and state assemblies, their exercise of the right to contest for the seats in the country's lawmaking bodies is very insignificant. The number of women parliamentarians in India has never exceeded 10% .and that of women administrators has never exceeded 12%. percent.

International Equity

As a sovereign, independent nation, India enjoys *equality of status in the comity of nations, in the UN and all other international bodies.* India complies with international law, various conventions, treaties, and declarations. However, as a developing country, India is faced with unequal treatment along with other developing countries at the hands of developed nations through the World Bank, IMF, and WTO. Similarly, India is also subject to exploitation by various multinational companies in matters of trade, business, environmental protection, intellectual property rights, and transfer of capital and technology. In the era of liberalization and globalization, all nations in the South are subjected to unequal treatment by countries of the North.

References

Agarwal, A., Narain, S., and Sen (1999). *Citizen Report*. New Delhi: Centre for Science and Environment.

Bahuguna, S. (1993). Development redefined. *Indian Journal of Public Administration*, 34. no. 3, 229–236.

Bava, N. (1984). *People's Participation in Development Administration in India*. New Delhi: Uppal.

Bava, N. (1993). *Development and the Social Science Method: An Interdisciplinary and Global Approach*. New Delhi: Uppal.

Bava, N. (1997). Towards an integrated theory of people's participation through NGOs in nation-building and development. In: Bava, N., ed., *Non-Governmental Organizations in Development: Theory and Practice,* 3–20, 255–274. New Delhi: Kanishka.

Bava, N. (1997). Environmental stewardship and sustainable development: Policy and administration in India. In: Jain, R.B., ed., *Environmental Stewardship and Sustainable Development,* 189–204. New Delhi: BRPC.

Bava, N. (1999). Environmental movements for sustainable development. In: Chaube, S.K., and Chakrabarty, B., eds., *Social Movements in Contemporary India,* pp. 161-189. Calcutta: Bagchi.

Bava, N. (2004). Panchayati raj: An Indian model of grassroots democracy and decentralized rural development. In: Mudacumura, G.M., and Haque, S.M., eds., *Handbook of Development Policy Studies.* New York: Marcel Dekker.

Census of India: 2001. New Delhi: Government of India.

Chaturvedi, T.N. (ed.) (1989). Special number on environment and administration. *Indian Journal of Public Administration,* xxxv, No. 3 (July–September).

Chaturvedi, T.N. (ed.) (1993) Special number on sustainable development of society: Imperatives and perspectives. *Indian Journal of Public Administration,* 34(3).

Chaubey, S.K., and Chakrabarty, B. (eds.) (1999). *Social Movements in Contemporary India.* Calcutta: Bagchi.

Dhanagare, D.N. (1993) Sustainable development, environment and social science research in India. *Indian Journal of Public Administration,* 34(3), 551–563.

Economic Survey, Government of India, Report 2002–2003, New Delhi: Government of India.

Fuwa, K. (1995). Definition and measurement of sustainability: The biophysical aspects. In: Munasinghe, M., and Shearer, W., eds., *Defining and Measuring Sustainability.* Washington D.C.: World Bank.

Gandhi, Indira (1972). *Address of The Prime Minister of India.* United Nations Conference on Human Environment, Stockholm, Sweden, June 5–16, 1972, UN Conference on Human Environment Report (1972), New York: United Nations, 1973.

Gann, N. (1993). Environment and development a search for an economic rethinking. *Indian Journal of Public Administration,* 34(3).

Holling, C.S. (1995). Sustainability: Cross-scale dimension. In Munasinghe, M., and Shearer, W., eds., In *Defining and Measuring Sustainability,* 65–70. Washington, D.C.: World Bank.

Lele, S. (1995). Coming to grips with biological issues in a social construct, or, how to talk about sustainability without being a social scientist. In: Munasinghe, M., and Shearer, W., eds., *Defining and Measuring Sustainability.* Washington, D.C.: World Bank.

Ministry of Environment and Forests, *Annual Report: 2000–2003, and 1994–1995,* New Delhi: Government of India.

Misra, R.P. (1993). Sustainable development: The ecological perspectives. *Indian Journal of Public Administration,* 34(3), 254–264.

Payne, R.A. (1995). Freedom and environment. *Journal of Democracy,* 6(3).

Pronk, J., and Haq, M. (1992). *Sustainable Development: From Concept to Action: The Hague Report.* New York: United Nations Development Program.

Roy, R. (1993). Sustainability of society: Imperative and perspective. *Indian Journal of Public Administration,* 34(3).

Schmandt, J. (1994). Water and development in semi arid regions. Paper presented at the XV World Congress, Berlin, International Political Science Association, Unpublished.

Shiva, V. (1988). *Staying Alive: Women, Ecology and Survival in India.* New Delhi: Kali for Women.

Shiva, V. et al. (1991). *Biodiversity: World Rainforest Movement.* Penang.

Special number on sustainable development and administration. *Indian Journal of Public Administration,* 35(3) (July–September 1989).

Special number on sustainable development of society: Imperatives and perspectives. *Indian Journal of Public Administration,* 34(3) (July–September 1993).

Sunday Hidustan Times, Delhi Edition, February 22, 2003.

Times of India, Delhi Edition, January 29, 31; February 3, 12; March 11; June 23–25, 27; July 4, 2003.

United Nations Development Program (1993, 2003). *Human Development Reports.* Oxford: Oxford University Press.

Utting, P. (1994). Social and political dimensions of environmental protection. In Dharam Gai, ed., *Development and Environment: Sustaining People and Nature.* Oxford: Blackwell, Institute of Social Studies.

Weider, E. (1977). The goals, strategy and environment of development. In Sharma, S.K. (ed.). *Dynamics of Development: An International Perspective,* Vol. 2. Delhi: Concept Publishing.

World Bank (1996). *World's Biodiversity and Agriculture: Implications for Conservation and Development.* Washington, D.C.: World Bank.

World Commission on Environment and Development (1987). Report on *Our Common Future.* New Delhi: Oxford University Press.

SUSTAINABLE DEVELOPMENT: NATIONAL AND REGIONAL EXPERIENCES

Chapter 12

Microfinance in Asia: Toward Economic Sustainable Development Policies and Strategies

Kathryn Gow

CONTENTS

Introduction

Across Asia and neighboring countries, there have been many microfinance schemes introduced in the past two to three decades. The majority of these schemes have improved the immediate lives of individuals and their families who have received the microcredit loans, with proven outcomes of better health, education, and housing (Carvajal, 1989; Chua, 1998; Fawcett, 1999; Sebstad and Chen, 1996). This chapter focuses on the goals, objectives, and strategies for microfinance schemes and the overarching policies that have allowed them to flourish. It further outlines suggestions for improving the facilitation for these schemes to play their role in alleviating poverty in Asia.

Defining Microfinance

Microcredit is a system of providing access to savings and more importantly credit to those people who cannot borrow money from the usual formal sources of credit because they are too poor and have no collateral. They are often women, and their only alternative (outside loans from families) has been to borrow cash from traditional moneylenders, and this in turn leads them to being exploited and locks them into the continuing cycle of poverty because of the very high interest rates.

Unlike the recent held China microbank lending initiatives (Saywell, 2000) in which the borrower has to pay back the loan or lose house or car held as collateral, microfinance for the poor (based on Grameen principles [Yunus, 1994]) does not generally ask for collateral. According to the Microcredit Summit Campaign, by the end of 2001, 2,186 institutions had made loans to 54,904,102 clients, over half of whom were among the poorest at the commencement of their loan program—a stunning 38.7% increase since the previous year (Lee (2003a, p. 8).

Lee (2003a) further noted that following the Microcredit Summit +5 meeting in New York in 2002, one of the directives of the commissioned papers was to focus on "influencing policies, regulations, and systems in favor of sustainable microlending" (p. 9). In terms of global policy, both the World Bank and the Consultative Group to Assist the Poorest (CGAP) have approached government policy makers to have interest rates, laws, and supervision requirements in countries such as Vietnam reviewed and updated (CGAP, 2002a).

At the government level, microfinance policies and strategies vary according to the state of economic development, and the strength of political and social relationships with international and regional trade. From the perspective of the World Bank, its World Bank Group's Microfinance

Institutional Plan 1999 addresses two major objectives: to reduce poverty and to help in developing financial sectors. Their action plan underscores the fact that a large section of the labor force in client countries is composed of microentrepreneurs, which are a vital economic force (The World Bank Group, 1999).

From that perspective, the World Bank adopted strategies that promote a supportive financial sector police and regulatory framework, facilitate capacity building, give operational assistance, disseminate best practice, and facilitate donor coordination. The proponents of CGAP believe that microfinance will contribute to the Millennium Development Goals by enabling the "poor to increase and diversify" their incomes; to "build human, social, and economic assets," and to improve their lives with "better nutrition, improved health, access to schooling" (CGAP, 2002b, p. 1), and a higher quality of roofing on their houses; to expand their small business enterprises; and to empower women.

More specifically, CGAP (2003a) lists several outcomes, which they align to both the strategies for, and outcomes of, microfinance. Such strategies include eradicating extreme poverty and hunger, achieving universal education, promoting gender equality and women's empowerment, and reducing child mortality while improving maternal health. CGAP (2003a) in its phase III strategy 2003–2008 has a vision of microfinance that incorporates supporting "the development of financials systems that work for the poor" (p. 5).

Other policy objectives on regulation and supervision issues come from CGAP (2002b), which sets out the objectives of prudential regulation such as (1) protecting the country's financial system by preventing failure of one institution from impacting negatively on others and (2) protecting depositors who are unable to monitor the financial health of the institution. Specific strategies include mapping financial services for the poor; advancing industry knowledge; providing technical advice; raising capital efficiently and effectively; working with networks; building industry knowledge; improving linkages between financial and nonfinancial programs and incubating new models; deepening poverty outreach; measuring social performance; building the information infrastructure; and developing financial reporting standards; building local expertise; engaging in multilateral policy consultations; supporting country-level policy dialogues; facilitating development of police and regulator standards; and developing technical tools, services, and training (CGAP, 2002b).

Microfinance and Poverty Alleviation

Since the mid-1950s, several Asian countries have used different kinds of poverty reduction strategies. Chowdhury (2001) cites CIRDAP's (Centre on Integrated Rural Development for Asia and Pacific) (1999) mapping of how these strategies have changed over five decades: from the development paradigm of growth through industrialization (in which community development was the poverty reduction strategy); to agricultural intensification and human capital development in the 1960s (when a trickle down approach was tested); through the 1970s (when the emphasis was on redistribution with growth and basic needs and integrated rural development); to the 1980s, during which the focus was on structural adjustments, private sector–led development (when the strategy was on growth, human resources development, safety nets and nongovernmental organizations [NGOs]); through to the 1990s (when the paradigm shifted more to human development and growth and thus the strategy encompassed labor-intensive growth, human resource development of the poor targeted programs, and safety nets).

Because most of the microfinance programs are conducted in rural areas, public policy on rural development has been a vital influence on the support, funding, and regulation of such poverty alleviation and rural development strategies (see Asian Development Bank, 2003). As Chowdhury (2001) points out, the "thrust now" is toward a target group approach, with emphasis on sustainability, equity (including gender equity), and environmental protection.

Microfinance in Economic Development

There are thousands of microfinance programs being conducted in Asia, some of which have been operating for over 20 years and some of which have only just been incubated in the past year. The issue of whether or not microfinance plays a strategic role in economic development depends on the economic level of the country in which it is operating, and the impact it has on a family in rural Bangladesh may be very different from a family in Malaysia or the Philippines.

As the author has observed in field studies, one of the major benefits of the presence of MFIs (microfinance institutions) in rural areas is that "it helps prevent the forced migration of rural people who go to the cities in search of work; the more people who leave a community, the more the remaining community suffers from the absence of that human resource and his/her income" (Gow, 2001a, p. 387). "The migration of some of the CARD members in the Philippines during the economic downturn was high and has detrimental effects on family and community life, both from a social and economic viewpoint" (Gow, 2001a, pp. 387–388). According to McGuire and Conroy (1998) both donors and governments, with the exception of Pakistan to that date, have given substantial funds to support the development of microfinance in Asia.

While the Grameen Bank (GB) has caught the attention of the popular press and indeed the cursory academic glance, there are many different types of microcredit and microfinance programs. In 1983, Professor Muhammed Yunus established the GB of Bangladesh for the purpose of poverty alleviation. The underlying assumption of the traditional Grameen model is that the rural poor just need access to credit to be able to climb out of poverty. Groups of five people meet at Center meetings each week (although this has been recently changed to fortnightly in many areas, since the Grameen Bank has reviewed its operations), and they make loan repayments, undergo training, and discuss a range of rules and ideas (Bornstein, 1996).

The GB generally has only loaned to women, and most Grameen Bank Replicas (GBRs) will also only lend to women. Although there has been some criticism of this practice (Teare, 1998) and some angst from the men affected and the male community as a whole, and keeping in mind that some MFIs involving men have been successful, the evidence is still weighted against men utilizing the loan monies to improve the lives of their families as a whole (Yunus, 1995).

In Malaysia, another success story was the Grameen Replica, Amanah Iktiar Malaysia (AIM). From 1986, under the initial guidance of David Gibbons and Sukor Kasim, AIM became so efficient in the business of microfinance that in 1996, the Malaysian government, with its goal of reducing the percentage of poor people in rural areas by 2001, loaned substantial sums of money to AIM (AIM, 1996).

Unfortunately, at about the same time that the Grameen Bank in Bangladesh was reported to be having significant problems with their program, problems in AIM began to come to light (see Conroy, 2002). Some of these related to computer technology and operational, financial, and managerial issues (Lee, 2003b, p. 3), as well as, apparently, a loss of the original vision and aims of the microfinance scheme for the poor. After considerable management reorganization, one of the original creators of AIM, Kasim, believes that sustainability is a priority and will be built into the strategy while "unsustainable area offices may have to be consolidated," and AIM will have to measure itself "against established standards in institutional financial self-sufficiency" (Lee, 2003c, p. 5).

Viability and Sustainability

Robinson (2001) is adamant that for microfinance programs to be viable, they must be self-sustainable. The poverty lending approach relies heavily on subsidies. She nominates the Bank Ryat Indonesia (BRI) in Indonesia as being a model to follow.

Along the same line, McGuire (1998a, p. 10) argues that "it is clear that at present most MFIs are not operating on a sound basis," and Baruah (2002, p. 28) contends that although short-term impacts are good in alleviating poverty, "long-term impacts like asset creation and the ability to withstand future economic or health-related stresses without falling back into poverty have not been widely observed."

Moreover, Dao (2001, p. 24) argues that "effective programs must reach large numbers of borrowers to demonstrate significant impact and cost effectiveness," echoing McGuire's (1998b, p. 1) admonition that we need to understand that if "microfinance is to make an important contribution to poverty reduction in the region, the microfinance sector will need to develop to the stage where it can reach large numbers of poor people on a sustainable basis." Renteria-Guerrero (Hassan and Renteria-Guerrero, 1997) had developed a formula in 1997 that enabled planners to calculate the likely viability of a credit program, and it would seem that such a formula should be part of every program plan. He gives a simple method for determining the breakeven point, which can be calculated thus: (Cost of Funds + other Annual Operating costs + Bad debts + Pilferage) × (1 + the annual rate of Inflation) = (the amount of loans to be disbursed annually × the rate of interest changed to loanees). However, CGAP (2003a) reports that there have been several NGO microfinance schemes that have achieved financial sustainability and have still reached the very poor with very small loan sizes, even in sparsely populated areas.

Whether or not modern technoanalysis, such as that proposed by Akroyd (1999), logical framework, would be of assistance in establishing the whole range of factors that might influence the outcome of the feasibility and sustainability of a new, or expanding, microfinance program remains to be explored. Akroyd (1999, p. 65) advocates that the tool should be used at each stage of the project cycle. "This approach accustoms planners to think in terms of logical causes and effects within a project hierarchy, and obliges them to consider the key assumptions and risks which underpin success."

Mosley (2001, p. 66) also provides a new formula for assessing poverty-oriented projects—poverty-elasticity of aid expenditure. That is, he uses the incomes from household budget surveys as major components of the poor's income, in order to calculate the poverty-elasticity of particular types of aid expenditure. However, it is not a simple concept, and readers are invited to study Table 7 in his article (available from Beech Tree Publishing, 10 Watford Close, Guildford, Surrey, GUI 2EP, UK).

GRET (Group de Recherche et d'Echanges Technologiques) in Vietnam (CGAP, 1996) and the Association of Asian Confederation of Credit Unions (1999) in Thailand have been critical of NGOs that do not think through the effects of their loan program on the local community at the macro level. Indeed Mosley (2001, p. 63) warns that if projects go wrong, microfinance can actually increase the vulnerability of the very poor, because it raises their levels of debt (CGAP, 2003b), thus leading them to the risk of losing their existing assets. Dao (2001, p. 19) also questions whether the poor should take out loans, if they cannot invest wisely or if they are already in debt. Indeed, Hoeskma, Gow, and Finlay (1998) found that in badly designed loan programs, some people had lost their houses and all that they owned before entering a well-prepared and monitored GBR (Grameen Bank Replica) program.

Another criticism relates to a lack of targeting of the loans, specifically to prospective entrepreneurs. Lapar and colleagues' study (1995, cited in Gaile and Foster, 1996, p. 7) of loan takers in the Philippines intimated that borrowers may in fact be more entrepreneurial than nonborrowers, and that is why they perform so well. Moreover, the Association of Asian Confederation of Credit Unions (AACCU) in Thailand would advocate that such loans should only be made available to people with latent or explicit entrepreneurial skills because funds are scarce, and in encouraging economic development, it is better to loan the money to people who will do something worthwhile with it and grow enterprises that go on to employ others in the community.

Certainly if applicants do not have an enterprising spirit and skills in agriculture or mariculture, or in small business products or services, or an ability to act as agents, then it is likely that they will not be successful in establishing a larger business, even if they have access to appropriate avenues of credit. The AACCU (1999, p. 1) emphasizes that it is important to accept that "not all poor have entrepreneurial competencies."

The reasons given for success of various microfinance schemes vary. Fawcett (1999, p. 3) explains that credit workers say that the loan recovery rate is high—usually more than 98%, and in some groups 100%—because of close monitoring of group activities, training, motivation, and the higher sense of responsibility that women display. Aid officials say that women who earn more contribute to better nutrition, schooling, and health care for their children (Fawcett, 1999, p. 3). But critics say the approach is unsuitable for remote hilly villages without access to transport or other infrastructure, involves high risks, and can prove an expensive proposition because interest rates can be as high as 25% (Fawcett, 1999). Dao (2001, p. 18) also believes that the selling interest rate is one factor that hinders microfinance outreach.

Although international donors fund such fledgling programs for 3 years and in some cases not until after the program has been running successfully for at least 3 years, the women's groups know that it takes 3 to 5 years at least for the program to become sustainable, when it is being conducted in very poor areas where there is no infrastructure and little funding for salaries and equipment (Gow, Moore, Hoeksma, and Wood, 2000). Furthermore, Gibbons (2003, p. 1), who has had a lot of "hands-on" experience in establishing, monitoring, training, and consulting with Grameen Bank replicas and in helping them turn around, believes that "shortage of capital is seriously constraining the outreach of microfinance to the poor in Asia."

Mayoux (2002a, p. 58) argues that financial sustainability is only one part of best practice and needs to be judged against the backdrop of criteria for empowerment and poverty alleviation. Indeed, Mayoux contends that diversity of thinking is needed and a shift away from the setting up of parallel specialized microfinance banks. She further argues that mainstream banks should fulfill their social responsibility, such as improving the links between microfinance and other institutions, so that they contribute to empowerment and the implementation of gender awareness training on an ongoing basis.

At a microlevel, there have been several responses to such social responsibility, and according to Chowdhury (2001, p. 3), the Bangladesh Rural Advancement Committee (BRAC), the largest national NGO in the Southern Hemisphere, is such an example. He refers to BRAC as a model of a civil society organization that has played an effective role in poverty alleviation and proved that it is possible to work with state agencies to achieve a common goal.

At a macrolevel, Vietnam is one of the few countries that have responded quickly to poverty alleviation through loans to the poor and have utilized the financial system to fulfill such social responsibility as Mayoux (2002a) advocated. Since the beginning of Vietnam's major economic reforms, the imperative for credit provision is really construed as an adjunct to other economic improvement strategies. One of the Vietnam government's policies is to alleviate poverty, and one strategy is to promote production activities by improving technology and financial access. Microfinance, through its twin goals of credit provision and savings capacities, is thus seen as one of the resources to achieve this aim (Dao, Nguyen, Tran, and Pham, 1999). The government believes that change at all levels of rural and urban economic improvement will increase the country's economic prosperity.

Working on changing their nation's laws about banking and finance has been a preoccupation with many microfinance institutions in Vietnam, the Philippines, and India. Fortunately, in Vietnam, where the government has been working exceptionally hard on its economic redevelopment policies and strategies, a number of laws have been changed or passed since Doi Moi (economic reform) was introduced in 1986. The Law on the State Bank of Vietnam (which, since 1995, has been responsible for the development of all financial institutions and thus influences credit to the poor [Dao, 2001]) and the Law on Credit Institutions (which, since 1998, has assisted rural credit needs) have been two key laws that have been passed. Together with the Civil Code (dealing with private credit markets) and the Cooperative Law (which, since 1995, has been responsible for banking and credit activities in both the formal and informal sectors), they have all aided rural finance. But there is still "no firm legal framework for microfinance" institutions (p. 10).

Dao (2001) outlines the three sectors to the Vietnamese financial system. Although one is the informal sector, consisting of moneylenders and others, the semiformal sector seems to fund microfinance programs. However, within the formal sector also there are the Vietnam Bank for the Poor (VBP), which was established in 1995 and gives loans to poor households, and the Vietnam Bank for Agriculture and Rural Development (VBARD), which is responsible for dispensing and recovering loans. These are state-owned commercial banks, but the People's Credit Funds (PCFs) and other credit cooperatives are owned by their members, who are mostly farmers.

The other formal sector banks, including the Rural Shareholding Banks (RSHBs) are generally not involved in microfinance, although some have loaned money to the poor. Dao (2001) reports that this formal outreach has assisted a large number of rural households. But, as in all countries, it is not clear how many of the "poorest of the poor" have benefited.

According to the VBP (Dao, 2001), the proportion of people under the poverty line decreased by 21% from 1993 to 1998, a rather remarkable feat in such a short time; and if one analyzes only the very-low-income households, 10% of them climbed above the poverty line within the same time frame. Interest levels in Vietnam range from 0.7% to 1.5% per month. The Vietnam Women's Union (VWU) and the Vietnam Farmers Union (VFU) along with the NGO programs generally charge up to 30% to 50% more than the other institutions, but are organized on a small scale (Dao, 2001). There is a move to transfer all such social and policy loan programs to a new type of policy bank, which will leave the commercial banks free to pursue free market principles.

Interestingly, on a more global scale, Goodwin (1998, p. 57) sets forth a number of recommendations for a policy about commercial banks' becoming engaged in microfinance. One of these is to allow small banks to become regulated, and this would lead the way for larger commercial banks to enter the microfinance market for the poor.

There is no doubt that the Vietnam government recognizes the important role that microfinance plays. Nevertheless, the Vietnamese government has no policy specifically about microfinance, and it is not alone with regard to this matter in Asia. However, there is a microfinance government plan outlined in the Hunger Eradication and Poverty Reduction (HEPR) program (Nguyen, 2001). According to Goodwin (1997), the Banking with the Poor Network (BWTP) is the only network that works toward making linkages between NGOs and MFIs and commercial banks to facilitate the capital flow in microfinance.

Gender, Equity, and Empowerment

The FAO/UNDP (2002, p. 23) recommends, among other initiatives, the increased access to formal credit for women as a way to equalize the gender imbalance in Vietnam. USAid, which provides loans for credit programs only in the nonformal sector, made one of the conditions of the sponsorship that the loans go to women borrowers. Poster and Salime (2002) criticized this dispersal scheme, claiming that it may have a negative impact on the household. The emphasis on loans to groups, and not individuals, arose out of USAid's belief that this leads to group solidarity (Poster and Salime, 2002), but solidarity also creates tensions. It may also be a misunderstanding of the Grameen circle approach.

Poster and Salime (2002) also believe that microfinance programs create too much work for women. This has certainly been expressed by groups who have been running the programs for more than 2 years (Thuy, 2000). Thus, from a feminist point of view, creating work for women through individual loans in the informal sector keeps them unprotected economically (Poster and Salime, 2002, p. 196).

Pearson (2000) asserts that the GB and its replicas are one of many forms of MFIs, and that it is quite possible for the microfinance system to be streamlined. This process will make the system less exhausting to administer and less time consuming for the managers of the project, which factors are of concern to the MFIs (see McLaughlin, 2002).

From the perspective of feminist empowerment and gender equity policies, Mayoux (2002b, pp. 246–247) does not agree that the strategies in the three paradigms, underlying the microfinance strategy, of financial self-sustainability, poverty alleviation paradigm, and the feminist empowerment paradigm, are always in the interest of women. She further argues that empowerment concerns are often ignored in the program designs; thus as well as having a negative effect on the women themselves, they could prejudice the financial sustainability of the projects.

Indeed, Coke (2000), in her survey of a GBR in the Visayas Region in the Philippines, concluded that the female loanee is limited by what is considered to be an acceptable activity for women and by their need to be involved in household production and, therefore, her choices in setting up a small business are limited. Along the same line, Todd (2002), in her review of microfinance schemes in the Philippines, concluded that the road out of poverty necessitates the development of a partnership between women and their menfolk, plus an adaptation to technology, because businesses would be more likely to be successful if they involved male activities.

According to the GEO (2000), loans from subsidized credit programs often fail to reach the poor and are used for consumption and often are not repaid (ADB, 1998). As Haynes and Avery (1996, p. 61) have highlighted, the finances of businesses and families are often entwined and therefore, even if their business secures a loan, then its impact may be mitigated by spending on household requirements.

However, there is another lobby that asserts that poor women have the right to spend such money in this way. Pearson (2001, p. 319) advocates that although there is a rule that women should use the money they borrow for business proposes and increase in income, women have a legitimate demand for money they can spend on basic reproductive needs, such as food, housing, education, health care, and transport, and not just productive commercial activities.

Microfinance Policy and Reality

It is useful to align the progress to date with the Millennium Development Goals specifically for the role of microfinance (CGAP, 2002b) in the reduction of poverty by 2005: helping to eradicate extreme poverty and hunger; achieving universal education; promoting gender equality and women's empowerment; and reducing child mortality, improving maternal health, and combating disease. Is the international community achieving these, and if we are not achieving them, we need to ask why not.

Setbacks

The fact that macroeconomic factors have a massive impact on even small microfinance projects needs to be kept in mind, as the International Monetary Fund and others interested in the world economic outlook do not believe that the East Asian growth after the 1997 crisis can achieve the predicted rapid productivity growth, a path that Vietnam has pursued since Doi Moi. Crafts (1999, p. 139) also warns that "there are downside risks to the East Asian 'developmental state' model." This means that in respect to policies relating to poverty alleviation goals and the expectation that schemes such as microcredit could lift people out of poverty within 5 years, or even 10 years, is no longer a reasonable goal.

There are also economic trends, unexpected natural disasters, and world events that have intervened in the plan to alleviate world poverty.

Notably there was the Bangladesh flood, which dramatically affected the GB's performance, although by all reports they have now restructured their systems (Gibbons, 2003) and moved to make significant changes that have turned around what could have been the death knell for one of the most amazing grassroots institutions ever implemented for the poorest of the poor.

Across Asian programs, the Asian economic collapse had a seriously negative impact on many of the microfinance programs and the poverty levels of the peoples involved, especially in countries such as Indonesia (see McGuire and Conroy, 1998). Although wars, droughts, and floods also affected several Asian countries for some time, additional disasters, such as sudden acute respiratory syndrome (SARS) and terrorist activities threatened to take a disastrous toll on aspects of economies such as Singapore and China, and to a lesser extent Vietnam (BizAsia, 2003).

The ongoing negative consequences of the increasing effects of HIV/AIDS disease (Economic and Social Commissions for Asia and the Pacific [ESCAP], Regional Commissions Development Update, July 2002) and the widespread effects of hard drug use have reduced the labor available in the 18- to 35-year-old range, leading to decreases in the living standards of people in many areas. Uncontrollable calamities of such proportion mean that more demands are made on aid funds than before, and billions of dollars have been diverted to the world threat of disease and death, annihilating whole villages, towns, regional areas, and even professional groups of people, such as teachers (Crawley, 2000; UNAIDS, 2000).

On a macrolevel, aid agencies have been well aware of international aid fatigue for more than a decade and rather than the problem lessening, it is actually becoming bigger, as we experience more and more wars, famines, and political unrest. People everywhere feel overwhelmed and ask themselves what is the point of contributing millions of dollars to causes and activities when within a few years all the good work may well have been undone and the people may return to their former, if not a worse, level of poverty and despair.

Although many institutions may become despondent and "give up the good fight," not so the GB. It fought back after the Bangladesh flood and restructed its loan systems so that it could help people to cope with this added burden of catastrophe. So, it is not surprising that faced with the additional impact of the Asian economic collapse and the drying up of its sources of sponsorship, it remodeled itself. Perhaps after all, the GB still works on its original model of action learning (Yunus, 1994).

Nevertheless, regardless of how much access a person has to credit facilities, there are still market forces at work that hinder or obstruct the improvement in their standard of living, such as lack of access to markets internally and externally. Anderson and associates argue (2002, p. 227) that 40% of the costs of the barriers to market access in developing countries are from industrial countries, but 60% are from within their own countries.

South Asia and some countries such as Laos and Vietnam have a critical level of rural poverty (Chowdhury, 2001), affecting more than 45% of rural people. According to Dao (2001, p. 1), there are still "a large number of poor and low-income households" excluded from access to microfinance.

Chowdhury (2001) argues that because the poor depend on small-scale agriculture microenterprise and the informal sector, then providing them with a conducive environment should be a key priority. Chowdhury does not believe that access to credit alone will pull this group out of poverty and proposes, as do others, strategies for old age pensions, insurance, social safety nets, minimum wage indexation, and improved labor standards and labor mobility.

In spite of the large number of programs being conducted in Bangladesh, it is still difficult for any of the microfinance institutions in Bangladesh to reach the 15% of people who make up the ultrapoor group who, according to Chowdhury (2001, p. 19), cannot be covered by the existing programs, because the very poor fear the risk of losing what little they already have by borrowing money. Nevertheless, it seems that BRAC is now attempting to target even this difficult-to-access group, with a great deal of support from "bilateral and multilateral donors."

Keeping Perspective

It seems that the role of microfinance as a tool to assist in economic development is often forgotten, as more and more is expected of this type of microeconomic activity. Perhaps the expectation that it could actually be used to move people quickly out of poverty and thence whole regions or countries, and even the country itself, into economic viability was poorly conceived and the role and capability of microfinance itself misunderstood and perhaps then even misused.

Although some projects and institutions indicate that they have become sustainable, they have not done this without seeking outside support of some type, whether that be to form itself into a chartered bank, a credit union, or a large NGO. On a microlevel, there is no evidence that a microfinance scheme can achieve significant outreach or sustainability without donor aid, or government assistance, or private enterprise endeavors (Morduch, 2000). Perhaps the real debate should be whether loan capital should only be given to people who, after their second loan, demonstrate a real capacity and competence to increase their businesses to employ other people in the villages and towns on an ongoing non-subsidized basis. On the other hand, who will set themselves up as judge and jury to decide if a home-based business is any less a contribution to a country's economic improvement than one that moves out to the community to employ others on a wider scale?

The debate about the role of microfinance in alleviating poverty on a large scale and in a sustainable capacity continues. However, if one asks the loanees from a successful, well-organized and sustainable microfinance program, they will tell you that they would rather have had the opportunity to add to their income generation and that this has led to positive outcomes for the family and the village and neighborhood. The success stories far outweigh the occasional stories of failure, and it is important that academic theorists and critics balance their knowledge about what actually happens by working in the field with the people they are studying, at all levels, over time and across several programs, in different countries.

Conclusion

From an economic development standpoint, there is no doubt that policies that facilitate microfinance schemes and institutions need to have strategies that ensure the review of the management and monitoring of such activities within an overarching conceptualization of sustainability. This means that considerations such as the likelihood of growth in the business and the predicted impact of its contribution spilling over into the economy of the village, town, or city in which it is instituted need to be analyzed at some stage in the allocation of funds to the individual, group, or enterprise. Indeed, there may be a second stage in which funds are only allocated to those individuals, families, or groups who can demonstrate entrepreneurial ability in order to achieve sustainable economic development.

However, from social, educational, and health development perspectives, there is no guarantee that if funds are restricted in the manner outlined, the recognized outcome measures of better health, housing, and education, together with women's greater income generation and subsequent increased economic purchasing power, will be achieved to the same extent that is occurring now in Asian countries.

References

ADB. (1998). Asian Development Bank Annual Report 1997. Manila: Asian Development Bank. http://www.adb.org/Documents/Reports/Annual_Report/1997/default.asp (accessed September 27, 2003).

AIM. (1996). *Laporan Tahunan 1996 Annual Report*. Kuala Lumpur: Amanah Ikhtiar Malaysia.

Akroyd, D. (1999). Logical framework approach to project planning, socio-economic analysis and to monitoring and evaluation services: A smallholder rice project. *Impact Assessment and Project Appraisal, 17*(1): 54–66.

Anderson, K., Dimaranan, B., Francois, J., Hertel, T., Hoekman, B., and Martin, W. (2002). The cost of rich (and poor) country protection to developing countries. *Journal of African Economies, 10*(3): 227–257.

Asia Times (2003). Singapore Airlines Fights to Reinvent Itself. Tony Sitathan. http://www.singapore-window.org/sw03/030528at.htm (accessed 21.01.04).

Asian Development Bank. (2003). *Use of ADF IX resources.* Asian Development Fund (ADF) ADF IX Donors' Meeting, Tokyo, 9–11 December 2003. http://www.adb.org/Documents/Reports/ADF/IX/Use_of_IX_resources_Tokyo.doc (accessed 21.01.04).

Baruah, B. (2001). How can we strengthen microcredit organizations? Newsletter of The Association of Women's Rights in Development. http://www.awid.org/publications/news/fall2001.pdf (accessed 28.09.05).

BizAsia. (2003). Singapore economy back in expansion mode. 22 October. http://www/bizasia.com/economy_/iv8cs/singapore_economy_back.htm (accessed 21.01.04).

Bornstein, D. (1996). *The Price of a Dream.* New York: Simon & Schuster.

Caravajal, J. (1989). Microenterprise as a social investment. In: *Microenterprises in Developing Countries.* London: Intermediate Technology.

CGAP. (1996, May). *Microfinance in Viet Nam: A collaborative study based upon the experiences of NGOs, UN agencies and bilateral donors.* Hanoi: Consultative Group to Assist the Poorest, United Nations Development Programme.

CGAP. (September, 2002a). *Consensus Microfinance Policy Guidance: Regulation and Supervision.* CGAP position paper. Consultative Group to Assist the Poor. The World Bank. Washington, D.C. http://www.cgap.org/assets/images/Policy%20Guidance%20on%20Regulation%20and%20Supervision%20in%20Microfinance.pdf (accessed September 27, 2003).

CGAP. (December, 2002b). CGAP Donor Brief, No. 9, Consultative Group to Assist the Poorest. The World Bank. Washington, D.C. http://www.cgap.org/docs/DonorBrief_09.pdf (accessed September 27, 2003).

CGAP. (January, 2003a). CGAP Phase III Strategy 2003–2008. Building financial systems that work for the poor. Consultative Group to Assist the Poorest; The World Bank. Washington, D.C. http://www.cgap.org/assets/images/CGAP%20III%20Strategy_forWeb.pdf (accessed September 27, 2003).

CGAP. (February, 2003b). CGAP Donor Brief, No. 10, Consultative Group to Assist the Poorest. The World Bank. Washington, D.C. http://www.cgap.org/docs/DonorBrief_10.pdf (accessed January 21, 2004).

Chowdhury, A.M. (2001). Role of the State and NGOs in Curbing Poverty in South Asia: The Bangladesh Case. Paper presented at the Japan Program/INDES 2001 Conference, Japan: Priorities and Strategies in Rural Poverty Reduction: Experiences from Latin America and Asia. http://www.iadb.org/int/jpn/English/support_files/RP%203%20Bangladesh%20Chowdjury.pdf (accessed September 20, 2003).

Chua, R.T. (1998). *The Performance and Sustainability of Two Philippine Micro-finance Institutions.* Brisbane: The Foundation for Development Cooperation.

CIRDAP. (1999). *Rural Development Report 1999.* Dhaka: Centre on Integrated Rural Development for Asia and Pacific.

Coke, R.N. (2000). Gender and Microfinance Business Choice: Evidence from the Philippines. http://schlbus.belmont.edu/fac/coker/rcoke1.pdf (accessed September 27, 2003).

Conroy, J.D. (2002). Microfinance in Malaysia: Time to rebuild. http://www.bwtp.org/publications/pub/AIM_paper.htm (accessed September 27, 2003).

Crafts, N. (1999). Asian growth before and after the crisis. *IMF Staff Papers, 46*(2): 139–165.

Crawley, M. (2000). Losing teachers: How AIDS undercuts education in Africa. *The Christian Science Monitor,* July 25. http://search.csmonitor.com/durable/2000/07/25/pls4.htm (accessed 26.09.05).

Dao, V.H. (2001). Informal credit market and micro-finance: Micro-finance sector in Vietnam. Priorities and strategies in rural poverty reduction: Experiences from Latin America and Asia. The Japan Program Working Paper Series. Paper 13. Presented at the Japan Program/INDES 2001 Conference, Japan. www.iadb.org/int/jpn/English/support_files/RP%2013%20-%20Vietnam%20Hung.pdf (accessed May 30, 2003).

Dao, V.H., Nguyen, X.N., Tran, T.Q., and Pham, M.T. (1999). Outreach diagnostic report: Improving low-income household access to formal financial services in Vietnam. Report to the Vietnam-Canada Rural Finance Outreach Project. Hanoi: Development International Desjardins. http://www.chs.ubc.ca/lprv/OutputPDF/ PovertyWorkshopBib_Apr02.pdf.

ESCAP. (July 2002). Regional Commissions Development Update. Twelfth Issue. Activities of the Economic and Social Commissions for Asia and the Pacific. http://www.un.org/Depts/rcnyo/newsletter/NL12/Activities%20%20ESCAP.htm (accessed September 27, 2003).

FAO/UNDP. (August, 2002). Gender differences in the transitional economy of Vietnam: Key gender findings: Second Viet Nam Living Standards Survey, 1997–1998. Report prepared by the Food and Agriculture Organization of the United Nations, Regional Office for Asia and the Pacific with UNDP Support for Policy and Programme Development. Hanoi: UNDP.

Fawcett, B. (1999). Small loans change lives. Extracted from a Reuters report. *Grameen Dialogue, 38*: 3.

Gaile, G.L., and Foster, J. (1996). *Review of methodological approaches to the study of the impact of microenterprise credit programs.* Report on Assessing the Impact of Microenterprise Services (AIMS) in conjunction with USAID's Office of Microenterprise Development. Washington, D.C.: USAID.

GEO (2000). Policy Responses—Asia and the Pacific. In: Global Environment Outlook 2000. United Nations Environment Programme. http://www.grida.no/geo2000/english/0166.htm (accessed May 19, 2003).

Gibbons, D. (2003). Reducing the capital constraint in India: A collaboration with ICICI Bank. *Credit for the Poor. Cashpor, Inc.—The Network for Credit and Savings for the Hard-Core Poor, 37*(1): 3, 7.

Goodwin, R. (1997). Key issues for profitable bank engagement in microfinance. Paper presented at the Asia Regional Conference on Sustainable Banking with the Poor, Fourth Asia-Pacific Regional Workshop, Bangkok, 3–7 November. Brisbane: Foundation for Development Cooperation.

Goodwin, R. (1998). *The Role of Commercial Banks in Microfinance*. Brisbane: Foundation for Development Cooperation.

Gow, K.M. (2001a). Microfinance as a component of sustainable economic development in Asia. In: Shanableh, A., and Chang, W.P., eds., *Towards Sustainability in the Built Environment*. Brisbane: Queensland University of Technology, pp. 382–391.

Gow, K.M., Moore, B., Hoeksma, M., and Wood, B. (2000). How access to credit changes lives for very poor women in Asia. Paper presented at the Gender and Indochina Conference. Bangkok, WARI (Women's Action and Research Initiative), February 26–28.

GRET. (1999). General presentation of GRET's Microfinance project in Vietnam, Notes on GRET given to the author at an interview with Nichola Perrin on April 23, 1999, Hanoi.

Hassan, M.K., and Renteria-Guerrero, L. (1997). The experience of the Grameen Bank of Bangladesh in community development. *International Journal of Social Economics, 24*(12), 1488–1523.

Haynes, G.W., and Avery, R.J. (1996). Family businesses: Can the family and the business finances be separated? Preliminary Results. *Entrepreneurial and Small Business Finance, 5*(1): 61–74.

Hoeksma, M., Gow, K., and Finlay, M, (1998). Preparing to conduct a successful microfinance loan scheme in rural Vietnam. *Development Bulletin, 46*: 56–58.

Lee, W.C. (2003a). Making a difference: The microcredit Summit +5. *Credit for the poor. Cashpor, Inc.—The Network for Credit and Savings for the Hard-Core Poor, 37*: 8, 9.

Lee, W.C. (2003b). Taking AIM in a new direction. *Credit for the Poor. Cashpor, Inc.—The Network for Credit and Savings for the Hard-Core Poor, 38*: 1, 3.

Lee, W.C. (2003c). An interview with Associate Professor Sukor Kasim, Managing Director of AIM. *Credit for the poor. Cashpor, Inc.—The Network for Credit and Savings for the Hard-Core Poor, 38*: 4–5.

Mammem, K., and Paxson, C. (2000). Women's work and economic development. *Journal of Economic Perspectives, 14*(4): 141–164.

Mayoux, L. (2002a). Women's empowerment versus sustainability? Towards a new paradigm in micro-finance programmes. In: B. Lemire, R. Pearson, and G. Campbell, eds., *Women and Credit: Researching the Past, Refiguring the Future*, 2nd ed. Oxford: Berg, pp. 319–324.

Mayoux, L. (2002b). Women's empowerment or feminization of debt? Towards a new agenda in African micro-finance. Discussion paper For a One World Action Conference. Sponsored by the UK Department for International Development. London, March 21 and 22. http://www.wccnica.org/pubs/microfinance_paper1.pdf.

McGuire, P.B. (1998a, June). *Second Tier Microfinance Institutions in Asia*. Brisbane: The Foundation for Development Cooperation.

McGuire, P.B. (1998b, February). *Policy and Regulation for Sustainable Microfinance: Country Experiences in Asia.* Brisbane: The Foundation for Development Cooperation.

McGuire, P.B., and Conroy, J.D. (1998). *Effects on Microfinance of the 1997–1998 Asian Financial Crisis.* Brisbane: The Foundation for Development Cooperation.

McLaughlin, D. (2002). Microfinance partnerships: Opportunities and challenges. *Development Bulletin, 57*: 27–30.

Morduch, J. (2000). The role of subsidies in microfinance: evidence from the Grameen Bank. *Journal of Development Economics, 60*(1): 229–248.

Mosley, P. (2001). A simple technology for poverty-oriented project assessment. *Impact Assessment and Project Appraisal, 19*(1): 53–67.

Nguyen, H.H. (2001). Hunger Eradication and Poverty Reduction (HEARR) Activities in the High Land Provinces with the Ethnic Minorities in 1993–1997: The Directive Solution in 1998–2000. Vietnam: MOLISA. http://www.undp.org.vn/projects/vie96010/cemma/ras93103/027.htm.

Pearson, R. (2000). Gender, Globalisation and Transition Economies. Paper presented at the Gender and Indochina Conference. Bangkok, WARI (Women's Action and Research Initiative), February 26–28.

Pearson, R. (2001). Continuity and change—towards a conclusion. In: B. Lemire, R. Pearson, and G. Campbell, eds., *Women and Credit: Researching the Past, Refiguring the Future,* 2nd ed. Oxford: Berg, pp. 319–324.

Poster, W., and Salime, Z. (2002).The limits of microcredit: Transnational activitism and the evolution of EU sex equality policy. In: N.A. Naples and M. Desai, eds., *Women's Activitism and Globalization: Linking Local Struggles and Transnational Politics.* New York: Routledge, pp. 189–219.

Robinson, M.S. (2001). *The Microfinance Revolution. Vol. 1: Sustainable Finance for the Poor.* Washington, D.C.: World Bank.

Saywell, T. (2000). Mrs. Wang gets a taste for credit. *Far Eastern Economic Review, 163*(17): 56–58.

Sebstad, J., and Chen, M. (1996). *Overview of Studies on the Impact of Microenterprise Services (AIMS).* Washington, D.C.: USAID.

Sitathan, T. (2003). Singapore airlines fights to reinvent itself. *Asia Times,* May 28. http://www/singapore-window.org/sw03/030528at.htm (accessed January 21, 2004).

Teare, P. (1998). Grameen woman blues. http://www.junius.co.uk/LM/LM90/LM90Grameen.htm (accessed April 3, 2003).

The World Bank Group. (1999). The World Bank Group's Microfinance Institutional Action Plan 1999. Microcredit Summit meeting of Councils, 24–26 June 1999. Abidjan, Cote D'Ivoire. http://www.wbln0018.worldbank.org/.../sme?openform&Rural+and+Microfinance/SMEs&Policies+&+Guidelines (accessed September 27, 2003).

Thuy, Le Thi. (2000). VWU's experience with grassroots women and microfinance. Gender and Indochina Conference. Bangkok: WARI (Women's Action Research Initiative), 26–28 February.

Todd, H. (2002). Off the pavement and out of retail: The secret of escaping poverty—and men are important too. *Cashpor, Inc.—The Network for Credit and Savings for the Hard-Core Poor. Credit for the Poor, 35*: 13–15.

UNAIDS. (2000). AIDS epidemic Update: December 2000. How is Africa coping with HIV? The body: An AIDS and HIV infor mation resource. http://www.thebody.com.unaids/update/cope.html (accessed 27.09.05).

Vyas, J. (2002). Banking with poor self-employed women. In: B. Lemir e, R. Pearson, and G. Campbell, eds., *Women and Credit: Researching the Past, Refiguring the Future,* 2nd ed. Oxford: Berg, pp. 145–165.

Yunus, M. (1994). *Grameen Bank as I See It*. Dhaka: Grameen Bank.

Yunus, M. (1995). *Grameen Bank: Experiences and Reflections*. Dhaka: Grameen Bank.

Chapter 13

Citizens' Participation in Neighborhood Revitalization

Patricia A. Hippler

CONTENTS

Introduction

Few places are more in need of sustainable development strategies than the nation's urban neighborhoods. For decades, families who have been financially able have left these once-vibrant neighborhoods for the greener pastures of suburban living. Business and industry that used to be concentrated in and around cities have dispersed jobs and economic opportunity to the suburbs as well. Buildings are run down and infrastructure is crumbling. Crime is up,[1] schools are struggling, and access to jobs and needed services is practically nonexistent. People remaining in these neighborhoods do so only because they cannot afford to move out. They have little hope for their future or for the future of their children.

The severity of the crisis has left community leaders and politicians scrambling for a quick fix, something that will turn their cities and their neighborhoods around quickly and effectively. Yet, more than 50 years after Congress passed its first urban neighborhood revitalization program, the Housing Act of 1949, many neighborhoods are worse off than ever. Subsequent government programs,[2] encompassing billions of dollars of investment, have at best achieved only limited success in very localized areas.

Yet, amid increasing poverty and a widening gap between the haves and the have-nots,[3] there are signs of progress. Little by little, some neighborhoods are being renewed—not by faraway bureaucrats or even local politicians but instead by the very citizens who live in these communities. Through a variety of tools, ordinary citizens are turning their communities around and generating optimism for the sustainable future. Make no mistake; these neighborhoods still have a long way to go. Their decline did not happen overnight, and neither will their revitalization. But a review of the literature shows that citizens' participation can be a valuable tool to change the future of the nation's neighborhoods by not only revitalizing them, but also sustaining that revitalization.

This chapter examines the value of a participatory approach to sustainable neighborhood revitalization. It begins by defining participation and discussing why many scholars and planners say it should be a component of sustainable development efforts. The chapter further outlines some of the more common tools to facilitate participation and examples of participation efforts in various cities across the country. It also includes an important discussion of the limits and challenges of participation, as well as some suggestions to overcome those challenges.

Defining Participation

Simply stated, *participation* is "the meaningful involvement of people in decisions that affect their lives" (Hanna, 2000, p. 399). A participatory system should be broad and open enough to allow everyone with a stake in the outcome to have his or her opportunity to be heard (Hanna, 2000). This view of participation is the ideal; however, from a practical standpoint, it may not be possible to engage every single affected person in the decision-making process. No matter how good the participatory system, sometimes the number of participants is too large to include everyone.

Similarly, even people who stand to be impacted by a decision may have no interest in being involved in the decision-making process. The problems facing neighborhoods are complex and multifaceted. Although a citizen may recognize the problem of high crime, for example, he or she may lack understanding of the many factors that contribute to the problem and therefore lack the capacity to attempt to solve it.

As such, information plays a very important role in the process of participation. Communities cannot build consensus around an idea without communicating with citizens about the impact. The simple act of sharing information, of working to educate people about any given idea or initiative, is a form of participation (Hanna, 2000). But information alone does not empower people to influence the decisions that affect them; they must, after receiving the information, have the opportunity to communicate their own ideas, concerns, or desires[4] (Hanna, 2000).

Rationale behind Participation

No one knows better the problems facing their community than the people who live there every day. On the basis of firsthand experience, many neighborhood residents can determine where financial or human resources are needed the most and will do the most good over the long term (Bramhall, 1992; Rubin, 2000). Of the many things that can be learned from past attempts at neighborhood revitalization, the most important is that there is no single solution that will work in every neighborhood. Each community has its own unique characteristics, physical attributes, and workforce makeup. These factors will figure prominently in determining the success and sustainability of any given revitalization strategy (Nowak, 1997).

Participation also helps bring out the potential of people in the neighborhoods through networking, teamwork, and other participatory processes (Haynes and Nembhard, 1999). When a few people take matters into their own hands, by volunteering time or donating money, they motivate others to do the same, thereby increasing the impact of community-based efforts (Bramhall, 1992).

Although Porter (1997) argues for a market-based approach and relegates government and citizens to a supportive role on the sidelines,[5] Haynes and Nembhard (1999) argue that citizens should be front-and-center in the effort not only to create job opportunities in their neighborhoods but also to ensure those opportunities match the needs and skills of residents—a vital component of any sustainable development effort. Current approaches tend to miss the link between jobs and social betterment; as a result people move out of the community when they can rather than use their skills to help others in their neighborhood move up (Haynes and Nembhard, 1999).

Another reason justifying citizens' participation is the poor record of success for traditional initiatives. Top-down approaches have failed our nation's cities, not only because they failed to involve affected people but also because they failed to recognize the depth and complexity of the cities' problems. Many traditional revitalization efforts have focused on neighborhoods as real estate markets (Nowak, 1997). They might give a community a facelift by building or renovating housing, or even bringing in new business. But if the people cannot afford the housing and are not qualified for the jobs, the effort has not truly helped anyone.

Neighborhoods need more than a facelift. Their very foundation has been shaken, and the only way to strengthen them is to rebuild their social systems by getting people together to work toward a common goal. Participation restores the sense of community that is at the heart of America's neighborhoods. It helps ensure the real needs of the community are being addressed in a way that coincides with the goals of the community at large (United States General Accounting Office, 1995).

Participation Tools

Social Capital

There are many options available to communities that wish to engage in participatory planning and problem-solving processes. Those neighborhoods with a strong foundation of social capital will more easily be able to mobilize citizens into action using these tools. Social capital is vital to the success of community-based revitalization efforts because it represents an already existing infrastructure of coordination and cooperation among citizen groups, usually based on common traits such as race or religion[6] (Silverman, 2001).

Community Development Corporations

One of the most prominent and long-used tools to facilitate community participation is Community Development Corporations (CDCs). According to a survey conducted in the mid-1990s for the National Congress for Community Economic Development (NCCED), the more than 2,000 CDCs around the country have produced more than 400,000 units of affordable housing, developed 23 million square feet of commercial and industrial space, lent $200 million to minority business enterprises, and created as many as 67,000 full-time, permanent jobs (Harrison and Glasmeier, 1997).

Today, CDCs are elaborate business-oriented organizations[7] (Blakely and Bradshaw, 2002). Although the organizations, most of which have formed since the 1960s, were originally very focused on changing the physical place in neighborhoods, they have evolved to address social concerns as well. They work to provide services such as child care, family support, health care, economic development, school reform, housing improvements and an array of quality of life activities (Naparstek and Dooley, 1997). According to Sullivan (in Naparstek and Dooley, 1997), CDCs work to bring about social change in a neighborhood by

> changing the ethnic composition of the residents; changing the attitudes of individual residents already there; changing the way individuals relate to one another; and changing the way the neighborhood and its residents interact with powerful people and institutions outside the neighborhood. (p. 5, Proquest)

It is their comprehensive, multifaceted approach—one that is sensitive to the needs of both business and human beings—that makes CDCs successful in creating jobs and alleviating poverty in low-income neighborhoods (Blakely and Bradshaw, 2002).

Governing Nonprofits

Another tool that has been used successfully is governing nonprofit organizations. These are nonprofit organizations that do not provide any specific service but instead form their goals and missions "on very broad social and political issues" and work to build coalitions among a broad range of groups (Hula, Jackson, and Orr, 1997, p. 1, Proquest). Governing nonprofits seem to operate on the theory of strength in numbers in that they recognize the value of bringing together people with broad, collective interests—groups that had been underrepresented or not represented at all—to get their voices heard (Hula et al., 1997). The authors reviewed the actions of three governing nonprofits, in Baltimore,[8] Detroit,[9] and Los Angeles,[10] and found the organizations all made an impact on the actions of government in their communities, to varying degrees.[11] Important to the success of these organizations is establishing working relationships with the existing political structure without being co-opted by strong mayors or other leading political figures.

Responsive Participatory Redesign

Fung (2001) discusses the merits of responsive participatory redesign (RPR) as a tool for planning and urban design that allows citizens to take the initiative to correct defects. Elements of RPR, such as "feedback loops" that enable citizens to respond to problems and suggest changes, could also be valuable in revitalization efforts. The bottom-up approach allows citizens to use their knowledge and ingenuity to change the shape of their neighborhoods (Fung, 2001). Fung focuses on spatial issues (as opposed to poverty or joblessness), and his assessment of RPR's role in the Chicago Alternative Policing Strategy (CAPS) demonstrates the impact spatial issues can have on community well-being and quality of life. The neighborhoods examined were able to take an active role in making their communities safer by working with police to cut down on local drug trafficking and reduce gang activity[12] (Fung 2001). Although these problems were small in scale on a citywide level, they had a noticeable impact at the neighborhood level and may have escalated had there not been a system in place for citizens to participate with law enforcement in a solution (Fung, 2001).

Government Programs and Initiatives

While locally generated initiatives without strong ties to government tend to be more successful at spawning neighborhood revitalization (Hula et al., 1997), government has attempted to harness the power of community participation in neighborhood revitalization as well. Among the most recent of those efforts are the Clinton administration's Empowerment Zones and Enterprise Communities programs. Enacted into law in 1993, the programs promised both funding tools and regulatory relief to a limited number of communities that could demonstrate broad support of a strategic plan by citizen groups, local governments, social service agencies, businesses, and universities (Peirce, 1994; Riposa, 1996). The six Empowerment Zone communities[13] would receive $100 million in funding for social services and a variety of other tax and financial incentives. According to a 1996 report from the United States General Accounting Office, the Empowerment Zones initiative was being implemented in different ways in the six communities,[14] but in each case, participation was playing a vital role in stakeholder communication and strategy development.[15]

Participation in Action

Minneapolis

A number of case studies demonstrate how participation is being used to help address both physical and social ills of neighborhoods over the long term. Minneapolis launched its Neighborhood Revitalization Program (NRP) in 1990 to put decision-making power in the hands of individual neighborhoods (Martin and Pentel, 2002). The goals were to build neighborhood capacity, to encourage cooperation among various levels of government and citizens, to involve citizens in rebuilding the services they need, and to restore a sense of place in the community (Bramhall, 1992). The program targeted all neighborhoods, both rich and poor. However, those that were historically the poorest received the most funding (Martin and Pentel, 2002). Citizens worked together to focus efforts on everything from economic development and park development to crime and security, and human services (Martin and Pentel, 2002). In the city's Whittier neighborhood, the community-based Whittier Alliance made construction of a new school its top priority. Giving citizens the opportunity to prioritize and address their collective concerns has helped increase people's sense of ownership in their community (Martin and Pentel, 2002).

Portland's Albina Neighborhood

After years of citizens being displaced by various attempts at urban renewal, Portland's Albina community embarked on a community planning effort in 1989 that involved more than 100 public and private entities (Bramhall, 1992). Citizens initiated the process and worked together to develop a plan that focuses on infill housing and rehabilitation, as well as creation of jobs (Bramhall, 1992).

Denver's Cole Neighborhood

Although Albina residents initiated their neighborhood revitalization effort, citizens in Denver's Cole neighborhood had to be persuaded (Bramhall,

1992). Once citizens realized they would have the financial support, as well as the support of business, they formed the Cole Coalition to rebuild their neighborhood through building maintenance and rehabilitation, tree plantings, and citizen patrols (Bramhall, 1992).

North Little Rock

Building trust through citizen participation has also helped North Little Rock, Arkansas, address ongoing decay of its neighborhoods and commercial areas. Following a murder in the downtown, citizens demanded a comprehensive effort to turn their city around (Baxter, 1995). As a result, the city turned to two federal initiatives for help, the Local Initiative Support Coalition and Main Street Program, and implemented programs to use volunteers to rehabilitate homes and buildings, develop skills through sports, and improve neighborhood safety with community policing (Baxter, 1995).

Indianapolis

In Indianapolis, Mayor Stephen Goldsmith was elected in part because of his plan to limit the scope of government and give political decision-making power to citizens. He was successful to some extent in that citizens and neighborhoods were mobilized and ready to act to improve their living conditions (McGovern, 2003). In some of the targeted neighborhoods, the city invested more than $1.5 billion in improving streets, sidewalks, and sewers (McGovern, 2003). Yet, the overall impact, measured in availability of affordable housing, has been small, caused in large part by the fact that he cut the size of government so much that most neighborhoods did not have the financial or human resources[16] they needed truly to make a difference (McGovern, 2003).

Challenges and Limits to Participation

Participatory systems are by no means simple to implement, nor are they a panacea for solving the many problems of declining neighborhoods. The Goldsmith case in Indianapolis demonstrates a few of the limits and challenges to participation as a tool for neighborhood revitalization. First and foremost, citizens cannot be expected to turn their neighborhoods around all by themselves. The problems facing neighborhoods are very complex and may require more than a group of citizens can achieve. They need the financial and intellectual support of experienced community leaders and developers to make their neighborhoods better places to live and work (McGovern, 2003; Nowak, 1997; Silverman, 2001). Another limitation, illustrated by the Goldsmith case as well as the Minneapolis case, is that lack of representation by certain groups in participatory efforts can lead to initiatives that may harm those groups. In both Indianapolis and Minneapolis, housing initiatives focused on new construction and rehabilitation, primarily in the form of turning rental properties back into single-family homes[17] (Martin and Pentel, 2002; McGovern, 2003). This may leave renters without affordable housing; therefore, it is important when developing a plan to ensure all interests are represented.

In some cases, government leaders may view citizen participation as a threat because it results in conflicting demands that destabilize government order because few of the demands could ever be met by government (Berry, Portney, and Thomson, 1993). Skepticism among citizens—especially those who have been struggling for so long to overcome poverty—leaves many people wary of getting involved with government (United States General Accounting Office, 1995). Many want to see results before they are even willing to participate (United States General Accounting Office, 1995). For communities that are able to organize, there is much red tape to negotiate on the path to obtain funding for initiatives to address the communities' various concerns; federal government is very compartmentalized (United States General Accounting Office, 1995), and, despite efforts to change, there is still limited coordination among agencies.[18]

Another challenge to successful participatory efforts is the difference in debate and decision-making style among established developers and citizens. The formal, bureaucratic style of decision making may drown out the voices of citizens who are more informal in their approach (Tauxe, 1995). In a case study involving growth in Mercer County, North Dakota, Tauxe found that local conventions for decision making carried less weight with those in power even though citizens using the local, informal means stood to be impacted most by the outcome. According to Tauxe, local business leaders and developers shared similar interests, and their opinions were "represented disproportionately over those of others who were not accustomed to leading in local politics"[19] (p. 7, Proquest).

Finally, Nowak (1997) notes that despite the successes of community-based development, it has only made a small dent in the overwhelming challenges facing neighborhoods:

> In most of America's low-income urban neighborhoods, even the best community-based development efforts function as managers of decline as much as catalysts of significant renewal … in the absence of other economic strategies, community-based initiatives cannot reverse the downward spiral. (p. 3, Proquest)

Overcoming Challenges and Limitations

Despite the challenges, it is clear participatory processes are a promising method to achieve neighborhood revitalization. Berry, Portney, and Thomson (1993) make three primary recommendations[20] for building effective citizen participation programs:

- Boards or other structures designed to facilitate participation must be given real authority, not just an advisory role.
- Existing government leaders and administrators must be willing to work with participation structures to implement ideas and initiatives. Incentives must be included to stop administrators from setting up the effort to fail as a means to protect their own turf.
- Participation efforts must be citywide, with each neighborhood represented, and to build credibility, programs should be offered to all citizens, not just low-income or minorities.

In addition, the authors suggest that participatory systems must have control over some financial resources, that neighborhood associations should have the means to communicate with all households in their areas a few times a year, that neighborhood association members should be included on other city boards with public representatives, that cities must establish effective means of communication with neighborhoods to keep them aware of issues that impact them, that volunteers leading neighborhood associations should be in place for relatively short periods of time, and that neighborhood associations should not become involved in political activities (Berry et al., 1993).

Conclusion

Citizen participation systems offer a promising opportunity for neighborhoods of all shapes and sizes in need of sustainable revitalization. Government at every level has tried to address the challenges facing neighborhoods—low-skill workers, overregulation, high building costs, high crime rates, dilapidated infrastructure, deteriorating public schools, and declining tax bases—but to no avail. Neighborhoods are simply too unique for a top-down approach to revitalization to be effective in every location over the long term. In response, more scholars and practitioners are turning to citizen participation for results.

Participation works because it allows citizens the opportunity to be involved in changing their own destiny. People who live in struggling neighborhoods know best the most pressing problems they face and can help direct money and other resources to address those problems. At the same time, a greater sense of ownership and community is generated, and thatonly enhances the impact of the revitalization effort.

Participatory efforts have achieved some success in big cities such as Los Angeles and Minneapolis, as well as in smaller areas such as North Little Rock, Arkansas, and the Cole neighborhood in Denver. In terms of the lessons learned, citizen participation systems, used in conjunction with financial and other redevelopment tools, can breathe new life into big cities and small towns across the nation.

Notes

1. Recent data show crime rates in the nation's largest cities have dropped slightly; however, crime rates are still very high in urban areas compared to those in suburbs and rural communities.
2. Other federal initiatives include the Demonstration Cities and Metropolitan Development Act of 1966, the Housing and Urban Development Act of 1968, the Community Development Block Grant program of 1974, Enterprise Zones in 1988, and Empowerment Zones in 1992.
3. Mudacumura (2002) highlights the income disparity, noting that the richest 20% of the world's population represent 82.7% of the total world income, and the poorest 20% represent just 1.4% of the total world income.
4. Hanna (2000) makes a case for information and indirect participation as valuable contributors to the participatory process. He urges recognition of these forms of participation and also points to the limitations in that information is sometimes provided as a means to "guide opinions and gain endorsement" of a project already decided on without the input of citizens.
5. Porter makes some valid points about the value of facilitating the growth of market forces rather than trying to change them, and of worker training programs that have business interests rather than social welfare interests at their center. But his implication that neighborhoods should just step aside for new business regardless of its potential impact ignores important community and quality of life issues.
6. Silverman examines the mobilization of social capital for neighborhood revitalization and points out the importance of paying attention to the underlying values of the group when attempting to involve them in a particular revitalization issue.
7. CDCs today work very closely with private, mainly small businesses, as well as the financial community. Their services now include joint ventures with entrepreneurs, housing development networks, and bank credit lines.
8. Baltimore's BUILD (Baltimoreans United in Leadership Development) works to help low-income neighborhoods in the city. Of the three governing nonprofits studied by Hula and associates, it was found to have the broadest community support and most significant impact.

9. New Detroit was created in the 1960s in response to civil unrest in Detroit. It has had some success in its mission of racial harmony and economic development.

10. Rebuild Los Angeles, or RLA, was formed after the riots that resulted from the verdict in the Rodney King beating case. It was created by government and thus continues to have close ties with the political establishment in the city, though it has had some success in drawing needed services back to distressed areas.

11. Refer to Hula and associates (1997) for a full discussion of the impacts of BUILD, New Detroit, and RLA.

12. The author studies three specific cases in the CAPS program. Residents in Rogers Park targeted three rental properties at the center of a drug-trafficking problem by opening the lines of communication with the landlord, adding new lighting, and arranging citizen patrols. At a transit authority bus stop, citizens fought gang activity by working with school and transit officials to prevent students from lingering at the stop. Finally, at Gill Park, the neighborhood helped stop drug activity by targeting patrols at peak times identified by citizens, enforcing loitering and curfew laws, and cleaning up the park by clearing trees and improving the facilities to attract more legitimate users.

13. The six Empowerment Zone communities are Atlanta, Baltimore, Chicago, Detroit, New York, and Philadelphia-Camden. From the 500 community applicants, 6 cities were designated Empowerment Zones, 2 as Supplemental Empowerment Zones, and 65 as Enterprise Communities, of which 4 were designated Enhanced Enterprise Communities. These communities also received considerable federal funding, though less than full Empowerment Zones.

14. Four of the six zones (Atlanta, Baltimore, Detroit, and New York) formed nonprofit corporations to administer the program; Chicago and Philadelphia are operating through city government.

15. At the time the report was issued, Empowerment Zone participants indicated via survey that community representation was a significant factor in aiding implementation of the program; however, the participation requirement also hindered some efforts because of a history of antagonism and distrust between local government and community leaders.

16. In his efforts to cut government, Goldsmith dismissed a number of the city's best planners and developers, who could have served as valuable resources to neighborhoods as they embarked on their revitalization efforts.

17. Some view the Minneapolis NRP effort as an attack on renters in the city. This example illustrates that self-interests can overtake broader city goals if equal representation is not achieved.

18. The report cites a number of initiatives that were being launched to help improve coordination, including Vice President Al Gore's National Performance Review and Department of Housing and Urban Development plans to consolidate 60 programs into 3.

19. As an anthropologist, Tauxe observed a series of public hearings in the mid-1970s as Mercer County's coal and energy industries were growing. She argues that current participatory systems will not be effective until decision makers become more culturally sensitive and are willing to take all people seriously.
20. See Berry and associates (1993, pp. 295–296).

References

Baxter, C. (1995). Partnerships: Good citizen/government relations. *Journal of Housing and Community Development, 52,* 34–36.

Berry, J.M., Portney, K.E., and Thomson, K. (1993). *The rebirth of urban democracy.* Washington, D.C.: The Brookings Institution.

Blakely, E.J., and Bradshaw, T.K. (2002). *Planning local economic development: Theory and practice.* Thousand Oaks, CA: Sage Publications.

Bramhall, B. (1992). Building people power in three cities. *Planning, 58,* 23–26.

Fung, A. (2001). Beyond and below the new urbanism: Citizen participation and responsive spatial reconstruction. *Boston College Environmental Affairs Law Review, 28,* 615–635.

Hanna, K. (2000). The paradox of participation and the hidden role of information. *APA Journal, 66,* 398–410.

Harrison, B., and Glasmeier, A.K. (1997). Why business alone won't redevelop the inner city: A friendly critique of Michael Porter's approach to urban revitalization. *Economic Development Quarterly, 11,* 28–38.

Haynes, C., and Nembhard, J.G. (1999). Cooperative economics—a community revitalization strategy. *Review of Black Political Economy, 27,* 47–71.

Hula, R.C., Jackson, C., and Orr, M. (1997). Urban politics, governing nonprofits and community revitalization. *Urban Affairs Review, 32,* 459–489.

Martin, J.A., and Pentel, P.R. (2002). What the neighbors want: The neighborhood revitalization program's first decade. *Journal of the American Planning Association, 68,* 435–449.

McGovern, S.J. (2003). Ideology, consciousness, and inner-city redevelopment: The case of Stephen Goldsmith's Indianapolis. *Journal of Urban Affairs, 25,* 1–25.

Mudacumura, G.M. (2002). Towards a general theory of sustainability: Bridging key development dimensions through a multi-paradigm perspective. Ph.D. dissertation, Pennsylvania State University, Harrisburg.

Naparstek, A.J., and Dooley, D. (1997). Countering urban disinvestment through community-building initiatives. *Social Work, 42,* 506–514.

Nowak, J. (1997). Neighborhood initiative and the regional economy. *Economic Development Quarterly, 11,* 3–10.

Peirce, N. (1994, May 16). Examining the new politics of empowerment zones. *New Orleans Times-Picayune,* p. B7.

Porter, M.E. (1997). New strategies for inner-city economic development. *Economic Development Quarterly, 11,* 11–17.

Riposa, G. (1996). From enterprise zones to empowerment zones: The community context of urban economic development. *The American Behavioral Scientist, 39,* 536–543.

Rubin, H.J. (2000). Economic partnering with the poor: Why local governments should work with community-based development organizations to promote economic development. *International Journal of Public Administration, 23,* 1679–1709.

Silverman, R.M. (2001). CDCs and charitable organizations in the urban south: Mobilizing social capital based on race and religion for neighborhood revitalization. *Journal of Contemporary Ethnography, 30,* 240–268.

Tauxe, C.S. (1995). Marginalizing public participation in local planning: An ethnographic account. *Journal of the American Planning Association, 61,* 471–481.

United States General Accounting Office. (1995). *Community development: Comprehensive approaches address multiple needs but are challenging to implement.* Washington, D.C.: Author.

United States General Accounting Office. (1996). *Community development: Status of urban empowerment zones.* Washington, D.C.: Author.

Chapter 14

Toward a Sustainable Rural Development in Africa: A Sociological Case Study of a World Bank Agricultural Development Project in Nigeria

Andrew A. Zekeri

CONTENTS

Introduction

During the last 30 years of the 20th century, the concepts of sustainable development and sustainability were adopted as developmental goals among academics and practitioners from numerous disciplines and nationalities. What was once considered an academic debate has moved to the center stage of development plans, and "sustainability" was the focus of discussion at the World Summit on Sustainable Development (WSSD) held in Johannesburg, South Africa, in September 2002. One of the goals of the WSSD was to influence the development agenda for the near future.

Contemporary trends in the rural areas of many African countries seem to demand bold initiatives in rural policy and a concerted effort in sustainable rural development policy. At the national and international levels, a comprehensive and effective rural policy has been an elusive goal, and sustainable rural development policy has become more of a rhetoric exercise than a reality. Still, some initiatives in rural development are under way in the first decade of the 21st century and others are on the horizon, especially in science and education.

A search for a sustainable rural development policy for Africa in the 21st century requires that we take stock, critically review previous rural developmental projects, and identify the pitfalls—the main agenda for this chapter. Such a review can give perspective and suggest directions for a new agenda to apply social science research and education in the search for sustainable development policy and administration.

The purpose of this chapter is to examine the impact of a World Bank Agricultural Development Project in Igalaland, Nigeria, on rural farmers and their farming system. The chapter will focus on adoption of recommended farm practices and reasons why the project failed to achieve its stated aims such as poverty alleviation and the augmentation of domestic output of agricultural products in Igalaland. Policy implications of the findings and lessons learned for sustainable rural development in the 21st century are presented.

Defining Sustainable Rural Development

This section outlines the basic sociological ideas or concepts that are used to analyze and interpret the collected data. The basic sociological concept used to analyze and interpret the data is sustainable rural development. Thus, this section underscores the meaning of sustainable rural development while highlighting its success and failure factors. The chapter further identifies some of the essential elements of sustainable rural development that are used as criteria for assessing the performance of the Ayangba Agricultural Development Project (AADP).

What Is Rural Development?

Rural development is a concept that has received widespread attention for the past 30 years among scholars in developing countries and donor agencies. Despite its popular use, there is a considerable disagreement among scholars about the meaning and definition of the term *rural development*. Some scholars equate rural development with agricultural development. For instance, the World Bank (1985, p. 3–4) conceives rural development as

> a strategy designed to improve the economic and social life of a specific group of people—the rural poor. It involves extending the benefits of development to the poorest among those who seek a livelihood in rural areas. This group includes small-scale farmers, tenants and the landless.

Similarly, Robert Chambers (1983) thinks that rural development should include rural women and children. To Chambers (1983, p. 147–148), rural development is a

> Strategy to enable a specific group of people, poor rural women and men, to gain for themselves and their children more of what they wanted and need. It involves helping the poorest among those who seek a livelihood in the rural areas to demand

and control more of the benefits of development. The group
includes small-scale farmers, tenants and the landless.

From the preceding definitions, one can infer that rural development
is a process that seeks to improve the living standard of the rural poor
by addressing the myriad problems from which they suffer. Therefore,
rural development is a process that involves not only agricultural development but the improvement of economic aspects of rural life. The
intention is to improve the lifestyle of the rural poor through increased
production and equitable distribution of resources (Chambers, 1993). Rural
development implies the process of improving the living standards of the
rural population in terms of material entities such as food and income
(Cernea, 1985; Chambers, 1997, 1993; Karamah, 2001; Miachi and Zekeri,
1997; Zekeri and Miachi 1996; Zekeri and Ochimana, 2000).

According to Uma Lele (1985), *rural development* is defined as improving living standards of the mass of the low-income population residing
in rural areas and making the process of their development self-sustaining
(1985, p. 20). Lele further contends that this simple definition has three
important features with substantial implications for ways rural development
programs are designed and implemented. These features are (1) improving
the living standard of the subsistence population, (2) including mass
participation, and (3) making the process self-sustaining. Self-sustenance
means involving the subsistence populations in development programs.

Sustainability

Sustainability became the watchword for development in the 1990s,
precisely because it is a multifaceted concept, having different meanings
for different players in international development arena (Conway and
Barbier, 1990; Munasinghe and Shearer, 1995; Pearce, 1993; Stone, 2003).
By far the largest and most powerful players in the search for sustainability
are the international development agencies, particularly the World Bank
and bilateral donors including the United States Agency for International
Development (Francis and Youngberg, 1990; Stone, 2003; Zekeri, 2002).
The World Bank has embraced the multifaceted concept of sustainability
as a framework to guide the search operational strategies to reduce poverty
(World Bank, 1997, 2002, 2003).

According to the Operation Evaluation Department (OED) of the World
Bank, sustainability includes the capacity of a project to continue to deliver
its intended quantitative and qualitative benefits over a long period (OED,
1986, p. 1). Along the same line, Honadle and Vansant (1985, p. 2) define
sustainability as

the percentage of project-initiated goods and services that is still delivered and maintained five years after the termination of donor resources, the continuation of local action stimulated by the project, and the generation of successor services and initiatives as a result of project built local capacity.

In this study, Honadle and Vansant's (1985) and Lele's (1985) definition is employed. Sustainable rural development means development aimed at improving living standards of the mass of the low-income population residing in rural areas and making the process of their development self-sustaining with the ability to preserve and defend their way of life after the project ends. *Sustainable rural development* as the concept is analyzed in this chapter also builds the capacity of rural residents to act effectively, to solve their common problems collectively by using local available resources, and to pursue their common interests after the project ends.

Success

The often-ambitious targets of the World Bank Rural Development Strategy have not been met. Some of the project approaches employed have been less successful, and in many cases the benefits seem unlikely to be sustained (Lele, 1985; World Bank, 1988). Despite the apparent attractiveness and theoretical advantages of integrated rural development projects, such projects often fail.

Failure Factors of Past Rural Development Projects

Professionals from the Western world are often in positions of carrying out cross-cultural projects with the avowed purpose of improving conditions in developing countries. The record is replete with major problems, unsuccessful projects, and often disenchantment on both sides of national boundaries. A major disappointment has been the failure of most rural development projects to benefit significantly the poor majorities in developing countries.

The failure occurred because the beneficiaries did not participate in projects aimed at their own development. Real development must be people centered instead of production oriented. In fact, some critics define beneficiary participation as integral to authentic development.

Viewed from the preceding definitions of sustainable rural development, earlier project analysis led to the conclusion that limited effectiveness of the rural development projects can be attributed to a combination of factors: ambitious project targets, lack of profitable technical packages, poor knowledge of the sociocultural environment and its impact on project interventions, scarcity of trained manpower, and inadequate planning and implementing capacity of national institutions (Cernea, 1985; Lele, 1985; Miachi, 1983; Miachi and Zekeri, 1997; Zekeri, 1989a, 2002; Zekeri and Ochimana, 2000). The human part of development projects was assumed to be infinitely malleable as long as profit per hectare was maintained. There was a failure to consider the social and cultural context of projects. This failure invited inappropriate design at best and led to projects that were ineffective and were not wanted by their supposed beneficiaries. Furthermore, expatriate technical assistance is a poor long-run substitute for local capability, even if it enhances efficiency.

The Case Study: Ayangba Agricultural Development Project

With the foregoing points of argument at the back of our mind, let us now examine some facts emerging from the AADP and test some our arguments against such facts. The AADP, located in Kogi State, was based on the design of the World Bank–supported projects in northern Nigeria at Funtua, Gusau, and Gombe (see Table 14.1). The project was part of the World Bank Rural Development Strategy, which sought to expand development efforts and resources for alleviating poverty in rural areas of less developed countries (World Bank, 1988). The Rural Development initiative was announced at the annual meeting by the bank's president in September 1973 and elaborated in a policy paper dated February 1975 (World Bank, 1988). The rural development strategy enabled the bank to shift the focus of development efforts toward smallholders, whose productivity and efficiency had previously not been well recognized.

The AADP was funded by a loan from the World Bank, and its staff played an important role in the design and management of the project. The objectives were to raise crop production by means of technical advice, supply of inputs, and provision of feeder roads; to raise livestock and fisheries production; to establish forestry plantations; to improve infrastructure by the provision of rural water supplies; and to aid institution building by the establishment of project headquarters at Ayangba (World Bank, 1985, 1988). The Rural Development Sector Policy Paper described the operational goals of the strategy as improved productivity, increased employment and thus higher incomes for target groups, as well as a minimal acceptable level of food, shelter, education, and health. In addition to the expatriates recruited by the World Bank, an independent project management unit was established under the Ministry of Agriculture and Natural Resources to execute the project.

Table 14.1 Agricultural Development Projects in Nigeria[a]

	Name	Loan Number	Loan Amount (US$M)	Approval Date	Project Costs (US$M)	Beneficiaries (Families)	Technical Assistance	
							Staff Years[a]	Consultant Months[b]
1	Funtua	1092	29.0	12/74	57.6	60,000	75	—
2	Gusau	1099	19.0	12/74	37.4	41,000	59	—
3	Gombe	1164	21.0	12/74	42.1	32,000	53	60
4	Lafia	1454	27.0	06/77	85.0	42,000	61	12
5	Ayangba	1455	35.0	06/77	114.0	105,000	78	28
6	Bida	1667	23.0	09/79	64.4	60,000	70	50
7	Ilorin	1668	27.0	09/79	64.4	90,000	65	125
8	Oyo North	1838	28.0	08/80	69.4	55,000	60	36
9	Ekita Akoko	1854	32.5	12/80	80.5	70000	75	30
10	Agr. Tech. Asst	2029	47.0	06/81	120.1	n.a.	318	72
11	Bauchi State	1981	132.0	04/81	350.6	280,000	240	71
12	Kano State	1982	142.0	04/81	482.2	430,000	210	164
13	Sokoto State	2185	147.0	06/82	498.7	482,000	125	108
14	Kaduna State	2436	122.0	06/84	194.0	430,000	157	125
15	Multi - State I[c]	2733	162.0	06/86	256.4	245,000	—	286
16	South Borno	2741	25.0	06/86	39.3	42,000	25	20
	Total		1,018.5		2,556.1	2,464,000	1,671	1,187

[a] For internationally recruited staff.

[b] For specialized consultancy services.

[c] Seven states: Anambra, Bendl, Benue, Cross River, Ano, Ogun, and Plateau.

Source: Rural Development: World Bank Experience, 1985–1986.

The Project Area

The project was located in Ankpa, Dekina, Bassa, and Idah, Ofu, and Omala Local Government Council Areas of the state, with about 150,000 farm families cultivating some 300,000 hectares (Miachi, 1983; World Bank, 1988; Zekeri, 2002; Zekeri and Miachi, 1996). This area was formerly known as the Igala Province. The people of the area are predominantly of the Igala tribe, though Bassa and Bassa Nge are also numerically important. The area is bounded to the north and west by the Benue and Niger rivers.

A complex of cropping system exists in the area because of the rainfall pattern and length of the growing season. The crops grown in the area are the long-season crops such as yam, cassava, cocoyam, and pigeon pea. Others are medium-length season crops such as rice, cotton, guinea corn, millet, maize, bambara nuts, and cowpea. Oil palm trees are widespread. Poultry, goats, and sheep are the most important animals in the area. There are few cattle, and pigs can be found only in particular communities.

As alluded to earlier, the World Bank loan was intended to assist the state and federal governments to finance an agricultural development project designed to increase crop production through improved farm practices and expanded extension services; the development of vital crop varieties, and roads; the provision of credit facilities, inputs required to increase production and farm incomes; as well as support for livestock, forestry, and fishery development. One other purpose of this chapter is to highlight experiences in a way that enables us to learn from it, so that foresight in design and implementation becomes clearer.

Research Methods

The case study draws on a series of independent studies conducted by colleagues and me in 1984, 1989, 1999, and 2000–2001 (see Miachi and Zekeri, 1997; Zekeri, 1989a, 1989b, 1990a, 1990b, 1992a, 1992b, 2002; Zekeri and Ochimana, 2000). A variety of methods were used in each of the studies. Open-ended in-depth interviews included approximately 110 individuals. Some participants were recruited through local churches, a public health center, and land development schemes in Iyale, Okura-Olafia, and Egume. Interview sessions were designed to give us qualitative understanding of how rural farmers viewed the agricultural project in their land. In addition, questionnaires were administered to 300 farmers in the area.

The questionnaire was designed to collect information on family size, age, gender, educational attainment, marital status, personal income from farming, size and location of farms, major crops, major type of yams, livestock raised, and opinions about the adoption of the AADP recommended farming practices and new crop varieties. The questionnaires, with explanatory cover letters, were sent to extension agents, veterinary officers, and home economic agents in the project area, who contacted the farmers. Of the 300 farmers, 214 were contacted and interviewed. The completion rate was 71%.

Measuring Adoption

Adoption of new farm practices was measured by actual use of farm practices. Respondents were asked to rate the extent to which they were using a series of AADP-recommended farm practices. Response categories were a great extent, somewhat, and not at all. They were also asked to note possible reasons for not using the practices. The findings to be presented later are based on focus group interviews, individual open-ended interviews, and analysis of survey results.

Neglect of Cultural Values

Respondents were asked, "In your opinion, do you think the AADP neglected the cultural values and preference of the Igalas?"

Results

Table 14.2 shows the respondents' socioeconomic characteristics. Most of the rural farmers who responded to the study were male. The majority (97%) of the overall sample were married. Education varied significantly. Of the respondents, 42% never went to school, 36% had adult education, and only 22% completed their primary education. None of the respondents had advanced education.

The majority had more than three farms that were larger than 14 acres. Most had an annual income from farming that is less than US$100.00. Crops grown were classified by seasons. Corn is the most grown rainy season crop in the area. In fact, more than 90% of the farmers grow corn. Moreover, the dry season crops grown in the area include corn, guinea corn, millet, and bambara nuts, grown by 13.3%, 50.3%, 22.7%, and 13.85%, respectively, of local farmers.

Table 14.2 Socioeconomic Characteristics of Respondents and Types of Crops Grown (*N* = 214)

	Percentage		*Percentage*
Gender		**Personal Income from Farming**	
Male	61	**Annually**	
Female	39	Under 1000 naira	34.7
Education		1000 to 2999 naira	57.6
Never went to school	42	3000 to 4999 naira	7.4
Adult education	36	**Rainy Season Crops**	
Class 7 passout	22	Corn	90.6
Marital Status?		Beans	5.0
Married	97	Millet	3.3
Divorced	0	Barbara nuts	—
Widowed	0	Mellon	—
Not married	03	**Dry Season Crops**	
Number of Farms Owned		Corn	13.3
One farm	28	Guinea corn	50.3
Two farms	37	Millet	22.7
Three farms	34	Barbara nuts	13.8
Size farms		Pigeon peas	—
1–5 acres	17.0	**Major Type of Yams**	
5–9 acres	11.6	White yam (Odoli)	88.7
10–14 acres	23.4	Yellow yam (Ogoma)	2.8
14 or more acres	48.2	Water yam (Ebina)	8.6

Adoption of Recommended Farm Practices

Table 14.3 shows the adoption of the AADP new farm technologies. Respondents were asked, "To what extent do you use the following AADP recommended farm practices?" The data showed that the majority (more than 60%) of the rural farmers are not using the recommended practices. More than 90% are not applying herbicides to control weeds or insecticides to control insects, treating seeds before planting, or treating seeds before storage; 88.5% are not using the improved breeding practices.

Reasons for Not Using the Recommended Farm Practices

Respondents were asked, "If you are not using any of the AADP's methods of farming, which of the following may be your reason?" The results are presented in Figure 14.1. About 94% felt that the main reason for not using the AADP farm practices was that the labor cost is too high. Around

Table 14.3 Are You Using the Following AADP Recommended Farm Practices? (*N* = 214)

	Not at All (Percentage)
Applying fertilizer to crops	61.5
Applying herbicide to control weeds	92.1
Applying insecticide to control insects	95.3
Treating seeds before planting	90.6
Treating seeds before storage	91.1
Taking good care of animals' health	87.9
Using improved breeding practices	88.5
Deworming animals	78.9
Keeping animals in good housing	73.4

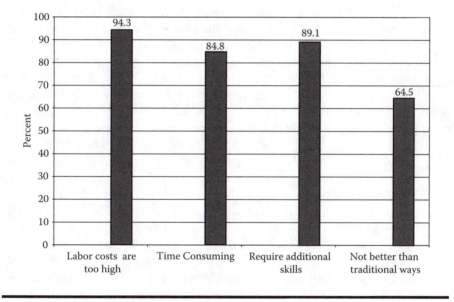

Figure 14.1 Reasons for not using the AADP recommended farm practices.

85% noted they were time consuming, and 89.1% felt they required additional skills. This is because farming in the project area is solidly and sensibly based on mixed cropping. Two thirds of the cultivated area is planted in crop mixtures, and virtually more than 90% of the grain cultivation takes place in mixed crop enterprises. In addition to greater efficiency in the use of hand labor, there are other substantial economic reasons for this. More than 64% noted that the AADP's recommended farm practices were not better than their traditional methods.

Table 14.4   "In Your Opinion, Do You Think the AADP Neglected the Cultural Values and Preferences of the Igalas?"

	Former AADP Employees	Farmers
Strongly agree	41.8	62.0[a]
Disagree	49.1	27.1[a]
Don't KNOW	9.1	10.7
Total percentage	100.0	100.0
Number	58	155

[a] Chi-square = 8.73 with 2 degrees of freedom. $P < .01$.

Cultural Values and Preferences

In the analysis for this section, respondents were divided into two analytic subgroups on the basis of their association with the project. The farmers were asked, "Were you an employee of the AADP or a ministry of agriculture posted staff member to the AADP?" Responses were dichotomized to separate AADP employees from non-AADP employees. Project employees had been full-time farmers before they were employed for the project. Non-AADP employees were full-time farmers who continued to depend on farming as their primary source of income. Of the 300 farmers, 214 (71%) returned completed questionnaires; among these, 59 (28%) were classified as "AADP employees." The remaining 155 respondents (72%) were classified simply as "local farmers."

The data in Table 14.4 show that the AADP neglected the cultural values and preferences of the Igala people. Of the rural farmers who were former employees of the AADP, 41.8% agreed that the AADP neglected their cultural values and preference, whereas 49.1% said the AADP did not. Of the 155 rural farmers who were not former employees of the AADP, 62% agreed that AADP neglected their cultural values and preferences, 27.1% disagreed, and 1.3% indicated that they do not know. Although the majority of the farmers indicated that the AADP neglected their cultural values and preferences, rural farmers who were not former employees were more likely than former employees to say so.

In-Depth Interviews and Observations

Thematic analysis revealed that the World Bank embarked on a major agricultural project to transform the traditional agriculture without prior discussion with Igala farmers. There was no effort to understand the traditional farmer first and then offer advice to meet his or her needs on the basis of that knowledge. The AADP was insensitive to the needs of the Igala farmers, and plans were developed in a vacuum without concern for traditional values. This condition led to the inappropriateness of recommendations.

The technology offered consisted of limited use of inorganic fertilizer, new varieties of maize, rice, cowpea, and cassava; use of seed-dressing chemicals and staking of yams. Recommendations were based on research findings that were not specific to the project area. The project management failed to explore the relevance of project recommendations to the traditional cropping pattern. For example, sole crop recommendations were advocated by the project despite the widespread use of mixed crops under traditional conditions. Further, the livestock component was ill conceived and has no impact on the farmers. It was based on production of pig and poultry breeding stock, and animal health and extension. The rural farmers showed no interest in receiving improved pigs for their own production because the majority of the people in the area do not eat pork.

Extension Approach

In its extension approach, the AADP also failed to appreciate the indigenous farming system. A mixed cropping system was predominant in Igalaland, but the AADP recommended sole cropping. Consequently, the sole crop packages recommended by extension staff were inappropriate, and Igala farmers quite rationally refused to adopt them because they did not fit their mixed cropping systems.

Yams were obviously the most important crop in the area in economic terms and should have been a major focus of extension activity; instead they were largely neglected. The AADP's agricultural instructors lacked the practical understanding of indigenous farming systems to communicate farmers' views and rationale for adopting and not adopting recommendations to extension and adaptive research policy makers. Furthermore, because the instructors were urban-oriented school leavers, their knowledge of agricultural principles and research was too shallow to allow them to advise individual farmers on how to adopt new inputs and practices.

Land Development Schemes of the AADP

One of the laudable programs of the AADP were the Land Development Schemes (LDS). The expatriates and project planners looked at the LDS as the project geese that would lay the golden eggs, viewing the schemes through the prism of their aims and objectives. The AADP operated 19 LDS.

Schemes were organized on the basis of one farm family for up to 3 hectares. Most farmers retain their own existing farms elsewhere. The schemes were operated on a communal basis, and the proceeds were to be shared among the members. The finding presented here is based on fieldwork and interviews with rural farmers (Zekeri and Ochimana, 2000).

The results of these groups' effort on Okura LDS were disappointing. Most of the programs of operations were ill planned and badly executed by the AADP officers. The tractor-hiring unit was a glaring example of this absurdity. Tractors were not hired out at the appropriate time, and other requests for aid were treated with neglect.

The failure of the scheme is also traceable to production problems. Decline in production due to late operations contributed immensely to the withdrawal of some members. The farmers were not given necessary education because of lack of visual aids from the AADP at the right time. It is common knowledge that out-of-time teaching is not appreciated by adult learners. If you teach an adult farmer how to plant when it is time for harvesting, he will term it useless. Thus, most of the rural farmers had a dubious attitude toward the LDS because the AADP senior officials had neglected to deal in a timely way with the Igala people.

Discussion

The AADP failed to achieve it objectives. There are no quantifiable benefits from the rural farmers' perspective. One major weakness dogged the AADP in Igalaland: the failure to deal with traditional agricultural issues and to appreciate how well these issues were already understood and, in some respects mastered, by the rural Igala farmers. Concretely, the failure to consider the social and cultural context of the project area led to inappropriate design and poor implementation of the project.

The findings presented illustrate a project's inadequate regard for, and consequent lack of fit with, existing sociocultural conditions. The AADP overoptimistically expected the rural farmers to adopt their maize variety, which does not fit the preexisting system of mixed cropping and consumption. Confronted with these situations, rural farmers gave priority to their traditional variety. Because the AADP cash crops not only were new to the local culture but also conflicted with existing priorities and other interests of farmers, they were not adopted. Most farmers chose to grow their traditional varieties of maize, rice, cowpea, and cassava. The AADP's recommendations were based on research findings from another area and were not specific to the project area.

The land development scheme of the AADP was also culturally insensitive. The cooperative cultivation that the AADP promoted did not work because it is was made up of strangers who had no prior basis for mutual trust. In Igalaland, cooperation is based on extended kinship. There was no careful social design for forging a community out of strangers and facilitating cooperative production.

From a sociological perspective, the valuable lessons from this case study include the following:

- Too much reliance should not be placed on the advice of foreign experts who do not understand the existing problems.
- Project design must take into consideration indigenous farming systems.
- There is a need to conduct extensive studies about the social organization, behavior, motivation, and traditional economic ties before initiation of and during the course of development projects.
- Rural development projects must not be thrown at rural farmers. We must make sure that the intended beneficiaries want it, know about it, and support it. The interests of rural farmers must be aroused and must be mobilized around the development objectives.
- Cultural values have to be understood and taken into account when agricultural development projects are designed. Traditional cultures do not rationalize in terms of scientific or western logic.
- Exclusive use of technology transfer to increase productivity and profit simply would not work.
- More attention must be paid to the knowledge and skills of African farming communities.
- The big questions are, How do farming communities think they can best be helped? What solutions do they recommend?

The possibility that Africa's farmers might know the right answers to their own problems a lot better than foreign experts should cross the minds of experts and of the governments who employ them. Much more attention must be paid to the knowledge and skills of African farming communities.

Implications for Sustainable Rural Development in the 21st Century

Sustainable rural development in Africa in the 21st century comes down to tailoring the design and implementation of projects to the needs and capabilities of rural people who are supposed to benefit from them. There should be greater reliance on indigenous social expertise, and more training in sociocultural engineering for international agency staff. The big question for the 21st century is, How do farming communities think they can best be helped? What solutions do they recommend? The possibility that African farmers might know the right answers to their problems a lot better than foreign experts should occur to foreigners and the governments who employ them.

Sustainable rural development requires rural fieldwork, and implementation and evaluation must be based on visits to villages and interviews with the affected people. As Cernea (1985) correctly warned, people must come first in any development project.

Sustainable rural development for Africa must have a socially informed and culturally appropriate design and implementation strategy. Cultural variability should be addressed with the help of professional sociologists and anthropologists. Sociological and anthropological analysis must be incorporated in project design from the beginning. The analysis of the AADP presents additional evidence to buttress this argument.

Conclusion

The future rural development projects for Africa need concrete people-oriented objectives, culturally attuned technologies, and social implementation strategies that count on the rural people's ability to perceive the problems to be solved. The case study of AADP shows that the development project did not develop grassroots structures to guarantee some form of sustainable rural development.

The main finding of this study underscores the general need for social engineering that takes into account the sociocultural characteristics of affected people while devising sustainable rural development strategies. To the extent possible, any project must have a socially informed and culturally appropriate design and implementation strategy.

There should be a recognition that any agricultural technology introduced must build on the existing farming knowledge, as well as the agroecological and socioeconomic constraints that farmers confront. This implies testing any proposed solution on farmers' fields, under farmers' conditions, using farmers' criteria of evaluation in combination with agronomic and economic measures of results.

From a sustainability standpoint, the AADP was not a sustainable development project. The expected project benefits at completion with respect to the crop and livestock were disappointing. There is no sustainability of benefits from physical infrastructure established under the project. The project grassroots contacts with local or indigenous organizations were weak, and the development intervention project was dominated by expatriates and few national elites. This neglect of the local development stakeholders had serious implications for the sustainability of this project's efforts in the studied area.

Considering the cultural values and preferences, the AADP introduced seed varieties that were hitherto unknown to the farmers. The latter became skeptical about the new varieties even though scientific research had proved that the improved varieties were better than the "traditional" varieties. The improved maize, for instance, is much bigger (wider, thicker, and longer) than the traditional type. But "traditional" cultures do not necessarily subscribe to scientific or Western logic. For any rural development project to be sustainable, it is necessary to learn from rural people. As Clark (1991, p. 6) contends:

> agricultural programes have often languished, not because of external finance, but because of the society's inability to absorb it effectively and the planner's inability to define an efficient social strategy for development. Money is not everything, and in some cases money is the least important contribution to change processes. The financial levers of development can never soundly substitute for the nonfinancial ones.

Development disasters can be avoided when rural people are actively involved in the design and implementation of the project. Concretely, the fiasco of the AADP-improved maize variety might have been prevented had national and foreign experts spent more time in the field talking to local farmers, taking advantage of their wealth of knowledge related to soils, seasons, plants, domestic and wild animals, farming practices, diet, cooking practices, social customs, and relations.

References

Cernae, Michael M. (1985). *Putting People First: Sociological Variables in Rural Development Projects*. New York: Oxford University Press.

Chambers, R. (1983). *Rural Development: Putting the Last First*. London: Longman Scientific and Technical.

Chambers, R. (1993). *Challenging the Profession: Frontiers for Rural Development*. London: Intermediate Technology.

Chambers, R. (1997). *Whose Reality Counts? Putting the First Last*. London: Intermediate Technology.

Clark, J. (1991). *Democratising Development: The Role of Voluntary Organizations*. London: Earthscan.

Conway, Gordon R., and Edward Barbier. (1990). *After the Green Revolution: Sustainable Agriculture for Development*. London: Earthscan.

Francis, Charles, and Garth Youngberg (1990). Sustainable agriculture: An Overview. In: Charles A. Francis, Cornelia Butler Flora, and Larry D. King, eds., *Sustainable Agriculture in Temperate Zones*. New York: Wiley, pp. 1–23.

Honadle, G., and J. Vasant. (1985). *Implementation for Sustainability: Lessons from Integrated Rural Development*. Conn.: West Hartford Publisher.

Kamarah, Umar I. (2001). *Sustainable Rural Development:Semantics or Substance? The Study of Rural Projects in North Western Sierra Leone (1985–1995)*. New York: University Press of America.

Lele, Uma (1985). *The Design of Rural Development: Lessons from Africa*. Baltimore: The Johns Hopkins University Press.

Miachi, Thomas A. (1983). Towards an effective agricultural development strategy for Nigeria: An anthropological case-study of a land development scheme in Western Benue State. A paper presented at the National Seminar on Quality of Life in Rural Nigeria, Federal Department of Rural Development, Lagos and The Agricultural and Rural Management Training Institute, Illorin, Nigeria. June 6–8.

Miachi, Thomas A., and Andrew A. Zekeri (1997). Rural Development in Africa: The Impact of World Bank-Assisted Rural Development Program in Igalaland, Nigeria. In: Ntam Baharanyi, Robert Zabawa, and Walter Hills (eds.), Natural Resources and the Environment: Community Development Issues, Proceedings of the 54th Annual Professional Agricultural Workers Conference, Tuskegee University, Alabama. pp. 185–195

Munasinghe, Mohan, and Walter Shearer (1995). *Defining and Measuring Sustainability: The Biogeographical Foundations*. Washington, D.C.: Distributed for the United Nations University by the World Bank.

Netting, Robert (1993). *Smallholders, Householders: Farm Families and the Ecology of Intensive, Sustainable Agriculture*. Stanford, Calif.: Stanford University Press.

Operations Evaluations Department (OED) (1985). *Sustainability of Development Projects: First Review of Experience*. Washington, D.C.: World Bank.

Pearce, David (1993). *Blueprint 3: Measuring Sustainable Development*. London: Earthscan.

Stone, Pricilla (2003). Is sustainability for development anthropologists? *Human Organization* 62(2): 93–99.

World Bank (1985). *Rural Development Sector Policy Paper*, Washington, D.C.: World Bank.

World Bank (1989). *Sub-Saharan Africa: From Crisis to Sustainable Growth: A Long Term Perspective Study*. Washington, D.C.: World Bank.

World Bank. (1988). *Rural Development: World Bank Experience, 1965–1986, Operation Evaluation Department*. Washington, D.C.: World Bank.

World Bank. (1991). *World Bank Report 1991: The Challenge of Development*. Oxford: Oxford University Press.

World Bank. (1997). Explaining the Measure of Wealth: Indicators of Environmentally Sustainable Development. *Environmentally Sustainable Development Studies and Monographs Series 17*. Washington, D.C.: World Bank.

World Bank. (2002). *Making Sustainable Commitments: An Environment Strategy for the World Bank*. Washington, D.C.: World Bank.

World Bank. (2003). *Sustainable Development in a Dynamic World: Transforming Institutions, Growth, and Quality of Life.* World Development Report 2003. Washington, D.C.: World Bank.

Zekeri, Andrew A. (1989a). World Bank agricultural development projects in Nigeria: Perceived benefits, opinion about adoption and appropriateness of technology by Western Benue farmers. Paper presented at the 86th Annual Meeting of the Southern Association of Agricultural Scientists (Rural Sociology Section), Nashville, Tennessee.

Zekeri, Andrew A. (1989b). World Bank agricultural development project in Nigeria: The Western Benue farmers' perception of neglected parameters. Paper presented at the Fifth Annual Conference of the Association for International Agricultural and Extension Education, Chevy Chase, Maryland.

Zekeri, Andrew A. (1990a). Development: Rectifying inequality or favoring the few? *Journal of Developing Societies* 6(2):241–251.

Zekeri, Andrew A. (1990b). Development: Rectifying inequality or favoring the few? Paper presented at the Annual Meetings of the Rural Sociological Society, Norfolk, Virginia.

Zekeri, Andrew A. (1992a). Benefits from agricultural development projects: another lesson from Nigeria. *Journal of Rural Studies* 8(3):303–308.

Zekeri, Andrew A. (1992b). Distribution of benefits from agricultural development projects in rural Nigeria. Paper presented at the Eighth World Congress for Rural Sociology, International Rural Sociological Association Meetings, University Park, August 11–16.

Zekeri, Andrew A. (2002). World Bank-Assisted Agricultural Development Projects in Nigeria and Technology Adoption: Another Lesson from Igalaland. A paper presented at the 99th Annual Meeting of Southern Association of Agricultural Scientists, Southern Rural Sociological Association Section, Kissimmee, Florida, February 3–5.

Zekeri, Andrew A., and Thomas A. Miachi (1996) Rural Development in Africa: The Impact of World Bank-Assisted Rural Development Program in Igalaland, Nigeria. A paper presented at the 54th Annual Professional Agricultural Workers Conference, Tuskegee University, Alabama, December 8–10.

Zekeri, Andrew A., and Tijani Ochimana (2000). Assessing the Success and Failure of the World Bank Land Development Schemes in Kogi State, Nigeria. A paper presented at the 58th Annual Professional Agricultural Workers Conference, The Tuskegee University Kellogg Conference Center, Tuskegee, December 3–5.

Chapter 15

Prisons: A Cautionary Tale of Rural Economic Development

David Walker

CONTENTS

Introduction

For at least two decades, depressed rural areas in New York, Texas, California, and other states have turned to prisons as an engine for local economic development. The trend was driven, in part, by changing public policies toward drug abuse, crime, and incarceration that resulted in an explosion in the number of state and federal prisoners after the mid-1970s. At the same time, traditional underpinnings of rural economies—including farming and resource extraction—were eroding. Rural communities began to tap the flood of money being spent on corrections. They had cheap, plentiful land to offer, and prisons offered the promise of low-skill jobs and a chance to rebuild distressed economies. The communities envisioned recession-proof prosperity and growth guaranteed by steadily increasing incarceration rates (and tougher sentencing laws), as well as multiplier effects to spur new businesses.

Between the vision and the reality, however, is a large gap. A growing body of research suggests that the tangible economic benefits of prison construction to host communities are negligible and may even be negative in some cases. Meanwhile, the social costs of hosting a prison remain largely overlooked in cost–benefit assessments because those costs are difficult to measure. Furthermore, the future prospects of rural prison economies are increasingly uncertain. The reason for that is a slowdown in incarceration rates brought on by declining crime rates, softening public attitudes toward crime and sentencing, and, most recently, state budget shortages that have made corrections spending levels difficult to sustain.

Prisons, in other words, have turned out to be unreliable engines of rural economic development at best. In retrospect, that is not surprising. The pursuit of prisons is a variation of the traditional "smokestack-chasing" approach to economic development, wherein communities compete to attract any business that is likely to produce jobs. Although that strategy seems logical, it has proved to be generally ineffective. One reason is that the jobs sought are not always appropriate for the local labor force or otherwise consistent with community needs, assets, and values. Another reason is that the price paid to "buy" jobs with tax breaks, land giveaways, and other incentives offsets (and in some cases exceeds) the economic contributions of those jobs. And finally, communities that focus on chasing jobs not only leave themselves vulnerable to external forces beyond their control, they tend to forgo the hard work of participatory, multidimensional approaches that build community assets and expand long-term economic development options. All of those factors have diminished the promise of rural prison building as a means of economic development. This chapter presents a cautionary tale against an outdated approach to economic development that remains all too common.

Theoretical Background

In their survey of recent economic development literature, Harold Wolman and David Spitzley (1999) cited four explanations for the increase in local economic development activity in the preceding two decades. Those explanations include the increase in international mobility of capital, slow economic growth on the national level, international economic restructuring (resulting in a shift of manufacturing jobs overseas), and cutbacks in aid from the national government. They assert:

> Local elected officials respond to the increasing unemployment and underemployment of their residents (voters) by trying to increase local employment opportunities. ... In the market for jobs, cities, states and other governmental entities seek to purchase jobs for their current or future residents.

Some economic development scholars argue that local economic development projects are spurred by a need to correct revenue imbalances brought about by external economic pressures (Wolman and Spitzley, 1999). In other words, local officials seek to correct budget shortfalls resulting from a loss of tax revenue caused by, say, the closure of a noncompetitive factory or mine.

From a political perspective, whether or not economic development initiatives achieve their goals may be immaterial. Wolman and Spitzley (1999) argue that politicians are concerned primarily with their electoral prospects, which they perceive to be driven by their association with innovative and publicly visible activities. Wolman and Spitzley cite Feiock and Clingermayer: "Whether a development actually provides tangible benefits is, perhaps relatively unimportant. What is important is that the use of these policies provides politicians with something for which they can claim credit."

Particularly in economically distressed areas, local officials are likely to be under public pressure to do something to attract economic activity, whether or not the effort is likely to be a success. And they are unlikely to bear any political costs of failure for at least two reasons. First, the actual monetary costs to a community of economic development initiatives are often hidden from public view and spread over many taxpayers. Second, the outcomes of economic development initiatives are unlikely to manifest themselves until long after the politicians responsible leave office. The result is that politicians have less to lose politically by investing in economic development initiatives that ultimately do not work than by forgoing opportunities because they appear unlikely to work (Wolman and Spitzley, 1999).

The traditional, reactive approach to economic development strategy of "buying" any available jobs underlies much rural prison construction. In recent years, though, scholars have been arguing persuasively for more holistic, participatory approaches. The idea behind the new approaches is to build social and economic capital to empower communities to solve local economic problems. This new approach is about making social change, not just about attracting jobs (Mudacumura, 2002). Scholars suggest, for instance, that problem solving and decision making include not just politicians and business leaders, but a broader spectrum of interested parties, including activists, community groups, and the unemployed. They argue for economic development initiatives that account for the social, cultural, environmental, and spiritual needs of communities, and not just the economic and political needs (Mudacumura, 2002). There is also a call to expand the traditional market perspectives (jobs gained, additional taxes raised) for evaluating economic development outcomes to include social factors such as job quality, security and safety, changes in income distribution and the poverty rate, and diversity of the economic base (Reese and Fasenfest, 1999). It is in the context of these nontraditional approaches to economic development that I undertake this study of rural prison construction.

The Rise of the Prison–Industrial Complex

Until the 1970s, the U.S. prison population held steady at fewer than 250,000 inmates. By 1980, the total U.S. prison population (local, state, and federal) had crept up to approximately 504,000 inmates. The number of inmates doubled to 1.1 million in 1990, then nearly doubled again to 1.9 million in 2000. As of June 30, 2002, there were slightly more than 2 million inmates in local, state, or federal prisons, according to the U.S. Bureau of Justice statistics (U.S. Bureau of Justice, 2003). The explosion in the U.S. prison population resulted from the antidrug and anticrime policies of the 1970s and 1980s. Those policies helped spawn the so-called prison–industrial complex, which the author Eric Schlosser (1998) describes as "a set of bureaucratic, political, and economic interests that encourage increased spending on imprisonment, regardless of the actual need."

Since the 1980s, politicians of all stripes have proclaimed themselves to be "tough on crime," if only to inoculate themselves from attacks by opponents. Michael S. Dukakis lost the 1988 presidential election partly because his opponent, George Bush, painted him as soft on crime. Bill Clinton, determined not to leave himself vulnerable to similar attacks in the 1992 presidential election, angered liberals with his tough positions on crime and bragged, "I can be nicked on a lot, but no one can say I'm soft on crime" (Mauer, 2002).

Although Clinton and other Democrats exploited the crime issue, it was Republicans who started the "Get Tough" movement that hardened public attitudes about crime and paved the way for tougher sentencing laws. Arizona Senator Barry Goldwater was one of the first Republicans to exploit middle-class fears of crime in an attempt to win votes in his 1964 bid for the presidency. Four years later, Richard Nixon campaigned on a "law and order" platform, when violent protests against the Vietnam War and recreational drug use were on the rise. Despite Nixon's rhetoric, though, the public still considered drug abuse a public health issue, not a criminal one, and Congress responded in 1970 by repealing most mandatory sentences for drug offenders (Schlosser, 1998). At the time, the national incarceration rate had been stable for more than 40 years, hovering around 100 prisoners per 100,000 people. The total federal and state prison population was also stable at approximately 225,000 inmates (Wray, 2000).

By 2000, the incarceration rate had risen to nearly 500 inmates per 100,000 citizens, and 1.9 million people were incarcerated. The tide started to turn first in New York, then in California. In January 1973, New York governor Nelson Rockefeller, a liberal Republican with an eye on the White House, called for mandatory life sentences without parole for every illegal drug dealer. He wanted to close plea bargain loopholes and subject even juvenile offenders to life sentences. The state legislature was unwilling to go that far, but within a few months, it did pass a series of tough drug laws. For instance, anyone convicted of possessing 4 ounces or more of an illegal drug, or of selling 2 ounces or more, faced a mandatory sentence of 15 years to life. The law also included mandatory sentences for many second felony convictions. Rockefeller then declared that New York had the "toughest anti-drug program in the country" (Schlosser, 1998).

Meanwhile, in California, the public was growing increasingly frustrated over the failure of prisons to rehabilitate criminals. Recidivism rates were high, and various incidents of prison violence had left a number of prison guards dead. In 1976, California Governor Jerry Brown signed a law that stated explicitly, "the purpose of imprisonment is punishment" (as opposed to rehabilitation, which was assumed until then). The law imposed a series of mandatory sentences and eliminated parole (Hallinan, 2001). As a result, California's prison population quadrupled from 1980 to 1994, and the proportion of the state budget that went to corrections rose from 2.3% to 9.8% without raising any outcry from the public, elected officials, or state bureaucrats (Mauer, 2002).

From California and New York, draconian prison-as-punishment policies spread nationally. By 1986, 37 states had enacted mandatory sentencing laws for drug crimes and other felonies. Congress had also begun to toughen federal sentencing laws. Federal legislation that had the most impact on incarceration rates included the Sentencing Reform Act of 1984, requiring anyone sentenced of a federal crime after November 1, 1987, to serve at least 85% of his or her sentence. Subsequently, federal drug laws did even more to swell prison populations. The Anti–Drug Abuse Act of 1986 and the Anti–Drug Abuse Amendments Act of 1988—propelled at least in part by sensational and frightening press accounts of the urban crack cocaine epidemic—imposed harsh mandatory sentences of 5 years or more for possessing or dealing even small amounts of drugs. As a result of those laws, the federal prison population swelled from 44,000 in 1987 to 140,000 in 2000 (Hallinan, 2001).

As prison populations soared, conditions inside state prisons deteriorated as a result of overcrowding and aging infrastructure. Prisoners began filing claims of mistreatment, and by 1984, 32 states and the District of Columbia had been forced to sign consent decrees to improve prison conditions. To that end, states released 17,000 prisoners early in 1984, and they were faced with the choice of releasing even more or building more prisons (Hallinan, 2001). By that time, though, releasing prisoners was becoming politically untenable, given shifting public attitudes toward crime and punishment. The stage was set for a new era of ambitious prison construction, which turned into a boon for politicians, private prison companies, and local governments.

The Prison Construction Boom

New York and California both began aggressive prison construction programs. Despite the public support for tougher sentencing laws, New York residents rejected a $500 million bond issue for new prison construction in 1981. Then-governor Mario Cuomo got around that problem by enlisting the Urban Development Corporation to construct prisons. Although it was a public agency (originally created to construct housing for the poor), it could legally issue bonds without voter approval (Schlosser, 1998). The state ended up spending more than $7 billion over the next dozen years constructing prisons. Of 29 new prisons constructed over the last 20 years in New York, 28 are located in economically depressed rural regions upstate. By 1992, 90% of state prison employees, state prisoners, and state expenditures for prisons were in those rural Republican districts, although Republicans accounted for less than 60% of the state senate (Feldman, 1993).

Daniel Feldman, former chairman of the New York State Assembly's correction committee, railed against New York's prison boom as "political pork" and asserted, "When Republicans cry, 'Lock 'em up!' they often mean, 'Lock 'em up in my District!'" (Feldman, 1993). Cuomo, a committed liberal, was also outraged by the profligate spending on prisons, calling it "stupid" and a waste of resources. But the state's tough sentencing laws gave him no choice but to construct more prisons, he said. To be sure, he gained politically from new prison construction, which conveniently protected him from accusations that he was soft on crime, on the one hand, and bolstered his political capital with upstate Republican legislators, on the other, by providing them with prisons for economic development (Schlosser, 1998).

Prison expansion in California was just as rapid. The state went from 12 prisons in 1983 to 33 prisons in 1998, with a projected need for 15 more prisons by 2006 if the state's inmate population continued to increase at a steady rate. As in New York, most of the new California prisons were located in economically depressed rural areas. The construction costs to taxpayers exceeded $4.5 billion, plus an additional $4 billion annually to operate the new prisons (Byrd, 1998). The spending certainly created jobs. From 1980 to 1995, the number of prison guards employed by California jumped from 4,000 to more than 23,000. Referring to the boom in prison spending, one state representative quipped, "We call it our Pentagon around here" (Jackson, 1995).

While state governments built prisons in New York, California, and elsewhere, private prison companies cropped up to meet the demand for more prison cells, particularly in the South. Initially, the private firms contracted to operate prisons owned by state and local governments, but then they began building facilities and running them as hotels—charging states a per diem rate for housing each prisoner. Private prison companies claimed that they could operate prisons more efficiently than government in the antigovernment, proprivatization climate of the Reagan era. State legislators seeking ways to cut costs were seduced by the promises of private prison companies, and Wall Street considered the private prison industry a sure bet for investors.

The first private prison company was Corrections Corporation of America (CCA), founded in 1983 by Republican Party activist Thomas Beasley. CCA won its first contract to run a county jail in Hamilton County, Tennessee, in 1984. Kentucky awarded CCA a contract to run a single state prison in 1986. The following year, the company won its first multifacility management contract, and the private prison industry burgeoned from there. CCA's revenues went from $14 million in 1986 to $55 million in 1990 to $129 million in 1994. The company now controls more than half of the private prison business. Its next largest competitor, Wackenhut Corrections, began operations in 1988. Wackenhut grew from $19 million in revenues in 1989 to $84 million in 1994, when it went public. In all, prison beds under ownership or management of private companies grew from 2,000 beds in 1987 to about 100,000 by 2001 (Mattera and Khan, 2001). Their growth has been concentrated in certain states.

Private companies were responsible for almost all of the prison expansion in Texas during the late 1980s and 1990s, for instance.

Yet, the private prison industry is now moribund. Studies by the Government Accounting Office (GAO) and others during the 1990s cast doubt on claims that private companies could operate prisons more efficiently (U.S. GAO, 1996). Scandals, escapes, and corner cutting also discredited the private prison industry, and speculative construction created a glut of private prison cells (Cook, 2001). Private prison companies have lost both money and investor confidence since 1999, and their future remains uncertain.

The Economic Development Opportunity

Almost immediately, rural communities seized on the prison construction boom as an economic development opportunity. Calvin Beale, senior demographer at the Economic Research Service of the Agriculture Department, told the *New York Times* in 2001 that 245 prisons had been constructed in 212 rural counties throughout the United States (out of a nationwide total of 2,290 counties) during the previous decade. Beale also reported that an average of 25 prisons per year opened in rural areas during the 1990s, up from 16 per year in the 1980s and 4 per year in the 1970s (Kilborn, 2001). Population rose by an average of 12% during the 1990s in the 212 rural counties where new prisons were built, compared to an average growth rate of 1.5% for the previous decade (Doyle, 2003). (Prisoners accounted for most of that population growth.)

Rural communities sought prisons to offset or reverse declines in agriculture, mining, and industry that eroded rural tax and population bases during the 1980s. Agricultural consolidation, recession, and the farm crisis of the 1980s put many midwestern farmers out of work, for instance. Likewise, the oil bust of the 1980s devastated the rural economies of states such as Texas, Oklahoma, and Colorado. The prison boom presented an opportunity for economically desperate communities to rebuild. After years of economic stagnation in Akron County, Colorado, for instance, the director of the local Chamber of Commerce observed that a prison "is not the ideal business, but at this point it is a step in the right direction" (Miniclier, 1999).

Prisons held out the promise of badly needed jobs—first for construction workers, then for prison guards. Beale estimates, for instance, that 10 prison guard jobs are created for every 30 prisoners (Duke, 2000). Prisons also had the potential to boost population, making communities eligible for a bigger share of population-based state and federal assistance. In addition to those benefits, rural communities were counting on prisons to stimulate other local businesses. For instance, restaurants and hotels might be built to accommodate inmates' visitors (because most inmates were from far-off urban areas). Such promises gave hope to economically depressed rural communities, and local officials, of course, were eager to attract any jobs they could. For instance, after a private prison opened in Folkston, Georgia, in 1998, the mayor observed:

> We're already getting a combined Flash Foods [convenience store] and a McDonald's, which is a first. There's talk that we're going to have a Burger King, ... You're talking 15 to 20 jobs at each of those places. They might not be as high paying as we'd like it to be, but they are jobs. (Cook, 1998)

From the perspective of state officials, rural communities were ideal locations for new prisons. The rural communities had readily available labor, and cheap, plentiful land. Rural communities offered little or no resistance to prison construction, unlike the less economically desperate suburban and urban residents, who were concerned about public safety and the effects of prisons on property values. (Because prisons are considered nonpolluting, they are almost never resisted on environmental grounds in either rural or nonrural areas.) As one New York corrections official put it, "If we had our druthers, we'd locate all of our facilities in the metropolitan area, because that's where most of our inmates come from ... but why spend thousand of dollars in scarce state resources trying to convince a community to take a facility?" (Smith, 1990).

In fact, rural communities around the country began clamoring and inevitably competing for prisons to spur their economies. Calvin Beale explained to the *Washington Post*, "If you have a prison come in with 1,400 prisoners, you're probably going to get 400 jobs out of that, and in a rural setting that's a lot of jobs. ... So they welcome these jobs, and they bid for them" (Duke, 2000). In New York, for instance, citizens of rural upstate districts lobbied key legislators for new prisons. Daniel Feldman (1993), the former state assemblyman, wrote:

> As a representative of a high-density urban district, I was surprised when my 1987 appointment as chair of the Assembly's correction committee produced a stream of letters, telegrams, and resolutions to my office from numerous upstate rural communities enthusiastically requesting prisons in their districts!

With so much competition for prisons, politicians wrangled to help their constituents. No doubt eager to claim job gains at election time, legislators ended up controlling the siting process through backroom deals.

New York's corrections commissioner said in 1990, "We give our list [of planned prisons] to the Legislature, and the next day I get back the list of where our prisons are going to be" (Smith, 1990).

Competition for rural prisons was certainly not limited to New York State. In Illinois, a number of communities competed for three new prisons in 1997. Some constructed billboards with proprison propaganda. One even produced a music video to get the attention of state corrections officials (Challos, 1997). In 1996, *USA Today* reported competitions for prisons in various states. Florida, for instance, had 15 towns on a waiting list for a prison, and each had pledged to donate land for the construction. Missouri had 12 communities competing for three prisons. One of the towns sent civic leaders to the state capital to pass out buttons and candied apples to state legislators, then finally won the bid for a prison after residents approved an $11 million bond issue to improve roads and other infrastructure for the prison. *USA Today* also reported a "stampede" of bidders for one of twelve jails for nonviolent felons in Texas. "They offered land, cash incentives and cut-rate deals on utilities," said Texas Department of Criminal Justice spokesman Glen Castlebury (Glamser, 1996).

Some towns spent significant sums of money to attract prisons. Abilene, Texas, offered incentives worth $4 million to the state to attract a prison in 1990. The package included a 316-acre site for the prison itself, 1,100 acres of adjacent farmland, new roads to service the prison, and housing for guards and prison executives, upgrades for communications and public works infrastructure, and even the use of a private plane for state officials (King, Mauer, and Huling, 2003).

Rural communities all over the country were offering a variety of inducements to attract prisons. Starting in the late 1980s, city, county, and state authorities issued various forms of tax-free bonds to subsidize the construction of private prisons. The subsidies were justified by the promise of jobs (Mattera and Khan, 2001). In some cases, the subsidies were in the form of tax-free municipal bonds that lowered the cost of the construction (tax-free bonds carry lower interest rates than other bonds). In other cases, bond issues enabled private companies to avoid construction costs altogether. The money was borrowed against future revenues from operations, and the host communities took possession of the prison when the principal plus interest was repaid. There were multiple prison construction bond issues in Mississippi, Florida, and Texas totaling $70 million or more for each one of those states. There were single bond issues ranging from $10 million to $70 million in Idaho, Indiana, New Mexico, Tennessee, Oklahoma, and Virginia (Mattera and Khan, 2001).

Do Prisons Pay?

There remains a widespread assumption, bolstered in part by the media, that prisons are an economic boon to rural areas. For instance, the *New York Times* asserted, "More than a Wal-Mart or a meat-packing plant, ... prisons ... can put a town on solid economic footing." It was an assertion extrapolated largely from anecdotal evidence from one Oklahoma town (Kilborn, 2001). In fact, press reports frequently presume the economic benefits of prisons on the basis of information provided by local officials. But actual data on the economic impacts of prisons are scarce, and the data that do exist cast some doubt on the conventional wisdom. In other words, prisons may contribute less to economic development than either critics or boosters of prisons believe.

Two recent quantitative studies of rural prisons suggest that economic impacts are neutral at best. Other assessments are mostly anecdotal, and decidedly inconsistent in their conclusions. For instance, the federal government's expert on rural prisons—Calvin Beale—has offered mixed assessments. In 1995, he stated in an interview that economic benefits of prisons do not always live up to the expectations of host communities and suggested on the basis of his own qualitative studies that some communities do not benefit at all (Larmer, 1995). But in 2000, Beale told the *Washington Post* that prison expansion "has been a major source of growth, of jobs, of economic development" for rural communities (Duke, 2000).

An example of a community that benefited from a prison is Appleton, Minnesota, which built a 500-bed prison in 1993 with $27 million in federal development funding. The prison was subsequently expanded to 1,300 beds, and it employed 400 people. In 1998, Appleton sold the prison at a profit to CCA. Appleton officials credit the prison with revitalizing the local economy, which had been declining since the 1970s as a result of farm failures. Officials report that in addition to providing jobs for local residents, the prison spurred local businesses and provided Appleton with revenues to undertake road and sidewalk repairs. However, local officials acknowledge that the prison jobs have high turnover rates and many prison employees live outside the local area (Doyle, 2002). The net benefits, then, may be somewhat less than what they appear at first glance. Absent any formal economic impact analysis, the net benefits of Appleton's prison are difficult to ascertain.

Malone, New York, has also benefited from three separate prisons built in the early 1990s, but once again, rigorous analysis is lacking. The data are mostly observational and self-reported. The prisons generated 1,600 jobs and an annual payroll of $67 million. Most of the employees live in Malone or the surrounding county. According to local officials, the prisons have attracted a furniture assembly plant and a textile company, in addition to new pharmacies, discount stores, and fast-food outlets. Local officials also attribute expansion of both a local hospital and a golf course to the economic boost brought about by the prisons. Costs included increases in water and sewer rates in order to expand those systems to accommodate the prison (Duke, 2000).

Although some depressed rural communities undoubtedly benefit from prisons, plenty of others fail to realize anticipated economic gains. In Connell, Washington, a tanning salon and an appliance store opened after a medium-security prison was built in 1992, but two grocery stores closed despite a slight increase in population. And a mall 30 miles away continued to draw business away from Connell (Glamser, 1996). Likewise, a medium-security prison in Crowley County, Colorado, failed to revive the local economy after it was built in 1987. Instead, most of the prison employees ended up living outside the county, while the prison overloaded the county sewer system and prisoners overloaded the local court system with lawsuits (Larmer, 1995).

In Folkston, Georgia, the private prison that opened in 1998 (mentioned earlier) generates $106,000 per year in additional property taxes. But contrary to the expectations of local officials, property values dropped, and new housing starts failed to materialize after the prison arrived. Furthermore, more than two thirds of the prison employees live in surrounding counties, and the prison has failed to meet expectations as a stimulus for new business. "Most of the dollars leave the county," says one board member of the Folkston-Charlton County Development Authority (B. Morris, personal communication, 2003).

Several recent studies suggest that the local economic impacts of prisons tend to be neutral at best. For instance, the Sentencing Project—which is generally critical of the prison–industrial complex—compared economic trends over the preceding 25 years in 14 rural New York counties—7 with prisons, and 7 without. The study, released in February 2003, concluded that there are no discernible differences in economic trends among the two groups, which were chosen for their geographic and demographic similarities. Unemployment figures for both groups moved in parallel and remained consistent with the state average, leading the researchers to conclude, "Residents of rural communities with one or more prisons did not gain significant employment advantages compared to rural counties without prisons." The researchers also found no significant difference in per capita income increases from 1982 to 2000. During that period, per capita income rose 141% in the rural counties without a prison, 132% in counties that hosted a prison, and 160% across New York as a whole (Ryan, Mauer, and Huling, 2003).

The authors of the Sentencing Project study suggested several possible explanations for their results. Those included prison employees living outside the host county, the inability of local residents to compete for jobs because of union requirements or lack of skills, the lack of infrastructure and local business capacity to keep prison expenditures local, and the lack of multiplier effects because the prisons are not integrated into the local economy (Ryan, Mauer, and Huling, 2003). Indeed, contractors from outside host communities win almost all prison construction contracts, because local contractors lack the expertise and financial capacity to undertake such large-scale projects. Provisions for prisons are bought primarily from national rather than local suppliers, so prisons tend to have little direct impact on the local economy. And prison guards in upstate New York, at least, often are from other communities because the most senior guards get the best jobs in the system—and those are perceived by guards to be in the upstate prisons.

Another study comparing Colorado counties with and without prisons yielded similar results to those of the study conducted in New York. Christopher Seti of the University of Colorado in Denver concluded that "economies of prison counties rarely outpace those of their nonprison neighbors" (Seti, 2001). Seti's study compared 10 rural counties—5 with prisons and 5 without. From 1991 to 1998, the difference in per capita income increase between the two counties was statistically insignificant. The study also compares state projections for per capita income and unemployment in 2005 for all the counties, and once again, the counties with prisons are not expected to fare any better on those indicators than counties without prisons. The primary weakness of the Colorado study, however, is that it does not compare economic data for the two groups of counties *before* the prisons were constructed. If the counties with prisons were significantly worse off economically as a group before prison construction than the nonprison counties, then positive economic impacts of the prisons would be hidden by Seti's design.

Not only does the most comprehensive study to date of the economic impacts of rural prisons cast doubt on the popular supposition that prisons provide economic benefits to their host communities, the researchers conclude that prisons even hinder economic growth in some instances (Hooks et al., 2004). The study, which is pending publication, was conducted by sociologists at Washington State University. Relying on U.S. Department of Commerce data from all of the approximately 3,100 counties in the contiguous 48 states, they examined public, private, and total employment growth between 1969 and 1994. They controlled for the effects of tax rates, state contributions to the local economies, education levels, employment profiles (e.g., the percentage of manufacturing and nonmanufacturing employees), and spatial autocorrelation (i.e., the effects of growth or decline in one county on surrounding counties). They found that rural counties *without* prisons had faster growth rates for total income and per capita income. They also found no evidence that prisons—established or newly built—contributed to employment growth in rural counties. In fact, in slowly growing counties, new prisons impede employment growth, the researchers found. (They suggest that may be because scarce resources are diverted from other development opportunities.) Prisons have simply not contributed significantly to the economic development of rural counties over the past several decades, the authors conclude (Hooks et al., 2004).

The Social Impacts of Rural Prisons

Although recent research examines the quantifiable economic impacts of rural prisons, the social impacts remain largely unexamined. There may be several reasons for that. Social impacts are more difficult to quantify and measure with reliability or validity. In field studies, confounding variables make it difficult to establish cause and effect with certainty. And local officials, at least, focus on traditional economic outcomes for which they can claim credit, such as job gains. They have little to gain politically by examining the social costs of economic development initiatives.

But costs accrue. Prisons change community demographics and dynamics. Mentioned in some press accounts are the increased burdens on law enforcement and courts resulting from an influx of prisoners to a community. Those burdens increase because infractions committed by inmates inside the prison must be prosecuted locally. Also, lawsuits frequently filed by prisoners over prison conditions and other matters are also matters of local jurisdiction. Residents of host communities logically end up paying those costs in the form of higher taxes, reduced services, or both.

Another issue is the impact of prison guard jobs on the community social fabric. Prisons do create jobs. But communities rarely weigh the safety, quality, turnover rates, or other negative attributes of those jobs, which put strain on individuals and families. Studies conducted in the late 1970s and early 1980s examined the effects of job stress in corrections. One study conducted in New Jersey found that physical symptoms of stress—including hypertension, heart attacks, and ulcers—were higher among prison guards than among police officers, whose occupations are considered to be among the most stressful of all. The study also found that correctional officers reported twice the divorce rate of other workers and abnormally high rates of alcoholism, drug use, and family problems (Howard, 1984). In addition to boosting health-care and social service costs, those social problems tend to diminish the social capacity and capital of communities. But rural communities rarely assess any of those costs either before or after a prison arrives in town.

Even more difficult to quantify for the purposes of cost–benefit analysis are the ethical and spiritual issues surrounding the use of prisons for economic development. Communities that host prisons are, in effect, trying to build their economies and profit by isolating and controlling other human beings. ("Convicts for commerce is how some rural areas refer to it," remarked the head of the rural affairs division of the Texas Department of Economic Development [Bauer, 2000]). Is it a moral arrangement or not? It can be argued that prison communities are providing a service by confining those people who are a threat to society, and that prisons have to be built someplace.

But the arrangement also turns host communities into beneficiaries of the prison–industrial complex and arguably buys off the community's more compassionate instincts. Host communities have a vested interest in punitive policies and laws that treat prisoners—even those who are not much of a threat to society—as valuable economic commodities.[1] That most prisoners are culturally "alien" individuals (black and Hispanic) from far-off urban areas arguably makes it easier for residents (most of them white) of the rural host communities to distance themselves from the moral uncertainties of their collective action. To the extent that prisons undermine compassion and contribute to social and cultural alienation, they degrade the social capital and capacity of rural communities. And that, in the end, is an economic development handicap.

Such handicaps are impossible to quantify, of course. The effects are perhaps best illustrated by example. Susanville, California, bet its future on a prison economy in the early 1990s as local mines and an army depot were closing, and the logging industry was in decline. A construction boom that began in 1995 eventually yielded three prisons with a total of 10,000 inmates. National retailers such as Wal-Mart, Taco Bell, and Blockbuster Video moved in. By traditional economic measures such as job gains, population gain, and wage gains, Susanville's economic development strategy has been a success. But many residents are ambivalent because of the social consequences of that strategy. Joelle Fraser (2000) described the town's transition in 1999:

> After the strip lengthened and the stoplights multiplied and many small businesses, unable to compete with Wal-Mart, quietly boarded their doors, Susanville is reminiscent of so many towns that have outgrown themselves and lost something in the process. But it is also unlike many small towns—there is the overwhelming presence of men with military haircuts and trim mustaches, the constant talk of prison scandals and

violence (eleven inmates have been killed or committed suicide since High Desert's opening), the clear division between locals and prison employees and inmate families. People complain about anonymity, about long lines at the bank, about traffic, about the rise in prices. The police department faces rising domestic violence, a 50 percent jump in juvenile delinquency and trade in hardcore drugs like heroin from gang members associated with the prison. The real estate community holds a glut of property because the new prison employees [are] not settling in like they were supposed to.... A new prison requires that the community adapt to a rapid leap in a specific kind of population—those drawn to and associated with the work of corrections, an industry for whom the raw material is the systematic incapacitation of hostile, despairing human beings, in this case over 10,000 of them.

Yet distressed rural communities continue to compete for prisons, despite the experience of other communities and mounting evidence that prisons are not an economic panacea. Eventually, these communities may be forced rather than persuaded to shift their economic development strategies away from prisons. The reason is that tectonic changes in state and federal corrections policies now threaten to divert money away from prison construction. Already, the prison boom is waning.

Public Opinion, State Budgets, and Diminishing Opportunities

Prison construction may cease to drive rural economic development because of softening public opinion toward crime and punishment and a budget crisis that has left states unable to continue to fund the draconian prison policies of the last three decades. Indeed, numerous states are now reforming their criminal justice policies in ways designed to reduce prison populations and the associated costs. In 2001 and 2002, 13 states enacted reforms to reduce their incarceration rates (Wilhelm and Turner, 2002). Other states are now exploring ways to reduce their own incarceration rates and corrections budgets. New prison construction is already slowing as a result: 11 new prisons opened in rural communities in 2001, compared with 38 in 1998 (Kilborn, 2001).

Shifting public opinion over the last decade has made sentencing reform possible. Various polls and studies reveal that the public no longer considers crime a pressing social issue. The Pew Research Center found, for instance, that the number of Americans who considered crime as the most important issue facing their communities dropped from 29% in 1994 to 12% in 2001 (Wilhelm and Turner, 2002). A Harris poll yielded similar results: in 1994, 37% of respondents said crime was one of the two most important issues facing government; when the survey was repeated in 2000, 11% of respondents said so.

Attitudes about incarceration have also softened. In a 1994 study by Peter D. Hart Research Associates, 48% of respondents favored addressing the underlying causes of crime, and 42% favored deterrence through tougher sentencing. When that survey was repeated in 2001, 65% of respondents said they favored addressing the underlying causes of crime, whereas 32% preferred harsher sentencing. The Hart studies also revealed changing opinions about mandatory sentencing laws, which 55% of respondents favored and 38% opposed in 1994. By 2001, 38% favored mandatory sentencing laws, and 45% opposed them (Wilhelm and Turner, 2002).

Changing attitudes have also been reflected at the ballot box in some states, most notably Arizona and California. In 1996, 65% of Arizona voters approved Proposition 200, a referendum to replace mandatory prison sentences for certain nonviolent drug offenders with supervised mandatory treatment. Legislators subsequently tried to rescind some of the provisions, so voters again supported three ballot measures in 1998 upholding the 1996 vote (Campaign for New Drug Policies, 2002). In 2000, 61% of California voters approved Proposition 36, a drug-sentencing reform referendum almost identical to Arizona's Proposition 200. To be sure, voters are not approving such referenda in all cases. Ohio voters rejected sentencing reform for nonviolent first- and second-time drug offenders in 2002 (*Columbus Dispatch*, 2002).

Meanwhile, state legislatures around the country have been taking up sentencing reform, mostly because states can no longer afford the costs of their punitive incarceration policies. Total expenditures (local, state, and federal) for corrections increased from $9 billion in 1982 to $49 billion in 1999, a 442% jump. Most of that money is spent by state governments, and more than half of the money ($24 billion) is spent to imprison nonviolent offenders, particularly drug users and dealers (U.S. Department of Justice, 2003). From 1980 to 2000, state and local expenditures for corrections rose by 600% (Wilhelm and Turner, 2002). On average, corrections accounted for 7% of state budgets in 2000 (Schiraldi and Greene, 2002). In Louisiana, where the state's prison population rose by 43%, and corrections expenditures rose by 45% between 1994 and 1999, the chair of the legislature's criminal justice committee told the Associated Press, "The people expect us to be tough on crime and they expect us to lock everybody up and throw away the key. And that's great as long as you've got a jail and you've got the finances. But we've come to a point where we just can't afford to keep doing it" (Wilhelm and Turner, 2002).

The primary reason states can no longer afford such policies is the state budget crisis that resulted from a slumping national economy and rising health-care costs. Budget shortfalls for fiscal 2002 in 40 states totaled nearly $40 billion—or about $1 billion on average for each state, according to the National Association of State Budget Officers. The situation has hardly improved since. Nearly every state is in fiscal crisis that is expected to continue, forcing states to cut spending to close the gap (National Association of State Budget Officers, 2003).

Whereas a few states (California among them) have avoided cutting their corrections budgets, many others are actively seeking ways to cut prison spending. Some of the solutions are short term. For instance, Ohio, Massachussets, and Illinois have closed some of their prisons, crowding the inmates into other facilities. Nebraska granted early release to more than 500 of its prisoners. Michigan has saved money by cutting prison staff positions. Still other states have adopted sentencing reforms intended to reduce their incarceration rates—and by extension, their demand for new prisons—in the long term. Connecticut, North Dakota, and Indiana have repealed mandatory minimum sentences for some nonviolent offenses, for instance. Idaho, Oregon, and Washington have increased treatment options for nonviolent drug offenders. Michigan has pared back its truth-in-sentencing requirements, so prisoners are eligible for parole sooner. Louisiana, Virginia, and Texas have expanded the number of inmates eligible for early release. Alabama and New Mexico have relaxed their habitual offender laws. North Carolina enacted alternative sentencing for many offenses. In addition to enacting sentencing reforms to reduce incarceration rates, Kansas enacted an early warning system: Whenever prisons are in danger of overflowing within 2 years, a corrections commission warns the legislature, which then explores additional reforms as a means of avoiding new prison construction. Partly as a result of that system, Kansas has avoided building any new prisons for more than a decade (Wilhelm and Turner, 2002).

Such reforms have led some observers to conclude that the "Get Tough" era may be coming to a close. To be sure, they are making the prediction cautiously; a sudden increase in violent crime rates, combined with intense media attention, could harden public opinion once again. Moreover, a return to economic prosperity could ease the pressure on state legislatures to cut corrections costs (Mauer, 2002). For now, though, the prison construction boom appears to be declining because of a changing political climate and a lack of money to keep it going. Rural communities pinning their hopes for economic salvation on prisons may have no choice now but to find new alternatives for economic development.

Conclusion and Recommendations

Public policy toward crime and punishment over the past 20 years has swelled prison populations and generated a flood of spending on new prison construction by state and federal governments. Depressed rural communities have seized the opportunity to compete for prisons with hopes of attracting jobs and rebuilding their economies. Such a strategy for economic development was predictable, given a long history of reactive economic development approaches and the electoral benefits for politicians in claiming credit for attracting jobs. As it turns out, though, prisons are not an economic development panacea for most rural communities. The economic benefits are usually significantly lower than predicted, and the infrastructure and social costs are often higher than expected. The result can be a narrow margin of benefit—or even no benefit at all. Still, rural communities persist because they perceive no other options. Too often, that is because they limit themselves to traditional supply-side approaches to economic development that emphasize "buying" jobs with land giveaways, tax breaks, and infrastructure improvements at taxpayer expense.

Rural communities may have more success by adopting new approaches, and they may finally be forced to do so by impending changes in public policy that could halt or even reverse the explosive growth in the U.S. prison population. New prison construction has already slowed. Competition for prisons among rural communities for prisons is likely to get stiffer and therefore more expensive. If demand for new prisons slows even more, they may cease altogether to be an option for rural economic development.

Such changes present rural communities with an impetus to engage in the hard work of community building to strengthen their resources and capacities. Rather than delegate the task of economic development to a small cadre of public officials and business leaders, these communities must engage in broad-based participatory problem solving that addresses community needs, assets, and values. To succeed, rural communities must build the knowledge and skills of individual members, build relationships and networks to foster collective action, and strengthen and link community institutions (Mudacumura, 2002).

Such activities are likely to result in community economic development options that the community may not have considered. For instance, citizens might make themselves less dependent on external economic forces by establishing a community business corporation to launch new worker-owned and -managed businesses that provide jobs, more equitable income distribution, and other economic and social benefits for the community. Community-building initiatives could also provide the community with unforeseen opportunities to participate in regional economic development activities. Community building could also make the community more attractive to a broad range of businesses, thereby breaking the dependence upon the least desirable enterprises—such as prisons.

Note

1. According to the *Washington Post*, for instance, advocates for reforming harsh sentencing laws in New York say their efforts are opposed "by some lawmakers whose small-town constituents don't want to stop the flow of inmates." See Lynne Duke, 2000. "Building a Boom behind Bars; Prisons Revive Small Towns, but Costs Are Emerging." *The Washington Post*, September 8.

References

Bauer, Esther M. (2000). An Earth without a future. *The Washington Post*, March 28.

Byrd, Gwynnae. (1998). With no room at the prison, what is the alternative? *Los Angeles Times*, November 29, p. 6.

Campaign for New Drug Policies. (2003). Fact sheet on 17 winning campaigns. Retrieved from www.drugreform.org

Challos, Courtney. (1997). Towns see prisons as freedom from economic woes. *Chicago Tribune*, March 31.

The Columbus Dispatch. (2002). Keep the lid on pot: Voters wisely reject ballot issues aimed at legalizing drugs. November 12, p. 8-A.

Cook, Rhonda. (1998). Charlton opens prison Monday with high hopes. *The Atlanta Journal Constitution*, August 2.

Cook, Rhonda. (2001). Struggling areas argue for new prisons. *Atlanta Journal Constitution,* February 28, p. 3B.

Doyle, Zanetta. (2003). Does crime pay? Pros and cons of rural prisons. *Economic Development Digest*. Retrieved from www.nado.org/pubs/july021.html

Duke, Lynne. (2000). Building a boom behind bars; prisons revive small towns, but costs are emerging. *The Washington Post*, September 8.

Feldman, Daniel L. (1993). 20 years of prison expansion: A failing national strategy. *Public Administration Review,* 53(6), 561–567.

Fraser, Joelle. (2000). An American seduction: Portrait of a prison town. *Michigan Quarterly Review*, 93(4), 774–797.

Glamser, Deeann. (1996). Towns now welcoming prisons. *USA Today,* March 13.

Hallinan, Joseph T. (2001). *Going Up the River: Travels in a Prison Nation*. New York: Random House.

Hooks, Gregory, Linda Lobao, Clayton Mosher, and Thomas Rotolo. (2003). The prison industry: Carceral expansion and employment in U.S. counties, 1969–1994. *Social Science Quarterly*, 85, 37–57.

Howard, Roberta L. (1984). *Stress Management for Correctional Officers and Their Families*. Washington, DC: The American Correctional Association.

Jackson, Derrick Z. (1995). A boom in the prison business. *The Boston Globe*, January 25, p. 13.

Kilborn, Peter T. (2001). Rural towns turn to prisons to reignite their economies. *The New York Times*, August 1.

King, Ryan S., Marc Mauer, and Tracy Huling (2003). Big prisons, small towns: Prison economics in rural America. The Sentencing Project. Retrieved from www.sentencingproject.org/news/ruralprisons.pdf

Larmer, Paul. (1995). Poor, rural places are magnets for prisons. HighCountry News.org, January 26. Retrieved from www.hcn.org/servlets/hcn.Article?article_id=1123

Mattera, Philip, and Mafruza Khan. (2001). Jail breaks: Economic development subsidies given to private prisons: Good jobs first. Retrieved from www.goodjobsfirst.org/jbstudy.htm

Mauer, Marc. (2002). State sentencing reforms: Is the "Get Tough" era coming to a close? *Federal Sentencing Reporter*, 15(1), 50–52.

Miniclier, Kit. (1999). Akron County ponders lockup as start-up. *The Denver Post*, February 23.

Mudacumura, G.M. (2002). Towards a general theory of sustainability: Bridging key development dimensions through a multi-paradigm perspective. Ph.D. dissertation, Pennsylvania State University, Harrisburg.

National Association of State Budget Officers. (2003). Fiscal survey of states, May 2002. Fiscal survey of states, November 2002. Fiscal survey of states, June 2003. Retrieved from www.nasbo.org/publications.php

Reese, Laura A., and David Fasenfest. (1999). What works best. In John P. Blair and Laura A. Reese (eds.), *Approaches to Economic Development*, pp. 278–291. Thousand Oaks, Calif.: Sage.

Schiraldi, Vincent, and Judith Greene. (2002). Reducing correctional costs in an era of tightening budgets and shifting public opinion. *Federal Sentencing Reporter*, 14(6), 332–336.

Schlosser, Eric, (1998). The prison-industrial complex. *The Atlantic Monthly*, 282(6), 51–77.

Seti, Christopher. (2001). Prisons and their effect on local economies: The Colorado experience. Center for Tax Policy Research, University of Denver.

Smith, R. (1990). Upstate: Give us all the prisons. *Newsday*, October 8.

US Bureau of Justice Statistics. (2003). Prison statistics. Retrieved from www.ojp.usdoj.gov/bjs/prisons.htm

US General Accounting Office. (1996). Private and public prisons: Studies comparing operational costs and/or quality of service. GAO/GGD-96–158.

Wilhelm, Daniel F., and Nichoals R. Turner. (2002). Is the budget crisis changing the way we look at sentencing and incarceration? *Federal Sentencing Reporter*, 15(1), 41–49.

Wolman, Harold, and David Spitzley. (1999). The politics of local economic development. In John P. Blair and Laura A. Reese (eds.), *Approaches to Economic Development*, pp. 225–260. Thousand Oaks, Calif.: Sage.

Wray, L. Randall. (2000). A new economic reality: Penal Keynesianism. *Challenge*, 43(5), 31–60.

Chapter 16

Sustainable Waste Management: A Case Study of the Bangkok Metropolitan Authority

Watana Luanratana and C. Visvanathan

CONTENTS

Introduction

The metropolis of Bangkok has an area of 1,568 square kilometers with a population of about 10 million registered and nonregistered residents. In its 50 districts comprising 2,000 communities, Bangkok generated about 9,500 tons per day of solid waste in 2002. The entire municipal solid waste management (SWM) is under the jurisdiction of the Bangkok Metropolitan Administration (BMA), which arranges for primary collection, transport, and disposal. At an estimated annual increase of 2.25%, the waste generation for 2007 would be 10,600 tons per day, and the trend would accelerate with the expansion of the urban boundaries and growth of urban population with the increased standards of living (BMA, 2000a). The scenario for the year 2000 indicated that of the total waste generated and collected, more than 90% was disposed of at the two landfill sites. Currently, the BMA has a simple system of SWM: collection and storage of discharged waste into roadside bins or enclosures in institutions and business centers from which compaction trucks collect and haul to the transfer stations for onward transportation to the landfill sites. During the entire stream, waste picking and scavenging (material recovery for recycle and reuse) occurs, contributing to only 8% reduction of the total waste. This is done either by the BMA collection and transport workers or by the informal sector collectors called Salengs, who visit door to door with carts, or by the waste pickers who scavenge from the roadside bins, transfer station heaps, and landfills (Figure 16.1).

The trend shown in Figure 16.1 requires change for effective SWM as BMA has had to cope up with several problems related to its environmental, social, financial, managerial, and administrative aspects. Some of the technical problems encountered are the spills of waste, dust problems during transport, and malodor from transfer stations and landfill sites. As a result, the affected citizens have made complaints to the BMA. Illegal dumping and disposal have hindered 100% waste collection (BMA, 2000b). Waste collectors and scavengers work in an unhealthy environment.

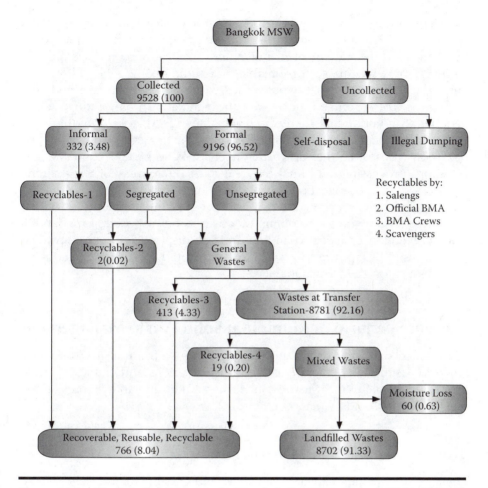

Figure 16.1 Municipal solid waste in Bangkok for 2000. Source: BMA (2000a).

Despite different acts, laws, and regulations for SWM, their implementation has been inadequate, with a lack of coordination and follow-up between the implemented schemes and the civic authority. Budget allocations have not been streamlined to suit all aspects of SWM; and collection of user fees covers only a minute fraction of the actual costs (BMA, 2000b). Lack of dissemination of public information hinders the overall management of the waste. There is large room for improvement in the SWM system, from upstream reduction in generation to downstream disposal. Incorporating the principles of cleaner production (CP) would allow an effective reduction of the waste generation as well as disposal in the landfills with a larger percentage of recovery of the valuables in the entire waste stream.

CP concepts would help minimize the problems and constraints faced by BMA for effective SWM in the metropolis. Bangkok can be considered as a large industry, generating products and wastes with citizens as the consumers. CP would begin at the industry, targeting reduction of waste by changes in the pattern of manufacture of its various products and the pathways by which these consumables reach the people who utilize them and generate waste. That would take care of the upstream with the awareness of the refuse reduction at the generating point and by segregation into components to recover valuables (recyclable, reusable, and repairable objects), biowaste (kitchen organic matter and yard waste), and hazardous wastes. Further downstream, changes in the collection systems, transport, processing, and final disposal must be addressed. Streamlining of the storage and collection (segregation based on properties of waste) would allow a change in the waste-processing techniques that would ultimately reduce the total volume of waste to be disposed at the landfill sites. Prevention of illegal dumping and self-disposal is a necessity. The present trend of rapid rise in waste quantity could be stabilized, reducing the pressure on the management.

Present Scenario of Municipal Solid Waste Management

BMA collects and transports the municipal refuse from all its 50 districts with its existing infrastructure to the transfer stations and employs private transporters to haul the waste for final disposal at the landfills outside the metropolitan boundary.

Waste Generation and Discharge

To estimate the per capita waste generation, Bangkok households are classified on the basis of income group, namely, A, B, and C. Table 16.1 summarizes the result of a detailed survey conducted at the On-Nuch transfer station. It is interesting to note that the per capita solid waste generation did not differ significantly between high- and low-income groups, at 0.425 kg per capita per day, whereas Visvanathan and Tränkler (2003) have reported that India and China range between 0.3 to 0.65 kg and 0.2 to 1.7 kg, respectively.

Waste Composition

The overall waste composition sampled on a wet basis indicated that kitchen waste dominated the total quantity, at about 51%; nonrecyclable (plastic and foam and paper) was the second largest at more than 24%. Other recyclables (plastic, foam, paper, metals, bottles, and glass) as

Table 16.1   Classification of Households and per Capita Waste Generation

Household Classification	Income Level (THB/month)[a]	Population (%)	Solid Waste Generation Rate (kg per capita per day)
A	30,000 and above	24	0.490
B	13,000 – 29,999	38	0.440
C	Below 12,999	38	0.400
Weighted average			**0.437**

[a] THB40 = US$1.

Source: Japan Bank for International Cooperation [JBIC] (2001).

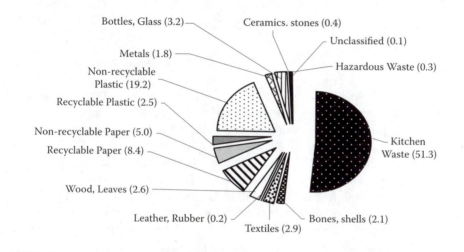

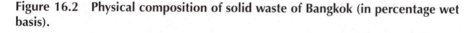

Figure 16.2   Physical composition of solid waste of Bangkok (in percentage wet basis).

indicated constituted almost 16%. The rest of the components were textiles, leather, wood, leaves, rubber, ceramic, and stones with a small percentage of recyclables (Figure 16.2). This clearly indicated a larger fraction of combustible waste, which under the existing circumstances could not be considered for incineration because of the higher moisture content in the kitchen waste and reduced calorific value. Meanwhile, a higher fraction of biodegradable waste indicates the attractiveness of the composition for adoption of composting techniques, but before selecting this treatment technology, proper upstream waste segregation schemes need to be chosen.

Collection and Transport

The responsibility of waste collection and transportation lies directly with the BMA. Currently there are 1,306 collection vehicles and a total crew of around 7,000 who make 1,780 daily collection trips to residential and commercial areas. These collection vehicles are used for hauling 9,500 tons of waste to the transfer stations. Each of these transfer stations, located at On-Nuch, Tharaeng, and Nongkhaem, handles about 3,500, 2,300, and 2,800 tons, respectively. In general, the transfer stations are overloaded; overloading leads to unsanitary conditions, which are due to stockpiling of excess waste despite continuous hauling to the landfills.

With the continuous increase in waste generation in BMA, it is important to investigate the collection system and crew efficiency. For example, in Kuala Lumpur municipality in Malaysia, 7,660 tons per day of waste is hauled with a fleet of 565 collection trucks (Levine, 1995); this figure indicates the lacunae in the collection system of BMA.

Disposal

Private transporters haul the wastes from the transfer stations using 20- to 30-ton trailers for final disposal at the designated landfill sites. The waste from On-Nuch is landfilled at Rachthewa; that from Nongkhaem and Tharaeng is hauled to the landfills at Kampangsaen 1 and 2. The first site with a capacity of 7.5 million cubic meters has been in operation since July 2000 and was projected to reach its capacity after 4 years; the Kampangsaen landfill has been expanded since November 2000. These landfills have been designed and operated more as impoverished dumpsites than as secured sanitary landfills, as required by the national waste disposal regulations.

Waste Processing

Waste processing and pretreatment become essential parts of the waste stream before the final disposal. At BMA, there exist no formal processing and treatment facilities, though there are potentials for a higher degree of processing based on the waste composition. The techniques used by BMA are material recovery at various stages and a pilot project for separate collection in some target waste generation units to allow recycling.

Recycling

Recycling of the waste reduces the waste quantity if it is practiced widely. There are two forms of recycling systems in operation, which can be considered as formal and informal sector operations. In the formal sector, the BMA transport crews collect all the valuables they can find in the waste stream and sell them to the waste shops during the regular waste collection shifts to obtain additional income. The Pollution Control Department (PCD) has estimated that such collections total about 413 tons per day, accounting for more than 50% recovery of the recyclable waste in the stream (BMA, 2002). The formal system uses 10 target groups (educational institutes, hospitals, department stores, hotels, religious centers, high-rise buildings, condominiums, housing estates, markets, and commercial centers) that have been initiated to practice source segregation.

In the informal sector, the most prominent recovery of recyclables is by Salengs, who make locality visits with their tricycles and collect materials from the households. About 2,100 Salengs operate in Bangkok and collect a total of about 332 tons of recyclables, which accounts for more than 40% of the recovered materials (JBIC, 2001). In addition, the scavengers at the transfer stations collect about 2% to 3% of the recyclables. As a whole, the present scenario indicates that the recycling rate is about 8% (766 tons) of the total waste stream with the participation of both the formal and informal sectors. The system saves the BMA about Thai baht (THB) 97 million per year at THB 350 per ton of waste.

The Recycle Promotion Drive by the BMA

As an initial step of reducing the total amount of solid waste generated, BMA focused mainly on the policy of waste recycling. In spite of the original target of 20% waste reduction through recycling by 2001, only 8% recycling was achieved even with the concerted efforts of the PCD and active local educational and media campaigns by nongovernmental organizations (NGOs) (Thailand Environment Monitor, 2003). The reduction of waste was aimed at adherence to the rule of 4 Rs—reduce, reuse, repair, and recycle. To allow such a system, source separation has been promoted with the use of separate colored bins: green for food wastes and other biodegradables; yellow for recyclable waste (bottles, plastic, glass, paper, aluminum cans, and other metals), and gray for the hazardous category of wastes (lightbulbs, dry cells, batteries, etc.) especially in commercial centers. The source separation activities are designed such that they are carried out by the BMA collection crews or Salengs, rather than by household owners. Though these recycle activities carried out by the BMA workers assist their monthly incomes, their working efficiency is significantly reduced in terms of garbage collection rate. Currently, the BMA is considering drafting a policy whether to prohibit or make this system of source separation official as an initiative to promote recycling (BMA, 2002).

Present Problems and Constraints

BMA is faced with increasing SWM problems that can be broadly categorized as waste-related environmental issues, management issues, and financial aspects issues. These issues are discussed in detail in the following sections.

Waste-Related Environmental Issues

The waste discharge rate has been increasing by about 2.25% annually mainly because of the population growth and the increase in urbanization and BMA's waste handling capacity has not kept pace with the trend (BMA, 2002). It does not collect 100% of the total generated waste, and illegal dumping and disposal are still practiced. The capacity of transfer stations is found to be inadequate to handle the incoming waste; the result is stockpiling, which creates significant environmental problems. The waste pickers and scavengers as well the BMA workers are at environmental health risks while handling the waste. The transport for final disposal at the landfill sites has been a cause of air pollution in terms of dust, odor, noise, fumes, and emission of landfill gases. These problems are due to the lack of institutional capacity in the sphere of technical management that would be able to remedy them. Another issue is the leakage of wastewater from the collection trucks and transfer stations. Leachate generated at the disposal sites leads to groundwater pollution for which treatment facilities are required.

Management Issues

Despite efforts by BMA to formalize the recycle system with source segregation by using several pilot projects, the SWM system is not fully integrated. BMA workers sort the recyclables during waste collection trips; that activity reduces their efficiency as they barely collect 5.33 tons per trip. However, their role is not formalized; nor is that of the Salengs who operate individually without any input from the civic authority. The existing regulations governing collection of waste and levying of fees and user charges are not well coordinated; therefore, strengthening of the management issues would be necessary. The actual SWM cost far exceeds the realization from the users, as seen in Table 16.2. For effective management, the participation of the private sector, NGOs, and community-based organizations (CBOs) would be necessary. The role of PCD for direction of municipal solid waste (MSW) activities should go hand in hand with the objectives of BMA to foster effective monitoring of the waste collection, transport, processing, and disposal. Further, publication by the

Table 16.2 Comparison of Expenditure and Collection of User Fees with Percentages for Years 1995–2000

Year	Collection Costs[a] THB/Ton	%	Disposal Costs[a] THB/Ton	%	Total Costs[a] THB/Ton	%	Collection Fees[a] THB/Ton	%	Deficit[a] THB/Ton	%
1995	416.02	68.59	190.48	31.41	606.50	100	25.78	4.25	580.72	95.75
1996	418.86	70.37	176.36	29.63	595.22	100	20.55	3.45	574.69	96.55
1997	419.94	74.23	145.82	25.77	565.76	100	20.45	3.61	546.31	96.56
1998	452.99	71.69	178.84	28.31	631.83	100	17.83	2.82	614.01	97.18
1999	553.84	77.24	163.17	22.76	717.01	100	17.67	2.46	699.34	97.54
2000	477.87	72.75	178.97	27.25	656.84	100	22.47	3.42	634.37	96.58

[a] THB40 = US$1.

From Bangkok Metropolitan Administration, 2002.

Department of Public Cleansing (DPC) of public information must be directed to more target groups to allow a reduction of the waste upstream rather than provide the downstream solution. BMA requires adequate professional and technical competency for effective management.

Financial Aspects

Another issue of concern for management are the budget allocations for the various activities related to SWM. Compared to that for the other municipal services, the financial allocation for SWM is in the range of 20% to 25%. Of this amount, 65% to 75% is spent on the collection and transportation activities, the remaining 25% to 35% is used for the final processing and disposal. This clearly indicates the processing and disposal sectors have received inadequate attention, lacunae in the overall management of these aspects of the waste stream are the result.

Table 16.2 indicates that the absence of budgetary provisions for processing and the levy on the users are far too highly subsidized (hardly 2.5% to 3%) with an annual fluctuation that could contribute to the ineffectiveness of the management, as well as cause deficit in the budget. More than 95% of the SWM costs are borne by BMA, at a total of more than THB 2 billion. The cost of disposal has been between 20% and 31% of the total management cost, indicative of a disproportionate expenditure for the collection. For effective management of the solid waste, the collection, processing, and disposal must be streamlined in the budgetary provisions. The user fees should be able to cover a larger fraction of the budget than the present one by applying the "Polluter Pays Principle," which would reduce the waste generated. It has been seen from practices in India and Sri Lanka that the involvement of the private sector in collection and transport has greatly increased the efficiency of the MSW system (Asian Institute of Technology [AIT], 2004). Another example of increased efficiency with the involvement of the private sector was reported in Kuala Lumpur, Malaysia, where the collection by the private sector was 8.5 tons per vehicle trip, whereas that by the public sector was only 5.7 tons per vehicle trip (Levine, 1995).

Sustainable Waste Management Strategies for BMA

The sustainable waste management approach of BMA should incorporate the basic principle of waste reduction, reuse, and recycling at the source to allow an upstream approach to the overall strategy for waste reduction. The fundamental approach would be to consider Bangkok as a large industry whose citizens are consumers to apply the CP principles that would dictate the production and supply of goods and services with environment-friendly norms. This strategy would minimize the waste at the producer's end rather than at the consumer's end with a stepwise follow-up on the downstream. In creating the strategy, the factors influencing the generation play an important role in the waste minimization plan that could be achieved by using legal and economic instruments, suasion, and appropriate collection, treatment, and disposal technologies.

Factors Controlling Waste

The primary factors that control the waste amount are the population and the income level of the citizens. The forecast for the waste amount is based on these two factors, though various other factors contribute to its precision. In terms of the factors considered later, the forecast for waste discharge and collection amount is given in Figure 16.3, which indicates a steady rise with nearly 15,000 tons per day by 2019.

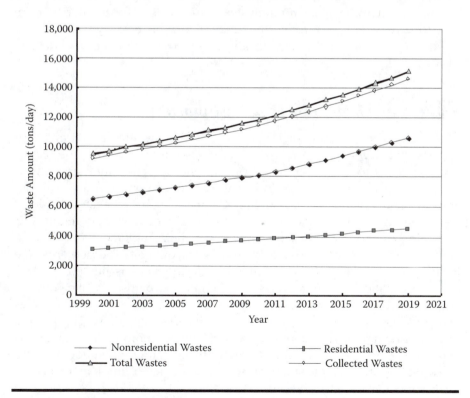

Figure 16.3   Forecast of waste generation and collection amount.

The present population estimate of Bangkok is based on the 1990 census, and the proposed waste management plan has forecasted an annual growth of registered and nonregistered residents by 1.53% until 2019; the growth of commuters has been assumed to be 1.47% (BMA, 2000b). On this basis, the forecast for waste discharge can be determined together with the income growth. Waste generation and collection up to 2019 show a smaller growth in the domestic waste component but a substantial growth in the nonresidential (industrial and commercial) waste sector. It has been found that the increase in per capita daily residential waste has been 0.4 to 0.425 kg, whereas the per capita nonresidential waste increase is from 0.467 to 0.902 kg, thus increasing the share of the latter sector from 54% to 68% within the period 1989 to 2000 (BMA, 2000b). This factor requires stabilization at the current level to allow a consolidated decrease in the otherwise uncontrolled growth of MSW in the metropolis.

The growth in income of an individual increases her or his consumption pattern and is related to the growth in gross domestic product (GDP). The present trend in Thailand indicates a rise by 2.5% for the period from 2000 to 2010 and by 3.4% for 2011 to 2020. The waste discharge is expected to grow by 2.25% for the first decade and 3.06% for the second decade (JBIC, 2001).

Waste Minimization by Legal Instruments

Waste minimization can only be achieved with the incorporation of CP options that target the upstream of waste generation. Keeping the factors controlling waste generation fixed on the one hand, minimization efforts should bring about a control in the waste generation with a down-the-line follow-up on the waste stream. Control can be facilitated by legal and economic instruments. BMA has a number of laws and regulations governing environmental management, but their implementation is centralized and enforcement by legal authorities is difficult. The power vested in the police for enforcement with fines and permits is limited by their lack of institutional arrangements and technical expertise. Public comprehension of the rules and regulations is lacking, without regular updates that could be achieved with effective multimedia campaigns. The present system of command and control (CAC) has limited enforcement. BMA has inadequate professional capacity with technical competency for the enforcement of the law, which causes complexities of implementation of environmentally sound practices.

Economic Instruments

Besides the legal aspects, economic incentives play a vital role. The legal instruments can only be effective with the provision of economic instruments in the form of municipal taxes and service charges for handling the waste. Another factor to control waste generation would be to levy taxes or duties on goods that generate waste, restrict use of excessive packaging material, and provide a deposit refund system for recyclables and reusables (plastic, glass, rubber, or metal containers and household appliances once out of service). Further, the production process of consumables may be monitored for environmentally friendly practices and provide market-based incentives (MBIs) of loans, tax relief, and grants to the producers for adherence to sound environmental practices. Strictures and fines for violating these norms and regulations would deter the producers from environmentally unethical practices.

Suasion

Sustainable management of the urban MSW would not be complete with only a legal approach and application of economic instruments without voluntary public participation and awareness among the polluters. The willingness to promote a sound environment goes a long way in the reduction of the waste, for which education of the masses through multimedia campaigns would be necessary to make the public realize its importance. Hence, public willingness to participate in the programs and projects initiated by BMA would enhance effective management and coordination of the activities. Changing of consumer habits and patterns from the existing ones would be difficult using only CAC and economic instruments but would be simplified if the public were persuaded to change, thereby paving the way for the reduction of generated waste.

Appropriate Technologies

The applicable technology is related to both upstream (generation, source segregation, collection, transport) to downstream (processing/treatment and final disposal) MSW. Generation of waste depends on the technological approach in the various sources of waste—the consumer goods. An integrated approach by the producer of such goods to reduce packaging would decrease the waste at the user's end. This in effect would be a CP technique. Source segregation when systematized to separate different categories of waste promotes recycling and reuse of valuables in the waste stream.

The kitchen and the yard wastes that constitute biodegradable waste can be segregated and processed as compost either in the backyard or by large-scale composting units or plants specifically functioning under the BMA umbrella and can provide useful products for agricultural use as soil conditioners or biofertilizers. Once the biodegradable and recyclable wastes are separated, the volume to be processed further would be reduced by more than half and could easily be handled using the existing infrastructure for processing—compaction at the transfer stations and disposal in landfills.

Introduction of incineration facilities by BMA would require further segregation of waste into combustibles and noncombustibles. The calorific value of BMA MSW has been found to be about 4600 kJ per kg (JBIC, 2001), which is much lower than the minimal value required for sustainable combustion (5024 to 5861 kJ per kg) (AIT, 2004). The removal of the biowaste component from the waste stream would drastically reduce the moisture content and increase the calorific value of the waste, allowing a self-sustaining combustion in the incinerator that would generate electricity as a useful by-product. Such a technical strategy would help in the reduction of the waste volume for landfills and minimize problems arising out of transport of waste, malodor, leachate, and landfill gases.

Waste Generation Control and Reduction Plan

The significant growth in waste discharge as forecasted (Figure 16.3) had made BMA set targets for waste reduction with control at the source by implementing the legal, economic, and technical instruments vis-à-vis CP options as indicated. The waste stream has two components, residential wastes and nonresidential wastes, of which the former quantity could be stabilized but could not be reduced drastically with the options cited. People's participation with an effective campaign for reduction of waste generation would help control the per capita waste generation.

However, this would not significantly reduce the total waste generation, as the population of the metropolis would be on the increase. The present 0.468 kg per capita per day domestic waste generation could be maintained at the same level by 2019, but in effect, the total volume of domestic waste would increase significantly with the population growth. This value is lower than the per capita generation in cities of most developing Asian countries (Visvanathan and Trankler, 2003). Hence, the priority focus for waste reduction should be in the nonresidential sector.

BMA has proposed a reduction target for waste discharge by 2019 from its nonresidential waste stream estimated at 1.157 kg per capita per day, which could effectively be reduced to 0.632 kg per capita per day by applying CP principles with stringent measures to control large waste discharges. Eventually, the measures could be expanded to include the medium- and small-scale waste discharges. Another step would be the recycle rule for the products that generate recyclable waste (household appliances, computers, mobile phones, electrical accessories), which should be routed back to the producers once the useful life is finished. Other waste products resulting from canning and packaging (cans, bottles and plastic trays) would have to be sent to the producers for recycling or reuse or to a recycling agency. Specific proposed scenarios for the waste reduction scheme are as follows:

- Charges to be levied on large-volume business or corporate waste based on the quantity per unit discharged
- Reduction in discharge by application of the reduction and recycle rule
- Institutional arrangements for the promotion of reduction and recycling

On the basis of BMA's proposed waste management plan, a recycle and reuse proposal for 15% of refuse has been put forward; the rest of the waste would be processed by composting, incineration, and disposal in sanitary landfills by 2019. Figure 16.4 indicates the various scenarios for the plan for integrated SWM in which waste is segregated from the generating source, residential and nonresidential sectors, into three categories (recyclables and reusables, biodegradable and nonbiodegradable), and for each category the processing and disposal criteria are outlined. The recyclables and reusables and the biodegradables would be removed from the waste stream at the beginning as a result of source segregation. The volume to be landfilled would be the processed household hazardous wastes, the incinerated residue, and the other nonbiodegradable wastes.

Sustainable Measures of Solid Waste Management

The efforts of BMA to incorporate CP through its proposed waste management plan would require additional sustainable measures based on the legal, financial, and technical instruments and motivation. These would exert control in the waste generation, a sound collection system, a market for recycling and reuse, dissemination of information and environmental education, and a monitoring system for the proposed activities and pilot projects.

The metropolitan management with certain regulations to control waste should require all large- and medium-scale generators to submit plans for waste reduction and reduce fancy packaging. It should promote recycling and resale of used goods, subsidize backyard or home composting, and

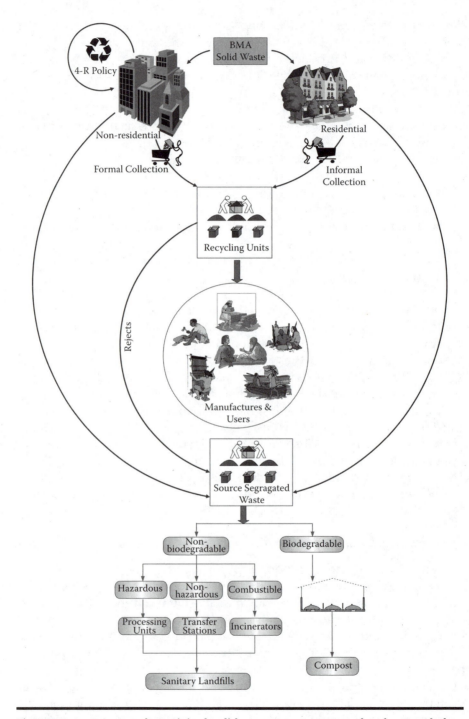

Figure 16.4 Integrated municipal solid waste management plan for Bangkok.

implement waste segregation at the source. Separation of large-scale organic wastes from such generation sources as hotels, restaurants, fast-food joints, and cottage food-processing units would provide resources for composting and hence reduce biowaste from the main stream.

Once the system is streamlined to that effect, an effective collection system would induce the polluters to segregate the waste. In addition, the informal sector waste collectors such as Salengs and scavengers should be registered under the BMA and the collection work by BMA crews should be formalized. At the same time, an awareness campaign on the benefits of source separation among the citizens would assist the collection system. The solid waste of Bangkok is the property of the BMA, and once the right to the ownership is given to the private sector with infrastructure support, its entry would make a difference in the SWM system, as indicated previously. The valuables in the waste stream would be attractive for private sector involvement that would make possible the establishment of recycling and resource recovery plants. This would significantly assist the SWM system for BMA as well as increase efficiency.

To begin recycling various types of waste a market would be necessary and BMA would be required to create it for the sustainability of the recycling units. Further, it should be able to provide certain subsidies in the form of collection, storage, and transport of the recyclables as well as land for establishing such units. A media campaign to encourage use of recycled goods and repair facilities would pave the way for reduction of waste that would otherwise accumulate in the main stream.

One of the keys to successful waste management is citizens' awareness of the environmental issues related to the garbage disposal. That could be achieved by disseminating information regarding the CP concepts of waste reduction, source segregation, recycling and composting technologies among the citizens along with the understanding of the adverse effects of the waste on human health, aesthetics, and the general environment.

All efforts to implement waste reduction strategies backed up by legal, economic, and technical measures would only partially fulfill the objectives or could even create a chaotic system without the effective monitoring of the waste stream. This system would not only collect statistics but also locate any lacunae in the SWM, which could be immediately remedied.

Conclusion

Municipal refuse is closely related to citizens' urban life: the industrial, corporate, and business activities of a city. The present scenario in Bangkok indicates the lacunae in the system of SWM by the metropolitan authority which are due to problems and constraints that limit 100%

collection and to lack of technologically sound methods for segregation, transport, and disposal.

Recognizing the facts and the loopholes within the system, BMA's policymaking body has proposed certain effective measures that incorporate principles of CP to reduce significantly the generation of refuse in the metropolis by targeting the sources, mainly the nonresidential sector, which includes the burgeoning industry, institutions, business centers, and corporate sector. These measures include reduction in the waste generation at the source with lesser consumption of packaging materials, stringent methods of resource utilization, and regulations governing the discharge of waste by large- medium- and small-scale dischargers.

The levy and collection of appropriate fees and discharge taxes should encompass all dischargers. Having more target groups for source segregation would allow a source-separated waste for further downstream processing. Inclusion of the small- and large-scale private sector participation, community participation, and involvement of the local NGOs would definitely prove a boon for BMA, providing for integrated SWM as shown in Figure 16.4.

The objectives of reducing total waste generation and increasing its processing by promoting recycling and composting would decrease quantities of trash at different stages in the waste stream. BMA has to secure active cooperation and understanding of its citizens while promulgating its plans for the desired objectives. Sharing of responsibilities by citizens, corporations, and administrative bodies would allow the establishment of an effective system that would cater to the urgent needs of sustainable development of the metropolis.

An analysis of the approaches to be adopted in the future with an understanding of the present scenario reflects BMA's people-oriented approach, which would encourage greater public participation through voluntary groups who could help with promotional materials and dissemination of information. The implementation of the proposed plan with its various approaches for CP concepts would achieve by 2019 a total per capita refuse discharge of 1.1 kg per capita per day (residential 0.468 kg and nonresidential 0.632 kg) by significantly reducing the nonresidential waste from the projected value of 1.625 kg per capita per day (without a plan). Bangkok would be generating a daily waste volume of 10,562 tons with CP options instead of 15,065 tons without the changed strategy (a reduction by 30% of the total discharge).

A recycling of 15% waste and composting of another 20% would further decrease the waste disposal amount to 6,865 tons (without incineration), ensuring longer life for the landfills. Introduction of incineration facilities would further decrease the landfilled waste by 20% to 25%. This objective could only be achieved by using the CP options in the upstream of waste collection, which begin with reduction among the population in consumption patterns and source segregation for reuse, recycling, and composting, instead of downstream reduction, as presently practiced. To achieve the objective, strengthening of the BMA infrastructure and its institutional capacity would required for sustainable development within the framework of the principles of CP for well-coordinated urban refuse management.

References

Asian Institute of Technology (2004). Comparative Study on Municipal Solid Waste Management, Asian Regional Research Programme on Environmental Technology, Environmental Engineering and Management. Bangkok, Thailand: AIT.

Bangkok Metropolitan Administration (2000a). Final Report on Study of Alternatives for Management of Commercial and Non-Hazardous Industrial Solid Waste. Bangkok, Thailand: BMA.

Bangkok Metropolitan Administration (2000b). Completion Report on Technical Assistance to the Bangkok Metropolitan Administration: Improvement of Solid Waste Collection Management, COWI-EP&T Associates, Ministry of Environment and Energy, Danish Cooperation for Environment and Development. Bangkok, Thailand: BMA.

Bangkok Metropolitan Administration (2002). Final Report on Solid Waste Management Study for Bangkok Metropolitan Administration, Sogreah. Bangkok, Thailand: BMA.

Japan Bank for International Cooperation. (2001). Solid Waste Management at On-Nuch, Special Assistance for Project Formation (SAPROF), Phase 1, Final, Bangkok, Thailand.

Levine, S.C. (1995). Private Sector Participation in Municipal Solid Waste Services in Developing Countries.Volume 1. The Formal Sector, Urban Management Programme, Urban Management and the Environment, UNDP/UNCHS/World Bank. Washington, D.C.: The World Bank.

Thailand Environmental Monitor (2003). A joint publication of the Pollution Control Department, Royal Thai Government, The World Bank, U.S. Asia Environmental Partnership, Japan Bank for International Cooperation and U.S. Agency for International Development. Retrieved from http://www.worldbank.or.th/monitor

Visvanathan, C., and Tränkler, J. (2003). Municipal Solid Waste Management in Asia: A Comparative Analysis, Proceedings of Workshop on Sustainable Landfill Management, 3-5 December 2003, Chennai, India.

Chapter 17

Multi-Regime-Regulation and Sustainable Development: A Study of the International Hazardous Waste Trade

Britta Meinke-Brandmaier

CONTENTS

Introduction

Hazardous waste disposal by Northern-based firms in the Third World began in the early 1980s. In order to avoid stringent regulations and higher costs, many firms producing the wastes started seeking management facilities beyond their national borders. To begin with, transboundary movements of hazardous wastes were a phenomenon of the industrialized world and were legitimized with free trade and labor sharing in waste disposal among states with the same economic and environmental standards (Rublack, 1993, p. 28). Increasingly, other countries became involved. In the mid-1980s, there were more signs of wastes being shipped to countries in Latin America, the Caribbean, and Africa (Valette and Spalding, 1990). The group of potential importing countries for hazardous wastes was thus joined by some of the poorest countries in the world, which suffered from falling "terms of trade," sinking export proceeds, and increasing foreign debts (Bartram and Engel, 1989: 116; Puckett, 1992, p. 95; Valette and Bernstorff, 1989, p. 26). These new "importing countries" usually lacked the financial, technical, legal, and institutional capacity for monitoring trade in hazardous waste and preventing illegal imports.

The United Nations Environment Program (UNEP) paid early attention to the problem of hazardous waste trade. It was difficult to quantify precisely the amount of hazardous waste generated, given considerable differences in definition among countries. UNEP estimated that 300 to 400 million tons of toxic waste was produced per year (Tolba, 1990, p. 3), and every year at least 30 million tons of toxic waste was transported across borders (Hilz, 1992, p. 20). The hazardous waste trade between industrialized and developing countries was estimated as making up at least 10% (Tolba, 1990, p. 4) of that 30 million tons.

In 1982, UNEP initiated action on the waste issue and began to draw up the "Cairo Guidelines on Environmentally Sound Management of Hazardous Wastes." The goal of these guidelines, though not legally binding, was to assist governments in the process of developing policies for the environmentally sound management of hazardous wastes (UNEP/GC.14/17, Annex II; UNEP, 1987). Parallel to the development of the Cairo Guidelines and in response to the growing trade in hazardous waste, the legal framework of the Organization of Economic Co-operation and Development (OECD) (Decision C [83] 180/Final, 23 I.L.M 214 [1984]) and the European Community (EC) (Regulation 84/631 EEC, OJ L 326 [1984]: 31) were expanded to apply to third countries as well (Decision

OECD/C[86]64/Final, 25 I.L.M 1010 [1986]; Regulation 86/279/EEC, OJ L 181 [1986]: 13).

These early attempts to control trade in hazardous waste were welcomed by the World Commission on Environment and Development (WCED). In its report "Our Common Future," the commission stressed the importance of three principles that were incorporated in these legal attempts: equally strict controls on shipments to third countries, prior notification to and consent from the country of final destination, and a guarantee of adequate disposal facilities in the recipient country (WCED, 1990, p. 272). The commission, however, did not consider these steps taken by industrialized countries as sufficient: "But as of now there is no effective mechanism either to monitor or to control hazardous waste trade.... Governments and international organizations must more actively support efforts to achieve an effective international regime to control the transfrontier movement of hazardous wastes" (WCED, 1990, p. 272).

International regimes are "sets of implicit or explicit principles, norms, rules, and decision-making procedures around which actors' expectations converge in a given area of international relations" (Krasner, 1982, p. 186). Regimes are a form of international institutions[1] that have been especially suitable for the organization of international environmental politics. In this chapter, I will show how international environmental regimes can contribute to sustainable development. I will argue that in some issue areas, states establish and maintain not only global regimes but also regional ones to ensure an effective protection of the environment. This is true for the issue area "international trade in hazardous wastes." After the Basel Convention on the Control of transboundary movements of hazardous wastes and their disposal (28 I.L.M 657 [1989]) was adopted in March 1989, 12 additional regimes and organizations to control the international waste trade at the regional level were established or further developed until February 1998. At the same time, the institutionalized policy of the contracting parties of the Basel Convention changed from control to prohibition of waste movements from industrialized countries to the less developed world ("change of a regime").[2]

In the following sections, I will describe and analyze this evolutionary development and show that the adoption of regional agreements banning the import of hazardous waste created the pressure necessary for the global regime to adapt. With the amendment decision to prohibit exports of hazardous waste to the less-developed world, the global regime (1) reestablished sovereignty for developing countries that were previously unable to control the import of hazardous waste into their territories and (2) moved the problem back to its source by forcing the industrialized world to deal with the hazardous waste it generated.

Efficient Control of the International Hazardous Waste Trade

Phase One: The Adoption of the Basel Convention

The Negotiation Process

In 1987, UNEP's Governing Council adopted a decision requesting the executive director to start drafting a global convention (UNEP/GC.14/30). Six working group meetings were necessary before the Basel Convention was ready for signature, and 96 countries, 50 international organizations, plus a number of nongovernmental orgaizations (NGOs) participated in one or more of these working groups.[3]

The preparation of the agreement in the working groups as well as the diplomatic conference in Basel were contentious and difficult. Two opposing groups of countries with different viewpoints were negotiating. On the one hand, there was the group of countries, among them most of the OECD nations, that generally wanted the international hazardous waste trade to continue to be legal. These countries nevertheless supported measures to control the scandalous traffic to developing countries. This group advocated regulation to control the international hazardous waste trade based on prior informed consent procedures, with the basic goal of being able to distinguish between legal and illegal shipments of hazardous wastes.

On the other hand, there was the group of African countries, principally supported by other developing countries that were confronted with the international trade in hazardous wastes that they could not control because these wastes were often labeled as harmless raw materials such as household wastes, building materials, or fertilizer. The African states became aware of the fact that it would be easy for the illegally operating "waste brokers" to fake their consent, taking into consideration the corruption of governments in most Third World countries.[4] The African countries, therefore, started to develop their own hazardous waste trade policy. The Council of Ministers (CM) of the Organization of African Unity (OAU) adopted a resolution and declared that "the dumping of nuclear and industrial wastes in Africa is a crime against Africa and the African people" (OAU/CM/Res. 1153 [XLVIII]). They favored a total ban on the waste trade (OAU/CM/Res.1199 [XLIX]) along with the group of environmental NGOs, the most important of them Greenpeace.

At the last working group meeting to prepare the convention, it became evident that the African negotiators had found little support among the other recipient states. The countries of Central and Eastern Europe and some of the more industrialized developing countries either did not want to risk their gains from hazardous waste imports or wanted to keep the door open for their own potential hazardous waste exports. With that, the African group was left alone and not able to carry through the goal of an outright ban (Lembke, 1991, p. 28).

The Basel Convention on the Control of Transboundary Movements of Hazardous Wastes and Their Disposal was adopted in March 1989 by 116 states (including the EC) represented at a ministerial conference in Basel. Nevertheless, the convention was only signed by 35 countries and the EC. Not a single African country was among them. Instead, the African nations announced at the conference they were going to draw up their own convention on hazardous wastes.

The Main Provisions of the Basel Convention

The provisions of the Basel Convention cover the generation, management, and disposal of hazardous wastes. *Wastes* are defined as "substances which are disposed of or are intended to be disposed of or are required to be disposed of by the provisions of national law" (Art. 2.1). *Disposal* is defined in Annex IV of the convention. Besides operations leading to final disposal of the wastes such as landfill and incineration (Annex IV A), the definition includes operations leading to resource recovery, recycling, reclamation, direct reuse, or alternative use (Annex IV B). Thus, wastes subject to recycling operations were also subject to the convention's provisions.

The scope of the convention includes two categories of wastes: *hazardous waste* and *other waste. Hazardous waste* is waste that belongs to any category in Annex 1 (waste streams and hazardous constituents), unless it does not possess any of the characteristics listed in Annex III (hazardous characteristics). Waste that is defined as, or considered to be, hazardous by domestic legislation of one or more parties involved in a movement of the waste in question is also hazardous for the purposes of the convention. *Other wastes* are household wastes and residues arising from the incineration of household wastes. They are not defined as hazardous wastes but are also included in the scope of the convention (Art. 1).

The Basel Convention binds the contracting parties to ensure that the generation of hazardous and other wastes is reduced to a minimum. Still, if the generation of hazardous waste cannot be avoided, it should, as far as compatible with environmentally sound management, be disposed of in the state of generation. The export of hazardous wastes is only allowed if the state of export does not have the technical capacity and the necessary facilities to dispose of the waste in an environmentally sound manner or the waste in question is required as raw materials for recycling or recovery industries in the state of import. The export of hazardous waste is forbidden when there is reason to believe the waste will not be managed in an environmentally sound manner.

Furthermore, the export of hazardous waste is generally prohibited within the area south of 60° south latitude (Antarctica), to contracting parties that established a national import ban for hazardous waste, and to noncontracting parties to the convention (Art. 4). Notwithstanding the ban to nonparties, the export of hazardous waste to noncontracting parties is allowed, when it would occur on the basis of bilateral, multilateral, or regional agreements, provided the provisions of such agreements or arrangements are no less stringent than those of the Basel Convention (Art. 11).

The convention, therefore, did not establish a ban on the waste trade. The export of hazardous wastes is based on the principle of "prior informed consent (PIC) in writing." The PIC procedure in writing means that a transboundary movement of hazardous waste may only take place after the states of import and transit have given their written consent to the states of export, on the basis of detailed information provided to them by that state (Art. 6). The Basel Convention was thus primarily an instrument for the international control of the hazardous waste trade.

Beyond that, the Basel Convention concentrates on combating illegal traffic in hazardous waste. A transboundary movement of hazardous and other wastes is deemed to be illegal traffic when it is carried out without notification, without consent of the state concerned, and with consent obtained from states concerned through falsification, misrepresentation, or fraud. Furthermore, export of hazardous wastes is seen as illegal traffic when the waste does not conform to the documents or when it is deliberately dumped. In cases of illegal traffic, the state of export has to ensure that the waste in question is taken back into the state of export or disposed of in an environmentally sound manner (Art. 9). The Basel Convention entered into force after the 20th ratification in May 1992.

Phase Two (March 1989 to December 1992)

The opposing viewpoints of North and South that emerged during the negotiation process determined the reactions to the convention. In the view of the less-developed states, especially the African countries, the Basel Convention did not constitute the appropriate legal basis for the regulation of the international trade in hazardous wastes. These countries still favored an outright ban, and many of them, including the 69 African, Caribbean, and Pacific (ACP) states, were successful in introducing this claim in the EC-ACP negotiations within the framework of the Lomé IV Convention (29 I.L.M 788 [1990]). The convention had, with Article 39, for the first time, a provision on the export of hazardous and radioactive waste. It states that "the Community shall prohibit all direct or indirect export of such waste to the ACP States while at the same time the ACP States shall prohibit the direct or indirect import into their territory of such waste from the Community or from any other Country."

Coinciding with the Lomé IV negotiations, the African countries tried to continue their own hazardous waste trade policy. Disappointed with the Basel negotiations, in which they could not secure an outright ban, the African nations agreed at a June 1989 OAU meeting to draft an African Convention on the transboundary movement of hazardous wastes (OAU/CM/Res. 1225 [L]). Three working group meetings were held to prepare and draft the Bamako Convention on the Ban of the Import into Africa and the Control of Transboundary Movement and Management of Hazardous Wastes within Africa (30 I.L.M 775 [1991]), which was signed by 12 African countries in Bamako, Mali, in early 1991. The Bamako Convention, developed with the help of UNEP, African experts, and representatives of Greenpeace (Clapp, 1994, p. 27), prohibited the import of all hazardous waste, for any reason, into Africa from noncontracting parties and expanded definition of hazardous waste to include radioactive waste as well (Art. 2).

The wording of the import ban for hazardous waste "for any reason" reflected Africa's wish to be protected from waste deals for recycling as well. Already in early 1991, it was obvious one of the major weaknesses of the Basel Convention was its hazardous waste definition. Although the annexes of the convention list properties of hazardous waste, the convention also recognized that potential hazards posed by certain wastes had not yet been determined and that all countries had different definitions of hazardous wastes.

As a consequence, not only the Basel but also the Lomé IV Convention were circumvented as soon as they were adopted by waste traders who relabeled their wastes as commodities bound for recovery operations. Although the PIC procedure of the Basel Convention applied to all waste, regardless of eventual destination, the provisions of the convention were difficult to enforce when hazardous materials were not labeled as waste. With the adoption of the Bamako Convention, however, the African states sent an important political sign. No longer would the African states accept the import of hazardous waste for any reason into the African continent (Clapp, 1994, p. 30; Godwin 1993, p. 202; Greenpeace, 1994, p. II-8; Kummer, 1994, p. 50).

The Lomé IV and Bamako Conventions counted as multilateral agreements on hazardous waste in the sense of Article 11 of the Basel Convention. The text of both conventions was sent to the Basel Convention Secretariat, which informed all contracting parties of the existing treaties and of the established import bans. Because the Basel Convention prohibited the export of hazardous waste to contracting parties that banned their import, the bans of the Lomé IV and Bamako Conventions became part of the global regime. Both agreements appeared to be partly successful. According to Greenpeace, the planned waste exports to Africa were already decreasing in 1991 (Bernstorff, 1991, p. 28; Greenpeace, 1994, p. II-4).

The member states of the OECD also reacted to the establishment of the treaty. After the Basel Convention was negotiated, the recycling industry, particularly the scrap-metal traders, found itself confronted with the huge potential trade restrictions. Scrap metals are often contaminated with small amounts of hazardous substances such as polychlorinated biphenyls (PCBs). In very low concentrations, however, they do not harm the environment or human health. Because of the hazardous constituents, the scrap-metal traders feared all scrap metals would theoretically be subject to the provisions of the Basel Convention. As a consequence, the export of scrap metals would be part of the complicated PIC procedure. Trade in these secondary raw materials would only be allowed with states that were Basel Convention parties or within a bilateral, multilateral, or regional agreement. After that, waste generators, transporters, and recyclers started to concentrate their efforts on facilitating the international movement of hazardous waste for the purpose of recycling (Rosencranz and Eldridge, 1992, p. 320).

With Decision C(92)39/Final "Concerning the Control of Transfrontier Movements of Wastes Destined for Recovery Operations" (OECD, 1993, p. 72–110), the OECD introduced a new recyclable waste classification scheme commonly known as the "red, amber, green" system. The scheme classified all recoverable wastes in one of three categories according to the degree of hazard. "Green"-listed waste is not subject to controls other than those governing commercial transactions. "Amber"-listed waste is subject to more extensive control; only "red"-listed waste is regulated in the OECD countries according to the provisions of the Basel Convention.

Greenpeace attacked the OECD approach. In the Greenpeace study "When Green Is Not: The OECD's 'Green' List As an Instrument of Hazardous Waste De-Regulation," Greenpeace examined the "green" list and concluded "that the OECD's so called 'green' list contains hazardous wastes," and that the decision to establish the three-tiered approach "was born, not as a result of real science, but as a result of intensive industry pressure" (Johnston, Stringer, and Puckett, 1992, p. 31). In addition to the threat to human health and the environment that was raised in not controlling this type of waste among OECD countries, Greenpeace feared international political and legal implications of the OECD decision in the context of EC legislation, the Lomé IV Convention, and the Basel Convention (Johnston, Stringer, and Puckett, 1992, p. 2).

The new Council Regulation (EEC) No. 259/93 of February 1, 1993, "on the supervision and control of shipments of wastes within, into and out of the European Community" (OJ L 120 [1993]: 13), with which the EC implemented the Basel Convention, established the OECD red, amber, green system to apply to recovery wastes. Contrary to the OECD decision, which applied to waste trade within OECD countries only, the EC regulation applied to third countries as well (Art 16). This created a legal conflict because the EC, as mentioned, had already agreed with non-OECD parties of the Basel Convention and with the ACP countries within the Lomé IV Convention to control hazardous waste as defined by the Basel Convention. If the EC or an EC country now exported a green-listed waste without control to a non-OECD Basel party or an ACP country, the EC or the EC country would be in violation of both conventions.[5]

Exporting as well as potential importing countries acted before the entry into force of the Basel Convention and tried to define their provisions through regional agreements in an attempt to influence the development of the regime. Therefore, the first conference of the Basel Convention parties, held in Uruguay in December 1992, was again marked by the ongoing conflict between these two groups. Recalling the Bamako and Lomé IV Conventions, the less-developed countries under the leadership of the G-77 again called for an outright ban.

In the meantime, this group had gained support from Agenda 21, a document containing a program for action for implementing the principles enunciated in the Earth Charter, both outcomes of the United Nations Conference on Environment and Development (Rio Summit or UNCED, 1992). The targets of Chapter 20 of Agenda 21, titled "Environmentally Sound Management of Hazardous Wastes," were the following: (1) preventing or minimizing the generation of hazardous wastes as part of an overall integrated cleaner production approach; (2) eliminating or reducing to a minimum transboundary movements of hazardous waste; (3) ratifying the Basel Convention; (4) ratifying and full implementation of the African Bamako Convention; and (5) eliminating the export of hazardous wastes to countries that prohibit such imports. In line with these targets, UNEP Executive Director Mustafa Tolba (UNEP/CHW.1/21: 2) and the Convention Secretariat also put forward proposals for a ban on hazardous waste exports to developing countries.

Confronted with this strong coalition, some OECD countries, including Switzerland, Denmark and two Eastern European countries, Poland and Hungary, announced their support for a full ban. Other OECD countries, among them six key industrial nations (United States, United Kingdom, Germany, Australia, Japan, and Canada) still opposed a ban. Although in the minority, this group was nevertheless very powerful. It warned the secretariat of the Basel Convention and UNEP it would not ratify the convention if it established a total ban for waste trade from OECD to non-OECD countries. The secretariat and UNEP, knowing an increased membership would give the convention greater legitimacy, were scared by this development (Clapp, 1994, p. 35; Puckett, 1994, p. 55; Vallette, 1993, pp. 2–3).

The Decision I/22, finally adopted at the conference, consequently did not establish a total ban but *requested* that industrialized countries prohibit transboundary movements of hazardous wastes for final disposal; transboundary movements with hazardous waste destined for recovery and recycling operations were allowed to take place in accordance with the provisions of the convention. In contrast, Decision I/22 *requested* developing countries to prohibit the import of hazardous wastes from industrialized countries (UNEP/CHW.1/24: 37–38). A decision on a full ban for the export of all kinds of hazardous waste from industrialized to the less-developed world was postponed to the next conference.

Phase Three (December 1992 to March 1994)

After the less-developed countries were unable to obtain a total ban at the first conference of the parties, many of them arranged or continued negotiations on regional agreements. The first group to start the process, which Greenpeace called the "cloning of Bamako," were the Central American countries. In December 1992, Costa Rica, El Salvador, the Republic of Guatemala, Honduras, Nicaragua, and Panama adopted the "Central American Regional Agreement on the Transboundary Movement of Hazardous Wastes" (UNEP/CHW.C.1/Inf.2). As did its prototype, the Bamako Convention, the Central American Agreement obliged its parties to prohibit the import of hazardous wastes in the territories of the Central American countries (Art. 2 and 3).[6]

The next group of countries were the contracting parties to the Barcelona Convention for the Protection of the Mediterranean Sea against Pollution (15 I.L.M 290 [1976]). At their sixth Ordinary Meeting in October 1989, they generally agreed to develop a protocol on the Control of Transboundary Movements of Hazardous Wastes (UNEP [OCA]/MED IG.1/5: Annex IV). A first draft of the protocol was written by Greenpeace (UNEP [OCA]/MED IG.2/3/Add.1) and mirrored the Bamako Convention to some extent. It also prohibited the export of all hazardous wastes, for any reason, from developed countries to developing countries, and the developing countries were prohibited from importing such wastes into their territories (Art. 6). As at the Bamako Convention, the definition of hazardous waste included radioactive waste as well (Art. 4). In October 1991, the contracting parties to the Barcelona Convention decided to establish a working group to prepare a protocol (UNEP [OCA]/MED IG.2/4,

Annex IV: 15). In October 1993, they furthermore agreed to support a total export ban for hazardous waste from developed to less developed countries under the Basel Convention (UNEP [OCA]/MED IG.3/5: Section 3).

In January 1990, the contracting parties to the Cartagena Convention on the Protection and Development of the Wider Caribbean Region (22 I.L.M 227 [1983]) agreed to take national and international action to control the transboundary movement of hazardous waste (UNEP [OCA]/CAR IG.6/6: Resolution 1, Annex IX). Greenpeace representatives then provided a complete analysis of the hazardous waste trade between industrial and Caribbean states and proposed the development of a legally binding instrument banning the import of hazardous waste (CEP Technical Report No. 7). In November 1992, the contracting parties agreed to ratify the Basel Convention first and to use its forum for paying attention to the specific problems of transboundary movements of hazardous wastes in the Wider Caribbean Region (UNEP [OCA]/CAR IG. 10/5: 5).

The next group of countries to act were the High Contracting Parties to the Lima Convention for the Protection of the Marine Environment and Coastal Area of the South-East Pacific (UNEP, 1994). At their fifth meeting in October 1991, Colombia, Chile, Ecuador, Panama, and Peru agreed to set up a legal working group to develop a protocol to prohibit transboundary movements of hazardous wastes and their disposal (CPPS/PNUMA/PSE/485–92: Decision 5). The text of the Draft Protocol on the Prohibition and Control of Transboundary Movements of Hazardous Wastes and Their Disposal in the South-East Pacific (CPPS/PNUMA/PSE/WG.4(92)/7), which was revised in July 1993, contained a ban on the import of hazardous and radioactive wastes (Art. 8).

The signatories to the Bukarest Convention on the Protection of the Black Sea against Pollution (32 I.L.M 1110 [1993]) also agreed in April 1992 to establish a legal instrument to control the transboundary movements of hazardous wastes. Article XIV of the convention states: "The Contracting parties shall take all measures consistent with international law and cooperate in preventing pollution of the marine environment of the Black Sea due to hazardous wastes in transboundary movement, as well as combating illegal traffic thereof, in accordance with the Protocol to be adopted by them."

After a proposal by the government of Papua New Guinea, the 22 heads of government of the South Pacific Forum (SPFS) agreed in August 1993 to negotiate a regional convention (SPFS [93]11: para. 50). The fragile ecosystems of island countries were under threat from proposals by companies in industrialized countries to use them as a "dumping ground" (Lawrence, 1995, p. 2), prompting the forum members to acknowledge "the urgent need to prohibit the importation (of wastes) ... into the region" (SPFS [93]11: para 59). A first draft of the regional convention, which was considered by the legal working group in March 1994, contained an import ban for all types of hazardous and radioactive wastes (SPFS [94]TOXIC.4).

The South East Asian states followed suit and decided at an interparliamentarian meeting of the Association of South-East Asian Nations (ASEAN) in September 1993 "to prohibit the import and transboundary movement of all hazardous wastes for any reason into the ASEAN countries, with a view to concluding a regional convention prohibiting the Importation and Transboundary Movement into ASEAN of Hazardous Wastes" (Kummer, 1994, p. 33; 1995, p. 121).

Likewise, the states of the Economic Commission for Latin America and the Caribbean (ECLAC) decided at a joint ECLAC/UNEP meeting in Santiago in November 1993 on the conclusion of a regional convention or protocol. It banned the import of any hazardous wastes into the region, including those destined for recycling (ECLAC/LC/R.1372: 20–21). The background to this initiative was the fear of the Latin American and Caribbean states that the already existing regional agreements prohibiting transboundary movements of hazardous waste to some regions "will probably force countries to seek new channels for international trade in those wastes, placing regions which lack such agreements in a vulnerable position" (ECLAC/LC/R.1372: 20).

In addition to these regional approaches, more and more states used their sovereign right to establish national import bans. By the time that the second conference of the parties to the Basel Convention took place in Geneva in March 1994, 103 countries of the world had said they would not accept imports of hazardous waste to their territories (Puckett, 1994, p. 55).

At the meeting, the G-77 and China, the Nordic countries (UNEP/CHW.2/CRP.4), and Greenpeace again called for a total ban on hazardous waste movements for all destinations from OECD to non-OECD countries. Even though most of the less-developed countries had agreed unilaterally or regionally on hazardous waste import bans, it became evident most of the developing countries did not have the funding to monitor and to enforce these bans. Therefore, these countries tried to impose a global ban within the framework of the Basel Convention, which could effectively support the national and regional import bans. Though contentious and difficult,[7] the negotiations ended successfully for this group of countries. The G-77 and China, firmly supported by the Central and Eastern European and Nordic countries, were able to introduce a complete ban in the framework of the Basel Convention against the wishes of the minority of opposing countries, mainly Canada, Australia, Germany, the Netherlands, Japan, Great Britain, and the United States.

Finally, the 64 contracting parties to the Basel Convention adopted Decision II/12 "to prohibit immediately all transboundary movements of hazardous wastes which are destined for final disposal from OECD to non-OECD states" (UNEP/CHW.2/30: 37). It was also decided "to phase out by 31 December 1997, and to prohibit as of that date, all trans-boundary movements of hazardous wastes which are destined for recycling or recovery operations from OECD to non-OECD states" (UNEP/CHW.2/30: 37).

Phase Four (March 1994 to September 1995)

With their "decision" to ban the waste trade between OECD and non-OECD countries, the contracting parties to the Basel Convention used a measure with ambiguous legal status.[8] To avoid discussion about the legal status of the ban decision and to guarantee its quickest implementation, proposals were made for a formal amendment of the convention at the third meeting of the conference of the parties. The first proposal was made by the governments of Denmark, Finland, Norway, and Sweden. It called for inclusion of the entire content of Decision II/12 into a new Article 4 A of the Basel Convention (UNEP/CHW.3/2). The second proposal was made by the Commission of the European Union and contained only a legally binding amendment to include the export ban for hazardous waste for final disposal into a new Article 4 A of the convention (UNEP/CHW.3/3).

The adoption of Decision II/12 raised a mainly technical question about hazardous waste. The contracting parties to the Basel Convention had to decide which waste is deemed to be hazardous and is thus part of the total export ban. This difficult task had been left to the Technical Working Group, one of the organs of the regime. Because it could not complete its work before the third conference of the parties to the Basel Convention, the working group recommended extending the mandate until the fourth conference (UNEP/CHW/WG.4/8/5: 5–7).

While the contracting parties of the Basel Convention tried to solve the formal and technical questions that were raised by the adoption of Decision II/12, the negotiations at the regional level continued. At the fourth conference of the parties to the Cartagena Convention for the Protection and Development of the Wider Caribbean Region, the majority of countries were of the opinion that the development of a regional protocol banning the import of hazardous waste was not necessary anymore. By ratifying the Basel Convention, all Caribbean states would thus be part of the total export ban for all sorts of hazardous waste from OECD to non-OECD countries. Therefore, the development of such a protocol was postponed until 1998–1999 with the basic goal of adopting regulations for the transboundary movements of hazardous wastes within the region (UNEP(OCA)/CAR IG. 11/10: 17; UNEP(OCA)/CAR IG.12/7).

In May 1995, the second meeting of technical experts including Greenpeace was held to develop a protocol for the protection of the Mediterranean from the transboundary movements of hazardous waste within the framework of the Barcelona Convention. Turkey pushed for a change of the terminology of the export ban from OECD to non-OECD countries. The new wording included first an export ban on hazardous waste to developing countries, and second, a ban on all imports of hazardous wastes for all non-EU countries. With these changes, Turkey, as a non-member of the EU, was protected from hazardous waste imports, and as a member state of the OECD, Turkey was obliged not to export hazardous waste to the developing countries (UNEP [OCA]/MED WG 79/4: 4–6).

In September 1995, the South Pacific states adopted the Waigani Convention, which included an obligation for Pacific Island developing parties to ban the import of hazardous and radioactive wastes from outside the region and an export ban for "other parties" (namely, Australia and New Zealand) for hazardous and radioactive wastes to all Forum Island states (Art. 4).

After the Technical Working Group of the Basel Convention started its work on the clarification of hazardous wastes, the EU Commission decided there was no reason to postpone the implementation of the export ban from OECD to non-OECD countries (Decision II/12 of the Basel Convention Parties). After this development, the Council of Ministers requested the commission in June 1995 to support an amendment of the Basel Convention by which the full content of Decision II/12 would be transformed into its legal body at the third meeting of the Basel Convention parties. With that, the commission had received a clear mandate for the negotiations at the third conference, and the member states of the EU, Denmark, Finland, and Sweden withdrew from their original proposal for a formal amendment of the Basel Convention. Consequentially, it was clear before the third conference started that the commission would support the amendment proposal, put forward by Norway (UNEP/CHW.3/2/Corr.2).

Because of the old conflict (trade versus ban), the negotiations about the proposals for a possible amendment were again difficult (Bernstorff, 1995). In the 17 months between the second and the third conferences, 24 additional states had ratified the Basel Convention, a fact that Greenpeace interpreted as support for the content of Decision II/12 (UNEP/CHW.3/34:1). The issue for the contracting parties to the convention was to decide under what circumstances and between which countries the trade in recyclable waste would be allowed. Finally, the contracting parties adopted Decision III/1 on an amendment to the Basel Convention. With the amendment, a new Article 4 A was inserted into the convention, which obliges the Annex VII countries (member states of the OECD and EU, Liechtenstein) to prohibit all transboundary movements of hazardous wastes destined for final disposal (Annex IV A) to states not listed in Annex VII. Furthermore, all transboundary movements of hazardous wastes destined for recovery, recycling, reclamation, direct reuse or alternative use (Annex IV B) from Annex VII to non–Annex VII countries was to be phased out by December 31, 1997, and prohibited as of that date. In addition, a new preambular paragraph 7bis stated the parties to the convention recognize "that transboundary movements of hazardous wastes, especially to developing countries, have a high risk of not constituting an environmentally sound management of hazardous wastes as required by this Convention" (UNEP/CHW.3/35: Decision III/1).

The formal amendment of the Basel Convention would enter into force between parties that accepted it on the 90th day after the receipt by the depository of their ratification by at least three fourths of the parties present at the third conference (Art. 17.5 BC). Together with Decision II/12, the export ban has legally binding effect. The Technical Working Group was instructed to give absolute priority to completing the work on hazard characterization and the development of lists and technical guidelines in order to submit them for approval to the fourth conference of the parties.

Phase Five (September 1995 to February 1998)

With Decision III/1, the Technical Working Group was requested to define the scope of the formal amendment of the Basel Convention. Between December 1995 and February 1998, the group developed two different lists (A: hazardous waste, B: waste not covered by the Basel Convention) as well as a procedure for a flexible adaptation of the lists to new scientific evidence, which were proposed for adoption at the fourth conference (UNEP/CHW.4/87: 11).

With the Directive 120/97/EEC of January 20, 1997 (OJ L 228 [1997]: 32), the EU implemented and ratified Decisions II/12 and III/1 of the Basel Convention parties. The new Article 16 includes an export ban for hazardous waste listed in Annex V (recycling, reuse, recovery). Exports of these wastes were only allowed until December 31, 1997. In addition, exports of hazardous wastes until the termination date are only permitted to member states of the OECD, to contracting parties of the Basel Convention, and to those countries with which the member states of the EU had concluded bilateral or multilateral agreements.

In September 1996, the Izmir Protocol on the Prevention of Pollution of the Mediterranean Sea by Transboundary Movements of Hazardous Wastes and Their Disposal was adopted within the framework of the Barcelona Convention (UNEP [OCA]/MED/IG.9/4). It included two bans. First, all parties ban the export to developing countries and second all non-EU countries ban all imports of hazardous wastes (Art. 5). The term *developing countries* was defined in Article 1 and included all countries that are not member states of the OECD.[9]

Between September 1995 and February 1998, Decisions II/12 and III/1 were implemented in two additional regions. The implementation of Decision III/1 by the EU had a tremendous effect, because already 15 of the 25 member states of the OECD at this time had ratified the formal amendment of the Basel Convention, but with the adoption of Decision III/1, the contracting parties of the convention had created a precedent. Only member states of Annex VII (member states of the OECD and EU, Liechtenstein) were obliged to prohibit the export of hazardous waste in non–Annex VII countries. Liechtenstein is not a member of the OECD or the EU. The inclusion of Liechtenstein in Annex VII, therefore, provided a mechanism by which other countries could apply for inclusion in Annex VII. On this basis, Monaco (UNEP/CHW.4/8), Israel (UNEP/CHW.4/9), and Slovenia (UNEP/CHW.4/CRP.1) proposed amendments of the Basel Convention at the fourth conference with the aim of including their countries in Annex VII.

The contracting parties decided at their fourth meeting to leave Annex VII unchanged until the amendment contained in Decision III/1 enters into force (UNEP/CHW.4/35: Decision IV/8). While the final decision on Annex VII was postponed, the lists A (hazardous waste) and B (waste not covered by the convention) that were developed by the Technical Working Group were adopted without much conflict. Consequentially, the Basel Convention was amended. With Decision IV/9, the lists A and B were transformed into the new Annexes VIII and XI.

With that, the regulatory framework of the convention developed from a framework to control transboundary movements of hazardous wastes to a framework of prohibition of hazardous waste movements between specified countries. In addition, the states knew precisely which hazardous wastes were covered by the ban. Therefore, it can be assumed that the majority of the contracting parties to the convention will increase efforts to ratify the amendment (Decision III/1). As of September 2005, 58 contracting parties (including the EU) had ratified the ban amendment.

International Regimes and Sustainable Development—An Analysis

Since the Basel Convention on the Control of Transboundary Movements of Hazardous Wastes and Their Disposal was adopted, the global regime has showed tremendous evolutionary development from a control regime to an instrument to ban the export of hazardous waste from industrialized countries to the less developed world. In other words, the goal of the regime changed from control to prohibition of transboundary movements of hazardous wastes between specified countries ("change of a regime").

A necessary precondition for the change of the Basel Convention was the pressure created at the regional level through the adoption of the hazardous waste import ban policy. Most of the developing countries were confronted with a strong need for additional action, and this action made a difference for them. Nationally or regionally adopted import bans provided these states with some additional protection from Northern firms' using them as dumping grounds for their hazardous waste. Or, in other words, by additional national or regional action to the global regime, these states achieved a better political outcome. Therefore, the policy innovation of a complete import ban diffused horizontally from the ACP to the African, then to the Central American, the South-East Pacific, the Black Sea, the South Pacific, the South-East Asian, and to the Mediterranean group of countries and can be explained by overlap of countries in different regional agreements and the existence of mediators such as UNEP or Greenpeace.

The global Basel Convention, however, provided the legal basis for developing countries to enforce the nationally and regionally adopted import bans for hazardous wastes by stating contracting parties to the convention are obliged to prohibit the export of hazardous wastes to the parties that have prohibited their import (Art. 4). Through this regulation, the adoption of additional policies at the regional level had an immediate effect, because for contracting parties they became part of the global regime (*Multi-Regime-Regulation*; Meinke, 2002). The Basel Convention parties were in principal legally forced to accept the national or regional import bans by other contracting parties of the convention, whether they wanted to or not. It is clear the probability that the OECD countries would accept a global hazardous waste export ban increased the more countries had adopted the complete import ban policy and the more countries had taken legal steps to halt hazardous waste imports.

With the amendment to the Basel Convention, the parties finally agreed it is useless to deal with the environmental problem of hazardous waste generation and trade without looking at poverty and international inequality, as already requested in the report of the WCED (1990). They finally had to recognize that transboundary movements of hazardous wastes to developing countries have a high risk of not constituting environmentally sound management as required by the convention. Moreover, the ban decision can be seen as an attempt to reestablish state sovereignty for those developing countries that were—because of poverty, corruption, lack of human capital, and unequal environmental standards—not able to protect their territories from importation of hazardous waste. In addition, the Basel ban is a measure to move the problem of hazardous waste back to its source: 90% of all hazardous wastes are generated in the industrialized world, which now agreed to take responsibility for their environmentally sound disposal instead of taking advantage of lower environmental standards in developing countries and shipping waste "out of sight, out of mind." In the long run, this could lead to price reality, which in consequence could create strong incentives for entrepreneurs to avoid hazardous generation in the first place. By moving the problem back to its source, incentives could be created for companies to introduce measures of "clean production" into their generation processes.Endnotes

Notes

1. An *international institution* can be defined as "a persistent and connected set of rules (formal and informal) that prescribe behavioral roles, constrain activity, and shape expectations" (Keohane 1989, p. 3). Institutions "may take the form of bureaucratic organizations, regimes (rule-structures that do not necessarily have organizations attached), or conventions (informal practices)" (Keohane, Haas, and Levy 1993, pp. 4–5).
2. Krasner originally distinguished between "change of a regime" and "change within regimes" (Krasner 1982, pp. 187–188). Because both possibilities were difficult to separate, regime analysts today refer to *change of a regime* if changes occur in the substance of the manner of how actors regulate an existing problem; *change within a regime* describes a situation in which some of the norms and rules of the regime are changed by actors in a given issue area (Meinke 2002, p. 48; Oberthür, 1997, p. 48).
3. See Reports of the Working Group Sessions: Preparatory Meeting (UNEP/WG.180/3), first session (UNEP/WG.182/3), second session (UNEP/WG.186/3), third session (UNEP/WG.189/3), fourth session (UNEP/WG.190/4), and fifth session (UNEP/IG.80/4, Annex I).
4. In one of the most cited examples, a local farmer in Koko, Nigeria, rented out his backyard for US$100 to an Italian waste trading firm. The firm unloaded 8,000 leaking barrels with more than 2,000 tons of toxic waste, which, while sitting in the hot sun, burst open and contaminated the land. The farmer was told the barrels contained fertilizer, but in fact they contained industrial waste laden with dangerous PCBs and asbestos fibers. After several villagers had stolen the empty barrels for water storage and subsequently become very ill, Nigeria forced Italy to take back the waste (Clapp, 1994, p. 20; Grefe and Bernstorff, 1991, p. 11).
5. In order to deal with this particular problem, a provision was introduced in which the commission was obliged to query all non-OECD countries as to whether they wanted to import "green"-listed wastes. If these countries did not respond within 6 months, the commission would provide the council with appropriate proposals (Art. 17).
6. The list of categories of hazardous waste of the Central American Agreement is similar to that of the Bamako Convention.

7. For a detailed description of the negotiation process, see Puckett and Fogel, 1994; Bernstorff, 1994; and Meinke, 2002.
8. Decisions do not have to be ratified to enter into force and are therefore extremely useful for the establishment of measures that should enter into force extremely quickly. They provide some politically and some arguably legally binding power over states that did not oppose the decision in question. Because Decision II/12 was adopted by consensus, one can say that the decision was legally and politically binding for the contracting parties to the convention at this time. Nevertheless, existing international agreements such as the Basel Convention cannot be legally amended by means of decisions.
9. However, for the provisions of the protocol, Monaco is obliged to fulfill the same provisions as the member states of the OECD; that means the export of hazardous wastes from Monaco to developing states is prohibited and Monaco is allowed to import hazardous wastes from member states of the EU.

References

Bartram, B., Engel, B. (1989). Ende des "Giftmüllkolonialismus"? Zur Baseler Konvention und ihrem Hintergrund. *Vereinte Nationen, 4,* 115–121.

Bernstorff, A. (1991). Der neue Müllkolonialismus. Abfallexporte der Industriestaaten. *Wechselwirkung, 52,* 24–31.

Bernstorff, A. (1994). Ächtung! Die Weltgemeinschaft will Giftmüllexporte der Reichen verbieten. *Die Friedenswarte 3–4,* 38–65.

Bernstorff, A. (1995). Exportverbot für Giftmüll soll rechtskräftig werden. UNEP-Konferenz wehrt Industrielobby ab. *Die Friedenswarte, 70,* 250–259.

Clapp, J. (1994). Afrika, NGOs, and the International Toxic Waste Trade. *Journal of Environment and Development 2,* 17–46.

Godwin, D.L. (1993). The Basel Convention on Transboundary Movements of Hazardous Wastes: An Opportunity for Industrialized Nations to Clean Up Their Acts? *Denver Journal of International Law and Policy, 22,* 193–208.

Greenpeace (1994). *Database of known hazardous waste exports from OECD to non-OECD countries.* Study prepared for the Second Conference of the Parties to the Basel Convention, Amsterdam: Greenpeace.

Grefe, C., Bernstorff, A. (1991). *Zum Beispiel Giftmüll.* Göttingen: Beck-Verlag.

Hilz, C. (1992). *The International Toxic Waste Trade.* New York: Van Nostrand Reinhold.

Johnston, P., Stringer, R., Puckett, J. (1992). *When Green Is Not: The OECD's "Green" List as an Instrument of Hazardous Waste De-Regulation.* A Critique and Scientific Review, Amsterdam/Exeter: Greenpeace.

Keohane, R.O. (1989). Neoliberal Institutionalism: A Perspective on World Politics. In R.O. Keohane, ed., *International Institutions and State Power: Essays in International Relations Theory,* Boulder, Colo.: Westview, pp. 1–20.

Keohane, R.O., Haas, P.M., Levy, M.A. (1993). The Effectiveness of International Environmental Institutions. In P.M. Haas, R.O. Keohane and M.A. Levy, ed., *Institutions for the Earth: Sources of Effective International Environmental Protection*, Cambridge, Mass.: MIT Press, pp. 3–24.

Krasner, S.D. (1982). Structural Causes and Regime Consequences. *International Organization, 36*, 185–205.

Kummer, K. (1994). Transboundary Movements of Hazardous Wastes and at the Interface of Environment and Trade. *UNEP Environment and Trade Series No. 6*, Geneva: UNEP.

Kummer, K. (1995). *International Management of Hazardous Wastes: The Basel Convention and Related Legal Rules*. Oxford: Oxford University Press.

Lawrence, P. (1995). Foreign Policy Interests and the Negotiation of Environment Conventions: The Waigani South Pacific Convention on Hazardous and Nuclear Wastes. Paper presented at the Conference on International Law and Australian Foreign Policy, Canberra, 10 July 1995.

Lembke, H.H. (1991). *"Umwelt" in den Nord-Süd-Beziehungen. Machtzuwachs im Süden, Öko-Diktat des Nordens oder Globalisierung der Verantwortung?* Berlin: Deutsches Institut für Entwicklungspolitik.

Meinke, B. (2002). *Multi-Regime-Regulierung: Wechselwirkungen zwischen globalen und regionalen Umweltregimen*. Wiesbaden: Deutscher Universitaets-Verlag.

Oberthür, S. (1997). *Umweltschutz durch Internationale Umweltregime. Interessen, Verhandlungsprozesse*. Wirkungen. Opladen: Leske+Budrich.

Puckett, J. (1992). Dumping on Our World Neighbours: The International Trade in Hazardous Wastes, and the Case for an Immediate Ban on All Hazardous Waste Exports from Industrialized to Less-Industrialized Countries. *Green Globe Yearbook*, 93–106.

Puckett, J. (1994). Disposing of the Waste Trade: Closing the Recycling Loophole. *The Ecologist 2*, 53–58.

Puckett, J., Fogel, C. (1994). A Victory for Environment and Justice: The Basel Ban and How It Happened. *Toxic Waste Trade Update 7.1*, 2–7.

Rosencranz, A., Eldridge, C.L. (1992). Hazardous Wastes: Basel after Rio. *Environmental Policy and Law 22/5/6*, 318–322.

Rublack, S. (1993). *Der grenzüberschreitende Transfer von Umweltrisiken im Völkerrecht*, Baden-Baden: Nomus.

Tolba, M.K. (1990). Foreword. In K. Kummer and I. Rummel-Bulska, ed., *The Basel Convention on the Control of Transboundary Movements of Hazardous Wastes and Their Disposal*. Nairobi: UNEP Environmental Library No. 2, pp. 3–4.

UNEP (1984). *Convention for the Production of the Marine Environment and Coastal Area of the South-East Pacific and Its Supplementary Agreements*, Nairobi: UNEP.

UNEP (1987). Cairo Guidelines and Principles for the Environmentally Sound Management of Hazardous Wastes. In *Environmentally Sound Management of Hazardous Wastes: Environmental Law Guidelines and Principles*. Nairobi: UNEP.

Valette, J., Bernstorff, A. (1989). *Der internationale Müllhandel.* Eine Bestand-saufnahme von Greenpeace. Hamburg: Greenpeace.

Valette, J., Spalding, H. (1990). *The International Trade in Wastes.* Washington, D.C.: Greenpeace USA.

Valette, J. (1993). Basel "Dumping" Convention Still Legalizes Toxic Terrorism. *Toxic Waste Trade Update, 6*, 3–5.

World Commission on Environment and Development (1990). *Our Common Future (The Brundtland Report),* Oxford: Oxford University Press.

Abbreviations

ACP	African, Caribbean, and Pacific
Art.	Article
ASEAN	Association of South East Asian Nations
CM	Council of Ministers
CRP	Conference Room Paper
EC	European Community
ECLAC	Economic Commission for Latin America and the Caribbean
Ed.	Editors
EEC	European Economic Community
EU	European Union
G-77	Group of G-77 and China
NGO	Nongovernmental Organization
OAU	Organization of African Unity
OECD	Organization for Economic Co-operation and Development
OJ	Official Journal of the European Community
para.	Paragraph
PIC	Prior Informed Consent
Res.	Resolution
SPFS	South Pacific Forum
UNEP	United Nations Environment Programme

Chapter 18

The Institutionalization of Poverty in the Third World: The Case of Grenada

Paul C. Mocombe

CONTENTS

Introduction

In an essay titled "How States Sell Their Countries and Their People," Thomas Klak and Garth Myers (1998, pp. 88–90) argue that the governments of countries such as Grenada, Barbados, St. Lucia, Jamaica, and Haiti, and many others in the Caribbean, are selling their countries and people to foreign investors in nontraditional export sectors, specifically through the establishment of export-processing zones (EPZs). The latter are labor-intensive manufacturing centers involved in the import of raw materials and the export of factory products. Such EPZs are believed to "attract manufacturers seeking bargain-priced and compliant labor as a cost-saving component of global commodity chains." Consequently, this leaves these countries and their citizens vulnerable to the demands of foreign manufacturers, who "are often prepared to relocate if provoked by social instability or by exogenous changes in trade policies or production methods."

Hence, Klak and Myers's (1998, p. 88) essay "is less concerned with the particularities of Caribbean countries that have led to their present situation and more concerned with the remarkable elements of sameness in their current development policies." The authors further contend that these policies are geared toward global investors to demonstrate that countries not only are neoliberal converts, but offer greater advantages, that is, cheaper labor, than the myriad others pursuing similar policies. "This [contemporary] global homogenization of development policy," which dates from the debt crisis of the 1980s, is also concerned with the homogenization of development policy, that is, the progressive development of national states and cultures along the lines of the Western nations. Klak and Myers (1998, p. 90) argue that such global homogenization "emerged from a confluence of three exogenously controlled factors ... massive foreign exchange shortfalls in less developed countries, the search by international investors for cost-saving components in manufacturing, and the spread of neo-liberal ideas that encourage open economies, foreign investment, and nontraditional exports." Those factors pushed the states to position themselves in the global economy.

Concretely, through the spread of neoliberal ideas, states are able to develop along the lines of the Western world (continuing the development project), and in that process, the adoption of neoliberal ideas is supposed to reenergize the "massive foreign exchange shortfalls in less developed countries" by enticing international investors, who are searching "for cost-saving components in manufacturing." It is further assumed that the wealth resulting from the profits maximized from cheap labor cost, will trickle down to the masses, who are interpellated into the global process as cheap laborers, whereby their earned wages from these investors will increase their standard of living.

Whereas many sociologists of development understand this process, "the global homogenization of development policy," through the structural (social) relations of ideological capitalism, which represents the continual historical (Western, mostly United States–dominated) attempt to institutionalize the world's people (localize their behavior, social relations, as agents of the Protestant ethic) into the world economy (globalization), could this amount to the practice (capitalism) of bourgeois culture as "enframed" by its structuring metaphysic, the Protestant ethic? One may suggest that the globalization process represents *global localization* (worldwide social integration into the metaphysics of bourgeois culture) or homogenization, through the practice (capitalism) of the Western bourgeois culture, as opposed to cultural heterogeneity within the capitalist (global) world system as *only* a governing *economic system*.

In other words, it is not enough to look at globalization within the framework of the global attempt to enlarge capitalist markets (through technology, the globalization of capital, decline of the nation-state, universalization of consumerism, etc.) as the structure of the process (Arrighi, 1994; Bell, 1976; Giddens, 1990; Harvey, 1989; Jameson, 1991; Kellner, 2001; Sklair, 2001) within which heterogeneous groups operate. Instead, social theorists must understand the globalization process within anthropological notions to grasp better the nature (structural) of resistance movements. This implies viewing globalization as the continual attempt to interpellate the world's masses into the relational logic, as "enframed" by its rigidified structure, of Western culture, the Protestant ethic, and resistance movements as ontologically grounded cultural structures, whose values and meanings diametrically oppose it.[1]

Therefore, it is not the relational logic of capitalism that structures the global movement. In fact, Max Weber (1958 [1904–1905]) demonstrated that logic is itself enframed within the larger social context or structure of signification of the Protestant ethic, but on the contrary, the practice of capitalism is determined by the structural relations of Protestantism and can only be negated by an opposing structuring ontology, not a denouement of its contradictory practices.

In other words, the Protestant ethic was understood as a set of irrevocable cultural values or structural terms, that is, materialized metaphors beyond logical or empirical proof—rationality, hard work, systematic use of time, and a strict asceticism with respect to worldly pleasures and goods—that gave rise to the contemporary capitalist practices that constitute modern societies and the existing configuration of power (i.e., social relations) within which contemporary power elites attempt to homogenize the world.

This chapter's position differs from both Marxist and non-Marxist structural interpretations of the constitution of modern society in that my analysis begins with the cultural conceptions that structured the practices that gave rise to the society; the former schools rationalize the structural terms from which they begin their analysis from the recursively organized practices Weber attributed to the Protestant ethic. Finally, my position assumes that it is only another irrevocable value system that can deter the onslaught of the Protestant ethic and the spirit of capitalism, not reason itself.

This chapter attempts to shed light on globalization and its necessary outcome—the institutionalization of poverty throughout the Third World—within the relational signs of the Protestant ethic, considering Ferdinand De Saussure's (1986 [1916]) analysis of the relational means by which terms in a structure are delimited. The author further interprets the impacts of globalization using the case of the Grenadian government, which has adopted forcibly this way of life.

The Global Context

Since the rise of the European merchant class (around the 16th century) as a global ruling class with their establishment of the American empire, their structuring ontology—that is, Protestantism and its practice, capitalism—have been the basis for all social action (Polanyi, 2001 [1944]). As no other structuring ontology has been able to displace it, it is no surprise then to suggest that their contemporary progenies (the upper class of owners and high-level executives in the "developed" parts of the world) also prescribe the rules of conduct that are sanctioned for social behavior in the world today (Arrighi, 1994; Bell, 1976; Giddens, 1990; Harvey, 1989; Jameson, 1991; Kellner, 2001; Sklair, 2001).

Thus, the upper class of owners and high-level executives, based predominantly in the corporate community of their most powerful home base, the United States, represent today's dominant class, whose various distributive powers lead to a situation in which their policies determine the "life chances" of not only local social actors but global ones as well (Domhoff, 2002). That is to say, "the routinized ways of acting in the United States follow from the rules and regulations needed by the corporate community to continue to grow and make profits" (Domhoff, 2002, p. 181). Globally, this action plays out through American-dominated institutions such as the World Bank, World Trade Organization (WTO), and International Monetary Fund (IMF), who prescribe fiscal, political, and social policies to countries in search of aid for development that homogenize social practices in order to fit with the ethos of the corporate community (Escobar, 1995; Nash, 2001).

Specifically, the IMF with the World Bank assume a de facto role of banker to the world, determining conditions by which states can obtain aid for development, that is, structural adjustment measures. These terms and conditions, in turn, homogenize human practices along lines that make it more viable for the practice of capitalism to take hold; that, from my structural perspective, amounts to making global social actors agents of the Protestant ethic working for the predestined (multinational corporations).

Many sociologists of development (McMicheal, 1996; Portes, 1997) have labeled this contemporary global trend *postdevelopmentalism* or *globalization under the auspices of neoliberalism*, a replacement of the old model of "state"-driven development policy (Keynesian economics). The latter dominated the early half of the 20th-century world and was interested in replicating the development pathways of developed countries. The globalization project, as was its predecessor (developmentalism), is still both an ideological force (i.e., a conceptualization of the world) and a material force (i.e., real transnational movements of capital and commodities). However, unlike developmentalism, the contemporary globalizing project redefines development as participation in the world market rather than development replication (technologically, economically, politically, and culturally) along the lines of the Western world (McMicheal, 1996, p. 279). That is, "alternatively, the globalization project seeks to stabilize capitalism through global economic management—this time [as in its colonial heydays] along the lines of [market] specialization, rather than replication" (McMicheal, 1996, p. 279).

From a historical structural perspective, it could be argued that "market specialization" neither negates nor inhibits the "replication" aims of agents of the Protestant ethic. Instead, in the postdevelopmental or globalization era, the homogenization of the plan for development becomes the continual aim of (foreign-trained) state bureaucrats operating through "ideological state apparatuses," of the law, education, and so forth, in order to determine their citizens as agents of the Protestant ethic, the structure of relations that underscores the practice of capitalism (Althusser, 2001; Mocombe, 2001).

In more empirical terms, this means that state governments, in signing agreements such as the Marrakesh Accord, establishing the WTO, and adopting the structural adjustment measures of the IMF and World Bank, serve as conduits through which the major Western powers homogenize the development policies as they force lesser-developed countries to adopt policies that are favorable to their "way of life." Thus, structural adjustment programs (privatization of state public assets, slashed social budgets, cut wages) are conceived to attract foreign investments and, as such, could serve as agents of the Western cultural ideology, that is, the Protestant ethic, a global aim with local implications (global localization).

Ironically enough, these structuring policies, as a result of their practical implications, appear to be value free (nonideological or cultural) and equated with reality and existence as such, on the basis of reason and rationality. In other words, all economic development aspects of neoliberal policies (free trade, cut wages, liberalization, privatization, and export expansion) are reasoned within the instrumental rational discourse (economics) that appears to have no basis in ideological or cultural suppositions. Indeed, proponents of the rational economic man contend that "human beings" are by "nature" self-interested social actors, who are only out to satisfy their economic wants and needs (Inkeles, 1959, 1960, 1969). Accordingly, Klak and Myers (1998, p. 5) see that "from this perspective globalization serves as a tool for investors to extract concessions from states, and for investors and states to extract concessions from workers and other citizens," a perspective that views social actors as rationally calculating self-interested agents, who make decisions based on their *freely* determined self-interest, as opposed to structurally determined and negated ones.

Along the same lines, the current structural adjustment measures and neoliberal policies that force global agents to organize recursively are a result of a structuring ideology that determines "market practices" in a particular way (capitalism). Simply looking at the practice of capitalism as both structure and practice of relations through which social actors rationally and recursively organize may appear to be exploitative and oppressive, particularly when rational individuals of the corporate community calculate how best to maximize their self-interest through the utilization of other rational individuals.

Yet, the Caribbean nations that are exploited and oppressed in such a social relation "buy into it," in spite of its exploitative and oppressive overtone (Klak and Myers, 1998). One would assume that if all are rational and attempt to maximize their self-interests, countries that find themselves exploited within the globalizing process would remove themselves from such a relation. But that has not been the case, as the Caribbean highlights; instead, all nations, despite the threat of capitalist practices to their ontological security, appear to be adopting similar patterns of development.

Paradoxically, globalization is understood through this structure of relations, that is, the synchronicity that determines and negates the practices of capitalism. Concretely, globalization must be understood not just through its practice of capitalism, but in terms of the ideological (cultural) structure (the Protestant ethic) that gives rise to these practices and makes them appear to be natural and immutable; for, as the irrational behavior of states who remain within the exploitative relation of global capitalism, I am arguing here, highlights, it is not reason or rationality that makes capitalism appear to be natural and immutable, and therefore acceptable. (For the most part, the masses in the structure of relations do not understand the scientific discourse that justifies the "observable" rational nature of humans. When they do, they brush it off as opinionated statements, for from the masses' viewpoint, "man" cannot completely understand God's will.) On the contrary, it is the metaphysical underpinning of the Protestant ethic with its rigidified precepts and concepts that Protestant social actors of the 16th century and since institutionalized and implemented into the material world that are beyond the scope of reason or human understanding. These precepts and concepts appear to represent the unchangeable nature of reality and existence, and as such to be outside humanity's grasp. This is the determining and negating factor.

Consequently, capitalist social practices are the rational means for living out these concepts, which presuppose social action. Thus, in order to understand the nature of things, in terms of capitalist practices, one must begin the analysis with Protestant precepts and concepts, not as structurationist Marxists and non-Marxists view the practices of the capitalist structure, as the *habitus* of individuals, an "embodied history, internalized as a second nature and so forgotten as history" (Bourdieu, 1990, p. 56). Social actors are instead self-reflective and consciously recursively organize themselves by the "ungroundable premises and unobservable substances" of the Protestant ethic. In this understanding, it is easy to account for agency within the globalization process, that is, structural movements and counter movements (cultural and metaphysical); that is, the aim of agents of one cultural structure (agents of the Protestant ethic) to condition all "other" structures within their ethos. Several anthropologists (Escobar, 1995; Nash, 2001) attempt to make sense of the contemporary nature of things (e.g., Why would nations adopt policies that exploit and oppress their workers and citizens?) by beginning their investigations precisely from this position. Could the WTO and other UN institutions (IMF, World Bank, etc.) represent cultural and structural institutions bent on homogenizing and normalizing human action toward a unified end, that is, agents who determine their own fate through diligent work? World systems theory or other Marxist and non-Marxist structural positions that view both the structure and practice of globalization as resulting from "rational" capitalism cannot accurately demonstrate, if all are rationally calculating agents, why certain social groups, communities, and so on, despite their best interest to do otherwise, adhere to the external rules and practices of global capitalism and others do not.

My argument here, in keeping with the anthropological position, is that the latter groups recursively organize their material practices by a structuring ontology with "ungroundable premises and unobservable substances" that diametrically oppose the structuring ontology of the Protestant ethic, whereas the former groups are already integrated into its ethos, which makes the adoption of neoliberal practical policies compatible with their ideals, which necessarily foster and integrate an acceptable understanding of poverty based on the structuring ontology of the Protestant ethic.

The Structure of Bourgeois or Capitalist Culture

The Protestant ethic, as Max Weber (1958 [1904–1905]) points out, represents what was understood (cultural conditions), that is, the set of values or structural terms—rationality, hard work, systematic use of time, and a strict asceticism with respect to worldly pleasures and goods—to give rise to the contemporary capitalist practices that constitute modern societies and by association the (ideological) mechanical solidarity we call American capitalist society and the existing configuration of power (i.e., social relations), within which agents of this worldview attempt to interpellate global social actors. This position differs from both Marxist and non-Marxist structural interpretations of the constitution of modern and American society in that my analysis begins with the cultural conceptions that structured the practices that gave rise to the society, whereas the former schools rationalize the structural terms from which they begin their analysis from the recursively organized practices Weber attributed to the Protestant ethic. These two viewpoints, as my structurationist (i.e., the conflation of structure, practice, and consciousness) approach implies, are inextricably linked (see Figure 18.1).

Weber defines a capitalistic economic action

> as one which rests on the expectation of profit by the utilization of opportunities for exchange, that is on (formally) peaceful chances of profit. Acquisition by force (formally and actually) follows its own particular laws, and it is not expedient, however little one can forbid this, to place it in the same category with action which is, in the last analysis, oriented to profits from exchange. Where capitalist acquisition is rationally pursued, the corresponding action is adjusted to calculations in terms of capital. This means that the action is adapted to a systematic utilization of goods or personal services as means of acquisition in such a way that, at the close of a business period, the balance of the enterprise in money assets (or, in the case of a continuous enterprise, the periodically estimated money value of assets)

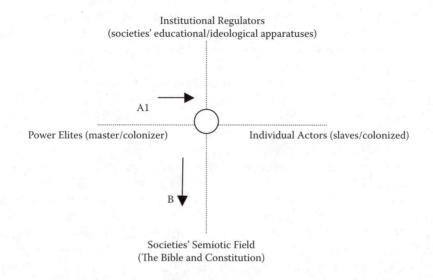

Figure 18.1 **Diagram representing the structure of bourgeois culture. Capitalist interpretations (Marxist, postmodernist, world system, and dependency theory) view the synchronic axis (horizontal line) as resulting from the practices of the diachronic axis (the vertical line). Specifically, the economic subjugation running along line A1 derives from the abstract laws of institutional regulators (movement of line B), which rigidify (i.e., reify) into the horizontal axis and are exported throughout the global (globalization).**

    exceeds the capital, i.e., the estimated value of the material means of production used for acquisition in exchange. (Weber, 1958 [1904–1905], pp. 17–18)

    Although this relationship appears paradoxical because Protestant beliefs did not embrace the idea of economic gain for its own sake, clearly this is an essential (and novel) component of capitalism. Weber's argument is that although capitalism had existed elsewhere in elementary form, it had not developed on anything like the scale seen in modern Europe. Its emergence was a result of the relatively wide endorsement of the idea of accumulating capital as a duty or end in itself. This, in itself, is an irrational attitude: There is no rational reason why we should choose work against either leisure or consumption.

    For Weber, religion provides the key to understanding this peculiarly modern orientation to everyday life, because religion entails a choice of ultimate values that cannot be justified on rational grounds. Once we have chosen such a value, however, we can pursue it by rational means: It makes sense to talk of rational and irrational ways of realizing an ultimate value. Weber's argument is that the rational pursuit of the ultimate values of the ascetic Protestantism characteristic of 16th- and 17th-century Europe led people to engage in disciplined work, and that disciplined and rational organization of work as a duty is the characteristic feature of modern capitalism—its unique ethos or spirit.

The crucial link to Protestantism is through the latter's notion of the calling of the faithful to fulfill their duty to God in the methodical conduct of their everyday lives. This theme is common to the beliefs of the Calvinist and neo-Calvinist churches of the Reformation. Predestination is also an important belief, but because humans cannot know who is saved (the elect) and who is damned, it creates a deep inner loneliness in the believer. In order therefore to create assurance of salvation, which is itself a sure sign (or proof) of election, diligence in one's calling (hard work, systematic use of time, and a strict asceticism with respect to worldly pleasures and goods) is highly recommended—so-called this-worldly asceticism. In general terms, however, the most important contribution of Protestantism to capitalism was the spirit of rationalization that it encouraged. The relationship between the two is deemed by Weber to be one of elective affinity (Marshall, 1998, pp. 534–535).

That affinity gave rise to the *economic* organization of modern society (Polanyi, 2001 [1944]), as the ideals (rationally calculating individuals attempting to prove their predestination, which was reflected in their economic gains) of Protestantism were rationalized into the world; that is, means (purposive–formal–rational action, i.e., the lived world) were established to facilitate the ends (substantive rationality) of Protestantism: economic gain for its own sake as a sign of one's election in a particular "calling," which "embedded" social or cultural relations in the economic system:

> Economic production is organized in a capitalist manner, with rationally calculating entrepreneurs [the predestined prosper]; public administration is organized in a bureaucratic manner, with juristically trained, specialized officials—that is, they are organized in the form of private enterprises and public bureaucracies. The relevant means for carrying out their tasks are concentrated in the hands of owners and leaders; membership in these organizations is made independent of ascriptive properties [today, maybe, but not the case for this type of society's early formation]. By these means, organizations gain a high degree of internal flexibility and external autonomy. In virtue of their efficiency, the organizational forms of the capitalist economy and the modern state administration establish themselves in other action systems to such an extent that modern societies fit the picture of "a society of organizations," even

from the standpoint of lay members. (Habermas, 1987 [1981],
p. 306)

Hence, in this Durkheimian, that is, *mechanical*, understanding of the
origins and organizational basis, that is, structure, of modern American
society, "the cultural struggle for distinction is intricately connected to the
economic distribution of material goods, which it both legitimates and
reproduces" (Gartman, 2002, p. 257).

> Weber's explanation refers in the first instance not to the estab-
> lishment of the labor markets that turned abstract labor power
> into an expense in business calculations, but to the "spirit of
> capitalism," that is, to the mentality characteristic of the purpo-
> sive-rational economic action of the early capitalist entrepre-
> neurs. Whereas Marx took the mode of production [i.e., the
> practice of Protestantism—economic gain for its own sake] to
> be the phenomenon in need of explanation, and investigated
> capital accumulation as the new mechanism of system integra-
> tion, Weber's view of the problem turns the investigation in
> another direction. For him the explanans is the conversion of
> the economy and state administration over to purposive–rational
> action orientations; the changes fall in the domain of forms of
> social integration. At the same time, this new form of social
> integration made it possible to institutionalize the money mech-
> anism, and thereby new mechanisms of system integration.
> (Habermas, 1987 [1981], p. 313)

Although "Marx starts from problems of system integration [an understanding of the practices, i.e., formal economic rationality, of Protestant-
ism], Weber from problems of social integration," these two analytic levels
should not be kept separate, for the "predestined" (white Protestant males)
by developing, and maintaining the control of, the capitalist market
economy and state (organization of a material resource framework along
the agential moments of the Protestant ethic, that is, the new mechanisms
of system integration) reified their practical consciousness, which they
rationalized with reality and existence as such, in institutions operating
through materialized metaphors beyond logical or empirical proof, on
ungroundable premises, on nonobservable substances, to direct (mechan-
ically and systemically) the agential moments (i.e., colonization of the
lived world) of social actors for the sole purpose of accumulating economic
gain (Marx's "ideological superstructure"), which became the aim of all
those interpellated into the order of things, that is, the "social relations

of production" (put differently, the spirit of capitalism, is the praxis—discursive practice—of the discourse of Protestantism).

Capitalist (Marxist and non-Marxist) interpretations of this symbolic social order (i.e., the semiotic field in the Figure 18.1) view its attempt to spread globally, that is, globalization, as a result of the inexorable rules of the social relations of production—horizontal axis in Figure 18.1—as determining social action (movement along the vertical axis). That is, it could be argued that social action (movement along the vertical axis) within globalization results from the rational abstract laws of capitalist economics, which sees human society and individuals as rational economic persons. While arguing about the Protestant ethic, along the horizontal axis, that is, the ideals of the Protestant ethic inexorable and natural laws and recursively organized through the spirit of capitalism (movement along the vertical axis), one may realize that it is not rationality (i.e., the rationally arrived at rules of economics) that governs the structure of relations and its attempt to interpellate the world's people, that is, globalization. In other words, the capitalist symbolic social order is maintained and reproduced not as a result of empirical observable forces (i.e., natural laws) that determine human action and interaction. On the contrary, the symbolic order and its recursively organized practices are a result of the practical consciousness of social actors who seek to exercise the Protestant ethic in the material world by institutionalizing the norms, values, proscriptions, and prescriptions by which all social actors must organize and reproduce their being in the world.

Global localization, therefore, falls in line with the structural logic of Ferdinand De Saussure (1986 [1916], p. 80), which posits that the synchronic axis (Protestantism) gives rise to the diachronic (i.e., historical) practice—vertical axis—capitalism, and globalization represents the means of localizing or structuring the global setting within the structure, or the discourse of Protestantism, through capitalist practices. So in essence, Protestantism is the reason for capitalist practices, and the latter does not change the former; that is why there is room for a "clash of civilizations," that is, a clash of "structuring structures," as the only means of deterring globalization.

Although both positions speak to the idea of reifying thought and are inextricably linked, the two approaches, in terms of methodology, diametrically oppose one another. The capitalist understanding argues for the social construction of reality, based on human instrumental rationality (i.e., the real is rational and the rational real), which would mean that the capitalist practices are objectionable if they violate and oppress constituted rational subjects.[2] The Protestant approach, on the other hand, suggests that the practices of capitalism are natural and immutable, based on an enframing ontology that stands outside the grasp of human instrumental rationality; that is why its constituted members would be compelled to live out, and have others live out, these practices regardless of their oppressive nature.

Essentially, the argument here is that to understand the phenomenon of globalization simply through the capitalist approach is inconclusive and must be approached through the Protestant ethic, for the former assumes and has its metaphysical grounding in the latter, not instrumental rationality. In other words, the structure of market capitalism and the global economy are not determined and negated by the contradictory relations inherent in capitalist practices. On the contrary, as Weber points out, it is the structuring ontology of the Protestant ethic, which in the Heideggerian (1971) sense of the word *enframes* all Western practices, that is determining.

The understanding of capitalism as determining structure and practice is the result of a theoretical error of the social sciences. That is, the grounding of the social sciences in Newtonian methodology—which emphasizes the empirical extrapolation, by a detached observer, of immutable laws of human nature—fails to account for the structure that makes human action observable (Chomsky, 1959). Capitalism, from this perspective, is the observable practice, and the structuring laws of capitalism become what are observed. But how can this be, if these laws, which are observed in "nature," must in turn be "taught" to human actors? There is an underlying contradiction within this nomothetic approach that suggests other forms of human action because the capitalist one must be taught. Could rationality suggest a capitalist behavior that further implies that capitalist rationality structures, in the Kantian sense, what is observed?

My argument answers this question in the affirmative and, therefore, argues that rationality begins with structural premises, which are ontological and by logical definition cultural. Rationality, in this sense, simply attempts to structure or transform these premises into the material world, whereby experience (human praxis) is no longer that of social actors encountering the material world but of their following rules of conduct, which are sanctioned in line with presupposed premises.

Accordingly, the argument here is that the cultural premises of capitalism are that of the Protestant ethic, and all thoughts within that structuring system are a result of the organization of its structuring ontology. That is why the contradictions of capitalist practices will not destroy the system—they are instead *actions* that can be remedied to avert destruction. The destruction of capitalist practices is contingent on clashes with alternative systems enframed in an irrevocable ontology (i.e., Islam, Catholicism, ecological crisis, etc.) that diametrically opposes that of the Protestant type (Huntington, 1996).

The Protestant Ethic as Bourgeois Culture

Whereas most sociologists of development view globalization within the structure of relations of capitalist ideology, my Weberian approach posits that globalization represents the attempt by agents of the Protestant ethic to homogenize the globe into their Protestant ideology. In other words, individualism, free trade, labor, democracy, market organization, commodity production, bureaucratic organization, and so on, promoted by the WTO, World Bank, UN, and others, are the praxis of the Protestant ethic, which translates into economic gain (accumulation of goods, wealth) for its own sake through organized (bureaucracy), lawless (free from human intervention), calculating (rationality), and economic competition (labor).

From a global standpoint, this means that countries subscribing to neoliberal policies are in essence adopting cultural reforms that will eventually transmogrify their cultural identity via the cultural praxis of Western Protestantism, that is, market capitalism.[3] In other words, the countries led by calculating (foreign-trained) state bureaucrats will begin to establish the most viable markets (which will interpellate their people or citizens as individuated calculating laborers in need of work for economic gain). The success of the established markets and the people will be reflected in their economic gain, which rests on the viability of these markets in competition, a matter of chance (predestination), and calculating rationality. When the viable markets usurp the infant market (for example, the banana industry of Grenada), such usurpation is the price of competition and the success of the more calculating competitor. Hence, it is up to each individual nation-state to make sure that the markets it opts for offer the best chance for economic gain.

From this perspective, poverty and its institution (class differentiation or stratification) are acceptable and necessary elements of the order of things, because the relational cultural–structural sign of the Protestant ethic is success through economic gain for its own sake. Because one never knows whether he or she is predestined or not (reason does not account for chance or predestination), economic gain—that is, wealth, lack thereof, or continuous work to the grave for wealth—is a necessary by-product of the Protestant cultural ideology.

Thus, working through poverty for economic gain for its own sake as a sign of success is a necessary part of adopting neoliberal policy enframed by the Protestant ethic. That is, when countries agree to adopt neoliberal economic policies (free trade, Intellectual Property Rights Agreement, governmentless competition, etc.), they agree to allow market competition—which may lead to the failure of individuals and markets—to be the determining factor in the organization of cultural praxis. Therefore, countries that sell their people through EPZs, for example, are simply attempting to find the most viable ways to obtain economic gain (by attracting foreign investment) in order to rid themselves of poverty by becoming as successful as are those who have made it, that is, those who have obtained economic gain for its own sake through calculating rationality and hard work (the United States and Western Europe).

But this is problematic, for these countries are already poor; that would mean that by adopting the neoliberal policies that force countries to structure their masses in a manner that allows for market competition, liberalization, and so on, their poverty is exacerbated and becomes a necessary (institutional) aspect of their national projects. Basically, the structure of globalization through its practice, market capitalism, not only makes poverty acceptable, but also necessary: The poor will get poorer and the rich will get richer (Klak, 1998).

The Grenadian Context

The case of Grenada in today's "global-localizing" process will serve as an example of the aforementioned theoretical points. One of the nine member states of the Caribbean Community (CARICOM), Grenada gained its independence from Britain in 1979. Five years after their independence, in a bloodless coup spearheaded by Maurice Bishop, the New Jewel Movement in Grenada attempted to reconstitute their society, which was for so long part of the British colonial heritage.

> The socialist program of the Peoples Revolutionary Government (PRG) was optimistic as well as idealistic. Several objectives were framed to thoroughly redevelop the island's economy: (1) construct the Point Salines International Airport to handle wide-bodies jets and invest in the infrastructure necessary for a restructured, locally owned tourism industry; (2) encourage growth of a mixed economy with three major institutional bases—state, cooperative, and private—with the state playing the leading role; (3) improve the standard of living through a comprehensive program aimed at upgrading social services and ensuring basic needs; and (4) diversifying overseas trade and diversifying the portfolio of foreign aid and assistance, particularly courting assistance and linkages with CMEA countries, including Cuba, and improving South-South cooperation. (Conway, 1998, p. 38)[4]

These objectives (in terms of points 2, 3, and 4), enframed within a Marxist political ideology, on the surface, appeared diametrically to oppose the Protestant colonial heritage that Great Britain institutionalized on the island. The socialist doctrine of the PRG was to institutionalize economic equality as opposed to the continued class stratification.

Thus, structured more along the lines of Catholicism and feudalism, Grenada's planned revolution appeared to undermine the structural ontology of the American empire, the progeny of Britain. Bishop's rhetoric was answered by the U.S. State Department with great displeasure. Whereas Bishop's principled stances were championed by the U.S. Congressional Black Caucus, the Republican administration was not amused. This led to a social revolution that lasted four years. Strife within the PRG culminated in a military coup and the assassination of Maurice Bishop and followers, thus providing an opportunity for the U.S. military and the Reagan administration to coordinate the invasion and occupation of that Windward "Spice Isle." Grenada was gradually admitted back into the fold, the airport was finished, tourist facilities were opened to foreign finance, and the national economy was to be open, export oriented, and dominated by foreign capital (39).

For the most part, the outcome of an "open economy" has led to global localization, the interpellation of social actors as agents of the Protestant ethic. When the PRG led by Maurice Bishop had overthrown the conservative regime of Eric Gairy, exports of agriculture and agriculture-based products contributed 80% or more of total domestic merchandise exports (Hickling-Hudson, 1988, p. 10). After the invasion in 1983, the openness of the national economy, which was then agriculturally dominated, made it susceptible to competition from larger and more global agribusinesses that drove the local markets out of business, in particular, the banana industry.

The U.S. Agency for International Development (USAID) provided more than $120 million in economic assistance from 1984 to 1993. Today, the U.S. economic assistance is channeled primarily through multilateral agencies such as the World Bank—in sectors that could eventually advance to the stage of generating new exports that would generate growth for the Grenadian economy, that is, tourism and other "service industries in which the need for technical expertise is high and which could be diffused through the rest of the economy, either by the formation of joint ventures or through strategic alliances between local firms and foreign-owned enterprises setting up business in the country" (Rampersad et al., 1997, p. 210). The citizens were trained to work diligently in these industries, for economic gain for its own sake.

In keeping with the imposition of the neoliberal practices, Grenada in 1993 was among the participants of the Uruguay Round of Multilateral Trade Negotiations (MTNs), which acceded to the provisions of the WTO (free trade, cut wages, privatization, austerity measures, and export expansion). According to the Grenada minister of finance, the medium-term goal of signing this pact "is to re-position the Grenadian economy as a more diversified, competitive and knowledge-based economy, thereby ensuring that the quality of life of all its citizens is permanently enhanced" (Boatswain, 2000). This, he continues, will be done through "sustained robust growth": "heightened activity in the construction and telecommunications sector; the sustained growth of the tourism sector; the continued expansion of the international services sector; and the resurgence of the agricultural sector."

In short, Grenada will attempt to specialize and to have its citizens work diligently in particular markets for economic gain. Moreover, fiscal reforms are expected, such as cutting government spending to 3% of GDP over the period 2000–2002, and liberalizing trade. Thus, robust growth and trade liberalization would lead to "poverty eradication and reduced unemployment," which are inextricably linked. Grenada's specialized sectors (tourism and service industries and agriculture) will essentially be targeted to create more jobs, thereby reducing poverty and enhancing the quality of life of all its citizens.

In 1998, the Grenada minister of finance remarked that "Grenada was ranked 52nd in the world with a medium human development status. Grenada has recorded improvements in most of the social indicators, including infant mortality, life expectancy and literacy. At the peak of the structural adjustment program in 1994, unemployment was 26.7%. At the end of 1999, our national rate of unemployment was 12.5%." "Notwithstanding these achievements," he continues, "the 1999 country poverty assessment for Grenada found that 32.1% of the persons surveyed fell below the poverty line, and 12.9% were identified as indigent." So he states, the aim of the government of Grenada, in light of these improvements and continual poverty, is to continue to work diligently toward economic gain, that is, expanding the aforementioned specialized sectors, for its own sake for the masses (interpellate them as workers after economic gain) so that poverty is eradicated, that is, "our citizens ... share in the benefits of growth" (Boatswain, 2000).

Essentially, these statements, enframed or reinterpreted within the linguistic structure of my methodological approach, underscore the obvious fact of Dr. Boatswain's statements: that the poor must work diligently through their poverty (poverty is institutionalized), and that work will eventually lead to economic gain and the eradication of their poverty. This seems paradoxical, as market growth, that is, job creation, the underlying aim of globalizing agreements such as the MTN, appears simply to attempt to institutionalize poverty through low-wage work, not eradicate it, given the need by the predestined (multinational corporations) to provide cost-saving jobs to the damned (poor) in order to maintain their piety (success as signified through economic gain for its own sake).

Conclusion

So what is it about self and society in the globalization era that compels states and their bureaucrats to buy into the idea that economic gain for its own sake, through work for those predestined by the grace of God, is the key to poverty eradication? In my view it is not enough to argue that the power of the globalizing nations, and their attempt to protect their economic way of life by any means necessary (world system approach), is the driving force behind the acceptance. This does not explain the particular acceptance of this worldview by those in particular situations despite the fact that in many instances this economic way of life is detrimental to a sense of development intended to eradicate poverty.

In order to understand the former point, it is necessary to look at the reasons that make this worldview compelling, that is, the metaphysical grounding—cultural structure—(Protestantism) of the spirit of capitalism; that is, the metaphysical or cultural structure of capitalism, Protestantism, makes it appear to be natural and immutable. That being the case (from the heydays of colonialism to today's globalization movement), its agents (social actors determined and negated by this structure) have been attempting to effect the ever-increasing encroachment of this reality on other realities throughout the globe. This process is done through the institutionalization of laws and ideas that govern the practices, that is, the spirit of capitalism, of the Protestant ethic. Hence whereas the Europeans, as Max Weber suggests, went from ideology to practice, the movement for other peoples of the world has been from practice to ideology. That is, by adopting the practices of the spirit of capitalism, a secular and rapacious version of the Protestant ideology becomes the governance of social actions in other realities (localization).

This characteristic of the globalizing process speaks to the illusion of reifying thought—"the idea," as Habermas observes, "that the differentiation of an objective world means totally excluding the social and the subjective worlds from the domains of rationally motivated agreement" (1984 [1981], p. 73). In this sense, "the worldview ... does not permit differentiation between the world of existing states of affairs, valid norms and expressible subjective experiences. The linguistic worldview is reified as the world order and cannot be seen as an interpretive system open to criticism" (Habermas, 1984 [1981], p. 71). And this is where the world system approach, among all other sociological approaches, finds its viability. "The pursuit of national 'competitiveness' within an increasingly bound global economy [i.e., reified structuring objective worldview] is consonant with the world-system approach and places this perspective in a theoretically privileged position to analyze current trends" (Portes, 1997, p. 354). Yet, "the postulate of a single universal unit of analysis is a major weakness since the level at which most development problems, dilemmas, and decisions take place is the intermediate one of nations and communities seeking to cope with the constraints of their particular situations" (p. 354). That means essentially that the perspective's Durkheimian "mechanical solidarity" approach cannot account for the ideological, that is, cultural and structural, resistance that anthropologists such as June Nash suggest serves as antisystemic movements. It must rely instead on the structural practices of capitalism, which are a result of "rationally motivated" abstract agreements, as determining and negating factors.

Hence, by refusing to budge from the level of capitalist structural motivations, world system theorists remain outside the understanding of what constitutes the nature of resistance to its contradictions, for clearly class struggle is not the basis. What needs to occur, as I have attempted to do here, is to view globalization and its politics of development within the anthropological notion of culture: that is, to understand globalization, as Arturo Escobar (1995) attempts to do, within the cultural structure (discourse, metaphysics, etc.) that structures its practice—capitalism—and its attempted homogenization of other (institutionalized) ontologies of human behavior through containment, that is, containing other discourses, cultural structures, metaphysics, and so on, through the practice of its own. Let it be known that world system theorists are correct to see this homogenization process as the underlying trend of the modern period. But their perspective fails to account for, or determine the nature of, the resistance faced by this worldview; instead the focus is on the contradictions of self-interests that the world system fosters. I believe the "true" resistances taking place around the globe, that is, the Zapatista movement, Islamic fundamentalism, ecological crisis, and liberation theology coming out of the Catholic Church, are ontological in nature, thereby hitting at the heart of "the spirit of capitalism," that is, the Protestant ethic, whereas world system posits the end of historical capitalism in its structural crisis, in a "clash of civilizations," a clash of structuring structures.

In other words, social change is not a result of the historical exhaustion of contradictory practices of a structure. On the contrary, social change is a result of the replacement of one structuring structure by another as a result of their encounter. In light of the fact that almost all social actors (globally, with the encroachment of capitalism into the Muslim world) have been interpellated into the structure of Protestantism via its practice, capitalism, it appears that the ecological crisis stands alone as the last remaining antisystemic structural ontology. Be that as it may, the aim of humanity should be the homogenization of the world so that all are the same one world political entity tackling the problem of sustainable development. As it stands now, the poor have to remain poor in order to deter the ecological crisis humanity is facing. This is unjust and immoral, for it implies, in keeping with the logic of the structure humanity finds itself in, that a few are worthy at the expense of the less worthy. Therefore, insomuch as I detest bourgeois culture for exactly this reasoning, I nonetheless, support all of humanity's aim to protest participation in it, given its attempt to usurp all of the material world's resources for its own aim—mainly economic gain for its own sake. If not the ecological crisis, surely this push for participation will bring about the fall of a pernicious worldview that by its very logic is destructive and exploitative.

Notes

1. This paradigmatic shift I am attempting is done in order to demonstrate the historicity of structuralism.
2. The Frankfurt school, especially Herbert Marcuse (1964), saw that the positivism of the Enlightenment project gave rise to the illusion of reifying thought; that is, science and its results became a new sort of metaphysics that "enframed" social practices; economics has rationalized market capitalism, which therefore represents the nature of reality and existence as such. I do not completely accept that argument, for it is my assumption that reason has not demystified the world, but on the contrary, has reasoned the myths into "reality" (practical reason). Thus, capitalism is the "reality" of the myth of Protestantism, its "enframing" ontology. I do not accept the Weberian understanding that the ever-increasing rationalization of the world necessarily leads to its demystification; on the contrary, for me, rationality only finds means for reaching the ends of an enframing ontology.
3. The loss of meaning characterizing the global setting, which is proposed by advocates of a postmodern break in history (Harvey, 1989; Jameson, 1991), for me represents precisely this move of transplanting practice, postindustrialism or consumerism, without its structural grounding.
4. CMEA is the "Council for Mutual Economic Assistance: former trading alliance among state socialist countries, including the Soviet Union, its allies, and Cuba; also abbreviated COMECON" (Klak, 1998, p. xiii).

References

Althusser, Louis (2001). *Lenin and Philosophy and Other Essays*. New York: Monthly Review Press.

Arrighi, Giovanni (1994). *The Long Twentieth Century*. London: Verso.

Balibar, Etienne, and Immanuel Wallerstein (1991). *Race, Nation, Class: Ambiguous Identities.* London and New York: Verso.

Bell, Daniel (1976). *The Coming of Post-Industrial Society.* New York: Basic Books.

Boatswain, Anthony (2000). Grenada's strategy for economic development, *CaribNews,* New York, p. 1.

Bourdieu, Pierre (1984). *Distinction: A Social Critique of the Judgement of Taste.* Cambridge, Mass.: Harvard University Press.

Bourdieu, Pierre (1990). *The Logic Practice,* Stanford, Calif.: Stanford University Press.

Chomsky, Noam (1959). Verbal behavior, *Language,* 35(1), 26–58.

Conway, Dennis (1998). Misguided directions, mismanaged models, or missed paths? Pp. 29–50 in *Globalization and Neoliberalism: The Caribbean Context,* Edited by Thomas Klak. Lanham, Md.: Rowman & Littlefield.

Domhoff, William G. (2002). *Who Rules America? Power & Politics,* 4th Edition. Boston: McGraw-Hill.

Escobar, Arturo (1995). *Encountering Development: The Making and Unmaking of the Third World.* Princeton, N.J.: Princeton University Press.

Gartman, David (2002). Bourdieu's theory of cultural change: explication, application, and critique, *Sociological Theory,* 20(2), 255–281.

Giddens, Anthony (1990). *Consequences of Modernity.* England: Polity Press.

Habermas, Jürgen (1984 [1981]). *The Theory of Communicative Action: Reason and the Rationalization of Society (volume 1).* Translated by Thomas McCarthy. Boston: Beacon Press.

Harvey, David (1989). *The Condition of Postmodernity.* Cambridge, Mass.: Blackwell.

Heidegger, Martin (1971). *The Question Concerning Technology.* New York: Harper and Row.

Hickling-Hudson, Anne (1988). Toward communication praxis: reflections on the pedagogy of Paulo Freire and educational change in Grenada, *Journal of Education,* 170(2), 9–38.

Huntington, Samuel P. (1996). *The Clash of Civilizations and the Remaking of World Order.* New York: Simon and Schuster.

Inkeles, Alex (1959). Personality and social structure. Pp. 249–276 in *Sociology Today,* edited by Robert K. Merton, Leonard Broom, and Leonard S. Cottrell, Jr. New York: Basic Books.

Inkeles, Alex (1960). Industrial man: the relation of status, experience, and value, *American Journal of Sociology,* 66: 1–31.

Inkeles, Alex (1969). Making men modern: on the causes and consequences of individual change in six developing countries, *American Journal of Sociology,* 75, 208–225.

International Monetary Fund (2002). *Grenada Statistics Yearbook.* Washington, D.C.: IMF.

Jameson, Fredric (1991). *Postmodernism, or the Cultural Logic of Late Capitalism.* Durham, N.C.: Duke University Press.

Kellner, Douglas (2002). Theorizing globalization, *Sociological Theory,* 20(3), 285–305.

Klak, Thomas (1998). *Globalization and Neoliberalism: The Caribbean Context.* Lanham, Md.: Rowman & Littlefield.

Klak, Thomas and Garth Myers (1998). How states sell their countries and their people. In Thomas Klak (Ed.), *Globalization and Neoliberalism. The Caribbean Context* (pp. 87–109). Lanham, Md.: Rowman and Littlefield.

Marcuse, Herbert (1964). *One-Dimensional Man.* Boston: Beacon Press.

Marshall, Gordon (1998). *A Dictionary of Sociology.* New York: Oxford University Press.

Marx, Karl (1992). *Capital: A Critique of Political Economy. Volume 1.* Translated from the third German edition by Samuel Moore and Edward Aveling. New York: International.

McMichael, Philip (1996). Globalization: myths and realities, *Rural Sociology*, 61(1), 274–291.

Mocombe, Paul (2001). A Labor Approach to the Development of the Self or "Modern Personality": The Case of Public Education. Master's thesis, Florida Atlantic University. Ann Arbor, Mich.: UMI.

Nash, June (2001). *Mayan Visions: The Quest for Autonomy in an Age of Globalization.* New York and London: Routledge.

Polyani, Karl (2001 [1944]). *The Great Transformation: The Political and Economic Origins of Our Time.* Boston: Beacon Press.

Portes, Alejandro (1997). Neoliberalism and the sociology of development: emerging trends and unanticipated facts, *Population and Development Review*, 23(2), 353–372.

Rampersad, Frank, et al. (1997). *Critical Issues in Caribbean Development: The New World Trade Order: Uruguay Round Agreements and Implications for CARICOM States.* Kingston, Jamaica: Ian Randle.

Saussure, Ferdinand de (1986 [1916]). *Course in General Linguistics.* Chicago: Open Court.

Sklair, Leslie (2001). *The Transnational Capitalist Class.* Cambridge: Blackwell.

Weber, Max (1958 [1904–05]). *The Protestant Ethic and the Spirit of Capitalism.* New York: Charles Scribner's Sons.

SUSTAINABLE DEVELOPMENT: CURRENT AND FUTURE CHALLENGES

Chapter 19

Implementing Sustainable Development Policies: A Theoretical Discourse

Gedeon M. Mudacumura

CONTENTS

419

Introduction

The purpose of development, in strictly economic terms, is the capacity of a national economy to generate and sustain an annual increase in its gross national product (GNP). A common alternative economic index of development has been the use of rates of growth of income per capita or per capita GNP to consider the ability of a nation to expand its output at a rate faster than the growth of its population (Todaro, 1996). Economic development theorists of the 1950s and early 1960s viewed the process of development as a series of successive stages of economic growth. The economic theory of development primarily focused on the right quantity and mixture of savings, investment, and foreign financial and technical assistance. The latter constituted all that was necessary to enable poor countries to become developed.

Because of their failure to take into account individual and contextual factors, the simplistic "one size fits all" development approaches never worked. Sorting out what is generalizable and what is situation-specific, identifying cause and effect linkages, and devising appropriate action strategies have been challenging tasks for development scholars. As a result, the state of the art in both the theory and the practice of implementing development policy in both North and South is still deficient (Brinkerhoff, 1996; Mudacumura, 2001). It is difficult to extract from the literature a coherent framework applicable to the task of meeting specific goals in particular settings probably because of the perceptions and experiences of practitioners, which have not been sufficiently explored and systematically related to the analytical literature (Boeninger, 1992).

This chapter looks at the development literature, exploring the challenges of implementing sustainable development policies in both developed and developing countries. Translating policy reforms and program intentions into results that ultimately produce benefits and better lives for citizens is the major concern shared by developing countries. In this context, Brinkerhoff (1996) highlights the importance of bridging the language and terminology gap between those who focus on the technical content of policy (theorists) and those who are involved with the implementation of policies and programs (practitioners). Bridging this gap is crucial for it may allow development of both wider and better understanding of implementation factors and the process linking policy goals to outcomes. Overlooking this point may lead to weak implementation, which hurts large numbers of people, particularly the poor living in countries struggling to promote better opportunities for growth and development (Brinkerhoff, 1996).

Policy makers and public managers face the challenge of sustaining policy reforms beyond the launch phase so that those policy changes, whose benefits rarely appear in the short term, can bear fruit. Public officials charged with implementation policy reforms face changes in their roles, severe institutional constraints, new interaction patterns with other public agencies and civil society, and pressure to show results. This chapter reviews the fragmented nonlinear nature of the policy process and elaborates on policy implementation in a multiorganizational context with no single entity in charge. The focus is on the crucial interactions of development organizations committed to various forms of social change and development leading to strong sustainable communities. The multiorganizational approach to policy implementation relies on the relationships among all the intervening organizations.

Scholars interested in developing countries have not taken advantage of the rich insights of interorganizational approaches to examine the implementation and development policy outcomes. The chapter alludes to issues of managing external relationships and interdependencies while ensuring that basic operating tasks are accomplished (Kiggundu, 1996). The concepts of strategic management that are useful and appropriate for improving implementation performance, are briefly discussed.

Recent experiences with a number of "wicked" policy problems have begun to suggest the viability, if not the necessity, of collaborative citizen–expert inquiry in solving a specific category of contemporary policy problems (Fischer, 1993). Current research on development policy implementation highlights the need for strong local leadership, competent local development institutions, and broad-based public and private sector participation (Brown and Covey, 1987; Gittell, 1990). The last part of the chapter discusses briefly a participatory research method that recognizes the relevance of local people's expertise in the implementation of sustainable development policies.

Before delving into the challenges of implementing sustainable development policies, some comments on the growth paradigm that was recommended as the panacea for problems of development are provided. The author also alludes to the human-centered development approach that many international development agencies have embraced

Overview of the Growth Paradigm

Researchers from the British Social Sciences Research Council (SSRC) asked carefully selected samples of 1,500 respondents three times in a period of 5 years the following question: There has been a lot of discussion about the quality of life recently; what do you think are the important things that make it up? The findings revealed that nonmaterial factors such as a good home life and a contented outlook were rated as important by more people than material factors such as the quantity of consumer goods.

Of the replies that can be put into one category or the other, 71% were about factors that have little or nothing to do with cash (Douthwaite, 1993). How do these findings fit with the prescribed economic growth paradigm, which underscores increasing production and consumption, with the intent of improving societal welfare?

Although Daly (1996) claimed that the economic growth paradigm has enriched the few, impoverished the many, and endangered the planet, Douthwaite (1993) argued that growth destroys jobs because its process depends on the introduction of labor-saving technology. Erroneously assuming that what works in developed countries should also work in developing countries and underestimating people's cultures are some of the main reasons for the ineffectiveness of the economic growth paradigm in less developed countries. Indeed, looking back over the years, Soedjatmoko (1985) underlined that in their preoccupation with growth and its stages and with the provisions of capital and skills, development theorists have paid insufficient attention to institutional and structural problems and the power of historical, cultural, and religious forces in the development process.

Similarly, early development theorists viewed development as an economic phenomenon in which rapid gains in overall and per capita GNP growth would "trickle down" to the masses (Todaro, 1996). During that period, development economists were giving secondary importance to problems of poverty, unemployment, and income distribution. Owens (1987) captured this concern when arguing how development has been treated as if it were nothing more than an exercise in applied economics, unrelated to political ideas, forms of government, and the role of people in society. Integrating the political and economic theory could lead to consideration of not just ways in which societies can become more productive but the quality of these societies, which are supposed to become more productive—the development of people rather than the development of things.

The proponents of limited economic growth emphasized that the growth paradigm, even if it was beneficial at one stage in human history, is downright damaging, and further attempts to push for more economic growth would produce much more harm than any benefits the expansion might bring (Douthwaite, 1993). The international community is becoming aware of the detrimental effects of an economic growth paradigm that might have broadened the gap between the rich and the poor. As Dwivedi (1994) put it, the golden age of the 1950s turned into the age of pessimism and disillusion by the 1980s. Nevertheless, the worldwide awareness displayed at the Earth Summit in 1992 demonstrated that no one group of nations could keep "progressing" while the majority remained hungry and poor.

Although developed countries' resources and knowledge are required to bring about remarkable development changes in developing countries, sustainable development will materialize only when people experiencing the socioeconomic hardships are actively involved in the design and implementation of policies that directly affect them. This idea implies ascertaining means and ways of building local capacity, an approach that many development agencies have embraced to enable local people to be active participants in the development of their communities.

Human-Centered Development

Most multilateral (World Bank, the United Nations Development Program [UNDP]) development agencies have realigned their development approaches to underscore the relevance of putting people at the center of all aspects of the development process. Such approaches are premised on the need to create a conducive environment for people, individually and collectively, to develop their full potential and to have a reasonable chance of leading productive and creative lives in accord with their needs and interests (Mudacumura, 2002).

According to the UNDP (1990), human development is conceived as both the process of widening people's choices and the level of their achieved well-being. The most critical ones are to lead a long and healthy life, to be educated, and to enjoy a decent standard of living. Additional choices include political freedom, guaranteed human rights, and self-respect.

The concept of human-centered development partly derived from the Brundtland Commission Report (1987) and partly from work done by many nongovernmental organizations (NGOs) over the past 30 years (Mudacumura, 2004b). Both sources place people at the center of development, advocate protection of life opportunities for current and future generations, and emphasize the respect for natural systems on which life depends. Growth in national production (gross domestic product [GDP]) is absolutely necessary to meet all essential human objectives, but studying how this growth translates or fails to translate into human development in various societies is very important, particularly in regions with high concentration of poverty.

Emphasizing the importance of putting people first, Schumacher (1977) reiterated the primacy of shifting the focus from goods to people. Drawing his lesson from historical records, Schumacher (1977) highlighted that real development does not start with goods; it starts with people and their education, organization, and discipline. Without these three, all resources remain latent, untapped potential. Similarly, the UNDP acknowledges that people are the primary assets, the real wealth of any nation. Aristotle also prioritized human development when warning against judging societies merely by such characteristics as income and wealth sought not for themselves but desired means to other objectives. He differentiated a good political arrangement from a bad one in terms of its successes and failures in facilitating people's ability to lead flourishing lives.

Along the same line, sociologists agree that people are the instruments and beneficiaries, as well as the victims of all development activities. Their active involvement in the development process is the key to success. Actually, putting people first in policies and investment programs for promotion of development, or for assistance in spontaneous development, is not a radical but a realistic call (Cernea, 1993).

The preceding discussions highlighted the current development philosophy, which recognizes economic growth as a means to achieve sustainable human development ends rather than an end in itself. But for development to be sustainable, there is a need to go beyond the logic of economics and to integrate other key development dimensions (Mudacumura, 2002). The critical role of people in implementing sustainable development policies cannot be overemphasized. The UNDP's broad-ranging human resource development strategy prepares people for productive participation in social and economic life. Civil society plays important roles in providing services and opportunities for development and in influencing government policies (UNDP, 1997). The following sections focus on the process of translating policy into results that ultimately improve the quality of life for citizens.

Policy Implementation: Content versus Process

The majority of the developing countries are confronted with the issue of successfully pursuing long-term reforms in democratizing environments; that involves not only knowing what direction to move in but also paying attention to how to get there, recognizing that policy implementation is as much process as it is content. The first generation of development scholars primarily focused on policy content, downplaying the process side. The policy implementation process is at least as political as technical and is complex and highly interactive. Besides technical analysis, it calls for consensus building, participation of key stakeholders, conflict resolution, compromise, contingency planning, and adaptation (Brinkerhoff, 1996). Related to both the technical and process aspects of implementation, the concept of participation is a major issue in implementing development policy that will be sustained over a long period.

Looking at the policy content, local input is indispensable for designing and carrying out policies that work. Despite its critical importance, scholars have not fully explored the conceptual definition of participation and its various levels in the context of implementing development policies. Jacob (1994) remarked that if increasing the level of participation is a critical objective for sustaining development, then a set of general criteria to guide the development of techniques for cross-national comparisons of levels of participation should be developed. An operational definition of participation within sustainable development would be a step toward meeting all of these requirements.

On the process side, participation is central to the state–society realignments associated with democratization and good governance. There is a growing international consensus that sound governance is essential in achieving sustainable development. Here, *governance* is defined as the exercise of political, economic, and administrative authority to manage a nation's affairs. It is the complex mechanisms, processes, relationships, and institutions through which citizens and groups articulate their interests, exercise their rights and obligations, and mediate their differences (UNDP, 1997). The notions of what constitutes good governance vary a great deal. Current literature on the role of the state does not contain a clearly defined and well thought through framework that identifies the elements that should be included in a comprehensive theory of governance.

Thus, the challenge facing all societies is to create a system of governance that promotes, supports, and sustains human involvement in the implementation of development policies. The UNDP and the United States Agency for International Development (USAID) have been at the forefront pushing for effective democratic forms of governance that prioritize active participation of all development stakeholders. These agencies have stressed that capacity building for effective and sound governance should be the primary means of alleviating poverty. In this context, the UNDP (1994) contends that the goal of governance initiatives should be to develop capacities needed to realize development that gives priority to the poor, advances women, sustains the environment, and creates needed opportunities for employment and other livelihoods.

Similarly, Drabek (1987) and Paul and Israel (1991) argue that international development agencies should concentrate their efforts on organizing and empowering poor populations. Emphasizing the importance of the participation of the poor in rural development, Nindi (1993) views cost reductions, greater efficiency, greater profits, job enrichment, happiness, solidarity, and community development as the main objectives of people's participation.

The USAID recently clarified the aim of all its programs: to build local capacity, to enhance participation, and to encourage accountability, transparency, decentralization, and empowerment of communities and individuals (Sholes and Covey, 1996). Most development scholars consider strengthening civil society and structuring the relationships between states and civil society as sine qua non conditions for effective implementation of development policies in developing countries (Bava, 2004; Mudacumura, 2001; Nel, 2004). In fact, governance transcends the state to include civil society organizations and the private sector, because all three are involved in most activities promoting sustainable development. The three must work synergistically, complementing each other's efforts in the implementation of sustainable development policies.

To improve development policy implementation while searching for an adequate approach for donors to assist developing countries in managing the implementation of reforms, the USAID initiated an applied research and technical assistance project in 1990. The Implementing Policy Change (IPC) Project undertook studies that concentrated on the implementation and management side of policy reform in more than 30 developing countries. In its second 5-year phase, which began in 1995, the IPC's unifying theme was the application of a strategic perspective, and associated toolkit, to policy reforms with the ultimate goal of building capacity for strategic policy management. The 10 years of applied research is a gold mine of a longitudinal data set that may be used to build more relevant comprehensive frameworks or models necessary to make sense of the existing implementation theories and knowledge.

Policy beneficiaries must take ownership both of the policy to be implemented and of any capacity-building efforts intended to enhance implementation. Unless concerned development stakeholders or groups of development organizations manifest the willingness to pursue the policy reform, externally initiated change efforts whether at the local, national, or international levels are likely to fail (Chambers, 1997; Mudacumura, 2001). Indigenous leadership, composed of dedicated policy champions, is a prerequisite for sustainable policy implementation. In fact, Crosby (1996) considers policy legitimation, constituency building, resource accumulation, organization design and modification, mobilization of resources and actions, and monitoring of the impact as critical tasks in policy implementation. Constituency building creates and mobilizes positive stakeholders in favor of the new policy; once constituency members have a stake in the change, they will be more likely to mobilize to defend their interests in the change. The proposed policy must have the support of key stakeholders to assure that the change can take place (Crosby, 1996).

Strategizing the Implementation

Kiggundu (1996) contends that the management of organizations in developing countries is characterized by reactive response to crises and firefighting behavior. This reactive stance can be reduced if managers and policy makers incorporate the concepts and techniques of strategic management into their implementation toolkits. Unfortunately, the actual practice of strategic management is very limited among public sector and NGOs often used as implementing agencies for development projects (Crosby, 1991; Land, 1995).

From a conceptual standpoint, strategic management consists of a set of leadership and managerial tasks that create the organization's charter or mission to give it the image of its unique wholeness, legitimizing that image; formulating strategies for effective achievement of the mission; communicating the organization's mission, management philosophy, and values; and managing the external environment to take advantage of emerging opportunities and to defend the organization against potential threats while providing leadership to other members of the organization (Kiggundu, 1989).

Thus, strategic management's systemic and integrated perspective could provide a framework to help development organizations to move beyond internal problems and pay more attention to external relationships and interdependencies, specifically considering stakeholders' concerns and the external environment's features. Focusing on the latter emphasizes the fact that sustainable organizational performance results from an ongoing process of adjustment to external factors and stakeholders over time (Crosby, 1992). It is commonly argued that managers in developing countries often shy away from the challenges of strategic management because of the complexities and uncertainties characterizing the environment in which they work, and because conventional strategic planning tools such as forecasting are often inadequate in reducing uncertainty and complexity to manageable levels. Austin and Kohn (1990) attribute this uncertainty to the overall quality of governance in these countries, and the dominant and often inconsistent role of government.

Implementing sustainable development policies is, however, a complex undertaking involving broad partnerships of organizations. Capacity to deal with that complexity can be enhanced by applying the tools and techniques of strategic management that incorporates an integrated managerial approach blending an outward-looking focus, forward-thinking leadership, stakeholder orientation, network building, and participatory decision making (Kiggundu, 1996; Mudacumura, 2001, 2004a).

Moreover, effective policy change often requires difficult changes in stakeholder coalitions, shifts in the structures and rules of implementing agencies, and new patterns of interactions. Interorganizational cooperation can generate information, mobilize resources, and produce solutions to problems that are intractable to the parties working alone (Wood and Gray, 1991). Adapting an interorganizational relations approach may make a difference in the implementation of sustainable development policies. In fact, Mandell (1988) suggested focusing the implementation research on the understanding of the relationships among intergovernmental actors with a concern for the problem of managing these relationships, and de Haven-Smith and Van Horn (1984) viewed the major thrust of an implementation framework constructed with interorganizational concepts as to explain conflict and its attendant consequences.

Such a framework would make sense when policy coordination is the central concern of implementation analysis. In fact, Hanf and Scharpf (1978) noted that policy implementation is influenced by a very complex web of relationships among the various actors of the different levels of government, and Dillion and Quinn (1980) emphasized the imperative call for coordinating the numerous policy stakeholders.

Interorganizational Relations

The view of implementation as an interorganizational concern is defined as macroimplementation that emphasizes the influence and power exercised by implementation actors in the policy environment. Espousing the concepts of intra- and interorganization suggests that no single theory of organizational model is likely fully to capture the complexity of development policy implementation. Development policy scholars are turning to an interorganizational framework, focusing on the fact that both the formulation and implementation of development policy increasingly involve different governmental levels and agencies, as well as interactions between public authorities and private organizations (Hanf and Scharpf, 1978; Mudacumura, 2001, 2002).

In light of the complexity of development policies, the increasing call for coordination underscores the imperative need for diverse development organizations to join the effort while implementing sustainable development policies. As Hanf and Scharpf (1978) remarked, efforts to deal with problems of coordination and integration in pluralistic decision systems will not be successful unless the cooperative undertakings through which coordination is sought are firmly rooted in the agreement and consent of those to be coordinated. This will occur only if the interorganizational framework focuses on comparative and relational properties of an interaction network (Mudacumura, 2001). The network, in this context, consists of organizational units that are interdependent in the sense that the ability of individual units to achieve their own objectives will depend not only on their own choices but also on those of others (Chisholm, 1998).

Several scholars agree about the difficulty of assessing the organizational interdependency. For instance, Pfeffer and Salancik (quoted in Menzel, 1987) maintain that interdependence is the reason why nothing

turns out exactly the way one wants it to, and looking at the interorganization perspective, Menzel (1987) contends that implementation outcomes are often unpredictable and largely the result of give and take
among organizations pursuing independent goals. This idea fits with
Berman's (1978) view that preordained outcomes are neither automatic
nor assured, and implementation is more like a disorderly learning process
than a predictable procedure. Similarly, Bardach (1977) argues that policy
implementation is much like an assembly process: putting together pieces
from different sources, with perhaps rather different objectives than those
originally intended, and then reshaping those pieces into a mechanism
capable of eventually producing the required results.

Currently, there is little agreement among policy scholars on a theory
of interorganizational implementation (Goggin et al., 1990; O'Toole, 1995),
and the research conducted has been heavily inductive (Mazmanian and
Sabatier, 1983). The cases of deductive approaches have focused on single
organizations or those characterized by a top-down compliance orientation
(Chubb quoted in O'Toole, 1995).

Focusing on innovations, O'Toole (1997) highlights converting good
ideas into steady, reliable streams of public action as what has been largely
missing in the complex issue of policy implementation. Considering innovative programs as patterns of activities to achieve a new goal or improve
on the pursuit of an established one, successful innovation requires
thinking through and solving puzzles regarding implementation. Because
much implementation develops in and through networks of interdependent actors, empirical scholarship has demonstrated that substantial challenges await those seeking to manage the effort and that significant
implementation performance gaps can be found (O'Toole, 1997).

Furthermore, in light of the implementation patterns that are composed
of many clusters of organizations or parts of organizations, assuming that
formal authority drives all the participation or that all the actors are
voluntarily motivated is not realistic (Hjern and Porter, 1981). Ultimately,
this requires development organization managers to broaden their horizon
and maintain close contacts with each other in the larger environment.
Rather than dealing with the activities of any single organization or
individual, managers must deal with the patterns of interactions within an
entire set of organizations (Chisholm, 1998; Knoke and Kuklunski, 1982;
Mudacumura, 2001). The challenging task is for development managers
to maximize the chances of reaching the goals of both the individual
organization and the network as a whole.

This latter view is consistent with institution building and strengthening
of civil society, the dominant themes advocated by most international
development agencies. According to Brown (1991), the development
process involves building social institutions, in the sense of structures,

customs, rules, and values, that enable all the people of a society to improve their quality of life in ways that are sustainable and just. Studies of grassroots development activity reveal strong relationships between the presence of local organizations and economic and social improvements (Esman, 1978; Morss et al., 1976). Creating and adapting institutions to fit evolving social demands are the greatest challenges in most of the less developed countries. Gray (1989) observed that linkages among diverse institutions allow organizations to deal with interdependence and turbulence associated with social and technical change.

Similarly, Levine and White's (1961) empirical study of interorganizational relationships pointed out three related factors that determine the interdependence of organizations: (1) the accessibility of each organization to necessary elements from outside the system, (2) the objectives of the organization and particular functions to which it allocates the elements it controls, and (3) the degree to which consensus exists among the various organizations. The underlying assumptions of the study were that all the essential elements needed by organizations are limited. Otherwise, if they were in infinite supply, there would be, in theory, little need for organizational interaction and for subscription to cooperation as an ideal. Consequently, under the conditions of scarcity, interorganizational exchanges are essential to implement effectively sustainable development policies, particularly when one takes into account the complexities surrounding development issues.

Facing a future of increasing complexity, Trist (1983) suggested trying self-regulation within interdependence and coined the concept of *interorganizational domains*, which are concerned with field-related organizational populations. He argued that an organizational population becomes field related when it engages with a set of problems, or societal problem area, that constitutes a domain of common concern for its members. Thus, interdependence in contemporary environment renders traditional policy implementation models dysfunctional. Complex societal problems require interorganizational collaboration to deal with them effectively.

Patterns of hierarchical and authoritarian decision making, typical in the administrative systems of most developing countries, are associated with institutional arrangements that encourage defection, distrust, exploitation, disorder, and stagnation (Brown, 1994). These patterns foster a competitive environment, which is not conducive to collaborative efforts in development policy implementation. A variety of new institutional arrangements for cooperative problem solving among development organizations have been created during the last two decades to work on problems of community development (Chisholm, 1997; Weisebord, 1992).

For instance, Putnam's (1992) work in a democratic society revealed patterns of decision making characterized by high levels of cooperation, trust, reciprocity, civic engagement, and collective well-being. Instead of competing, citizens cooperate and make collegial decisions with each other. Collegial decision making fosters strong civil societies, the latter a prerequisite for strong governments (Bratton, 1989; Esman and Uphoff, 1984; Putnam, 1992). Failure to build democratic and pluralistic systems in which citizens do not feel compelled to cooperate not only compromises the likelihood of implementing sustainable development policies but also could jeopardize the potential for poor countries to increase their stock of social capital. The latter includes informal associations, institutions that support cooperative action, and norms of tolerance and trust.

The Italian experience suggests that social capital is rooted in hundreds of years of civic association and organization (Putman, 1992). The analysis of developing countries' experience with alliances proved that organizations work together even if they have long histories of conflict and power struggles. As opposed to hundreds of years of civic association and organization in Europe, Brown (1994) noted that African alliances have developed the institutional arrangements and attitudes associated with higher levels of social capital in relatively short period of time. Did these African alliances result from a straight application of Western interorganizational relations theories? What are the key determinants of such alliances?

Oliver (1990) identified six critical contingencies of relationship formation recognized as generalizable determinants of interorganizational relationships across organizations, settings, and linkages: necessity, asymmetry, reciprocity, efficiency, stability, and legitimacy. The theory and research that have addressed the tentative predictions of interorganizational relationships assumed that organizations consciously enter into relations for specific reasons within the constraints of a variety of conditions that limit or influence their choices.

Furthermore, Oliver (1990) argues that mandates from higher authorities may provide the impetus for interorganizational relations that otherwise might not have occurred voluntarily. Do these relationships last longer? Are they conducive to cooperation among organizations mandated to link? Research on developing countries' alliances is still in the initial stage and has not fully explored these questions. Although preliminary findings reveal some variant of interorganizational relations, such as interagency cooperation or coordination as a potential strategy for improving institutional performance (Honadle and Cooper, 1989; Rondinelli, 1983), it was observed that interorganizational relations can have high costs in staff time spent in meetings and dealing with paperwork (Chambers, 1983). He concluded that with maximal coordination, staff time would be completely taken up in meetings and arrangements and the output would be nil.

Bearing in mind that bureaucratic and interagency rivalry is commonplace in developing countries, the cost of maintaining interorganizational linkages can also be seen in terms of the power individual agencies give up in the process. The resource dependence model of interorganizational relations postulates that organizations will be powerful relative to others to the extent that they control resources needed by others and can reduce their dependence on others (Provan et al., 1980). On the other hand, some evidence suggests that the effect of interorganizational relations on organizational effectiveness is positive (Njoh, 1997). Similarly, Warren (1967) conceptualized the interorganizational relations in terms of cooperation and coordination through resource exchange and provided evidence demonstrating that such relations are positively related to organizational effectiveness. Molnar and Rogers (1982) restricted the concept of organizational environment to organizations with which a given agency must interact in order to fulfill its goals and found evidence similar to Warren's.

Using different concepts and reaching the same conclusion is an indication of the inconclusiveness surrounding the relationships between interorganizational relations and organizational effectiveness. Looking at the policy implementation in light of these opposing views, Njoh's (1997) empirical study in a Sub-Saharan African country provides strong evidence that development organizations that interact frequently with others in the same policy domain are likely to be more effective than those that either interact infrequently or do not interact at all. This finding may motivate development administrators to emphasize the interorganizational relations among development organizations, which closely work with different policy actors in the implementation of sustainable development policies.

The policy actors range from international development agencies supplying the necessary financial and technical resources to rural grassroots organizations composed of dedicated peasants eager to participate actively in the formulation and implementation of the policies geared at improving their socioeconomic well-being. But to what extent do current policy implementation models best suit the needs of the resource-supplying agencies and policy recipients? Do these models foster an ongoing learning process that allows development policy stakeholders to deal effectively with the implementation problems encountered? These questions deserve particular attention and are discussed next.

Policy Implementation Models

Williams (1971) defined *policy implementation* as an inquiry seeking to determine whether an organization can join men and material in a cohesive organizational unit and motivate them in such a way as to carry out the organization's stated objectives. Crosby (1996) and other policy implementation scholars view implementation as not necessarily a coherent, continuous process; instead, it is frequently fragmented and interrupted. With the evolution of the implementation research, two major schools of thought developed: top-down and bottom-up. A quick review of the implementation literature highlights the extent to which the proponents of the two schools of thought embraced divergent orientations in their analysis of policy implementation; contradictory conceptual definitions and implementation recommendations resulted. To produce knowledge that leads to a body of generalizable principles, Matland (1995) recommends converging the two perspectives, tying the macrolevel variables of the top-down models to the microlevel variables of bottom-up models.

Considering the implementation research from the global perspective with the intent of building a universal body of knowledge, policy scholars across the nations may achieve more by learning from each other and adapting or adjusting the conceptual frameworks to their specific research environments. Although Berman (1978) views the emerging field of implementation analysis as lacking a conceptual framework for conducting generalizable research on what goes wrong with social policy and, more importantly, on how to improve policy performance, Menzel (1987) sees the implementation research as robust with ideas intended to explain why policies fail or succeed. Unfortunately, neither a dominant person nor a single theoretical framework has emerged so far (Williams, 1980), and cumulative research is as scarce in implementation analysis as it is in other disciplines of social sciences (Hjern, 1982). The following section outlines some of the implementation models discussed in the literature.

Blueprint Model

The blueprint model consists of following a set of prescribed steps beginning with problem specification and concluding with postproject evaluation. The major characteristic of this model is the designed-in-advance solution to the identified problem. The devised plan typically specifies objectives, target to be reached, outputs to be produced, a predetermined time frame, the level of resources required, and an implementation timetable that constitute a blueprint subject to minimal changes. For instance, the majority of international development agencies could be criticized for presenting "ready-made" solutions that are not adapted to individual country circumstances. Concretely, critics argue that the World Bank is reluctant to consider alternatives to the models and solutions that it outlines in policy advice and documentation (World Bank, 2003). Giving priority to structure and control and minimizing adjustments during implementation do not necessarily lead to desired outputs. One may wonder why the proponents of this model assume that the suggested solution would not be susceptible to major adjustments during the implementation phase and that policy beneficiaries may not call for radical policy changes.

Developing countries' policy makers and resource-supplying agencies should realize that failure to produce outputs as planned frequently begins a vicious cycle of tighter controls, followed by more pressure for results and greater degrees of failure (Leonard, 1987). Furthermore, the designed-in-advance solution may be irrelevant by the time of implementation. Let us illustrate this point with the following scenario.

$$T(-1) \rightarrow T(0) \rightarrow T(1) \rightarrow T(2) \rightarrow T(3)$$

For illustration purposes, $T(-1)$ represents the starting point in time when people experience a specific problem. At $T(0)$, the problem is identified and called to the attention of policy makers. A policy is formulated at $T(1)$, implemented at $T(2)$, and ideally evaluated at $T(3)$. In both developed and developing countries, several months or years may elapse between problem identification and policy implementation. Considering the lag between problem identification and policy implementation, it would be less ingenious to assume that the design-in-advance solution at $T(1)$ is still appropriate to solve the original problem that existed before $T(-1)$. Furthermore, recalling the dynamic nature and the complexity of societal problems, the design-in-advance solution may most likely be irrelevant by the time of the policy implementation. This critical issue is often overlooked in the discourse of sustainable development policy implementation.

There is a need to build a feedback mechanism that can inform policy makers and policy implementers whether the suggested policy and the implementation approaches effectively take care of the identified problem. Such a feedback mechanism may lead to a clear understanding of the policy process, thus allowing researchers to devise sound and pragmatic implementation models.

Process Model

Contrary to the blueprint model, the process model starts with the assumption that not enough is known in the preimplementation stage. The cornerstone of this model is its flexibility to merge design and implementation throughout the life of the project, allowing modification and adaptation as knowledge about the specific environment is acquired. Each design iteration represents an experimental solution, to be tested and then redesigned on the basis of accumulated learning in the face of the uncertainty and complexity that characterize sustained socioeconomic development (Brinkerhoff, 1996).

The process model falls in line with the organization development (OD) approach, which, instead of identifying ideal solutions a priori, assists policy implementers in iteratively developing second or third best solutions that all major policy actors can agree on over the life of the reform. Concretely, the OD emphasizes a collective problem-solving approach, which builds strategic planning and management capacity along with technical skills, key aspects of human resource development that contribute to sustainable human development (White, 1990). Conceived to develop new and creative organizational solutions and the organization's self-renewing capacity, the OD process underscores the need for community members to work collaboratively with policy implementers, thus bringing about the desired societal changes.

Top-Down Model

The proponents of the top-down model see implementation as concern with the degree to which the actions of policy implementers and target groups coincide with the goals specified in the policy decision (Mazmanian and Sabatier, 1983). Defining implementation as the carrying out of the policy decision usually embodied in a statute, top-downers consider centrally located actors as most relevant to producing the desired effects (Matland, 1995). The question, however, becomes how these actors achieve the expected outcomes from unclear and ambiguous policy. Another critical remark relates to the policy beneficiaries, whose role in the policy implementation is rarely acknowledged. Could focusing primarily on those aspects of the policy implementation process controllable by centrally located actors who adopt policies or mandates yield successful implementation results?

In their quest to develop generalizable policy advice, top-downers who tend to study relatively clear policies have concentrated their efforts in identifying the variables that can be manipulated at the central level (Matland, 1995). Developing a comprehensive set of recognizable patterns in behavior across different policy areas is not only a challenging task, but also a less likely endeavor when one recalls the timeliness and specificity of development problems. Overlooking this requirement and intentionally paying less attention to politicoadministrative realities of the policy process may make any further solutions or advice less relevant.

Despite the top-downers' recommendations to make policy goals clear and consistent, to limit the extent of change necessary, and to place implementation responsibility in an agency sympathetic with the policy's goal (Mazmanian and Sabatier, 1983), changing the policy makers' ingrained behavior of being ambiguous while enacting policies is beyond policy researchers' control. In fact, Matland (1995) remarked that attempting to insulate inherently political subject matter from politics could lead to policy failure. Top-downers are also criticized for failing to consider the views of the target population and the service deliverers, whose knowledge and expertise of the true problems is indisputable (Chambers, 1997; Stiglitz, 1998).

Bottom-Up Model

Contrary to top-downers, who place more emphasis on the centrally located actors, bottom-uppers argue that a more realistic understanding of implementation can be gained by looking at a policy from the view of the target population and the service deliverers (Berman, 1978; Hjern and Porter, 1981). Specifically, centrally located actors devise a government program at the macroimplementation level while local organizations (microimplementation level) react to the macrolevel plans, develop their own programs, and implement them (Berman, 1978). Considering that contextual factors within the implementing environment often dominate the rules embodied in the policy decision, local level implementers must customize the policy to local conditions to minimize the risks of failures.

Similarly, it is worth recalling that the people directly affected by development problems should be the key stakeholders in policy implementation processes. Focusing on local actors, Hjern (1982) mapped a network that identifies the relevant implementation structure for a specific policy at the local, regional, and national levels. Among other findings, he noted that program success depends in large part on the skills of individuals in the local implementation structure who can adopt policy to local conditions.

Backward and Forward Mapping

Recognizing the urgent need to reconcile the merits of the top-down and bottom-up frameworks, Elmore (1982) devised the backward and forward mapping approach. Forward mapping consists of stating precise policy objectives, elaborating detailed means–ends schemes, and specifying explicit outcome criteria by which to judge policy at each stage; backward mapping consists of stating precisely the behavior to be changed at the lowest level, describing a set of operations that can ensure the change, and repeating the procedure upward by steps until the central level is reached (Elmore, 1982).

Conceived to provide policy designers with possibilities to choose policy instruments on the basis of the incentive structure of target groups, Matland (1995) sees the main advantage of the backward and forward mapping approach as allowing policy designers to incorporate microimplementers' and target groups' views in planning any implementation strategy. Symbolic implementation characterized by high policy ambiguity and conflict offers the opportunity to restructure the way resolutions are developed, with the high level of ambiguity allowing the outcomes results to vary across sites. In this particular stance, the local coalitional strength determines the outcomes, and the policy course is determined by the coalition of actors at the local level who control the available resources (Matland, 1995).

Successful implementation of any policy requires implementers to seek support beyond their own organizations. The advocates of the models discussed—top-down, bottom-up, backward and forward mapping—do not approach implementation from the multiactor implementation perspective. They basically follow the linear type of reasoning, overlooking the impacts that other organizations in the surrounding environment might have on the process and the outcomes. O'Toole (1997) reiterates the relevance of focusing on analytical and practical questions regarding policy implementation in multiorganizational settings that consist of dense policy spaces; complicated, often cross-cutting public problems; and political systems in which power and often authority are shared among several units.

Dealing effectively with development policy implementation challenges requires multidisciplinary researchers to gear their thinking toward a grounded development policy implementation approach that bridges the positivist and postpositivist theoretical tenets. While the positivists' advocacy of pursuing a clearly defined objective implied little contribution from the recipient, underestimating the citizens' points of view is the root cause of the poor implementation of development policies.

It is worth recalling that early development economists reinforced the separation between expert and client by predicating their policy recommendations on objective economic relationships pursued by rational actors, requiring little knowledge of the policy beneficiaries and the political climate in which public policy makers operate. Banfield (1980) referred to this economic policy analysis as a form of "metaphysical madness" predicated on the dangerous delusion that the policy scientist can supplant the politician. This metaphysical madness is grounded in pseudosophisticated methods that treat what are fundamentally political problems as technical puzzles. To bridge the gulf between policy experts and policy beneficiaries, recent research has focused on the participatory approach, discussed next.

Participatory Approach

Given the fact that none can claim to understand with certainty the intricacies of development policy implementation processes, reducing the distance between policy experts and citizens may allow development scholars to be understood as concerned members of the broader community (Mudacumura, 2001). Dryzek (1989) further charges that most policy knowledge in any number of fields is in the exclusive hands of experts, superseding and, hence, undermining the democratic ethos.

Emerging experiences are beginning to suggest that participatory research may hold the key to solving specific categories of societal problems. It should be emphasized that social scientists have attempted to advance a collaborative inquiry as a response to the crisis of professions and its practical manifestations (Fisher, 1993). Such collaborative inquiry, rather than providing technical answers designed to resolve or close off political discussion, has the task of empowering citizens, allowing them to examine their own interests and to make their own decision (Hirschhorn, 1979).

Empowerment is here conceived as a process by which individuals gain mastery or control over their own lives and democratic participation in the life of their community (Zimmerman and Rappaport, 1988). The President's Council on Sustainable Development (PCSD, 1997) claimed that true participation means giving people the opportunity to take part in the initial phases of planning, not just the ratifying decisions that have been made, or commenting on plans that have been drafted; Zimmerman and Rappaport's research highlights that the individual experience of empowerment includes a combination of self-acceptance and self-confidence, social and political understanding, and ability to play an assertive role in controlling resources and decisions in one's community.

Increasing citizens' participation in the articulation, formulation, and implementation of sustainable development policies is most likely to improve their self-esteem and confidence (Mudacumura, 2002). Citizen expertise is not the key requirement for making constructive suggestions, but people's willingness to express their perceptions in an open public policy forum organized by government analysts is the main prerequisite of effective policy implementation.

Conclusion

This chapter provided a brief overview of development issues with particular emphasis on policy implementation challenges while emphasizing the shortfalls of the early economic development models, which failed to put people at the center of the development process. The debate surrounding the effective implementation of development policy is far from being resolved. But a growing number of implementation studies suggest that interorganizational interactions could improve the likelihood of achieving effective policy implementation.

Moreover, the chapter looked at various theoretical implementation frameworks, highlighting the shortfalls of each model and underscoring the active participation of policy beneficiaries in the implementation of development policies as the determinant factor leading to sustainable communities in which people work together to produce a high quality of life. These communities flourish because they build a mutually supportive, dynamic balance among social well-being, economic opportunity, and environmental quality (PCSD, 1997).

From a research standpoint, development policy scholars and practitioners dealing with complex development problems should take seriously the epistemological implications of a participatory research approach, which taps into the wealth of knowledge of those affected by development problems. Applying such an approach may minimize the constraints that can impede the effective implementation of sustainable development policies.

References

Austin, J.E., and Kohn, T.O. (1990). *Strategic Management in Developing Countries: Cases Studies.* New York: The Free Press.

Banfield, Edward C. (1980). Policy Science as Metaphysical Madness. In R. Goldwin, ed., *Bureaucrats, Policy Analysts, Statesmen: Who Leads?* Washington, D.C.: American Enterprise Institute.

Bardach, Eugene. (1977). *Implementation Game.* Cambridge, Mass.: MIT Press.

Bava, N. (2004). Development as Multi-Dimensional Concern. In: G. Mudacumura and S. Haque, eds., *Handbook of Development Policy Studies.* New York: Marcel Dekker.

Berman, Paul. (1978). The Study of Macro- and Micro-Implementation. *Public Policy* 26(2): 157–84.

Boeninger, Adgardo. (1992). Economic Policy Change and Government Processes. In G. Lamb and R. Weaving, ed., *Managing Policy Reform of the World Bank: Asian Experiences.* Washington, D.C.: Economic Development Series, The World Bank.

Bratton, M. (1989). Beyond the State: Civil Society and Association Life in Africa. *World Politics* 41(3): 407–30.

Brinkerhoff, Derick W. (1996). Process Perspectives on Policy Change: Highlighting Implementation. *World Development* 24(9): 1395–1401.

Brown, David L. (1991). Bridging Organizations and Sustainable Development. *Human Relations* 44(8): 807–31.

Brown, David L. (1994). *Creating Social Capital: Nongovernmental Development Organization and Intersectoral Problem Solving*. Boston: Institute of Development Research.

Brown, David L., and Covey, Jane G. (1987). *Development Organizations and Organization Development: Toward an Expanded Paradigm for Organization Development*. Boston: Institute for Development Research.

Cernea, Michael M. (1993). The Sociologist's Approach to Sustainable Development. *Finance & Development* 33(4): 11–13.

Chambers, Robert. (1983). *Rural Development: Putting the Last First*. New York: Wiley.

Chambers, Robert. (1997). *Whose Reality Counts? Putting the First Last*. Bath, England: The Bath Press.

Chisholm, Rupert F. (1997). Building a Network to Foster Economic Development. *International Journal of Public Administration* 20(2): 451–477.

Chisholm, Rupert F. (1998). *Developing Network Organizations: Learning from Practice and Theory*. Reading, Mass.: Addison-Wesley.

Crosby, Benjamin L. (1996). Policy Implementation: The Organizational Challenge. *World Development* 24(9): 1403–15.

Crosby, B.L. (1991). Strategic Planning and Management: What Are They and How Are They Different? Technical Note No. 1, Implementing Policy Change Project. Washington, D.C.: USAID.

Crosby, B.L. (1992). Management and the Environment for Implementation of Policy Change, Parts 1 and 2. Technical Notes 4 and 5, Implementing Policy Change Project. Washington, D.C.: USAID.

Daly, H.E. (1996). *Beyond Growth, the Economics of Sustainable Development*. Boston: Beacon Press.

de Haven-Smith, Lance, and Van Horn, Carl E. (1984). Subgovernment Conflict in Public Policy. *Policy Studies Journal* 12: 627–42.

Dillion, Robert J., and Quinn, Robert E. (1980). Interorganizational Systems. *Public Productivity Review* 4: 63–83.

Douthwaite, Richard. (1993). *The Growth Illusion: How Economic Growth Has Enriched the Few, Impoverished the Many, and Endangered the Planet*. Tulsa, Okla.: Council Oak Books.

Drabek, A.G. (1987). Development Alternatives: The Challenge for NGOs. *World Development* 15 (Supplement): 9–15.

Dryzek, John S. (1989). Policy Science of Democracy. *Polity* 22: 97–118.

Dwivedi, O.P. (1994). *Development Administration: From Underdevelopment to Sustainable Development*. New York: St. Martin's Press.

Elmore, Richard F. (1982). Backward Mapping: Implementation Research and Policy Decisions. In Walter L. Williams, ed., *Studying Implementation: Methodological and Administrative Issues*. Chatham, N.J.: Chathman House.

Esman, M.J. (1978). Development Administration and Constituency Organization. *Public Administration Review* 38(2): 166–72.

Esman, M.J., and Uphoff, N.T. (1984). *Local Organizations: Intermediaries in Rural Development*. Ithaca, N.Y.: Cornell University Press.

Fischer, Frank. (1993). Citizen Participation and the Democratization of Policy Expertise: From Theoretical Inquiry to Practical Cases. *Policy Sciences* 26: 165–87.

Gittell, Ross. (1990). Managing the Development Process: Community Strategies in Economic Revitalization. *Journal of Policy Analysis & Management* 9(4): 507–31.

Goggin, Bowman, Lester, and O'Toole. (1990). *Policy Implementation: Toward a Third Generation.* Glenview. Ill.: Scott Foresman/Little Brown.

Gray, B. (1989). *Collaborating: Finding Common Ground for Multiparty Problems.* San Francisco: Jossey-Bass.

Hanf, Kenneth, and Scharpf, Fritz W. (1978). *Interorganizational Policy Making: Limits to Coordination and Central Control.* Beverly Hills, Calif.: Sage.

Hirschhorn, Larry. (1979). Alternative Service and the Crisis of the Professions. In John Case and Rosemary C.R. Taylor, eds., *Co-ops, Communes and Collectivities: Experiments in Social Change in the 1960s and 1970s.* New York: Pantheon, pp. 153–93.

Hjern, Benny. (1982). Implementation Research—the Link Gone Missing. *Journal of Public Policy* 2(3): 301–8.

Hjern, B., and Porter, D.O. (1981). Implementation Structures: A New Unit for Administrative Analysis. *Organization Studies* 2: 211–37.

Honadle, George, and Cooper, Lauren. (1989). Beyond Coordination and Control: An Interorganizational Approach to Structural Adjustment, Service Delivery and Natural Resources Management. *World Development* 17: 1531–41.

Jacob, Merle. (1994). Toward a Methodological Critique of Sustainable Development. *The Journal of Developing Areas* 28(2): 237–52.

Kiggundu, Moses N. (1989). *Managing Organizations in Developing Countries: An Operational and Strategic Approach.* West Hartford, Conn.: Kumarian Press.

Kiggundu, Moses N. (1996). Integrating Strategic Management Tasks into Implementing Agencies: From Firefighting to Prevention. *World Development* 24(9): 1417–30.

Knoke, Davis, and Kuklunski, James H. (1982). *Network Analysis.* Sage University paper Series on Quantitative Applications in the Social Sciences. Beverly Hills, Calif.: Sage.

Land, A. (1995). Management Audit and Self-Assessment in the Public Sector: Lessons from Capacity Development Exercise in Zambia. ECDPM Working Paper 95-3. Maastricht: European Center for Development Policy Management.

Leonard, D.K. (1987). The Political Realities of African Management. *World Development* 15: 899–910.

Levine, Sol, and White, Paul E. (1961). Exchange as a Conceptual Framework for the Study of Interorganizational Relationships. *Administrative Science Quarterly* 5: 583–601.

Mandell, Myrna P. (1988). Intergovernmental Management in Inter-Organizational Networks: A Revised Perspective. *International Journal of Public Administration* 11(4): 393–416.

Matland, Richard E. (1995). Synthesizing the Implementation Literature: The Ambiguity-Conflict Model of Policy Implementation. *Journal of Public Administration Research and Theory* 5(2): 145–74.

Mazmanian, Daniel A., and Sabatier, Paul A. (1983). *Implementation and Public Policy.* Glenview, Ill.: Scott/Foresman.

Menzel, Donald C. (1987). An Inter-Organizational Approach to Policy Implementation. *Public Administration Quarterly* 11(1), 3–16.

Molnar, Joseph J., and Rogers, David L. (1982). Inter-Organizational Relations among Development Organizations: Empirical Assessment and Implication for Inter-organizational Coordination. Unpublished paper, Center for Agricultural and Rural Development, Iowa State University of Science and Technology, Ames, Iowa.

Morss, E.R., Hatch, J.K., Mickelwait, D.R., and Sweet, C.F. (1976). *Strategies for Small Farmers Development*, Vols. 1 and 2. Boulder, Colo.: Westview.

Mudacumura, Gedeon M. (2001). Networking Development Organizations to Foster Global Sustainable Development. *International Journal of Economic Development*—On-line Journal Vol. 3(1). Retrieved from http://www.spaef.com/IJED_PUB/v3n1.html

Mudacumura, G.M. (2002). Towards a General Theory of Sustainability: Bridging Key Development Dimensions through a Multi-Paradigm Perspective. Ph.D. diss., Pennsylvania State University, Harrisburg.

Mudacumura, Gedeon M. (2004a). Participatory Development Policy Design: Integrating Instrumental and Democratic Rationality. In G. Mudacumura and S. Haque, eds., *Handbook of Development Policy Studies*. New York: Marcel Dekker.

Mudacumura, Gedeon M. (2004b). Role of Non-Governmental Organizations in Rural Development. In G. Mudacumura and S. Haque, eds., *Handbook of Development Policy Studies*. New York: Marcel Dekker.

Nel, Heather. (2004). The Impact of Globalization on the Development Role of Local Government in South Africa. In G. Mudacumura and S. Haque, eds., *Handbook of Development Policy Studies.* New York: Marcel Dekker.

Nindi, B.C. (1993). Dilemmas of Development in Rural Institutions in Sub-Saharan Africa. *Journal of Eastern African Research & Development* 23: 140–50.

Njoh, Ambe J. (1997). *Inter-Organizational Relations and Effectiveness in Planning and Administration in Developing Countries: Toward a Strategy for Improving the Performance of Development Policy Organizations.* London: Edwin Mellon.

Oliver, Christine. (1990). Determinants of Inter-Organizational Relationships: Integration and Future Directions. *Academy of Management Review* 15(2): 241–65.

O'Toole, Laurence. (1995). Rational Choice and Policy Implementation: Implications for Inter-organizational Network Management. *American Review of Public Administration* 25(1): 43–57.

O'Toole, Laurence J., Jr. (1997). Implementing Public Innovations in Network Settings. *Administration & Society* 29(2): 115–38.

Owens, Edgar. (1987). *The Future of Freedom in the Developing World: Economic Development as Political Reform.* New York: Pergamon Press.

Paul, S., and Israel, A. (1991). *Nongovernmental Organizations and the World Bank.* Washington, D.C.: The World Bank

President's Council on Sustainable Development. (1997). Sustainable Communities Task Force Report. Washington, D.C.

Provan, Keith G., Janice M., and Kruytbosch, Carlos. (1980). Environmental Linkages between Organizations. *Administrative Science Quarterly* 25: 200–25.

Putnam, R.D. (1992). *Making Democracy Work: Civic Traditions in Modern Italy.* Princeton, N.J.: Princeton University Press.

Rondinelli, Dennis. (1983). *Development Projects as Policy Experiments: An Adaptive Approach to Development Administration.* London: Methuen.

Schumacher, E.F. (1977). *Small Is Beautiful: Economics As If People Mattered.* New York: Harper Perennial.

Sholes, Rebecca, and Covey, Jane. (1996). *Partners for Development: USAID and PVO/NGO Relationships.* Boston: Institute for Development Research.

Soedjatmoko. (1985). *The Primacy of Freedom in Development.* Lanham. Md.: University Press of America.

Stiglitz, Joseph. (1998). *Towards a New Paradigm for Development: Strategies, Policies, and Processes.* Geneva: UNCTAD.

Todaro, Michael P. (1996). *Economic Development.* New York: Addison-Wesley.

Trist, Eric. (1983). Referent Organizations and the Development of Inter-Organizational Domains. *Human Relations* 46(7): 777–802.

UNDP. (1990). *Human Development Report.* New York: Oxford University Press.

UNDP. (1994). *Human Development Report.* New York: Oxford University Press.

UNDP. (1997). Reconceptualizing Governance. Discussion Paper. New York: Division of Public Affairs, United Nations.

Warren, Rolland L. (1967). The Inter-organizational Field as a Focus for Investigation. *Administrative Science Quarterly* 12: 396–419.

Weisebord, M. (1992). *Discovering Common Ground.* San Francisco: Berrett-Koehler.

White, Louise G. (1990). *Implementing Policy Reform in LDCs: A Strategy for Designing and Effecting Change.* Boulder, Colo.: Lynne Rienner.

Williams, W. (1971). *Social Policy Research and Analysis: The Experience in the Federal Social Agencies.* New York: American Elsevier.

Williams, Walter. (1980). *The Implementation Perspective.* Berkeley: University of California Press.

Wood, D.J., and Gray, B. (1991). Toward a Comprehensive Theory of Collaboration. *Journal of Applied Behavioral Science* 27(2): 139–62.

World Bank. (2003). *Sharing Knowledge Innovations and Remaining Challenges.* Report of the Operations Evaluation Department (OED). Washington, D.C.: World Bank.

Zimmerman, Marc A., and Rappaport, Julian. (1988). Citizen Participation, Perceived Control, and Psychological Empowerment. *American Journal of Community Psychology* 16(5): 725–50.

Chapter 20

The Political Economy of Sustainable Development: The Governance Perspective

Anthony Barclay

CONTENTS

Introduction

In a little over a decade, sustainable development has increasingly stimulated interest among development practitioners, scholars, and politicians. The concept has been referred to as a development paradigm, an anthropocentric moral imperative, and a vision. Several others see it merely as "buzzwords" and a "utopian" concept that is inherently limited in its applicability to poverty-stricken countries. Along with these perceptions there is a plethora of varied definitions and interpretations. Notwithstanding, there appears to be a common theme among them that relates to a concern for improving people's present and future quality of life. In this chapter, the quality of life is referred to as *human development*, which is defined as the ability for people to lead a long and healthy life, to acquire knowledge and skills and the opportunity to utilize them, as well as to have access to productive resources needed for a decent standard of living (UNDP, 1996). Implicitly, it involves the production, distribution, and utility of goods, services, and social capital with a value system embedded in the entire process.

The focus on sustainable development began to emerge when intellectual momentum shifted from the perception that development was simply an economic process measurable in economic aggregates such as gross domestic product and gross national product. This shift engendered a new view of development as a holistic process comprising socioeconomic, financial, and ecological policies; effective governance and an enabling sociopolitical environment having the requisite human and institutional capacity to perform appropriate tasks effectively and efficiently with a view to improving the quality of life. Development, so defined, should be people centered, equitably distributed, and environmentally and socially sustainable (UNDP).

In most less developed countries, the pursuit of human development has been and remains exceedingly challenging because of the complexity of the issues, the peculiarities of contexts, and the enormity of the constraints. Considering the situation in these countries, and if sustainable development is to have any substantive operational significance, it must be defined more concretely to reflect contextual and spatial specificity. Otherwise it would serve only as an abstraction of limited pertinence to comprehending the dynamics and profound complexities of the issues concerning the improvement of human development. Consequently, its relevance to developing strategic actions to address these issues may be of little or no essence to the process.

This chapter is intended to contribute to the dialogue on the relevance of the sustainable development concept to improving human development. The chapter accepts the notion that seeking such relevance is best facilitated when it is considered within a specific context. Thus, sustainable development is discussed in the context of governance with reference to African countries in general and Liberia in particular within a political economy framework.

The rationale for discussing sustainable development in a governance context is predicated on the pivotal role of governance in the sustainable development process. According to the World Summit on Sustainable Development's Plan of Implementation, the basis of sustainable development are sound environmental, social, and economic policies; democratic institutions responsive to the needs of the people; the rule of law; anticorruption measures; gender equality; and an enabling environment for investment (WSSD, 2002, p. 1). Governance is a fundamental part and parcel of this basis.

The chapter is organized into six sections. After this introduction, the second section seeks to provide an effective operational meaning of sustainable development. It also discusses governance and political economy as its contextual feature and framework for discussion with a focus on the institutional aspect of sustainable development. The third section presents an overview of the sustainable development challenges faced by most African countries. The fourth section discusses the Liberian situation, as a case study to provide an empirical content. This section is based largely on secondary information and the author's experience. It is limited in terms of statistical techniques for determining causal relationships. Nevertheless, it provides a credible indication through which one may be able to understand the dramatic downward spiral of Liberia's socioeconomic conditions and the imperative for recovery along a path of sustainable development. The next section provides brief preliminary insights of an evolving institutional framework in which sustainable development, defined and placed in a specific context, may be relevant to this imperative. The final section provides concluding remarks.

Conceptual Clarity and Context

The recent popular usage of the concept and its proliferation originated in the 1980 World Conservation Strategy document of the World Conservation Union. In the document, the conditions for development to be sustainable are articulated in the following statement:

> For development to be sustainable it must first take account of social and ecological factors, as well as economic ones; of the living and nonliving resource base and of the long-term as well as the short-term advantages and disadvantages of alternative actions. (IUCN, 1980, cited in Dalal-Clayton and Bass, 2000, p. 7)

Later, the use of the concept became more prominent after the publication of the Brundtland Report in 1987. In this report, *sustainable
development* is defined as "development that meets the needs of the
present without compromising the ability of future generations to meet
their own needs" (WCED, 1987, p. 8). The report notes that it involves
"a process of change in which the exploitation of resources, the direction
of investment, the orientation of technological development and institutional change are all in harmony and enhance both current and future
potential to meet human needs and aspirations" (WCED, p. 46). From
these definitions, it would seem that the essentials for achieving sustainable
development are fluid and fraught with generalities so much so that it is
not easily amendable to defining policy prescriptions, investment criteria,
and operational mechanisms.

A review of the literature suggests that sustainable development in less
developed countries requires effective governance; a dynamic and
enabling international environment supportive of international cooperation, particularly in the areas of finance, technology transfer, debt, and
trade; and full participation of these countries in global decision making.
It is said also to require peace, security, stability, and respect for human
rights (WSSD, 2002); respect for cultural diversity (Maser, 1999; UNESCO,
2003); an ecologically balanced system (Urbanska, Webb, and Edwards,
2000); and ethics (Newton, 2002).

With such a wide array of requirements for achieving sustainable
development, it is therefore understandable that the meaning and interpretation of sustainable development have also been expanding. Daly
(1996) observes that the way to render any concept innocuous is to expand
its meaning to include virtually everything. He further states that by 1991,
the phrase had acquired such cachet that everything had to be sustainable.
Nevertheless, he argues that most important concepts are not subject to
analytically precise definitions and contends that they are largely dialectical. From this view, in the case of sustainable development, he feels that
one could still give content to and enhance the analytics of the concept.
His clarification of the concept integrates sustainability, sufficiency, equity,
and efficiency. Implicitly, he suggests that sustainable development
involves activities that strive for "sufficient per capita wealth that is
efficiently maintained and allocated, and equitably distributed for the
maximum number of people that can be sustained over time under these
conditions" (Daly, 1996, p. 220). In his clarification of this definition, he
provides an interesting analysis on the issues of the inherent limitations
of growth, the meaning of development, and the criteria for sustainability.
An in-depth discussion of these issues, however, falls beyond the scope
of this chapter.

A review of other perceptions of sustainable development can provide insight. Guimaraes (2003) suggests that what determines the quality of life in any given community and hence its sustainability is the synergy of the relationships among population, organization, environment, and technology. He explains each of these factors as follows: The population factor includes size, composition, density, and demographic dynamics. The organizational factor involves social organizations, aspirations, values, culture, production, and consumption patterns; social stratification; and pattern of conflict resolution. The environmental factor involves the physical and built environment, environmental process and services, and natural resources. The technological factor involves innovation, technical progress, and energy use.

The concept is also defined by the Canadian Ministry of Indian and Northern Affairs (INAC) as a long-term focus that seeks to preserve and enhance economic, social, and natural capital to improve the quality of people's lives and ensure a continuing legacy for the future; a coordinated and integrated approach to decision making, incorporating social, economic, and environmental considerations; and recognition of the interdependence of domestic and global activities. Barbier (1987) interprets sustainable development as a process whose objective is to reduce the absolute poverty of the world's poor through providing lasting and secured livelihoods that minimize resource depletion, environmental degradation, cultural disruption, and social instability.

Other scholars and organizations have advanced additional definitions that they believe are more operational. Warhurst (1998, p. 3), citing Serageldin (1996), states that as a working concept, sustainable development may be defined as "a process whereby future generations receive as much capital per capita as, or more than the current generation has available." He explains that capital includes natural capital, physical (or produced) capital, and social (including human) capital, the measurement of which together may be considered as forming the basis of sustainable economic development and growth. He further indicates that in this process, a transformation occurs in which some natural capital would be depleted and changed into physical capital, which in turn would depreciate, but that with technology, more efficient replacements would be generated.

UNDP (1994) describes sustainable development as a process for realizing human development "in an inclusive, connected, equitable, prudent and secured manner" (cited in Bansal and Howard, 1997, p. 16). In essence, slightly expanding on what Warhurst adapted from Bansal and Howard by including the inclusive factor, one may deduce that the key elements of sustainable development are (1) inclusiveness, involving and encouraging the participation of the people; (2) connectivity, embracing ecological, social, and economic interdependence; (3) equity, ensuring fairness within and across generations and species; (4) prudence, exercising duties of care and prevention, technologically, scientifically, and politically; and (5) security, ensuring safety from chronic threats and protection from harmful disruption.

Ohiorhenuan and Ohiorhenuan (1998, p. 31) define sustainable development from an institutionalist perspective by focusing on the key words *sustainability* and *development* and by integrating the preservation of the ecosystem and social capital. They indicate that sustainability is "the attribute of enduring without giving way and that the sustainability of a thing or process lies in its continuity through time." Utilizing Pearce, Barbier, and Markandya's (1990) portrayal of development as a vector of desirable social objectives and explicitly factoring in the requirement that the ecosystem be preserved, they define sustainable development as a process in which the development vector increases monotonically over time.

From a further review of their discussion, one may argue that irrespective of sustainable development's being a process or an outcome, it must endure over time. From an institutionalist perspective, whatever causes the process or outcome to endure must be appropriate, and effectively managed and maintained. In addition, they argue that external conditions that impact on sustainable development must remain favorable "not as an absence of change, but rather the maintenance of (relative) stability in the presence (of these) conditions and/or continuous throughput" (Ohiorhenuan and Ohiorhenuan, 1998, p. 31). The authors further point out that the applicability of the concept is contingent on the specific domain of intervention such as the global domain, the national domain, and the subnational domain.

The preceding perceptions provide only a snapshot of the varied interpretations of the sustainable development concept. A more detailed review of the literature suggests that these perceptions are intended to suit specific purposes such as social aspirations and political consensus. Others reflect specific domains of certain sectors and disciplines such as economics, environment, and sociology. In the economics realm, definitions are mixed in terms of the central or integral role of growth in the process with divergent views on the "limits" or "no limits" of growth. It can be defined as having two components—the meaning of development and the conditions necessary for sustainability. In general, the definitions reflect a concern with the integration of social, economic, and environmental factors in decision making. The concept is also viewed as a process and as an outcome.

The thrust of this chapter is concerned most with the process dimension. The essence of achieving an outcome is through a process. Moreover, the outcome, in the context of sustainable development, should not be viewed as static but rather as a dynamic phenomenon. Given the evolving needs of human development, there can be no end point or final state of sustainable development. What is important is achieving meaningful progress in creating and sustaining a positive impact on human development in the sustainable development process. From this perspective, and on the basis of the integration of three factors—economy, society, and environment—emphasis is placed on identifying strategic actions through which the process can be expedited.

It must be recognized, as Dalal-Clayton and Bass (2000, p. 9) observe, that in situations in which integration of the three factors is not possible, the process should involve "making alternative choices and negotiating trade-offs." They correctly assert that such factors as peace and security, prevailing economic interests, political systems, institutional arrangements, and cultural norms will undeniably influence policy decision making and negotiations. The governance of this process, with particular emphasis on the institutional aspects, is critical.

The term *institution* according to Ohiorhenuan and Ohiorhenuan (1998, p. 30) may refer to "a socially recognized human organization providing a valued service" as well as "a matrix of socially sanctioned norms and rules of conduct governing individual and group behavior—'the rules of the game.'" The "rules of the game" include not only regulations, laws, policies, and legal decisions from a court of law, but also the rules and policies governing the behavior and practices of those who make and apply those rules. The latter is particularly relevant to administrative law and procedure, electoral laws, and civil service regulations. In addition there is the constitution, the rules that guides all rule making and establishes the legitimacy of individuals' and organizations' actions. Utilizing institution as conceived previously serves as a mechanism through which results-oriented strategic actions may be taken to realize objective sustainable development outcomes.

Moreover, there is an inherent political dimension in the process that goes beyond formal political systems, which should not be ignored. This is generally referred to as the *political will* or *political commitment*. These terms refer to both the psychological attributes of politicians as well as an outcome of objective reality determined by a political playing field (Kelegama and Parikh). The psychological attributes would explain why politicians act differently in similar situations. The outcome perspective would explain why irrespective of which politicians are in power, they act virtually the same. The recognition of these realities justifies the governance context and political economy approach for this chapter.

Considering the issues discussed previously and utilizing Ohiorhenuan and Ohiorhenuan's (1998) explanation of sustainability, we may derive a perception of sustainable development that reflects an action and results orientation. From this perspective, sustainable development may be defined as a continuous process of preserving and enhancing the production, distribution, and utility of economic, social, and natural capital to improve the status of the current and future human development. The process involves multiple mechanisms and domains of intervention in which political and institutional factors are critical for policy decision making, implementation, evaluation, and follow-up actions. To ensure its enduring element, the political and institutional factors must be managed to adjust appropriately to possible changes for the maintenance of stability and an enabling operating environment. Thus, this will require appropriate institutions, effective leadership, and a results-oriented management capacity. A long-standing debate is on determining what is required to achieve this desired state of affairs.

Governance and Political Economy

To explore answers to the preceding issues one must first consider that the factors mentioned—appropriate institutions, effective leadership, and results-oriented management capacity—are attributes of governance. As is sustainable development, governance is a concept that is widely used in the development literature with a variety of meanings and interpretations. An in-depth discussion of these definitions is beyond the limits of this chapter. However, because it is an issue of concern, a brief discussion of the concept is necessary for contextual clarity.

The increasing use of the concept began when it was diagnosed that barriers to structural adjustment were due not only to the substance of policies, but also to the policy environment. Thus, governance became associated with democracy, culture, and institutional characteristics that cover several issues. Frischtak (1994, p. 1) explains this further:

> Institutional building and design; the nature and transparency of decision-making procedures; interest representation and conflict resolution mechanisms; the limits of authority and leadership accountability—all of which ultimately concern the very essence of the polity—are frequently identified as governance issues and fill the expanding agenda of what can be called the political economy of structural adjustment.

Depending on a particular definition of governance, the use of the concept has been criticized as being overly prescriptive to a particular political system, insensitive to African culture, and beclouded with subjectivity when used as "good" governance. To avoid these criticisms, Shihata (1990) views governance as the provision of universal and abstract rules, the institutions that enforce them, and the predictable mechanisms to regulate conflicts over both rules and their enforcement. In her discussion of governance deficiencies, Frischtak (1994) describes governance as a process of coordinating the aggregation of diverging interest to promote policy that can credibly be taken to represent the public interest. It appears that, as Kruiter (1996) observes, the definition, usefulness, ethnical connotation, and political dimensions of the concept are still evolving.

Generally, as indicated, governance involves institutions, laws, rules, regulations, policies, and enforcement mechanisms in pursuit of specified objectives. To derive a working definition of governance for this chapter, Landell-Mills's (1991) definition of governance is useful. Explicitly incorporating the institutional dimension, governance refers to the legitimate and calculated use of authority and power in the exercise of control over society and the management of its resources intended to achieve shared or agreed development goals through appropriate institutional mechanisms. In the process, it is expected to promote accountability, transparency, rule of law, participation, and other factors that engender and nurture an enabling institutional and socioeconomic environment. This definition dovetails with Martin's (1994) observation that it encompasses the nature and functioning of the state institutional and structural arrangements, decision-making processes, policy formulation, implementation capacity, information flows, leadership effectiveness, and the nature of the relationship between the rulers and the ruled.

It may, therefore, be argued that the success or failure of the sustainable development process largely rests on the quality of institutions and the political environment. The importance of institutions and the political environment, however, does not repudiate the critical role of other traditional factors, land, labor, and capital, in the sustainable development process. The focus is being placed on the political environment and institutions, because the governance of all other factors of production operates through institutions in a political environment. This political environment characterizes the interaction of different individuals and groups in society seeking to influence public policy for socioeconomic development or to promote the lack of it in pursuit of their own interests. The dynamics involved is referred to as the *political economy*. It is within this framework that the challenges of sustainable development are discussed.

The Challenge of Sustainable Development in Africa

Africa is said to be the least developed continent despite its rich endowment of natural resources and a considerable trained caliber of human resources including those in the diaspora. It is believed that these resources could make a meaningful developmental impact if their preservation, enhancement, and utility were facilitated in a manner most advantageous to African human development. This would lead to a change in Africa's production pattern from primary production and export of raw materials to industrial production of semifinished and finished products. It would contribute to the retention and further development of its trained and experienced human resources rather than accelerate the continuous brain drain. Exercising effective control and management of these resources would lead to opportunities for improved livelihoods of the people and ultimately to a higher quality of life. Unfortunately, poverty, in all its dimensions, is most prevalent in Africa and is particularly pronounced in Sub-Saharan Africa.

As noted in Balogun (2003), Sub-Saharan Africa's literacy rate is 60%, which is significantly below the developing countries' average of 73%. Life expectancy at birth is about 48.8 years, whereas it is over 60 years in all other regions. About 46% of people in Sub-Saharan Africa live below the income poverty line of less than US$1 a day. Compared to East Asia, the Pacific, and Latin America, this percentage is 15% below the poverty line. Access to electricity, telephones, other telecommunication services, pipe-borne water supply, and sanitation facilities is all appallingly low relative to that of most other regions in the world. In terms of civil and other conflicts that further exacerbate the state of poverty, about 40% of Sub-Saharan African countries have experienced at least one such conflict over the last 40 years. UNDP (2002; p. 17) notes that about 1.5 million persons died as casualties of war over the period 1990 to 1999 in Sub-Saharan Africa. This amount is significantly higher than the casualties recorded for other regions.

The situation is even worse, given that it has generally regressed in recent years. This is reflected by UNDP (2002, p. 13) in its observation that

> the lives of (Sub-Saharan Africans) very poor people are getting worse. The share of people living on US$1 a day was about the same at the end of the 1990s—47% as at the start. Thus, because of population growth, the number of poor people in the region has increased. And while most of the world has increased the share of children who are immunized against the leading diseases, since 1990 immunization rates in Sub-Saharan Africa have fallen below 50%.

Africa is also faced with major environmental issues. These issues include pollution, particularly that affecting freshwater resources and marine life; coastal erosion and other land degradation; scarce water resources; droughts; and floods (Nana-Sinkam, 1995). Moreover, the pattern of African livelihood pressurizes the natural resource base so greatly that its sustainability is often threatened. Generally, in the context of sustainable development, striking and maintaining a balance in the use and preservation of environmental resources as well as minimizing the impact of environmental damages to Africa caused by Western and other countries are daunting challenges Africa currently faces.

This general state of affairs has largely been attributed to a host of factors, some of which are more relevant than others in certain areas. These factors include the historical legacies of slave trade, colonialism, and external intervention in the internal affairs of these countries for ulterior economic and political motives, including the Cold War machinations and manipulations. The problems are also caused by the imposition of ill-conceived structural adjustment programs and a crippling debt burden. On the internal sociopolitical front, the causes are attributed to political authoritarianism, the military intervention into politics, poor management of conflicts, self-aggrandizement by the political leadership, patrimonial dynamics of African politics, human rights violations, and ethnic rivalries. The causes may also be attributed to a poorly developed civil society. Most civil societies in Africa are not sufficiently capacitated to participate substantively in public affairs, demand high-quality public services, and effectively hold public officials accountable (Gyimah-Boadi, 1997).

From an institutional perspective, the lack of adequate institutional capacity and an unconducive socioeconomic and political governance environment also contribute to the current state of affairs in African countries. In most of these countries, the institutional systems lack well-defined and effectively implemented regulations, procedures and processes that minimize the domination and manipulation of the system by political cliques. In cases where they exist, they are regarded as mere academic administrative instruments and therefore are blatantly ignored with impunity. In general, the system is largely characterized by ineffective utilization of human resources, poor communication, overcentralization of authority, corruption, political patrimony, ad hoc adherence to policies and procedures, and a pervasive lack of transparency and accountability.

These factors cause institutional failures, which in turn contribute to poor policy implementation. This situation has immensely contributed to large transaction costs, political and economic uncertainties, civil crisis, and ultimately unsustainable growth and development. Ayittey (1998, p. 4) underscores this general view in his statement that "the absence of key institutions lies at the heart of Africa's intractable woes and interminable conflicts."

There have been attempts to address these institutional issues over time through various reforms. Balogun (2003) categorizes these reforms as First Generation Reforms, Structural Adjustment Reforms, and Internally Driven Reforms. He indicates the First Generation Reforms were instituted in the early postindependence period with the declared objectives to equip the public service institutions inherited from the colonial administration for the postindependence challenges of nation building and economic modernization. Particular emphasis was, however, tacitly placed on ensuring the loyalty of the civil service to the political leadership rather than the state. To address the issue, he further explains that several commissions, including the Ndegwa Commission in Kenya, the Udoji Commission in Nigeria, the Mills-Odoi Commission in Ghana, and the Wamalwa Commission in Swaziland, proposed the installation of management programs considered most modern at the time.

These measures produced very limited or no institutional performance improvement. The results were generally ascribed to halfhearted or absent political commitment; the disconnect among the reforms' dominant concerns and performance, productivity, and efficiency; and the administrative and political leaders' preoccupation with the capture and retention of power, authority, and wealth.

The Structural Adjustment Reforms, although basically not concerned with typical institutional reform issues, affected institutional public service delivery capacity. This was especially pronounced in the education and health sectors as well as other areas that directly impact on poverty alleviation. Moreover, the Structural Adjustment Program reforms led to the dismantling of public service institutions without providing any viable alternatives (Adedeji, 1992, cited in Balogun, 2003, p. 12). They also aggravated the ethics and accountability crisis in the civil service of many African countries. This period engendered a phenomenal increased incidence of moonlighting, inflation of contract prices, bribery, and other forms of corruption (Nti, 1989).

Recognizing the virtual lack of success in these reforms a few countries introduced the Inward-Oriented Institutional reforms. These reforms were identified, planned, designed, and introduced in a participatory manner to address specific problems. They included measures to inculcate the ethos of professionalism, dedication, accountability, transparency, and attitudinal changes. In some countries the application of information and communication technologies (ICT) was introduced to enhance the personnel management system, including improved remuneration structures and other incentives linked with performance. Moreover, some countries have embraced democratic norms in which changes in government are achieved through constitutional means and conflicts are resolved peacefully rather than through various forms of systemic violence. According to UNDP (2002, p. 63), the last two decades of the 20th century saw a historic shift in the global spread of democracy as about 81 countries, of which 29 were in Sub-Saharan Africa, took steps toward democratization. In several cases these reform measures and attitudinal changes have been encouraging, but there is still substantial room for improvement in terms of economic and social quality of life.

Liberia: A Case of Unsustainable Growth and Development

During the decades of the 1950s and 1960s, Liberia's economic performance was appreciably high. In terms of the real gross national product (GNP) growth index, Liberia's performance, using 1954 as a base year, was second to Japan's, as Liberia had an index measure of 175 as compared to Japan's 180 (UNDP/Liberia, 2000). In comparison with Korea, according to Lindenberg (1999: 11) over the period 1965 to 1987, Liberia ranked 58th in per capita GNP (US$642), while South Korea ranked 56th (US$687) among 120 countries on the basis of data and country coverage by the World Bank. By 1987, Korea had emerged as one of the world's highest developing countries in terms of growth and human development as measured by the Physical Quality of life Index (PQLI). Korea's per capita GNP increased from US$687 to US$2,690 and was ranked among the top 30 nations of the world. Liberia's performance, in contrast, significantly declined. Its per capita GNP fell from US$642 to US$450 and was ranked among the lowest 30 countries on the PQLI scores. Comparative rankings on the Human Development Index reflect similar stark disparity. In 1994, Korea is ranked 101 and Liberia 144 on a scale of 1 to 173 (UNDP, 1994). Currently, these differences have considerably widened with Liberia's situation' exacerbated by the colossal devastation caused by its civil wars.

Empirical studies have suggested that such difference in performance among countries may be ascribed to endogenous and exogenous factors. For example, a study by Lindenberg (1999, pp. 29–36), referred to earlier, identifies the following factors:

> Endogenous Factors
> *Natural endowment*—Examples include mineral production, population size, and population density.
> *Cultural and ethnic endowment*—Variables include ethnic, racial, and religious diversity and region.
> *Baseline human resource endowments*—These are conditions resulting from earlier social investments such as initial levels of literacy, life expectancy, and infant mortality.
> *Political and economic institutional context and continuity*—This refers to the type of political regime and economic

system. Long-term continuity refers to the percentage of time democratic regimes were in office and measures of political instability such as nonprogrammed changes of presidents or prime ministers.

Exogenous Factors

Natural disasters—The number of earthquakes, volcanic eruptions, droughts, and floods, as examples.

External military interventions.

External economic influences—Changes in terms of trade, export product, and market concentration.

Access to foreign flows—Annual average total debt, average debt service, and average aid.

The Lindenberg study, utilizing statistical analysis, suggests that among the endogenous factors, initial human resource base and its institutional context were the most important determinants of human development. For economic growth alone, the endogenous factors that mattered were low political instability and regional, ethnic, and linguistic homogeneity. Because economic growth, in the context of this chapter, is intrinsic to human development, the determinants of human development would include those that are considered specific to economic growth as well as the regeneration and prudent utility of environmental resources.

For exogenous factors, the study suggests that the terms of trade, export product mix, and access to foreign resources inflows are pertinent to human development but were not significant in explaining the differences in countries' performances.

To understand Liberia's dismal human development performance, it would be helpful to explain its circumstances in the context of the relevant endogenous and exogenous variables, as discussed previously. Liberia is endowed with lucrative natural resources and human capital that compare favorably with other countries that have a relatively higher status of human development. Liberia's population is heterogeneous. It is characterized by (1) 16 major indigenous ethnic groups and (2) descendants from Africans who were sold by fellow Africans or abducted to serve as slaves in the United States, referred to as *Americo-Liberians,* and immigrants from the West Indies and other parts of Africa referred to as *Congo people* (Barclay, 1999, p. 299; Liberty, 2002, p. 271). Although there has been considerable integration of the population through intermarriages and other social interactions over time rendering the ethnic characteristics less explicitly defined, integration was a major problem in the initial period of Liberia's evolution. One of Liberia's past presidents, Arthur Barclay, in the early part of the last century, attested to this problem:

> The Liberian nation is to be made up of the Negro civilized to
> some extent in the United States and repatriated, and of the
> aboriginal tribes. At present it is composed of a small number
> of civilized and a large number of aboriginal communities in
> varying degrees of dependence. The problem is how to blend
> these into a national organism, an organic unity. (Starr, 1913,
> cited in Liberty 2002, p. 257)

Other problems during the initial stage of statehood included (1) a
governing elite, many of whom were inexperienced in national leadership
or lacked the requisite capacity; (2) severe financial constraints due to the
nation's nascent operational resource base; and (3) imperialistic incursions
by major European countries that threatened the sovereignty of the state.

The governing elite, in the early period of statehood, largely comprised
the Americo-Liberians. Later the Congo people were amalgamated in the
regime. Given their relative small size, homogeneity, and cohesion, as
well as their being the major players in establishing the state as Liberia,
this group dominated the political and economic domains of the state's
apparatus. For fear of being marginalized and in some cases because of
pure bigotry, the ruling elite maintained an "exclusionary" governance
policy. Later this was changed to a "gradual absorptive" policy in which
other ethnic groups became part of the ruling elite. Over the years this
oligarchic regime became generally known as Congo people. This group
has been blamed for every shortcoming of the political system, every
failure in public policy, and every inequity in the society, irrespective of
the complexity of the causes or how recent the emergence of the awareness of or the ability to deal with them (Berg, 1970). What has not been
relatively highlighted was the critical role this group played in safeguarding
Liberia's sovereignty and national dignity. The following quote succinctly
explains the situation and its ethnic implication: "The emigrant leadership
of the 1890–1930 years was composed of educated politicians, not professionals, technocrats or intellectuals. They had one political objective as
a group: to keep Liberia free" (Liberty, 2002, p. 228).

In spite of the "colonial naivete of their minds," these men took on
again and again the British and French and never went down to igno-
minious defeat. Their greatest triumph would be in the 1930 to 1935
period when, faced with League of Nations sanctions and almost certain
mandation, they adroitly rode out the storm.

Liberty also notes that it was because of these eventful trying times
that W. E. Burghardt Dubois (1933, p. 683) wrote:

> Indeed the record of peace, efficiency and ability made by this
> little poverty-stricken settlement of the rejected and despised,

sitting on the edge of Africa and fighting the world in order to be left alone, is, despite querulous criticism, one of the most heartening efforts of human history. (cited in Liberty, 2002, p. 229)

Liberty further explains:

It was this kind of triumph, not any kind of innate feeling of superiority, which jelled emigrant paramount determina- tion—the sheer will to survive at all cost—that kept emigrant ethnicity at the apex of the Liberian ethnic pyramid. It was these experiences that created the *esprit de corps* of that stratum in this century that made it reluctant to share power with others who challenged or denigrated the passage through the difficult years. (Liberty, 2002, p. 229)

The ruling elite was thus successful in safeguarding the nation's sov- ereignty but alienated the majority of the population. Moreover,because of the lack of resources, the complexity of the issues, and the overall capacity deficiencies, the evolving needs for strengthening the human resource base and other attributes of human development remained largely unrealized. The opportunities for civil society's participation in the nation- building process were also very limited and highly skewed toward those having connections to the ruling elites. In essence, initial investment in the human resource base was rather limited and cannot be compared with that of Japan and Korea. Moreover, focus on maintaining ethnic cohesion of a minute section of the population fueled dissension and served as a breeding ground for problems that were to emerge later. This is a brief account of the ethnic factor in Liberia's evolution and impact on human development up to 1950.

During the 1950s and 1960s, as noted earlier, Liberia achieved phe- nomenal economic growth. This was due largely to the high demand and the attractive world market prices for rubber and iron ore, the country's main export commodities at that time. Unlike in Japan and Korea, this growth was not effectively utilized and managed to develop a vibrant human resource base, effective institutional mechanisms, and strategic structural reforms to serve as an adequate sustainable foundation for enhancing human development. This does not imply that there were no attempts toward this end. There were indeed relative increased educational opportunities, improved health facilities, and administrative reforms. What should be inferred here is that the results were less than the situation deserved and the people expected.

The situation worsened in the mid- and late 1970s because of external economic factors, specifically, escalating oil prices and a global recession that culminated in depressed prices and demand for Liberia's export commodities. These exogenous factors led to a deterioration of whatever progress was previously achieved. Economic growth fell to less than 1%, and previous economic and social progress began to dissipate. This in turn led to economic hardships with a disproportional adverse effect falling on those who were not directly responsible for the general situation or in the best position to cope with it. The situation set in motion sociopolitical upheavals fueled by ideologically inspired revolutionaries.

Ultimately, the situation led to military coup and subsequently internecine upheavals and full-fledged civil war. Although the explicit causes of the civil war may be due to other multiple factors in addition to those implicitly referred to in this chapter, the situation rendered all semblance of governance incapacitated (Barclay, 1999). In his reflections on the military rule in Liberia, Sawyer (1988) provides a succinct account of the decadence of governance during that time. His observations reveal that laws forbidding criticisms of the government were strictly enforced, arbitrary arrests escalated, and the writ of habeas corpus was selectively applied. He further notes that opposition party leaders were prohibited from consulting and were restricted in their travel in and out of the country; the Supreme Court arbitrarily debarred lawyers who questioned its judgment; and the legislature threatened to ban organizations that disagreed with government policies or actions. Furthermore, he notes that freedom of the press was suppressed. Generally, his account suggests that not only were government institutions affected but so were those of the civil society and the private sector. Thus, Liberia fell into a governance crisis of unparalleled historical proportions.

During the war (1989 to 1997) and the period of the regime that was elected immediately after the war (1997 to mid-2003), environmental concerns were heightened. It is reported that gold and diamond mining and the extraction of logs were major sources of financial support for the rebels. Mining activities increased the rural communities' vulnerabilities to malaria and various water-borne diseases. The rate of log extraction raised alarming signals on the rapid depletion of forest reserves and its environmental consequential effects. Regarding logging operations, Hofstatter (2001) notes:

> Liberia will likely have no forest reserves within the next ten years because of the destructive rate at which logs are being extracted. The fact that there is virtually no forest management nor replanting of trees means that the social, economic and ecological impacts of this trade will have severe long term

implications for the future of Liberia and its people. The plants and animals species that live in these forests will have their habitats destroyed and may face extinction. Unique and rare species of vegetation and trees are disappearing rapidly. (Hofstatter, 2001, p. 7)

The overall situation, as discussed previously, suggests that the evolution of the circumstances and efforts toward improvement in Liberia's economic and social conditions have been, to a large extent, inimical to the path of sustainable development. Policies and strategic actions to preserve and enhance the production, distribution, and utility of economic, social, and natural capital have been relatively ineffective in some cases and nonexistent in others. The next section discusses how the institutions of governance may have contributed to the state of unsustainable growth and development.

An Institutional Perspective on Sustainable Development in Liberia

From the perspective of a socially recognized organization providing a valued service, institutions may be categorized as statal and parastatal organizations, civil society organizations, and private sector organizations. The discussion here focuses on the former. At the outset, it must be noted that these organizations operate within the overall governance authority of the state. In the Liberian context, the state is constitutionally sanctioned in terms of governance as having a democratic system of government with three independent branches: the executive, the judicial, and the legislative. These branches are to serve as checks and balances in the governance of the state. People are expected to serve in these branches by rules and regulations including free and fair elections for certain positions. The government, through its institutional apparatus, is constitutionally required to ensure an impartial application of the law, a guarantee for responsible and accountable freedom and human rights, and the decentralization of political authority and decision making as well as conditions to facilitate the efficient functioning of markets. It is also required to facilitate the improvement of human development.

In practice, this system of government has been more symbolic than substantive. The multiparty system of government became virtually a one-party system. Elections have rarely been free and fair. The independence of the three branches of government became compromised by the dominance of the executive branch, in which the presidency became paramount.

Other state institutions responsible for economic growth and human development and all of their attributes were severely constrained by the lack of adequately qualified and motivated human resources, unclear internal standards, and recently woefully inadequate incentives. The institutions were also plagued by inept management practices and systems that were highly susceptible to political patrimony, arbitrary decision making, and an unpredictable response to crisis situations. In some cases, the appropriate "rules of the game" were in place, but the ability or the commitment to enforce these rules consistently and transparently was weak. UNDP/Liberia (2002, p. 26) lends support to this general perspective in its observation that

> the doctrine of separate but equal branches of government adopted from the United States and enshrined in the Liberian Constitution has not worked in practice as expected. The absence of a vibrant multiparty system made the incumbent President the key player in legislative matters and a strong influence on administrative and judicial matters. Given its pre-eminent and wide discretionary power, the Presidency incrementally encroached into the other branches of governance and appropriated a wide range of administrative, judicial and political initiatives. Other factors responsible for the weakness of administrative governance included the absence of a code of conduct for public officials and the lack of effective systems for recruitment, training, compensation and promotion of civil servants.

Adding to the preceding factors, Conteh and associates (1999) suggest that the tripartite issues of unfair distributive justice, national identity crisis, and inequality contributed to the malaise in national governance. Thus confidence in the system became increasingly eroded.

According to the Liberian Presidential Task Force on Policy Adjustment Report (Government of Liberia, 1993, p. 4), some of the other major inhibiting factors that have depressed public sector efficiency, outputs, and confidence were the following:

■ Nepotism and corruption in the appointment, promotion, and compensation of public servants and officials as a result of the absence of a set of objective criteria and enforceable civil service structure and regulations

■ Moonlighting, hustling, and misuse of public facilities on the part of many public workers in search of means to augment personal disposable income permitted by the absence of clearly defined terms of reference, reporting procedures, performance and evaluation schemes, and a public accountability system

■ Overlapping and uncoordinated functions among the various ministries and agencies as well as conflicting operational procedures in the implementation of public policies and programs

The other aspect of institutions as defined in the context of this chapter deals with individual and group behavior and socially sanctioned norms and rules of conduct governing such behavior. It would appear that just as national development was hampered by governance constraints, personal development was constrained by the lack of internal maturity and emotional strength and the disintegration of principle-centered behavior. There are, however, notable exceptions. As Fahnbulleh (2002, p. 1) observes, "There are well-meaning and conscious Liberians who have done great deeds and are capable of doing greater things provided the circumstances and conditions are present." Although the roots of the negative behavioral patterns may have some historical roots, the situation in more recent times has become rampant.

The shift into near anarchy during the military coup in 1980 and its reign heightened people's perception of government positions as avenues for the accumulation of fast and vast wealth. This lingering perception is apparently being unwittingly institutionalized. Many officials in the recent political regimes seem to act as if the country were their personal domain, with each having institutional and administrative sections as prized fiefdoms that they were entitled to exploit for personal gain. Because of weak enforcement mechanisms, lack of political commitment, precise performance standards, and an ethical code of conduct, many individuals and groups overstep their limits of authority remorselessly. A code of conduct should have been established as stipulated in the Liberian 1986 revised constitution. According to Article 90 of that constitution:

■ No person, whether elected or appointed to any public office, shall engage in any other activity, which shall be against public policy or constitute conflict of interest.

■ No person holding public office shall demand or receive any other prerequisites, emoluments or benefits, directly or indirectly, on account of any duty required by government.

■ The Legislature shall, in pursuance of the above provision, prescribe a code of conduct for all public officials and employees, stipulating the acts, which constitute conflict of interest or are against public policy and the penalties for violations. (cited in Banks and Woterson, 2003, pp. 3–4)

This code of conduct has yet to be established and institutionalized. When this code is established along with effective enforcement mechanisms and capacity, it will serve as a disincentive to those persons who embrace the belief that the avenue to public jobs that provide opportunities for corruption is a resort to arms. It will also serve as a deterrent to public officials who believe that they can enrich themselves at the expense of the nation and not have to account for such practices (Banks and Woterson, 2003).

On the issue of leadership, there appeared to be a pattern whereby many of those in the higher echelon of the political hierarchy received cooperation from their staff and the general public not because these leaders were trusted, respected, or honored but rather because they had coercive and utility power as opposed to legitimate power and authority. Coercive power is the creation and use of fear and threats in getting things done. Utility power is characterized by the "What's in it for me?" syndrome. This is basically a situation in which people strive to satisfy their bosses or even the public, with an expectation of rewards, which could be promotion, inclusion in an inner cycle, job security, or material and pecuniary benefits. Their services are therefore not necessarily based on principles or the objectives of the organization. Under such leadership, there are abundant lip service loyalty and superficial commitment (Covey, 1991). Generally, this situation did not provide an enabling environment for sustainability.

Many of Liberia's institutional leaders during the last two decades fell into the preceding category. Nevertheless, there is now a glaring need to focus on getting things accomplished through enthusiastic cooperation based on the institutional heads' character, competence, motivational attributes, and genuine commitment to a principle-centered cause or objective. This is what characterizes legitimate power and authority.

From the preceding discussion one may conclude that although Liberia is endowed with considerable mineral resources, fertile land, and human capital, albeit less than adequate, the institutional capacity necessary to develop further, deploy, and utilize these resources has been lacking. These institutional failures, in many cases, served as disincentives for stimulating innovation, production, and investment. They adversely affected the development and efficient functioning of a market economy and contributed to continued overreliance on the production and export of raw materials as the economy's impetus for growth. They also adversely affected the nurturing of democratic practices, personal integrity, principle-centered leadership, and other virtues of human dignity. Instead, they provided incentives for corruption, social and economic dishonesty, and other unscrupulous, antisocial norms. These vices and misguided policies generated partly by institutional failures became pervasive and were apparently virtually institutionalized, albeit informally. This situation immensely contributed to unsustainable growth and development that ultimately resulted in Liberia's downward spiral to its current state of calamitous socioeconomic decline, political instability, and recurring civil wars.

Toward an Evolving Institutional Framework for Sustainable Development

To develop a meaningful framework for sustainable development from an institutional perspective in the context of Liberia and countries facing similar circumstances, it may be necessary to begin from a conceptual basis. This section provides only preliminary insights. These insights should be followed by in-depth empirical studies and institutional analysis to which more substantive elements may be added to ensure a strategic action and results orientation.

As indicated in the discussion, Liberia currently faces a desperate situation and enormous challenges. This framework is intended not to facilitate recovery and rehabilitation because this would mean putting Liberia on a path to its prewar conditions, factors of which contributed to the current situation. Nevertheless, one must consider the need to address the immediate security issues but with a view to placing Liberia along a sustainable development path. The framework should therefore be structured to reflect emphasis on substantive innovative institutional reforms that would serve as sustainable preventive and remedial measures to institutional failures rather than an emphasis on the violent removal of personalities.

The organizing principle of the framework is that it must reflect a holistic view of the sustainable development process as well as the various sectoral issues relevant to political, economic, social, and environmental concerns. It must also reflect a comprehensive geographic coverage, specific domains for intervention, broad-based participatory mechanism, and alternative sources of national-ownership-assured support. It must be user friendly for identifying and analyzing critical issues, assessing strengths and needs, formulating and implementing policies, identifying who should do what and why, as well as monitoring, evaluating, and facilitating responsible follow-up actions.

The framework should have several components to address specific concerns related to improving governance institutional performance. First, it should have mechanisms through which institutions acquire values and stability. Values should reflect socially accepted norms relevant to enhancing integrity, justice, accountability, and competence. Stability should reflect not necessarily maintenance of the status quo, but rather the capacity to adapt to changing socioeconomic circumstances without losing sight of the national development objectives. Other components should include (1) constitutional reforms to minimize and control, but not to incapacitate the authority of the presidency, and (2) capacity building.

The capacity-building component should be comprehensive, involving education, skills development, systems management, organizational structures, procedures and processes, performance management, motivation, teamwork, and leadership. It should have an incentive system review mechanism and other factors relevant to facilitate the retention and effective utility of the existing and built capacity. It should also involve, with special emphasis, personal development, stressing character strengthening, moral responsibility awareness, and attitudinal changes to stimulate and enhance conformity with constitutional and socially sanctioned norms. The framework must ensure that enforcement mechanisms, characterized by fair and transparent punitive measures, must be institutionalized and applied without discrimination. Finally, the framework should embrace Balogun's four pillars of agency governance: (1) the role of civil society in holding public agencies to account, (2) a pattern in the exercise of political power, (3) the professional and ethical basis of managerial and leadership authority, and (4) the credibility of the prevailing rules regime.

Conclusion

The concept of sustainable development is now widely used in the development literature, national and organizational strategic plans, and political speeches. It has been interpreted to mean different things for different purposes. This chapter has discussed the concept with a view to providing an operational perception and to exploring its relevance and applicability to improving human development now and in the future.

Using Liberia as a case study, this chapter attempted to illuminate Liberia's socioeconomic retrogression and the possible relevance of the sustainable development concept to its recovery. The intended recovery is perceived to be not to the country's previous status, but along a sustainable development path with a view to improving human development.

The concept is considered most relevant when couched in a governance context from an institutional perspective. From this view, it is asserted that institutional failures contributed to the current state of the country's socioeconomic development. Recognizing the inherent interplay of power politics and the personal dynamics of the political economy, the chapter provided brief preliminary insights on an institutional sustainable development framework. In addition to the traditional organizational reform measures and institutional performance mechanisms, the chapter suggested the pursuit of innovations that would ensure the effective implementation of appropriate strategies for inculcating a value system, promoting institutional stability, and undertaking constitutional reforms and capacity-building programs for institutional strengthening. It further suggested that capacity building should place a special focus on personal development. This is considered important so that progress and achievement may be realized not by the personalization of the issues, but rather by individual and groups' character, competence, and genuine commitment. This would be a people-centered approach to institutional development.

Acknowledgment

Dr. Anthony Barclay is currently Human Development Advisor at the ECOWAS Secretariat in Abuja, Nigeria. Special thanks go to Dr. Gene Ogiogio, Ms. Paddy Mutimusakwi, and Mrs. Catherine Mlingwa of the African Capacity Building Foundation in Zimbabwe for their kind assistance. The views expressed in this paper are those of the author and do not necessarily reflect the views of ACBF, ECOWAS, or those who rendered assistance. The author may be contacted at yalcrab77@yahoo.com.

References

Adedeji, Adebayo. (1992). Institutional Dimension in the Policy Process. In: Matahaba, G., and Balogun, M.J., eds., *Enhancing Policy Management Capacity in Africa*. West Hartford, CT: Kumarian Press. Cited in M.J. Balogun, 2003.

Ayittey, George B. (1998). Africa's Failed Renaissance. http://c:vnet.org/journal/issue9/ftgayitt.html (accessed August 29, 2003).

Balogun. M.J. (2003). Performance Management and Agency Governance for African Development: The Search for Common Cause on Excellence in the Public Service. *DPMN Bulletin*: 10(3). http://www.dpmf.org/bulletin-may-03/performance-mgt-balogun.html (accessed August 23, 2003).

Banks, Philip A.Z. III, and Woterson, Cletus S. (2003). "The Challenges Posed for Liberia." *The Perspective,* September 2003, pp. 1–4.

Bansal, P., and Howard, E. (1997). *Business and the Natural Environment*. Boston: Butterworth-Heinemann. Cited in Warhurst,. 1998. p. 3.

Barbier, E. (1987). The Concept of Sustainable Economic Development. Environmental Conservation. Cited in Indian and Northern Affairs, Canada, Sustainable Development, 2003. http://www.ainc-inac.gc.ca/sd/what is_e.html (accessed September 2, 2003).

Barclay, Anthony. (1999). Consolidating Peace through Governance and Regional Cooperation: The Liberian Experience. In: Adedeji, Adebayo, ed., *Comprehending and Mastering African Conflicts: The Search for Sustainable Peace and Good Governance.* London and Ijebu-Ode: Zed Books/African Centre for Development and Strategic Studies, pp. 297–316.

Berg, Elliot. (1970). "Politics, Privilege and Progress in Liberia." *Liberian Studies Journal,* 2(2), pp. 173–183.

Canadian Ministry of India and Northern Affairs (INAC). (2002). Sustainable Development Strategy, 2001–2003, Ottawa.

Conteh, Al Hassan et al. (1999). Liberia. In: Adedeji, Adebayo, ed., *Comprehending and Mastering African Conflicts: The Search for Sustainable Peace and Good Governance.* London and Ijebu-Ode: Zed Books/African Centre for Development and Strategic Studies, pp. 297–316.

Covey, Stephen R. (1991). *Principle-Centered Leadership.* London: Simon and Schuster.

Dalal-Clayton, B., and Bass, Stephen. (2000). National Strategies for Sustainable Development. The Challenge Ahead, IEED Discussion Paper. http://www.nssd. net/working/Issues.html (accessed 10 March 2003).

Daly, Herman E. (1996). *Beyond Growth.* Boston: Beacon Press.

Dubois, W.E.B. (1933). Liberia, the League, and the United States. *Foreign Affairs,* 9, July.

Fahnbulleh, Boima. (2002). "Soul." *The Perspective,* March, pp. 1–5.

Frischtak, Leila L. (1994). Governance Capacity and Economic Reform in Developing Countries. World Bank Technical Paper, Number 254, Washington, DC: World Bank.

Government of Liberia. (1993). "Presidential Task Force on Policy Adjustment and Institutional Reform, Preparatory and Programming Framework (Phase 1)." June.

Guimaraes, Roberto P. (2003). "The Politics and Ethics of Sustainability" as a New Paradigm for Public Policy Formation and Development Planning. *International Journal for Education Development,* pp. 1–28. http://www. spaef.com/ IJED_PUB/3 3/3_guimaraes.html (accessed March 2003).

Gyimah-Boadi, Emanuel. (1997). Civil Society in Africa: The Good, the Bad, the Ugly. http://www.civnet.org/journal/issue1/egboadi.htm (accessed December 29, 2003).

Hofstatter, Benjamin. (2003). Liberia: Trade, Environment and Conflict. http://www. american.edu/TED/ice/liberiadiamonds.htm (accessed September 16, 2003).

IUCN/UNEP/WWF. (1980). "The World Conservation Strategy: Living Resources Conservation for Sustainable Development." Gland, Switzerland.

Kelegama, Saman, and Parikh, Kirit. (no date). Political Economy of Growth and Reforms in South Asia. Draft Paper. Institute of Policy Studies, Colombo, Sri Lanka and Indira Gandhi Institute of Development Research, India.

Kruiter, Ange. (1996). *Good Governance for Africa: Whose Governance?* Maastricht: ECDPM.

Landell-Mills, P., and Serageldin, I. (1991). Governance and the External Factor. Washington, D.C.: World Bank.

Liberty, Clarence E. Zamba. (2002). *Growth of the Liberian State: An Analysis of Its Historiography*. San Francisco, CA: The New World African Press.

Lindenberg, Marc M. (1999). *The Human Development Race. Improving the Quality of life in Developing Countries*. CA: ICS Press.

Martin, D.C. (1994). The Cultural Dimension of Governance. A discussion paper. In: Proceedings of the World Bank Conference on Development Economics, pp. 325–341.

Maser, Chris. (1999). *Ecological Diversity in Sustainable Development: The Vital and Forgotten Dimension*. Port St. Lucie, FL: St. Lucie Press.

Nana-Sinkam, S.C. (1995). Land and Environmental Degradation and Desertification in Africa. http://www.fao.org/docrep/X5318E/x5318e00.htm (accessed February 2004).

Newton, Lisa H. (2002). *Ethics and Sustainability: Sustainability and the Moral Life*. Englewood Cliffs, NJ: Prentice-Hall.

Nti, James. (1989). The Impact of the Economic Crisis on the Effectiveness of Public Service Personnel. In: Balogun, M.J., and Mutahaba, Gelase, eds., *Economic Restructuring and African Public Administration*. West Hartford, CT: Kumarian Press. Cited in Balogun, 2003.

Ohiorhenuan, John F.E., and Ohiorhenuan, Lily A. (1998). An Institutionalist Perspective on Sustainable Development. In: Ohiorhenuan, John F.E., and Wayen, John A., eds. *Challenges and Prospects for Sustainable Development in Africa*. New York: UNDP, pp. 19–49.

Pearce, D.W., Barbier, E.B., and Markandya, A. (1990). A. *Sustainable Development*. London: Earthscan. Cited in Ohiorhenuan and Ohiorhenuan, 1998.

Sawyer, A. (1988). *Effective Immediately: Dictatorship in Liberia, 1980–1986: A Personal Perspective*. The Netherlands: The Africa Centre.

Serageldin, I. (1996). Sustainability and the Wealth of Nations: First Steps in an Ongoing Journey. Environmentally Sustainable Development Studies and Monograph No. 5. Washington, D.C.: World Bank.

Shihata, I. (1990). "Issues on Governance." In Borrowing Members … the Extent of Their Relevance under the Bank's Article of Agreement (mimeo). Cited in Frischtak, 1994.

UNDP. (1994). Human Development Report, UNDP. New York: Oxford University Press.

UNDP. (1996). Human Development Report, UNDP. New York: Oxford University Press.

UNDP. (2002). Human Development Report, UNDP. New York: Oxford University Press.

UNDP/Liberia. (2000). *NHDR* (National Liberian Human Development Report). Liberia, Monrovia:UNDP/Liberia.

UNESCO. (2003). Cultural Diversity, Biological Diversity and Sustainable Development. A Concept Note for UNESCO Forum.

Urbanska, K.M., Webb, N.R., and Edwards, P.J. (2000). *Restoration Ecology and Sustainable Development*. New York: Cambridge University Press.

Warhurst, Alyson. (1998) "Developing a Sustainable Economy: Towards A Pro-Active Research Agenda." A desk study prepared for Economic and Social Research Foundation, April. http://www.sussex.ac.uk/units/gec/pubs/reps/dssuseco.htm (accessed March 2003).

WCED. (1987). *Our Common Future*. Oxford: Oxford University Press.

WSSD (World Summit on Sustainable Development), (2002). Plan of Implementation, Advanced unedited copy, September.

Chapter 21

Technology Assessment in the Journey to Sustainable Development

Getachew Assefa and Björn Frostell

CONTENTS

Introduction

Technologies have been in use since the Neolithic revolution and intensively used since the industrial revolution. With the growth of world population and the limited resources available, the application of technologies will continue to increase in line with the quest for commensurate carrying capacity of the Earth. The rapid evolution of science and technology has so far been accompanied by increased energy and resource consumption and environmental pollution. However, these negative impacts of technology or technical systems were not widely recognized until some time later.

Specifically, after the first United Nations (UN) Conference on Human Environment, held in Stockholm in 1972, undesirable impact of technologies gained significant recognition. Among the list of areas for priority action put up by the conference were the need for understanding and controlling the changes man produced in the major ecological systems, the need for accelerating the dissemination of environmentally sound technologies and for developing alternatives to existing harmful technologies, and the need to avoid commitment to new technologies before adequately assessing their environmental consequences.[1]

Different approaches, methods, frameworks, and tools were proposed to assess different impacts of technical systems. Technology Assessment (TA) is just one of those that have won institutional recognition since their inception. The Congressional Office of Technology Assessment (OTA) in the United States was founded in 1972 with the aim to study technological change and provide early indications of the probable positive and negative impacts of the applications of technology.

The rethinking and change of ideas regarding approaches and concepts developed since the 1960s and 1970s called for different revitalization efforts in terms of both the discussions involved and the instrument for action required. These changes are results of imbalances among the outcome and expectations, contemporary requirements, practicality and feasibility, lack of comprehensiveness, and so on.

Two events of interest in this regard were the closing of OTA, 23 years after its establishment by the U.S. Congress, and the second UN Conference in Rio de Janeiro on Environment and Development in 1992, 20 years after the Stockholm Conference.

One of the reasons for OTA's closing was related to methodological issues. In the words of an insider, OTA, "had difficulty in developing and sharing successful approaches to assessment, either at the tactical level of specific techniques or at the conceptual level" (Wood, 1997). The *tactical level* refers to specific data collection and research methods.

The *conceptual level*, also called *midlevel methodology*, provides a common conceptual frame of reference for many studies.

The 1992 UN Conference on Environment and Development, also called the Rio Summit, institutionalized the theory and practice of *sustainable development*, first coined in 1987 in the Brundtland Report, with ecological, economic, and social considerations. In making sustainable development operational, human activities at different levels should be checked for compliance with these three considerations to fulfill the needs of present and future generations. Checking compliance requires compilation of different types of information. A variety of decision tools, everything from physical tools and computer-based tools to methods and procedures, can be used for gathering and analyzing information for assessment of any technical system.

At the conceptual level or midlevel, a TA with an established framework is of paramount importance for assessing sustainability of technologies. The three dimensions of sustainability can be addressed with the aid of TA tools. In other words, the number of areas of TA that are normally expressed in the form of multiple categories can be recategorized into ecological, economic, and social dimensions. Furthermore, one possible and cost-effective way of reinforcing conventional TA from the sustainable development point of view at the tactical level is the use of well-established tools, methods, and concepts of systems analysis in an integrated manner. There is a consensus among users and developers of assessment tools that there are already sufficient systems analysis tools that deal with at least the ecological and economic dimensions. Resources and efforts should, thus, be siphoned toward integrating, combining, and enhancing existing tools.

The integration or combinations of existing tools and concepts to account for the three spheres of sustainability in a coherent way is required. There is not sufficient knowledge derived from the experience of working with such integrated tools. Integrated tools provide a framework for cross-fertilization of component tools. This cross-fertilization reinforces the capacity of each individual tool in structuring, analyzing, and partially or fully evaluating different impacts of technologies. Combining existing tools is useful in avoiding problem shifting and compensating for weaknesses in some tools in a given decision-making situation (Wrisberg et al., 2002).

In the following sections, the concept of TA is discussed at the general level in a wider perspective, followed by a discussion on limitations associated with conventional TA. Current activities at the international level are also presented. These sections are based on a survey of literature on conventional TA. Finally, some discussions on how the terms *tech-*

nology and *technology assessment* are used in the remaining sections is given.

Technology Assessment

Different authors and authorities have defined TA in a variety of ways. Armstrong and Harman (1980) presented four different definitions that reflect a wide variety of views. They distilled five points that could be identified as underlying features in the different definitions. Three of these features are relevant to the scope of this chapter:

■ A useful TA should produce a comprehensive, even-handed evaluation and comparison of valid alternative choices.
■ TA should provide specified stakeholders with comparisons of the broad range of advantages and disadvantages of the alternatives.
■ TA as a multidisciplinary effort requires participation of social as well as physical scientists.

The United Nations Environmental Program (UNEP) broadly defines TA as "a category of policy studies, intended to provide decision-makers with information about the possible impacts and consequences of a new technology or a significant change in an old technology. It is concerned with both direct and indirect or secondary consequences, both benefits and disadvantages, and with mapping the uncertainties involved in any government or private use or transfer of a technology. TA provides decision-makers with an ordered set of analyzed policy options, and an understanding of their implications for the economy, the environment and the social, political and legal processes and institutions of society" (CEFIC, 1997). TA is useful when a new technology is introduced or when an existing technology is significantly modified. In other words, it can be used for new or already implemented technologies.

According to Durbin and Rapp (1983), TA is not a completely new phenomenon. It was performed implicitly and on an intuitive basis, not explicitly and by means of methodology, even before the establishment of OTA in the United States in 1972. The traditional way was related to the primary goals of engineering efficiency and economic profit. Despite this history, however, TA originated as part of the formal scenery in the United States (Durbin and Rapp, 1983). The purpose of TA then was to serve as a basis for policy formulation, and it had a strong link to decision making.

The term *technology assessment* is used in a variety of contexts that differ largely in scope and depth. The problem of dealing with a variety of issues that are rather many and complex has motivated Brooks (1994) to develop TA typologies. In order to develop these typologies, he formulated eight dimensions of TA.

The dimensions of technology assessment as formulated by Brooks, with modified examples, were as follows:

1. The degree of specificity of the object of assessment (e.g., the use of buses in a specific place in Sweden, the use of buses in general, or the use of biogas buses in particular).
2. The scope of the system included (e.g., the bus as an artifact, the bus with its whole set of supporting systems, including highways, oil refineries, fuel stations, insurance companies, repair shops, bus factories).
3. The degree of confinement to hardware and technical characteristics (e.g., including emissions, fuel efficiency, driving performance, but not legal systems, insurance, policing, licensing systems, etc.)
4. The type of impact categories (e.g., environmental, health, safety, ecological, economic, social, psychological).
5. The geographical and temporal scope of impacts considered (e.g., local, regional, short-term, intergenerational impacts, long-term ecological productivity)
6. The degree to which the likely political and behavioral responses are explicitly considered (e.g., responses to alternative policy prescriptions for the sociotechnical system being assessed).
7. The degree of "neutrality" aimed at in the assessment (e.g., assessment designed to gather evidence in support of an already chosen policy; assessment designed to evaluate and compare the consequences of alternative policies; assessment designed to explore, in as value-free a way as possible, the probable or possible consequences of a continuation or likely evolution of existing trends).
8. The stage of development in the "life cycle" of the technology being assessed (e.g., at the research and development [R&D] stage, already beginning to be deployed, already deployed on a large scale; the challenge is to regulate or alter it to reduce its secondary impact). This dimension, of course, greatly affects the degree of foresight required and the resultant uncertainties, and the kind of evidence that can be assembled.

In the effort to put all the discussions around TA types and tools required for each type in context, an extensive literature attempts to categorize and explain the aims of different types of TA. Brooks classified TA into five types, primarily using the first three dimensions listed. These types of TA are project assessment TA, generic TA, problem assessment TA, policy assessment TA, and global problematique TA.

Project assessment TA is concerned with a concrete project such as a thermal energy plant or the actual plan for construction and testing of a prototype of a new power plant. The novelty or extent of previous experience with the technologies to be employed or the degree of previous experience with the particular type of environment in which they are to be deployed is important. Depending on the extent that a project presents special challenges either because of the novelty of the technology used or of the unprecedented problems of a new environment, project assessment may spill over into the next category, generic TA, which must rely more on theoretical insights derived from science and less on cumulative practical experience with the technology in operation.

Generic TA focuses on a general class of technologies without reference to a particular project or a particular site, environment, or social setting.

In problem assessment TA, the approach is to examine a broad problem area such as commercial air transport and assess a variety of technologies as well as nontechnical measures that might be used to cope with the problem.

Policy assessment TA is very similar to problem assessment TA, except that it takes greater account of nontechnological alternatives to achieving social goals for whose realization new technology is only one of many options.

In a global problematique TA a number of closely interrelated social, political, economic, and technical problems coexist and are difficult to attack piece by piece, and the resulting cluster of problems affect the world as a whole considered as a single system. What makes the "problématique" different from other forms of TA or problem assessment is that no single scientific report, no single decision, and no single nation will have the last word. The management of the problématique has to be a cumulative process of "social learning" with, ultimately, very wide participation of virtually all the stakeholders.

It is clear to see from the preceding discussion that TA has a strong link to the *last word* or decision making.

The Institute for Technology Assessment and Systems Analysis (ITAS) in Karlsruhe, Germany, distinguishes among three types of TA with different starting points: project-induced TA, problem-induced TA, and technology-induced TA (Berg, 1994). From the point of view of TA objectives, four TA types can be identified: awareness, strategic, constructive, and back-casting, all of which may aim at either analysis or intervention (van Den Ende et al., 1998). Other authors who discussed different types of TA were Wad and Radnor (1984) and Berlozink and Van Langenhove (1997).

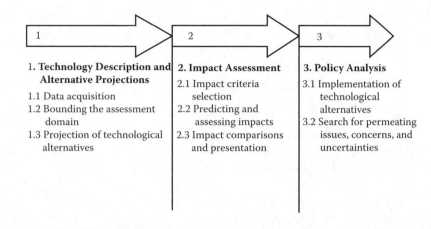

Figure 21.1 The three functional elements of the TA process. (Based on Armstrong and Harman, 1980.)

Armstrong and Harman (1980) divided TA exercises into three steps: Technology Description and Alternative Projections, Impact Assessment, and Policy Analysis (see Figure 21.1). Each step has its own components, as depicted in Figure 21.1. The impact assessment step is the central part of the whole process. The more value-laden policy analysis step relates the impact assessment to the concerns of the society (Durbin and Rapp, 1983). The impact assessment step is further discussed as follows.

The *impact criteria selection* (Durbin and Rapp, 1983) substep, also known as *impact identification* in other literature, is structured in seven categories: economic, legal, environmental, institutional, social, political, and technological (other technologies than the one under assessment). Armstrong and Harman (1980) treated this issue by discussing four different approaches of defining and structuring impact criteria and mentioned a typical breakdown of the impacts into five categories: economic, sociological, legal, environmental, and technical. It is not clear whether the order of listing implies the order of priority given to the categories. TA works that cover part of the categories listed with different degree of specificity and detail and, with different spatial coverage, are available.

Tools and methods enter the TA scene under the latter two steps of impact assessment, namely, *predicting and assessing impacts* and *impact comparisons and presentation*. Armstrong and Harman (1980) formulated a different grouping of impact assessment techniques.

Those tools dealing with predicting and assessing impacts are grouped as follows:

1. *Established tools from the scientific disciplines involved in TA.* Input–output analysis, cost–benefit analysis, and the air–water diffusion model are examples of this group of tools. These tools were especially related to the primary goal and intent of the technology.
2. *Methods of futurology and systems research.* Some of the TA tools falling under this class are expert opinion (Delphi), analogy, quantitative models, conceptual models, trend analysis, cross-impact analysis, and scenarios.
3. *Techniques for social impacts.* Quantitative measures, morphological analysis, expert opinion, and polling are techniques used to account for social impacts of technology.
4. *Tools focusing on organization of the impact assessment process.* Unlike the preceding three groups of tools, this group deals with the coordination of the process of impact assessment. Examples of such tools are expert opinion synthesis, predictive models, and ad hoc systems analysis.

The grouping shown is not to be taken as a clear-cut categorization because some tools fit into more than one category.

Those tools dealing with the next step of impact comparison and presentation or evaluation of impacts on a common scale and organization of impact presentation are categorized as follows:

1. Tools for subjective (social and political impacts) and objective (physical and economic) impacts: The tools dealing with subjective impacts include public polls, stakeholder representatives, public review synthesis, the project team as public substitute, and sample alternative viewpoints. For those impacts that are relatively objective such as environmental impacts, comparisons and presentations in terms of emission quantities, from measurements or calculations, are possible.
2. Methods for quantifiable and nonquantifiable impacts: For quantifiable impacts, numbers are used; for the nonquantifiable ones, words and pictures are the alternatives.
3. Approaches for evaluating and summarizing comparisons: Methods of summarizing that use common physical units whenever possible or otherwise unitless scales can be employed.
4. Ways of organizing the presentation of impacts: Impact presentation can be organized on the basis of interest groups, technological choices, relevance trees, and other categories.

Henriksen (1997) made an extended presentation of a toolkit of technology assessment techniques. The techniques are divided into nine groups: economic analysis (11^2), decision analysis (9), systems engineering and systems analysis (7), technological forecasting (6), information monitoring (4), technical performance assessment (9), risk assessment (5), market analysis (4), and externalities–impact analysis (6).

TA Issues and Worldwide Activities

When the Congress closed OTA in 1995, after production of a number of TA reports during its 23 years of existence,, one of the issues raised by its critics was related to methodology problems. There are strong tendencies in the literature that indicate the absence of consensus on different issues related to operating TA. Ludwig (1997) and van Eijndhoven (1997) described the controversy around the concept as "TA dilemma." Ludwig expressed the most common claim made against TA as lack of sufficient methodology. Durbin and Rapp (1983) pointed to this problem as the "vague scientific and methodological status of TA." With regard to disciplinary organization of impact criteria, Armstrong and Harman (1980) recognized that TA suffered from relatively poor coordination, integration, and overall balance.

TA has also been criticized as "nonparadigmatic" and, therefore, by inference, not cumulative (Brooks, 1994). In a survey of actual TA projects in the United States, Rossini and associates (1978) found that TA practitioners, at least in the first years, seldom used any of the quantitative techniques that had been widely advocated in the theoretical literature; quantitative tools were not favored. Wad and Radnor (1984) pointed out that in fact specialists preferred to rely on their own judgments and intuition in the selection of approaches and in the design of the TA. These problems had a surpassing impact on the credibility and reproducibility of TA studies. A well-defined paradigm would offer a common language, making it easier to compare different TA studies than is the case with intuitive practices.

On the other end of the discussion, some objected to the attempt to have a common methodology, labeling it as "reducing TA to a formula" (Blair, 1994). While recognizing the merit of allowing each specific TA to determine the methodology, this claim should not overshadow the importance of developing a methodology on the basis of which TA studies can be carried out on a comparative level.

Over the years, TA has had different definitions of varying emphasis. TA devoted considerable attention to presenting the public and stakeholder group attitudes toward technology and its impacts (Armstrong and Harman, 1980). According to the same source, assessment of social impacts was the central feature of TA. The European Chemical Industry Council

(CEFIC, 1997) showed that TA originally concerned itself with the assessment of the political and socioeconomic impacts of new technologies but later included environmental dimensions as well. Even later on, the environmental dimension was present only to a limited extent.

Despite the demise of OTA and the criticism targeted at TA, the interest and engagement in it did not disappear. The solutions to global problems that threaten the notion of sustainable development can be realized with the help of technology. The indispensability of TA arises from the need to avoid unwise and unfounded decisions in selecting the right technology (Ludwig, 1997). Different activities are going on at different levels, including efforts of restoring OTA (Dietz, 2002; Hutton, 2001). For further readings on the post-OTA world of TA, refer to Bimber and Guston (1997) and Hill (1997).

A number of countries have a separate body that deals with issues of TA, such as the Danish Board of Technology. This board is an independent body established by the Danish Parliament in 1995 and is the successor of the Technology Board, which was set up as a statutory body in 1986. The Norwegian Board of Technology is an independent office for TA established by the Norwegian government in 1999.

Some such bodies in other European countries (e.g., Berg, 1994) are Rathenau Institute of the Netherlands, the former Netherlands Organization for Technology Assessment; Parliamentary Office of Science and Technology of Great Britain; Parliamentary Office for Evaluation of Scientific and Technological Options in France; the German Parliamentary Office of Technology Assessment and Center for Technology Assessment (CTA) at the Swiss Science and Technology Council. Within the European Union (EU) these bodies have formed a partnership through European Parliament Technology Assessment (EPTA).

At the global level, the International Association for Technology Assessment and Forecasting Institutions (IATAFI), sponsored by the UN, was established in 1993 with a secretariat in Bergen, Norway. The aim of the association is development of international cooperation among institutions that work with assessment and forecasting of new technologies. The institutions share knowledge, methods, data, and other essential information.

Within the UN, UNEP has been driving a TA program called Environmental Technology Assessment (EnTA). As defined by this program, EnTA is a process that can assist decision makers in making informed choices that are compatible with sustainable development by examining and describing the environmental implications of new technologies. It also provides information that provides public policy makers, nongovernmental organizations, and the general public with better information about technology choice decisions (UNEP/IETC, 1997). EnTA, despite its focused name, covers a number of TA areas other than environmental impact.

Revisiting Technology and TA

In light of the broad context discussed previously at the general level and as exercised internationally, there is a need to delimit how the terms *technology* and *technology assessment* are used here. *Technology* in this context implies any technical system that can result in or be well described in terms of energy and material flows in line with the photosynthesis analogy. As materials (water and carbon dioxide) and energy (solar radiation) produce the biomass in the biosphere through photosynthesis, different types of materials and energy produce the technomass in the anthroposphere through technology.

In other words, all technical systems for which the energy and material flows within themselves and from and to the environment are not insignificant enough to be neglected are part of the technology domain under discussion. *Technology* in this case is defined as hard and soft means to transfer, transport, and transform materials and energy in a given economy. Manahan and Turner and associates took this line of technology discussion. Manahan (1999) discussed technology as the ways in which humans do and make things with materials and energy. On the other hand, Turner and colleagues (1994) viewed economic activity as a process of transforming materials and energy.

This activity of processing materials and energy is in concurrence with shaping, forming, manufacturing, producing, or generating a product or a service of an economic value. Good examples in this regard are the technologies used in the production and manufacturing of different chemicals, waste management, fuel and energy production, and operating transport systems.

The discussion regarding TA is limited to the part of the conventional TA that deals with the hardware and technical aspects of impacts of technology. Ethical, legal, and political aspects of wider perspective are outside the scope of this chapter. Unlike conventional TA and UNEP's EnTA, only the impact assessment part makes up the TA concept discussed here. The policy analysis step of traditional TA is beyond the scope of the TA discussed here.

This tactical-level TA comprises the assessment of ecological impacts in terms of emissions to the environment and depletion of resources (primary energy) and economic impacts in terms of traditional financial costs and environmental costs and social impacts. In a nutshell, TA in this context uses a conceptual framework defined by the three dimensions of sustainability: ecological, economic, and social dimensions. In this regard, TA was redefined as the evaluation of an object, function, or sequence of functions—created by human society to assist in achieving a goal—with respect to sustainability in comparison to other solutions providing the same function(s) (Eriksson and Frostell, 2001). The technology is assessed from the perspective of a certain defined setting within which it is supposed to operate at the microlevel. TA is important in relation to the operational level of sustainability, because sustainability in its practical sense demands measurement and performance comparison.

A systematic combination of different tools of systems analysis and other relevant tools is of advantage in developing a TA tool that can deal with the ecological, economic, and social impacts of technology. This kind of tool can be referred to as a *technology sustainability assessment* (TSA) tool.

TA and Sustainable Development

The world political and social order in the 1970s and 1980s, which witnessed the major part of the TA years, was different from the order that has prevailed since the beginning of the 1990s. The discussions on the knowledge and development landscape of this new era, which characterize the last decade of the last century and the beginning of the new century, are dominated by the notion of sustainable development. Catching up with this new order, it is no wonder that there are some attempts at discussing TA in the context of sustainable development (CEFIC, 1997, and Ludwig, 1997). The synthesis of such attempts and the distillation of the TA literature, in light of the new order, boil down to the need to recategorize the impacts assessed into ecological, economic, and social impacts.

Combining systems analysis tools developed in different disciplines with a considerable magnitude of integration of ideas and concepts leads to a tool that can address the ecological, economic, and social aspects in an integrated fashion. Once such a tool is well developed, it can function as a TSA tool (Figure 21.2). The realization of such a tool demands a considerable degree of coordinated efforts from both social and natural scientists.

Conventional TA was dominated by qualitative methods from social sciences. Quantification was limited to cost–benefit economic analysis (Durbin and Rapp, 1983). The inspiration from the efforts made to develop sustainable development indicators to measure social phenomena around the mid-1990s implies the importance of quantitative analysis in social sciences, to say nothing of natural science types of problems. Sustainability

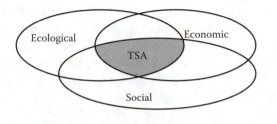

Figure 21.2 A technology sustainability assessment (TSA) tool that can address ecological, economic, and social impacts of a technology in an integrated fashion.

indicators can, thus, be useful for testing the relevance, quality, and quantity of various actions, including application of technologies, in terms of principles of sustainable development. The World Resources Institute (WRI) emphasizes "measuring sustainable development" by using material flow analysis together with other metrics for environmental and social factors (WRI, 2002). Different institutions and authorities use sustainability indicators based on a theme-by-theme (ecological, economic, and social) approach. Development of tools for social indicators that are able to win global consensus in order to have integrated performance indicators based on the integration of ecological, economic, and social indicators is needed.

Most of the literature on TA focuses on the assessment of a technology at the macrolevel, in relation to higher levels of political decision making. However, not all social impacts and ecological impacts attract the same degree of attention from political decision-makers; nor do investments on individual technologies at the microlevel have the political importance for high-level political decision-makers that they have for individuals at lower levels. The focus in conventional TA is on new technologies that surpass local scale considerations. This exercise has a risk that "old" or "familiar" technologies with less novelty and complexity pass easily through the screens of contemporary TA exercises. In order to avoid such a risk and observe the "think globally and act locally" concept, a microlevel TA exercise is better suited. Macrolevel technology assessment as exercised since the OTA years should be zoomed in to meso- and microlevel technology assessment practices. On the other hand, the micro- and mesotechnology performance should be related to the macrolevel performance of regional to global technological systems.

Combination of Tools of Systems Analysis

This section starts with a discussion on combinations of different tools of systems analysis. This is followed by a description of three such tools that are combined to develop a systematic TA tool that deals with the assessment of the ecological and economic sustainability of technologies.

In the quest for an improvement in TA exercises, there are a number of assessment tools with different features and bases that can be combined. Because the extent of issues covered in TA naturally requires the application of a range of tools, combination is considered to be helpful for resource-efficient and comprehensive assessment work.

According to Brattebø (2001), assessment tools can be based on *quantitative* or *qualitative* tradition. The *quantitative* group are required because, more often than not, one cannot manage what one cannot measure. Among these are material and substance flow analysis (MFA–SFA), life cycle assessment (LCA), and life cycle costing (LCC). The *qualitative* group is a logical complement of the first because one cannot measure all parameters in numbers. These include interviews, scenario analysis (forecasting and back-casting), panels, and consensus conferences. It is impossible to make such classifications in a clear-cut manner because there are qualitative elements within the quantitative tools, and vice versa.

Discussions concerning possibilities of combining different tools have been going on at different levels. Combination of tools is important in both avoiding problem shifting and compensating for weaknesses in tools (Wrisberg et al., 2002). The peculiarity of each tool causes each single approach to produce only a partial contribution to the assessment work. Often, it is the combination of several of them that represents the real tool that can be advantageously used by decision-makers (Aresta and Caroppo, 2002). The integration of different assessment techniques or tools is, thus, the most appropriate approach for tackling environmental, economic, and social issues (Cowell et al., 1997).

Specific studies and discussion focusing on integrating LCA with other tools have also been made. In a document that discussed different decision support tools and their relationship with LCA, CHAINET[3] emphasized two specific points to be addressed—namely, integration and harmonization of LCA with other tools and cross-fertilization between tools—to help identify whether there are features of LCA that can be exploited elsewhere, and vice versa.

The list of tools that can potentially be combined in the search for a powerful assessment tool becomes even larger according to UNEP's EnTA program. Environmental management tools such as Environmental Impact Assessment (EIA), Life Cycle Assessment (LCA), and Risk Assessment (RA) are considered by UNEP to be similar but separate from TA (UNEP, 2002). While the European Chemical Industry Council (CEFIC) regards them as part of a broad range of TA tools (CEFIC, 1997), Ludwig (1997) gives a relatively structured picture of how different tools and methods called "instruments of TA" relate to each other. These include EIA, LCA, environmental management and audit scheme (EMAS), and ecobalance (EB).

The combination of systems analysis tools in the same computer-based tool enhances its position in providing information regarding different dimensions of the assessment. A tool of this kind is different from a toolbox with a number of separate tools because it systematizes the whole approach, allowing the tools to cross-fertilize.

While recognizing the advantage of investigating the potential of combining a number of different systems analysis tools, the authors' firsthand experience confines the following discussion to the tools of MFA–SFA, LCA, and LCC.

Material and Substance Flow Analysis (MFA–SFA)

Material Flow Analysis, or Material Flow Accounting, or Material Flux Analysis (MFA) refers to accounts in physical units (usually in terms of tons) that comprise the extraction, production, transformation, consumption, recycling, and disposal of flow of substances and materials. MFA covers approaches such as Substance Flow Analysis (SFA) and bulk Material Flow Accounting (b-MFA). Both approaches use the principle of material balances. Further, Wrisberg and colleagues (2002) consider Material Input Per Unit of Service (MIPS) as a function-oriented variant of MFA.

Fischer-Kowalski (1997) discussed the history of MFA, using a literature review of societal metabolism, since the mid-19th century across various disciplines such as biology, ecology, sociology, cultural anthropology, and social geography. Of great significance, however, Baccini and Brunner developed the concept of MFA for assessing the anthropogenic metabolism of regions in the early 1980s. They combined existing scientific methods and new approaches to connect and interrelate soil, water, and air with the anthroposphere in a holistic manner. Quite often cited in the literature is their book *Metabolism of the Anthroposphere* (Baccini and Brunner, 1991).

Udo de Haes and coworkers (1997) distinguished three phases of carrying out MFA–SFA:

1. Goal and system definition
2. Inventory and modeling
3. Interpretation

The goal should be explicitly defined because the system boundary and other accompanying aspects are related to it. Examples of possible goals of MFA–SFA modeling can be data acquisition and generation, error-checking procedure, and identification of missing flows.

The inventory and modeling phase concerns the computation of the flows and stocks for a given year. This computation can use three types of modeling: bookkeeping, static modeling, and dynamic modeling. In bookkeeping, a flowchart for the given system with all stocks, flows, and processes both in society and in the environment is developed. Then, for the given period of time, empirical data are collected and attributed to the flows and stocks. The static modeling describes a static condition, apart from possible changes in the immobile stocks and from changes outside the given system. The core point here is the development of one consistent mathematical structure that makes it possible to specify relations among the different flows and stocks within the system. In a dynamic model, the process equations include time as a variable. In this way, not only the long-term equilibrium of a certain regime but the road to this equilibrium and the time required to reach it can be calculated.

In the third phase, the interpretation phase, MFA–SFA results expressed in terms of mass of flows and accumulations of the material or substance under study are used in different ways. If the analysis is generally directly related to the toxic or other specific polluting character of a single material or substance, mass flow is enough. In the case that a number of substances are studied and the result becomes too great to handle on a mass basis, an aggregation is required. For further readings on MFA–SFA refer, for example, to van der Voet and associates (1995).

Life Cycle Assessment (LCA)

Life cycle assessment (LCA) is a method for analysis and assessment of the environmental impacts associated with a product, service, or activity throughout its entire life cycle (e.g., ISO, 1997). LCA can be seen as both a procedure and a model. It has a step-by-step procedural framework:

1. Goal definition and scoping
2. Inventory analysis
3. Impact assessment
4. Interpretation

In the goal definition and scoping step, the purpose and scope and level of detail of the study, the basis for comparison or the functional unit, and the procedure for data collection and handling of data quality are defined.

The second step of inventory analysis results in a list of quantitative inputs and outputs to and from the system under assessment. The inventory table is made up of material and energy requirements, products, coproducts, waste, and emissions that cross the system boundary. The important point in determining inventory is establishment of boundaries between the studied system and both the environment and other product systems by using a logical cutoff procedure (Ekvall, 1999).

The third step in LCA, impact assessment, consists of selection and definition of environmental impact categories, classification (assigning of resource and emission data to relevant categories), and characterization (quantification and aggregation of the classified data using substance- and category-specific conversion factors).

Impact valuation, a part of the third step in which the environmental impacts are translated into a single-value parameter, is an optional element according to the international standard (ISO) 14040 standard. Impact valuation involves normalization, grouping, and weighting.

In the last step of LCA, interpretation, the validity of the results is examined against the goal of the study using different techniques such as sensitivity analysis for checking data uncertainties and effect of methodological choices. This data quality analysis is described as mandatory in comparative assertions.

The need to differentiate among different types of LCA is emphasized in the literature. This is helpful in understanding the discussion around methodologies, guidelines, and standards and interpreting results. Ekvall (1999) surveyed the literature on LCA and showed that two types of LCA can be distinguished under different terms: an LCA with an accounting perspective, called *retrospective*, and an LCA modeling the effect of changes, called *prospective*. In delimiting the system boundary in a prospective LCA, the main question is whether a process or a subsystem is relevant to the change under consideration. Expanding the system also includes other subsystems outside the core that can be affected by the change. Further readings on LCA can be found in, for example, ISO (1998, 2000).

Life Cycle Costing (LCC)

The discussions in this section concerning life cycle costing are entirely based on Wrisberg and coworkers (2002). Life Cycle Costing (LCC) is a tool that looks at the entire life cycle of a product, process, or activity and calculates the entire life cycle costs, which include all internal costs and plus external costs, incurred throughout the entire life cycle. The internal costs include conventional costs and less tangible, hidden, indirect company costs. Conventional costs are the ones that appear in typical company accounts for use in process control, product costing, investment analysis and capital budgeting, and performance evaluation. They include both annual operational costs such as labor, material, and product transportation, and one-time capital costs such as new equipment and buildings, engineering and design for new installations, and utility connections. The less tangible, hidden, indirect company costs tend to be less measurable and quantifiable, frequently are contingent or probabilistic in nature, and often are obscured by placement in an overheads account. For example, they include environmental permitting and licensing, reporting, waste handling, storage, and disposal. External costs are those for which a company, at a specified time, is not responsible, in the sense that neither the marketplace nor regulations assign such costs to the firm; they address emissions and resource use and their environmental and human health effects. LCC places a monetary value on those impacts. Simplified LCC does not include all external costs.

LCC aims at the analysis of the processes in connection with a given function, as does LCA. The type of system definition is therefore function oriented. Environmental impacts in comprehensive LCC can be translated into monetary metric at three stages. These are initial interventions (e.g., emission of kilograms of SO_2), "midpoint" effects (e.g., increased acidity in water bodies), and impacts on end points (e.g., the fish kills and loss of biodiversity resulting from increased acidity). LCC uses different costing approaches and techniques that vary in terms of the point in the impact chain where the impacts are assessed.

Several methods are available for valuing physical impacts in monetary terms. The methods involve assuming or creating a fictitious market in order to gather the value that individuals might assign to an externality (contingent valuation), examining behavioral responses that are, or might be, influenced by an externality (e.g., hedonic pricing), or analyzing the implicit value placed on pollution abatement by society through the actions of its regulatory agencies (e.g., regulators' revealed preferences).

Three types of quantitative data are required in LCC. These are data on internal costs, data on external environmental effects (in physical or monetary units), and data for valuation of environmental impacts if they are not already in monetary terms. For further readings on LCC refer to the reference list in Wrisberg and associates (2002).

The TA discussion in this section is mainly concerned with the tactical level of methodology without reference to a specific method of combination. The fact that conventional TA is "nonparadigmatic" and noncumulative, as mentioned by Brooks (1994), can partly be taken into account by developing a combined TA tool using such well-established concepts and standardized tools. The role of each of the component tools is briefly described as follows.

The use of the concept of MFA–SFA within the TA allows the possibility of recognizing the potential accumulation of toxic substances or depletion of resources, and identification of the most effective point of control of harmful concentrations and flows. MFA–SFA is a robust tool in a number of policy questions (Wrisberg et al., 2002).

With regard to LCA, Ekvall (1999) pointed out its strong points: a LCA is established among decision-makers, has structured procedure and ISO, and is an established platform for methodological development and harmonization (SETAC[4]-UNEP). From the perspective of the methodological deficiencies of conventional TA, the use of tools with LCA as a building block enhances the position of the TA tool. LCA also has the merit of avoiding problem shifting (Wrisberg et al., 2002) from one stage in the life cycle to another, from one sort of environmental issue to another, and from one location to another.

LCC is suitably used for comparing technical systems that provide the same function but that may have different costs of investment, operating, and maintenance and importantly different environmental performance that can be interpreted in monetary terms. Use of LCC in a TA tool enhances the economic assessment capability of the latter. The advantage of simplicity that LCC offers in the form of a single indicator can be useful with respect to decision making.

Multidisciplinary requirements are also part of the discussion in TA. Groot (1992) stated that multidisciplinary projects simply require everyone to do his or her own thing. Perhaps a project coordinator or manager is needed to glue the final product together, but the pieces are fairly clear of disciplinary size and shape. Interdisciplinary efforts, on the other hand, require more or less integration of the disciplinary contributions. In combining tools, an interdisciplinary interaction with sufficient knowledge concerning the weaknesses and strengths of the tools is important.

Computer-Based TA Tool

The assessment work required for making sound decisions regarding sustainable development entails collection, processing, and analysis of large amounts of information. This information can be qualitative or quantitative. Computers are powerful tools in analysis of complex information once a ready-made algorithm is available in digital form.

With development of softwares and hardwares capable of processing large magnitudes of both quantitative and qualitative data with reasonable speed and ease in presenting results in a comprehensible format, computer-based TA will remain the dominant type of TA tool. The advantages and limitations of such computer-based tools are discussed in the following from the perspective of the authors' experience of developing and using a Swedish computer-based tool known as ORWARE. It is a combination

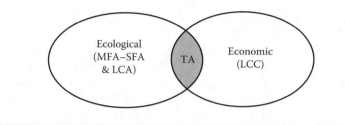

Figure 21.3   A TA tool as a combination of MFA–SFA, LCA, and LCC.

of MFA–SFA, LCA, and LCC that addresses the ecological and economic impacts of technologies, not social impacts (Figure 21.3).

The Advantages

In order to analyze any problem, for example, one associated with a technological system, one needs knowledge about the structure of the system or data about the system. Models are an appropriate possibility for structuring knowledge. In light of different aspects of methodology, issues, and tools of TA, a computer-based TA tool can be seen as a model concept that can contribute to the development and practice of systematic TA.

This contribution is discussed in terms of the combination of component tools and the inherent positive features of the Swedish computer-based TA tool—ORWARE. Generally every quantitative LCA involves MFA–SFA data for producing LCI data but all data in a multiple MFA–SFA are not part of LCI. Hence, MFA–SFA and LCA are treated in this case as two distinct parts.

The quantitative nature of MFA–SFA, LCA, and LCC enhances both measuring and understanding of issues addressed. The MFA–SFA describes the static situation of different material or substance flows between different subsystems in a defined system. The tool handles a large number of physical flows and may therefore be characterized as a multidimensional material and substance flow analysis. Normally, MFA–SFA is often used in relation to macrolevel applications at a region or city level. In this case, however, the same principle and methodology are used at a relatively microlevel of processes and technologies and process and technology chains.

The MFA–SFA modeling is important specifically with regard to flows that are not characterized using LCA methods into impact categories. Examples in this case are heavy metal flows. The use of MFA–SFA facilitates the task of tracking down specific substances of interest. Recycling issues and stock issues within the different technological systems can be identified using the information from the MFA–SFA model. Emissions such as NO_x are also of interest in terms of the absolute value of the amount emitted because of regulation requirements, and so on. The material flow modeling generates data on such emissions from the technology system.

The flows of pollutants and in some cases nutrients between parts of the systems under study, and later their final destination in any of the three compartments of the natural environment, namely, air, water, and soil, are mapped using the MFA–SFA part.

In addition to the role MFA–SFA plays in locating and displaying the amount of different flows and emissions for self-enabled analysis, it provides inputs to the other two conceptual tools incorporated: LCA and LCC. The MFA–SFA part maps the flow of each material and substance inside and outside the system. It is possible to pick any one of the flow steams corresponding to any vector element at any point along the technology chain for an ad hoc assessment.

The use of multidimensional MFA–SFA renders immunity to the limitations of conventional MFA–SFA that deals with a single material or substance. Such limitations are associated with the inability to avoid shifting of problems to other materials or substances. Although the MFA–SFA modeling is static, the interaction of the different substances and hence the formation and consumption of different substances are modeled using formation coefficients. For noninteracting substances, their coordinate is modeled in terms of both the process streams they flow through and their destination (air, water, or soil) after leaving the system.

The LCA part uses most of the data, not all, generated by MFA–SFA and processes it further into different ecological impact categories. In other words, the MFA–SFA carried out on different substances contained in emission and effluent streams is translated to relevant impact categories using standard LCA methodology. The life cycle modeling is carried out for all the chains of technologies through which the feedstock passes until the final product joins its final recipient in the environment. As the main feedstock is processed along the technology chain, relevant emissions and effluents occurring during the course of the process are characterized into impact categories. The flows of materials and energy required for running the technology chain are followed from "cradle to grave." The emissions and effluents associated with the cradle-to-grave life cycle of the material and energy inputs are also characterized into impact categories.

In the LCC part, the operating cost of the technology system, the investment costs, and other costs of maintenance and demolition or management of demolition waste are considered. However, these costs make up the internal-cost part of the LCC only. Unlike the cost consideration of conventional cost–benefit analysis (CBA), LCC includes external costs. In calculating the external costs, LCC uses the emission data from the MFA–SFA modeling (Figure 21.4).

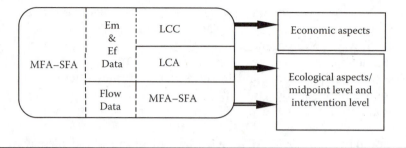

Figure 21.4   The use of MFA–SFA, LCA, and LCC in ORWARE.

The *midpoint level* in Figure 21.4 refers to the impact categories of LCA, whereas the *intervention level* implies the data directly provided by the MFA–SFA part (e.g., emission and resource depletion data).

While the LCA classifies the emissions leading to the same type of impact and aggregates into impact categories (midpoint level); the LCC translates the mass of each emitted substance into monetary terms. It is not necessarily the case that exactly the same type of emissions are used by both LCA and LCC because there is a difference in the level of knowledge reached with regard to the tools and the scientific and social thinking underlying them. The LCC used includes both internal and external costs. The external-cost dimension of LCC covers both extractions and emissions.

The information from the LCC complements the information from LCA in two ways. In the first place, it provides an economic dimension of the assessment of the building phase of the physical structure, the magnitude of which is otherwise left out as negligible from the point of view of LCA. Second, it serves as an economic variety of characterization of the emissions along the life cycle. In this case, emissions from both the core system, just covering the system under study, and the external system, including upstream and downstream units, are accounted for separately or in aggregated form.

In general, MFA–SFA, LCA, and LCC complement each other, enhancing the capacity of a combined tool in terms of the quality of the TA-related information generated. They also cross-fertilize in systematizing the whole work of assessment of the ecological and economic impacts of technical systems.

Positive features of a computer-based TA tool in light of TA are its quantitative, even-handed, and holistic features and, as mentioned earlier, its structured result presentation. Because the tool uses and produces quantitative data, it makes it easier to add, compare, and identify parts of the life cycle with significant ecological and economic implications and to specify what can be gained by alternative chains of technologies that fulfill the same function. This is true in terms of both ecological and economic impacts at both system and subsystem levels.

A computer-based tool provides even-handed analysis and structured handling of input and output data, covering both ecological and economic dimensions, consistently and coherently. This is important because it allows reference to previous results in a comparable way and helps identify important factors that steer different aspects of the technical system. It is not easy to do so when analyses are performed in a non-even-handed way. Although this facet seems trivial, the absence of an appropriate tool in the impact assessment part of conventional TA has precipitated criticism.

The systems perspective involved in using the concepts of core system and compensatory system gives the opportunity to have insight into different sectors at the same time and provide understanding on how they influence each other in a holistic manner. The cross-fertilization of MFA–SFA, LCA, and LCC aids in determining the weak points along the chain of technologies in terms of ecological, economic, and technical performance.

Use of computer-based tool facilitates structured presentation of huge amounts of data and complex information. This includes the input data, the model made up of different submodels, the generic data used in LCA and LCC, the mathematical equations of partitioning and transfer coeffi-cients and, importantly, the output data. MATLAB® SIMULINK® is used as a graphic interface for the modeling part, allowing the possibility of visualizing and analyzing the modeled systems. The results can be saved in MATLAB® for future retrieval; the main result presentation is done in Microsoft® Excel. Both the ecological and economic output data are displayed both in tables and in different diagrams in such a way that cause–effect relations can be traced. Because the assessment is done in terms of scenarios, bar diagrams that show each impact category with each bar corresponding to a scenario provide one possible method of presentation. Such result presentation is possible for both core systems and the total system that includes the compensatory system (see Figure 21.5).

All impact categories can be collected into the same bar diagram or a radar diagram. The latter provides an axis for each ecological or economic impact category with lines connecting the axes through points correspond-ing to the values of the relative impacts of each scenario (see Figure 21.6).

The Limitations

Despite the positive features mentioned, such a tool suffers from different levels of limitations. The problem with using computer-based tools in TA applications can be categorically identified as specific and general. The

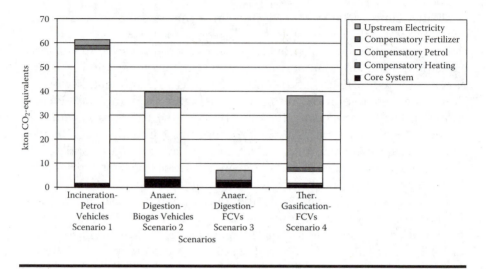

Figure 21.5 Example of core and compensatory system result presentation in ORWARE. (From Assefa et al., 2002.)

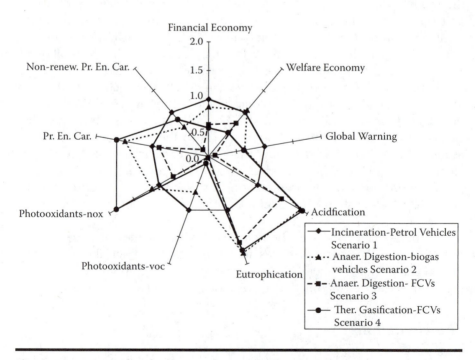

Figure 21.6 Example of radar result presentation in ORWARE.

specific problem is related to assessment of technologies that are still at R&D stage. This involves the use of data about technologies for which no real-life experience is available. The uncertainty in acquiring such data through estimation, inference, and extrapolation from other technologies is a limitation. The problem emanates from the prerequisite that the technology should be described in terms of material and energy flows.

The general problems are those associated with the relationship between the model and the reality modeled and data quality at different levels and the component tools. In addition to the data-intensive nature and quality problem of LCA, some inherent weaknesses in today's LCA concept can be mentioned. One limitation is related to effects such as rebound effects whereby an increase in economic activity resulting from cost-efficient changes offsets the savings obtained through the original change. A second weakness is associated with the underlying assumption that when a demand for a material increases in the life cycle investigated, the production of that material is increased by the same amount (Ekvall, 2002).

Moreover, only known and quantifiable ecological impacts are considered in LCA (Wrisberg et al., 2002). This limits the scope of the assessment. LCC may be compromised by the confidentiality of data for economic processes. Another limitation lies in the problems incurred with monetarization of physical impacts that do not exist on the market. The uncertainty is highly dependent on the question at stake and the data and models used.

Knowledge and Decision-Making Dimension

Combining the tools of systems analysis in a TA tool is an attempt to inject a relatively objective and scientific basis into the impact identification and analysis part of TA while keeping the policy part open for other important considerations. With an increased objective and scientific component, TA has a potential to provide knowledge that can serve as a basis for exercising sound decision making in the journey to sustainable development.

In terms of inspirations from discussions on LCA and knowledge and requirements of decision-making processes from Ekvall (1999), the potential contribution of TA in making sound decisions can be pointed out. Ekvall identified constraints in making sound decisions, namely, lack of knowledge, limited capacity for information processing, and conflicting goals. TA is capable of producing information regarding the ecological and economic and social performance of chain of technologies from a systems perspective.

The relative performance obtained from comparisons of alternatives will continue to exist in a transition period until improved knowledge paves the way for better options. Sustainability indicators are examples of relative performance. With improved knowledge and with experience from working with relative performance, it will be possible to develop absolute performance metrics. Preceding this development, our knowledge should enable us to define and characterize an absolute sustainable level of each type of capital or the total capital, depending on whether weak or strong sustainability draws global consensus.

On the political front, commitment and determination of decision makers are required as a driving force. The information about performance after validation in relation to appropriate methodologies leads to knowledge of varying importance. Specifically those involved in the R&D of technologies require knowledge that is beyond the traditional knowledge referred to as "knowledge of how to do or make things" by Edwin Layton. The problem with limited capacity of information processing implies the need to make result presentations handy without a need for further processing. The familiarity of different sections of society including decision makers with the component tools combined with a reasonable degree of integration facilitates the role it can play in the decision-making world. According to CHAINET (2002), LCA is one of the tools that have received much attention from both the scientific world and the policy makers. Ekvall (1999) pointed out that LCA is established among decision makers. This feature would enhance the decision-making relevance of TA tools that contain LCA methodology.

However, the reliability of such TA tools would, by and large, depend on improved knowledge on how to deal with data gaps, data uncertainties, and data qualities. The knowledge we currently have does not provide us with conclusive evidence on whether a given technology is sustainable or not in absolute terms. We will have to continue for years to come, if not decades, with less-is-better- or much-is-better-type assessments.

If the finding that knowledge is currently doubling every year and will double every 73 days by 2020 (Bosseau, 1998) holds and has a direct relevance, we are in a better position to address the knowledge gaps that lurk behind efforts of checking the impacts of technologies in our journey to sustainable development.

Notes

1. Stockholm 1972—Brief Summary of the General Debate (http://www.unep.org/).
2. Numbers in brackets indicate the number of techniques under each group.

3. European Network on Chain Analysis for Environmental Decision Support.
4. The Society of Environmental Toxicology and Chemistry.

References

Aresta, M., and Caroppo, A. (2002) *An Introduction to the Environmental Life-Cycle Assessment (ELCA)*. Metea Research Center, University of Bari, Italy. http://www.metea.uniba.it/CEEDES/lca.pdf (accessed December 26, 2002).

Armstrong, J.E., and Harman, W.W. (1980) *Strategies for Conducting Technology Assessments*. Westview Press, Boulder, Colorado.

Assefa, G., Björklund, A., Eriksson, O., and Frostell, B. (2002) ORWARE: An Aid to Environmental Technology Chain Assessment. *Journal of Cleaner Production*, 13(3), 265–274.

Baccini, P., and Brunner, P.H. (1991) *Metabolism of the Anthroposphere*. Springer-Verlag, Berlin.

Berg, I.V. (1994) *Technology Assessment in Europe: A Documentation of TA Research Establishments*. Kernforschungszentrum Karlsruhe, Karlsruhe, Germany.

Berloznik, R., and Langenhove, L.V. (1998) Integration of technology assessment in R&D management practices. *Technological Forecasting and Social Change*, 58, 23–33.

Bimber, B., and Guston, D.H. (1997) Introduction: The end of OTA and the future of technology assessment. *Technological Forecasting and Social Change*, 54, 125–130.

Blair, P.D. (1994) Technology assessment—current trends and the myth of a formula. http://www.wws.princeton.edu/~ota/ns20/blair_f.html (accessed December 22, 2002).

Bosseau, D.L. (1998) Where are we now? Some thoughts about expansionism. *Journal of Academic Librarianship*, 24(5), 390–391.

Brattebø, H. (2001) Formal education in industrial ecology. In: The Science and Culture of Industrial Ecology. The International Society for Industrial Ecology, The Netherlands November 12–14, 2001. www.yale.edu/is4ie/images/Brattebo.pdf (accessed December 22, 2002).

Brooks, H. (1994) Technology assessment. In: J-J. Salomon, F.R. Sagasti, and C. Sachs-Jeantet (eds.). *The Uncertain Quest: Science, Technology, and Development*. United Nations University Press, Tokyo.

CEFIC. (1997) Technology assessment: A tool towards sustainable chemical industry. European Chemical Industry Council, Brussels, http://www.cefic.be/position/st/pp_st03.htm (accessed December 22, 2002).

CHAINET. (2002) Life cycle assessment (LCA). http://www.leidenuniv.nl/interfac/cml/chainet/ (accessed December 26, 2002).

Cowell, S.J., Hogan S., and Clift, R. (1997) LCANET theme report: Positioning and applications of LCA. Centre for Environmental Strategy, University of Surrey, Guildford, England. http://www.leidenuniv.nl/interfac/cml/lcanet/ftheme1.htm (accessed December 22, 2002).

Dietz, F. (2002) Office of technology assessment could return. *Mechanical Engineering*, 124(4), 24.

Durbin, P.T., and Rapp, F. (1983) *Philosophy and Technology*. D. Reidel, Boston.

Ekvall, T. (1999) System Expansion and Allocation in Life Cycle Assessment with Implications for Wastepaper Management. Doctoral thesis. AFR Report 245. Göteborg, Sweden: Department of Technical Environmental Planning, Chalmers University of Technology, Sweden.

Ekvall, T. (2002) Cleaner production tools: LCA and beyond. *Journal of Cleaner Production*, 10(5), 403–406.

Eriksson, O., and Frostell, B. (2001) An approach to sustainability assessment of energy systems. In: S. Silveria (ed.). *Building Sustainable Energy Systems: Swedish Experiences*. Swedish National Energy Administration, Stockholm, Sweden.

Fischer-Kowalski, M. (1997) Society's metabolism—origins and development of the material flow paradigm. In: S. Bringezu, M. Fischer-Kowalski, R. Kleijn, and V. Palm. (eds.). *Regional and National Material Flow Accounting: From Paradigm to Practice of Sustainability*. Proceedings of the ConAccount workshop January 21–23, 1997, Wuppertal Special 4, Wuppertal Institute for Climate, Environment and Energy, Leiden, The Netherlands.

Groot, W.T. de. (1992) *Environmental Science Theory: Concepts and Methods in a One-World, Problem-Oriented Paradigm*. Elsevier, London.

Henriksen, A.D.P. (1997) A technology assessment primer for management of technology. *International Journal of Technology Management*, 13(5/6), 615–638.

Hill, C.T. (1997) The Congressional Office of Technology Assessment: A retrospective and prospects for the post-OTA world. *Technological Forecasting and Social Change*, 54, 191–198.

Hutton, K. (2001) Return of the Congressional Office of Technology Assessment? National Council for Science and the Environment. http://csf.colorado.edu/forums/cnie/current/ (accessed December 22, 2002).

ISO. (1997) Environmental management—life cycle assessment—principles and frame work. ISO 14040:1997. European Committee for Standardisation CEN, Brussels.

ISO. (1998) Environmental management—life cycle assessment—goal and scope definition and inventory analysis. ISO 14041:1998. European Committee for Standardisation CEN, Brussels.

ISO. (2000) Environmental management—life cycle assessment—life cycle interpretation. ISO 14043:2000. European Committee for Standardisation CEN, Brussels.

Ludwig, B. (1997) The concept of technology assessment—an entire process to sustainable development. *Sustainable Development*, 5, 111–117.

Manahan, S.E. (1999) *Industrial Ecology: Environmental Chemistry and Hazardous Wastes*. Lewis, London.

Rossini, F.A., Porter, A.L., Kelley, P., and Chubin, D.E. (1978) *Framework and Factors Affecting Integration within Technology Assessments*. Georgia Institute of Technology, Atlanta.

Turner, K.R., Pearce, D., and Bateman, I. (1994) *Environmental Economics: An Elementary Introduction.* Harvester Wheatsheaf, New York.

Udo de Haes, H.A., van der Voet, E., and Kleijn, R. (1997) Substance flow analysis (SFA), an analytical tool for integrated chain management. In: S. Bringezu, M. Fischer-Kowalski, R. Kleijn, and V. Palm (eds.) *Regional and National Material Flow Accounting: From Paradigm to Practice of Sustainability. Proceedings of the ConAccount Workshop,* January 21–23, 1997, Wuppertal Special 4, Wuppertal Institute for Climate, Environment and Energy Leiden, The Netherlands.

UNEP. (2002) Environmental technology assessment. United Nations Environment Program. http://www.unep.or.jp/ietc/supportingtools/enta/ (accessed December 22, 2002).

UNEP/IETC. (1997) Work-book for training in environmental technology assessment for decision makers. Technical Publication Series no. 5. UNEP International Environmental Technology Centre, Osaka/Shiga, Japan.

Van den Ende, J., Mulder, K., Knot, M., Moors, E., and Vergragt, P. (1998) Traditional and modern technology assessment: Toward a toolkit—a research methodology and learning strategy for social impact assessment. *Technological Forecasting and Social Change,* 58, 5–21.

van der Voet, E., Klein, R., van Oers, L., Heijungs, R., Huele, R., and Mulder, P. (1995) Substance flow analysis through the economy and the environment. Part 1. System definition. *Environmental Science and Pollution Research,* 2(2), 89–96.

van Eijndhoven, J.C.M. (1997) Technology assessment: Product or process. *Technological Forecasting and Social Change,* 54, 269–286.

Wad, A., and Radnor, M. (1984) Technology assessment: review and implications for developing countries. *Science Policy Studies and Documents* No. 61. Paris: UNESCO.

Wood, F.B. (1997) Lessons in technology assessment: Methodology and management at OTA. *Technological Forecasting and Social Change,* 54, 145–162.

WRI. (2002) Global topics: Resource and materials use. World Resources Institute. http://www.wri.org/ (accessed December 26, 2002).

Wrisberg, N., Udo de Haes, H.A., Bilitewski, B., Bringezu, S., Bro-Rasmusse, F., Clift, R., Eder, P., Ekins, P., Frischknecht, R., and Triebswetter, U. (2002) Demand and supply of environmental information. In: N. Wrisberg and H.A. Udo de Haes (eds.). *Analytical Tools for Environmental Design and Management in a Systems Perspective: The Combined Use of Tools.* Kluwer Academic, Boston.

Chapter 22

Industry and Sustainable Development in 18 Developing and Transition Economies

Ralph Luken and Nadejda Komendantova-Amann

CONTENTS

Introduction

The 1992 United Nations Conference on Environment and Development (UNCED) recognized that sustainable development would require countries to "build upon and harmonize their various sectoral economic, social and environmental policies and plans." Spurred by UNCED, most developing country governments have made efforts to draw up national sustainable development strategies (NSDSs). The Johannesburg Plan of Implementation, approved at the World Summit on Sustainable Development, called for the completion of NSDSs and the beginning of their implementation.

In its preparatory activities for the 5-year review (Rio+5, 1997) of the Earth Summit, the United Nations Industrial Development Organization (UNIDO) evaluated the NSDS-related efforts of most developing countries. The evaluation focused on the extent to which the various integrated frameworks and country profiles took into account the potential impact of industry (defined as the manufacturing sector) on social and economic development and addressed the potentially negative impact of industry on environmental quality and resource utilization.[1] UNIDO found little information on the positive impacts of industry in these strategies and profiles—except, as one might expect, in national development plans—in spite of the fact that the weighted average of manufacturing value added

(MVA) in gross domestic product (GDP) in all developing countries is approximately 25%.[2] It also found little information about the impacts of industry on environmental quality in the more explicit environmental frameworks, such as National Conservation Strategies and National Environmental Action Plans, and next to nothing in these documents about the positive impacts of industry or efforts to integrate environmental concerns into industrial development.

A more recent assessment that addressed industry-related issues to some extent was the International Forum on National Sustainable Development Strategies organized by the UN in Accra, Ghana, in October 2001 (UNDESA, 2002). It discussed the experiences up to that time in formulating NSDSs. It highlighted a number of obstacles in the realization of these strategies such as the inability of many countries to develop a clear approach to the issue or to create effective assessment mechanisms; a proliferation of policies, activities, and institutions focusing on different sustainable development concerns but with little coordination among ministries or agencies; and the inadequate sharing of the experience gathered.

The forum stressed, among other things, the need to make better use of such integrated approaches to development that already exist in a country rather than create new initiatives and capacities; to involve all stakeholders, using effective coordination and networking systems, in all phases of the process; to promote equity and local empowerment; to make progress through concrete projects that are realistic in terms of financial, human, and institutional resources; and to include mechanisms for both process and outcome and impact assessments as an integral part of the NSDS process.

At the forum, 12 developing and 4 developed country experts described sustainable development planning experiences in their countries.[3] Only some of the expert reports mentioned key industry-related issues—the importance of industry in achieving sustainable development, industry participation in the sustainable development planning process, and industry-specific sustainable development policy measures. Six of the 12 reports acknowledged the importance of industry, 6 mentioned industry participation in the sustainable development process, and 1 described industry-specific sustainable development policy measures. Only the report from China mentioned all three issues. None of the reports attempted to assess the impact of industry on sustainable development since the initiation of the NSDS process with the Rio Conference.

Given the dearth of information about the role of industry in sustainable development, UNIDO as part of its preparatory activities for WSSD requested national experts in 18 developing and transition economies to report on the extent to which recent changes in industrial, environmental, and technology policies have more closely aligned industrial development objectives with sustainable development objectives. The experts were also requested to assess the impact of industry (manufacturing in particular) on sustainable development, roughly over the period 1990 to 2000, to report on obstacles encountered in enhancing the positive and reducing the negative impacts of industry on sustainable development, and to put forward proposals for enhancing the contribution of industry to sustainable development.

The 18 national reports are from Bolivia (Cadima and Aguirre, 2001), Cameroon (Tekeu and Noumsi, 2001), Chile (Urzu, 2001), China (Huijiong, 2001), Colombia (Escobar, 2001), Cote d' Ivoire (Ahossane, 2001), Czech Republic (Moldan, 2001), Egypt (Mobarak, 2001), Ethiopia (Malifu, 2001), Indonesia (Hasnain and Nazech, 2001), Nigeria (Imevbore, 2001), Pakistan (UNIDO, 2001a), Philippines (UNIDO, 2001b), Sudan (Awad, 2001), Tunisia (Nafti, 2001), Turkey (Erer, 2001), Vietnam (Sam, 2001), and Zimbabwe (Guarjena, 2001).

This chapter draws on the 18 national reports and international data sources to accomplish three tasks. First, the chapter will characterize the impact of industry on sustainable development in these 18 countries. We had hoped to use data in the 18 national reports as well as international data sources for this task. However, the economic, social, and environmental data in the 18 national reports were limited and primarily qualitative in nature. As a result, the assessment draws only on data available from international organizations. The characterization will list available and industry-relevant data on all three dimensions of sustainable development, social, economic, and environmental; then elaborate on trends in a few of identified parameters to give a sense of what happened on each of the three dimensions over the period 1990 to 2000 and present an integrative index using a methodology similar to the one used by UNDP in constructing the Human Development Index (HDI) (UNDP, 2003).

Then the chapter will summarize the perceptions of the country experts about the obstacles to enhancing the socioeconomic impacts and mitigating the negative environmental impacts of industry on sustainable development. Next it will present the country experts' proposals for enhancing the contribution of industry to sustainable development. Finally, it will put forward their proposals for steps that are needed for assessing the contribution of industry to sustainable development.

Sustainable Development in the Manufacturing Sector

An increase in industrial output (defined as manufacturing value added [MVA]) has two major consequences for sustainable development. On the one hand, it contributes to social and economic development by contributing to the gross national product (GNP), increasing employment and incomes, and generating tax revenue that can support social services. On the other hand, it puts additional pressure on the environment in terms of both increased inputs into the production process (environmental withdrawals) and potential discharge of pollutants (environmental releases) unless appropriate environmental measures are taken by industry.

The sources of information for this characterization are the World Bank's World Development Indicators (2003), the International Labour Organization's Yearbooks of Labour Statistics (2000, 2002), and UNIDO's Industrial Statistics Database (2003).

Economic Development

Several indicators are available for characterizing the economic contribution of industry to sustainable development; unfortunately data availability is a problem for using some of them. The more promising indicators for which data are complete for most countries are listed in Table 22.1.

Absolute Outcome Measure: MVA per Capita in 2000 (US$ 1995)

Using data for the year 2000, one can benchmark the 18 countries on the basis of MVA per capita and roughly assign them to three different groups: the countries with comparatively high MVA per capita, the countries with the medium MVA per capita, and the countries with low MVA per capita (Table 22.2). The country with the highest MVA per capita is the Czech Republic (US$1,440), and the country with the lowest MVA per capita is Ethiopia (US$7).

Dynamic Outcome Measure: Percentage Change in MVA per Capita in the Period 1990 to 2000

Using data for the years 1990 and 2000, one can compare the relative improvement in MVA per capita among the 18 countries and roughly assign them to three groups: significant progress, some progress, and no progress (Table 22.3). The country with the greatest percentage change in MVA per capita was China (410%) and the country with the lowest (negative) change in MVA per capita was Colombia (28 %).

Table 22.1a   Manufacturing-Related Sustainable Development Statistics

Country	MVA per Capita in 2000 (US$ 1995)[a]	% MVA per Capita Change 1990–2000[a]	MVA in 2000 (US$ 1995, millions)[a]	% MVA Change 1990–2000[a]	% Change of MVA/GDP 1990–2000[a]
Bolivia	156	10	1,290	40	-3.0
Cameroon	83	-2	1,230	18	-3.6
Chile	774	36	11,700	60	-16
China	210	410	382,100	250	25.5
Colombia	310	-28	13,100	-13	-30.0
Cote d'Ivoire	2	-5	2,130	38	1.2
Czech Rep.	1,440	10	14,800	9	-0.2
Egypt	229	52	14,610	84	20.5
Ethiopia	0	12	440	25	-0.7
Indonesia	271	60	55,900	84	25.3
Nigeria	12	-11	1,570	18	-11.0
Pakistan	75	14	12,360	46	-1.0
Philippines	263	4	19,890	29	-4.0
Sudan[a]	24	27	770	43	–
Tunisia	459	45	4,390	70	7.4
Turkey	564	33	38,660	55	8.6
Vietnam	67	133	5,296	173	34
Zimbabwe	102	-26	1,290	-9	21.6

a   UNIDO data.

Table 22.1b   Manufacturing-Related Sustainable Development Statistics

Country	Mfg. Exports (% of Merchandise Exports) in 1990/2000[a]	% Medium- and High-Tech Goods in 1985/1998[a]	Mfg. Employment in 2000 (thousands)[b]	Mfg. Employment (% of Total Employment) in 1990/2000[b]	Mfg. Employment (thousands) in 1990/2000[c]	% Change of Mfg. Employment in 1990/2000[b]
Bolivia	4.7/29	–/5.0	320	16.1/15.2	35/51	46
Cameroon	8.5/5	0.2/1.8	–	–	50/53	6
Chile	11.3/16.2	2.4/6.3	780	16.1/14.3	298/305	2
China	71.6/88.2	4.1/36.6	80,430	13.5/11.3	53,040/44,700	–16
Colombia	25.1/34	5.6/8.9	1,190	23.8/20.2	488/454	–6
Cote d'Ivoire	19/14.5	–	–	–	36/51	42
Czech Rep.	88/88.3	–/51.9	1,320	29.6/27.7	1577/1260	–19
Egypt	42.5/37.1	0.7/8.8	2,210	13.0/13.2	1077/1210	4
Ethiopia	6.8/9.8	–/0.1	–	–	82/95	16
Indonesia	35.5/57.1	1.9/15.5	11,520	13.7/16.3	2650/4474	69
Nigeria	2.5/0.2	1.5/0.1	–	–	–	–
Pakistan	7.9/84.7	7.9/9.2	4,230	17.7/11.0	584/562	–4
Philippines	37.9/91.7	–	2,790	9.7/9.6	1109/1073	–3
Sudan	69.1/77	–	–	–	–	–
Tunisia	67.9/81.2	15/15.5	–	–	251/342	36
Turkey	76.8/88.7	18.2/23.5	3,380	14.8/17.4	975/1168	20
Vietnam	18.7/28.1	–	3,293	–	891/1541	36
Zimbabwe	38.6/38.4	18.7/15.3	–	–	184/148	–20

a UNIDO data.
b ILO data.
c UNIDO data.

Table 22.1c   Manufacturing-Related Sustainable Development Statistics

Country	% Female Employment in 1990–2000[a]	Energy Use per Unit of MVA 2000 (toe/million US$)[b]	BOD per Unit of MVA 2000 (ton/million US$)[b]	% Change in Energy Use per Unit MVA 1990–2000[b]	% Change in BOD per Unit MVA 1990–2000[b]
Bolivia	11.5	731	3.5	40	5
Cameroon	2.9	463	1.7	379	–38
Chile	13.9/13.8	772	2.7	18	–29
China	19/21.7	875	5.3	–60	–71
Colombia	25/19.9	996	5.0	53	31
Cote d'Ivoire	5.6	106	–	19	–
Czech Rep.	35.9/27.6	–	–	–	–
Egypt	10.2/9.1	976	4.6	–21	–47
Ethiopia	–	363	–	5	–
Indonesia	12.4	496	4.9	–7	–30
Nigeria	–	–	–	414	–
Pakistan	14.1	1,542	3.7	17	–34
Philippines	12.8/12.5	504	4.8	44	–30
Sudan	5.3/–	406	–	245	–
Tunisia	–	429	–	–31	–
Turkey (1999)	9.8/ 9.7	383	1.2	12	–30
Vietnam	–	1,745	–	–31	–
Zimbabwe	12.8	779	6.6	–12	–3

[a] ILO data.
[b] IEA and WDI.

Table 22.2   Groups of Countries According to the Level of Development of the Manufacturing Sector

Highly Developed (US$)	Medium-Developed (US$)	Least-Developed (US$)
Czech Republic (1,440)	Colombia (310)	Cameroon (83)
Chile (774)	China (303)	Pakistan (75)
Turkey (564)	Indonesia (271)	Vietnam (67)
Tunisia (459)	Philippines (263)	Sudan (24)
	Egypt (229)	Nigeria (12)
	Bolivia (156)	Ethiopia (7)
	Cote d'Ivoire (133)	
	Zimbabwe (110)	

Source: WDI.

Table 22.3   Dynamic Measure: Percentage Change in MVA per Capita, 1990–2000

Countries with Significant Positive Change in MVA per Capita (1990–2000) (%)	Countries with Positive Change in MVA per Capita (1990–2000) (%)	Countries with Negative Change in MVA per Capita (1990–2000) (%)
China (210)	Sudan (27)	Cameroon (–2)
Vietnam (133)	Czech Republic (10)	Nigeria (–11)
Indonesia (60)	Bolivia (10)	Zimbabwe (–26)
Egypt (52)	Philippines (4)	Colombia (–28)
Tunisia (45)	Czech Republic (10)	
Chile (36)	Cote d'Ivoire (2)	
Turkey (33)	Ethiopia (0)	

Source: WDI.

Assessment

The countries with the highest MVA per capita in 2000 were the Czech Republic, Chile, Turkey, China, and Tunisia. Of these countries, four also showed significant improvements in MVA per capita, a result that confirms the observation that those countries that were relatively well off in 1990 continued to be so during the 1990s. Within the medium MVA per capita grouping, Egypt and Indonesia maintained their relative position based on performance during the period 1990 to 2000, whereas Colombia and Zimbabwe deteriorated. Within the low MVA per capita grouping, two of the countries (in terms of performance between 1900 and 2000) improved, but not enough to put them in the medium MVA per capita grouping.

Other economic indicators of manufacturing performance, such as percentage changes in MVA and in manufacture of medium- and high-tech goods, are consistent with the two indicators. For example, three of the countries in the high MVA per capita group (China, Indonesia, and Turkey) significantly increased their manufacture of medium- and high-tech goods between 1985 and 1998. Conversely, most of the countries in the least developed group (Cameroon, Pakistan, Nigeria, and Ethiopia) showed only a small increase or even a negative change in the manufacture of medium- and high-tech goods between 1985 and 1998.

Employment

Identifying appropriate measures here is difficult for both conceptual and statistical reasons. On one hand, increases in manufacturing employment are viewed as a positive change; on the other hand, decreases in employees per unit of MVA (or its converse) are seen as increased productivity. Nor are the data nearly as complete or consistent as are economic indicators.

There are three sources of employment data for manufacturing—World Development Indicator (WDI) Database, International Labor Organization (ILO), and United Nations Industrial Development Organization (UNIDO). The WDI reports only industry employment, which includes mining and quarrying (ISIC2 [International Standard Industrial Classification]), utilities (ISIC4), and construction (ISIC5), as well as manufacturing (ISIC 3), whereas both ILO and UNIDO report on manufacturing employment. The ILO data are more comprehensive as they include employment in both the formal and informal sectors, but not as complete as the UNIDO data. Consequently, we have used the ILO data to estimate manufacturing employment as a percentage of total employment and UNIDO data to estimate percentage change in number of employees in the manufacturing sector.

Absolute Outcome Measure: Manufacturing Employment as a Percentage of Total Employment

The latest years for which data on manufacturing employment as a percentage of total employment are available are 1999 or 2000, as indicated in Table 22.4. Data are available for only 10 of the 18 countries. As can be seen in Table 22.4, the countries fall roughly into two groups—those with industry employment over 15% of total employment (five countries) and those with less than 15% (five countries).

Table 22.4   Manufacturing Employment as a Percentage of Total Employment in 2000

Industry Employment More than 15%	Industry Employment Less than 15%
Czech Republic (27.7)	Chile (14.3)
Colombia (20.2)	Egypt (13.2)
Turkey (17.4)	China (11.3)
Indonesia (16.3)	Pakistan (11)
Bolivia (15.2)	Philippines (9.6)

Source: ILO.

Table 22.5   Dynamic Measure: Percentage Change in Manufacturing Employment

Countries with Significant Positive Change in Number of Mfg. Employees (1990–2000) (%)	Countries with Positive Change in Number of Mfg. Employees (1990–2000) (%)	Countries with Negative Change in Number of Mfg. Employees (1990–2000) (%)
Indonesia (69)	Cameroon (6)	Zimbabwe (–20)
Bolivia (46)	Egypt (4)	Czech Republic (–16)
Cote d'Ivoire (42)	Chile (2)	China (–17)
Tunisia (36)		Colombia (–6)
Vietnam (36)		Pakistan (–4)
Turkey (20)		Philippines (–3)
Ethiopia (16)		

Source: UNIDO.

Relative Outcome Measure: Percentage Change in Manufacturing Employment, 1990 to 2000

There are UNIDO data for manufacturing employment for 16 of the 18 countries assessed in this report. In looking at Table 22.5, one sees that in seven countries employment in manufacturing increased significantly, in three countries it increased, and in six countries it decreased, in some cases dramatically so.

Assessment

Given the incompleteness of the data on manufacturing employment, we could assess the consistency of the employment data and compare them with the economic data for only a limited number of countries. There is no discernible relationship between female employment and either manufacturing employment as a percentage of total employment or as percentage change in employment between 1990 and 2000. Three of the six countries (Indonesia, Tunisia, and Turkey) that had a significant positive change in the number of employees in the manufacturing sector also achieved a significant change in MVA; the three countries, Bolivia, Ethiopia, and Sudan, had a relatively modest change in MVA. Four of the six countries (Philippines, Colombia, Czech Republic, and Zimbabwe) that had a negative change in the number of employees in the manufacturing sector recorded only moderate or even negative change in MVA.

Environment

In writing this chapter, we searched for internally consistent global data on environmental withdrawals by and environmental releases from the manufacturing sector (ISIC3). Whereas manufacturing-related environment data are relatively robust for developed countries, for developing countries they are not. Here the data are fragmented and of uneven quality as there are no international organizations systematically collecting and vetting resource use or pollutant release data for the manufacturing sector. The United Nations Environment Programme (UNEP) focuses its efforts for the most part on environmental quality (ambient conditions) data and not its precursors, pollutant releases that affect environmental quality (UNEP, 2002). There is no international organization responsible for collecting and vetting water use data by the manufacturing sector. The Food and Agricultural Organization of the United Nations has estimated freshwater withdrawals for industry for approximately 1990 and 2000 on the basis of data from several years and several sources (FAO, 2003). The only exceptions to this bleak picture are energy use and associated CO_2 emissions collected and vetted by the International Energy Agency (IEA, 2002) and organic matter effluents estimated by the World Bank (World Bank, 2002). Consequently, our 18-country comparison is limited to two parameters—energy use as an indictor of changes in environmental withdrawals and biological oxygen demand (BOD) discharge as an indicator of changes in environmental releases.

Energy Use

Absolute Outcome Measure: Energy Use per Unit of MVA

Using IEA data for the year 2000, one can compare 16 of the 18 countries on the basis of energy use per unit of MVA and assign them to three

Table 22.6   Energy Use per Unit of MVA, 2000

Low Energy Use per Unit of MVA (toe/million US$)	*Medium Energy Use per Unit of MVA (toe/million US$)*	*High Energy Use per Unit of MVA (toe/million US$)*
Cote d'Ivoire (110)	Bolivia (730)	Pakistan (1540)
Ethiopia (360)	Chile (770)	Vietnam (1740)
Turkey (380)	Zimbabwe (780)	
Sudan (410)	China (870)	
Tunisia (430)	Egypt (980)	
Cameroon (460)	Colombia (1000)	
Indonesia (500)		
Philippines (500)		

Note: toe = tons of oil equivalents.
Source: IEA/UNIDO

different groups: low, medium, and high energy use per unit of MVA (Table 22.6). The picture that emerges suggests that a moderate level of energy use per unit of MVA (approximately 400 to 1000 toe per unit of MVA) is necessary to be classified as a highly developed country (see Table 22.2). In some cases energy use per unit of MVA is either too low, contributing to a low level of industrialization, or too high, probably one of the factors contributing to excessive costs of production.

Dynamic Outcome Measure: Percentage Change in Energy Use per Unit of MVA

Using data for the years 1990 and 2000, one can compare the relative improvements in energy use per unit of MVA among the 16 countries and assign them to three groups (Table 22.7). In this case, one can see decreases in energy intensity of production among all three categories of energy use per unit of MVA. The high increases in energy intensity of production occurred only in countries with relatively low energy use per unit of MVA.

Assessment

Five of the six countries with decreases in energy use per unit of MVA experienced significant increases in MVA per capita and relatively high percentage increases in MVA between 1990 and 2000. One of the other two countries (Zimbabwe) with a decrease in energy use per unit of MVA

Table 22.7 Percentage Changes in Energy Intensity of Manufacturing, 1990–2000

Decrease in Energy Use per Unit of MVA (%)	Moderate Increase in Energy Use per Unit of MVA (%)	High Increase in Energy Use per Unit of MVA (%)
China (–60)	Colombia (53)	Cameroon (379)
Tunisia (–32)	Philippines (44)	Sudan (245)
Vietnam (–31)	Bolivia (40)	
Egypt (–21)	Cote d'Ivoire (19)	
Zimbabwe (–12)	Chile (18)	
Indonesia (–7)	Pakistan (17)	
	Turkey (12)	
	Ethiopia (6)	

Source: IEA, UNIDO.

Table 22.8 BOD Use per Unit of MVA, 2000

Low BOD Discharge per Unit of MVA (ton/million US$)	Medium BOD Discharge per Unit of MVA (ton/million US$)	High BOD Discharge per Unit of MVA (ton/million US$)
Turkey (1.2)	Bolivia (3.5)	Colombia (5.0)
Cameroon (1.7)	Pakistan (3.7)	China (5.3)
Chile (2.7)	Egypt (4.6)	Zimbabwe (6.6)
	Philippines (4.8)	
	Indonesia (4.9)	

Source: WDI, UNIDO.

experienced a negative change in MVA and MVA per capita, reflecting the overall decline in economic activity due to the political situation.

Organic Pollutants

Absolute Outcome Measure: BOD Discharge per Unit of MVA

Using WDI data for the year 2000, one can compare 11 of the 18 countries on the basis of BOD per unit of MVA (tons of BOD per 106 US$ of MVA) and assign them to three different groups: low, medium, and high BOD discharge per unit of MVA (Table 22.8).

Table 22.9   Percentage Changes in BOD Intensity of Manufacturing, 1990–2000

Decrease in BOD Discharge per Unit of MVA (%)	*Moderate Decrease in BOD Discharge per Unit of MVA (%)*	*Increase in BOD Discharge per Unit of MVA (%)*
China (–71)	Indonesia (–30)	Bolivia (5)
Egypt (–47)	Philippines (–30)	Colombia (31)
Cameroon(–38)	Turkey (–30)	
Pakistan (–34)	Chile (–29)	
	Zimbabwe (–3)	

Source: WDI, UNIDO.

Dynamic Measure: Percentage Change in BOD per MVA, 1990 to 2000

Using data for the years 1990 and 2000, one can compare the relative changes in BOD discharge per MVA among the 11 countries (Table 22.9). In this case, one can see decreases in BOD intensity for 9 out of the 11 countries and increases in BOD intensity for 2 countries. The significant decrease in BOD per MVA in China, Egypt, and Pakistan over the period reflects a significant reduction in the absolute level of industrial organic pollutant release in those countries.

Assessment

Three of the countries with a significant decrease in BOD intensity (China, Egypt, and Pakistan) experienced a high growth in MVA and MVA per capita during the period, suggesting that improvements in environmental and economic performance were compatible. Also, four of the countries with a modest decrease in BOD intensity (Chile, Indonesia, Philippines, and Turkey) experienced a high growth in MVA and MVA/capita. Lastly, one of the two countries with an increase in BOD intensity (Bolivia) experienced positive growth in MVA and MVA/capita and the other (Colombia) experienced negative growth in MVA and MVA/capita.

There are no discernable relationships between levels of BOD intensity and energy-use intensity in either 1990 or 2000 or between changes in BOD intensity and energy-use intensity.

Integrative Measure

The UNDP Human Development Index (HDI) (UNDP, 2003) is a summary measure of human development. It measures the average achievement in a country for a given year on three basic dimensions of human development. These are life expectancy at birth, knowledge (combines adult literacy and enrollments), and standard of living (GDP per capita in terms of purchasing price parity). Before the HDI is calculated, an index for each dimension is created. These indexes are minimal and maximal values (goalposts), for example, the minimal and maximal values for life expectancy at birth, 25 years, and 85 years, respectively. Performance in each dimension is expressed as a value between 0 and 1. The HDI is then calculated as a simple average of the dimension indexes, giving a one third weighting to each dimension. The HDI assessed performance for 175 countries in the latest assessment.

A similar but more modest exercise was done for a Sustainable Industrial Development Index (SIDI) (see Table 22.10). The SIDI measures the average achievement in a country for a given year on three basic dimensions of

Table 22.10   SIDI[a] for 1990 and 2000

Country	1990	2000
Bolivia	0.230	0.130
Cameroon	0.305	0.308
Chile	0.320	0.338
China	0.043	0.150
Colombia	0.227	0.085
Cote d'Ivoire	—	—
Czech Rep	—	—
Egypt, Arab Rep.	0.094	0.112
Ethiopia	—	—
Indonesia	0.106	0.103
Nigeria	—	—
Pakistan	0.118	0.093
Philippines	0.129	0.097
Sudan	—	—
Tunisia	—	—
Turkey	0.568	0.606
Vietnam	—	—
Zimbabwe	0.175	0.116

[a] SID index = $1/3$ (MVA per unit of BOD) + $1/3$ (MVA per capita) + $1/3$ (MVA per employee).

industrial development—MVA per capita, employment, and environmental performance. It is not as refined as the HDI in this chapter as we did not attempt to set minimal and maximal values on the basis of data for only 18 countries (and then only a subset of those countries, given data limitations). Instead it just combines all three measures. We tried different variations with two of the parameters—employment per MVA versus MVA per employment and BOD per MVA and MVA per BOD. One variation is reported here just to show the results. The relative gains are consistent for China and Indonesia, as is the relative loss for Zimbabwe. However, the changes between the two periods for Egypt and Turkey do not appear to be reflective of the actual situation. Another apparent limitation is the relative ranking of the countries in 2000. It would seem that Cameroon would have a lower aggregate score and that China should have a higher aggregate score. Perhaps this situation would change if minimal and maximal values were included, as they were for the HDI. However, such an attempt was beyond the scope of this effort.

Major Constraints and Obstacles

The country reports describe many and varied obstacles that have hindered the pursuit of sustainable development since the Earth Summit. It is not possible to describe them in detail in this chapter. Rather, the chapter extracts country-specific observations on five generic categories—development and implementation of policies and regulations, economic, technology, human resources, and industry awareness and participation (Table 22.11).

Policies and Regulations

- *Bolivia:* The design of environmental norms and regulations has not taken into account the technical and economic limitations of enterprises. As a result, only a small number of enterprises have obtained and implemented an environmental license.
- *China:* National ministries often pursue inconsistent policies. For example, there exists a policy that sets a low price for water at the same time there is policy that promotes conservation of water. This lack of coordination and cooperation among leading government institutions decreases effectiveness of environmental laws. In addition, the period of implementation of regulations is so short that enterprises are simply unable to comply with them.

Table 22.11 List of Obstacles and Constraints to Sustainable Development

Country	Policies and Regulations	Economic Constraints	Technology	Human Resources	Industry Awareness and Partici-pation
Bolivia	+			+	+
Cameroon			+		
Chile		+	+		+
China	+				+
Colombia		+	+		
Cote d'Ivoire			+		+
Czech Rep.	+	+		+	+
Egypt	+				
Ethiopia	+	+	+		+
Indonesia				+	
Nigeria	+	+			
Pakistan		+	+		
Philippines		+			
Sudan			+	+	
Tunisia	+	+			
Turkey		+			+
Vietnam		+	+		
Zimbabwe		+		+	

- *Cote d'Ivoire:* The national action plan for Agenda 21 has been formulated, but not effectively implemented. Relevant ministries are still resolving sectoral differences that stand in the way of maximizing synergies and minimizing conflicts. The ministries implementing international environmental agreements see them as only environmental efforts rather than as instruments for promoting sustainable development.
- *Czech Republic:* Environmental considerations are not sufficiently integrated into development strategies. There is an insufficient definition of property rights for natural resources that leads to excessive resource utilization. The Polluter Pays Principle has not yet been fully applied.
- *Egypt:* Environment laws have been formulated, but not successfully implemented, because of geographical and sectoral fragmentation in decision making. There are too many agencies involved, and they do not systematically cooperate with each other. As a result,

wholly unrelated decisions on industrial development in specific regions are made; negative impact on the environment results.

- *Ethiopia:* Laws and regulations prohibiting pollution and creating occupational standards either are in the pipeline or do not exist at all. In the cases in which regulations have been promulgated, they are not being enforced.
- *Nigeria:* The restriction on land ownership makes investments in Nigeria unattractive (i.e., investors cannot own the land on which they build factories).

Economic Constraints

- *Chile:* The export-oriented liberalization policy has not accelerated development of the manufacturing industry and not resulted in industrial restructuring. The progressive tariff system used by some developed countries discourages high-value-added export.
- *Colombia:* Weak domestic consumption has resulted in the production of the cheapest products rather than those with higher value added. The financial weakness of many firms has limited their ability to address environmental issues.
- *Ethiopia:* Because of lack of finances, many firms cannot invest in more productive and cleaner technologies. They are only concerned about survival. Import of contraband goods has hampered the performance of large enterprises such as the textile sector. Weak domestic demand has forced enterprises to cut costs, thereby depriving them of the revenues needed to invest in newer technologies.
- *Nigeria:* The dependence on crude oil as the major single export commodity is not economically sustainable.
- *Pakistan:* Sanctions imposed by the international community and cuts in development assistance programs have caused serious financial difficulties.
- *Philippines:* Former trade protectionist regimes made the country dependent on the export of primary products, thereby putting great pressure on the environment. A highly protectionist domestic regime, a limited domestic market, and lack of competition have limited the incentive to invest in new machinery.
- *Tunisia:* Small and medium enterprises have not been able to adjust to the conditions of the open economy. These enterprises are characterized by structural weaknesses, undercapitalization, low productivity, old equipment, and lack of qualified specialized staff.

- *Zimbabwe:* High inflation rates and cash flow difficulties have caused shortages of the foreign exchange needed to import production inputs, machinery spare parts, and fuel. This situation seriously affects the operations of the manufacturing industries when there are breakdowns of equipment. In addition, the declining purchasing power of the population due to high inflation rates and unemployment has decreased domestic consumption.

Technology Limitations

- *Bolivia:* There is a general lack of incentives for the manufacturing sector to improve the competitive and innovative capacities. Only one third of enterprises invest in technology development, innovation projects, and modernization.
- *Cameroon:* There is still a lack of information about new technologies.
- *Chile:* The suppliers offering cleaner technologies are underdeveloped. This underdevelopment leads to an imbalance of information about available goods and services, which in turn increases transaction costs.
- *Colombia:* The main obstacle to technology upgrading is a general resistance to any kind of change in Colombian enterprises.
- *Cote d'Ivoire:* There is no national policy for promotion of science and technology. Most enterprises are operating with old technology and lack the financial resources to upgrade it.
- *Czech Republic:* There is insufficient support for the uptake of environmentally sound technologies. Research about advanced technologies was seriously eroded as a result of the political changes in the 1990s. Another problem is that small and medium enterprises lack both information about and the resources to purchase cleaner technologies.
- *Ethiopia:* The transfer of new technologies is limited by the absence of an appropriate patent law.
- *Pakistan:* Major constraints to technology upgrading are lack of information on cleaner technologies, sources of funding, and access to markets that sell environmentally sound technologies.
- *Tunisia:* Less than one third of enterprises have participated in the industrial upgrading program supported by the European Union (EU). And within this number, most are the leading enterprises in the sector. The rate of small and medium-size enterprises participating in the upgrading of industrial program still remains very low.

■ *Turkey:* There is the lack of an information network that industry can use to access information about and services for tackling environmental problems.
■ *Vietnam:* The industrial sector is dominated by heavy industry with an obsolete technology base.

Human Resources

■ *Bolivia:* Another problem is the absence of qualified personnel. The human resource units in the few firms that have them are not dedicated to training but mainly to recruitment and administration.
■ *Indonesia:* Qualified personnel and current expertise are largely concentrated only in some manufacturing subsectors.
■ *Tunisia:* Enterprises lack the human resources to integrate environmental considerations into their operations, a serious obstacle to their competitiveness in new markets.
■ *Zimbabwe:* The qualified labor force has diminished as a result of the economic and political problems.

Industrial Awareness and Participation

■ *Bolivia:* There is lack of involvement of enterprises in the development of policies and environmental norms. The enterprises have not been consulted in the design and formulation of legal norms that affect their activities. As a result, the norms are implemented incorrectly by enterprises.
■ *Chile:* Public authorities still do not provide sufficient information on sustainable development issues.
■ *China:* The traditional Chinese planning process does not involve enterprises in the formulation of policies and strategies.
■ *Cote d'Ivoire:* The lack of understanding of the concept of sustainable development and its realization at different levels are the main obstacles to the realization of sustainable development policies and strategies.
■ *Egypt:* The interaction between industry and government agencies in policy formulation is limited.
■ *Ethiopia:* For the most part, public officers, employers, and workers are still not aware of the concept of sustainable development. For example, many industries still do not opt for environmental management systems and workers misuse safety equipment, including by selling it.

■ *Tunisia:* Very few enterprises have participated in the formulation of environmental laws and regulations.

Overview of Obstacles and Constraints

Obstacles for development and implementation of sustainable development policies and strategies exist at the levels of ministries and enterprises. On the level of ministries, decisions are often made by different groups and are fragmented and not coordinated. Often decisions are made from a sectoral point of view that leads to insufficient implementation of such laws and norms by enterprises. On the enterprise level, the business plan for implementation of strategies is often weak. One reason is that enterprises are often not involved in the process of development and adoption of industry- and environment-related policies and regulations. Even if laws were developed and adopted, enforcement issues remain because of the absence of appropriate sanctions.

Economic obstacles are both external and internal to the countries. A major external obstacle are tariff systems that discourage high-value-added exports and force the export of low-valued products, which have limited employment and wage possibilities. Even when free trade zones are created with an economically stronger partner, such as between North Africa and the EU, most domestic enterprises are threatened because of their structural weaknesses, undercapitalization, low productivity, and lack of qualified staff. Major internal obstacles are the lack of competition among domestic producers and a limited domestic market that discourages the rates of investment needed to increase output and improve productivity.

The existence of old polluting industry in many developing and transition economies is a serious obstacle to sustainable development. There is a lack of information about environmentally sound technologies (ESTs) as well as the financial resources to acquire them, particularly in small and medium-size enterprises. Some countries lack special policies and strategies for the promotion of ESTs, and others have policies that actually discourage the uptake of ESTs

In many transition economy countries, political changes caused an erosion of the research base of the industry.

Many countries still lack qualified engineers who are willing to work with industry. Moreover, only a few firms invest in training and development of human resources.

The lack of awareness of sustainable development issues is present on all levels, from ministries and employers to workers. This lack leads to the situation in which sustainable development issues are simply not a matter of concern.

Recommendations for Further Actions and Priorities

Policies and Regulations

- *Bolivia:* It is necessary to pursue a new development scenario that will consider solidarity and cooperation as equally important forces in sustainable development. On the level of policy making, it is required to establish strategies that are based on holistic views and take into account complexities and interdependence of factors of sustainable development.
- *Cameroon:* Planning of the sustainable development strategy should be done in a more efficient way. The strategy needs to include legislative and regulative proposals for implementation of the strategy. Cameroon needs to build a more exhaustive and ambitious action plan for sustainable development.
- *Chile:* New policies need to be devised and implemented that take into account social concerns (increased unemployment) to complement the economic reforms, which have focused almost exclusively on improving resource and energy use.
- *China:* There is a need for policy changes that balance the scale economies of large enterprises and the employment effects of small and medium-size enterprises.
- *Colombia:* It is urgent to increase the efficiency of public institutions, modernize the judiciary system, and develop institutions on the local level.
- *Cote d'Ivoire:* Ivorian industry strategy should necessarily take into account the changes relative to globalization of the economy and the new role of international trade. On this account, the industrial strategy will continue to be based on achieving two strategic objectives: the implementation of the industrial upgrading program in order to improve the competitiveness of production units and the mainstreaming of environmental considerations in production and consumption systems.
- *Czech Republic :* Coordinating the plans of the Czech Confederation of Industry and Transport with the government, parliament, labor unions, and international community is required, as is the promotion of regional development.
- *Ethiopia:* The government needs to finalize three environmental proclamations, the Industrial Environmental Policy and Strategy, the Pollution Control Regulations, and the Environmental Impact Assessment Guideline.

■ *Indonesia:* The government must recognize environmentally sound performance as a critical component of good corporate governance now that Indonesian industry is under pressure to reform business practices and to compete successfully in the global economy.
■ *Nigeria:* In order to attract foreign investors to develop industry in Nigeria, it is necessary to reform land ownership laws.
■ *Zimbabwe:* Strengthening of the institutional capacity for development of planning and economic management is recommended.

Economic Development

■ *Bolivia:* The reversal of the import–export gap and Bolivia's place in a global economy require a transformation of the manufacturing sector through the elimination of institutional obstacles, increased competitiveness and productivity, and new higher-value-added products.
■ *China:* Growth of the service sector should be encouraged because of, among other reasons, its importance to the manufacturing sector. Research, design, accounting, consultancy service, information collection and dissemination, and goods distribution are inseparable from an efficient and effective manufacturing system, especially in a global knowledge-based society, and should be promoted.
■ *Czech Republic:* Industry should be restructured with the aim of increasing productivity, competitiveness, and orientation to ecoefficiency and gradual decrease in the consumption of natural resources, particularly nonrenewable resources.
■ *Egypt:* In order to integrate Egypt into the global economy, it is necessary to remove several barriers such as taxation, custom tariffs, and logistics charges for shipping and aviation transportation.
■ *Nigeria:* The growth of non–oil industry activities should be encouraged with foreign direct investment. Special efforts are necessary to eliminate unnecessary taxes that stifle initiative, to remove excessive regulatory constraints, and to promote confidence in the stability of the business environment.
■ *Vietnam:* An increase in foreign direct investment is needed to accelerate Vietnam's integration into the global economy.

Technology Development

■ *Czech Republic:* Important prerequisites for long-term sustainability in the country are the stabilization and gradual decrease in consumption of natural resources and particularly of nonrenewable resources. The most relevant task for the forthcoming years is the transition to ecoeffective, preventive, and partnership approaches, which would lead to waste minimization.

- *Egypt:* It is recommended that the private sector invest more in research and innovation.
- *Indonesia:* Greater efforts are needed to promote cleaner production and the transfer of environmentally sound technologies.
- *Pakistan:* Industrial outreach centers are needed for promoting not only cleaner production but also more advanced environmentally sound technologies, pollution control, and environmental management.
- *Philippines:* Additional incentives are needed to encourage more efficient processes and cleaner production and firms' adoption of international environmental management standards.
- *Tunisia:* Information technologies and the establishment of technology parks (*technopoles*) are needed to promote higher-value-added industries.
- *Vietnam:* An effective ban on the import of obsolete technologies is needed.

Human Resources

- *Colombia:* New employment opportunities should be created in both urban and rural areas by strengthening small and medium enterprises.
- *Nigeria:* On-the-job training and enhanced human capacity building should be provided with the objective of increasing the number of skilled managers and technicians. There is a need for specific programs to increase the participation of women in industry and to remedy gender discrimination.

Industry Awareness and Participation

- *Egypt:* The channels for communication and interaction between the government and private sector should be strengthened.
- *Ethiopia:* The state and civil society alliance in the service of sustainable development such as the National Commission on Sustainable Development should be strengthened.
- *Philippines:* A continuous dialogue between the public and private sectors is required, as well as the establishment of a national roundtable on industrial policy and environmental protection.

- *Tunisia:* It is necessary to increase the awareness of small and medium-size enterprises regarding raw material conservation, water and energy savings, and ecoefficient practices, with a view to improving their economic and environmental performance and to developing their internal capacity for adopting and managing environmentally sound technologies.
- *Turkey:* An expanded partnership between the state and private sector enterprises is needed to raise awareness of the need for environmentally sound production.

Overview of Priorities for Future Action

National sustainable development strategies should be part of the socio-economic development strategies in order that environmental objectives are on a par with more conventional economic objectives, such as increased employment, import substitution, and export promotion.

In most countries, industry should be restructured in order to increase productivity, competitiveness, and ecoefficiency. It is important to reorient the industry to production of the high- and medium-value-added goods and to expand the role of the service sector, which can provide basic support services for the manufacturing sector.

Manufacturing extension centers should offer integrated support packages for cost reduction, improved product quality, and uptake of environmentally sound technologies. For human development, programs for education and on-the-job training should be established and financed in order to increase the productivity of work and to increase employment possibilities in sectors manufacturing high- and medium-value-added goods.

For effective policy making, it is essential that all relevant parties, such as trade unions, civil society organizations, and representatives of business, participate in the decision-making process, preparation of plans and strategies, and formulation of realistic implementation measures.

Conclusion

Two major conclusions emerge from our review of the progress of 18 developing and transition economies in pursuing sustainable development with regard to the manufacturing sector over the period 1990 to 2000. First, there is a lack in most countries of basic data about environmental withdrawals (resource use) and environmental releases (pollutant discharges) as well as important social parameters needed to characterize their performance. Most countries have yet to undertake at-source monitoring and reporting on the most basic sustainable development indicators more than 10 years after the Earth Summit. Second, in spite of data limitations, it is possible to think that some countries have made remarkable progress in their pursuit of sustainable development. For example, China and Egypt managed to achieve high growth in the manufacturing sector and significant reductions in energy use and discharge of organic pollutants. In addition, Egypt increased employment in the manufacturing sector, and China managed to offset, to some extent, employment losses in state-owned enterprises with employment gains in privately owned enterprises. Other countries have made notable progress, such as Chile, Tunisia, and Turkey. Others, such as Colombia and Zimbabwe, have lost ground.

In reflecting on the obstacles and constraints described in the national reports, we were struck by two findings about the manufacturing sector that reinforce the more general findings of the International Forum on National Sustainable Development Strategies (see introductory section) and the ideas of the World Bank on the three key functions of an effective institutional environment.[4] First, most national reports state that there has been either little or inadequate participation of the manufacturing sector in the sustainable development planning and implementation efforts. Second, most national reports describe significant institutional and sectoral barriers impeding the formulation of a clear and implementable strategy that would enhance the contribution of industry to sustainable development.

In looking at the full national reports and the recommendations for future actions and priorities, we found ourselves returning to the observations described previously. First, in reviewing the full reports, we could find limited quantitative or even qualitative data on environmental quality and any additional economic or social data other than what we could locate in international data sources. Only a few of the countries are collecting at-source data on industrial resource use and pollutant discharge, such as China, Czech Republic, and Turkey. Without understanding the problems confronting a country, mobilizing industry and governments to take action is difficult. It should come as no surprise that the three countries that have been "picking up signals" are the ones making significant progress in pursuing sustainable development.

Second, most of the reports, some more emphatically than others, acknowledged the importance of industry participation in formulating and implementing sustainable development strategies. Dialogue and trust among the various participants are essential if sustainable development strategies are to become more than words on paper.

Third, better and in cases even basic integration of social and environmental considerations into industrial development strategies and policies is seen as necessary. More effective policy integration requires improved coordination, cooperation, and coherence (Luken and Hesp, 2003). The reports describe some promising examples of coordination and cooperation among various policy domains and their respective institutions aimed at reducing environmental pressure and more broadly at achieving sustainable development. However, much more needs to be done.

In reflecting on the logjam in moving forward with sustainable development efforts for the manufacturing sector, one is struck by the need for a Sustainable Production Initiative (SPI) that would link existing capacities to pursue simultaneously developmental, environmental, and technological objectives. This new initiative would differ from past efforts in three ways. First, the SPI requires national governments to make a case for pursuing sustainable development with the manufacturing sector. There is an amazing amount of information of both a qualitative and a quantitative nature available that is not being used to construct an overall picture of the sustainable development situations in most countries.

Second, the SPI would secure the active involvement of the industrial sector in the process of formulating NSDSs, in putting together a 10-year framework for sustainable production, as called for at WSSD; in achieving realistic improvements in the command and control regulatory programs; and in building firm-level technology upgrading programs. Third, the SPI would be a private sector–led initiative, most likely undertaken by the leading national industrial association, which would work with governmental, industrial, and environmental ministries. Industry and governments would have clearly defined roles and responsibilities within the SPI.

Notes

1. In the International Standard Industrial Classification (ISIC), industry includes mining and quarrying (ISIC2), manufacturing (ISIC3), electricity and gas (ISIC4), and construction (ISIC5). UNIDO's work is all related to manufacturing. In this book, the terms *industry* and *manufacturing* are synonymous.
2. UNIDO Industrial Statistics.
3. Bolivia, Brazil, China, Costa Rica, Cuba, Ghana, Jamaica, Nepal, Nigeria, Philippines, South Africa, Uganda, and Yemen.
4. These three categories are similar to those identified in World Bank (2003), "Sustainable Development in a Dynamic World," "World Development Review 2003," Washington, D.C. According to the World Bank, the three key functions of the institutional environment in promoting human well-being are picking up signals, balancing interests, and executing and implementing solutions (p. 37).

References

Ahossane, K. (2001). Manufacturing industry and sustainable development in Cote d'Ivoire. In: R. Luken, J. Alvarez, and P. Hesp, eds., *Developing Countries Industrial Source Book,* Vienna, UNIDO, pp. 35–38.

Awad, N.M. (2001). Industry and sustainable development in Sudan—achievements and prospects. In: R. Luken, J. Alvarez, and P. Hesp, eds., *Developing Countries Industrial Source Book,* Vienna, UNIDO, pp. 82–85.

Cadima, P.C., and Aguirre, C.B. (2001). Industry and sustainable development in Bolivia—achievements and prospects. In: R. Luken, J. Alvarez, and P. Hesp, eds., *Developing Countries Industrial Source Book,* Vienna, UNIDO, pp. 6–11.

Erer, S. (2001). Industry and Sustainable Development in Turkey: Achievements and Prospects. In: R. Luken, J. Alvarez and P. Hesp, eds., *Developing Countries Industrial Source Book,* Vienna, UNIDO, pp. 93–97.

Escobar, C.A. (2001). Industry and sustainable development in Colombia. In: R. Luken, J. Alvarez, and P. Hesp, eds., *Developing Countries Industrial Source Book,* Vienna, UNIDO, pp. 30–34.

Food and Agricultural Organization of the United Nations (FAO) (2003). Water Resources, Development and Management Service. AQUASTAT. Rome, FAO.

Guarjena, R. (2001). Industry and sustainable development in Zimbabwe. In: R. Luken, J. Alvarez, and P. Hesp, eds., *Developing Countries Industrial Source Book,* Vienna, UNIDO, pp. 105–111.

Hasnain, S.A., and Nazech, K.M. (2001). Industry and sustainable development in Indonesia—achievements and prospects. In: R. Luken, J. Alvarez, and P. Hesp, eds., *Developing Countries Industrial Source Book,* Vienna, UNIDO, pp. 58–63.

Huijiong, W. (2001). Sustainable industrial development overview of China—current and future perspectives. In: R. Luken, J. Alvarez, and P. Hesp, eds., *Developing Countries Industrial Source Book,* Vienna, UNIDO, pp. 23–29.

Imevbore, A.M.A. (2001). Industry and sustainable development in Nigeria —achievements and prospects. In: R. Luken, J. Alvarez, and P. Hesp, eds., *Developing Countries Industrial Source Book,* Vienna, UNIDO, pp. 64–69.

International Environmental Agency (2002). *Energy Statistics of Non-OECD Countries 1999–2002.* Paris: IEA.

International Labor Organization (2000). *Yearbook of Labour Statistics,* Geneva, ILO.

International Labor Organization (2002). *Yearbook of Labour Statistics,* Geneva, ILO.

Luken, R., Alvarez, J., and Hesp, P. (2001). *Developing Countries Industrial Source Book,* Vienna, UNIDO.

Luken, R., and Hesp, P. (2003). *Sustainable Development and Industry? Reports from Seven Developing and Transition Economies.* Cheltenham, England and Northampton, Mass., Edward Elgar.

Malifu, E. (2001). Development of the manufacturing sector in Ethiopia. In: R. Luken, J. Alvarez, and P. Hesp, eds., *Developing Countries Industrial Source Book,* Vienna, UNIDO, pp. 51–57.

Mobarak, A. (2001). The challenges of sustainable development in Egypt. In: R. Luken, J. Alvarez, and P. Hesp, eds., *Developing Countries Industrial Source Book,* Vienna, UNIDO, pp. 46–50.

Moldan, B. (2001). Industrial development in the Czech Republic in the light of sustainable development. In: R. Luken, J. Alvarez, and P. Hesp, eds., *Developing Countries Industrial Source Book,* Vienna, UNIDO, pp. 39–45.

Nafti, R. (2001). Industry and sustainable development in Tunisia—achievements and prospects. In: R. Luken, J. Alvarez, and P. Hesp, eds., *Developing Countries Industrial Source Book,* Vienna, UNIDO, pp. 86–92.

Sam, D.V., Ha, T.H., Hao, D.H., Nhan, T.V., Nhan, H.T., Toan, P.K., and Duc, L.M. (2001). Vietnamese national industrial overview. In: R. Luken, J. Alvarez, and P. Hesp, eds., *Developing Countries Industrial Source Book,* Vienna, UNIDO, pp. 98–104.

Tekeu, C., and Noumsi, S. (2001). Industry and sustainable development in Cameroon—achievements and prospects. In: R. Luken, J. Alvarez, and P. Hesp, eds., *Developing Countries Industrial Source Book,* Vienna, UNIDO, pp. 12–16.

United Nations Department for Economic and Social Affairs (2002). *Report on an Expert Forum on National Sustainable Strategies for Sustainable Development.* Meeting held in Accra, Ghana 2001, New York, United Nations.

United Nations Development Programme (2003). *Human Development Report 2003,* New York and Oxford, Oxford University Press, Technical Note 1, pp. 340–346.

United Nations Industrial Development Organization Report for Project NC/PAK/97/018—industrial policy and the environment in Pakistan: Industry and sustainable development in Pakistan. (2001a). In: R. Luken, J. Alvarez, and P. Hesp, eds., *Developing Countries Industrial Source Book,* Vienna, UNIDO, pp. 70–75.

United Nations Industrial Development Organization Report for the Project NC/PHI/97/020—industrial policy and the environment in the Philippines: Industry and sustainable development in the Philippines. (2001b). In: R. Luken, J. Alvarez, and P. Hesp, eds., *Developing Countries Industrial Source Book,* Vienna, UNIDO, pp. 76–81.

United Nations Industrial Development Organization (2003). *Industrial Statistic Database,* Vienna, UNIDO.

Urzua, O. (2001). Development of manufacturing industry and sustainable development in Chile. In: R. Luken, J. Alvarez, and P. Hesp, eds., *Developing Countries Industrial Source Book,* Vienna, UNIDO, pp. 17–22.

World Bank (2003). *Sustainable Development in a Dynamic World,* World Development Review 2003, Washington, D.C.: World Bank.

World Bank (2003). *World Development Indicators 2003,* Washington, D.C.: World Bank.

Chapter 23

Toward Sustainable Tourism: Moving Beyond Ecotourism

Graham Miller and Tracy Berno

CONTENTS

Introduction

This chapter reviews the changing conceptualizations of the tourism industry, particularly as they relate to sustainable tourism (ST). It is argued that having identified the potentially negative environmental impacts of tourism and having moved beyond a simple recognition of the economic benefits of tourism, development planners now need to advance again beyond the reactionary interpretation that ST is synonymous with ecotourism. This requires a more sophisticated understanding of the tourism industry that integrates the industry with other sectors of the economy and seeks further stakeholder involvement to promote sustainable development (SD). The chapter concludes by presenting a discussion of the need to facilitate this conceptual shift through the development of indicators that can assist in monitoring whether tourism is moving toward or away from sustainability.

Tourism: A Dynamic Concept

Tourism has a lengthy and dynamic history. Through graffiti on the pyramids in Egypt, there is evidence of travel for leisure purposes dating back to a time when the pyramids would have been contemporary structures. Tourism has evolved from being predominantly the domain of the rich and privileged and the "Grand Tour" to an age of mass tourism. The post–World War II era saw an unprecedented growth in international tourism. This rapid growth was predicated on socioeconomic changes in the more developed countries. Changes such as higher incomes, better income distribution, longer paid holidays, improvements in transportation technology, and a decline in travel costs provided the means for people to travel in numbers never before realized (Cooper et al., 1993). Further encouraging the growth of the phenomenon was a very positive image of tourism development conveyed by the advocacy platform and the willingness of the World Bank and other institutions to fund tourism projects (Pleumarom, 1994).

In 1950, there were 25 million international tourist arrivals. This figure increased to 692 million in 2001 and is predicted to reach 1 billion by the year 2010 (World Tourism Organisation [WTO], 2003). Over the 50 years from 1950 to the present, tourist arrivals have grown at an average annual rate of 7%, while the receipts from tourism have grown at an average annual rate of 12% to reach US$463 billion at current prices (WTO, 2003).

Currently, tourism is the world's largest economic sector and its economic importance is indisputable. Tourism is one of the top five export categories for 83% of all countries in the world and the main source of foreign exchange for at least 38% of countries. By the late 1990s, international tourism and international fare receipts accounted for approximately 8% of total export earnings on goods and services worldwide. Total international tourism receipts (inclusive of international fares) amounted to an estimated US$532 billion, surpassing all other international trade categories. Tourism is the only international trade in services in which the less developed countries (LDCs) have consistently had surpluses compared with the rest of the world. Between 1980 and 1996, LDCs' positive balance in the travel account rose from US$4.6 billion to US$65.9 billion. This was driven primarily by the growth of inbound tourism to countries in Asia, the Pacific, and Africa (WTO, 2003).

International tourism, with its emphasis on the exploitation of "free" resources (sun, sea, sand, and friendly people), has become an attractive option for economic development for LDCs. From the birth of mass tourism in the 1950s, the tourism industry has largely been seen as an economic panacea and mostly bereft of environmental, social, or political impact. Tourism, unlike other development options such as manufacturing, mining, or forestry, was widely perceived to be a clean and renewable industry. Zierer (1952, cited in Cohen, 1978, p. 218) states confidently, "A notable characteristic of the tourism industry is that it does not, or should not, lead to the destruction of natural resources."

Because it drew on "free" natural, historical, social, and cultural resources, tourism was also thought to be less capital intensive in its requirements for development. Tourism was seen to have potential to be a major driving force for economic development in many LDCs because of its large potential multiplier and spillover effects on the rest of the economy and its generation of jobs for unskilled and semiskilled workers (Archer 1985). Particularly for LDCs with limited exploitable natural resource bases, tourism was seen as a viable development option offering an important opportunity for economic diversification (WTO and IHRA, 1999). Convinced by the economic benefits of the industry, the World Bank was an enthusiastic supporter of tourism development and loaned nearly $500 million to tourism projects between 1969 and 1979 (Lanfant and Graburn, 1991). Stankovic (1979, p. 25) characterizes the effusive views of tourism, opining, "tourism ... can, more than many other activities, use and valorise such parts and elements of nature as are of almost no value for other economic branches and activities." Bartelmus (1994) refers to this neoclassical view as an "empty-world" approach because of the way the environment and humans are excluded from consideration; such an exploiattive approach to natural resources was typical of the age before Carson's seminal *Silent Spring* (Carson, 1966).

In addition to the numerical growth of tourism, there has been an increasing spread of tourism to encompass almost all the reaches of the globe. This has been accompanied by a diversification of the tourism product from the traditional sun, sea, and sand offering. Concomitant with this quantitative and qualitative rise, from the mid-1960s, there emerged a growing disquiet about the level and type of negative impacts the industry effected.

Among tourism academics, the unquestioning acceptance of tourism as a panacea was replaced in the 1970s and early 1980s by an era of the critique. By the early 1970s, the potential negative impacts of tourism were being considered (see, for example, Young, 1973). These early critiques of tourism as a development tool focused primarily on the negative sociocultural impacts (deKadt, 1979), but as international tourism continued to grow exponentially, that negative impacts were effected on the societies, environments and economies of destinations became apparent as well.

Along the same lines, Plog (1974, p. 4) cautiously observed that "destinations carry with them the potential seeds of their own destruction, as they allow themselves to become more commercialized and lose their qualities which originally attracted tourists." Among the many epoch-marking works, Budowski (1976) and Cohen (1978) focused on the environmental impacts of tourism; Cohen (1972), deKadt (1979), Doxey (1975), and MacCannell (1976) the sociocultural impacts; Britton (1982) and de Kadt (1979) the political consequences; Bryden (1973) questioned the previously unchallenged economic value of tourism.

While the critiques of the 1970s raised awareness of the potential impacts of tourism, the response adopted by the protagonists of the industry during the mid-1980s was described as *adaptive* (Jafari 1989). The initial response to these negative impacts involved a series of initiatives undertaken by public sector bodies to attempt to manage tourism through visitor management techniques. These initiatives were designed to ameliorate the worst of the impacts in the short term. Overall, these were small-scale, localized initiatives that did not attempt to change the nature of tourism as a whole (Swarbrooke, 1999). They were, nevertheless, the precursors of ST.

This promulgation of alternative forms of tourism seemed reactionary rather than adaptive and gave rise to the vilification of mass tourism (Butler, 1990; McElroy and de Albuquerque, 1996; Smith and Eadington, 1992; Turner and Ash, 1975). Mass tourism came to be synonymous with unsustainable practices, seen as being responsible for the deleterious effects of tourism on environments and societies. As a consequence, with the emphasis on small-scale developments, community involvement, and the preeminence of environmental protection, the rise of alternative tourism and "ecotourism" was seen as championing a sustainable way forward (Wight, 1993).

The idea that there is one type of tourism that is an alternative to mass tourism demonstrates the intellectual weakness of alternative tourism and hints at the value of the concept more as a marketing tool to attract higher-spending tourists than as a useful conceptual contribution. Further, in prioritizing the environment, the most sustainable forms of tourism risked being overlooked because of the ideological filters through which tourism development was viewed during this period. In particular, the propensity to use the term *ecotourism* synonymously with *sustainable tourism* displays an inadequate understanding of both terms as not all forms of ecotourism are sustainable, and not all ST takes place in natural areas. It could even be suggested that an ecotourist can be more demanding than the mass tourist, who may not desire to visit endangered species in remote locations (Berno and Bricker, 2001). Additionally, the needs and wastes of the mass tourist may be more readily planned for and managed in large numbers, incorporating economies of scale (Wall, 1997).

The relationship between ST and ecotourism has to be critically evaluated with a recognition that the latter can be diametrically opposed to the former (Swarbrook, 1999; WTO and UNEP, 2000). For tourism to be sustainable, all forms of tourism (not just elite forms of alternative tourism) must move toward the goal of sustainability (deKadt, 1979; Krippendorf, 1987; WTO and UNEP, 2000). The "alternative tourism" approach is further dismissed in an essay by Butler (1990: p. 41), who confirms that, "mass tourism need not be uncontrolled, unplanned, short term or unstable. Green tourism is not always and inevitably considerate, optimising, controlled, planned and under local control."

Wheeller (1994, p. 10) describes the concept of ecotourism as "an altruistic, even noble concept hijacked for commercial and material purposes," and this is a view supported by Wight (1993), who believes increasingly ecotourism is little more than an exercise in "greenwash" to attract more customers. Indeed, it is the problem of numbers that identifies a further intellectual weakness of ecotourism. Wheeller (p. 92) sums up the conundrum: "We have, on the one hand, a problem of mass tourism growing globally, out of control, at an alarming rate. And what is our answer? Small-scale, slow, steady, controlled development. They just do not add up."

Moreover, as Swarbrooke (1999) pointed out, if there continues to be a value-based distinction made between "good" tourism (the so-called alternative forms of tourism) and "bad" tourism (mass tourism), potentially tourism could become a divisive force in society. Indeed, even at a destination level, many areas unable to afford alternative tourism rely instead on the economic returns of mass tourism to help meet developmental needs. Mowforth and Munt (1998) cite the example of Belize's ambition to develop into the world's premier ecotourism destination, which had to be tempered when insufficient revenue was generated through this small-scale approach.

By the beginning of the 1990s, the tourism debate entered a period typified by a need for knowledge about the different forms of tourism and their potential impacts (Jafari, 1989). This position was achieved by recognizing that any type of tourism could potentially be sustainable, as believed by the early advocates of tourism, or not sustainable, as suggested by the cautionary writers of the 1970s. Butler (1990, p. 41) comments, "To promote one form of tourism as a solution to the multiple problems which can be caused by extensive and long term development is somewhat akin to selling nineteenth century wonder medicines."

However, many of the definitions of ST continue to focus on the relationship between tourism and the natural environment, emphasising "alternative" or "eco" forms of activities. These initiatives have been important in highlighting the need to evaluate tourism critically and have suggested practical ways to address some of the negative social and environmental impacts of tourism development. Techniques such as environmental impact assessment, environmental auditing, pollution control, and recycling are all useful advancements made from the aim of promoting environmental conservation (Twining-Ward, 2002). Yet they are not enough to address in a comprehensive manner the overall sustainability of tourism. Hunter (1995, p. 164) refers to this as a "pick and mix" approach to ST that values one aspect of sustainability over others. No single type of tourism is inherently more sustainable than another. To suggest otherwise precludes comprehensive critical consideration of the issues.

Additionally, a single focus on environmental issues related to tourism fails to consider the much broader range of stakeholders that have an interest in promoting and maintaining tourism as a means for SD. As will be seen, this narrow focus on the environmental aspects of tourism is derived from a narrow interpretation of what ST is.

Reconceptualizing Sustainable Tourism

As Berno and Bricker (2001, p. 10) observed,

> although a very commendable ideal, sustainable tourism is fraught with other challenges, both in terms of definition and operationalization. Tourism is a complex and fragmented phenomenon that despite its critical role in the global economy does not conform to classical definitions of industry and product. Its organization and administration are complex and the needs of different stakeholder groups are conflicting. Given this context, how can tourism be sustainable, and what is it that should be sustained?

Tourism's sustainability argument developed in parallel (Bramwell and Lane, 1993) with the broader SD debate. Emerging from this debate were two clear interpretations, one concerned with sustaining the advancement of the tourism industry, the other more closely linked with the developmental literature, concerned with tourism's contribution to sustaining development in a wider society. Butler (1993, p. 29) characterizes this first interpretation of ST as "tourism which is in a form that can maintain *its* viability in an area for an indefinite period of time" (emphasis added). The essential element to this definition is that tourism is concerned to maintain "its" viability over an indefinite period. This is clearly the definition of ST that has been developed by those in the tourism industry, and not the definition that has crossed from the developmental literature, although it is equally clear that a tourism industry that is not sustained is not in a position to contribute to SD.

Alternatively, Butler (1993, p. 29) describes tourism in a SD context as "tourism which is developed and maintained in an area in such a manner and at such a scale that it remains viable over an indefinite period and does not degrade or alter the environment (human and physical) in which it exists to such a degree that it prohibits the successful development and well-being of *other activities and processes*" (emphasis added). Godfrey (1998, p. 214) also identifies the link between self-sustaining tourism and tourism in a SD context: "ST is thus not an end in itself, nor a unique or isolated procedure, but rather an interdependent function of a wider and permanent socioeconomic development process."

Tourism is an integrated system in which the constituent parts are linked. Therefore, a change in one part affects the other parts. As such, tourism must be approached holistically. The need to tie firmly the sustainability of the tourism industry to the success of other industrial sectors is central to the reconceptualization of ST. In many ways, ST is about the competition for and distribution of finite resources. A balance must be struck between tourism and other existing, and potential activities. Trade-offs between sectors may be necessary if the greater good of SD is to be achieved (Berno and Bricker, 2001; Wall, 1997). As Hunter (1995, p. 161) states, "It is a truism that no set of delineated human endeavours comprising one socioeconomic sector, such as tourism, can ever exist in total isolation from other sectors." Similarly, almost a decade before, Getz (1986, p. 31) had warned tourism planners "not to act in isolation from other social, economic and environmental planning. There is a tendency to think of tourism planning as a separate problem, narrowly defined to include only marketing and visitor services. Existing theory and knowledge about the possible multitude of impacts of tourism completely discredits that approach."

The frequency of these warnings suggests that tourism has indeed become dissociated from other industrial sectors in terms of its aims and consideration of its impacts, preferring instead to target attention on matters relating directly to its business area. Jenner and Smith (1992), in identifying the interdependence of tourism and the environment, recognize the impact of tourism on the environment and the impact of other industries on tourism but fail to address the reciprocal problems tourism can cause for other industries. The common word *sustainable* belies the different goals of ST and SD, which are not necessarily the same.

Clarke (1997, p. 228) is also indicative of this separatism and feeling that the proprietorial tourism industry is in competition with other industries for the scarce resources necessary: "The tourism industry must protect *its* assets" (emphasis added). This may be the view of private industry, and in order to sustain the tourism industry, it is axiomatic that resources be secured before the concern for losing them is considered. Further, it is to be assumed that one industry is only concerned with its own industry, although for an industry reliant on so many intangible factors this is a myopic approach and one that is ultimately doomed.

The concept of ST was embraced by the industry with minimal consideration of the theoretical link between the concept of SD and the particularities of the context of tourism. As Harrison (1996, p. 72) stated, "By combining development (inevitably a value laden concept) with sustainability (which is allegedly nonoperational and reformist) we thus arrive at the doubly vague concept of SD, only then to focus on one aspect of this dubious process—that of ST."

The concept of ST is variously interpreted as a process of tourism development or an outcome of tourism development. This lack of consensus on its meaning and application has led to the suggestion that "defining sustainable development in the context of tourism has become something of a cottage industry in the academic literature of late" (Garrod and Fyall, 1998, p. 199). There has been an almost unquestioning acceptance that the principles and objectives of SD can be applied to tourism. As a result, fundamental questions about tourism's role in development in general, and the validity of the concept of ST in particular, have not been addressed adequately (Berno and Bricker, 2001).

For Hunter (1995) the view of ST as concerned with sustaining the tourism industry is the "dominant paradigm," one in which a "tourism-centric" view is taken of sustainability. Within this view, Healey and Shaw (1994) believe that there is a preference for the economic over the environmental, and Craik (1995) places the environment above sociocultural matters for consideration. Yet, what is central to the criticism is that "the general SD debate is somehow external to the process of interpreting ST" (Hunter 1997, p. 856). One reason for this interpretation of ST must in part be caused by the commercial sector's input into muddying the ST concept, whereas the industry was absent to a greater extent from the more abstracted SD debate.

Harrison (1996) argues that the phrase ST has just become a label with no meaning that is attached to any product the tourism industry wishes to sell. Wall (1997) is similarly critical, believing that the phrase is often used as a marketing gimmick to create an illusion of clean and green products (Wickers, 1992). Krippendorf (1982, p. 140) opines, "So long as the short-sighted tourism companies can reckon with increasing growth rates, that is all they are interested in. Those who are only concerned with the short-term, as most of them are, feel that the consequences of growth are insignificant." Yet there is some evidence to suggest that local residents and tourism consumers are increasingly forcing the industry to change direction and accept to a greater extent the impacts of tourism on the tourism industry, although the problem of public goods still stifles concerted action (Haywood, 1993). However, the dominant paradigm does ensure that the tourism industry is largely not concerned with the impacts on unrelated industries.

Muller (1994) believes that the tourism industry needs to strike a balanced approach on the thorny path to SD. Muller's (1994, p. 132) "magic pentagon," presented in Figure 23.1, shows that the five elements identified need to be held in approximation to each other: "The target situation is balanced tourism development,"

Muller (1994, p. 133) continues: "The tourism development we aim for is economically productive, socially responsible and environmentally conscious. We are prepared to cease pursuing further development when it

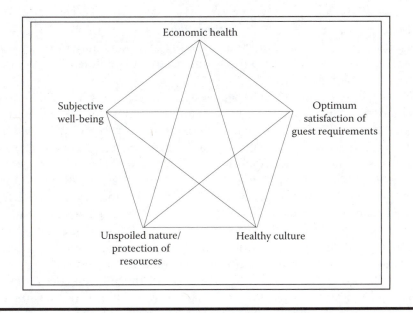

Figure 23.1 The magic pentagon. (From Muller, 1994.)

leads to an intolerable burden for our population and environment. We want to avoid the pitfalls of economic imperatives." The problem with such a statement is again that the tourism-centric nature is evident rather than the contribution that tourism can make to SD. The tourism industry may be best placed to provide employment at the expense of balance, resulting in an industry that is not sustainable (in terms of being in balance) on its own but increases sustainability in a society as a whole.

Where there is need for balance, then it is across industries, rather than within an industry. Urry (1990, p. 23) reminds us that "the more exclusively an area specializes in tourism, the more depressed its general wage levels will be." When the industry is considered in isolation, as Clarke (1997) highlights, the opportunity costs of tourism are not considered, with the result that tourism is promoted, literally, at all costs. UNEP (1995, p. 30) recognizes this risk:

> We want to counter the danger of one-sided economic devel-
> opment and over dependence on the tourist trade. We support
> the strengthening of agriculture and small-scale trade as well
> as their partnership with tourism. We strive for a qualitative
> improvement of jobs in tourism. We also continually explore
> all possibilities for the creation of new jobs outside the tourist
> trade.

Butler (1998, p. 28) endorses this view: "To talk of ST in the sense that tourism could (and should) achieve SD independently of other activities and processes is philosophically against the true nature of the concept, as well as being unrealistic."

This "whole economy" perspective (Harris and Nelson, 1993) requires the kind of holistic planning that Bramwell and Lane (1993), Inskeep (1991), Gunn (1994), and Getz (1986) among many others, call for. However, this assumes a level of control over the planning process that is unrealistic. Berno and Bricker (2001) observe that there are several inherent challenges in applying the holistic principles of SD to tourism. These include the nature of the tourism industry and product, the frag-mented fashion in which decisions about tourism are made, and the diverse and often conflicting interests in tourism development held by a broad range of stakeholders. Critical decisions about tourism development are made at local, national, regional, and international levels.

Despite the apparent vertical integration of these levels, decisions are often made in a mutually exclusive fashion, with little or no consultation or collaboration. Governments, nongovernmental organizations (NGOs), and various professional and industry organizations, which often have diverse and conflicting interests in tourism development, further overlay this organizational structure. Further, within each of these levels exists the "plant" that tourism comprises (i.e., commercial enterprises that provide services such as accommodation, transportation, and tour operations). Finally, the tourists, the "consumers" of the tourism "product," constitute the demand side of tourism. They enter the system with their own unique and diverse ranges of motivations, attitudes, and values. Each one of these components and levels in the tourism system must be considered in the operationalization of SD practices.

Also playing a critical role in ST development is the distribution of power and control influencing the nature of development within the industry. With the increase in transnational corporate (TNC) interest in tourism and the emergence of global alliances in all aspects of the tourism product (e.g., airlines, hotels, tour operators), it is not clear where the power and control lie to promote and enforce sustainable practices. The profit-driven, immediate economic return orientation of the tourism industry is often in direct conflict with the need to protect the social and environmental resources that are under increasing pressure.

Finally, the interests and needs of the different stakeholders in tourism must also be taken into consideration. Stakeholders in tourism are a broad range of participants who have both rights and responsibilities within the system. Swarbrooke (1999) has identified six main stakeholder groups that have an interest in tourism: the public sector (supragovernmental organizations, national governments, local bodies, and quasi-governmental organizations), the tourism industry, voluntary sector organizations, the host community, the media, and the tourists themselves.

Clearly, there is a need for partnership and cooperation among these various interests in tourism. However, it must be appreciated that these different interest groups have a variety of goals in relation to tourism development. Applying key principles for ST to this scale of participants, and their varying needs is extremely complex and difficult to control. Hardin (1968) illustrated the problem of this lack of control with the result that the common good was reduced in favor of individual gain.

For Murphy (1984), this is analogous to the decline in collective community and a move toward an individualistic society. This also parallels the divide between tourism that contributes to SD and tourism that is concerned with sustaining its own industry. If strict control cannot be exerted at the planning level over the developments within that area, then it becomes difficult to argue that tourism is making a deliberate contribution to SD. This leaves the potential for the tourism industry still to make positive contributions to SD, but only when doing so coincides with the goal of ensuring the profitability of the tourism industry.

Stakeholder Involvement

Simmons (1994, p. 98) contends that because of changing consumer demands for a greater cultural component to their holidays, there is greater recognition by the private sector of the needs for local involvement in the tourism industry and states that "residents of destination areas are being seen increasingly as the nucleus of the tourism product." Although this provides a commercial rationale for stakeholder involvement, Murphy (1984, p. 171) states, "Input from concerned community groups could provide a balance to the ST objectives of the business sector, and possibly encourage greater variation and local flavour in future projects." Moreover, Pigram (1990, p. 6) believes, "Undoubtedly, decision making in the tourism sphere would benefit from public input," and Craik (1995, p. 93) adds, "Consultative processes are central to the successful development and implementation of viable development strategies and policies."

Perhaps the most important way greater stakeholder involvement seeks to achieve ST is through enhancing the place-specific knowledge of those managing the development. Stankey (1999) contends that public involvement and genuine participation are crucial to the whole tourism development process. Marien and Pizam (1997, p. 165) concur: "ST cannot be successfully implemented without the direct support and involvement of those who are affected by it. Therefore, evaluating a community's sensitivity to the tourism development is the first step in planning for sustained tourism development." For Wall (1997, p. 46) the importance of local differences to the achievement of ST means that the problems must be tackled at a local level: "While most would agree that if tourism is to contribute to SD it must be economically viable, environmentally sensitive and culturally appropriate, the forms which this might take are likely to vary with location. This in turn means that it will be very difficult to come up with useful principles for tourism development which are true for all places and all times."

Traditionally, stakeholders have been understood to be local residents, but this approach risks excluding valuable expert contributions on the basis of where that contribution originates. Clearly, such a position is fatuous, especially when many projects are blighted by local residents' lack of expertise to make a useful contribution. Tosun (1999) refers to the difficulty residents of developing countries face in trying to contribute to tourism projects developed by slick outsiders with vast resources.

If a stakeholder can be considered as anyone affecting or affected by a tourism project, then the range of actors is determined by how broad the definition of *tourism* is cast. Similarly, if ST is understood to be concerned only with sustaining the tourism industry, then stakeholders will be drawn only from a narrow range. Conversely, tourism that contributes to SD will enable a much broader range of actors, such as that suggested by Swarbrook (1999), to be reasonably considered to be stakeholders. Hence the need is not just to integrate tourism with a broader range of industrial sectors, but through a reconceptualization of ST to allow a greater integration of stakeholders within any tourism development.

Further weaknesses associated with local involvement center on the lack of knowledge and awareness of local residents about the tourism industry. Simmons (1994, p. 106) argues that the knowledge of the public is "at best barely adequate to instil confidence in the soundness of their contribution," reflecting Lucas (1978, quoted in Keogh, 1990): "if full information is not available on issues under consideration, opportunities or even rights to participate become meaningless." Joppe (1996, p. 476) goes further, believing that because of the way the consultation process is stacked against the residents, "citizen participation rarely has an effect on decision making," with the result that residents are reluctant to engage further in the process.

The complete absence of stakeholder involvement clearly represents a problem for tourism development, but achieving only partial stakeholder involvement can also be difficult. The most widely cited problem is one of power and the structures that enable or prevent a true representation of the views of locals and a spread of the benefits. For example, Hall (1994) refers to the "big men" of Samoa who dominated the apportionment of tourism's benefits to their own benefit. Fernando (1995) provides an excellent, although depressing account of the problems of developmental work conducted in Sri Lanka and organized through community involvement. The difficulties lie in those people deKadt (1979) refers to as "culture brokers" and by Nunez (1977) as "marginal men." These are members of the community who quickly rise to prominence in the project often because of language ability, entrepreneurial talent, or current position within the community, and as such can be seen to perform essential tasks. However, in the case of Sri Lanka, as those involved with the development become richer, they sought to expand the project, using what Nettenkoven (1979, p. 143) in another case describes as "an inexhaustible source of misunderstanding and false information."

Through greater stakeholder involvement not only are managers made aware of the locally specific issues; the process of drawing together disparate stakeholders is also beneficial in creating mutual understanding. Hence, there is a benefit of not only the product of stakeholder involvement, but also the process. Yet, despite these benefits, there are few examples of stakeholder involvement in tourism development; reflecting the economic and environmental bias ST has come to represent. For tourism to be able to claim with greater conviction that it is contributing to the SD of the destination, there is an urgent need to create greater stakeholder involvement.

Moving beyond Conceptions: Indicators of Sustainable Tourism

Perhaps the greatest criticism to be leveled at the sustainability debate has been the difficulty in operationalizing the principles once identified. This chapter concludes by suggesting that if tourism is to become more sustainable in the future, it needs to develop indicators to allow managers to monitor its impacts more accurately. In measuring SD and developing Indicators of Sustainable Development (ISD), the list of acronymic organizations involved is long and impressive. The European Environment Agency (EEA), United Nations Environment Programme (UNEP), United Nations Development Programme (UNDP), the World Bank, World Watch Institute, International Institute of Sustainable Development (IISD), New Economics Foundation (NEF), United Nations Commission for Sustainable Development (UNCSD), and WTO (World Tourism Organisation) are the main supragovernmental organizations; representation at the national and subnational levels would lengthen the list significantly.

The need for measurement has an ever-increasing resonance in society, with a seemingly endless desire to measure the previously unmeasured and to compare the performance of different providers of service. Schools are monitored for the value they add, health services for the standard of care they provide, and transport for the punctuality and quality of provision. The seeming truism that "what gets measured gets managed" and increased need for transparency of investment and consumer involvement have fueled much of the impetus to measure what may previously have been considered too subjective. Yet, despite this, Weaver and Lawton (1999, p. 21) in their review argue that "attention to the indicators issue in the tourism literature has not been as great as one might expect, considering its pivotal role in the sustainability monitoring process."

The lack of indicators to measure sustainability has been acknowledged by many. For example, in the United Kingdom, the Countryside Commission (1995, p. 9, now the Countryside Agency; quoted in Butler 1999, p. 17) state from a developmental perspective, "a commitment to monitoring is essential. Without any commitment to measuring impact on either a qualitative or quantitative basis, it is impossible to decide whether one is moving towards ST or away from it." Yet the EEA concedes of its own indicators "in the view of the agency ... (they) have had little success in arriving at meaningful tourism indicators" (quoted in DCMS, 1999). Goodall and Stabler (1998, p. 296) concur: "The principles underpinning sustainability may be seductively appealing, but there is a gray area between acceptance of these principles and their translation into workable environmental objectives or standards. Indeed, the range of appropriate indicators for measuring environmental performance is not clear-cut." For Muller (1994) the goal should simply be to make a start in measuring impacts at whatever level and in whatever way possible. Thus, although the goal should be perfect indicators, if a start, however imperfect, is not made to achieve greater disclosure of information relating to the impacts of tourism, then there will be no development of the concept.

Developing indicators of ST is an approach that fits well with the goal of increased stakeholder involvement. Place-specific knowledge can be added to the development as an identification of what sustainability means in a certain location. Twining-Ward (2002) provides an excellent account of how indicators of ST were developed through stakeholder participation in Samoa and the benefits, not just of the product, but of the process of linking disparate groups. However, it is inevitably the case that programs of indicators need funding and the danger exists that the end set of indicators may reflect not what is truly important to the destination, but instead to the funding organization (Miller, 2001). This is the politics of the real world, and, although desirable, it would be naïve to believe that this should not be the case. Yet such a position does not detract from the valuable information indicators of ST can provide to a range of actors able to promote ST, and as such their further development should be encouraged.

Toward Sustainable Tourism: Moving beyond "Eco"

This chapter has shown how the understanding of the tourism industry has shifted from regarding it as an economic panacea to recognizing the impacts that can occur. Out of this paradigm shift emerged the concept of ST.

Albeit with good intentions, unfortunately that the concept of ST was embraced with little consideration given to the theoretical linkages between SD and the problematic of the context of tourism. As a result, many questions regarding tourism's role in development and how the concept of ST can be operationalized (Garrod and Fyall, 1998; Hunter, 1995, 1997) remain unanswered. ST has been accused by some as being an inadequate concept, raising more questions than it can answer.

Given the importance of tourism to the world's economy, all serious thinkers would accept that it is in the best interests of tourism to ensure the longevity of the resources (natural, social, and economic) on which it depends (Manning and Dougherty, 1995). However, because of the complexity of the tourism industry and product and the fragmented way in which tourism is organized, achieving ST poses many challenges. Despite these significant challenges, tourism remains one of the most significant phenomena in contemporary society, and one that will continue to grow in size and economic importance. In order to address these inherent challenges, ST needs to be viewed as a holistic concept, involving the need to maintain global competitiveness for the long term, while equipping the industry to deal with immediate opportunities and challenges. ST, if it is to be achieved, must move beyond just the environment (the "eco" or "greening" of tourism) and encompass a range of innovative principles and practices.

Conclusion

This chapter has stressed the need for a more sophisticated appreciation of the value of the tourism industry to meet developmental needs if a broader perspective of what is ST is taken. Hunter (1997, p. 864) summarizes: "ST must be regarded as an adaptive paradigm capable of addressing widely different situations, and articulating different goals." One way that such an appreciation can occur is through the development of indicators of ST. This can provide managers with basic information that will assist them to promote more sustainability in the broadest sense. The risk of promoting a "technical" solution such as indicator development is that the moral argument for promoting ST may become lost amid the pursuit of data and targets. Yet it is possible that the provision of data will help to convince even the most empirical of tourism developers and further serve to increase understanding about the benefits, and limitations, of the tourism industry to promote ST. In the words of Butler (1998, p. 31):

> Inevitably any form of [tourism] development can only be judged sustainable or unsustainable after a long period of operation, when it can be ascertained if the demands of the activity have not prejudiced the needs of what were future generations when the development began.

References

Archer, B. (1985). Tourism in Mauritius: An Economic Impact Study with Marketing Implications. *Tourism Management*, 6(1): 51–60.
Bartelmus, P. (1994). *Environment, Growth and Development: The Concepts and Strategies of Sustainability*. London: Routledge.

Berno, T., and Bricker, K. (2001). Sustainable Tourism: The Long Road from Theory to Practice. *International Journal of Economic Development*, 3(3): 1–18.

Bramwell, B., and Lane, B. (1993). Sustainable Tourism: An Evolving Global Approach. *Journal of Sustainable Tourism*, 1(1):1–5.

Britton, S.G. (1982). *Tourism and Underdevelopment in Fiji*. Development Studies Centre, Canberra: Australian National University.

Bryden, J.M. (1973). *Tourism and Development: A Case Study of the Commonwealth Caribbean*. Cambridge: Cambridge University Press.

Budowski, G. (1976). Tourism and Conservation: Conflict, Coexistence or Symbiosis? *Environmental Conservation*, 3: 27–31.

Butler, R. (1990). Alternative Tourism—Pious Hope or Trojan Horse? *Journal of Travel Research*, 28(3): 40–45.

Butler, R. (1993). Tourism—An Evolutionary Perspective. In: Butler, R.W., Nelson, J.G., and Wall, G., eds. *Tourism and Sustainable Development: Monitoring, Planning, Managing*. Department of Geography Publication 37. Waterloo, Canada: University of Waterloo, pp. 27–43.

Butler, R. (1998). Sustainable Tourism—Looking Backwards in Order to Progress. In: Hall, M., and Lew, A., eds. *Sustainable Tourism: A Geographical Perspective*. Harlow, England: Longman, pp. 25–34.

Butler, R. (1999). Sustainable Tourism: A State-of-the-Art Review. *Tourism Geographies*, 1(1): 7–25.

Carson, R. (1966). *The Silent Spring*. London: Penguin.

Clarke, J. (1997). A Framework of Approaches to Sustainable Tourism. *Journal of Sustainable Tourism*, 5(3): 224–233.

Cohen, E. (1972). Towards a Sociology of International Tourism. *Social Research*, 39: 164–182.

Cohen, E. (1978). The Impact of Tourism on the Physical Environment. *Annals of Tourism Research* 5(2): 215–237.

Cooper, C., Fletcher, J., Gilbert, D., and Wanhill, S. (1993). *Tourism Principles and Practice*. Essex, England: Longman.

Craik, J. (1995). Are There Cultural Limits to Tourism? *Journal of Sustainable Tourism*, 3(2):87–98.

DCMS (1999). Sustainable Tourism Indicators Workshop. May 7 and June 3, DCMS, London.

DeKadt, E. (1979). *Tourism—Passport to Development?* Oxford: Oxford University Press.

Doxey, G.V. (1975). When Enough's Enough: The Natives Are Restless in Old Niagara. *Heritage Canada*, 2(2): 26–27.

Fernando, S. (1995). Theory and Practice of Participatory Development at Grassroots Level: Fact and Fiction in Sri Lanka. In Schneider, H., and Libercier, M.H., eds., *Participatory Development: From Advocacy to Action*, Paris: OECD, pp. 171–183.

Garrod, B., and Fyall, A. (1998). Beyond the Rhetoric of Sustainable Tourism? *Tourism Management*, 19(3): 199–212.

Getz, D. (1986). Models in Tourism Planning: Towards Integration of Theory and Practice. *Tourism Management*, 7(1): 21–32.

Godfrey, K. (1998). Attitudes towards Sustainable Tourism in the UK: A View from Local Government. *Tourism Management*, 19(3): 213–224.

Goodall, B., and Stabler, M. (1998). Principles Influencing the Determination of Environmental Standards for Sustainable Tourism. In *Tourism and Sustainability: Principles and Practice*. Wallingford: CAB International, pp. 279–304.

Gunn, C.A. (1994). *Tourism Planning*, 3rd ed. London: Taylor & Francis.

Hall, C. (1994). *Tourism and Politics: Policy, Power and Place*. Chichester, England: Wiley. .

Hardin, G. (1968). The Tragedy of the Commons. *Science*, 162: 1243–1248.

Harris, J.E., and Nelson, J.G. (1993). Monitoring Tourism from a Whole Economy Perspective: A Case from Indonesia. In Nelson, J.G., Butler, R.W., and Wall, G., eds. *Tourism and Sustainable Development: Monitoring, Planning and Managing*, Department of Geography Publications Series. Waterloo, Canada: University of Waterloo, pp. 179–200.

Harrison, D. (1996). Sustainable Tourism: Reflections from a Muddy Pool. In Briguglio, L., Archer, B., Jafari, J., and Wall, G., eds. *Sustainable Tourism in Islands and Small States: Issues and Policies*. London: Pinter, pp. 69–89.

Haywood, K. (1993). Sustainable Development for Tourism: A Commentary with an Organisational Perspective. In Nelson, J.C., Butler, R., and Wall, G., eds. *Tourism and Sustainable Development: Monitoring, Planning and Managing*. Waterloo, Canada: University of Waterloo, pp. 233–241.

Healey, P., and Shaw, T. (1994). Changing Meanings of "Environment" in the British Planning System. *Transaction of the Institute of British Geographers*, 19: 425–438.

Hunter, C. (1995). On the Need to Re-Conceptualise Sustainable Tourism Development. *Journal of Sustainable Tourism*, 3(3): 155–165.

Hunter, C. (1997). Sustainable Tourism as an Adaptive Paradigm. *Annals of Tourism Research*, 24(4): 850–867.

Inskeep, E. (1991). *Tourism Planning: An Integrated and Sustainable Development Approach*. New York: Van Nostrand Reinhold.

Jafari, J. (1989). An English Language Literature Review. In Bystranowski, J., ed. *Tourism as a Factor of Change: A Socio-Cultural Study*. Vienna: Centre for Research and Documentation in Social Sciences, pp. 17–60.

Jenner, P., and Smith, C. (1992). *The Tourism Industry and the Environment*. London: The Economist Intelligence Unit.

Joppe, M. (1996). Sustainable Community Tourism Development Revisited. *Tourism Management*, 17(7): 475–479.

Keogh, B. (1990). Public Participation in Community Tourism Planning. *Annals of Tourism Research*, 17: 449–465.

Krippendorf, J. (1982). Towards New Tourism Policies. *Tourism Management* 3(3): 135–148.

Krippendorf, J. (1987). *The Holidaymakers: Understanding the Impact of Leisure and Travel*. London: Heinemann.

Lanfant, M., and Graburn, N, H. (1991). International Tourism Reconsidered: The Principle of the Alternative. In Smith, V., ed. *Tourism Alternatives: Potential and Problems in the Development of Tourism.* Philadelphia: University of Pennsylvania Press, pp. 88–112.

MacCannell, D. (1976). *The Tourist: A New Theory of the Leisure Class.* London: Macmillan Press.

Manning, E.W., and Dougherty, T.D. (1995). Sustainable Tourism: Preserving the Golden Goose. *Cornell Hotel and Restaurant Administration Quarterly,* April: 29–42.

Marien, C., and Pizam, A. (1997). Implementing Sustainable Tourism Development through Citizen Participation in the Planning Process. In Wahab, S., and Pigram, J., eds. *Tourism Development and Growth: The Challenge of Sustainability.* London: Routledge, pp. 164–178.

McElroy, J.L., and de Albuquerque, K. (1996). Sustainable Alternatives to Insular Mass Tourism: Recent Theory and Practice. In Briguglio, L., Archer, B., Jafari, J., and Wall, G., eds. *Sustainable Tourism in Islands and Small States: Issues and Policies,* London: Pinter, pp. 47–60.

Miller, G. (2001). The Development of Indicators for Sustainable Tourism: Results of a Delphi Survey of Tourism Researchers. *Tourism Management,* 22(4): 351–362.

Mowforth, M., and Munt, I. (1998). *Tourism and Sustainability: New Tourism in the Third World.* London: Routledge.

Muller, H. (1994). The Thorny Path to Sustainable Tourism Development. *Journal of Sustainable Tourism,* 2(3): 131–136.

Murphy, P.E. (1984). *Tourism: A Community Approach.* London: Methuen.

Nettenkoven, L. (1979). Mechanisms of Intercultural Interaction. In DeKadt, E., ed. *Tourism—Passport to Development?* Oxford: Oxford University Press, pp. 135–145.

Nunez, T. (1977). Touristic Studies in Anthropological Perspective. In Smith, V.L., ed. *Hosts and Guests: The Anthropology of Tourism.* Philadelphia: University of Pennsylvania, pp. 207–216.

Pigram, J. (1990). Sustainable Tourism—Policy Considerations. *Journal of Tourism Studies,* 1(2): 2–9.

Pigram, J., and Wahab, S. (eds.) (1997). Sustainable tourism—unsustainable development. In *Tourism Development and Growth: The Challenge of Sustainability.* London: Routledge, pp. 33–49.

Pleumaron, A. (1994). The Political Economy of Tourism. Ecologist, 24(4): 142–147.

Plog, S. (1974). Why Destinations Areas Rise and Fall in Popularity. *Cornell Hotel and Administration Quarterly,* 14 (4): 55–58.

Romeril, M. (1989). Tourism and the Environment—Accord or Discord? *Tourism Management* 10(3): 204–208.

Simmons, D.G. (1994). Community Participation in Tourism Planning. *Tourism Management,* 15(2): 98–108.

Smith, V.L., and Eadington, W.R. (1989). *Tourism Alternatives: Potentials and Problems in the Development of Tourism.* Philadelphia: University of Pennsylvania Press.

Stankey, G.H. (1999). The Recreation Opportunity Spectrum and the Limits of Acceptable Change Planning Systems: A Review of Experiences and Lessons. In Aley, T., Burch, W., Conover, B., and Fields, D., eds. *Eco-System Management: Adaptive Strategies for Natural Resource Organisations in the 21st Century.* Philadelphia: Taylor & Francis, pp. 173–188.

Stankovic, S.M. (1979). A Contribution to the Knowledge of the Protection of Nature and Tourism. *Tourist Review,* 34(3): 24–26.

Swarbrooke, J. (1999). *Sustainable Tourism Management.* Wallingford, U.K.: CABI.

Tosun, C. (1999). Towards a Typology of Community Participation in the Tourism Development Process. *Anatolia: An International Journal of Tourism and Hospitality Research,* 10(2): 113–134.

Turner, L., and Ash, J. (1975). *The Golden Hordes: International Tourism and the Leisure Periphery.* London: Constable.

Twining-Ward, L. (2002). Monitoring Sustainable Tourism Development: A Comprehensive, Stakeholder-Driven, Adaptive Approach. Ph.D. dissertation, University of Surrey.

UNEP (1995). Environmental Codes of Conduct for Tourism: Technical Report #29. UNEP, Paris.

Urry, J. (1990). *The Tourist Gaze.* London: Sage.

Wall, G. (1997). Sustainable Tourism: Unsustainable Development. In Wahab, S., and Pigram, J., eds. *Tourism Development and Growth: The Challenge of Sustainability.* London: Routledge, pp. 33–49.

Weaver, D., and Lawton, L. (1999). Sustainable Tourism: A Critical Analysis. Research Report One, Gold Coast, Australia, Co-operative Research Centre for Sustainable Tourism.

Wheeller, B. (1991). Tourism's Troubled Times: Responsible Tourism Is Not the Answer. *Tourism Management,* 12(1): 91–96.

Wheeller, B. (1994). Egotourism, Sustainable Tourism, and the Environment—A Symbiotic, Symbolic or Shambolic Relationship. In Seaton, A.V., ed., *The State of the Art.* West Sussex, England: John Wiley & Sons, pp. 645–654.

Wickers, D. (1992). Whither Green? *Sunday Times,* 5th January.

Wight, P. (1993). Ecotourism: Ethics or Eco-Sell? *Journal of Travel Research,* Winter: 3–9.

World Tourism Organization (WTO) (2003). Tourism Highlights. Retrieved from http://www.world-tourism.org.

World Tourism Organization (WTO) and International Hotel and Restaurant Association (IHRA) (1999). Tourism and sustainable development: The global importance of tourism. Background paper #1. Geneva: United Nations Department of Economic and Social Affairs.

World Tourism Organization (WTO) and United Nations Environmental Programme (UNEP) (2000). International year of ecotourism 2002. Brochure.

Young, G. (1973). *Tourism: Blessing or Blight?* Harmondsworth, England: Penguin.

Chapter 24

An Assessment of Health Care System Reform in Post-Soviet Transitional Economies

Patricia A. Cholewka

CONTENTS

Introduction

From 1991 through 2001, the newly independent nations of the former Soviet Union operated within the first decade of their independence with inherited Soviet-style health care systems. Upon gaining their independence, and with their history of politically oppressed societies that stifled entrepreneurial thinking, inexperienced health care managers were unprepared for changing these once centrally administered command economies.

Their health care systems, judged by Western health care management models, were incapable of meeting patient care standards that were already being addressed within the dynamic, business-oriented and consumer-driven environments of more established democratic countries. They were burdened by a lack of funding for advanced medical technology, outdated clinical practice standards and administrative protocols, lack of comparable academic knowledge and unbiased research base, and an entrenched bureaucracy that perpetrated a static health care culture focused on therapeutics instead of disease prevention. During the first decade of this transition process, programs promoted by international donor organizations from the United States (United States Agency for International Development [USAID]), World Bank (WB), and European Union (EU) to restructure these health care systems met with considerable barriers and proved disappointing in changing entrenched behavior by practitioners and administrators alike.

The purpose of this chapter is to present a brief retrospective review of some of the intrinsic constraints influencing resistance to health care system change, anticipated changes to these systems, and actual program outcomes. Discussion will be within the context of determining the appropriateness of these new programs for restructuring these inherited systems. The intent is to profile both unresolved and ongoing health care system issues that should be acknowledged now so that reform policies can be developed to realize sustainable health care system improvement programs in the future.

Background

Inherited Constraints Influencing Resistance to System Change

The newly independent nations and regions of the former Soviet Union include Albania, Armenia, Azerbaijan, Belarus, Bosnia, Herzegovina, Bulgaria, Croatia, Czech Republic, Estonia, Georgia, Hungary, Kazakhstan, Kyrgyz Republic, Latvia, Lithuania, the former Yugoslav Republic of Macedonia, Moldova, Poland, Romania, Russian Federation, Slovakia, Slovenia, Tajikistan, Turkey, Turkmenistan, Ukraine, and Uzbekistan. These nations initiated their socioeconomic reforms from somewhat different macroeconomic conditions and have followed somewhat different strategies regarding the timing of and approach to these reforms (Blejer et al., 1993).

Although many are now showing more positive economic growth a decade after the initiation of economic reforms, there is marked variations in economic performance with prospects getting less favorable as one moves across the region from west to east (The World Bank Group, 2002). Within this economic restructuring, these nations are also faced with reforming their health care systems, which were once operated within a centrally planned, hierarchically structured economy that appropriated and used resources, including facilities, equipment, supplies, and personnel, without consistent accountability standards regarding how, when, for, and by whom these resources were used (Cholewka, 1999a). Their initial attempts at developing a more open and democratic socioeconomic and political environment, on a foundation of inherited economic conditions along with a legacy of misreported health care outcomes, confronted them with new health management challenges (see Table 24.1) (Cholewka, 2004).

However, these challenges presented new opportunities for improving diagnostic and treatment modalities to improve the quality of health services, professional education, and system organization and management. The structure and function of their health care system, based on institutionalization, that is, hospitalization and medical specialization, needed to change. The hospital (known as a *polyclinic*) now had the role of enhancing health outcomes rather than simply processing (treating) patients with mental and physical diseases and releasing them into the community without planned follow-up care. Hospitals could no longer be managed in isolation from society, and the wider health system and policy makers now had the responsibility to define broader health care goals that the health care system had to meet (Healy and McKee, 2001).

Anticipated Program Outcomes by Western Donor Organizations

The financial resources of these nations were, and continue to be, both inadequately and inappropriately allocated to satisfy the demand for health and social services. The declining health status of the population post independence revealed and confirmed that the return on investment of the Soviet-style health care system was low. It was determined that if this

Table 24.1 Legacy of Soviet-Style Health Care Services in Central and Eastern Europe

Issues	Health Care System Pre Independence
Health status of population	High mortality and morbidity rates due to nutritional, behavioral, and environmental risk factors
Policy making and system management	Emphasis on therapeutic (medical) versus prophylactic model
	Centralized financing and administration
	Poor professional practice and ethical standards
	Lack of response to local and community needs (system based on dependent beneficiaries versus informed consumers)
	Emphasis on institutionalized (hospitalized) care and continued proliferation of specialized health care facilities and personnel
	Lack of emphasis on behavioral and mental health services
	Universal access touted but access to system only to groups and individuals designated as politically and ethnically expedient
Structure	Centrally planned and administered system by Moscow, Russia
Function	Ineffective and inefficient
	Highly bureaucratic with widespread corruption
	Lack of focus on continuous monitoring of health care services for quality improvement
Resources	Statistical norms for structure, function, and financing set by central government
Training, research, and development	Isolation from global influence for academic, clinical practice, and research standards
	Noncompetitive and arbitrary funding for state-sponsored research, facility maintenance and construction, staff education, and technological improvements
Financing	Budget set and resources controlled by central government in Moscow, Russia; emphasis on most expensive level and manner of care—that of hospitalization and medical specialization

Adapted from World Health Organization (2002). The World Health Report 2002: Health Systems: Improving Performance (pp. 12–17, 31, 83, 89). World Health Organization: Geneva, Switzerland.

situation were not changed, without a healthy workforce and reduced tax burden, enterprises could not become viable and contribute to macroeconomic development and growth. Thus, the productivity of the health sector, that is, production of favorable results or outcomes in an efficient and effective manner, is an integral part of these nations' economic turnaround. Therefore, strategies that simultaneously addressed the reality of constrained economic resources and the need to create a more economically efficient health care system had to be found (Cholewka, 1999b).

The purpose of health care sector reform initiatives, as conceived by Western donor organizations (namely, the EU, WB, and USAID), was to introduce local leaders to new ways of operating their systems based on Western market-oriented management models and principles (Commission of the European Communities, 1997), then, in collaboration with system leaders, adapt programs to their systems to improve the efficiency and effectiveness of their outmoded centrally planned and controlled Soviet-style system model. Concern centered on the declining health status of the population of the countries of the former Soviet Union and the effect of this deterioration in public health on the global population. One of the goals of health care sector reform was to restructure the social contract so citizens would become "informed consumers" rather than dependent beneficiaries: that is, to improve the efficiency and effectiveness of health system operation so that a government's guarantees regarding health care would be durable and sustainable (Cleland, 1998).

Although the Soviet Union had started to replace health sector central planning in the 1980s with devolution of budgetary and managerial responsibility to the local level, these changes created a whole new set of intersectoral relationships and organizational functions for which local leaders were not adequately trained. Western public health observers were already reporting rapidly growing rates of otherwise preventable communicable diseases such as anthrax, gastrointestinal diseases, and tuberculosis; chronic diseases of their aging populations; high-risk behavioral conditions such as human immunodeficiency virus–acquired immunodeficiency syndrome (HIV/AIDS) and other sexually transmitted diseases, as well as diseases associated with substance abuse such as alcoholism and chronic obstructive pulmonary disease (WHO, 2000).

In general, many of the following elements were incorporated into health care system restructuring programs for the nations of the former Soviet Union:

■ Strengthening capacity of the role of governmental and quasi-governmental institutions, particularly with respect to the new functions of the Ministries of Health (MOH) and health care services reimbursement system (Health Insurance Funds). Changes in this sphere involved not only decentralization but also separation of the payer and provider roles so that the same government agency no longer had a monopoly on both payment and provision of services.

- Promoting the concepts of "money follows the patient" and "patient choice," that is, payment based on patient's choice of health care provider based on patient satisfaction for the quality of health care services received.
- Promoting new forms of provider payment with establishment of performance-based incentives (a "pay for performance" ethic).
- Restructuring and downsizing health care delivery systems—from polyclinics (hospitals) and specialization to primary care physician management.
- Introduction of management systems utilizing information technology, where feasible, for financial management (planning, control, accountability); human resources (building human capacity); clinical care (professional and organizational development); and quality improvement (efficiency and effectiveness of health care services).
- Supporting the privatization of state-owned health care facilities; entrepreneurial initiatives in establishing health care service agencies and private physician and dental practices; nongovernmental organizations (NGOs); and professional associations.
- Encouraging democratization and "transparency" of the health care system including the education of consumers about their role within the health care system (Dixon, Langenbrunner, and Mossialos, 2002; Cholewka, 1999; Cleland, 1998, p. 2).

System Restructuring Outcomes

Under this general restructuring plan, the health care sector managers (Ministries of Health and organizational leaders) now tried to adjust Western models of health care management to their systems. This was expected to be a long-term process meant to build local capacity for problem solving and self-determination. It was also thought that local "ownership" of the change process would lead to a paradigm, or mindset, change that would also encourage the demand for knowledge and continuing innovation by both practitioners and patients alike (Cholewka, 1999a; Cleland, 1998).

As the postindependence reformers became more influenced by national and global issues related to the establishment of more democratic institutions, they were learning that there needed to be an intersectoral exchange of information with health care systems other than their own for initiating and maintaining effective change strategies. As in the West, they began to see that hospitals cannot be managed in isolation from society; that policy makers have a responsibility to shape health care goals;

Table 24.2   Status of Soviet-Style Health Care Services in Central and Eastern Europe Post Reform Efforts

Issues	Health Care System Post Independence
Health status of population	Country-specific mortality and morbidity rates still high More emphasis on primary care and preventive services
Policy-making and system management	Still need for provision of services based on public expectations and needs, i.e., community, home care, and mental health services to address diseases of aging population, posttraumatic stress disorders due to socioeconomic changes and unresolved historical traumatic occurrences, and health risk behaviors Inadequate information management system for financial and management accountability, monitoring, and evaluation of national and local system operations
Structure	Centrally planned and funded by national Ministries of Health and administered by local governments and organizational managers
Function	Lack of consistent monitoring of health care services; improvements at behest of organizational managers Emphasis on keeping health care personnel and specialists employed in polyclinics Lack of ongoing intersectoral collaboration Inherent system corruption
Resources	Effective managerial and administrative accountability system lacking resource allocation and management
Training, research, and development	Emphasis still on institutionalized care (hospitalization) although primary care is being encouraged Need for trained mental and community health personnel More outside influence in establishing standards for nursing and physician education, clinical practice, research standards, and professional autonomy and associations
Financing	More local control of budgeting process National insurance funds set up to finance system with fee-for-service payments by patients Current or new health programs funded and operated by international donor organizations (NGOs)

Adapted from World Health Organization (2002). The World Health Report 2002: Health Systems: Improving Performance (pp. 23–72, 83, 89). World Health Organization: Geneva, Switzerland.

and that health care facilities must meet the needs of the patient population. Unfortunately, as were the other sectors of these Soviet-indoctrinated societies, they were, and continue to be, faced with much entrenched corruption (see Table 24.2) (Cholewka, 2003).

Corruption—Main Organizational Change Constraint

Corruption is very often framed as a problem of leadership not setting a good example. *Corruption* can be defined as the abuse of public office for private gain that can take place in state, private, and quasi-private activities. It can be classified into four main types: bribery, theft, bureaucratic corruption, and misinformation (Gray and Kaufmann, 1998). Within the post-Soviet countries, it was found by Western donor organizations, such as the World Health Organization (WHO), WB, and USAID, that it was very difficult, if not impossible, to carry out economic, social, political, legal, and ethical reforms in an environment of corruption and an ingrained mistrust and paranoia of the West. Change required political will at the national level and determined leadership at the local (community) level to develop and implement change strategies. All parties involved in this effort would have to assume the responsibility to make changes work.

Ideally, these restructuring strategies would charge leadership directly to initiate government reforms with accountability to realizable goals set by stakeholders within a specific, and presumably workable, time frame. This meant that within a more democratic environment, goals should include interdisciplinary communication with external donor organizations, nongovernmental organizations (NGOs), local and national governments, health care providers, as well as the community, in order to identify and correct system inefficiencies, enhance productivity, apply technology to government operations, and finance and procure cost-effective resources and service contracts.

The objective was for national governments to manage the provision of safe, efficient, and effective health care services as defined by the needs of the populace at the community level. However laudable these reform efforts were, refusal of Western donor organizations to confront the basic political ideology of the Soviet Union that had spawned the present political and socioeconomic legacy of these countries caused a misdiagnosis of entrenched socioeconomic culture and a failure to anticipate the depth, scope, and type of health care reform efforts needed. For example, improving mental health services requires acknowledging the political abuse of psychiatry by the Soviet authorities (Jenkins, 2001); the Soviet Union was excluded from the World Psychiatric Association for using "psychiatric facilities" to incarcerate political dissidents. "The organisational culture has been heavily influenced by the structural power embedded in the central blueprint of socialism. This has ensured that attitudes of dependence are entrenched in eastern European psychiatry [and those within the health care systems]" (Jenkins, 2001, p. 17).

In the post-Soviet transitional economies, a more progressive medical discourse emerged that tried to explain the legacy of the existing health care system, that is, its structure, function, administration, financing, service distribution, and, especially, its health care outcomes. The reality of high rates of ill health of post-Soviet citizenry (a result of ineffectiveness) and lack of resources (a result of inefficiency) of the health care system could be interpreted as the result of a long history of system corruption, a prevailing pattern of protecting self-interests, and political exploitation under Communist rule that disregarded the human rights of its population (WHO, 2000, p. 31).

With the dissolution of the Communist Soviet regime, health care policy objectives were focused on the formation of a restructured health care system based on democratic values of equity and social justice. Although these values were touted by the Soviet authorities, their actual realization was never fully achieved. Western donor organizations suggested cures that were either "political," that is, prescribing how to develop new participatory (democratic) forms of governance, or "rational," that is, prescribing ways to create interdisciplinary unity and coherence within the system. However, even with these Western prescriptions for change, there were more and more reported incidents of poor outcomes of health care services and mismanagement, indicating that it was easier to prescribe new values and ideas than to implement them.

An anticipated outcome of these health care reforms, that is, the creation of a new health care "culture," varied by country and health care system. Whereas some systems were able to innovate and increase capacity for cooperation and service delivery, others continued to experience internal struggles, inefficiency, and other effects of corruption and mismanagement (Blejer et al., 1993; The World Bank Group, 2002). This situation was initially interpreted as a gap between the central capacity for planning and policy shaping and the local capacity to manage and implement these restructuring programs. Increasing problems of ineffective program interpretation and implementation were blamed on the need for a more systematic knowledge of how the values of equity and justice were actually being transformed into new administrative practices within a democratic and market-oriented political model. And, more and more, the focus was put on the establishment of a "civil society" and emphasis on programs that would establish a society based on the "rule of law." However, models for reform were copied after Western models often out of context and without consideration of the fact that resource levels in the East were five to ten times lower that in the West, and that management capacity was severely limited relative to the demands of Western-style financing and more democratic management systems (Ho and Ali-Zade, 2001).

Influence of Corruption on System Restructuring

According to Ensor and Duran-Moreno (2002), it is imperative to distinguish between societies where corruption is endemic and a cross-sectoral problem those in which isolated instances of corruption are the norm, because corruption, the root cause of unsuccessful reform efforts, is harder to eliminate if it is institutionalized within structures that cross sectoral boundaries. They divide these countries into four distinct groups based on criteria used by Transparency International and the Heritage Foundation to measure the general levels of corruption in societies. These groups include (1) societies with relatively low black market and corrupt activity, including most of northwestern Europe; (2) societies with a moderate level, including the southern part of Western Europe and one or two "Western-leaning" Central or Eastern European countries, such as Hungary; (3) those with a moderate to high level, including the more developed Commonwealth of Independent States (CIS) countries; and (4) those with a high level, including the less developed CIS countries and the poorer Eastern European countries (Ensor and Duran-Moreno, 2002, p. 117). These authors believe that health sector corruption mirrors general societal corruption and suggest that where corruption is strongly embedded, the level of all types of corrupt activity is likely to be high and the health care sector will also be affected (Ensor and Duran-Moreno, 2002).

It is still apparent that these initiatives have not been totally effective, and it is imperative that more research be undertaken to determine the conditions that promote systems of management oriented toward the ethos of democracy and community service and which conditions function as impediments to such development. It is becoming more and more apparent that Western donor organizations misdiagnosed the pre- and post-Soviet health care system and that their interventions, based on a misunderstanding of underlying presenting symptoms and their own political interpretation, led reforms that were too extensive, too rapid, and ill conceived. Short-term, thoroughly planned (incorporating specific organizational, socioeconomic, and cultural factors), and successfully completed programs on a smaller scale should have been initiated to ensure positive reinforcement and sustainability.

Trust: A Factor in Improving Post-Soviet Health Care Systems

A simple underlying assumption that should have been made was that *trust* may have been a crucial factor in the attempt to build a national health system that fulfills the West's expectations for equity, accessibility, and quality. *Trust* is defined as the total confidence in the integrity, ability, and good character of another.

Trust is built over time by those in authority who are (or are perceived to be) credible, reliable, believable, dependable, responsible, honorable, honest, ethical, principled, moral, and incorruptible. It should have been assumed that trust would make cooperation and mobilization of resources and capacities easier and that distrust or lack of trust would make it harder. Post-Soviet society can be characterized as a "low trust society" because of the repressive means planned by the Communist Politburo (central governing authority) that were carried out by the state political police known as the Cheka (also known as the Narodnyi komissariat vnutrennikhdel [NKVD] and the Komitet gosudarstvennoi bezopasnosti [KGB]).

For more than a half century, the Cheka (NKVD, KGB) instituted and maintained within the populace a culture of fear, terror, and distrust of one another and their government through policies of manipulating information for creating suspicion about fellow citizens and encouraging reporting on family and friends for various economic rewards. By using tactics of espionage, torture, imprisonment in "death" (work) camps, exile, starvation, and liquidation (including genocide), they forcibly instilled an ideology of total, unquestioning fealty to the Soviet state that was unacceptable to most of the population (Courtois et al., 2000).

Thus a legacy of individual survival based on a distrust of others, self-preservation, and corruption was born, developed, and nurtured and became deeply ingrained in the Soviet system and permeated virtually every aspect of work including the keeping of productivity statistics at all levels (Applebaum, 2003). The results of this legacy remain, to varying degrees, within the socioeconomic culture of post-Soviet countries to this day. The word *tufta*, which translates very imprecisely as "swindling the boss," was heard in most of the languages of the old Warsaw Pact, and the Communist era proverb "They pretend to pay us, and we pretend to work" was commonly used (Applebaum, 2003, p. 350).

Therefore, it would have been crucial to ask how trust could be built into public administrative systems of the post-Soviet countries and which factors would promote this development. However, there is a need for more research showing how Western management models that differ in social, political, and administrative structures and processes might condition the building of trust in these countries.

Within the Soviet Union rules were set and arbitrarily enforced by both the central government and local authorities dictated by political circumstance. However, within the framework of a more open and democratic society, delegation is combined with a system of clear rules, supervision, and accountability. Members of a democratic society or organization are expected to perform and to contribute toward commonly set goals. Within these health care systems, there is a need both for more leadership with accountability on one hand and for more democracy and open debate through team building and team problem solving on the other (Cholewka, 2001; Donabedian, 1980; McLaughlin and Kaluzny, 1994).

For successful and sustainable reform efforts, the building of a strong managerial capacity is needed to gather, interpret, and use quantitative and qualitative data to compare performance to goals. In this way, the management process is used to make behavior more accountable to stated goals and use feedback, learning, discipline, and reward, and thus, build trust by staff that rules are uniformly applied and followed by all. For example, the manager of the information management or quality management department within a health care organization would use this information to provide feedback on spending patterns and to discuss why some departments or facilities are spending too much and others too little on particular functions. This would prioritize functions, safeguard patient safety and confidentiality, and focus on staff for training or other correction actions by management.

The real and major continuing problem of program ineffectiveness stems from the fact that the Western donor organizations did not, and still do not, have an adequate understanding of the political and socioeconomic "culture" instituted by the Soviet Communist system that promoted a common identity of all with the "state." This feeling of belonging to a totalitarian society that monitored and controlled every aspect of their lives—socially, economically, and politically through brutal enforcement methods that discouraged individualized behavior—would be hard to extinguish to build an allegiance to a new culture of democracy in such a short time (Cholewka, 1999a). Although identity and loyalty are conceived to be rather strong within sections of particular health care professional groups, building loyalty to a new system that promises to give these groups more professional autonomy could conceivably be successful—but only if those within these groups see an opportunity for their own self-interests (Cholewka, 2003, 2004). There is no doubt, however, that the existence of fragmented and opposed identities is detrimental to any attempt to promote the sharing of new and unfamiliar goals, values, or visions of a restructured society. Sustained attempts to build such a common identity must be embraced and supported by leadership. It takes time to rebuild health care systems (subsystems) while rebuilding whole societies.

Conclusion and Recommendations

The purpose of this chapter was to examine both unresolved and ongoing health care system issues that should be acknowledged now so that reform policies can be developed to improve current and future health care systems. After more than a decade of health care system reorganization attempts, the following areas were again identified by Western donor organizations, such as EU, USAID, and WB, for future intervention: activities related to financing health care, improving the continuum of care, improving quality of health services, mobilizing citizens and communities for better health, and advancing public health (Cholewka, 2004).

Although macroeconomic reform has been ongoing during this postindependence period, a full ten years' effort was not extended to health care system management change strategies. This stemmed, in part, from a lack of political will by Western donor organizations to seek accountability for program success. There is another big problem in changing the way in which the health care system functions because it is based on the medical model. Even in Western societies, the medical model of health care is not easy to change. It is hierarchical and based on the diagnosis and treatment of patients under the auspices and direction of the physician as chief provider of health care services and arbiter of the patient's progress and continuum of care through the health care system. It creates tensions with other professional staff and, in particular, in relation to the allocation of economic resources for patient care. It is important to solve this by using an interdisciplinary decision-making process that is incorporated in the Continuous Quality Improvement (CQI) model that is now advocated in Western health care systems in order to include in the care process the expertise of other health care practitioners, including nurses and patient advocacy groups (Cholewka, 1999a, 1999b, 2001; Donabedian, 1980; McLaughlin and Kaluzny, 1994).

The first few years of independence were critical for international donor organizations for determining how the health care sector was actually funded, structured, and operated. Soviet reports abounded and centrally set goals were supposedly met, but all data and reported outcomes were subject to political bias and therefore suspect—considering observable versus theoretical results. But, in fairness, when Western economists from international economic development organizations such as EU, WHO, USAID, WHO, and WB started to investigate and analyze the functioning of the post-Soviet health care systems, they found that there was no reliable and consistent information to use that could accurately compare them with Western models based on an open, participatory, democratic management style that encourages entrepreneurial economic activity and conforms to standards for accountability to stakeholders, that include government, payers, clients, providers, and investors.

It was also found that health care workers were neither educationally nor psychologically prepared to assume management roles equal to those of their Western counterparts. Because of this paucity of useful information and the Western practitioners' misunderstanding of the extent of socialistic

philosophy throughout these societies, programs based on Western management models were mistakenly instituted within these health care systems. Therefore the pace of transition by these nations was underestimated.
It was presumed that changes would be more rapid and spontaneous
because these systems were considered much like those in the West; that
is, the population was purported to be very educated and literate and a
basic economic infrastructure was present, and the population robust.

However, corruption, a major constraint to socioeconomic reform,
impeded change efforts. Corruption was, and still is, endemic and there
still is an ingrained distrust of Western methods (Applebaum, 2003; Conquest, 1990; Courtois et al., 2000; Ensor and Duran-Moreno, 2002; Hirschler, 2001; Thomas, 2001; WHO, 2000). Therefore, openness to a more
democratic system of governance was, and still is, very difficult to develop
and maintain (Cholewka, 2003).

The economic effects of corruption within the health care system
compromise the ability of the system to deliver efficient and effective
high-quality services to those most in need of them, and health status of
the population is affected. Diverting public monies (potential health care
resources) to private hands through corrupt practices is detrimental to
entrepreneurial activity of practitioners establishing independent practices
and building a strong private economic sector that encourages competition
and chances for practice improvement. Corruption in the health care sector
also impacts macroeconomic growth and international status as it reduces
economic development through a loss of international investment. If these
continuing impediments to health care system change are not confronted,
the development of sustainable programs for change will not occur at the
pace and scope anticipated by Western donor organizations.

References

Applebaum, A. (2003). *Gulag: A history*. New York: Doubleday.

Barr, N. (Ed.) (1994). *Labor markets and social policy in Central and Eastern
Europe: The transition and beyond*. Washington, DC: Oxford University
Press.

Bird, R.M., Ebel, R.D., and Wallich, C.I. (Eds.) (1995). *Decentralization of the
socialist state: Intergovernmental finance in transition economies*. Washington, DC: The World Bank.

Blejer, M.I., Calvo, G.A., Coricelli, F., and Gelb, A.H. (Eds.) (1993). Eastern Europe
in transition: From recession to growth? Proceedings of a conference on
the macroeconomic aspects of adjustment, cosponsored by the International Monetary Fund and the World Bank. Washington, DC: The International Bank for Reconstruction and development/The World Bank.

Cholewka, P.A. (1999a). *Comparative analysis of two healthcare organizations in post-Soviet Lithuania and Ukraine: Implications for continuous quality improvement.* Ann Arbor, MI: UMI.

Cholewka, P.A. (1999b). Reengineering the Lithuanian healthcare system: A hospital quality improvement initiative. *Journal for Healthcare Quality*, 21(4), 26–37.

Cholewka, P.A. (2001). Challenges to institutionalizing sustainable total quality management programs in healthcare systems of post-Soviet countries. (E-Journal). International *Journal of Economic Development*, Pennsylvania State University (www.spaef.com/IJED_PUB/).

Cholewka, P.A. (2003). Ten years of health systems transition in Central and Eastern Europe and Eurasia. *Journal for Healthcare Quality*, 25(2), 46–49.

Cholewka, P.A. (2004). Factors affecting sustainable healthcare management programs in post-Soviet transitional economies. In G.M. Mudacumura and M.S. Haque (Eds.), *Handbook of Development Policy Studies*. New York: Marcel Dekker.

Cleland, C.F.(1998). Health care system transformation in the NIS: Practical concepts, tools and techniques developed through ZdravReform 1993–1997. Abt Associates, Inc., funded by the United States Agency for International Development. Retrieved January 1, 2004, from ZdravReform Program CD-ROM.

Commission of the European Communities. (1997). Agenda 2000. Vols. 1 and 2. *The challenge of enlargement.* Brussels: Author.

Conquest, R. (1990). *The great terror: A reassessment.* New York: Oxford University Press.

Courtois, S., Werth, N., Panne, J., Paczkowski, A., Bartosek, K., and Margolin, J. (2000). *The black book of communism: Crimes, terror, repression.* Cambridge, MA: Harvard University Press.

Dixon, A., Langenbrunner, J., and Mossialos, E. (2002). Facing the challenges of health care financing: A background paper for USAID Conference: Ten years of health systems transition in Central and Eastern Europe and Eurasia (pp. 1–25). Washington, DC: USAID.

Donabedian, A. (1980). *Explorations in quality assessment and monitoring. Vol. 1. The definition of quality and approaches to its assessment.* Ann Arbor, MI: Health Administration Press.

Ensor, T., and Duran-Moreno, A. (2002). Corruption as a challenge to effective regulation in the health sector. In R. Saltzman, R. Busse, and E. Mossialos (Eds.), *Regulating entrepreneurial behavior in European health care systems* (pp. 106–124). Philadelphia: Open University Press.

Gray, C.W. and Kaufman, D. (1998). Corruption and development. *Finance and Development*, March 1998, pp. 7–10.

Healy, J., and McKee, M. (2001). Implementing hospital reform in Central and Eastern Europe and Central Asia. *Eurohealth*, 7(3), 1.

Hirschler, R. (2001). Interview with Nick Stern, senior vice president and chief economist of the World Bank. *Transition Newsletter*, 12(4), 1–4.

Ho, T., and Ali-Zade, N., (2001). Eastern hospitals in transition. *Eurohealth*, 7(3), 8–14.

Jenkins, R., (2001). Mental health reform in Eastern Europe. *Eurohealth*, 7(3), 15–21.

McLaughlin, C.P., and Kaluzny, A.D. (Eds.). (1994). *Continuous quality improvement in health care: Theory, implementation, and applications.* Gaithersburg, MD: Aspen.

The World Bank Group (2002). ECA Regional Brief. Retrieved from http://www.worldbank.org/eca/

Thomas, S. (2001). Petty corruption in the wild, wild east. *Transition Newsletter*, 12(4), 5–6.

World Health Organization (2000). The world health report 2000: Health systems: Improving performance (p. xv). Geneva, Switzerland: World Health Organization.

CONCLUSION: ALTERNATIVES AND RECOMMENDATIONS

Chapter 25

The World Bank's New Urban Strategy: An Assessment from Development Ethics

Stephen G. Schwenke

CONTENTS

Introduction

For many people, life is extremely tough in the urban areas in the less developed countries of the world (the South). The severity of poverty and the deprivation of opportunities in the urban South constitute a profound moral challenge even if seldom considered from such a perspective. To a large extent, the rich and powerful in the South and in the more advanced, industrialized and postindustrial economies of the world (the North) ignore or tolerate this degradation of human dignity; there exists a tacit acceptance of two very different standards for human dignity—one for "them" and one for "us."

Is it morally permissible to maintain distinct and inferior standards for people just because they are poor? If not, who would enforce a more equitable standard? Are there moral obligations that we have—as individuals and governments, North and South—to overcome deprivation and uphold a more uniform standard of dignity in the urban South? And why has so little been said, when discussing urbanization in the South, concerning such moral dimensions?

Those questions can be answered in several different ways, yet for those most severely affected by poverty and loss of dignity, each answer will be inadequate. Perhaps this inadequacy arises from our unfamiliarity with moral questions; it is uncommon, after all, to frame our analyses from a moral perspective. For most of us, moral vocabulary is thin, and moral voice appears to lack rigor. More importantly, it is conventional wisdom that narrow self-interest prevails, and that human beings lack motivation consistently to act on moral principles and precepts—even those that they and the vast majority of us hold in common. For example, if asked, we reject as morally unacceptable the thought that young poor children in the cities (North and South) are suffering and dying as a result of neglect, lack of nutrition, and disease. Yet, measured by the content of our public policies, the limited scope of our official foreign assistance, and the paucity of our charitable donations and social programs, we have chosen to live with that reality rather than demand that adequate resources be brought to bear.

Until recently, overt moral vocabulary was seldom part of any urban development dialogue, and the premise of value neutrality or value-free technical thinking dominated urban planning theory and practice. Overcrowding, unsafe buildings, lack of clean water and air, dismal sanitary standards, widespread unemployment and underemployment, lack of a reasonable means to obtain clear titles to property, unchecked environmental degradation, scarcity of parks and recreational resources, embedded corruption in government, and widespread insecurity—these problems of urban development and local governance affect North and South, but with far greater intensity in the South (Johns Hopkins University, 2001, p. 1). Such problems were to be solved, so it was assumed, through the application of appropriate technology and scientific methods. Starting in the 1950s, urban planners and development experts formulated powerful techniques of probability theory, modeling, and statistics and advocated that the application of these tools was the correct response to such problems in the urban environment. Not all were convinced, as noted by Jane Jacobs in her scathing attack on American city planning techniques of the 1960s:

> By carrying to logical conclusions the thesis that the city, as it exists, is a problem in disorganized complexity, housers and planners reached—apparently with straight faces—the idea that almost any specific malfunctioning could be corrected by opening and filling a new file drawer. (Jacobs, 1961, p. 437)

In the late 1960s, American and European planners and those involved in urban development policy and urban governance gradually began to tackle such challenges as urban amenity, social equity, and community. Despite this tentative expansion of horizons, urban growth and development remained conceptually rooted in the premise of top-down management and pragmatic problem solving, planning, and design, in which the rule of law, the weight of authority, and the influence of experts would shape cities to conform to an imposed master plan.

Planners and city managers in the North viewed themselves as expert authorities, whose role and duty were to impose their (probably well-intentioned) vision of urban growth on the residents and stakeholders of the city. These planners and city managers were hardly value neutral—they gave to their work their middle-class sensibilities and high standards of education—and often failed to connect with the on-the-ground realities and values of the poor. For those poor people facing a daily challenge of survival, the sensibilities and concerns of these middle-class, financially secure planners and managers were alien, yet the poor—the stakeholders of such development initiatives—were not invited to participate in deciding on urban development priorities.

The situation was, and to a considerable extent still is, further exacerbated in the South, where governments (almost always at the national level) engaged urban advisers from the North, adding a cultural barrier to distance the planner and the people further. Colorful, beautifully drafted, and elegantly framed master plans adorn the walls of many municipal offices in the South, yet the value of these expensive exercises in top-down, expert-led, and nonparticipatory urban development rarely extends beyond the creation of engaging wall decorations. In the author's project experience throughout the South, in national Ministries of Local Government and in many municipalities, from the city of Quelimane, Mozambique, to Alaminos Town in northwest Luzon in the Philippines, unimplemented urban master plans adorn walls and gather dust on shelves. While the dust gathers, unplanned urban growth continues almost exponentially.

Clearly the top-down, expert-dominated approach to urban development has not served the South well. Urban development plans—often unrealistic in their assumptions—remain unimplemented. Building codes—intended to ensure safe structures—are ignored or blunted by corruption. The voices of those most in need, the urban poor, remains unarticulated and silent. Local governments seem to lack compassion, or at least lack vision leading to a more effective governance role (Laquian, 2002, p. 99). Are there moral arguments of sufficient traction and strength to motivate those with resources, knowledge, and power—in the North and the South—to approach urban development more effectively, with a concern for social justice, popular participation, with care and compassion and a commitment to honoring human dignity?

The World Bank possesses significant resources, knowledge, and power and purports to represent the interests of all of its member countries, North and South. What kind of a response to these moral questions should we expect from the World Bank?

The New Urban Strategy

The International Bank for Reconstruction and Development—best known as the World Bank—is concerned with the growing development challenges of urbanization in the South. Under the organizing vision of achieving "the livable city," the World Bank has recently taken several significant policy and programmatic steps addressing the impact of urbanization in the South—most notably the publication in 2000 of a new World Bank strategy on urban development and local governance, *Cities in Transition—World Bank Urban and Local Government Strategy* (the "New Urban Strategy").

The New Urban Strategy was created as a result of the World Bank's realization that "urban development activities could and should have a greater impact in raising the living standards of the poor and promoting equity" (World Bank, 2000, p. 4). The World Bank updates its ongoing urban development mission through the New Urban Strategy, observing that cities and towns offer a distinctive and "dynamic development arena" that can model a "microcosm of sustainable development for the country" (World Bank, 2000, pp. 5–6).

The New Urban Strategy, with its evocative vision of "the livable city," claims linkages to the major strategic objectives of the World Bank: improving development effectiveness, increasing the participation of civil society, forging partnerships, and reducing corruption. As the World Bank defines *livable* in *the livable city* ideal—that notion at the conceptual center of the New Urban Strategy—the strategy comes closest to an overt, explicit reference to the moral dimensions of urban development and governance:

> If cities and towns are to promote the welfare of their residents and of the nation's citizens, they must be ... *livable*—ensuring a decent quality of life and equitable opportunities for all residents, including the poorest. (World Bank, 2000, p. 8)

Livable is a vague but encompassing term, a label of opportunity under which stakeholders might find space to pack their bundle of qualitative development priorities. *Decent* and *equitable* are unmistakably normative; they are an invitation extended to the stakeholders in individual cities and towns to engage in a rich dialogue concerning the meaning of these terms. And for *the livable city* to emerge, a rich dialogue is needed—yet nowhere in the New Urban Strategy is a formula or recipe to be found to achieve this ideal.

The New Urban Strategy seeks change, yet it has significant weaknesses in terms of incentives, involvement of stakeholders, and whom it excludes. Although the livable city vision offers inspiration, the New Urban Strategy fails to provide sufficient incentives to *motivate* positive changes in the urban environments of the South. Although it advocates participatory urban planning methods and argues for the inclusion and representation of all groups in urban society in urban governance processes, the New Urban Strategy provides inadequate guidance on the desirable form and purpose of participation. No surprise then that in practice the World Bank demonstrates only the most superficial—and ineffectual—commitment to participation.

The New Urban Strategy also establishes a policy of triage, setting selective criteria for assisting cities and towns, while excluding the vast majority of cities and towns in the South from World Bank assistance. The World Bank seeks to help[1] only those cities and towns who already have demonstrated a genuine desire to improve and who can meet certain standards that assure lenders that their monies will be applied effectively. Although the desire to avoid wasteful or ineffectual resource transfers is understandable, the resulting abandonment of those cities and towns suffering under repressive, corrupt, incompetent, inefficient, and unrepresentative local governments raises deep moral concerns.

The New Urban Strategy ought to demand much more of its own institution, the World Bank. The potential for this institution to provide some measure of beneficial leadership, advocacy, and positive influence to improve the development prospects for all cities and towns in the South remains largely unrecognized and unfulfilled.

The New Urban Strategy makes no overt reference to the many ethical concerns and moral obligations of urban development to which some of the previous criticisms refer. Specifically, the moral duties and obligations of the World Bank and of governments in the South remain obscure in the New Urban Strategy. A government's essential moral duty to ensure that those people most affected by urban development have a voice in decisions that affect them is not convincingly discussed. And the New Urban Strategy differentiates between who should receive its assistance and who should not without offering a morally acceptable justification.

Does it really matter whether the New Urban Strategy fails as a policy instrument to motivate beneficial change in the cities and towns of the South? Are the demands of urbanization really that morally compelling?

Urbanization in the South

The rapidity, scale, and intensity of urban growth in the South are alarming.[2] More than 50% of the population of the South is expected to be living in urban environments by the year 2015. By 2030 the projections jump to 60% of the world's population, or 4.9 billion people living in cities—and nearly all of that population growth will be in the cities of the South (Johns Hopkins University, 2001, p. 1).

Present-day conditions in the urban South, where a significant proportion of existing urban populations are impoverished, are hardly salutary. According to a recent *World Resources Report*, "An estimated twenty-five to fifty percent of urban inhabitants in developing countries live in impoverished slums and squatter settlements, with little or no access to adequate water, sanitation, or refuse collection" (World Resources Institute, 1998, p. 3). "A fifth of the world's population currently lives in cities where the air is unhealthy to breathe" (USAID, 2001, p. 1). Degraded urban environmental quality of this severity gravely threatens human health and well-being (Max-Neef, 1992, p. 49; World Resources Institute 1998).

The capacity of cities in the South to cope with such rapid growth is typically weak. In 1987, the World Commission on Environment and Development declared that simply to maintain the conditions from 1987 until 1997, the developing world would need to increase by 65% its capacity to produce and manage its urban infrastructure, shelter, and services (Johns Hopkins University, 2001, p. 2). This obviously has not happened. As presently resourced, this burgeoning urban growth is beyond the control or management of any government, South or North, national or local. New urban growth is largely unplanned or poorly planned—more than half of all new houses in cities in the South are built without formal approval, on unserviced sites (no or minimal infrastructure), and without clear title to the land (World Bank, 1998, p. 18).

The result is increasing deficits in the provision of even basic infrastructure and social services, a situation further exacerbated by the spatial implications of territorial isolation of the poor within cities in the South. The slums and squatter areas of the poor are often located on the urban fringe, in periurban areas, or in isolated pockets in inner city locations—all areas that receive significantly less in the way of formal urban infrastructure and services than do the more affluent neighborhoods.

The ability of urban governments to cope with rapid growth depends in large measure on their competence, authority, and motivation to act, and their resources. Although decentralization of governance is a growing trend in the South (United Nations Development Programme [UNDP], 2000b, p. 8), many developing countries still retain considerable power at the national level over the affairs of cities (World Bank, 2000, p. 50). Where decentralization has yet to occur, municipal "governance" exists in only a limited form that is neither institutionally structured nor popularly expected to provide civic leadership, generate governance policies, carry out integrated strategic thinking on quality of life issues, or offer opportunities for effective and significant local participation in local affairs (Laquian, 2002, p. 101). In cities and towns such as these—by far the rule and not the exception in the South—the role of urban government is limited to a very few service-delivery functions and remains highly dependent on centralized national-level controls, financial disbursements, and top-down management policies (Laquian, 2002, p. 121).

The development needs of the urban South are now urgent. Clearly the urban agenda deserves greater prominence at the World Bank, but why should ethics find a place on that agenda?

Ethics and Urban Development

Traditionally, those wishing rigorously to evaluate the reasonable range of ethically desirable or permissible actions apply rational reasoning skills within the structure of one or more leading ethical theories. In doing so, they hope to call attention to those actions that (1) lead to optimal consequences (utilitarianism), (2) accord well and are consistent with universalizable principles (Kantian ethics, human rights approaches), (3) result in the most freedom and opportunity for human flourishing (capabilities approaches), (4) best reflect the ideals of the just society (social contract theory), (5) reflect our essential human interdependence and allow for the expression of our caring and compassionate natures to influence social behavior (feminist ethics), or (6) flow from the virtuous character of those entrusted with decision-making authority (virtue ethics). Each of these approaches leads to important insights that—if heeded—may guide urban development beneficially.

The New Urban Strategy, however, makes no reference to any of these normative theories, or overtly to any ethical concerns. Utilitarianism remains the unspoken—and largely unexamined—ethical framework of classical economics, on which the World Bank is grounded. The New Urban Strategy ignores this one potential source for ethical reasoning and makes no reference to maximizing utility or utilitarian precepts of distributive justice. Similarly, although the World Bank is officially related to the United Nations, and the United Nations is the champion of the Universal Declaration of Human Rights, the New Urban Strategy ignores yet another potential opportunity to ground itself in a highly persuasive moral theory; there is no mention of human rights within the New Urban Strategy.

On the face of it, this may seem unremarkable. The direct linkage between urban development in the South and a guiding framework of human rights may not seem obvious. Yet linkages do and should exist; the development challenge confronting cities in the South certainly can—and perhaps should—be viewed as a human rights challenge. The UNDP's human rights approach, articulated in the Human Development Report 2000 (HDR 2000), supports this *urban development–human rights* connection in its general contention that "human rights and human development share a common vision and a common purpose—to secure the freedom, well-being and dignity of all people everywhere" (United Nations Development Programme, 2000a). Others too have recognized this *urban development–human rights* connection. For example, the principle that urban residents ought to enjoy at least a set of basic urban rights guides the *European Urban Charter* (1993). According to the charter, this basic set of rights includes

> the right to protection from aggression; from pollution; from a difficult and disturbing urban environment; the right to exercise democratic control of their local community; the right to decent housing, health, cultural opportunity and mobility...It is one of the responsibilities of local and regional authorities to protect such rights through the development of appropriate strategies. (Congress of Local and Regional Authorities of Europe, 1993, p. 5)

Human rights is but one of several leading moral approaches in development ethics. Nobel Laureate economist and philosopher Amartya Sen, in his *Development as Freedom* (1999), offers persuasive guidance to development thinking in general, based on another moral theory—the capabilities approach—which he pioneered. Arguably any of the leading moral theories, if applied during the formulation of the New Urban Strategy, would have raised important concerns and possibly suggested new directions in urban policy and strategy. The close linkage of the World Bank and the United Nations, however, and the large body of international law and conventions make a particularly strong case for considering a human rights–based moral theory in the context of any World Bank strategy or policy document. This chapter will, therefore, concentrate on this one moral theory: the human rights approach of the UNDP.

Would the quality of international assistance to cities and towns in the South benefit from consideration of human rights? More specifically, would the New Urban Strategy benefit from human rights theory as articulated in the UNDP's human rights approach, which is featured in the HDR 2000 (United Nations Development Programme, 2000a)?

But why should the World Bank consider *any* of the offerings of development ethics? What of the argument of those who contend that *no* moral theory of any kind has a place in public policy?

Objections to Moral Theory

There is resistance—often unarticulated but very much in evidence—in many policy circles to inclusion of moral analyses. Many objectors claim that moral issues are largely arbitrary and subjective in nature, and that attending to moral issues in governance processes, for example, in a participatory forum, is fraught with procedural or practical difficulties. In practice, this objection has merit. The stakeholders of urban development, however, should have a say in the policies, plans, and interventions that directly affect them, and the attention now placed on participatory development reflects this emphasis.

Yet moral issues, if raised at all in participatory workshops, are seldom addressed explicitly in a rigorous, unrushed manner through deliberations, reasoned justifications (and challenges to these justifications), and dialogue addressed at reducing disagreements and at consensus building. It is arguable that common models of participatory practice largely ignore moral issues, or at best channel moral concerns into narrow outlets such as vision statements.

Morality is not, however, arbitrary, as the systematic and critical study of moral beliefs, values, and concerns—ethics—makes abundantly clear. In ethics, our values and beliefs are organized into various (and to some extent, competing) systems, each of which exhibits coherence more or less internally, each more or less matching our considered judgments and deeply held beliefs (Goulet 1995, pp. 26–27; Griffin, 1996, pp. 8–17). In this way, individual moral concerns are given context, so that they can be argued from a systematic, well-reasoned set of relationships based on principles that in turn can be argued and justified. It is not practical or appropriate, however, to use the limited time and resources of a participatory workshop on urban development to justify a complete ethical theory (much less compare it to other contending theories, from first principles). Instead, various process tools can be derived from several well-established theories within the field of development ethics.

These tool-based approaches, currently receiving significant attention from development ethicists around the world yet still at a conceptual stage, arguably could be applied in a time-constrained structured participatory process without preliminary philosophical justifications, using language accessible to a diverse range of stakeholders. In the interim, and at a less sophisticated level, participatory practices are improving in ways that foster much richer exchanges of ideas, values, and constructive criticism.

A second objection to involving moral analyses is the claim that attending to moral concerns risks upsetting the status quo by challenging the existing economic and power relationships within any given society, for example, by questioning who has authority and why, how goods are distributed, and who is accountable to whom. This potential to pose "awkward questions" to those in power may serve as sufficient (but not publicly stated) reason for politically insecure city leaders to avoid a participatory approach.

Challenging the status quo, however, is often a central feature of a moral approach to development; the existence of widespread poverty, corruption, injustice, and the lack of universal respect for human dignity demand such a challenge. A moral approach offers some fresh insights into the means and ends for—and possibly even the necessary motivation for—changing the status quo in ways that lead to more just, compassionate, and decent societies, or to bolster the protection of the status quo when it is judged to be reasonably just. Changing the status quo need not be immediately radical or revolutionary—for example, progressive positive change toward sustainable development through the assertion of human rights–based claims, fulfilled over time, may be sufficient. The fulfillment of such claims will, however, *ultimately* entail radical changes to the status quo.

A third common objection to including moral analyses in urban development and governance is the concern that moral issues must be addressed and deliberated by participants who exhibit moral virtues, and that such participants may be few in number. If this claim were accepted, it would be difficult to imagine any society's moral progress over time. The leadership of morally virtuous persons is not unimportant—such leadership may deeply inspire and motivate others to be sensitive to social injustices and receptive to the deliberation of moral issues—but virtuous moral leadership is not a necessary condition.

The institutionalized commitment of social, political, or religious institutions to moral principles goes some distance to introducing the moral approach to the urban development process. If the participants in that process are able to accept the credibility of an ethical framework—such as a human rights–based framework—and a way can be found to apply this (such as through a derived set of participatory process tools) to the urban development agenda under discussion, then the necessary requirement for a wise and virtuous person to preside over the proceedings no longer pertains.

A fourth objection is that asserting values in public policy, whether within a participatory forum or through other operations of governance, is inappropriate because values vary in their moral justifications, from the universal to the relative. This dichotomy between the universal and the relative is a venerable old chestnut of philosophical debate, and a great deal is written and argued in the literature on this subject (Nussbaum, 2000, pp. 48–49). The growing consensus is that even diverse cultures and values systems already accept that many values—as expressed in practice—are *de facto* universal and fundamental to human nature (Booth, 1999, pp. 58–64). Examples include the values all cultures place on basic security against threats of injury and violence, the basic right to access to adequate sustenance to maintain a healthy human life, the common obligation to ensure that all enjoy clean water and air, the very human need to be treated as a person possessing dignity and worth, and the need to exercise choice and some degree of freedom in the major decisions affecting one's life (Ignatieff, 2001,[3] p. 54–57). Even with a wide overlap of common values between cultures, there is no compelling reason not to make space for local culture, tradition, and context significantly to influence and shape the implementation of development initiatives responsive to these universal values.

Finally, some people object to morally based approaches to urban development on the basis that the *qualitative* and nonempirical nature of moral values makes them impractical in the public policy and development context (Klitgaard, 1988, p. 11). This, however, is a superficial argument. Measuring moral performance may be more difficult than monitoring amoral criteria through gathering empirical data and identifying trends. But empirical data can say a great deal about the changes in achieving morally desirable goals, and the presentation of such data in participatory workshops can be informative. An extensive amount of work is being done around the world to identify appropriate empirical indicators that measure quality of life.[4] The degree to which national laws reflect internationally recognized human rights principles is measurable. Qualitative factors in the experience of poverty, the enjoyment of basic freedoms and opportunities, and the prevalence of respect for human dignity all are subject to meaningful evaluation through a variety of techniques, from focus groups to surveys. The claim that moral issues should not influence public policy or be raised in participatory workshops because they are troublesome to monitor and evaluate speaks more of a failure of political will or methodology than of a basic fault inherent in ethics.

Development Ethics, Human Rights, and the New Urban Strategy

No explicit human rights frameworks or considerations specifically based on human rights informed the formulation of the New Urban Strategy.[5] Many of the conceptual weaknesses of the New Urban Strategy are directly traceable to this lack of a human rights—or equivalent—ethical framework.

Development ethics fosters a reflective capacity in the consciousness of development theorists, practitioners, and decision makers, with respect to definitions of *development* and *sustainability*, and more generally how development is conceived, evaluated, described, and understood in particular situations (Goulet, 1995, pp. 37–52, 85–88). For example, development ethics, when associated with human rights conceptions, clarifies relationships between a moral rights claim maker and a duty bearer and invites a deliberative process regarding where one's moral obligations lie and to what extent these pertain to any given subject.

Development interventions informed by development ethics articulate the moral dimensions of the development agenda. Although they run some risk of entrenching opposing viewpoints, development interventions informed by development ethics can illuminate, resolve, and diminish conflicting development interests through structured, normative "quality-of-life" focused processes. This is perhaps most clearly seen in one tangible product of the participatory urban development planning process—the development of a vision statement (Ames, 1998). A vision statement is the articulation by representative stakeholders of the ultimate ends and fundamental means of urban development for their situation. The New Urban Strategy would be much improved, on this basis, were it to advocate (and, in implementation, provide the requisite funding for) deliberative participation of a character that would provide the opportunity for such an articulation of means and ends.

Effective popular participation in urban development and governance processes is a necessary but not sufficient condition to the pursuit of the livable city ideal (World Bank, 2000, pp. 56–57). Certainly political leaders, civil servants, and all stakeholders constantly need to improve their conceptual and management skills, their abilities to integrate technical approaches across many sectors with the quality of democratic processes and political leadership. Stakeholders also need to improve their participatory skills, to learn to be wary of the manipulations of self-interested but rhetorically gifted participants, and to achieve their own public voice. The door must be kept open to innovations and creative new approaches to urban problems. Even with all of this, the goal of a sustainable, livable city cannot be credibly pursued without explicit attention to moral values.

Human rights approaches, and specifically the UNDP's human rights approach contained in the HDR 2000, are prominently cited in the literature of development ethics. Unlike the New Urban Strategy, HDR 2000 advocates inclusive democracy and the empowerment of poor people based on human rights principles. Attention to human rights helps to provide structure to deliberative participation by isolating certain values and rights that are not subject to trade-offs (except—if it can be morally justified—in extreme circumstances). HDR 2000 observes that human development almost always involves sacrificing some interests of some stakeholders in the name of achieving "the common good," but human rights places limits on the extent to which any individual should bear losses to support the development goals of the larger community—a particularly important protection for the poor. The New Urban Strategy contains no such protections.

Human rights theories, such as HDR 2000, also provide a carefully articulated example—based on international human rights conventions and common ethical principles—for stakeholders in the urban development process to agree more easily on their own localized set of shared values. Among such values are distributive justice, the obligations of those holding public office to be accountable stewards of the common good, the rights and duties of popular participation, the prerequisite of human security to all human development, and the equitable inclusion of women in the participatory process.

Such values often run aground against the jagged unforgiving rocks of entrenched power; power retains its historical place as a central factor in development and human social relations. Under human rights thinking, social institutions are conceived not as mechanisms for moderating power—bargaining between competing interests (which favors the powerful over the poor)—but more as the internalization of agreed-upon and shared moral values as described in the form of collaboration. This assertion directly challenges the New Urban Strategy's market-based advocacy of *competitiveness*. *Collaboration* in urban development does not attract equivalent World Bank support in the New Urban Strategy.

Without human rights protections, it can be argued, only the goodwill of the powerful—or the perception of some larger self-interest by the powerful—will motivate those with wealth and power to attend to the just distribution of the benefits of development. The New Urban Strategy calls for a "dignified standard for the poor that permits them to share the resources of society" (World Bank, 2000, p. 47). Permitting the poor to share has little force as an appeal to those who hold power and leaves the action "to permit" with those who have control of the resources. Human rights thinking, in contrast, not only makes a moral demand for a share, but for a *fair* share—to opportunities, to access to economic resources, to security, to political expression, to freedom—appropriate to protect and respect the human dignity that all people are entitled to simply by being human beings (Shue, 1996, pp. 103–110).

When the powerful are not inclined to respect basic human rights protections or allow for a fair share, the disadvantaged do have recourse to national human rights laws—where these exist and are enforced—or, failing that, to the international human rights regime. In specific instances, these appeals may prove to be ineffectual, but the existence of a larger body of rights-based moral and legal protections offers some hope, and occasionally some relief, over and above reliance on the disposition of those in power to exercise benevolence or civic duty (Ignatieff, 2001, p. 22). The New Urban Strategy ought to embrace this human rights–based method of counterbalance to the misuse of power that thwarts legitimate urban development interests.

An approach based on a human rights framework can serve a constructive—and motivational—role in the achievement, through both competition and collaboration, of good development and good governance in the burgeoning cities and towns of the South. Fundamentally, claims grounded in a human rights framework have moral resonance with the majority of people concerned in the development of a city or town—stakeholders—and effectively initiate, empower, motivate, and sustain stakeholder participation throughout the lengthy, demanding development process (Shue, 1996, pp. 13, 30, 39, 74–77). These motivational drivers are not present in the New Urban Strategy.

Although motivation is a necessary condition to achieve social justice and improve quality of life, motivated people must also be empowered to act. Human rights provide this empowerment, giving stakeholders a strong moral claim to more than spectator or beneficiary status in participatory processes. Empowered people ask the *when* and *by whom* questions when considering development alternatives (Shue, 1996, pp. 71–78). The prospect of securing and sustaining the freedom and right to participate, which the UNDP's human rights approach demands, provides a strong motivation for stakeholders to consider themselves empowered to initiate and sustain deliberative participation in urban development, planning, and governance (Shue, 1996, pp. 71–78). And, as HDR 2000 observes, one of the best means for securing and sustaining stakeholder participation is through a process of democratization and local autonomy. This perspective ought to be incorporated into the New Urban Strategy.

The achievement of human rights is an inherently worthy goal and an appropriate urban development objective, especially when the pursuit of the progressive realization of human rights derivatively reflects the long-term aspiration of stakeholders. At the very least, there are some human rights—for example, Henry Shue's basic rights of subsistence, security, and certain liberties (Shue, 1996)—that are essential to development and should be advocated in all development strategies. Sen, one of the authors of HDR 2000, argues in that report that the domain of human development must encompass the expansion of choice for capabilities that people hold to be especially valuable—including guaranteed human rights. This is a much richer concept of development than that offered by the New Urban Strategy.[6] Sen and the other authors of HDR 2000 further argue that human well-being is linked to the achievement of seven essential freedoms:

1. Freedom from discrimination—for equality
2. Freedom from want—for a decent standard of living
3. Freedom from being thwarted in self-realization—for the realization of one's human potential
4. Freedom from fear—with no threats to personal security
5. Freedom from injustice
6. Freedom from repression—for participation, expression and association
7. Freedom from exploitation—for decent work (United Nations Development Programme, 2000a, p. 31)

In HDR 2000, Sen carries his argument further, linking these seven freedoms to the enhancement of certain human capabilities. Conceptually, this combination of human rights–based freedoms and capabilities is a broader and more persuasive articulation of development than the *sustainable, livable city* model of the New Urban Strategy and offers far more tangible guidance to any deliberative participation process affecting urban development and governance.

Human rights protections offer an important means to the goal of respecting human dignity—a goal most people hold to be deeply valuable (Ignatieff, 2001, p. 164). HDR 2000 argues that the achievement of human rights protections as an objective of development requires the pursuit of a human rights approach to development—for example, an assertion by poor people that they are entitled to be treated in a manner appropriate to the recognition of their human dignity.

HDR 2000 further observes that such attention to human rights, as a means to respect and protect human dignity, in turn requires a fundamental shift in development strategies. That required shift applies to the New Urban Strategy as well. It must place a much greater emphasis on·fostering deliberative participation and accepting the moral obligation to be responsive to the development aspirations of all people—and not just those in the few World Bank–selected cities.

Conclusion

In the South, the attainment of the goal of the *livable city* appears even more remote than it is in the North. Public participation is seldom conceived by the local political leadership as a process to involve stakeholders in working toward deliberative agreements (and disagreements) about the ends and means of a livable city. The concept of the livable city, at best, is simply assumed—without discussion—to be a shared and universal goal, yet in reality it translates into very different priorities among and between politicians, civil servants, business people, the poor, men and women, the unemployed and underemployed, academics, professionals, and so forth. Although there is often significant commonality among such interest groups in the identification of issues, the ranking of priorities varies—sometimes greatly. Without an opportunity for deliberation, in which views can be openly challenged and justifications offered, stakeholders are denied the opportunity to reevaluate their priorities and concepts and work with others to forge agreements that (most) everyone can accept.

An appreciation of societal values and cultural norms is also important to effective public participation and responsible urban governance. When confronted with ingrained cultural or social constraints, an interest group might become more conscious of social cleavages and hence become more entrenched and intransigent. But the alternative is also true; such an interest group might change its stated priorities. Zulu women in South Africa—when consulted outside earshot of Zulu men—will allocate priorities quite differently than when consulted in gender-mixed assemblies. Mayors of small towns in the Philippines—often outspoken, passionate advocates for their constituents in meetings with their peers—will avoid an "unseemly" public conflict in formal meetings with high-ranking provincial officials, even if it means that their silence will pave the way for policies that run directly counter to their espoused interests (Schwenke, 1995, pp. 6–8). Central governments, often with the technical advice of international experts, have been seen to impose a top-down image of the livable city that is alien to local sensibilities (Peattie, 1995).

In practice, progress toward an ideal like the World Bank's vision of the livable city suffers through lack of a local interpretation of this vision. Cribbed ("boilerplate") language and ethical clichés can usefully camouflage action opposed to genuinely ethical development. Instead, active stakeholder participation in formulating a consensus on both common development goals and the means to achieve them—that city's sense of its livable city ideal—is essential. If it is possible through participation to articulate such an ideal, the active and strategic pursuit of the ideal still remains dependent on the ability of the local governments. At this stage, the competence, integrity, and motivation of the political leadership of that city or town is a major determinant of success; if a mayor or a majority of city councilors share the livable city ideal—which ideally they participated in shaping—the mission of that city's government may become oriented to achieving the vision set by the leadership.

On rare occasions, an inspired and able political leader may possess his or her own vision of the livable city, achieved outside a participatory process (or when such a process fails to achieve positive results), around which he or she then builds a consensus. A classic case is the positive impact on development of the visionary leadership of Mayor Jaime Lerner in Curitiba, Brazil. Mayor Lerner visualized a city based on cooperation and partnership, characterized by attractive public spaces (commercial areas, parks), excellent access to public transport and social services (child care, health care, etc.), effective poverty alleviation, and a beneficial relationship between urban and rural interests. He thought of many cost-effective and innovative ways to achieve these goals, such as creating a pedestrian-only downtown, making vast improvements in a public bus system, involving the poor in recycling of trash in exchange for basic foodstuffs, and creating a park system that doubled as a groundwater drainage system in times of flooding. The city now thrives and has moved significantly closer to the livable city ideal, not initiated but now "owned" by a large number of stakeholders there.

The livable city ideal is at least a set of morally relevant standards by which citizens and others may evaluate their city in terms that speak to their own quality-of-life aspirations and concerns. As such, the World Bank's new Urban and Local Government Strategy ought to be amended explicitly to recognize universal human dignity, to embrace openly a

process of moral analysis within governance processes, and to institutionalize popular participation based on the principle at the center of deliberative democracy—the moral equality of all persons. In this manner, each
city might gradually move toward an explicit, integrated, and localized
articulation of the livable city ideal, influencing development strategies
and governance processes qualitatively and providing the essential motivation for sustained beneficial change.

Notes

1. Much of the World Bank's urban assistance is now channeled through a
   collaborative institutional venture with the United Nations, known as The
   Cities Alliance.
2. This trend is already acknowledged through various statistical analyses of
   a wide number of international institutions, development agencies, think
   tanks, and academic centers. Examples include the World Bank, the United
   Nations, USAID, DFID, the Central Intelligence Agency, International Council for Local Environmental Initiatives, Population Information Program at
   the Center for Communication Programs of the School of Public Health at
   the Johns Hopkins University, the Overseas Development Institute (UK),
   and the Woodrow Wilson International Center for Scholars.
3. Michael Ignatieff is the principal author. Amy Gutmann provided an introduction and served as overall editor, and she coordinated very short follow-
   up commentaries by K. Anthony Appiah, David A. Hollinger, Thomas W.
   Laqueur, and Diane F. Orentlicher.
4. For example, see a wide variety of applications as featured in *The Quality
   of Life* (1993) edited by Martha Nussbaum and Amartya Sen, Clarendon
   Press, Oxford.
5. Christine Fallert Kessides, urban economics adviser in the Urban Development Division at the World Bank, interview by author, April 6, 2001.
   Amy Nolan, former consultant to the Urban Development Division, interview by author, March 28, 2001. Dr. Timothy Campbell, adviser in Urban
   Development Division, interview by author, April 19, 2001.
6. The New Urban Strategy does not make reference to any specific definition
   of development, but the World Bank strongly associates development with
   economic growth and poverty reduction.

References

Ames, Steven C. (1998). *A Guide to Community Visioning: Hands-On Information
     for Local Communities*, rev. ed. Chicago, IL: American Planning Association
     Planners Press.
Booth, Ken. (1999). "Three Tyrannies." In Tim Dunne and Nicholas J. Wheeler
     (eds.), *Human Rights in Global Politics*. Cambridge: Cambridge University
     Press.

Congress of Local and Regional Authorities of Europe, European Urban Charter (1993). Retrieved from http://www.radaeuropy.sk/english/documents_coe/congres_local_reg/clrae.html

Goulet, Denis. (1995). *Development Ethics: A Guide to Theory and Practice*. New York: The Apex Press.

Griffin, James. (1996). *Value Judgement: Improving Our Ethical Beliefs*. Oxford: Clarendon Press.

Ignatieff, Michael. (2001). In Amy Gutmann (ed.), *Human Rights as Politics and Idolatry*. Princeton, NJ: Princeton University Press.

Jacobs, Jane. (1961). *The Death and Life of Great American Cities*. New York: Vintage Books, Random House.

Johns Hopkins University. (2001). *Population Reports*. Population Information Program, Center for Communication Programs, School of Public Health, Baltimore: Johns Hopkins University.

Klitgaard, Robert. (1988). *Controlling Corruption*. Los Angeles: University of California Press.

Laquian, Aprodicio A. (2002). Urban Governance: Some Lessons Learned. In Joseph S. Tulchin, Diana H. Varat, and Blair A. Ruble (eds.), *Democratic Governance and Urban Sustainability*. Washington, DC: Comparative Urban Studies Project, Woodrow Wilson International Center for Scholars.

Max-Neef, Manfred A. (1992). *From the Outside Looking In: Experiences in Barefoot Economics*. London: Zed Books.

Nussbaum, Martha C. (2000). *Women and Human Development: The Capabilities Approach*. Cambridge: Cambridge University Press.

Peattie, Lisa. (1995). *Rethinking Ciudad Guayana*. Ann Arbor: The University of Michigan Press.

Schwenke, Stephen. (1995). Where Image Collides with Reality: Planning in the Philippines. *Planners' Casebook* Winter 1995.

Sen, Amartya. (1999). *Development as Freedom*. New York: Alfred A. Knopf.

Shue, Henry. (1996). *Basic Rights: Subsistence, Affluence, and U.S. Foreign Policy*. Princeton, NJ: Princeton University Press.

United Nations Development Programme. (2000a). *Human Development Report*. New York: Oxford University Press.

United Nations Development Programme. (2000b). *The UNDP Role in Decentralization & Local Governance*. New York: UNDP and the German Federal Ministry for Economic Cooperation and Development.

USAID. (2001). *Making Cities Work*. Washington DC: The Office of Environment and Urban Programs, United States Agency for International Development.

World Bank. (1998). *Development and Human Rights: The Role of the World Bank*. Washington, DC: The International Bank for Reconstruction and Development.

World Bank. (2000). *Cities in Transition: World Bank Urban and Local Government Strategy*. Washington, DC: The International Bank for Reconstruction and Development.

World Resources Institute. (1998). *World Resources 1998–99: A Guide to Global Environment*. New York: Oxford University Press.

Chapter 26

Private and Public Sector Interfaces: Prerequisites for Sustainable Development

Lucio Munoz

CONTENTS

Introduction

This chapter introduces a framework that allows one to state the necessary and sufficient conditions for the existence of long-term full human-rights-friendly development and to describe the dilemmas that are generated when moving away from full human rights friendliness, locally and internationally.

The framework is generally based on whether or not development processes are fueled by the interaction of local or international human-rights-friendly businesses or governments. This allows us to appreciate the structure of development processes when interacting business and government actions are considered to be human rights unfriendly, partially human rights friendly, or totally human rights friendly. The chapter first describes the main human rights interfaces of businesses and governments to point out the need to work toward the promotion and implementation of proactive private–public human-rights-friendly development models that are based on the notion of self-interest regulation consistency. Then the possible human-rights-friendly business models and government models are listed to point out the nature of a possible full human-rights-friendly development model or sustainable development model.

In short, this chapter shows, using qualitative comparative theoretical tools, how business self-interest can be framed to be human rights friendly through effective monitoring and enforcement. It further highlights the dilemmas generated when relaxing local and international monitoring and enforcement mechanisms partially or totally.

Businesses and Human Rights Interfaces

Different business environments and motives can have different impacts on human rights, and there is growing interest in ensuring that businesses have the greatest positive impact on human and social rights possible or have higher levels of responsibility, morality, and accountability in their actions. Different business environments are here conceived as different business goals locally and internationally (e.g., economic only, ecoeconomic only).

In other words, there is increasing interest today in ensuring that the human rights dimensions of business development (e.g., social and community responsibility) are included in the decision-making and benefit sharing processes. Indeed, Sacks (2002) indicates that global development processes have an unavoidable moral dimension, which may explain why the inclusion of the social interface within the ecoeconomic decision making process in countries belonging to the Organisation for Economic Co-Operation and Development (OECD) is now gaining increasing momentum (OECD, 2000).

It is commonly accepted that sometimes business motives and environments fail to fulfill any moral, social, or ecological dimension and corrections are needed. For example, Saha and Parker (2002), without directly advocating the replacements of markets by state intervention, point out that regulation of markets is justified sometimes when markets do not reach the poor. Ensuring that markets reach the poor is relevant to poverty reduction strategies, as it is known that income disparities affect the environmental quality of production and consumption. In fact, it has been observed that rich people have the tendency to demand a healthier environment (Khan, 2002) and can afford better technologies, but poor people are limited in what they can buy or get or have. Also, inconsistencies between local and nonlocal levels of business regulation can lead to moral and ethical dimensions. For instance, O'Byrne (2003) points out that mismatches between nation-state and international laws are the sources of major human rights concerns.

Thus, markets and trade have very strong implications socially, environmentally, and economically for both rich and poor people in developed and developing countries and lead to moral or ethical dilemmas when the issues of trade flows and the promotion of human rights are considered. For example, the issue of whether or not countries that respect human rights should trade with those countries that do not respect them used to be settled with a policy of no trade, at least officially. However, now trade take place officially between countries regardless of human rights records, as the case of the United States and China shows, and that is seen as a clear ethical dilemma around international relations (Morris, 2002). And the current globalization process is apparently bringing the moral dilemmas of trade and social, economic, and environmental rights to a boiling point at which direct confrontation among relevant stakeholders, those who set policy, and those who oppose policy, is increasingly becoming the norm. Bigman (2002) indicates that international organizations such as World Trade Organization (WTO) can no longer meet without attracting the forces opposing the globalization agenda to their meeting places.

The main business and human rights issues can be categorized as follows: self-interest versus altruistic action; ineffective versus effective threats; non-human-rights-friendly products versus human-rights-friendly products; and voluntary compliance versus inflexible regulation. The main elements of these sources of discourse as well as current tendencies are discussed in the following.

Self-Interest versus Altruistic Action

Recently, the traditional view that businesses must pursue only their selfish interests if they are to be profitable is being questioned on sustainability grounds; corporations are being encouraged now to follow a more community-responsible approach. Henderson (2001) points out that corporations are under pressure to put more value on meeting the needs of society in general than on meeting the pure needs of stakeholders, and he feels that this approach will backfire on markets and social welfare in the long term as it is inconsistent with the true nature, profit seeking only, of businesses. Others see the more altruistic or community-centered behavior of corporations as consistent with current public expectations (Loizides, 1995).

The move today appears to be toward more corporate social and local responsibility, in terms of human rights and concerns of the communities affected by business actions. This is now being presented as a good business ethic that is also profitable (Conklin et al., 1991).

Ineffective versus Effective Threats

If corporations operate in an environment where nonmarket pressures (e.g., human rights and labor laws) or market pressures (e.g., consumer power and stakeholder participation) are weak or ineffective, such as in the case of developing countries, they will tend to display more unsustainable development patterns. The World Development Report (WDR, 2003) indicates that to promote growth that is socially and environmentally responsible, we need to create efficient institutions supported by a process based on equality and inclusion. Corporations in developed countries tend to behave in more environmentally friendly ways, probably because they are operating under more effective nonmarket and market threats. This appears to be reflected in the reported positive link between good government and institutions and financial performance (Azfar and Cadwell, 2003).

Today, a trend to provide effective and clear threats to influence international corporate behavior appears to be developing. For example, to ensure proper corporate ethics internationally, it is being proposed that international investment agreements be made in binding ways that are consistent with the promotion of sustainable development programs (UNCTAD, 2001a).

Non-Human-Rights-Friendly versus Human-Rights-Friendly Products

If the cost of ensuring that the goods and services produced are human rights friendly is included in their pricing, then the competitive behavior of businesses is affected. For example, Conklin and associates (1991) point out that maintaining cost competitiveness is one of the relevant sustainable development challenges in Canada, given that competitors may be operating in weaker regulatory environments and could sell the same product at lower prices. Differences with respect to economic environments or cost of doing business in different countries and localities are increasingly determining the allocation and concentration of corporate activity (Mintz, 2001).

Today, producing and selling goods consistently with sustainable development principles appear to be an important part of corporate strategies. Making such products may help corporations to develop new markets or reinvent old markets (Loizides, 1995) or help them to portray a cleaner attitude and behavior to society (OECD, 2002).

Voluntary Compliance versus Inflexible Regulation

Proponents disagree on which is the better way to police company behavior, voluntary compliance or binding instruments. Tayeb (1992) points out that international business actually transforms societies during the process of moving and producing goods and services, and that may justify the protection of vulnerable industries in less developed countries. And OECD (2002) indicates that voluntary business actions are seen as weak as they are not legally enforceable. However, regulation should support economic processes while ensuring the inclusion of environmental and social concerns.

Today, preference seems to be given to a combination of voluntary compliance and regulation to guide business behavior. For example, OECD (2001a) points out that its members are using more a combination of regulatory, economic, and social instruments and voluntary compliance to support environmental policies.

Governments and Human Rights Interfaces

The important role that governments play in regulating social and human rights and market activity is widely recognized, and when rights and market processes do not work, government intervention is required. For example, Seo (2000) calls on all governments to work together to help developing countries find sustainable development ways, given that uncontrolled markets fail to improve poor countries' socioeconomic conditions.

Countries and governments have the responsibility to seek the protection of human rights and economic and business well-being (Morris, 2002), internally (local accountability) and externally (global accountability), and this responsibility is increasing in importance with the current trend towards globalization. Johansson (2002) uses the freedom house index to underline that political and democratic ideas are increasingly becoming global.

Public and private sectors will probably work even more closely in the future as the path toward sustainability is increasingly making business sense. One indication of this willingness for close collaboration may be the fact that there is a clear tendency toward what is being called *sustainable banking* (Pronk, 2001), and therefore, toward profitable opportunities for all development stakeholders. The trend may explain why governments appear to be working hard at improving their local and international social and environmental images by increasingly showing more willingness to incorporate social and environmental issues and regulations in their decision-making process.

There are four negative images affecting government and human rights issues that are commonly expressed: the pro–big business image, the corruption-prone image, the weak institutional image, and the conservative policy image. All or some of these negative images appear to be driving the agenda and actions of those seeking a more just global economic system (Broad, 2002) or are seen as problems that may explain why globalization processes have not reached the poor, especially the rural poor, in the Third World (Bigman, 2002). In the following, the main factors underlying these negative images and current tendencies to improve them are discussed in general terms.

Pro–Big Business Image

It is known that in order to attract investment and new businesses or to retain past investment and businesses to support their economic agenda, governments tend to take a probusiness attitude or provide a good business environment. But providing a favorable business environment usually implies that corporations can do whatever they want (Madeley, 1999). As stronger or richer governments or segments of society should be expected to be better prepared to be successful in the free-for-all liberal model, then we should not be surprised when seeing the poorest governments or segments of society left out of the development and globalization process. This is because the effectiveness of the participants or the right to participate in the process is determined by how much economic power each of them has; big business can then participate and the poor and grassroots people are excluded (AS, 1998).

Today, governments are under pressure to ensure that their partnerships with corporations do not leave the losers and the poorest behind and that they lead to fair development. Bartoli (2000) points out that development has a human dimension besides growth, and Mandle (2003) indicates the need to care for those displaced.

Corruption-Prone Image

When governments make decisions, economic, social, and environmental, under conditions that lack accountability, transparency, impartiality, and inclusion mechanisms, then the seeds and images of corruption are present. Corruption undermines the foundations of democracy by opening possible ways to misuse public resources and power and by destroying public confidence in the public decision-making process (OECD, 1999). Hence, as indicated by the Commonwealth Secretariat (CS, 2000a), corruption is in general terms a result of bad governance and it can occur anywhere bad governance is present. Today, there is a lot of interest in promoting good governance and inclusion and in eliminating corruption worldwide. For example, in December 2001 there was a forum involving countries that are members of OECD and of the Organisation of American

States (OAS), focused on promotion of good government principles (OECD 2001b), and now the World Bank has made eradicating government corruption an important element of its development strategy (CS, 2000b).

Weak Institutional Image

Strong government institutions are needed to ensure fair development processes, yet institutional weakness is widespread in developing countries. Therefore, the ability of these governments to face corporate power and to protect their countries, especially the poor, from exploitation is very limited. Mullen (1999) lists weak institutional capacity as one of the factors seriously affecting the ability of the state to protect society and to implement propoor development strategies. Madeley (1999) points out that exploitation can result from implementing efficiency programs that are not accountable to communities, and hence under weak institutional capacity corporate abuse appears more likely.

Hence, the challenge is to build human, economic, social, political, and cultural capacity (James, 1998), especially now that countries are being encouraged to implement home country measures designed to attract foreign direct investment and business activity within their boundaries (UNCTAD, 2001b).

Conservative Policy Image

Governments have been traditionally very conservative when making development decisions, allowing very little or no stakeholder inclusion. They use top-down control approaches that are unconnected with local community concerns or marginalizing (Dalal-Clayton et al., 2003). Recently, stakeholder participation or inclusion has been an underlying characteristic of sustainable development initiatives worldwide. There are practical and ethical reasons for adding participatory approaches to development programs (Malvicini and Sweetser, 2003). It is believed that inclusion and empowerment make conservative policies more flexible, efficient, and socially acceptable. For example, the Asian Development Bank recently made institutional changes to ensure more participation and ownership (Malvicini and Sweetser, 2003), and donors, nongovernmental organizations (NGOs), and government officials are increasingly calling for more participatory development processes (Dalal-Clayton et al., 2003).

Private–Public Human-Rights-Friendly Development

Reactive Behavior

The perception that businesses and governments had in the recent past that products and services produced in human-rights-friendly ways could not be profitable put them in a reactive mode every time social, economic, and environmental groups pressed them to include human rights concerns in their decision-making process. This reactive mode appears to have been justified or encouraged by the perception that pressure groups and stakeholders were heterogeneous and not well enough organized to act effectively and to be feared. For example, Mandle (2003) points out that in 1999 nobody outside the protestors' camps seriously thought or expected that the antiglobalization movement could be able to affect the WTO meeting in Seattle as much as they did.

However, recent concerted and very strong local and international social action through what is being called *citizen backlash* (Broad, 2002) appears to have convinced businesses and governments that they cannot be only in a defensive or reactive mode forever, and most find ways to adjust the business as usual approach. These antiglobalization and anti-market movements and protests are inducing a need to devise some sort of socioenvironmental responsibility and ethics framework to guide corporate and government actions, locally and internationally. For example, pressure groups have pushed corporations toward corporate environmentalism (Jones and Baldwin, 1994) or addressing of the environmental impacts of industrialization (Stone and Washington-Smith, 2002).

Proactive Behavior

By incorporating human rights and social concerns in production activities and reflecting them in the pricing of their goods and services, businesses can escape the attention of pressure groups while practicing human rights responsible–behavior by using it as a marketing tool. There is a tendency now to see environmental issues as excellent business opportunities (Sainsbury, 2000) and to use environmentally friendly and sustainable behavior as an effective competitive and financial strategy (Jeucken, 2001) or as future cost saving or benefit generating activity, especially in less developed countries (Khan, 2002), where tackling environmental issues may be cheaper. Now pressure on governments and corporations is increasing on issue of using some basic levels of social protection to prevent market and social failures, such as the call of trade unions to establish a social clause to protect basic labor rights (Van Rozendaal, 2002) or calls for humanizing the behavior of corporations and the market (Alexander, 1997) or the nature of globalization (Bartoli, 2000).

Need for Self-Interest and Regulation Consistency

Even when acting proactively, we need to ensure that we create a market system (M) in which there is self-interest (S) regulation (R) consistency to ensure full human-rights-friendly development. Such a market system can be considered a sustainable market, expressed as follows:

$$M = S.R$$

The preceding model simply says that for a market (M) to be sustainable, it is necessary and sufficient to have regulation (R) that is consistent with self-interest (S). This is important because without regulation (M1 = S.r), then self-interest will lead to market failure number one: a situation in which a sustainable market does not exist because it is fully dominated by self-interest. Similarly, if we have regulation that is inconsistent with self-interest (M2 = s.R), then inconsistent regulation will lead to market failure number two: the state in which a sustainable market does not exist because it is fully dominated by regulation. Hence, the model suggests that a sustainable market exists only when there is self-interest and regulation consistency, and under those conditions we should expect that responsible self-interest would prevail. This idea of responsible self-interest appears to be consistent with the notion of the civilized market (Alexander, 1997), where it is asked that a characteristic of real persons, *responsibility*, be used to effect the separation of business and society. Therefore, we need to have regulatory systems that are flexible enough to transform pure self-interest into responsible self-interest. The qualitative comparative terminology used in this chapter to present these ideas is listed in Table 26.1.

Methodology

First, a simple model that allows one to classify businesses in terms of local and international levels of human rights compliance is introduced to point out the conditions for the existence of full human-rights-friendly businesses. Second, a simple model that helps to group governments in terms of local and international levels of monitoring and enforcement is presented to introduce the necessary and sufficient conditions for full human-rights-friendly governments. Third, the notion of full human-rights-friendly and -unfriendly development is discussed. Fourth, the local and

Table 26.1   Qualitative Comparative Terminology

M	= Market
S	= Self-interest
R	= Regulation
B	= Human-rights-friendly business
B*	= Fully human-rights-friendly business
b	= Human-rights-unfriendly business
b*	= Fully human-rights-unfriendly business
BL	= Human-rights-friendly business locally
bL	= Human-rights-unfriendly business locally
BI	= Human-rights-friendly business internationally
bI	= Human-rights-unfriendly business internationally
G	= Human-rights-friendly government
G*	= Fully human-rights-friendly government
g	= Human-rights-unfriendly government
g*	= Fully human-rights-unfriendly government
GL	= Human-rights-friendly government locally
gL	= Human-rights-unfriendly government locally
GI	= Human-rights-friendly government internationally
gI	= Human-rights-unfriendly government internationally
D	= Human-rights-friendly development
D*	= Fully human-rights-friendly development
D1*	= Fully human-rights-friendly development locally
D2*	= Fully human-rights-friendly development internationally
d	= Human-rights-unfriendly development
d*	= Fully human-rights-unfriendly development
d1*	= Fully human-rights-unfriendly development locally
d2*	= Fully human-rights-unfriendly development internationally
d1	= Human-rights-unfriendly development locally
d2	= Human-rights-unfriendly development internationally

international dilemmas of relaxing the full human-rights-friendly development model are described. And finally, some relevant conclusions are provided.

Human-Rights-Friendly Business Model

The following human-rights-friendly business model (B), based on whether or not businesses comply with human rights locally (BL) or internationally (BI) or both, can be stated as:

$$B = BL + BI$$

The four possible types of businesses that can be derived on the basis of the model are presented in detail in the following.

Total Human-Rights-Unfriendly Businesses

When businesses do not respect local and international human rights laws at the same time, they are considered to be total human-rights-unfriendly businesses, which can be expressed as:

$$B1 = bL.bI = b *$$

These types of businesses are simply not concerned about the incorporation of their local and international social externalities in their business environment.

Locally Oriented Human-Rights-Friendly Businesses

When businesses do not respect international human rights laws but respect local laws, they are considered to be locally oriented human-rights-friendly businesses, which can be expressed as

$$B2 = BL.bI$$

These types of businesses are only concerned about recognizing their social responsibilities at home, not abroad.

Internationally Oriented Human-Rights-Friendly Businesses

When businesses do not respect local human rights laws but respect international laws, they are considered to be internationally oriented human-rights-friendly businesses, which can be expressed as

$$B3 = bL.BI$$

These type of businesses are interested only in dealing with market promotion abroad, not in meeting their local social responsibility.

Total Human-Rights-Friendly Businesses

When businesses do respect local and international human rights laws at the same time, they are considered to be total human-rights-friendly businesses, which can be stated as

$$B4 = BL.BI = B*$$

These types of businesses are really concerned about the incorporation of their local and international social responsibilities in their business environment.

Human-Rights-Friendly Government Model

In terms of whether or not governments monitor and enforce human rights violations locally (GL) or internationally (GI) or both, the following human-rights-friendly government model can be indicated:

$$G = GL + GI$$

The four possible types of governments that can be derived from the model are described in detail in the following:

Total Human-Rights-Unfriendly Governments

When governments do not monitor and enforce local and international human rights laws at the same time, they are considered to be total human-rights-unfriendly governments, which can be stated as

$$G1 = gL.gI = g^*$$

These types of governments are not able or not willing to implement their local and international human rights responsibilities.

Locally Oriented Human-Rights-Friendly Governments

When governments do not monitor and enforce international human rights laws but monitor and enforce local laws, they are considered to be locally oriented human-rights-friendly governments, which can be expressed as

$$G2 = GL.gI$$

These type of governments are only interested in monitoring and enforcing local social responsibility, not in ensuring international human rights compliance.

Internationally Oriented Human-Rights-Friendly Governments

When governments do not monitor and enforce local human rights laws but monitor and enforce international laws, they are considered to be internationally oriented human-rights-friendly governments, which can be expressed as

$$G3 = gL.GI$$

These type of governments are only interested in monitoring and enforcing international standards, not in ensuring local human rights compliance.

Total Human-Rights-Friendly Governments

When governments do monitor and enforce local and international human rights laws at the same time, they are considered to be total human-rights-friendly governments, which can be stated as

$$G4 = GL.GI = G^*$$

These types of governments are able and willing to implement their local and international responsibilities related to ensuring human right law compliance.

The Full Human-Rights-Friendly Development Model

A full human-rights-friendly development model (D*) is one in which all businesses comply fully with human rights laws and all governments monitor and enforce effectively those laws at the same time as expressed in the following:

$$D^* = B^*G^*$$

The model described is the ideal sustainable development model in which both businesses and governments interact in consistent ways that lead to a state of full human rights friendliness: Self-interest and regulatory consistency is the rule.

Notice that in the model (D*), government monitoring and enforcement have to be consistent with business self-interest. Also, it is important to point out here that this model indicates that self-interest can be constrained, regulatory threats are effective, flexible regulated compliance exists, and human-rights-friendly products prevail in the market. Moreover, this model implies also that governments could then have a socially responsible image, an anticorruption image, a strong institutional image, and a progressive policy image.

By substituting B* with BL.BI and G* with GL.GI in this model, we get

$$D^* = (BL.BI)(GL.GI)$$

The model clearly shows that for development to be fully human-rights-friendly businesses must comply with local and international laws (BL.BI) and governments must monitor and enforce local and international laws (GL.GI) at the same time.

Reorganizing the terms in this model leads to the possibility of separating it into a local and an international component as follows:

$$D^* = (BL.GL)(BI.GI)$$

The explanation shows that the sufficient and necessary condition for having full human-rights-friendly development (D*) is the presence of local full human rights friendliness (BL.GL) and of international full human rights friendliness (BI.GI) at the same time.

Human Rights Dilemmas

The models shown can be used to point out the possible different types of human rights dilemmas that can be generated when moving away from full human-rights-friendly development conditions (D*). To facilitate the presentation, dilemmas are divided into general and specific, and each is separated into institutionally and locationally led dilemmas as follows.

Institutional Failure–Led General Dilemmas

In terms of the model (D* = B*G*), there can be three types of general dilemmas induced by institutional failure: when businesses are not fully human rights friendly but governments are; when governments are not fully human rights friendly but businesses are; and when both businesses and governments are not fully human rights friendly at the same time.

Please notice that (D* = B*G*) implies that if we eliminate government human rights friendliness fully or partially from the equation, then there would not be full human-rights-friendly development (D*) as local or international business self-interest would lead sooner or later to a total or partial market failure in the absence of regulation.

Institutional Failure–Led Specific Dilemmas

Assuming that full government human rights friendliness is the norm (GL.GI), then there can be partial and full business failures. Partial business failures take place when businesses are not human rights friendly locally or internationally. And full business failure takes place when businesses are fully human rights unfriendly. Under the conditions of business unfriendliness described, one can expect to see voluntary compliance as a difficult task as self-interest under ineffective regulatory threat would be irresponsible, leading to the continuation or increased production of human rights-unfriendly products and services.

If we assume that full business human rights friendliness is the rule (BL.BI), then it is possible to have partial and full government failures. Partial government failures take place when governments are not human rights friendly locally or internationally. And full government failure can take place when governments are fully human rights unfriendly.

Under the conditions of government unfriendliness pointed out, one can expect to see the worsening of negative governments' images, such as the pro–big business, corruption, weak institutional capacity, and conservative policy images.

It is worth emphasizing that the ideal model $D^* = (BL.BI)(GL.GI)$ implies that full business human rights friendliness requires full government human rights friendliness if the goal is to achieve full human-rights-friendly development (D^*).

Locational Failure–Led Specific Dilemmas

Assuming that full international human right friendliness prevails (BI.GI), then there can be partial and full local failures. Partial local failures take place when businesses or governments are not human rights friendly locally. And full local failure takes place when businesses and governments are both human rights unfriendly locally at the same time.

If we assume that full local human right friendliness is present (BL.GL), then there can be partial and full international failures. Partial international failures take place when businesses or governments are not human rights friendly internationally. And full international failure takes place when both businesses and governments are both human rights unfriendly internationally at the same time.

Conclusions

It has been shown by qualitative comparative means that businesses and governments can be grouped by their level of human rights friendliness.

Only when businesses and governments interact in full human-rights-friendly ways at the same time can full human-rights-friendly development (D*) materialize. And this implies that achieving sustainable development requires reaching a state of self-interest and regulation consistency. It has also been shown that departures from full human-rights-friendly development (D*) lead to general and specific institutionally and locationally driven dilemmas in which businesses or governments or both at the same time are in some form of human rights unfriendliness.

Hence, the ideal solution to resolving all human rights dilemmas at the same time is the establishment and promotion of a full human-rights-friendly development process locally and internationally at the same time; probably, the United Nations would be the ideal body for assuming this responsibility.

References

Alexander, Ivan. (1997). The Civilized Market: Corporations, Convictions, and the Real Business of Capitalism. Oxford, England: Capstone.

Asia DHRRA Secretariat (AS). (1998). The Impact of Globalization on the Social-Cultural Lives of Grassroots People in Asia. Jakarta, Indonesia: Grasindo.

Azfar, Omar, and Charles A. Cadwell. (2003). Market Augmenting Government: The Institutional Foundations of Prosperity. Ann Arbor: The University of Michigan Press.

Bartoli, Henri. (2000). Rethinking Development: Putting an End to Poverty. Paris: Economica.

Bigman, David. (2002). Globalization and the Developing Countries: Emerging Strategies for Rural Development and Poverty Alleviation. New York: CABI.

Broad, Robin. (2002). Global Backlash: Citizen Initiatives for a Just World Economy. Oxford: Rowman and Littlefield Publishers, Inc.

Commonwealth Secretariat (CS). (2000a). Fighting Corruption: Promoting Good Governance. London: Commonwealth Secretariat's Publication Unit.

Commonwealth Secretariat (CS). (2000b). Promoting Good Governance: Principles, Practices, and Perspectives. London: Management and Training Services Division.

Conklin, David W., Richard C. Hodgson, and Eileen D. Watson. (1991). Sustainable Development: A Manager's Handbook. Ottawa: National Round Table on the Environment and Economy.

Dalal-Clayton, Barry, David Dent, and Olivier Dubois. (2003). Rural Planning in Developing Countries: Supporting Natural Resource Management and Sustainable Livelihoods. Sterling, VA: EarthScan.

Henderson, David. (2001). Misguided Virtue: False Notions of Corporate Social Responsibility. London: The Institute of Economic Affairs.

James, Valentine Udoh. (1998). Capacity Building in Developing Countries: Human and Environmental Dimensions. Westport, CT: Praeger.

Jeucken, Marcel. (2001). Sustainable Finance and Banking: The Financial Sector and the Future of the Planet. London: EarthScan.

Johansson, Jonas. (2002). Globalisation and Democracy. In: Ole Elgstrom and Goran Hyden, eds. Development and Democracy: What Have We Learned and How? London: Routledge.

Jones, L.R., and John H. Baldwin. (1994). Corporate Environmental Policy and Government Regulation. London: JAI Press.

Khan, Shahrukh Rafi. (2002). Trade and Environment: Difficult Policy Choices at the Interface. New York: Zed Books.

Loizides, Stelios. (1995). Corporate Involvement in Community Economic Development: Options, Benefits and Key Success Factors. Ottawa: The Conference Board of Canada.

Madeley, John. (1999). Big Business, Poor Peoples: The Impact of Transnational Corporations on the World Poor. New York: Zed Books.

Malvicini, Cindy F., and Anne T. Sweetser. (2003). Modes of Participation, Experiences from RETA 5894: Capacity Building and Participation Activities II. Regional and Sustainable Development Department. Manila: Asian Development Bank.

Mandle, Jay R. (2003). Globalization and the Poor. Cambridge: Cambridge University Press.

Mintz, Jack M. (2001). Most Favored Nation: Building a Framework for Smart Economic Policy. Toronto: C.D. Howe Institute.

Morris, Susan C. (2002). Trade and Human Rights: The Ethical Dimension in U.S.-China Relations. Burlington, VT, USA: Ashgate.

Mullen, Joseph. (1999). Rural Poverty, Empowerment, and Sustainable Livelihoods. Brookfield, VT, USA: Ashgate.

O'Byrne, Darren J. (2003). Human Rights: An Introduction. London: Longman.

Organisation for Economic Co-operation and Development (OECD). (1999). Public Sector Corruption: An International Survey of Prevention Measures. Paris: OECD.

Organisation for Economic Co-operation and Development (OECD). (2000). Towards Sustainable Development: Indicators to Measure Progress. Paris: OECD.

Organisation for Economic Co-Operation and Development (OECD). (2001a). Environmental Performance Reviews: Achievements in OECD Countries. Paris: OECD.

Organisation for Economic Co-Operation and Development (OECD). (2001b). Public Sector Transparency and Accountability: Making it Happen. Paris: OECD.

Organisation for Economic Co-Operation and Development (OECD). (2002). Five OECD Case Studies. Paris: OECD.

Pronk, Jan. (2001). Foreword. In: Marcel Jeucken, ed. Sustainable Finance and Banking: The Financial Sector and the Future of the Planet. London: EarthScan.

Sacks, Jonathan. (2002). The Dignity of Difference: How to Avoid the Clash of Civilizations. New York: Continuum.

Saha, Suranjit Kumar, and David Parker. (2002). Globalisation and Sustainable Development in Latin America: Perspectives on a New Economic Order. Northamton, MA: Edward Elgar.

Sainsbury, Lord. (2000). International Science and Technology Co-operation for Sustainable Development: A Developed Country Perspective. In: International Science and Technology Co-operation: Towards Sustainable Development. Paris, France: OECD.

Seo Jung Uck. (2000). International Science and Technology Co-operation for Global Sustainability. In: International Science and Technology Co-operation: Towards Sustainable Development. Paris: OECD.

Stone, Hilary, and John Washington-Smith. (2002). Profit and the Environment: Common Sense or Contradiction? West Sussex, England: John Wiley & Sons.

Tayeb, Monir H. (1992). The Global Business Environment: An Introduction. London: Sage.

United Nations Conference on Trade and Development (UNCTAD). (2001a). Environment. New York: United Nations.

United Nations Conference on Trade and Development (UNCTAD). (2001b). Home Country Measures. New York: United Nations.

Van Roozendaal, Gerda. (2002). Trade Unions and Global Governance: The Debate on a Social Clause. London: Continuum.

World Development Report (WDR). (2003). Sustainable Development in a Dynamic World: Transforming Institutions, Growth, and Quality of Life. Washington, DC: The World Bank.

Chapter 27

Foundation Principles Governing Accounting: Revisiting the Representation of Business Activities

Kala Saravanamuthu

CONTENTS

Introduction

This chapter evaluates accounting's contributions to the development of analytical tools that should promote the innovation and implementation of sustainable practices. The underlying connection between information and the decision-making process has come a long way since March and Simon's theorization of management's bounded rationality (March, 1994; March and Simon, 1993; Simon, 1957, 1976) tempered the excesses of economic rationalism in making decisions. It can no longer be assumed that "better" information will always result in greater optimality. This chapter adds an ethical dimension to March and Simon's satisficing decision processes. It builds on management reflexivity that occurs when they are faced with disconfirming bits of information about an event or transaction (Giddens, 1991).

Information here refers to analytical data. Its representation of any event is, in turn, related to how sustainable performance is defined. It involves rethinking how accounting represents business performance because management decisions could either (further) aggravate or mitigate the impact of business activities on the fragile socioecological environment, which has already been ravaged by organizational practices (that have prioritized economic growth above everything else). Society does not have the luxury of postponing ethical issues until a later date when it has generated "enough" money. This argument has been used to rationalize the unethical economic rationality that has shaped societal "progress" thus far:

> For at least another hundred years we must pretend to ourselves and to everyone that fair is foul and foul is fair; for foul is useful and fair is not. Avarice and usury and precaution must be our gods for a little longer still. For only they can lead us out of the tunnel of economic necessity into daylight. (Keynes, 1930, quoted in Schumacher, 1973, p. 22)

Two areas will be examined in this critique: first, the ethics behind the various definitions of sustainable development; second, accounting's contribution to the sustainability debate, which is critiqued in proposing a way forward.

In researching the meaning of *sustainability*, it quickly becomes obvious that there are a number of competing interpretations with regard to the meaning and implications of sustainability. It is argued that competing interpretations are essentially manifestations of the underlying dialectic of sustainability: It is a dialectic that represents attempts by (competing) interest groups either to maintain the status quo (in terms of distribution of power and wealth) or to influence the direction of reform in favor of certain alternative interests, so much so that even efforts with an emancipatory focus are not united in their prioritization of needs. At the extreme, there are two opposing worldviews: namely, ecocentric worldviews (with environment-centered sustainability) and anthropocentric perspectives (with human-centered sustainability) (Eckersely, 1992).

The second question regarding the construction of sustainability feedback is set against this backdrop of ambiguity over the meaning of the term: That is, what sort of information should be provided to management to guide them in deciding between options A and B? Essentially the question of type of information to be produced takes the debate full circle to the presumption underlying the original question: To whom are management accountable under an ethos of sustainable development?

Therefore, this chapter is not an enunciation of all the wonderful mathematical manipulations that reprocess interdisciplinary measures of sustainability. Instead it is a social analysis that is located at the beginning of the measurement exercise. It raises the fundamental but prickly question of to whom the organization (and its management) are accountable. This is achieved through a review of competing definitions of *sustainability*. The third section then draws on ECOMAC, an European study of environmental management accounting practices (Bartolomeo et al., 1999), to ask whether accounting is living up to contemporary societal expectations: that is, to engender socioenvironmentally conscious decisions.

Further, as the concept of sustainability is much broader than ECO-MAC's environmental accounting,[1] a social dimension will be included through a brief review of the most recent Global Reporting Initiative (GRI) (2002). The GRI is an attempt to incorporate sustainability into another subarea of accounting, financial reporting. Before proposing a framework to address any resulting gaps (between accounting's innovations and societal expectations), the fourth section sheds more light on the inconsistency between accounting and other social disciplines (namely, law and land management) with regard to the perceived responsibility of property owners toward the larger community. The fifth section develops the ethical groundwork for the accounting framework that is put forward in the sixth section.

Defining Sustainable Development

The United Nations (UN) definition of sustainability is based on the presumption of open-ended accountability that extends beyond the legal boundaries of limited liability of a public company:

> Sustainable development is development that meets the needs of the present without compromising the ability of future generations to meet their own needs. ... Development involves a progressive transformation of economy and society. ... But physical sustainability cannot be secured unless development policies pay attention to such considerations as changes in access to resources and in the distribution of costs and benefits. Even the narrow notion of physical sustainability implies a concern for social equity between generations, a concern that must logically be extended to equity within each generation. (World Commission on Environment and Development, 1987, p. 43)

The UN's concern for the larger community (beyond the immediate economic interests of shareholders) is not new: It was raised by Berle and Means (1967), who revealed a rift between management and shareholders of large companies that contributed to social disasters such as the Great Depression. Their third recommendation calls for passive shareholders to relinquish their hold on management; it would relieve managers from the burden of having to prioritize economic growth needs over community needs unambiguously. Concern for the larger community has also emerged in more recent times in industry attempts to deflect stricter social regulations by regulating itself.

For instance, in the late 1990s, the main players in the commercial banking sector in Australia released their own "social charter" in an attempt to counter allegations of economic single-mindedness; banks have been reporting higher levels profits while continuing to charge higher fees and charges. Consequently, industry stands accused of exploiting corporate social responsibility reporting to camouflage the perpetuation of business-as-usual practices. Tokar (1997), Chatterjee and Finger (1994), and Athanasiou (1996) provide additional international examples of how "greenwash" rhetoric is used to distort and manipulate the sustainability message at corporate, national, and global levels.

Although the preceding illustrations may be portrayed as well-intended but ineffectual voluntary attempts at self-regulation, business in Australia (for instance) has been less than welcoming of an independent body's attempt to undertake the task of monitoring corporate social credentials through its Reputex Index. The index is calculated on a survey of social and environmental performance of Australia's top 100 companies. As in the Standard & Poor's or Moody's ratings, companies are rated from AAA to D for corporate social responsibility (McIntyre, 2003a, p. 11). Companies and market advocates have balked at this initiative, arguing that the methodology is flawed, political and subjective:

> The index is an exercise among civil society activists who wish to appropriate the resources of corporations for their own purposes. ... It has little to do with corporate goodness, it has a lot to do with increasing the power of NGOs to impose their agendas, which include the appropriation of property and further regulation of corporations. (G. Johns, as reported in McIntyre, 2003b, p. 10)

> Directors are paid to save the company, not the planet. ... More important, expecting companies to become foot soldiers in someone's self-declared moral war mistakes the role of companies and threatens economic freedom. (Albrechtsen, 2003, p. 13).

The property rights concern raised is a serious one as it reflects the extent of an organization's responsibility to the larger community and the environment. Despite the ambiguous nature of the term, sustainability is here to stay. Even though it makes the proponents of individual property rights uncomfortable, business has acknowledged the inevitability of impending changes to the corporate scorecard. A member of the World Business Council for Sustainable Development, the political voice for leading corporations, states:

> on the subject of sustainability ... there is indeed a connection—a strong one—among the triple bottom lines of economic, social and environmental performance. ... market forces apply not only to profit and loss and the creation of wealth, but to other factors that profoundly affect the quality of our lives. I think it's fair to state the case in rather stark terms ... that in the future, companies that are not sustainable—in the fullest sense of that term—will not be operationally or financially successful. It's doubtful they will even survive. That's why this topic has a special urgency for all of us. (Stavropoulos, 2000, p. 1)

Attempts to capture the spirit of sustainability in the form of "Triple Bottom Line" measurements have been attributed to John Elkington (1997). He warns of the public relations nightmare for producers that are not seen to adhere to the sustainability ethos in a society (that is better informed about the debate over economic and social priorities) because society is not as willing to embrace changes to its consumption patterns (J. Elkington, in McIntyre, 2003a, p. 11). Thus, a dialectical power struggle emerges from the ambiguity over sustainability: There are on the one hand,

- An informed community that is unable to effect significant change directly but has the potential to galvanize sufficient public pressure on organizations to change their habits
- And, on the other hand, the business world, which has the power to manipulate the sustainability agenda with its greenwash rhetoric of corporate environmental stewardship but that runs the danger of public backlash should a social or environmental disaster occur.

This dialectic of sustainability implies that no one group of subject actors should be demonized or hailed as representing the only way forward. It is a much more fluid situation in which information presented to the competing interest groups empowers them to shift the balance of argument (and power). The questions that then arise are what type of information should be produced and what is its intended impact on the recipients (be they management or external organizational constituents).

In searching for answers, the scope of the discussion in this chapter will be limited to accounting information, even though the accounting discipline is only one of several sources of measurements. Although all forms of signification shape the evolution of society's norms and practices, accounting has a significant impact on management decisions because it has traditionally been recognized as a means of assessing organizational performance. The accounting framework exists in the form of formalized, relatively uniform rules and assumptions about the world "out there." The conventional accounting framework is based on the presumption that the numbers constructed should reflect an organization's stewardship responsibility to shareholders only, hence, Albrechtsen's (2003) indignation that the directors are being held accountable to nobler causes.

It is obvious from the discussion on the definition of sustainability that the dilemma of "extent of responsibility" is central to the construction of information. Any 21st-century accounting framework cannot continue to adhere unproblematically to the 19th-century presumption that prioritizes business interests alone (Previts and Merino, 1998). Here this core assumption is examined in following subdisciplines of accounting: financial and management accounting. The former refers to external accounts provided to shareholders and other external organizational constituents as part of the firm's stewardship responsibility. It is governed by the accounting profession's standards and legislative disclosure requirements that seek to ensure uniformity and fairness in reporting. It is an inherently political process, and any changes to reporting requirements will consequently occur more slowly than in the management accounting domain. Here a financial accounting response to the multiple stakeholder ethos of sustainability will be considered through the GRI (2002).

Since 1997, the Coalition for Environmentally Responsible Economies and the United Nations Environment Program (UNEP) have published three globally applicable guidelines on accounting for sustainability. The aim is to raise sustainability reporting to the same level of acceptance and consistency as financial reporting in the long term (UNEP, 2001).

Management accounting refers to all types of information provided to management (that is, users within an organization) to assist in making decisions and to plan as well as to measure performance (and thus manage costs and revenues). Changes instigated by the sustainability debate are more likely to impact on management accounting before financial accounting. Here a management accounting study that was carried out in Europe to ascertain how companies addressed their information requirements, ECOMAC, will be used to shed light on the economic–environmental tensions in implementing sustainable practices. *ECOMAC* stands for *ecomanagement accounting as a tool of environmental management.* It was conducted under the auspices of the Environment and Climate Programme (Human Dimension of Environmental Change) of the European Commission (DG XII)[2] (Bartolomeo et al., 1999). It identifies the following activities as central to management accounting systems: bookkeeping, budget setting and control, capital budgeting, product costing, and performance measurement.

Management Accounting and Sustainability Debate

This section reviews management accounting's sustainability contributions before considering that of financial accounting. But first, ECOMAC's definitions of sustainability:

▪ Radical improvements in environmental performance—a minimum "factor four" reduction in environmental impact for the delivery of final goods and services to customers according to some estimates (von Weizsacker, Lovins, and Lovins, 1997).

- Increased "ecoefficiency" through the development of new products and processes which can create more economic value per unit of environmental impact (DeSimone and Popoff, 1997; Fussler and James, 1996).
- A long-term perspective in decision making, with greater emphasis on the impacts of decisions on future generations.
- A greater degree of internationalization of the external environmental costs of business (Rubenstein, 1994).

(*Source:* Bartolomeo et al., 1999, p. 19)

These expectations primarily prioritize preventative or front-end measures (instead of mopping up the spills at the end of the production pipeline). In this regard, it is very much in line with the call for a radical rethink of production methods and consumption behaviors (Economic & Social Research Council, 2000; World Scientists, 1992). Despite these well-intended directions, it will be argued here that the final interpretation of sustainability is very much the product of the dialectic between economic and socioenvironmental priorities. This tension is very much evident in the definition of a term, *ecoefficiency*, coined by the World Business Council for Sustainable Development in 1991:

> Ecoefficiency is achieved by the delivery of competitively-priced goods and services that satisfy human needs and bring quality of life, while progressively reducing ecological impacts and resource intensity throughout the life-cycle to a level at least in line with the earth's estimated carrying capacity. In short, it is concerned with creating more value with less impact. (World Business Council for Sustainable Development, 2000, p. 4)

There is every danger this win–win message could be little more than greenwash rhetoric unless the conventional understanding of terms such as *value* is radically changed in keeping with concern for socioenvironmental priorities. The question then is, How much of the conventional "dollar first" logic is entrenched in the accounting framework that underpins these innovations?

The Logic Underpinning the Accounting Framework

Revealing the underlying logic requires an examination of the fundamental building blocks of the conventional accounting framework. The foundation is represented by accounting's categorization of business activities in the balance sheet and income statement: namely, assets, liabilities, equity, revenue, and expenses. *Assets* are defined as economic benefits controlled as a result of past transactions or events, and *liabilities* are future sacrifices of economic benefits. Similarly, *revenues* are inflows, enhancements, or savings from outflows of economic benefits. *Expenses* represent consumption or losses of future economic benefits (Parker and Porter, 2002). It is argued that these definitions privilege economic over socioenvironmental concerns (Previts and Merino, 1998; Tinker, 1985).

Consequently, the notion of cost, which is an extension of accounting's building blocks, is also similarly partisan in its construction because it prioritizes economic benefits. Yet ECOMAC's innovations in (the financial aspects of) management accounting are essentially attempts to extend this very notion of cost to environmental concerns! For instance, the definition of *environmental costs* in one of the ECOMAC case studies, the Philips Deutschland's glass factory in Aachen, is as follows:

> The operational environmental costs of an organization equal the monetary value of goods and services sacrificed for environmental protection measures as well as for the absence of such measures. The operational environmental costs are net costs, therefore any monetary gains achieved through measures for environmental protection have to be subtracted. (Becksmann and Bouma, 1999a, p. 134)

ECOMAC also uncovered a variation of the cost theme, which is presented as an extension of the zero waste ethos of the quality management era:

> The essence of categorising costs according to the principle of quality, lies in the importance of prevention. The ideal is zero defects; this can only be reached by preventive actions. ... The relationship between preventive environmental costs and the costs of failure (such as waste disposal and air purification) signifies the financial side of going for zero waste. (Bouma and Wolters, 1999a, pp. 127–128)

It is argued here that even the well-intentioned efforts to prevent unsustainable practices are flawed because "environmental quality" is premised on the economic orientation of cost. In responding to pressures of globalization, the ECOMAC case studies display a (pseudo)sustainability ethos, which is shaped by the focus on quality. It is characterized by (1) a focus on controlling and reducing costs under all circumstances, and (2) a presumption that sustainability involves long-term continuous improvements, and (3) requires the environment to be wholly integrated into the business. But the holistic intentions (that is, 2 and 3) are undermined by the focus on costs (in 1). So, it is not surprising that the study shows that

> one major issue will always be the control and containment of the environmental costs attached to company's activities. For that matter, it is important for companies to know their environmental costs. All the case studies, in different ways, deal with these. (Bouma and Wolters, 1999a, p. 113)

Ultimately, the inherent economic orientation of the conventional cost measures means that it is important for companies to know *the impact of their activities on the environment*, instead of the conventional "costs" per se because the conventional accounting framework is inward looking in defining the extent of organizational responsibility toward society and the environment. The 21st-century framework should move away from the economic orientation of business priorities and place the social–environmental and economic goals on an even footing. Otherwise it will result in business-as-usual practices that are camouflaged by greenwash rhetoric. This problem has been highlighted by ecologists Pimm (1997) and Costanza and associates (1997), who illustrate the (ridiculous) extent to which the cost efficiency ethos costs is used to justify the continued exploitation of the biodiversity:

> The most profitable strategy for harvesting whales is to convert all of them quickly into money in the bank. Even the most stingy savings account produces interest income faster than whales reproduce themselves. ... Maximizing profits demanded that the slow-moving, inshore-feeding species were first hunted to extinction, before whalers tackled species whose capture required more advanced technology. The appropriately named right whales did go first, the "wrong" whales followed at ever shorter intervals. Generally, only species that grow faster than money in the bank should be harvested sustainably. (Pimm, 1997, p. 231)

So, although the ECOMAC survey reveals that

- 53% of respondent firms had integrated formal environmental policy goals into their "business-economic policy goals"
- 56% had an "environmental management system" in operation
- 24% were in the process of introducing such a system (Bartolomeo et al., 1999, p. 25)

this chapter uses ECOMAC's detailed findings (discussed later) to cast doubts over the appropriateness of cost-based environmental feedback in promoting sustainability (Saravanamuthu, forthcoming).

Investigation Evaluation

ECOMAC found a healthy move toward preventative management practices across all industry sectors: 44% to 53% of measures used were preventative ones. ECOMAC also found that management accounting is "is increasingly recognised as an important tool in environmental management," and its significance is expected to increase in the future (Bouma and Wolters, 1999b, p. 108). These authors argued that "the more intensely measures have an impact on the primary process, the stronger they will affect a company's cost structure" (p. 108). The increased reliance on extending conventional management accounting concepts to implement the sustainability agenda is a worrying development. The authors admit that this (partisan) framework would fit snugly into "economic selection criteria such as Net Present Value or Return on Investment," thus allowing "environmentally focused investment" to be assessed in terms of its profitability. Although this critique does not knock back the need for including economic considerations in evaluating investments, there is very real danger that a partisan model will cause it to dominate the sustainability criteria (cf. Giddings et al., 2002).

Further, ECOMAC reveals that the most popular primary assessment technique in making short-term decisions is the payback method: 35% of European respondents use it. In contrast, White and Savage (1995) studied the U.S. Environmental Protection Agency (EPA) and concluded that return on investment (ROI) is the most common investment criterion. But the European companies are using a longer payback period than firms using payback in the United States. Within Europe, firms in the United Kingdon and Italy have placed more importance on payback than the Dutch and German firms.

An integrated, holistic analysis of investments will be better able to reflect a more realistic impact of business activities on nature. But holism is not a trait of cost reliant tools (such as net present value [NPV], ROI, and payback) that unproblematically prioritize economic benefits above all other concerns. Perhaps a (single) holistic measure is not feasible at this stage because the accumulated (scientific) knowledge about how humans, the natural biodiversity, vegetation, and natural forces impact on each other, and are shaped by each other is at best patchy (Ehrlich, Ehrlich, and Holdren, 1997 in Daily, 1997; Heywood, 1995).

Allocation of Overhead Costs

Conventional accumulation of costs includes an arbitrary allocation of common or overhead costs. That is, costs are allocated to the cost centers where they are incurred to prevent distorting the cost–price data and subsequent management decisions. However, the nature of environmental costs does not permit this criterion to be applied in any logical or coherent manner:

> This [allocation based on where the cost is incurred] ... is not possible for some environmental costs, such as the cost of environmental administration. Here, nobody can determine, which part of the environmental administration cost is caused by each production step (p. 139). ... While for some environmental cost it can be determined, for which process and product they were incurred, for others, this is almost impossible. (Becksmann and Bouma, 1999a, p. 140)

Further, conventional allocation methods, which were rejected as inappropriate in the 1990s, are used to assign environmental overhead costs. The main activity used to allocate environmental costs has been labor hours (33% of respondents in Europe, and 55% in the United States), followed by production volume (24% in Europe and 53% in the United States). The European study cautions that several of their case studies (such as Cartiera Favini and Philips) reveal that these methods of allocation "may result in environmental costs being allocated to processes or products which do not in fact generate them" (Bartolomeo, Bennett, and James, 1999, p. 27), in direct contradiction to the fundamental principle of cost allocation.

The study uses the case study of the firm Italiana Petroli to argue for the application of activity-based costing (ABC) to generate cost information and data for environmental risk management purposes (Bouma and Wolters, 1999a, p. 125). Although the move away from profit maximization per se to risk management is a welcome relief, whether ABC is the best means of encouraging sustainable management is doubtful. Armstrong (2002) argues that the emergence of ABC as a costing and management tool has coincided with the introduction of cost efficiency strategies in (traditionally white-collar) service centers. Applied recklessly, ABC could result in loss of staff expertise, reduce staff morale, and cause the firm to be less competitive in the long run. Therefore, is this revamped conventional cost tool the best the accounting profession has to offer for the sustainability challenges of the 21st century?

Environmental Costs

The Philips Glass factory at Aachen and Sony Deutschland reveal that any definition of environmental costs has to be plant specific because of the unique circumstances and priorities surrounding each case, so much so that the study concludes that, "so far neither literature nor practice offers a generally accepted definition for the term 'environmental costs'" (Becksmann and Bouma, 1999b, p. 143). It raises a political question: In whose interests are costs being accumulated?

For instance, in the case of Sony Germany, the firm did not produce the products but was responsible for distributing and servicing them. Strictly, not all the environmental costs connected to the products are influenced by Sony Germany (Becksmann and Bouma, 1999b, p. 151). Does this mean that the firm's responsibility should not extend to the environmental impact of its subcontractors, who supply the products that constitute one of the company's revenue lines? If no responsibility is assigned (on the basis of strict legal entity boundaries), then it would follow that companies such as Nike and GAP (which sell designer apparel at premium prices) may not be held accountable for the sweatshop working conditions of the factories in Asia, where the apparel is produced. Does society today allow the veil of legal ownership to obscure the extended responsibility to exploited workers? Public outcry against such practices would indicate that it does not and it has (incidentally) resulted in these firms' adopting an internal social charter (British Broadcasting Corporation, 2000).

Signifying Environmental Parameters

It should not be surprising that ECOMAC has exposed "considerable doubts about the reliability of much environmental and environmental-related data within companies." This is because "direct measurement" of many of the environmental parameters is "often impossible or unduly expensive, so data has to be derived from other parameters, e.g. measuring inputs and outputs to estimate losses," resulting in high margins of error. The problem has been aggravated in large companies, where data are collected at different levels and in different locations (including different countries) (Bartolomeo, Bennett, and James, 1999, p. 28).

The ECOMAC study has identified the emergence of "neofinancial" data, that is, productivity data that are expressed in physical instead of financial numbers (Bartolomeo, Bennett, and James, 1999, p. 40). This form of representation makes little difference to the critique here because the physical numbers are little more than proxies for the logic of cost efficiency (Saravanamuthu and Tinker, 2003).

On the financial accounting front, the most recent formulation of sustainability reporting guidelines, GRI (2002), considers "boundary research" to be a "critical reporting issue" in sorting out the "intimate relationship between the organization and the larger economic, environmental and social systems within which it operates" (p. 26). It identifies stakeholders' information needs as extending beyond "direct employees and financial data" (GRI, p. 39). Despite these claims, its operational boundaries are based on "financial control, legal ownership, [and] business relationships" (GRI, p. 26). Its stakeholders "typically" include communities, customers, shareholders, suppliers, trade unions, workforce, business partners, local authorities, and NGOs (GRI, p. 40). It is important that GRI's stakeholders be holistically defined to allow social reform. GRI's current list of stakeholders also reflects a predominantly human-centered approach, with little acknowledgment of biodiversity in recovering and sustaining the health of the environment.

To recap, ambiguity surrounds the idea of sustainability because there is comparatively little knowledge about the holistic interconnections between humans and nature. What is obvious is that past interaction has resulted in high levels of social and environmental degradation, and society as a whole cannot continue as it has over the last century. But proceeding in a sustainable manner cannot occur in an information vacuum. On the other hand, precise information cannot be produced because of the lack of knowledge about interconnectedness, and hence sustainability.

The following section locates this critique of accounting's innovations in the broader context of developments in legal and land management practices.

Accounting Innovations: Legal and Land Management Practices

Reeve (2002) argues that the notion of property shapes and is shaped by several factors including demographic and political changes (Braden, 1982); the actions of the state (Castle, 1978), as well as technological and economic factors (Barzel, 1989). Here it will be demonstrated that the way in which common law distinguishes between public and private interests in ascertaining the rights and responsibilities of landholders is not unrelated to the state of the environment and a sense of responsibility for the wider community.

Common law determines the "quantum of socially permissible power exercised" (Gray and Gray, 1988, p. 16) in respect to a socially valued resource through one of three criteria: property in fact, property in right, and property as a responsibility. The method used has far-reaching implications as to where the boundary between public and private interests is located. For instance, for two centuries the native Australians have been denied land rights because the property as a right criterion had been used to uphold the presumption of *terra nullis* (that is, Australia has been deemed to be unoccupied even though it had been occupied by aborigines).

However, the case of *Mabo v. Queensland (no. 2)*[3] applies the criterion of property in fact and recognizes aborigines' spiritual and cultural connection with the land. Similarly, although property as a responsibility has been less widely acknowledged in the past, it is the most likely means of effecting the sustainability ethos because under this criterion, property rights are regarded as a bundle of sticks. Each stick represents one utility of land such as occupancy, or aesthetic value. Each stick is subject to state regulation, making property "no more than a defeasible privilege for the citizen" (Gray and Gray, 1998, p. 40).

This shift is mirrored in ecologically oriented land management practices. Hardin (1968) had foreseen the effect of an expanding human population on nature when he issued his infamous warning about the "tragedy of the commons" (p. 1245). He argues for private property to be used as a vehicle to avert the overextension of the natural resources (to the point where nature's chemical and biological recycling processes are unable to cope with the pollutants produced by an increasing population). But today, the ecologically oriented biosphere logic reverses this argument: It calls for a cooperative approach to land utilization regardless of individual property rights because there is a need to match land utilization with (bands of) soil type, which stretches beyond the boundary of any single farm (Brunckhorst, 2000). The farming community in general acknowledges this reality. A survey carried out by the Australian Bureau of Statistics (2002) shows that nearly 30,000 farms have changed land practices to manage or prevent salinity. Of the farmers, 66% identified farm sustainability as the main reason for changing practices, and 56% ranked "improved environmental protection" as their second aim, with 54% ranking "increased productivity" as the third objective.

Presently, there is an inconsistency. Farming communities (which are at the front line of land degradation) and the common law have acknowledged the need to embrace a wider sense of responsibility of ownership, whereas the conventional accounting framework maintains the notion of individual property rights and responsibility only to those who have a monetary interest in it. The next section puts forward a proposal to take advantage of this inconsistency to encourage an ethical approach to making decisions that are in keeping with the sustainability ethos of the 21st century.

Tenets of Ethical Decision Making

The inconsistency between accounting's representation of business reality (based on the rights of equity ownership) and the grassroots interpretation of property (as represented by contemporary case law and biosphere management) may be restated as follows: accounting simplifies the interconnectedness between humans and nature into a predominantly economic relationship, while the more socially grounded disciplines of law and land management struggle to reflect the ·holistic nature of the relationship. It is argued here that accounting should embrace the·uncertainty surrounding holistic interconnectedness (that underpins the idea of sustainability) instead of reducing it to a single dimension of cost-based economic growth. The ECOMAC study reveals the benefits of holistic accounting: Share prices of firms with good environmental records have outperformed the market average and have lowered the cost of capital for the reporting firm (Blumberg, Korsvold, and Blum, 1997, cited in Bartolomeo, Bennetta, and James, 1999, p. 44).

How does this inconsistency translate into sustainable management actions? Giddens (1991) notes that inconsistent interpretation of reality triggers reflexivity in the thought processes of an individual. Kholberg (1984; Barger, 2000; Power, Higgins, and Kohlberg, 1989) develops this reflexivity into three levels of moral development: Moral development begins at level one in which a child identifies strongly with social norms. Level two sees the emergence of interpersonal awareness in the form of moral reciprocity. In level three (or the postconventional level) the actor's reasoning and actions are based on the critical examination of principles underlying the norms. There are two stages within each level as reflected in Table 27.1.

The level of development necessary to transform conflicting evidence into ethical decision occurs in level three. Unfortunately, it has been dismissed as a theoretical end point because it has been difficult to verify

Table 27.1 Kohlberg's Stages of Moral Development

Level	Stage	Social Orientation
Preconventional	1	Obedience and punishment
	2	Individualism, instrumentalism, and exchange
Conventional	3	"Good boy and good girl"
	4	Law and order
Postconventional	5	Social contract
	6	Principled conscience

From Barger, 2000.

(Outhwaite, 1994). It is argued here that empirical evidence is scarce as there are few individuals who make it to this category—they are the Gandhis and Martin Luther Kings of this world. Their lived experiences provide the evidence sought, and here the chapter turns to Gandhi's lectures and writings for guidance.

Gandhi's actions were informed by the Advaitic Vedic philosophy, which is based on the premise that humans and nature are intrinsically interconnected. Knowledge about the holistic connections is not spelled out. The holistic connections are learned as an individual embarks on the path of ethical living, a path that became Gandhi's life journey as he selflessly strove to free oppressed Indians from British imperialism. Space constraints do not permit a detailed narration of his life experiences (see Saravanamuthu, 2003, for details). The point made here is that Gandhi's ethical progression to Kohlberg's level three emerged from his "experiments with (an ambiguous) truth" (Gandhi, 1995, 1993). The term *experiments* implies that truth is not absolute and static. The nonabsolute outcome of experiments encourages an individual to be more receptive to alternative perceptions of actuality, thus freeing one from the conventional (economic) depictions of the challenges of the 21st century. Otherwise, alternatives that challenge the status quo would be regarded as "impossible" strategies and would be dismissed out of hand (Krishnamurti, 1978).

Gandhi's experiments with truth also rebut the popular assertion that sustainable information has to be accurate and precise (cf. Albrechtsen, 2003). It is not possible to produce such information because of the ambiguity surrounding human–nature interconnectedness. Supposedly "accurate" accounting information has traditionally been produced. The operative word is *supposedly*, because accounting's claims to represent business activities fairly have been steadfastly debunked by critical theorists over the last two decades.

It is argued here that such specificity is unnecessary if the aim is to create thinking, reflexive individuals who arrive at ethical decisions despite the ambiguity surrounding sustainability. The following section puts forward an accounting application that strives to bridge theory and practice.

Linking Theory and Practice

The previous section suggests an ethical approach to decision making to fill the void caused by the uncertainty over sustainability, and the different sustainability interpretations between accounting and other grassroots approaches (including common law and land management disciplines). It recognizes that values and judgment play an increasingly important role in the current climate of ambiguity about what constitutes societal progress. These values emerge as decision makers are faced with inconsistent bits of information about the interconnected reality out there.

The inconsistent bits of information should become part of a 21st-century accounting framework. It is similar to Macintosh and Baker's (2002) heteroglossic set of accounts. Arguing that the current form of accounting information is a monological commodified perspective that encompasses agency theory, transaction cost analysis, neoclassical economics, and efficient markets research, the authors assert that accounting should capture the richness of the complex reality "out there" by granting competing perspectives equal expression in the accounts. This is a move away from a single, harmonious, but distorted representation of performance. The benefit of such unstructured representation of reality is found in the role that Gandhi's experiments with truth played in his moral development.

In essence, the way forward is to construct information to assist in risk management rather than in the blind pursuit of absolute financial outcomes (that is, immediate levels of profit). Risk management strategies acknowledge and accommodate uncertainty and ambiguity as part of the decision process. When intertwined with norms about sustainable development, it adds an ethical dimension to management decision making.

The seeds of this form of decision making have been identified in one of ECOMAC's case studies: that is, SGS-Thompson Microelectronics' "environmental investment" decisions. Its investments are not subject to "the usual financial criteria" (Bouma and Wolters, 1999a, p. 123, Table 3.3.6): Conventional cost information is calculated, but it is used as one of several sources of information. These other sources of information could be physical, nonfinancial numbers representing scientific calculations about emission levels, water quality, biodiversity in the soil, and so forth. The investment evaluation process begins with a (non-cost-based) analysis of the environmental impact of the proposed project. Here, it is also advocated that the concept of cost should not be extended to "environmental costs" (defined as per the ECOMAC study) because doing so would reduce the holistic management of social and environmental issues to

> expenses that are wholly and/or partly incurred to protect the environment; costs of inefficiency in the sense that it results in wastage of resources; intangible costs such as impact on reputation; external costs such as welfare of community; and opportunity costs of little or no environmental protection. (Bartolomeo, Bennett, and James, 1999, p. 48)

Therefore it would reinforce the preponderance of the logic of profit over the sustainability ethos.

The key is not to allow the partisan logic of cost efficiency (embedded in the conventional accounting framework) to sidetrack the innovation of sustainable management practices at a time when there is no clear predefined way forward because of the ambiguity surrounding the idea that humans and nature are interconnected. Innovation could be sidetracked if managers are unable to access alternative performance measures to legitimize sustainable practices. Even though it is not possible to state how the social, economic, and environmental priorities should be managed, it has clear advantages over accounting's traditional emphasis on economic goals.

The existence and acceptance of complementary and competing alternative measures allow greater discussion and exchange to occur before a judgment is made on how to proceed. The dissonance that emerges when inconsistent realities are depicted by competing measures is healthy and encourages reflexive scrutinization of assumptions underlying different perceptions of reality. It should result in the progression up Kholberg's hierarchy of ethical behavior in decision making.

Conclusion

The concept of sustainability that underpins the proposals for corporate social responsibility is an ambiguous one. Its ambiguity results in the dialectic between players attempting to camouflage business-as-usual practices and those genuinely striving for sustainability in operational matters. So, it is not surprising that less than 50% of ECOMAC's respondent firms were integrating environmental management processes in their "product design, distribution, use/consumption or disposal stages of the [product] life cycle" (Bartolomeo, Bennett, and James, 1999, p. 25).

In proposing a way forward, this chapter has drawn on the UN's definition, the findings of a European management information systems survey, the most recent financial stewardship reporting exposure draft, as well as common law judgments to centralize the role of property rights in the debate over sustainability. It is argued that failure to extend responsibility of individual property rights would reinforce the logic of cost efficiency over social and environmental needs at a time when there is crying need to address socioenvironmental degradation.

Notes

1. Sustainability implies reevaluating social, environmental, and economic priorities (Giddings et al., 2002).

2. ECOMAC attributes national attempts to orientate accounting practices towards sustainability as attempts to endorse the principles of sustainable development that were defined by Agenda 21 at the 1992 Rio Earth Summit. The fieldwork that was carried out in 1996 and 1997 comprised of a survey of 84 European (small, medium, and large) companies and 15 company case studies of mainly large international enterprises. The study examined how companies were using or intended to use "environmental costs and benefits figures in support of their decisions, and what they have been doing to remedy the limitations of conventional management accounting in this area" (Bartolomeo et al., 1999, p. 9).

3. *Mabo v. Queensland (no. 2)* (1992) 175 CLR 1 as cited in Gray and Gray (1998, p. 37, 26).

References

Albrechtsen, J. (2003). Corporate credibility takes a dive in ratings. *The Australian, April 16*, p. 13.

Armstrong, P. (2002). The costs of activity-based management. *Accounting, Organizations and Society, 27*, pp. 99–120.

Athanasiou, T. (1996). *Divided Planet: the Ecology of Rich and Poor.* Boston: Little, Brown.

Australian Bureau of Statistics. (2002). 4615.0 New ABS survey shows farmers are combating salinity. Media Release December, 11 2002, Australian Bureau of Statistics. Retrieved from http://www.abs.gov.au/Ausstats/abs@ns.../5F3C11FC21EC1AC7CA256C8B00758CC

Barger, R.N. (2000). A summary of Lawrence Kohlberg's stages of moral development. University of Notre Dame. Retrieved from http://www.nd.edu/~rbarger/kohlberg.html

Bartolomeo, M., Bennett, M., Bouma, J.J., et al. (1999). *Eco-Management Accounting.* Dordrecht: Kluwer Academic.

Bartolomeo, M., Bennett, M., and James, P. (1999). The Ecomac framework. In Bartolomeo, M., Bennett, M., Bouma, J.J., et al. (eds.), *Eco-Management Accounting*, pp. 13–80. Dordrecht: Kluwer Academic.

Barzel, Y. (1989). *Economic Analysis of Property Rights.* Cambridge: Cambridge University Press.

BBC (2000). NIKE and GAP—no sweat. Documentary Panorama film broadcast on SBS Television, Australia on March 6, 2001.

Becksmann, T., and Bouma, J.J. (1999a). Defining environmental costs for the Philips Glass factory in Aachen. In Bartolomeo, M., Bennett, M., Bouma, J.J., et al. (eds.), *Eco-Management Accounting*, pp. 129–142. Dordrecht: Kluwer Academic.

Becksmann, T., and Bouma, J.J. (1999b). Defining environmental costs for Sony Deutschland. In Bartolomeo, M., Bennett, M., Bouma, J.J., et al. (eds.), *Eco-Management Accounting*, pp. 143–157. Dordrecht: Kluwer Academic.

Berle, A., and Means, G. (1967). *The Modern Corporation and Private Property.* New York: Harcourt, Brace & World. (First edition, 1932).

Birkin, F., and Woodward, D. (1997a). Introduction. *Management Accounting (UK)*. Series: Management Accounting for Sustainable Development. June, pp. 24–26.

Birkin, F., and Woodward, D. (1997b). From economic to ecological efficiency. *Management Accounting (UK)*. Series: Management Accounting for Sustainable Development. July/August, pp. 42–45.

Birkin, F., and Woodward, D. (1997c). Stakeholder analysis. *Management Accounting (UK)*. Series: Management Accounting for Sustainable Development. September, pp. 58–60.

Birkin, F., and Woodward, D (1997d). The eco-balance account. *Management Accounting (UK)*. Series: Management Accounting for Sustainable Development. October, pp. 50–52.

Birkin, F., and Woodward, D (1997e). Accounting for sustainable development. *Management Accounting (UK)*. Series: Management Accounting for Sustainable Development. November, pp. 52–54.

Birkin, F., and Woodward, D (1997f). A zero-base approach to accounting for sustainable development. *Management Accounting (UK)*. Series: Management Accounting for Sustainable Development. December, pp. 40–42.

Blumberg, J., Korsvold, A., and Blum, G. (1997). *Environmental Performance and Stakeholder Value*. Geneva: World Business Council for Sustainable Development.

Bouma, J.J., and Wolters, T. (1999a). Developments in eco-management accounting: An analysis of the case studies. In Bartolomeo, M., Bennett, M., Bouma, J.J., et al. (eds.), *Eco-Management Accounting*, pp. 111–128. Dordrecht: Kluwer Academic.

Bouma, J.J., and Wolters, T. (1999b). Environmental management and management accounting: A survey among 84 European companies. In Bartolomeo, M., Bennett, M., Bouma, J.J., et al. (eds.), *Eco-Management Accounting*, pp. 81–109. Dordrecht: Kluwer Academic.

Braden, J. (1982), Some emerging rights in agricultural land. *American Journal of Agricultural Economics, 64*, no. 1, pp. 19–27.

Brunckhorst, D.J. (2000). *Bioregional Planning: Resource Management beyond the New Millennium*. Amsterdam: Harwood Academic.

Castle, E. (1978). Property rights and the political economy of resource scarcity. *American Journal of Agricultural Economics, 60*, pp. 1–9.

Chatterjee, P., and Finger, M. (1994). *The Earth Brokers: Power, Politics and World Development*. New York: Routledge.

Costanza, R., d'Arge, R., de Groot, R., et al. (1997). The value of the world's ecosystem services and natural capital. *Nature, 387*, pp. 253–260.

Daily, G.C. (ed.) (1997). Introduction: What are ecosystem services? In *Nature's Services: Societal Dependence on Natural Ecosystems*, pp. 1–10. Washington, D.C.: Island Press.

DeSimone, D., and Popoff, F. (1997). *Eco-Efficiency—the Business Route to Sustainable Development*. Cambridge, Mass.: MIT Press.

Eckersley, R. (1992). *Environmentalism and Political Theory: Toward an Ecocentric Approach*. London: University College London Press.

Economic & Social Research Council. (2000). Summary: What have we learnt about sustainable production and consumption? In the Global Environmental Change: Re-thinking the Questions programme, UK. Retrieved from http://www.gecko.ac.uk/doc-c/coredoc-c-summary.html

Ehrlich, P., Ehrlich, A., and Holdren, J. (1977). *Ecoscience: Population, Resources, Environment*. San Francisco: Freeman.

Elkington, J. (1997). *Cannibals with Forks: The Triple Bottom Line of 21st Century Business*. Oxford: Capstone.

Fussler, C., with James, P. (1996). *Driving Eco-Innovation*. London: Pitman.

Gandhi, M.K. (1993). *Gandhi: An Autobiography: The Story of My Experiments with Truth*. Boston: Beacon Press.

Gandhi, M.K. (1995). *Truth Is God*. Compiled by R.K. Prabhu. Ahmedabad: Navajivan.

Giddens, A. (1991). *Modernity and Self-Identity*. Sanford, Calif.: Stanford University Press.

Giddings, B., Hopwood, B., and O'Brien, G. (2002). Environment, economy and society: Fitting them together into sustainable development. *Sustainable Development, 10*, pp. 187–196.

Global Reporting Initiative (2002). Sustainability reporting guidelines. Boston: Global Reporting Initiative.

Gray, K., and Gray, S.F. (1998). The idea of property in land. In Bright, S., and Dewar, J. (eds.), *Land Law: Themes and Perspectives*, pp. 15–51. Oxford: Oxford University Press.

Hardin, G. (1968). The tragedy of the commons. *Science, 162*, pp. 1243–1248.

Heywood, V. (ed.) (1995). *Global Biodiversity Assessment*. Cambridge: Cambridge University Press.

Kohlberg, L. (1984). *Essays on Moral Development*. Vol. 2. *The Psychology of Moral Development*. San Francisco: Harper & Row.

Krishnamurti, J. (1978). *The Impossible Question*. Harmondsworth, England: Penguin Books.

Macintosh, N.B., and Baker, C.R. (2002). A literary theory perspective on accounting: towards heteroglossic accounting reports. *Accounting, Auditing and Accountability Journal, 5*(2), pp. 184–222.

March, J.G. (1994). *A Primer on Decision Making: How Decisions Happen*. New York: Free Press.

March, J., and Simon, H. (1993). *Organizations*. Cambridge, Mass.: Blackwell.

McIntyre, P. (2003a), Reputation ratings: the new company yardstick. Advertising and marketing supplement, *The Australian,* April 24–30, p. 11.

McIntyre, P. (2003b), Hewson's swipe at reluctant corporates. Advertising and Marketing supplement. *The Australian,* April 24–30, p. 10.

Outhwaite, W. (1994). *Habermas: A Critical Introduction*. Cambridge: Polity Press.

Parker, C., and Porter, B. (2002). *Australian GAAP*. Melbourne: Parker Publishing.

Pimm, S.L. (1997). The value of everything. *Nature, 387*, pp. 231–232.

Power, F.C., Higgins, A., and Kohlberg, L. (1989). *Lawrence Kohlberg's Approach to Moral Education*. New York: Columbia University Press.

Previts, G.J., and Merino, B.D. (1998). *A History of Accountancy in the United States: A Cultural Significance of Accounting*. Columbus: Ohio State University Press.

Reeve, I. (2002), Property rights and natural resource management. *Institute for Rural Futures, Occasional Paper 2002/1*. University of New England, Armidale, Australia.

Rubenstein, D. (1994). *Environmental Accounting for the Sustainable Corporation: Strategies and Techniques*. Westport, Conn.: Quorum Books.

Saravanamuthu, K. (2003). Rethinking individual property rights in accounting for sustainable development. Proceedings of Interdisciplinary Perspectives on Accounting Conference, Madrid. Retrieved from http://zoltar.uc3m.es/~confer/index.html

Saravanamuthu, K. (2004). What is measured counts: Harmonized corporate reporting and sustainable economic development. *Critical Perspectives on Accounting*, 15(3), pp. 295–302.

Saravanamuthu, K., and Tinker, T. (2003). Politics of managing: The dialectic of control. *Accounting, Organizations and Society, 28*, pp. 37–64.

Schumacher, E.F. (1973). *Small Is Beautiful: Economics As If People Mattered*. New York: Harper & Row.

Simon, H. (1957). *Models of Man: Social and Rational*. New York: John Wiley & Sons.

Simon, H. (1976). *Administrative Behavior: A Study of Decision-Making Processes in Administrative Organization*. New York: Free Press.

Stavropoulos, W. (2000). Building a sustainable enterprise: doing business in a world with nowhere to hide. Speech delivered at the Sustainable Business Forum, San Mateo, California, March 28. Available in the World Business Council for Sustainable Development Speech Library. Retrieved from http://www.wbcsd.ch/Speech/s82.htm

Tinker, T. (1985). *Paper Prophets: A Social Critique of Accounting*. New York: Praeger.

Tokar, B. (1997). *Earth for Sale: Reclaiming Ecology in the Age of the Corporate Greenwash*. Boston: South End Press.

UNEP. (2001). Global Reporting Initiative. Retrieved from http://www.uneptie.org/outreach/reporting/gri.htm

von Weizsacker, E., Lovins, A., and Lovins, H. (1997). *Factor Four: Doubling Wealth, Halving Resource Use*. London: Earthscan.

White, A., and Savage, D. (1995). Budgeting for environmental projects: a survey. *Management Accounting (USA), October*, pp. 48–54.

World Business Council for Sustainable Development (2000), Eco-efficiency: creating more value with less impact. Retrieved from http://www.wbcsd.ch/DocRoot/02w8IK14V8E3HMIiFYue/EEcreating.pdf

World Commission on Environment and Development. (1987). *Our Common Future*. Oxford: Oxford University Press.

World Scientists. (1992). Warning to humanity. Retrieved from http://www.newdimensions.org/article/warning.html

Chapter 28

Critical Impacts of Inequality on Sustainable Development

M. Shamsul Haque

CONTENTS

Introduction

In both the academic sphere and the practical policy circle, the idea of "sustainable development" has gained considerable attention for various reasons, such as the failure of traditional development models to achieve their promised objectives, greater awareness of the adverse impact of rapid industrial progress, and worldwide concern about environmental disasters such as nuclear accidents, oil spills, global warming, land degradation, deforestation, biodiversity loss, and ozone depletion (Haque,

2000; Hempel, 1996). The growing significance of environmental sustainability can be observed from some of the major international events held in recent decades, including the United Nations (UN) Conference on the Human Environment (1972), UN Conference on Environment and Development (1992), World Summit for Social Development (1995), and World Summit on Sustainable Development (2002). The crucial nature of sustainable development was reinforced when the delegates from all nations made the following declaration: "We, the representatives of the peoples of the world, assembled at the World Summit on Sustainable Development in Johannesburg, South Africa from 2–4 September 2002, reaffirm our commitment to sustainable development" (WSSD, 2002).

From these global events or occasions attended by government representatives, nongovernment organizations, journalists, and academics from countries all over the world, there emerged some major conventions and protocols for the environment and sustainable development such as the Vienna Convention for the Protection of the Ozone Layer (1985), the Montreal Protocol on Substances that Deplete the Ozone Layer (1987), the Framework Convention on Climate Change (1992), the Convention on Biological Diversity (1992), the Convention to Combat Desertification (1994), and the Kyoto Protocol (1997) (Haque, 2000). To enforce these conventions and protocols, there are international institutions such as the UN Environment Programme, the UN Commission on Sustainable Development, the Inter-Agency Committee on Sustainable Development, and the Secretariat of the Convention on Biological Diversity (Haque, 2000). At the regional and national levels, there have also been numerous conferences and workshops as well as environmental laws and institutions (ministries, agencies, commissions, associations) guided by the ethos of sustainable development.

Despite these international, regional, and national initiatives; legal provisions; and institutions, the goal of sustainable development remains largely unrealized, especially in terms of the continuing environmental disasters and ecological disorders in different parts of the world (UNEP, 1997). In terms of deforestation, nearly 90% of the original forests have been cleared in some regions, and the world lost about 20% of its tropical rain forest in the mid-20th century (Brown, 1991; Haque, 2000). In the 1990s, the loss of the world's tropical forest was about 15.6 million hectares per year (Sheeran, 2004). There is also an alarming condition of diminishing biodiversity; according to one estimate, if there is no serious remedial measure, the world may lose 25% (60,000) of its plant species by 2025, and about 69% of its marine fish stocks are already under the threat of being depleted (see UNPF, 2001).

In terms of the emissions of greenhouse gas (carbon dioxide), the total emissions reached as high as 26.4 billion metric tons in 1992 (the year of the Earth Summit in Rio) and increased by 4% in the late 1990s and became quite alarming (Leisinger, 1998). About 75% of such carbon emissions is from burning fossil fuels, and the remaining 25% is caused by deforestation (Sheeran, 2004). Because of increasing emissions of this greenhouse gas, there is a growing concern about the climate change; it is observed that the planet's average surface temperature increased by about 0.6°C during the 20th century (higher than predicted), and it is estimated that by the end of the 21st century, global temperature may rise by 1.4°C to 5.8°C (Sheeran, 2004). This global warming is likely to increase serious natural catastrophes such as sea-level rise, storms, flooding, and loss of plant and animal species (UNPF, 2001). Another indicator of the growing threat to sustainability is the problem of land degradation caused by soil erosion, salinization, and desertification. Each year, 6 million hectares of the world's land is severely affected by soil erosion, 20 million hectares by desertification, and millions more by salinization, which significantly reduce the crop yields and often make cultivation unprofitable (Brown, 1991; Haque, 2000).

In addition, because of the increasing emissions of ozone-depleting gases such as chlorofluorocarbons (CFCs), the ozone layer over the South Pole is being eroded; serious health disorders and crop losses may result (Haque, 2000). On the other hand, the increasing emissions of sulfur dioxide from coal-fueled factories and power plants may worsen the problem of acid rain in regions such as East Asia (Leisinger, 1998). Another challenge to sustainability is the rapid increase in the use of nonrenewable resources such as energy; from 1990 to 1995 the global demand for energy increased by 9%; the developing world's energy use is expected to increase from 32% in 1995 to 41% in 2015 (Wilkening, von Hippel, and Hayes, 2000). These are some of the major indicators of the continuing environmental problems and ecological disorders that pose serious threats to sustainable development.

The preceding paradoxical scenario of the growing threats to sustainable development, despite the increasing international and national initiatives to achieve such development, implies that in articulating these initiatives, there are problems with the diagnosis of the causes of unsustainability. In this regard, it is mentioned by Redclift (1988) that the current "managerialist" initiatives tend to fail to address the actual "causes" of the situation. In articulating the aforementioned conventions, protocols, rules, and institutions for environmental sustainability, the common tendency is to focus on factors such as population pressure, industrialization, urban expansion, and excessive consumption as the main causes of unsustainable development. However, there is inadequate attention paid to the existing structures of inequality within and between nations, which are considered by this author the most primary cause of unsustainability. It is already stressed by some scholars that the principle of equality should be central to any definition of sustainable development (Taylor, 2002). Unfortunately, as Flint and Danner (2001) point out, in much of the literature on sustainable development, the significance of equality is hardly understood and usually given little attention.

The main contention in this chapter is that although there are many apparent causes behind unsustainable development presented by various scholars and experts (some of these causal explanations are discussed later), it is the severe forms of inequality prevalent in societies and global structures that constitute the most critical challenge to sustainability. The chapter also attempts to demonstrate that inequality may even be considered one of the most critical factors to activate or intensify the other causes of unsustainability (e.g., population and consumption) often discussed in existing literature. In other words, to a certain extent, it is possible to interpret the structures of inequality as "the cause of causes" behind the prevalent problems of unsustainable development. However, before explaining the adverse impacts of inequality, the chapter presents some of the most common causal interpretations in this regard.

Causes of Unsustainability: Common Views and Explanations

In the existing literature, although there are conceptual controversy and diversity, according to one of the most widely cited definitions, *sustainable development* is "development that meets the needs of the present without compromising the ability of future generations to meet their own needs" (WCED, 1987, p. 8). In general, almost all interpretations of sustainability are related to environmental or ecological concerns, especially about how the continuity of development activities, needs satisfaction, and living conditions across generations may be disrupted or constrained by rapid resource depletion, land degradation, air and water pollution, climate change, biodiversity loss, natural disasters, and so on. However, a major part of the literature is about the factors that cause these unfavorable environmental conditions and thus pose threats to the realization of sustainable development. As mentioned earlier, some of the common causal factors that are claimed to affect sustainability are population pressure, industrial growth, urbanization, energy-intensive technology, wasteful consumption, and intensive cultivation (ADB, 2001; GOI, 1998).

First, one of the most common explanations of the problem of sustainable development is the global population pressure caused by high birth rates in various regions and countries, especially in the developing world. In line with the population theory of Thomas Robert Malthus

(1766–1834), which draws attention to the implications of population growth for the environment and long-term survival (Preston, 1996), it is argued that the expansion of population is a major cause leading to a more intensive use of resources (especially land), increased consumption and production of goods, more pollution of air and water, and larger volume of waste disposal, which constitute a threat to environmental sustainability (Corson, 1994). This explanation has gained prominence as a result of the rapid expansion of the world population (which is expected to reach 12.5 billion by 2050), coinciding with the worsening ecological conditions (Haque, 1999a). It has been mentioned that in the 20th century, as the world population increased to 6.1 billion, the global use of water and the emissions of carbon dioxide also multiplied (UNPF, 2001). One example is Southeast Asia, where the increasing population pressure has allegedly led to the worsening situation of pollution and the degradation of the coastal environment (Soegiarto, 1994).

Second, there is a widely discussed argument that environmental unsustainability is worsened by the excessive level of consumption, which is "central to the environmental crisis" (Ramphal, 1992). It is observed that consumption requires the production and processing of commodities by using natural resources (e.g., land, water, ore, energy); involves the building of factories that often use toxic materials; and, in some cases, produces waste and pollutants (e.g., use of cars) (Robbins, 1999, pp. 209–210). In illustrating the linkage between consumption and the environment, Shiva (2000, pp. 70–71) provides a specific example of consumption in restaurants; the process of preparing and serving foods begins with "intensive breeding of livestock and poultry," which causes land degradation, deforestation, and water contamination. In general, the modern process of producing agricultural consumption goods requires irrigation, fertilizers, and pesticides that worsen land degradation, salinization, waterlogging, and so on (GOI, 1998).

Third, the process of industrialization and technological advancement is also considered a common factor affecting environmental sustainability in most countries. In this regard, the adverse impacts of industrial growth are so well known that according to Nudler (1986, p. 61), "The destructive action of industrialism over the environment has been so convincingly shown that it hardly requires further comment." Recently, the rapid pace of industrialization, which involves intensive use of energy, water, iron, cement, timber, and chemicals, has intensified the greenhouse effect, water contamination, resource depletion, and thus ecological degradation (GOI, 1998). In addition, the advancement in technologies has intensified the process of ecological disorder by enabling industries to exploit natural resources at a faster and greater rate. For example, compared to traditional manual tools and techniques, there are now more powerful electric mining excavators, much larger oil supertankers, more efficient processes of producing fertilizers, and much faster vehicles to transport hazardous chemicals.

Fourth, there are studies on how the expansion of urbanization and urban lifestyle has led to worsening environmental problems. In this regard, it is specified that the process of urbanization means greater use of energy-intensive transport, water supply, recreational facilities, and so on. In general, urban population consumes more industrial goods, practices wasteful consumption behavior, and has more exposure to consumerist ideology through media (Jorgenson, 2003, p. 381). In addition, because of overcrowding, most large cities of the world are now experiencing the problems of unmanageable wastes, polluted air, and contaminated water. However, the rate of urban expansion has become more intensive in recent decades. In Africa, the percentage of population living in urban areas increased from 20% to 35% between the 1960s and the 1990s; in Asia and the Pacific, the rate of increase in urban population was 3.2% per year between 1990 and 1995; and in Europe, North America, and Latin America, about 70% of the total population are already living in cities (UNEP, 1999).

Finally, there is a common tendency among many scholars to blame the whole market system for endangering environmental sustainability. Under the dominance of markets, the single-minded motivation to maximize profit at a faster rate leads to patterns of production and consumption that are harmful to the ecological system. Profits are often made by degrading soil through commercial cultivation, polluting water through industrial wastes, endangering public health by using hazardous chemicals, expanding destructive consumerism through massive advertisement, and so on. In the current age, because of the globalization of markets, many developing countries are moving away from the traditional environment-friendly lifestyle and embracing consumerism, which represents an emerging serious challenge to sustainable development (Haque, 1999a; Sachs, 1992). It is often mentioned that in comparison with the Eastern cultural traditions based on the principle of harmony with nature, the Western market-based consumption culture is often detrimental to nature and its environmental sustainability, although there are controversies over such a cultural interpretation of environment–market relations.

Inequality as a Most Critical Factor Affecting Sustainable Development

After examining the existing explanations of factors causing unsustainable development (e.g., population, consumption, industrial growth, urbanization, and profit-driven market), this section of the chapter explains why the structures of severe inequality represent a more central cause behind this unsustainability and how the detrimental impacts of the preceding causal factors themselves are reinforced by such inequalities. Although the concept of sustainability puts greater emphasis on intergenerational equity in sharing resources and satisfying needs, it seems to be quite indifferent to the prevalent intragenerational inequalities in most societies (Anand and Sen, 1994; Haque, 2000). Before exploring the implications of existing inequalities for sustainable development, it is necessary to mention that because of space limitations, the focus of this chapter is specifically on economic inequality (not racial or gender inequality) between classes or income groups as well as between nations.

In terms of class inequality, it has been estimated from earlier studies that in the developing world as a whole, only 3% of landowners own 80% of agricultural land; in Latin America, only 1% of landlords own and control 40% of arable land; and in Africa, 75% of the population do not have control over even 4% of the land (Haque, 1999a). In recent years, the income gap between the rich and the poor significantly expanded worldwide; while the share of global income for the richest 20% consistently increased, it declined for the poorest 20% from 2.3% in 1960 to 1.1% in 2003 (Bhattacharya, 2003; Leisinger, 1998). The ratio of the average income of the richest 20% to that of the poorest 20% changed from 3:1 in 1820 to 30:1 in 1970 to 60:1 in 1990 to 86:1 in 2000 (Bhattacharya, 2003). Given this worsening trend, it is not surprising that the world's 2.8 billion poor survive on less than $2 a day (World Bank, 2001).

In terms of cross-national inequality, it was found that 22% of the world's population living in developed nations shared nearly 83% of the global gross domestic product (GDP), whereas 78% of the population living in developing countries accounted for 17% of the GDP (Haque, 1999a). In fact, the annual income gap between developed and developing countries has consistently widened; between 1960 and 1995 this gap tripled from $5,700 to $16,168 (Leisinger, 1998). On the other hand, the number of transnational corporations increased from 7,000 to 40,000 between 1970 and 1995, and about 90% of them are from developed nations (Karliner, 1997). Some of these corporations are financially very powerful: Of these corporations 500 account for 80% of the world's foreign investment and 70% of its trade, and the revenues of only two corporations (General Motors and Ford) amount to more than the total GDP of all Sub-Saharan African countries (Bhattacharya, 2003; Haque, 2004). The income of some corporate tycoons surpasses the combined income of many poor countries. It was observed in 1999 that the total income of the world's top 200 billionaires ($1135 billion) was nearly eight times the total income of about 582 million people ($146 billion) in poor countries (Mitra and Jeyaseelan,

2001). In terms of asset ownership, the three richest men, Bill Gates, Warren Buffet, and Paul Allen (all Americans), own assets that are equal to assets owned by 600 million people in the 48 least developed countries (Bhattacharya, 2003). These are just a few examples of the extent of inequalities between social classes and between nations that seriously affect the possibility of sustainable development.

First, underlying the population pressure as a threat to sustainable development is the structure of extreme economic inequality within the population in many societies that intensifies such a threat. More specifically, the serious income gap in most cases implies the coexistence of extreme poverty and affluence, which leads to a lopsided or uneven pattern of consumption behavior that adversely affects environmental sustainability. With regard to poverty, it is suggested that inequality worsens the condition of poverty, which, in turn, causes unsustainability, especially because the poor rely more heavily on natural resources because they can hardly afford resources from sources such as markets (GOI, 1998). More specifically, because of the extreme inequality in land ownership mentioned, most landless farmers in the developing world are often compelled to clear the forests to gather fuel wood and gain some cultivable land, and to practice overcultivation in order to survive (Haque, 2000). In Africa, for instance, the worsening situation of inequality and poverty has led to more intensive overcropping and overgrazing (Haque, 1999a; James, 1996). All these desperate farming activities contribute to further land degradation and deforestation. Because in Asia and the Pacific, countries with the highest density of poor people are the worst victims of environmental degradation, and it is stressed by Jalal (1993, p. 12) that "poverty alleviation and environmental protection generally go hand in hand, as income gap and environmental stress are closely linked."

On the other hand, extreme economic inequality also implies the greater affluence of the rich, which is equally detrimental to sustainable development, especially because of their conspicuous lifestyle and consumption behavior. It is found that domestic income inequality affects the levels and patterns of consumption (Jorgenson, 2003), and that the affluent elites are more likely to use (sometimes overuse) expensive but hazardous industrial goods such as private cars, refrigerators, air conditioners, aerosols, and building materials (Haque, 1999a; Simonis, 1990). Both the production and the consumption of these luxurious goods involve the intensive use of energy, emissions of greenhouse and ozone-depleting gases, and toxic pollution of the atmosphere, which are highly damaging to the ecological system. More recently, a new breed of educated rich in developing countries are more interested in recreation such as tourism and golf, for which many countries have converted tropical forests into luxurious parks, have used scarce land to create golf courses, and so on

(Bryant and Parnell, 1996; Langhelle, 2000). This brief analysis shows that extreme economic inequality in society reinforces a pattern of consumption behavior among both the poor and the rich, which is quite detrimental to environmental sustainability.

Second, beyond the impact of domestic inequality discussed earlier, international economic inequality also poses a serious threat to sustainable development. The scenario of how the environment is affected by internal inequality is played out at a much greater scale at the global level as a result of the alarming situation of inequality among various countries, especially between developed and developing nations. Historically, the structure of global inequality created under the colonial rule, in fact, intensified the exploitation of nature and the ecological system in the colonized regions and countries (Gowdy, 1994). The situation of poverty in developing countries, which puts pressure on the environment, is not only caused by their internal inequality, but worsened further by the unequal and exploitative world system (Cooper, 1995). It is suggested by Jorgenson (2003, p. 376) that "unequal relationships between countries in the world system enable more powerful countries to externalize the environmental and ecological costs associated with their domestic consumption of raw materials and produced commodities."

More importantly, under the existing international economic system characterized by extreme inequality, there are disproportionate sharing of resources, consumption, and environmental degradation between developed and developing countries. For example, 20% of the world population living in developed countries use 80% of world resources, account for 86% of global consumption spending, and produce 70% of the world's solid waste (Leisinger, 1998; UNDP, 1998). On the other hand, 80% of the world population in developing countries consume only 20% of global resources (Furst, 2001). The proportions of global resources consumed by the richest fifth and the poorest fifth of the world population are, respectively, 45% and 5% of meat and fish, 58% and 4% of energy, 84% and 1.1% of paper, and 87% and 1% of vehicles (UNDP, 1998). The population of advanced industrial countries accounts for the consumption of 70% of the world's energy, 75% of metals, 80% of fertilizer, 92% of cars, 74% of electricity, and so on (Haque, 1999a).

In terms of pollution, 20% of the world population (mostly from developed nations) accounted for 63% of the global emissions of carbon dioxide in 1995, and the United States alone was responsible for nearly 25% of such carbon emissions (UNPF, 2001). According to one study, the amount of per capita carbon emissions per year is 10.2 tons in Germany, 20.5 tons in the United States, and only 1 ton in Africa and South Asia (Leisinger, 1998). With regard to deforestation, it is found that a nation's share of the global deforestation depends largely on its position in the structure of the world capitalist system, and in the developing world, it is often caused, among other factors, by the expansion of livestock ranching to produce meat and export it to developed nations (Burns et al., 2003). Thus, because of extreme international inequality, there are "unjust" consumption and pollution between developed and developing countries, which seriously affect the prospect for sustainable development (Furst, 2001). It is estimated that in entire lifetime, a child born in any developed nation is likely to account for more consumption and pollution than that of 30 to 50 children combined in developing countries (UNPF, 2001). The preceding arguments and indicators show that although international agencies and experts often regard the population increase in poor countries as one of the most serious threats to sustainability, it is the structures of interclass and international inequalities in ownership, consumption, and pollution that pose a serious challenge today. In fact, population growth itself is often affected by inequality, because the fertility rates are known to be much higher among poor families and countries (Wolf, 1996).

Third, although the processes of rapid industrialization and urbaniza-tion adversely affect the environment (discussed earlier), the processes themselves are largely shaped by internal and international inequalities. With regard to industrial growth, it is widely recognized that in most Western nations, it was the preindustrial or precapitalist structure of inequality that led to an immense amount of wealth accumulation and thus generated the drive for industrial production for faster and larger surplus value. On the other hand, economic inequality also creates demand for luxurious industrial goods (e.g., automobiles, electronic appliances) among the rich guided by the pleasure-seeking principle of consumerism. In the case of developing countries, the structure of international inequality and backwardness (both real and perceived) led the launch of massive industrial development plans and the investment in large industrial projects, often with financial and technical assistance from developed countries. This urge for imitating advanced industrial nations and closing the international economic gap has been most evident in various Asian countries, where the rapid pace of industrialization in the 1990s led to a significant increase in energy consumption (UNEP, 1999).

Similarly, the process of urbanization, which has adverse implications for the environment, is also largely shaped and affected by economic inequality. For instance, the expansion of urban population is often the outcome of extreme rural inequality that enables the affluent rural elite or their children to migrate to big cities for a more luxurious lifestyle and compels the unemployed rural poor or the landless to join the urban underclass just for survival. In addition, there is more macrolevel inequality between urban and rural areas in terms of infrastructure, service access, and economic opportunities, which attract people to embrace urban life, especially in developing countries, where resources are disproportionately used for urban development at the expense of rural impoverishment (Burns et al., 2003). Under this structure of severe urban–rural inequality, in many countries, the rural economy has been transformed to produce cash crops for urban consumers, which usually require modern cultivation based on intensive use of irrigation and pesticides that often cause land degradation. On the other hand, the expansion of urban population leads to an increasing consumption of energy, use of automobiles and electric appliances, production of toxic waste, and pollution of air and water. In the urban area itself, there is inequality between the elite and the underclass, and most of these environmentally damaging activities and outcomes are largely related to the luxurious lifestyle of affluent urban elites. The point, in short, is that although rapid urbanization adversely affects environmental sustainability, to a great extent, the root cause of such urbanization and environmental degradation lies in the structures of inequality within and between urban and rural areas.

Fourth, the forms of economic inequality at the local, national, and international levels that threaten environmental sustainability are a crucial part of the world capitalist system based on uneven ownership, income, and consumption. It is explained by some authors that under the unequal world system, developing countries or peripheries are externally dependent, and thus vulnerable to the penetration of foreign capital, which distorts internal class structure, concentrates land ownership, and perpetuates income inequality in these countries (Burns et al., 2003, p. 361; Jorgenson, 2003, p. 380). These interclass and international inequalities shaped by the world capitalist system also affect the global structure of consumption that causes environmental unsustainability. In this regard, Andrew K. Jorgenson in his empirical study finds that "consumption levels are largely a function of a country's position in the core/periphery hierarchy of the world system. ... The core-periphery model of exploitation provides useful explanations of different environmental and ecological outcomes" (Jorgenson, 2003, p. 375). With regard to the process of environmentally hazardous urbanization, it is suggested that this process is also reinforced by the core–semiperiphery–periphery structure under the world capitalist system. This world system enhances urbanization worldwide as its international trade and exchange pass through many territories, and thus, it expands urban population, reinforces urban–rural inequality, worsens hazardous consumerism, and so on (Burns et al., 2003, p. 365).

In addition, the process of industrialization has been intensified under the world system based on international inequality in wages and prices, especially low wages and cheap raw materials in poorer nations, which has led to a significant increase in foreign investment in various industries and projects in developing countries (Khor, 2000). In recent years, under the neoliberal mode of world capitalism that encourages free trade and unconstrained foreign investment and ownership, there has been a proliferation of foreign companies in poorer nations where environmental regulations hardly exist. Such foreign investment in hazardous industries is enhanced further by the globalization of capital, technology, and information that represents an essential feature of the current capitalist system itself. Beyond worldwide industrial expansion, this deeply globalized capitalist system has allegedly worsened the condition of interclass and international inequality in ownership, income, and consumption (Mitra and Jeyaseelan, 2001), which is presented in this chapter as a primary challenge to sustainable development.

Finally, the structure of inequality not only affects environmental sustainability, it also greatly determines who suffers most and least from environmental degradation or unsustainable development. For instance, because of extreme social inequality in the developing world, according to the World Bank (1992, p. 30), "the poor are both victims and agents of environmental damage. About half of the world's poor live in rural areas that are environmentally fragile, and they rely on natural resources over which they have little legal control." Even in many developed countries, because of various forms of inequality and deprivation, the poor and the powerless suffer most from environmental and ecological disorders. In the United States, there is a serious problem of "environmental racism," because the landfills, hazardous waste sites, and polluting industries are usually built around the communities inhabited by the poor and minorities (e.g., African Americans, Native Americans, Hispanics, and Asians), who cannot afford expensive housing and are perceived to be too weak and passive to resist (see Flint and Danner, 2001).

At the international level, the structure of economic inequality and dependence has enabled the core or developed nations to externalize their polluting industries and production sites to the periphery or developing countries (Burns et al., 2003). Although this process reduces environmental damage in the former, it causes serious problems in the latter. By producing and exporting various consumption items (e.g., timber, oil, and cash crops) for affluent countries such as Japan and the United States, many poor countries suffer from environmental problems such as land degradation and pollution (Crabbé, 1997). It is also mentioned that the geographical separation of consumption (in developed nations) and production or harvesting (in poor countries) may often mask the environmental effects of the current global economy (Novek and Kampen, 1992). Moreover, because of international inequality and dependence, many developing countries have become the victims of waste dumping by developed nations. It is observed that developed nations are trying to dump nearly 29 million tons of toxic wastes in various African countries; that Australia dumped over 8.5 thousand tons of wastes and 1.3 million scrap batteries in certain developing countries; and that countries such as India, China, Indonesia, and the Philippines have become the major destinations for the waste dumping by the OECD countries (Bhattacharya, 2003). Because of global inequality in poverty and affluence, poorer countries accept being the targets of dumping of wastes by rich nations often in exchange for some small amounts of money, although it causes them to suffer from environmental degradation and unsustainability.

Concluding Remarks

In this chapter, it has been stressed that in order to achieve sustainable development, it is imperative to overcome the causes of unsustainability. It is also explained that although some of the common interpretations of these causes or factors (e.g., population pressure, industrial growth, urban development) have been widely known, the role played by the structures of inequality (among classes and nations) in causing unsustainable development as well as activating those common factors is often downplayed. The current emphasis on intergenerational equity fails to address these interclass and international inequalities, which need to be seriously addressed because the initiatives based on other causal explanations have not had much result. Some critics even argue that these common interpretations or the "popular paradigms" of sustainable development themselves have done greater harm to nature; many organizations and experts may have benefited from huge grants offered in the name of natural conservation and sustainability, but nature itself has hardly gained from them (Soule, 2000).

In any case, in order to be serious about resolving the problem of unsustainability by mitigating internal and international inequalities, some major policy options could be tentatively outlined. First, there is an immediate need to address the alarming condition of inequality and poverty, especially in developing countries, by adopting land reforms, redistributing income, generating employment, and reforming the service sectors (e.g., education, health, housing) in favor of the landless and the poor (Guimaraes, 2001; Hossain, 1995). As Jalal (1993, p. 7) mentions, sustainable development will "remain a dream unless problems of poverty alleviation and control of environmental degradation are dealt with simultaneously." In addition to these structural reforms, all sections of society, especially the marginalized low-income citizens, should be genuinely consulted and their voices taken into account in making decisions about issues that affect their lives, including the environment (Holmen, 2001).

Second, at the international level, there must be a basic change in the prevalent structure of extreme economic inequality among nations, especially between developed and developing countries. Although the demand of developing countries for a New International Economic Order, which emerged in the 1970s, has largely been forgotten, a similar but more effective collective strategy should be pursued by these countries in order to articulate their demand for a greater share of global income, more favorable terms of trade, fairer distribution of environmental costs and benefits, and so on. In line with this argument, some authors suggest the overall transfer of funds and subsidies from affluent nations to poor countries, which may reduce global poverty and inequality, diminish people's excessive consumption in rich countries, and alleviate environmental degradation in developing countries (Auty and Brown, 1997).

Third, there should be more effective international laws and institutions to enforce globally agreed environmental standards and ensure compliance with such standards by all nations, including the big powers such as the United States and China. Although there are some major conventions and institutions, mentioned earlier, they have not had much success, perhaps because of their lack of coordinated effort as well as their lack of power to oblige the global powers, especially the world's biggest polluters such as the United States, to comply with major environmental agreements and legislation such as the Rio Declaration and the Kyoto Protocol (Haque, 2000; Lemonick, 1997). More potent laws and institutions need to be adopted in order to put them above any particularistic national interests.

Fourth, beyond the enforcement of international laws and institutions, it is essential to change the consumption pattern, especially in developed countries, drastically by educating people, generating awareness through alternative media, and imposing negative incentives such as heavy consumption tax on hazardous industrial goods. Public education and awareness can be related to nutrition knowledge, dangers of modified foods and chemicals, adverse impacts of obsessive consumerism, and significance of ecological health (Haque, 1999b; Leisinger, 1998). To discourage hazardous consumption, heavy tax or duty should be imposed on private cars and certain electronic appliances, and strict regulations should be followed in relation to the polluting factories, packaging industry, and advertising agencies. On the other hand, it is necessary to take measures to improve the living standards of the rural poor, ensure the satisfaction of their basic needs, encourage people to use ecology-friendly technology, and so on (Dreze and Sen, 1995; Furst, 2001).

Finally, the adoption and implementation of the measures mentioned for environmental protection and sustainability require committed leadership and devoted policy makers. Unfortunately, because many political leaders and top officials themselves often gain from economic inequality, believe in industrial and urban expansion, and are fond of expensive imported goods, they may not take any drastic remedial measures in this regard. Thus, there is a need for such committed leadership to emerge in both developed and developing countries for undertaking genuine initiatives to redistribute land, reduce income gaps, adopt effective environmental protection laws and institutions, regulate industrial growth, and create public awareness at both the national and international levels in order to achieve sustainable development.

References

Anand, and S., A. Sen (1994). Sustainable Human Development: Concepts and Priorities. Occasional Paper, July. New York: Human Development Report Office, UNDP.

Asian Development Bank (ADB) (2001). *Asian Environment Outlook 2001*. Manila: ADB.

Auty, R.M., and K. Brown (1997). "An Overview of Approaches to Sustainable Development," in Richard M. Auty and Katrina Brown (eds.), *Approaches to Sustainable Development*. London and Washington: Pinter.

Bhattacharya, P. (2003). Back to the future: Urbanization, globalization and consumerism. IndiaNest.com. Retrieved from http://www.boloji.com/opinion/0051i.htm

Brown, L.R. (1991). "The New World Order," in Worldwatch Institute (ed.), *State of the World, 1991*. New York: W.W. Norton.

Bryant, R.L., and M.J.G. Parnell. (1996). "Introduction," in Michael J.G. Parnell and Raymond L. Bryant (eds.), *Environmental Change in South-East Asia*. Oxford: Routledge.

Burns, T.J., E.L. Kick, and B.L. Davis (2003). "Theorizing and Rethinking Linkages between the Natural Environment and the Modern World-System: Deforestation in the Late 20th Century." *Journal of World-Systems Research 9*(2): 357–390.

Cooper, P.J. (1995). "Inside-Out Management: Public Administration, Sustainable Development, and Environmental Policy," in U.N. Department for Development Support and Management Services (ed.), *Implementing Sustainable Development*. New York: United Nations.

Corson, W.H. (1994). "Changing Course: An Outline of Strategies for a Sustainable Future," *Futures 26*(2): 206–223.

Crabbé, P.J. (1997). Sustainable Development: Concepts, Measures, Market and Policy Failures at the Open Economy, Industry and Firm Levels. Occasional Paper No.16, October. Ontario: Industry Canada.

Dreze, J., and A. Sen (1995). *Indian Economic Development and Social Opportunity*. Oxford: Oxford University Press.

Flint, R.W., and M.J.E. Danner (2001). "The Nexus of Sustainability & Social Equity: Virginia's Eastern Shore (USA) as a Local Example of Global Issues," *International Journal of Economic Development*, 3(2).

Furst, E. (2001). "Global Resource Consumption, Environmental Space and Ecological Structural Change: Implications for Sustainable Development from the Perspective of North-South Relations," *International Journal of Economic Development, 3*(2).

Government of India (GOI) (1998). *Economic Survey 98–99*. New Delhi: Ministry of Finance, Government of India.

Gowdy, J.M. (1994). "Discussion Papers: Progress and Environmental Sustainability," *Environmental Ethics 16:* 41–55.

Guimaraes, R.P. (2001). "The Politics and Ethics of 'Sustainability' as a New Paradigm for Public Policy Formation and Development Planning (I)," *International Journal of Economic Development 3*(3).

Haque, M.S. (1999a). "The Fate of Sustainable Development under the Neoliberal Regimes in Developing Countries," *International Political Science Review 20*(2): 199–222

Haque, M.S. (1999b) *Restructuring Development Theories and Policies: A Critical Study*. Albany: State University of New York Press.

Haque, M.S. (2000). "Environmental Discourse and Sustainable Development: Linkages and Limitations," *Ethics & the Environment 5*(1): 1–19.

Haque, M.S. (2004). "The Growing Challenges of Globalization to Self-Reliant Developing in Developing Countries," in Gedeon Mudacumura and M. Shamul Haque (eds.), *Handbook of Development Policy Studies*. New York: Marcel Dekker.

Hempel, L.C. (1996). *Environmental Governance: The Global Challenge*. Washington, D.C.: Island Press.

Holmen, H. (2001). "The Unsustainability of Development," *International Journal of Economic Development 3*(1).

Hossain, K. (1995). "Evolving Principles of Sustainable Development and Good Governance," in K. Ginther, E. Denters, and Paul J.I.M. de Waart (eds.), *Sustainable Development and Good Governance*. Norwell, Mass.: Kluwer Academic.

Jalal, K.F. (1993). Sustainable Development, Environment and Poverty Nexus. Occasional Paper, Asian Development Bank. Manila: Asian Development Bank.

James, V.U. (1996). "Introduction: Planning for Sustainable Development in the Third World," in V.U. James (ed.), *Sustainable Development in Third World Countries*. Westport, Conn.: Praeger.

Jorgenson, A.K. (2003). "Consumption and Environmental Degradation: A Cross-National Analysis of the Ecological Footprint," *Social Problems 50*(3): 374–394.

Karliner, J. (1997). *The Corporate Planet: Ecology and Politics in the Age of Globalization*. San Francisco: Sierra Club Books.

Khor, M. (2000). Globalization and the South: Some Critical Issues. Discussion Paper No. 147, April. Geneva: United Nations Conference on Trade and Development.

Langhelle, O. (2000). "Sustainable Development and Social Justice: Expanding the Rawlsian Framework of Global Justice," *Environmental Values 9*: 295–323.

Leisinger, K.M. (1998). "Sustainable Development at the Turn of the Century: Perceptions and Outlook," *International Journal for Sustainable Development 1*(1): 73–98

Lemonick, M.D. (1997). "Turning Down the Heat," *Time, 150* (26), December 22.

Mitra, A., and M.A.J. Jeyaseelan (2001). "Civil Society, Globalization and Sustainable Development," *Seminar (India), 507,* November.

Novek, J., and K. Kampen (1992). "Sustainable or Unsustainable Development? An Analysis of an Environmental Controversy," *Canadian Journal of Sociology 17*(3): 249–273.

Nudler, O. (1986). "The Human Element as Means and Ends of Development," in K. Haq and U. Kirdar (eds.), *Human Development: The Neglected Dimension.* Islamabad, Pakistan: North South Roundtable.

Preston, S.H. (1996). "The Effect of Population Growth on Environmental Quality," *Population Research and Policy Review 15*(2): 95–108.

Ramphal, S. (1992). "In a North-South Gap, Seeds of Environment Discord," *International Herald Tribune,* January 24, p.4.

Redclift, M. (1988). "Sustainable Development and the Market: A Framework for Analysis," *Futures* December, pp. 635–650.

Robbins, R. (1999). *Global Problems and the Culture of Capitalism.* Boston: Allyn & Bacon.

Sachs, W. (1992). "Introduction," in W. Sachs (ed.), *The Development Dictionary: A Guide to Knowledge as Power.* London: Zed Books.

Sheeran, K. (2004). "Equity and Efficiency in International Environmental Agreements: A Case Study of the Kyoto Protocol," in Gedeon Mudacumura and M. Shamul Haque (eds.), *Handbook of Development Policy Studies.* New York: Marcel Dekker.

Shiva, V. (2000). *Stolen Harvest: The Hijacking of the Global Food Supply.* Cambridge Mass.: South End Press.

Simonis, U.E. (1990). *Beyond Growth: Elements of Sustainable Development.* Berlin: Ed. Sigma Bohn.

Soegiarto, A. (1994). Sustainable Fisheries, Environment and the Prospects of Regional Cooperation in Southeast Asia. Paper presented at the Nautilus Institute Workshop on Trade and Environment in Asia-Pacific, September 23–25, 1994, East-West Center, Honolulu.

Soule, M.E. (2000). "Does Sustainable Development Help Nature?" *Wild Earth* 10(4): 56–64.

Taylor, J. (2002). Sustainable Development: A Dubious Solution in Search of a Problem. Cato Policy Analysis Series, No. 449, Washington, D.C.: The Cato Institute.

United Nations Development Programme (UNDP) (1998). *Human Development Report 1998. New York: Oxford University Press.*

United Nations Environment Programme (UNEP) (1997). *Global Environmental Outlook—1.* London: Oxford University Press.

United Nations Environment Programme (UNEP) (1999). *Global Environment Outlook 2000.* London: Earthscan.

United Nations Population Fund (UNPF) (2001). *The State of World Population 2001.* New York: UNPF.

World Commission on Environment and Development (WCED) (1987). *Our Common Future*. Oxford: Oxford University Press.

Wilkening, K., D.V. Hippel, and P. Hayes (2000). "Sustainable Energy in a Developing World: The Role of Knowledgeable Markets," in P.S. Chasek (ed.), *The Global Environment in the Twenty-First Century*. Tokyo: United Nations University Press.

Wolf, C. (1996). Population Growth and Intergenerational Justice. Presented at APA Pacific Division Meeting, Society for Philosophy and Public Affairs, Spring.

World Bank (1992). *World Development Report 1992: Development and the Environment*. New York: Oxford University Press.

World Bank (2001). *World Development Report (WDR) 2000/2001: Attacking Poverty*. New York: Oxford University Press.

World Summit on Sustainable Development (WSSD) (2002). *The Johannesburg Declaration on Sustainable Development*. Johannesburg, South Africa: WSSD. Retrieved from http://www.johannesburgsummit.org/html/documents/summit_docs/1009wssd_pol_declaration.htm

Index